KENT HEARTH TAX

ASSESSMENT

LADY DAY 1664

THE BRITISH RECORD SOCIETY
HEARTH TAX SERIES VOLUME II

KENT ARCHAEOLOGICAL SOCIETY
KENT RECORDS VOLUME XXIX

in association with
UNIVERSITY OF SURREY ROEHAMPTON

JACKET INFORMATION FOR HEARTH TAX VOLUMES

General

The fireplaces illustrated on the jacket come from various parts of England and Wales and reflect a wide social spectrum from the major gentry (Little Moreton Hall) to yeoman farmhouses (Valley Farm; Glencoyne). Unfortunately, few seventeenth-century fireplaces in small, single-hearth houses and cottages survive unaltered, and it has proved impossible to find suitable illustrations of them. However, the simple timber chimney and fireplace of Tŷ-Mawr, the brick one at Valley Farm, and the cooking hearth of Glencoyne, are typical of the period and could have been found in many smaller houses and cottages.

DESCRIPTIONS

Front jacket

Top Left

Little Moreton Hall, Cheshire. Decorative fireplace in the chamber over the porch. The house was owned by the powerful Moreton family, whose wealth was based on land. The fireplace is part of the late sixteenth-century additions to the medieval house. By the seventeenth century there were around twenty fireplaces. © Jeremy Milln.

Top Right

Wickens, Charing, Kent. Fireplace with plaster overmantel in the chamber over the parlour. The house was built around 1600 by the Dering family, who were minor gentry. Six hearths were charged in the hearth tax of 1664. © Sarah Pearson.

Bottom Left

Valley Farm, Flatford, Suffolk. A late-medieval yeoman's house; in the sixteenth century a brick fireplace and ceiling (now removed) were inserted into the open hall. By the late seventeenth century a second stack with one, or possibly two, fireplaces had been added to heat the adjacent cross wing. © John Walker.

Bottom Right

Tŷ-Mawr, Castell Caereinion, Montgomeryshire. An open-hall house built in 1461. In the sixteenth century a half-timbered fireplace was added, and later an upper floor inserted (now removed). Tŷ-Mawr means 'great house', and although probably a long-house, with animals at one end, and only one hearth in the 1660s, this was a dwelling of high status in the region. © Peter Smith.

Outside back jacket

Glencoyne Farm, Ullswater, Cumbria. A rare surviving open fire, complete with hearth furniture, set within a typical northern firehood. The large space was lit by its own window, to the right of this photograph of *c*.1900. The house received its present form in 1629. It was owned by a family called Harrison, one of whom was taxed on three hearths in 1674. Reproduced by courtesy of the Museum of Lakeland Life, Kendal, Cumbria.

The Initial Ashford Hearth Tax Return, 1662
A register of certificates signed and marked by the householders stating the number of
hearths in their houses. CKS: U1107/01 folio 2r.

KENT HEARTH TAX ASSESSMENT LADY DAY 1664

Edited by
DUNCAN HARRINGTON

With an Introduction by
SARAH PEARSON

Computing Editor
SUSAN ROSE

Published by The British Record Society
c/o Patric Dickinson
The College of Arms
Queen Victoria Street
London EC4V 4BT
ISBN 0 901505 43 9

in association with

The Kent Archaeological Society
The Museum
St Faith's Street
Maidstone
Kent ME14 1LH
ISBN 0 906746 45 0

*The Societies and University wish to
express their gratitude to the
Pilgrim Trust for a grant to cover digital mapping
and the British Academy and Marc Fitch
Fund for assistance towards
publication of this volume.*

Printed in Great Britain

CONTENTS

List of Plates

List of Maps

List of Tables and Figure

PREFACE

We have much pleasure in introducing this, the second of the series of Hearth Tax volumes to be produced by the Roehampton Hearth Tax Centre and the British Record Society, in association with county record societies. There may well be some twenty volumes in the series. The Roehampton Centre is also, with the assistance of a grant from the Heritage Lottery Fund, having microfilm made of the Hearth Tax listings in the Public Record Office, which is, in turn, making copies of the relevant portions available to every appropriate local record office in the country. This should be completed in 2001. The work of transcription of Hearth Tax records from microfilm is already progressing in a considerable number of counties.

It is also intended to provide the volumes with scholarly introductions complete with maps and tables so that the volumes can be of the greatest use to social and economic historians working on a national canvas as well as to the local historians of the counties concerned. We have a particular interest also in stressing that the Hearth Taxes should throw light on the buildings about which they give such austere information. It is a long time now since the work of Fox and Raglan on Monmouthshire housing followed by Maurice Barley's *English Farmhouse and Cottage*, W. G. Hoskin's essay on the 'Great Rebuilding', and Bob Machin's corrective to it, made historians aware of vernacular housing as part of the evidence they should use. In the 1970s contemporary housing seemed to be accepted as part of the historical vocabulary. However, this part of the dictionary of historical tools seems to have been forgotten again. It is our hope in this series to focus attention once more on housing as necessary evidence in interpreting the past. We are also certain that these volumes will be greatly used by family historians since the Hearth Taxes and their indices are ideal for finding lost ancestors.

Since the population of England had reached five and a quarter millions by the mid-seventeenth century, the number of heads of households to be listed for taxation purposes was enormous. The Hearth Tax records of the 1660s and the 1670s are therefore so huge that their wholesale analysis has been beyond the scope of even the most enterprising individual, although much historical research has already been based on them. After the pioneering work of C. A. F. Meekings, Tom Arkell has done most to make the tax accessible to us. Professor Keith Wrightson, who is writing the introduction to the Durham volume in this series, has already used Mr Arkell's material on the Hearth Taxes for as many types of settlement as possible to establish the abnormality, in terms of extreme poverty, of his coal-mining *Whickham 1560-1765*. Dr Christopher Husbands, who has also done much to make the Hearth Taxes accessible to us, wrote in 1992, 'much of the potential of the Hearth Tax to provide a general framework for the socio-economic history of the later seventeenth century still remains to be exploited at both local and national levels'.

It is this potential which we are now exploiting in these volumes. We hope to end with maps showing the distribution of population, in terms of the density of households taxed and exempted, and of wealth in terms of the number of hearths, for the whole of England and Wales.

We are therefore very pleased that Mr Duncan Harrington has been generous enough to release his gigantic transcript of the Quarter Sessions assessment of Kent for Lady Day 1664, checked against the Exchequer duplicate. We thank him for many hundreds of hours of work. Our interest in revivifying housing as a necessary tool for historians makes us particularly glad that Sarah Pearson, formerly of the Royal Commission on Historical Monuments, and past President of the Vernacular Architecture Group, has been willing to write the historical introduction. We hope the volume will be a model for the series.

Margaret Spufford, Director
Susan Rose, Computing Editor

Centre for Hearth Tax Studies
University of Surrey Roehampton

Michaelmas 2000

ACKNOWLEDGEMENTS

This volume could not have been produced without the work of a great many people. The transcription was undertaken over a period of years by Duncan Harrington, who also wrote an introduction to the manuscripts, and compiled the indices. A general introduction to the hearth tax, to be included in all the hearth tax volumes, was written by Nesta Evans. The introduction to the hearth tax in Kent was contributed by Sarah Pearson, who also compiled the parish-borough list. Mike Shand of Glasgow University digitised the computerised base map of hundreds, and Phillip Judge drew the regional and parish maps. The transcript was turned into a database by Paul Ell and his colleagues at Belfast University, and Susan Rose turned the database and base map into the tables and proportional maps. Finally, Terry Lawson had the unenviable task of making the work of so many people consistent. Margaret Spufford oversaw the whole project from beginning to end, encouraging and advising all the contributors.

Duncan Harrington would like to acknowledge some financial assistance from the Marc Fitch Fund and from the estate of Sidney H. Titford towards computerising the text. He would also like to thank the staff of the Public Record Office and the Centre for Kentish Studies for their help during the research for this paper, especially Aidan Laws who kindly facilitated some editorial desk space during the time-consuming task of checking the Exchequer duplicates and constables' returns and to Kath Topping who, in the very early days provided photocopies of the Quarter Sessions document, and in more enlightened times facilitated a microfilm being made at his expense.

Sarah Pearson would like to thank the many people without whom it would have been impossible to undertake a rapid survey of so many seventeenth hearths in the county. In the first place, nothing could have been achieved without the willingness of so many owners to show her their fireplaces. Work on the three case study parishes would not have been possible without the detailed local knowledge of several people who generously made their research available and arranged access to many buildings. In Charing, Pat Winzar and the Palaeography Group of the Charing and District Local History Society provided transcripts of numerous wills and probate inventories relating to people in the parish. In East Peckham, Margaret Lawrence made available a wide variety of documentation and organised visits to many buildings. In Goodnestone, Julian Plumptre and Frances Smith helped to arrange access to a number of properties, and Jane Andrewes and David Eaves kindly lent copies of their unpublished theses, which were invaluable in placing the Goodnestone material in context. The rapid survey of Boughton Monchelsea, undertaken partly with this project in mind, was arranged by Paul and Olive Hastings and members of Boughton Monchelsea parish council. Peter Guillery was extremely helpful in discussing the building of small houses in the new towns of north-west Kent, and Charles Bain Smith arranged a day looking at seventeenth-century houses in Deal. Elizabeth Parkinson patiently answered innumerable queries on the administration of the hearth tax; Paul Cullen and Anne Reeves set the author right on various place-name matters; Jill Eddison assisted in sorting out Romney Marsh boundaries; Frank Panton helped to unravel the difficult ward, borough and parish situation in Canterbury; and Anthony Poole discussed a number of problems in correlating the hearth tax with other documentation in the Benenden area. An earlier version of the introduction benefited greatly from the perceptive and constructive comments of Jane Andrewes, Nesta Evans, Peter Kidson, Margaret Spufford and Joan Thirsk, and the final version has been much improved by Terry Lawson's sharp eyes.

GENERAL INTRODUCTION

By Nesta Evans

This volume is part of a series of county hearth tax returns which are being published jointly by the British Record Society, County Record Societies and the University of Surrey Roehampton, under the direction of the Roehampton Centre for Hearth Tax Studies. The aim is to publish at least one hearth tax return for every English and Welsh county which has not already one in print. The purpose of the series is to make available a major original source for late seventeenth-century economic and social history for anyone interested in this period. All the results will be tabulated and mapped. At the same time, a re-examination and re-listing of all the E179 documents in the Public Record Office is being undertaken, and those counties currently available in the search rooms will also become available on the P.R.O. web site. This introduction is intended to point out some of the ways in which hearth taxes can be used by historians of all kinds.

The best recent guide to the hearth tax returns is in Kevin Shürer's and Tom Arkell's *Surveying the People*.[1] Arkell's clear exposition of the hearth tax legislation is essential reading for anyone wishing to come to grips with this complicated source. His chapter includes the printed instructions issued to collectors of the tax in 1664, followed by a specimen return for Old Windsor.[2] The originals are in the Public Record Office.[3] There are also excellent introductions to several published returns, especially that to the Nottinghamshire returns.[4]

In order to avoid unnecessary duplication of effort, it is intended that the background to early modern taxation and following description of the administration of the hearth tax should be used in

[1] *Surveying the People*, ed. by Kevin Shürer and Tom Arkell (Oxford, 1992).
[2] Arkell, 'Printed instructions for administering the Hearth Tax' in *Surveying the People*, pp.38-64.
[3] PRO: E179/265/30; *Calendar of Treasury Books*, VII, pp. 1362-7.
[4] *Nottinghamshire Hearth Tax 1664:1674*, ed. by W. F. Webster with an introduction by J. V. Beckett, M. W. Barley and S. C. Wallwork, Thoroton Society Record Series, 37 (Nottingham, 1988). Other examples are: *Derbyshire Hearth Tax Assessments 1662-70*, ed.by D. G. Edwards, Derbyshire Record Society, 7 (1982); C. A. F. Meekings, *Dorset Hearth Tax Assessments, 1662-1664* (Dorchester, 1951); T. L. Stoate, *Cornwall Hearth and Poll Taxes 1661-1664* (Bristol, 1981), and *Devon Hearth Tax Return, Lady Day 1674* (Bristol, 1982); P. Styles, 'Introduction to the Warwickshire hearth tax records', *Warwick County Records: Hearth Tax returns*, 1 (1957).

the introduction to all volumes in the series. It first appeared in the volume to Cambridgeshire.[5] Where local circumstances vary, this description has been modified.

Early modern taxation

Regular direct taxation in the form of income tax did not exist before the late eighteenth century. In the Tudor period two medieval taxes, the fifteenth and the lay subsidy, were still in use. The former was a quota tax raised from communities, while the latter was levied on individual wealth usually assessed on land or goods, but also on wages in 1523-4.[6] Both medieval and Tudor subsidy records have been analysed by historians.[7] Until the hearth taxes of the later Stuart period no other taxes were sufficiently comprehensive to be as useful as the Lay Subsidy of 1523-4 for the study of economic and local history.[8] Dr Husbands wrote in 1987 that 'alone amongst the mid and late-seventeenth century taxes, the hearth tax allows historians to draw general comparative conclusions about local economies'.[9]

Subsidies continued to be used in the early Stuart period. Charles I introduced the much disliked Ship Money, but, as its threshold was high, its records are much less full than those of the subsidies. Taxation was heavy during the Civil War and Commonwealth, but its records are few. Another new tax at this time was the Excise, first introduced in 1643 and revived at the Restoration to compensate the Crown for the loss of taxes such as feudal dues and the revenue from the Court of Wards. Between 1641 and 1702 a number of poll taxes were levied. The first, in 1641, was raised to enable Charles I to pay off the Scottish army occupying parts of northern England. The next poll tax, in 1660, was similar in that its purpose was to pay the arrears due to the army and navy as a necessary step to their disbandment.[10] Two useful studies of seventeenth-century taxation are C. D. Chandaman's study of the post-Restoration public

---

[5] *Cambridgeshire Hearth Tax, Michaelmas 1664*, ed. by Nesta Evans, British Record Society, Hearth Tax Series I (London, 2000).

[6] Richard Hoyle, *Tudor Taxation Records* (London, 1994), pp.1-3.

[7] R. E. Glasscock, *The Lay Subsidy of 1334*, British Academy Records of Social and Economic History, n.s. 2 (1975); John Sheail, *The Regional Distribution of Wealth in England as Indicated in the 1524/5 Lay Subsidy Returns*, ed. by R.W. Hoyle, List and Index Society, Special Series, 28. 1 and 28. 2, and 29. 1 and 29. 2 (Kew, 1998).

[8] Unfortunately, as discussed below, p. xxxiii, the lay subsidy returns for Kent are very imperfect.

[9] C. Husbands, 'Regional change in a pre-industrial economy: wealth and population in England in the sixteenth and seventeenth centuries', *Journal of Historical Geography*, 13 (1987), 348-49.

[10] T. Arkell, 'An examination of the Poll taxes of the later seventeenth century, the Marriage Duty Act and Gregory King' in *Surveying the People*, p. 142. Pre-1660 tax returns are listed in J. Gibson and A. Dell, *The Protestation Returns 1641-42 and other contemporary listings* (FFHS, 1995), and for 1660-on in J. Gibson, *The Hearth Tax and other later Stuart Tax Lists and the Association Oath Rolls* (FFHS, 2nd edition, 1996).

revenues, and M. J. Braddick's research on the rise of the 'tax state' based on the two counties of Cheshire and Norfolk.[11]

The Administration of the Hearth Tax

The English hearth tax was a major source of government revenue levied twice yearly at Lady Day and Michaelmas from 1662 to 1689. Between 1666 and 1669 and from 1674 to 1684 the collection of the tax was farmed out, and from 1684 to 1689 it was carried out by a Commission which managed both the Excise and the Hearth Tax. Very few returns of named taxpayers survive from these three periods, although some lists of the sums of money collected exist.

Most of the surviving returns for 1662-66 and 1669-74 are to be found in the Public Record Office. It was only during these years that the documents had to be returned to Quarter Sessions and central Government. The hearth tax was administered county by county, and two copies of each return were made, one of which was enrolled for Quarter Sessions while the other was sent to the Exchequer. It is the latter which are now in the Public Record Office. Far fewer of the Quarter Sessions' copies have survived, and those which do, like the assessment published here for Kent, are to be found in county record offices and other local archive repositories.[12]

Initially the returns consisted of the assessment lists of taxpayers with the number of their hearths, and a separate return of the sums actually collected.[13] However, from Michaelmas 1664 to Lady Day 1666 and from Michaelmas 1669 to Lady Day 1674 the returns generally combined the assessment with the return of money collected. The returns were made to the Exchequer for auditing, and all those which survive in the Public Record Office are catalogued under E179, together with the records of other taxes. Since 1995, a major relisting of all taxation records held in this class has been in progress, and many documents, which previously were not easily identifiable, have been made accessible.

Meekings and Styles[14] agreed that Sir William Petty was 'one of the progenitors'[15] of the new tax, but the former pointed out that the idea was not original, for similar taxes were already being levied in France and the United Provinces. Petty, who was one of those

[11] C. D. Chandaman, *English Public Revenue 1660-1688* (Oxford, 1975), and M. J. Braddick, *Parliamentary Taxation in Seventeenth-Century England* (Woodbridge, 1994).

[12] The Irish hearth tax returns have survived for the 1660s for about half the counties, but the rest are lost. In 1691 the Scottish Parliament introduced a hearth tax which, like the Irish hearth taxes, continued to be levied until the late eighteenth century.

[13] Arkell, 'Printed Instructions' in *Surveying the People*, p. 41.

[14] Meekings, *Dorset*, and Styles, *Warwickshire.*

[15] Meekings, *Dorset*, p. xii.

supporting the introduction of new kinds of taxes, set out the arguments in favour of the hearth tax in his 'Treatise of Taxes and Contributions', written in 1662.[16] Petty's 'Treatise' provides evidence of contemporary discussion of the principles and theory of taxation. The events of the years leading up to the Civil War had shown that reform of taxation was a necessity. After the Restoration, the three main sources of ordinary revenue were customs and excise, and the hearth tax. Direct taxation was reserved for extraordinary expenditure such as financing war. Petty regarded the hearth tax as a form of excise, on the grounds that the number of hearths in a house could be seen as a reflection of the occupier's purchasing power. Householders, on the other hand, saw the hearth tax as a levy like the poll tax, but a permanent one.

Samuel Pepys wrote in his diary on 3 March 1662: 'I am told that this day the Parliament hath voted 2s per annum for every chimny in England, as a constant Revenue for ever to the Crowne'.[17] The Act did not receive the royal assent until May. The hearth tax was introduced in 1662[18] as part of the financial settlement of the Restoration and continued to be levied twice a year at the rate of one shilling per hearth each six months until 1689. Like the Excise, this new tax was intended to finance the conduct of normal government business by the king.

Macaulay propagated the traditional Whig view of the hearth tax as oppressive, but this was not entirely accurate. William II ordered its abolition as a political move to gain popular support, but a few years later he found it necessary to replace it with the almost equally obnoxious Window Tax. On 8 March 1689 John Evelyn wrote in his diary 'The Hearth Tax was remitted for ever: but what intended to supply it, besids great Taxes on land: is not named'.[19] It is ironic that at the point when the hearth tax was abolished, it was at last being efficiently administered and producing the long hoped for yield.[20]

The 1662 Act made existing local officials responsible for the collection of the tax under the supervision of justices of the peace, the clerk of the peace and the sheriff. Householders were given six days notice to make a written and signed return of their fire hearths and stoves. Kilns, blowing houses, stamps, furnaces, and private ovens in houses already charged were exempted from the tax, but blacksmiths'

[16] *Economic Writings of Sir William Petty*, ed. by C. H. Hull, 2 vols (Cambridge, 1899).

[17] *The Shorter Pepys*, ed. by Robert Latham (London, 1985), p. 183.

[18] 14 Charles II, c.10.

[19] *The Diary of John Evelyn*, ed. by Guy de la Bédoyère (Bangor, 1994), p. 364.

[20] *Derbyshire Hearth Tax Assessments, 1662-70*, ed. by D. G. Edwards, Derbyshire Record Society, 7 (1982), p.xiii.

forges and bakers' ovens were not. No instructions were given about returns from illiterate householders, a fact which caused difficulties in Kent.[21] These returns were collated by the petty constables before being enrolled at Quarter Sessions as the assessment for the tax. The high constables were only involved in the collection of the money raised by the hearth tax, which remained a separate process from the assessment until the revising Act of 1663.

Within four months of its introduction Pepys was writing, on 30 June 1662, about the discontent created by the new tax: 'They clamour against the Chimny-money and say they will not pay it without force'.[22] One of the chief reasons for the dislike of the new tax was the right given to constables to check the returns by entering houses, although only in the day time.

The collectors of the tax were permitted to subtract a poundage from the money they collected: twopence in the pound for petty constables, a penny for high constables, and fourpence for sheriffs, from which a penny had to be paid to the clerk of the peace. This was an inadequate reward for the amount of work involved, and probably goes some way to explain the disappointing financial returns from the first collection at Michaelmas 1662. Meekings mentions a memorandum criticising the manner in which the tax was levied under the 1662 Act. It can be found in PRO E179/159, and although undated 'may be safely placed in June or July 1663'.[23] It is particularly critical of the arrangements for collecting the tax, recommending the use of 'constant receivers' in the place of local amateur officials. The lack of control over these is a major reason for the low returns in the early years of the tax. In the seventeenth century there was no means of accurately forecasting the yield of taxes, and in 1662 the House of Commons overestimated the yield of the hearth tax.

The 1663 Act 'for the better ordering & collecting the Revenue arising by the Hearth Money'[24] concentrated on under-assessment rather than on failures in collecting the tax. The checking process was supposedly tightened, and petty constables were instructed to write their assessments in a book or roll in two columns headed 'chargeable' and 'non-chargeable', giving the names and hearths of both those liable and not liable to the tax and identifying the owners and hearth numbers of empty properties. An extra check was introduced at hundred level, as these books or rolls had to be checked by the high

---

[21] See below, pp. civ-cv.
[22] *Shorter Pepys*, p. 210.
[23] *Surrey Hearth Tax 1664*, ed. by C. A. F. Meekings, Surrey Record Society, 17 (1940), pp. xxv-xxvi.
[24] 15 Charles II, c.13.

constable before being signed by the justices of the peace. The clerk of the peace had to make a county copy of the enrolled new assessment, as well as the Exchequer duplicate. This new assessment was generally used for the Lady Day 1664 collection. No attempt was made to reform the sheriff's administration of the tax and this led to the failure of the 1663 Act.

When Charles II opened the new session of Parliament on 21 March 1664, he pointed out that the revenue from the hearth tax had declined and added 'Men build fast enough'. The King asked Parliament to 'let Me have the Collecting and Husbanding of it by My own Officers; and then I doubt not but to improve that Receipt, and will be cozened of as little as I can'.[25] The new Act became law on 17 May 1664.[26] Clarendon was impressed by the new Act and in his autobiography called it 'a very good additional bill for the chimney money, which made that revenue much more considerable'.[27]

One of the principal features of the new Act was the replacement of the sheriffs by specially appointed receivers. Their salary was one shilling in the pound, but this included the payments they had to make to sub-collectors. They had to deposit bonds as security against default in the King's Remembrancer's office; the amount of security was based on the value of the 1662 assessment.

The receivers were appointed by the Exchequer Commission set up to administer the 1664 Act; it also instructed the Exchequer auditors to make copies of the 1662 assessments for the receivers and to send them a set of printed instructions setting out the procedures for the assessment, collecting and accounting.[28] These instructions show that the government was determined to tighten Exchequer control over the administration and collection of the hearth tax with the aim of improving its yield. With a few exceptions there was one receiver for each county and most county towns were joined to their county. A number of military men were appointed to receiverships, and it is probable that this was intended as a compensation for their losses in the Civil War.[29] A discussion of the complex situation in Kent can be found below under the introduction to the manuscript.[30]

It was intended that the new officials should use the Lady Day 1664 assessment as a working document, but in fact it was the original assessment made in 1662 which was used. It was realised too late that

[25] *Lords Journals*, XI, p. 583.
[26] 16 Charles II, c.3.
[27] Meekings, *Dorset*, p. xviii.
[28] Arkell, 'Printed instructions' in *Surveying the People*, pp. 41-54, 55-64.
[29] Calendars of Treasury Books, 1667-8.
[30] See below, pp. cviii-cx.

the most recent returns would not reach the Exchequer in time for them to be copied out and sent to the receivers for the Michaelmas 1664 collection. The instructions sent with the 1662 assessment urged the receivers to 'endeavour to procure ... Copies of the Taxation for the half year ended 25th of March 1664'.[31] Most of the receivers failed to do this and were faced with using instructions which referred specifically to the Lady Day 1664 return. Not surprisingly, this led to the failure of the attempt to achieve national uniformity in the returns, and accounts for the variations found in printed returns from different counties. A further difficulty for the receivers resulted from their late appointment, which led to them being unable to make their first assessment until after the date when the Michaelmas 1664 collection was due. As a result they had to collect the money retrospectively, and their assessments became a combined assessment and return.[32]

The system of collection was stricter under the 1664 Act than it had been under the two earlier Acts. Self-assessment by occupiers was replaced by collection by the Receiver's officers, often called 'Chimney Men'. They were to collect the tax from each house, and could levy the duty by distress on the goods of anyone who refused to pay after one hour. When a distress was made the petty or parish constable had to be present, and an appeal against taking a distress could be made to one justice of the peace. Anyone who violently resisted the chimney men could be sentenced to a month's imprisonment by a single justice. Although the constables were no longer the collectors of the tax, they, and the chimney men, were given the right to search every house once a year to find 'what Fire Hearthes or Stoves are increased or decreased since the former Certificate'.

One of the intentions of the Hearth Tax Act of 1664 was to prevent landlords from escaping payment of the tax by dividing a house into tenements, and then letting them to poor tenants. In 1663 this had been seen as a problem in some parts of Kent.[33] The 1662 Act had stipulated that if a house was worth not more than twenty shillings a year on the full improved rent, the occupant was exempt from paying the tax unless he owned land or tenements worth over twenty shillings a year, or land, tenements, or goods of the value of at least £10. Sir William Petty saw it as essential to the success of the hearth tax that landlords should be made responsible for its payment when their tenants were excused through poverty. Petty called the tax 'an "Accumulated Excise" levied on a necessary commodity closely related

---

[31] Arkell, 'Printed instructions' in *Surveying the People*, pp. 51-3.
[32] *The Glamorgan Hearth Tax Assessment of 1670*, ed. by Elizabeth Parkinson, South Wales Record Society (Cardiff, 1994), pp. xiv-xv.
[33] See below, pp. l, lii-liii.

to a man's general consumption and not "a particular Excise upon but one onely commodity, namely Housing".[34] After the new Act of 1664 there are many references in the fourth column of the return to landlords who have let the land away from the house, or have divided a house into several dwellings occupied by tenants exempt from the tax. Where this happened the landlord had to pay the tax. The owners of empty houses were also named, as were absentee owners of land or houses. A few owners lived outside the county.

Further modifications to the earlier Acts were concerned with liability to pay. Although this does not concern the Lady Day return published here, after May 1664, everyone with more than two hearths had to pay even if otherwise entitled to exemption. If the owner had let the land away from the house, so reducing its value to under twenty shillings, or if he sublet to poor tenants exempt from the tax, it was he who paid; and anyone moving into a new house was liable for the whole six months tax due at the succeeding Lady Day or Michaelmas. Beckett mistakenly stated that all houses with *two* or more hearths were to be taxed, regardless of the standing of their occupants.[35] This led him to suggest 'a social acceptance that the less prosperous members of society were generally to be found in one-chimney houses'.[36] It is true that the majority of those exempt from paying hearth tax lived in one-hearth houses, but by no means all did so, particularly in Kent where, before the new Act of 1664, exempt households often included those with three, four, or even more hearths. It is therefore likely that there are regional variations in the proportions of taxpayers and exempt living in households of different sizes.[37]

In spite of the reforms it appears that the tax continued to produce less than was expected. On 3 September 1665, Pepys was worrying about where the money would come from to pay the fleet should the Dutch attack: 'it is said that at this day our Lord Treasurer cannot tell what the profits of Chimny money is; what it comes to per annum - nor whether that or any other part of the Revenue be duly gathered as ought'.[38] The Lord Treasurer was Thomas Wriothesley, second Earl of Southampton.

The new administration of the hearth tax did not achieve what had been hoped of it, for the receivers took even longer than had the sheriffs to clear their accounts. The effects of the plague outbreak in 1665-6 and the Dutch war of 1665-67 may also have had some bearing

[34] Hull, *Economic Writings*, I, p.94.
[35] Webster, *Nottinghamshire*, pp. ix, xi.
[36] Ibid., p. xxv.
[37] See below, pp. li-lii.
[38] *Shorter Pepys*, pp. 520-1.

on these delays. This is probably one of the main reasons why the hearth tax was farmed out in 1666. The farming out of the collection of the tax from Lady Day 1666 to Lady Day 1669 'proved to be a total failure', and was made worse by the destruction of the Hearth Tax Office in the fire of London.[39] These three years are the period of what Braddick called 'hearth tax disorders', marked by riots against the tax in a number of counties.[40] From 1670 the administration of the tax was far more efficient than it had been earlier. The receivers, who administered the tax from Michaelmas 1669 to Lady Day 1674, and their sub-collectors, were under the firm control of the office of the Agents for the Hearth Tax.[41] The final period of the hearth tax, from Michaelmas 1684, was the most successful in terms of sums raised. Hitherto, the annual return had averaged £150,000 a year, but in its final years the yield rose to £216, 000 per annum.[42] Its continuing unpopularity led to its abolition early in the reign of William and Mary, who were anxious to win support for their rule.

One major change in the instructions for 1684 was the requirement to list the names of inhabitants, and empty houses, in topographical order.[43] This was rightly seen as the best way of preventing evasion of the tax and omissions from the lists. Had this been done when the Exchequer was in charge of administering the hearth tax, modern historians could use the returns to follow the collectors' routes. These are exceptions, for this was already possible in Warwickshire in the early 1670s, as well as for the 1678 return for the City of Worcester, which is 'virtually a gazetteer of all the households in the city in 1678'.[44]

The hearth tax lists need to be used with care, for the deceptively simple information contained within them is full of inconsistencies. Some of these arise from the changing administration of the tax, together with the differing interpretations of the rules within the separately administered counties and cities. By the fifth collection at Michaelmas 1664, the rules had been changed twice, together with a change of officials and some change of administrative areas. By the time of the Michaelmas 1670 collection, the increasing standardisation was not necessarily reflected in the county lists, which still showed an inconsistency in recording those not liable. In addition,

[39] Arkell, 'Printed instructions' in *Surveying the People*, p. 43.
[40] Braddick, pp. 252-66.
[41] Ibid., p. 44.
[42] Ibid., p. 44.
[43] Tom Arkell (pers. comm., 1999) suggests this may not be an innovation, but a continuation of the innovations mentioned below. Elizabeth Parkinson (pers. comm.) has found evidence that topographical listing was a pre-1684 innovation in Middlesex.
[44] Arkell, 'Printed instructions' in *Surveying the People*, p. 53, quoting Meekings and others.

the surviving documents represent different stages of the collection procedure: assessments of taxpayers, returns of those who had paid, and fair copies of working papers compiled by many individuals, to name but a few. A discussion of the changing administration of the tax with its resultant effect on the recorded data is the subject of a forthcoming thesis.[45]

[45] E. Parkinson, 'The Administration of the Hearth Tax 1662-6', forthcoming doctoral thesis, the University of Surrey Roehampton. We are grateful to Elizabeth Parkinson for providing this paragraph.

THE KENT HEARTH TAX RECORDS: CONTEXT AND ANALYSIS

By Sarah Pearson

HISTORICAL BACKGROUND

The Administrative Boundaries used for the Hearth Tax in Kent

Since pre Conquest times the administrative unit in Kent for judicial and taxation purposes was the lathe. By the seventeenth century their number had been reduced to five: Sutton at Hone in the west, Aylesford and Scray, running north-south, across the centre of the county, St Augustine in the north-east, and Shepway in the south-east, covering much of Romney Marsh and adjoining areas. The lathes were divided into hundreds, of which, in 1664, there were sixty-four. Below the hundreds were the parishes or boroughs (Map 1). But some of Kent lay in separate jurisdictions. The major one was the group of Cinque Ports and their associates, which had always claimed exemption from county taxation, and are seldom included in county returns. In addition there was the City and County of Canterbury, and several liberties, including the liberty of Romney Marsh, which spread over the eastern half of the marsh, incorporating the whole hundred of Worth. These are mapped and identified on Map 1. A few of the smaller liberties were included in the hearth tax for Lady Day 1664, but the majority were not, and have therefore not been published here. However, Tenterden and Canterbury City and County, which were separately assessed, have been published here as appendices.[46]

The partial nature of the coverage means that the 1664 returns do not provide a complete picture of the county.[47] In addition, there are considerable problems in correlating the information with known places. The unit for collection by the borsholder or petty constable was

---

[46] The list of jurisdictions which were not included in the assessment for Lady Day 1664 can be found in Appendix II. For the Tenterden and Canterbury City and County assessments, see Appendices III and IV.

[47] In 1664 the Exchequer received payment for 8944 hearths in the Cinque Ports, and for 2695 in the City and County of Canterbury (see below pp. cix-cx and Appendix V). Together these covered most of the missing areas. Calculating the number of hearths which were not charged, and the number of households overall, cannot be precise. But on the basis of the figures from other older towns in the county (see p. xxxii, n. 61 and Table 1), it is likely that approximately 15,519 hearths in 5000 households, or 18 per cent of hearths and 16 per cent of households in the county, were not included in the Quarter Sessions returns.

either the parish or the borough. Where the final division was by
parish, the boundaries can probably be determined with some
accuracy. But in many hundreds the smallest unit was the borough, and
neither hundreds nor boroughs were necessarily coterminous with
ecclesiastical parishes. Ecclesiastical parishes may extend into two or
more hundreds (compare Map 1 with Map 13), and a borough may
cross a parish boundary. The boroughs have nothing to do with
ecclesiastical administration but are related to the earlier manorial
pattern of the county, in which the centre of the manor tended to lie in
the earliest settled region in the north, with outlying properties
elsewhere, notably in the marshes and Weald to the south. The result
was that medieval manors in Kent were seldom compact, but held
parcels of land in a number of places. The history and complexity of
the landholding pattern need not concern us here,[48] but it had
repercussions for taxation, for some of the outlying lands became
boroughs which were taxed with the hundred in which the original
manorial centre lay. An example is the borough of Kingsnorth, which
physically lies in Ulcombe parish south-east of Maidstone, in the
hundred of Eyhorne, but as late as 1664 was accounted part of the
hundred of Faversham several miles to the north. Another case, very
typical of the Weald, is the parish of Headcorn, which was divided
between the hundreds of Barkley, Calehill, Cranbrook and Eyhorne,
and included a detached portion of the hundred of Tenham, which also
lies on the north coast. Since the boroughs were used for administering
taxes, what mattered was not so much their boundaries, which are
seldom precisely known, but who lived within them.[49] Thus correlating
parishes with hearth tax units, and mapping the county for purposes of
analysing the tax, is extremely difficult.

The problems created by the use of hundreds and boroughs
were apparent even in the seventeenth century, for by that time these
administrative units were already all but obsolete. In the mid
seventeenth century, Sir Roger Twysden of *Roydon Hall* in East
Peckham parish was one of the justices of the peace for the southern
half of the lathe of Aylesford, and in September 1663 and January 1664,
in the notebook which he kept relating to his activities as a J.P., he
grumbled bitterly about the necessity to collect the tax in boroughs,

---

[48] See K. P. Witney, *The Jutish Forest* (London, 1976); A. Everitt, *Continuity and Colonization: the
Evolution of Kentish Settlement* (Leicester, 1986); F. R. H. Du Boulay, *The Lordship of
Canterbury* (London and Edinburgh, 1966); Michael Zell, *Industry in the Countryside*
(Cambridge, 1994), pp. 10-15.

[49] The only early borough map so far discovered for Kent is a 1742 map of Headcorn borough
which lies in Headcorn parish, but is accounted in Tenham hundred (CKS: U390 P). This, like
many other boroughs forming detached portions of hundreds, is mapped on the 1st edn 6in.
O.S. map.

and claimed he had tried, to no avail, to get the tax collected by parish in a more logical fashion. He was particularly concerned about the borough of Oxenhoath in West Peckham parish, which physically lay within his jurisdiction but was to be collected by the Commissioners for the northern half of the lathe since, despite lying seventeen or eighteen miles away, it was accounted part of the hundred of Hoo. In his view the taxpayers might very well escape paying, just as they often escaped watching and warding and other duties - though in fact the twenty-one households in the borough paid up, and did not escape on this occasion.[50] In the tables and distribution maps in this volume information from detached boroughs, such as Oxenhoath, have been recorded and totalled within the hundred in which they physically lie, for only then can any sense be made of the pattern of hearths across the county.

Collection by hundred and borough makes it extremely difficult today to publish the information from the Kent hearth tax in meaningful tabular or map form. One problem is that it is not easy to locate all the boroughs. Many of them have names which are no longer used; not only are they missing from modern maps, but they were also not mentioned by Hasted in the late eighteenth century, and are not found in sources for place names in Kent.[51] A second problem is that even if the boroughs could have been mapped, they are too small for purposes of statistical analysis, while the hundreds, which have therefore been chosen as the main working unit, are often on the large side. Thirdly, although the hundreds have been shown on maps since the seventeenth century, most of the early maps are somewhat schematic in outline and do not include the detached portions, which are critical in analysing the hearth tax. Thus the hundred boundaries used for the base map in this volume have been taken from the first edition six inch Ordnance Survey maps, surveyed between 1853 and 1870, preceding the rationalisation of the later nineteenth century when the detached portions of both ecclesiastical parishes and hundreds were reassigned.[52] Even so, it should be noted that by this time there had already been changes to both hundred and parish outlines. Some places are shown in one hundred on the map, but are included in another in the hearth tax, and some detached boroughs could not be found at all. To help the modern reader, a list correlating boroughs, parishes and hundreds and noting the most obvious discrepancies is

---

[50] Notebook of Sir Roger Twysden as justice of the peace, 1635 -72, CKS: U47/47 01, pp. 59-60.

[51] E. Hasted, *The History and Topographical Survey of the County of Kent*, 12 volumes (1797-1801, 2nd edn reprinted Canterbury, 1972); J. K. Wallenberg, *The Place-Names of Kent*, (Uppsala, 1934).

[52] These changes are discussed in the Victoria History of the Counties of England, *Kent*, III (London, 1932), pp. 356-70.

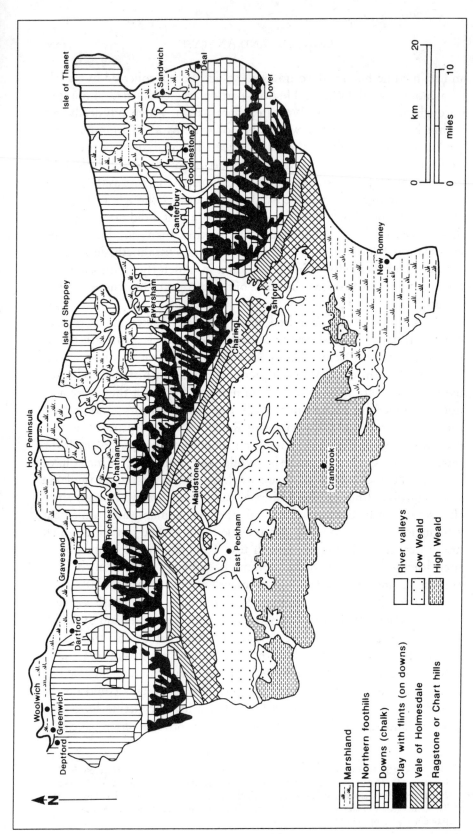

MAP 2 The Geographical Regions of Kent

Partially based, with kind permission, on the map of geographical regions of Kent in *The Medieval Houses of Kent* (fig. 3), published by RCHME (HMSO 1994).

included as Appendix VII.

The Regions of Kent

The historic county of Kent had just under 1,000,000 acres and was the ninth largest in England.[53] It is a county of contrasts and all writers remark upon the diversity and variety of the landscape.[54] Its geology and soils form east-west bands (Map 2), each influencing the pattern of agriculture, industry and society. The long coastline and various estuaries provided opportunities for fishing and harbours from which produce could easily be transported to feed the growing city of London. The north coast is fringed by good grazing marshes, to the south of which lies excellent agricultural land: to the east, and on the Hoo peninsula further west, rich loams produced some of the best grain growing conditions in England, with large open fields separated by few hedges. In the middle of the north coast the soils were eminently suited to growing hops and fruit. Further south, the land rises to the North Downs, the soil remaining suitable for arable cultivation almost to the top, where surface clay-with-flints makes agriculture difficult. Here poorer grazing was mixed with woodland, much of it coppiced for a variety of purposes. Descending from the scarp of the Downs, a string of settlements lay on the spring line bordering the narrow and fertile Vale of Holmesdale floored with gault clay. This in turn is quickly succeeded by the sandstone of the greensand ridge, known as the ragstone or Chart hills. To the south east of Maidstone quarrying was an important industry, and in this central section of the county the greensand ridge and its southern slopes have some of the best soils in the South-East for mixed arable, fruit and pastoral farming; to east and west the land is less productive, and was more likely to be pastoral. In places there were heathy commons, or the deer parks of the wealthy. To the south again, the heavy clays of the Low Weald were primarily pastoral, although all areas grew some crops. The High Weald beyond is a region of woods and small streams, studded with small enclosed fields, both its timber and water power being turned to advantage in the cloth and iron industries which developed in the fifteenth and sixteenth centuries. Finally, Romney Marsh lies in the south-east corner of the county, an

---

[53] C. W. Chalklin, *Seventeenth-Century Kent* (London, 1965), p. 7; VCH, III, p. 358.

[54] Chalklin, *Seventeenth-Century Kent*, pp.73-109; S. G. McCrae and C. P. Burnham, *The Rural Landscape of Kent* (Wye College, 1973), pp. 52-6, 113-20; A. Everitt, 'The making of the agrarian landscape of Kent', *Archaeologia Cantiana*, 92 (1976), pp. 1-31; J. Thirsk, 'The Farming Regions of England', in *The Agrarian History of England and Wales*, ed. by J. Thirsk, 4 (Cambridge, 1967), pp. 55-64; and B. Short, 'The South-East: Kent, Surrey and Sussex' in *The Agrarian History*, 5 i (1984), pp. 270-313.

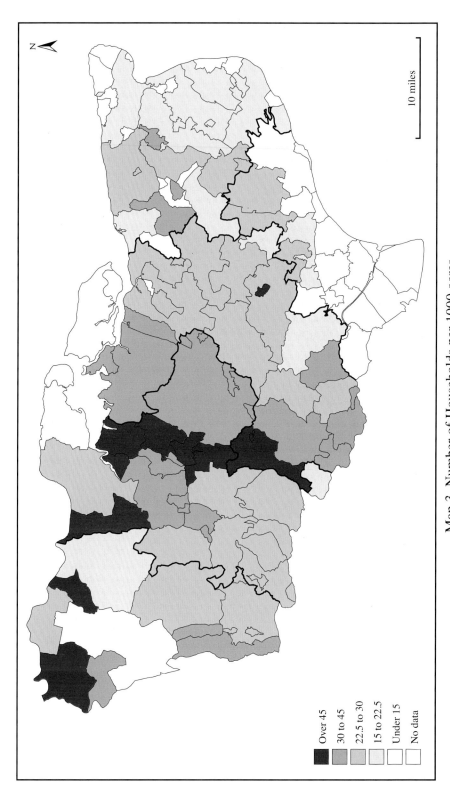

Over 45

30 to 45

22.5 to 30

15 to 22.5

Under 15

No data

10 miles

Map 3. Number of Households per 1000 acres

unhealthy area which nonetheless provided superb grazing for fattening the livestock of farmers living in other parts of Kent.

The Hearth Tax as an Indication of the Density of Population

The early settlement history of the county, and the landholding patterns to which it gave rise, were inextricably woven into determining how population and employment developed in the various regions. In the early Middle Ages the manorial centres in the north were characterised by large and closely managed arable farms which, despite many changes, in essence survived into the seventeenth century. Initially the northern manors had extended their lands southwards to take advantage of abundant pasture and woodland. But gradually the south was permanently settled, and as lordship in the Weald was always light, this became a landscape of independent pastoral farmers, many of whom came to be engaged in various aspects of cloth production centred on Cranbrook in the High Weald (Map 2). The rise of prosperity in the Weald, brought about by the cloth industry in particular, can be seen in the changing distribution of population and wealth between the fourteenth and sixteenth centuries.

Comparison of the population figures, gleaned from the 1377 poll tax and mid sixteenth-century surveys, shows how the distribution of the population changed over two hundred years.[55] In the fourteenth century, population was densest along the north coast and around Maidstone. Central Kent and Romney Marsh had their fair share of people, but the least densely populated regions seem to have been the High Weald, west Kent, and the grain growing area to the east. The mid sixteenth-century figures are partial and difficult to interpret, particularly as no returns survive for the diocese of Rochester, west of the Medway. In the rest of Kent, population was still dense along the central section of the north coast and in the vicinity of Maidstone, while the north-east remained sparsely populated. But big changes had occurred in Romney Marsh, where few people were living by then, and in the High Weald, which by the mid sixteenth century was among the most densely populated areas of all.

In line with the rest of the country, the population of Kent grew rapidly during the later sixteenth and early seventeenth centuries. From around 80 - 90,000 in the mid sixteenth century it had risen to an estimated 130,000 in 1603, and to around 160,000 by the 1670s.[56] The sources for these figures are various. The 1664 hearth tax is among

---

[55] S. Pearson, *The Medieval Houses of Kent: an Historical Analysis* (RCHME, London, 1994), pp. 14-15, where full references are given.

[56] M. Dobson, 'Population, 1640-1831', in *The Economy of Kent, 1640-1914*, ed. by A. Armstrong, (KCC, Woodbridge, 1995), p. 11.

TABLE 1. HEARTHS IN TOWNS[1]

Town	Total entries[2]	Total hearths	1 hearth households No	1 hearth households %	2 hearth households No	2 hearth households %	3-4 hearth households No	3-4 hearth households %	5-9 hearth households No	5-9 hearth households %	10 + hearth households No	10 + hearth households %	Exempt households No	Exempt households %	Exempt hearths No	Exempt hearths %	Empty houses No	Empty houses %	Population[3]
Ashford	268	687	84	31.3	96	35.8	53	19.8	32	11.9	3	1.1	115	42.9	168	24.5	11	4.1	1139
Bromley	104	277	28	26.9	54	51.9	10	9.6	7	6.7	5	4.8	50	48.1	82	29.6	-	-	442
Chatham	437	1431	43	9.8	176	40.3	136	31.1	72	16.5	10	2.3	134	30.7	264	18.4	-	-	1857
Cranbrook	287	582	135	47.0	87	30.3	45	15.7	19	6.6	1	0.3	164	57.1	225	38.7	-	-	1220
Dartford	303	903	57	18.8	122	40.3	77	25.4	38	12.5	9	3.0	71	23.4	109	12.1	6	2.0	1288
Deptford	999	3270	115	11.5	369	36.9	342	34.2	141	14.1	32	3.2	337	33.7	721	22.0	97	9.7	4246
Gravesend[4]	553	1729	128	23.1	226	40.9	87	15.7	92	16.6	20	3.6	127	23.0	231	13.4	41	7.4	2350
Greenwich	659	2540	81	12.3	259	39.3	140	21.2	135	20.4	44	6.7	96	14.6	181	7.1	40	6.1	2801
Maidstone	802	2616	171	21.3	278	34.7	183	22.8	145	18.1	25	3.1	402	50.1	721	27.6	2	0.2	3409
Milton-next-Sittingbourne	206	551	50	24.3	69	33.5	63	30.6	23	11.2	1	0.4	65	31.6	101	18.3	12	5.8	875
Rochester	712	2378	123	17.3	224	31.5	219	30.8	121	17.0	25	3.5	250	35.1	468	19.7	35	4.9	3026
Sevenoaks	185	587	52	28.1	81	43.8	28	15.1	16	8.6	8	4.3	78	42.2	116	19.8	-	-	786
Tenterden	97	300	21	21.6	41	42.3	19	19.6	12	12.4	4	4.1	45	46.4	85	28.3	3	3.1	412
Tonbridge	142	354	47	33.1	50	35.2	30	21.1	13	9.2	2	1.4	70	49.3	107	30.2	4	2.8	603
West Malling	128	328	47	36.7	35	27.3	29	22.6	15	11.7	2	1.6	38	29.7	50	15.2	8	6.2	544
Westerham	161	508	46	28.6	58	36.0	28	17.4	22	13.7	7	4.3	85	52.8	145	28.5	-	-	684
Woolwich	280	775	48	17.1	121	43.2	76	27.1	30	10.7	5	1.8	35	12.5	49	6.3	13	4.6	1190
Totals	**6323**	**19816**	**1276**	**20.2**	**2346**	**37.1**	**1565**	**24.8**	**933**	**14.8**	**203**	**3.2**	**2162**	**34.2**	**3823**	**19.3**	**272**	**4.3**	

[1] Defining towns has never been easy, and the ones in this table are those which occur in the 1664 hearth tax and are accepted as towns by Chalklin in Armstrong, *The Economy of Kent*, pp. 205-13 and Appendix IIIA. Canterbury City, which was not included in the Quarter Sessions returns, and does not contain exemptions, is not strictly comparable with the other towns and is therefore discussed separately in Appendix V.

[2] Those entries which are left blank (e.g. 24 examples in Rochester) have been counted in this table as having one hearth.

[3] The population figure is the total number of households in 1664 multiplied by 4.25, the multiplier used in Armstrong, *Economy of Kent*, Appendix IIIA.

[4] Milton-next-Gravesend has been included with Gravesend, for as Hasted, *History of Kent*, III, p. 319 indicates, East Street in Gravesend, and the east side of High Street, lie in the parish of Milton. I am grateful to Terry Lawson for drawing this to my attention. The considerable discrepancy between the population calculated here and that listed in Armstrong, *Economy of Kent*, Appendix IIIA, may mean that Milton was not included in that figure.

them, but given its incomplete nature, it cannot be used on its own. By the later seventeenth century the population had ceased to grow, and the next estimate, for 1700, shows a drop to 150,000. Although the 1664 hearth tax only records a moment in time, it can be used to illustrate some of the changes which were taking place during the seventeenth century. Map 3 shows the density of households per 1000 acres in 1664. The lowest population densities, with fewer than fifteen households per 1,000 acres, lay on the fringes of the county, in the marshes and their hinterlands. In addition, the rural areas of east Kent were generally thinly populated, as they had been since the Middle Ages. In contrast, a central band running from the north coast to the Sussex border had over thirty households per 1000 acres. The northern half had always been densely settled, but the population of the southern half had grown during the sixteenth century as people flocked into the High Weald to work in the cloth industry. Although by the later seventeenth century the industry was in decline and people were moving away to find work elsewhere, it is clear that many still remained.[57] At the same time, the population along much of the north coast had increased as the London fringes expanded and the naval and dockland towns began to employ more and more people, so that some of the northern hundreds further west had over forty-five households per 1000 acres.[58]

Kent has normally been considered an agricultural county, and in the Middle Ages there were few towns in the county apart from Canterbury, Maidstone, Rochester and the Cinque Ports. But during the sixteenth and seventeenth centuries the situation changed. Proximity to London and the Continent, and the opportunities for ports and docks provided by the extensive coastline, gave rise to significant urban growth around the Thames and the Medway. By the end of the century one third of the population lived in towns, both old and new, and this is where the highest population densities of all are to be found.[59]

The northern towns have not been distinguished from their hinterlands in Map 3, but the urban population has been shown in more detail in Table 1. This indicates that the largest concentration in the 1664 hearth tax occurs in Deptford, where many of those living in the 999 households found employment connected with the Royal

---

[57] P. Clark, 'Migration in England during the late seventeenth and early eighteenth centuries,' *Past and Present*, 83 (1979), 57-90; M. J. Dobson, 'The last hiccup of the old demographic regime: population stagnation and decline in late seventeenth and early eighteenth-century south-east England', *Continuity and Change*, 4 (1989), 395-428.

[58] D. C. Coleman, 'Naval dockyards under the later Stuarts', *Economic History Review*, Ser. 2, 6 (1953-4), 134-55; Dobson, 'The last hiccup'.

[59] Chalklin, 'The towns', in Armstrong, *Economy of Kent*, p. 206

Naval Dockyard and a number of private yards involved in overseas trade. If, as has been suggested, each urban household averaged 4.25 persons, then the population of the town was somewhere in the order of 4246, a number which is estimated to have risen to 6625 by 1676, when it was not much lower than the 7431 estimated for Canterbury at that date.[60] Unfortunately, the figures for Canterbury in 1664 are incomplete, but the density of households in Westgate hundred, which included parts of the City, is one of the highest in the county, with sixty-six households per 1000 acres. In 1664 the next most populous town was Maidstone, with 802 households, and this was followed by Rochester, with 712. Maidstone was the centre for business and trade for a large part of central Kent, while Rochester was a cathedral city of long standing, and also benefited from the growing naval dockyard at Chatham. Chatham had 437 households and Gravesend, which likewise had a flourishing port, had 553. Greenwich, with 659 households, was rather different from the other northern towns, for it not only had a number of private docks, but it had a palace and became an attractive and fashionable place of residence for the many wealthy people who were moving out of London at this time. The older ports of Dover and Sandwich, although not included in the 1664 figures, were probably of much the same size, with between 500 and 700 households.[61] Cranbrook, meanwhile, had only 287 households. The 1664 hearth tax seems to catch the moment when the older urban centres were being overtaken by the new towns,[62] for by 1700 not only Deptford, but also Chatham and Greenwich, had overtaken Maidstone, Rochester, Dover and Sandwich.[63] A number of smaller towns, made up of 100 - 300 households, are scattered throughout the county.

---

[60] 4.25 is the multiplier used for the towns in Armstrong, *Economy of Kent*, Appendix IIIA, from which the 1676 figure for Deptford and Canterbury are taken. But see this volume, Appendix V for alternative figures for Canterbury.

[61] The numbers are based on the 1676 population figures in Armstrong, *Economy of Kent*, Appendix IIIA. However, alternative figures may be arrived at from the total number of hearths charged in these towns in 1662 (see below, p. cx). At that date, 2208 hearths were charged in Dover and 2033 in Sandwich. On the basis of the figures in Table 1 it appears that on average 25 per cent of hearths (not households) in the older towns were not charged, so that the chargeable hearths, multiplied by 4/3, suggest total hearth numbers of 2944 and 2711. Table 1 also suggests that in towns as a whole the average number of hearths per household was 3.1, from which it may be inferred that there were roughly 950 households in Dover, and 875 in Sandwich. The disparity between these figures and those arrived at using the Compton Census could be accounted for by the fact that the areas covered by the two calculations were different. Thus great caution should be taken in using any of these figures.

[62] The 'new' towns as used here, in which the number of hearths exempted averaged only 15 percent, are Chatham, Dartford, Deptford, Gravesend, Greenwich and Woolwich.

[63] Armstrong, *Economy of Kent*, Appendix IIIA

The Hearth Tax and the Distribution of Wealth

Population density and wealth are often considered to be closely related, and up to a point the relationship can be demonstrated in Kent. In 1334 the lay subsidy shows that the wealthiest part of the county was the most densely populated central section of the north coast, in the hundreds of Milton, Tenham and Faversham. This was followed by the central part of the county around Maidstone, and by the north-east, which was relatively wealthy despite the low density of population. West Kent and other parts of the east came third; while most of the High and Low Weald were classed among the poorest areas of England. Two hundred years later, the Tudor subsidies of the early sixteenth century show that the wealthiest part of the county, returning over 60 shillings per square mile, was a broad swathe across central and north-east Kent, between Maidstone and Thanet, stretching in the centre as far south as Tenterden. The High Weald to the south-west of Tenterden hundred, the downland area south of Canterbury, and most of the north-west, returned over 50 shillings per square mile, leaving only the western Weald, together with Romney Marsh and the eastern half of Shepway lathe, in the vicinity of Folkestone, returning less. The greatest change was in the situation of the High Weald. By the 1520s, despite the fact that some documents are lost and there are no figures for the Cinque Ports (which seriously distorts the figures for the east), Kent was among the wealthiest counties of England.[64]

Map 4, which illustrates the number of hearths per 1000 acres, should give some idea of the distribution of wealth in 1664, and it would certainly be the aspect which concerned the Exchequer. One might expect that hearth numbers would reflect the agriculture of the county. But whereas the agriculture largely follows the topography, as illustrated in Map 2, changing from arable and fruit in the north, through corn and sheep, to corn and cattle, to the primarily pastoral land of the south,[65] these east-west bands are hardly reflected in the distribution of hearths shown in Map 4. Instead the county is divided into zones which run from north to south rather than east to west, very much in line with the distribution of households shown in Map 3. The west is the most varied area, probably because urban and rural regions were undergoing very different experiences. The developing

---

[64] The 1524/5 lay subsidies, which are usually used to indicate wealth, are very incomplete for Kent, and it is only possible to get an idea of the overall amounts of tax paid in the different regions. For the details see Sheail, *Regional Distribution of Wealth*, 28 (1998), pp. 105-08, 159-67. For comparison of the subsidies, see summary and references in Pearson, *Medieval Houses*, pp. 12-14.

[65] G. Mingay, 'Agriculture' in Armstrong, *Economy of Kent*, fig. 5; B. Short in Thirsk, *Agrarian History*, 5 i, pp. 270-313 and fig. 9.i.

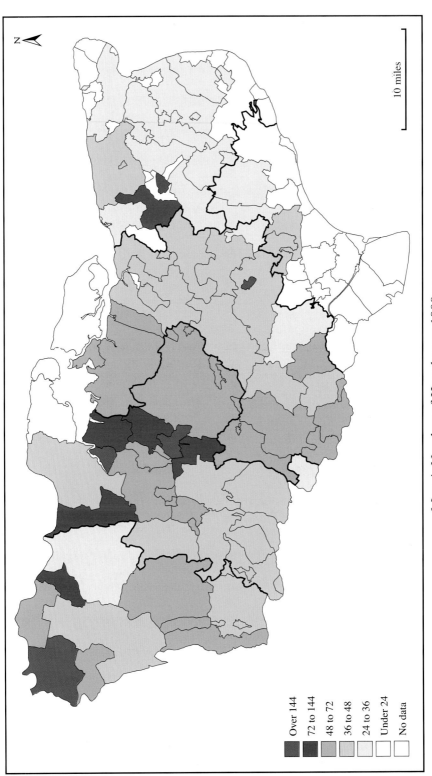

Over 144

72 to 144

48 to 72

36 to 48

24 to 36

Under 24

No data

10 miles

N

Map 4. Number of Hearths per 1000 acres

towns of the north and north-west, which unfortunately are not here distinguished from their hinterlands, had the greatest density of hearths, with the whole of Blackheath hundred registering over 144 hearths per 1000 acres, and several others having over 72 hearths per 1000 acres. The same high numbers apply to the region between Maidstone and Chatham. This is followed by parts of the south-west, and again by a striking north-south swathe in the centre of the county. In these areas the high number of households shown in Map 3 is mirrored by 48 - 72 hearths per 1000 acres. The change to both population and wealth in the central High Weald since the Middle Ages can be almost wholly put down to the rise of the cloth industry, which began in the fifteenth century, and peaked in the sixteenth. At the top, it produced a number of wealthy clothiers, at the bottom it provided a living for a growing and dependent population. By 1664 its heyday was over and considerable poverty was reported around Cranbrook, but there was still a very high density of houses and hearths in the region.

To either side of the central section are large areas with 36 - 48 hearths per 1000 acres, again stretching from north to south. Apart from the Hoo peninsula and the Isle of Sheppey, the lowest density of hearths lies in east Kent. Lowest of all are the Downs behind Dover and Folkestone and the fringes of Romney Marsh, which had never shown much sign of wealth, largely because the good grazing for which the area was famous tended to be owned by those who lived away from the unhealthy marshes. However the downland, dipslope and lowlands further north, which had returned 50 or more shillings per square mile in 1525, also had under 36 hearths per 1000 acres. Of course, the map would not be quite the same if the Cinque Ports were included, for there would be high numbers in Dover, Sandwich and the more urbanised parts of the Isle of Thanet. But rural east Kent, both north and south, is marked by fewer hearths per 1000 acres than most of the rest of Kent. This seems to reflect the disparity of wealth and population noted in earlier periods, although comparison of Maps 3 and 4 indicates that a few of the rural hundreds in the east, such as Downhamford, Kinghamford and Loningborough, had a low density of hearths despite a relatively high density of households;[66] a situation which was probably accounted for by a high proportion of single-hearth houses. Thus in this region, in 1664 as at earlier periods, wealth and population did not necessarily go hand in hand.

---

[66] M. Dobson, *Contours of Death in Early Modern England* (Cambridge, 1997), fig. 2.3, illustrates a relatively high population in the same part of east Kent in 1676.

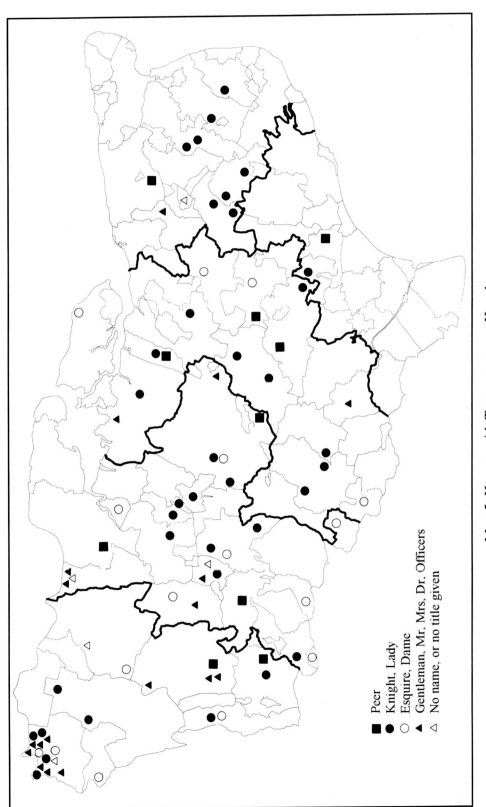

Map 5. Houses with Twenty or more Hearths

Peer

Knight, Lady

Esquire, Dame

Gentleman, Mr, Mrs, Dr, Officers

No name, or no title given

If one breaks this down a little further, it begins to make more sense. Soils in Kent are extremely varied, and the east-west bands of the topographical map do not give rise to uniform agriculture across the county: there is, in fact, generally less high-quality agricultural land to the west of the Medway than to its east; the Chart hills and High and Low Weald all divide into three, with better quality soils in the centre than to either side; the central area, particularly north of the Downs, became famous for its good fruit-growing soils, and much of the best arable land in the county lies in the north-east. These factors, allied with the effects of industry and differences in landholding, probably lie behind the patterning visible in Map 4. As early as the Middle Ages, analysis of surviving houses suggests marked differences between the west, centre and east of the county, with the greatest number of large, high-quality, dwellings lying in a north-south band across the centre of Kent.[67] Although the sixteenth-century growth of industry in the High Weald and the seventeenth-century urbanisation of the north-west meant that the distribution had changed to some extent, hearth numbers, which reflect the size of the houses they heat, show a very similar pattern.

To explore these issues further, Tables 2 and 3, on pages lix – lxi, tabulate the numbers of households and hearth numbers by hundreds, and Maps 5 - 10 plot their distribution across the county.

Houses with Twenty or more Hearths

The number of people with more than twenty hearths was never great. Map 5 illustrates eighty-five households with twenty or more hearths listed in the returns.[68] The symbols on the map have been placed in approximately the correct positions within each hundred, and they show a reasonably even spread, with noticeable gaps only round the north, east and southern borders, where there may have been a few more in the areas for which there is no data. Of these large houses, ten were owned by peers, and as Kent was never a county of aristocratic landowners, this represents nearly all the properties they owned in the county. They range from the eighty-five hearths belonging to the Earl of Dorset at *Knole*, on the edge of Sevenoaks, and the sixty of Viscount Strangford at *Westenhanger Castle* in Stanford parish, to the Earl of Leicester's more modest twenty-one hearths at *Penshurst Place*,

---

[67] Pearson, *Medieval Houses*, pp. 123-25

[68] The 85 excludes Sir Nicholas Crispe (Eltham) who had 27 hearths in tenements, Mr Thomas Browne, Warden of the College, or Trinity Hospital, in East Greenwich, who had 30 hearths, and also the 27 hearths of Dr Turner, Dean of Christ Church Canterbury (Westgate), since the Christ church precincts physically lie in the City and County of Canterbury. For discussion of the Canterbury situation see Appendix V.

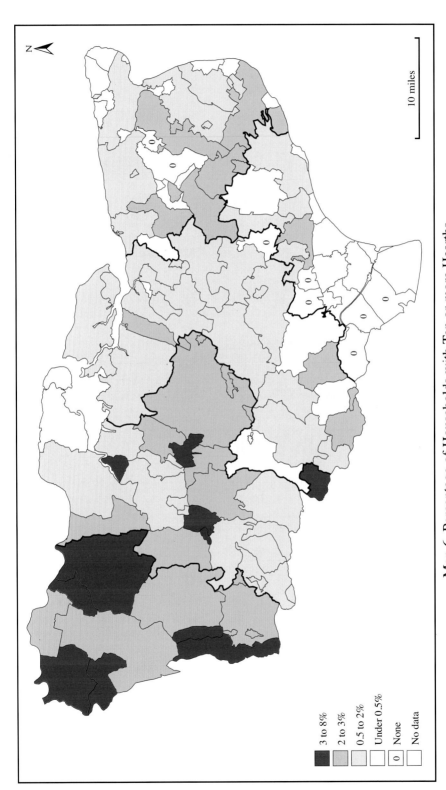

10 miles

Map 6. Percentage of Households with Ten or more Hearths

Penshurst. Both Leicester and Strangford also had second homes within the county. Thirty-five houses belonged to knights and baronets, or their widows. These included the homes of many of the older county families, among them some of the most notable figures in county politics during the seventeenth century, such as Sir Roger Twysden of *Roydon Hall*, East Peckham, Sir Edward Dering of *Surrenden Dering* in Pluckley and Sir Thomas Peyton of *Knowlton Court*, Knowlton.[69] Sixteen belonged to esquires or their widows. A few of these likewise came from well-established, if slightly less prominent, families, such as the Digges of *Chilham Castle*, Chilham and the Harts of *Lullingstone Castle*, Eynsford; but they also included a number of new men, some of whom had played prominent roles in the events of the 1640s, like Thomas Blount of *Wricklesmarsh* in Charlton, or held important posts after the Restoration, like Philip Packer of *Groombridge Place*, Speldhurst. However, many were virtually unknown. Below these lay nineteen properties belonging to the families of mere gentlemen or officers, plus three houses whose occupants are untitled, and two more which had no named occupant.

The geographical distribution of these groups varies. While the homes of the peers are spread across the county, those of the baronets and knights tend to be grouped in the region around Maidstone and on the northern edge of the Downs in east Kent. In 1640 the eastern part of the county together with the Weald were the heartlands of what Everitt has termed the 'indigenous gentry' whose families were established before 1485, and at least 50 per cent of those around Maidstone belonged in the same category.[70] Only a few of the more prominent members of these old county families had mansions with twenty or more hearths, the majority making do with between six and eighteen. William Boys Esquire of Hawkhurst, with twenty-one, was the only member of his extensive family to exceed twenty, and Sir Henry Oxinden, of the senior branch of the Oxinden family, lived in Wingham in a house with only seventeen hearths, his relatives having even fewer. In contrast, one of the mere gentlemen had as many as forty-eight hearths, and one officer had forty. The majority of the large gentry houses lay in the western lathe of Sutton at Hone, where over half the gentry families, including knights and baronets, had arrived since 1603.[71] Many of the largest houses are clustered in Blackheath hundred, reflecting the arrival of gentry and merchants who had moved from London into Deptford and Greenwich, with another

[69] A. Everitt, *The Community of Kent and the Great Rebellion, 1640-60* (Leicester, 1966), pp. 323-4, Appendix VI.
[70] Ibid., p. 37.
[71] Everitt, *loc. cit.*.

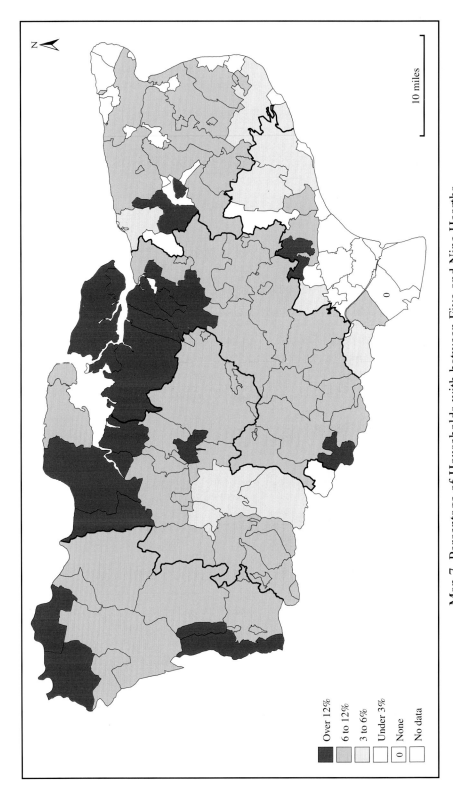

Map 7. Percentage of Households with between Five and Nine Hearths

Over 12%

6 to 12%

3 to 6%

Under 3%

None

0

No data

10 miles

N

little group further down the Thames in Milton-next-Gravesend. Apart from these concentrations in the north-west, houses with twenty or more hearths were not a feature of the towns. Five lie within Canterbury City, but there was only one house of this size in both Maidstone and Rochester.[72] The majority of the larger houses outside the north-west were country seats, and their location reveals the whereabouts of the lands of the aristocracy and wealthier gentry.

Households with Ten or more Hearths

Map 6 is based on 589 houses, or 2 per cent of the total number of houses listed in the tax. It illustrates houses with ten or more hearths, and includes the information about the larger houses plotted in Map 5, so the pattern of distribution is not markedly different. The emphasis on large houses in the western lathe of Sutton at Hone on the fringe of London is clear, likewise their relative paucity in all three eastern lathes, although there are reasonable numbers in the parishes between Canterbury and Dover where many of the older county families had their seats. The region around Maidstone also has a fair proportion of houses with more than ten hearths. The only area where there is a significant difference between the two maps is the southern part of the Weald along the Sussex border, where Map 6 has concentrations not present in Map 5. In fact, the actual number of houses here with between ten and nineteen hearths is small: only four in Little Barnfield, and six each in Selbrittenden and Tenterden. Likewise the high proportion in Littlefield, to the north-west of the Weald, represents only seven houses which may be seen as part of the general scattering of larger properties in the Maidstone area. In contrast, several hundreds in the east of the county had only one or two houses this size (see Table 2), and some, indicated by a zero on the map, had none at all.

Many of these houses were owned by people with titles, and it is worth considering what the hearth tax reveals about the gentry and their homes in 1664. Just under 1700 names listed in the tax returns are titled, from peers down to mere gentlemen and officers. There is, as might be expected, a variation in the average number of hearths in the dwellings of peers, knights, esquires, and gentlemen and officers. Some of the names are repeated, for many wealthy individuals owned houses for rent, and paid tax for their tenants or when the house was empty. The following calculations have therefore left out obvious repetitions, houses that are marked as empty, and those with four hearths or less,

---

[72] For Canterbury see Appendices IV and V. In Faversham, there was not a single house of this size in 1671 (P. Hyde and D. Harrington, *Hearth Tax Returns for Faversham Hundred 1662-1671* (Lyminge, 1998), pp. 50-7.

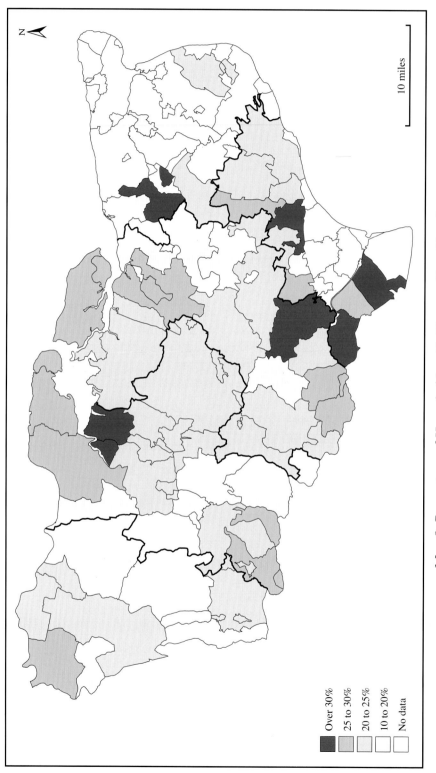

Map 8. Percentage of Households with Three or Four Hearths

Over 30%

25 to 30%

20 to 25%

10 to 20%

No data

10 miles

N

which are often empty or clearly not main residences. On the other hand, in order to increase the statistical sample the widows of each rank have been included. On this basis, peers had an average of 34.9 hearths, knights an average of 18.2 hearths, esquires, 13.1, and gentlemen, including officers, 8.5. The general downward trend is not surprising, but the Kent figures are interesting when compared with those from other counties.[73]

Knights in seven other counties had average hearth numbers ranging from 23.6 - 14.4, with the Kentish knights, at 18.2, coming towards the bottom of the scale, surpassed by those of Norfolk, Oxfordshire, Surrey and Derbyshire, and on a par with those of Dorset. Esquires had an average ranging between 14.9 and 9. The Kent esquires, with an average of 13.1, were nearer the top, although they were surpassed by those in Surrey, Oxfordshire and Norfolk. Finally, the gentry of the seven counties had on average between 8.1 and 4.8 hearths, so the average for the gentry of Kent, at 8.5, exceeded those found elsewhere.[74] This impression, of relatively few men of high rank and outstanding wealth but many men of the middle sort, is not only apparent in the returns for the gentry, but is indicated by the fact that 120 of the 589 people charged on more than ten hearths had no title at all.

Households with between Five and Nine Hearths

In many ways the map of houses with ten or more hearths needs to be viewed in relation to both of the next two. Map 7 illustrates the proportion of houses with between five and nine hearths, which accounted for 11 per cent of houses in the county. The naval and dockyard towns of the north coast, and the ports which carried Kentish produce to London, all had their share of these properties. They were again numerous in the extreme north- west, but also formed over 12 per cent of houses in towns such as Gravesend, Chatham, Rochester, Sittingbourne, Milton-next-Sittingbourne and Faversham and their environs (see Table 1). In most of central Kent, except for

---

[73] The comparison is based upon the list published in N. Cooper, *Houses of the Gentry, 1480–1680* (New Haven & London, 1999), pp. 6, 347-50. Cooper excludes all houses with four hearths or less, on very much the same grounds as those used here. This was also the figure used by Gregory King in the 1690s when calculating the number of gentry in England. Cooper's counties are Derbyshire, Dorset, Norfolk, Oxfordshire, Surrey, Warwickshire and Westmorland.

[74] Cooper, *loc. cit.*, excludes men designated 'Mr', basing his figures solely on those termed 'Gent'. But to do so in Kent would mean excluding the majority of the gentry in the north-west of the county. In Blackheath hundred, for example, 218 men are termed 'Mr', and only four are designated 'Gent'.

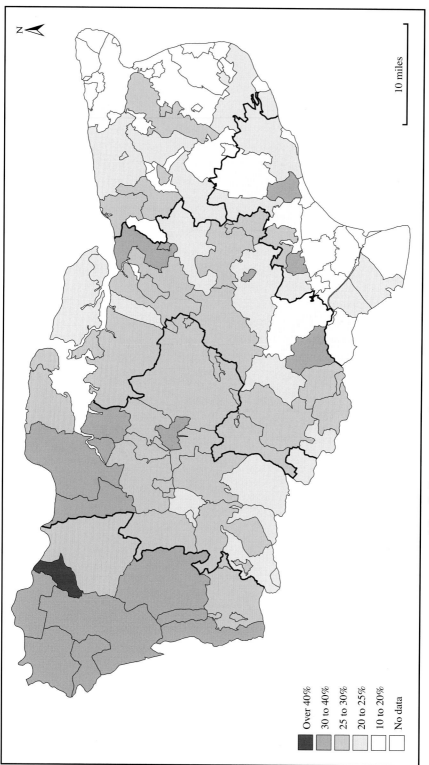

Over 40%
30 to 40%
25 to 30%
20 to 25%
10 to 20%
No data

10 miles

N

Map 9. Percentage of Households with Two Hearths

one or two hundreds in the Medway valley and Low Weald where larger houses had predominated, 6-12 per cent of houses were of this size. The cloth making region around Cranbrook had a number of larger properties, and Zell has suggested that when the traditional, high-quality and expensive broadcloths of the Kentish Weald fell out of fashion during the seventeenth century, the wealthy clothiers simply turned their attention to their other source of income: their farms. Cattle rearing was an important business in the region, and those who had a stake in the land could continue to prosper, shielded from the worst effects of the collapsing cloth industry.[75] The surnames of wealthy sixteenth-century clothiers in the Cranbrook, Staplehurst and Biddenden areas, such as Buckland, Gibbon, Sharpe, Sheffe and Taylor, turn up in 1664 paying tax on eight, nine, ten or even eleven hearths. Whether these families were still in the clothing trade or not, they were certainly still able to live in high-quality houses. Houses with between five and nine hearths also formed between 6-12 per cent over most of the north-east, but were rarer further south where several hundreds had under 6 per cent. Newchurch hundred in Shepway and Preston hundred in the lathe of St Augustine had only one house each in this category. In both cases this was the largest house in the district.

Some entries with sizeable numbers of hearths were inns. These are seldom identified by name, but where they are they tend to have between five and nine hearths, as in Tonbridge where Richard Rootes had nine hearths at the *Crowne*, and in Beckenham where Richard Kinge had seven at the sign of the *George*. Innholders were often gentlemen, and some gentry with ten or more hearths may have run particularly large establishments. This is perhaps especially true in the northern ports where inns must have been numerous.[76] However, the only gentleman who is readily identifiable as a landlord is Robert Knowler, gent., with six hearths at the *Maypole* in Haw borough in the parish of Herne.

Households with Three or Four Hearths

Over the county as a whole the proportion of households with three or four hearths is 22 per cent (Map 8). The highest proportions lie in the centre of the county. In the central lathes of Aylesford and Scray they form 20 per cent or more of the properties in the majority of hundreds, with between 31 and 35 per cent in some of the southern hundreds, such as Oxney and Street (see Table 3). However, it does not

---

[75] Zell, *Industry in the Countryside*, p. 245.

[76] Chalklin in Armstrong, *Economy of Kent*, p. 209, notes the exceptionally numerous inns in Gravesend, where the hearth tax shows there were plenty of sizeable properties but not a single named inn.

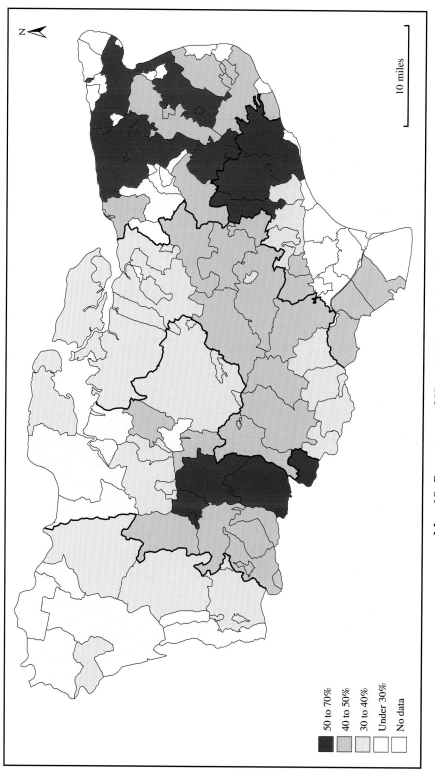

Map 10. Percentage of Households with One Hearth

50 to 70%
40 to 50%
30 to 40%
Under 30%
No data

follow that these proportions necessarily indicate high numbers in absolute terms, for by and large they represent the largest dwellings to be found, and thus form a higher proportion of the total than in hundreds where larger houses were commoner. Along the central part of the north coast the percentages tend to be between 21 and 29, but they need to be combined with the higher proportion of larger houses with between five and nine hearths to indicate a much more widely distributed high standard of living. In Sutton at Hone to the north-west, where there were so many larger houses, the number with three or four hearths is proportionally lower. The lathe of St Augustine in the north-east is the only lathe to have a below average figure for three and four hearths, at 21 per cent, and if the hundred of Westgate, which includes part of the city of Canterbury, is removed, the overall average for the lathe drops to 18 per cent, giving a more accurate picture of the small number of larger houses in the rural areas of north-east Kent. In some hundreds, such as Kinghamford in the Downs, and the small hundred of Preston, only 12-13 per cent of houses have this number of hearths. Nonetheless, no part of Kent drops below 10 per cent, a figure which has been included in the key to facilitate comparison with other parts of England.

Households with One or Two Hearths

While the maps of houses with three or more hearths may be taken to indicate where the better-off members of society predominated, those illustrating one and two hearths, and the people who were exempted from paying the hearth tax, tell us more about the less well off. In many counties two-hearth houses are already accounted as the homes of the relatively well-to-do. The question of their wealth, and of the sort of houses they actually lived in, will be dealt with later, but in a general sense we may take it that they lived in less favourable circumstances than those with more fireplaces. Over the county as a whole 29 per cent of households had two hearths and 36 per cent had one.

Map 9 shows the distribution of two-hearth houses. The pattern of distribution is not very different from those showing more. There is the same concentration in the west and north: over 30 per cent of houses in most hundreds along the north coast from Chatham and Gillingham westwards had two hearths, and similar percentages occur in some of the western hundreds further south. Much of the rest of central Kent, around Maidstone, along the central section of the north coast, and in the High Weald around Cranbrook, had proportions between 25-30 per cent. Only the areas bordering Romney Marsh, and most of north-east Kent, had under 25 per cent, with many of those

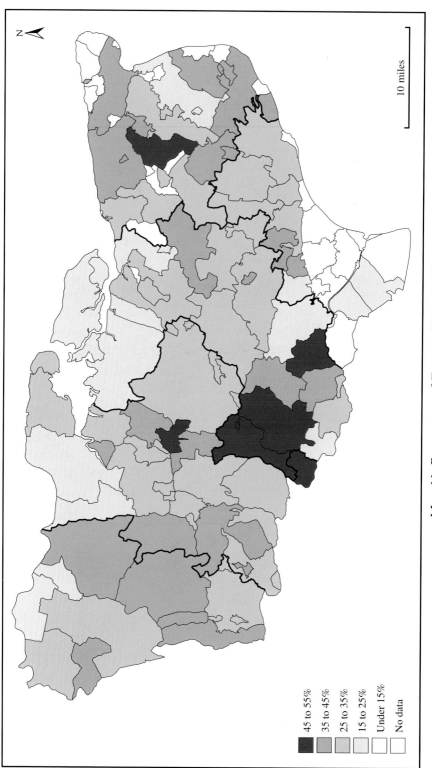

Map 11. Percentage of Exempt Households

45 to 55%
35 to 45%
25 to 35%
15 to 25%
Under 15%
No data

10 miles

N

hundreds having only 10-20 per cent. Again, nowhere in Kent falls into the 'under 10 per cent' category.

Map 10, illustrating the proportion of households with single hearths, is almost an inversion of Map 9. In the north-west, where the number of two-hearth households was highest, the number with single hearths is lowest, with under 30 per cent in many hundreds: in other words, there were fewer houses with single hearths than with two hearths. The situation in central Kent is more mixed, with many hundreds having only 30-40 per cent of houses taxed on single hearths, although four hundreds to the south-west of Maidstone returned 50-60 per cent in this category. In east Kent, 50-60 per cent of houses in the majority of hundreds have just a single hearth, and two, Preston and Ringslow in the far north-east, have between 60-70 per cent. In terms of the nation as a whole it may be significant that so few hundreds have such high percentages of single hearths, but within Kent what these maps bring out clearly is the contrast between the well-heated properties of the north-west, and the simpler and colder houses of the north-east.

Exemptions

Map 11 shows the distribution of those people who were exempted from paying the tax. This is a tricky area to understand. In theory, in accordance with amendments to the original Act, exemption from the tax was granted to all who did not contribute to church or poor rates by reason of their poverty or the smallness of their estates; or to tenants who lived in houses worth less than twenty shillings a year, unless they owned land, tenements or goods valued at £10 or more. Arkell, working in Warwickshire, found that in practice the closest correlation lay between those who were exempt from the tax and those who paid £1 or less in rent. In addition, hearths of an industrial nature, including private ovens or furnaces in kitchens, brew houses, bakehouses and wash houses, were not charged.[77] From 1663 the exemptions were to be listed separately, and this was clearly done in a 'Not Chargeable' category in the Lady Day 1664 return for Kent.[78] From May 1664, after the Lady Day collection published here, no one with more than two hearths was supposed to be exempt, a ruling which must have caused further complications in Kent.[79]

---

[77] For more details see above, pp. xvi-xvii.

[78] 15 Charles II c.13; Arkell, 'Printed instructions', in *Surveying the People*, pp. 39-41. For the Warwickshire evidence see T. Arkell, 'The incidence of poverty in England in the later seventeenth century', *Social History*, 12 (1987),. 23-47.

[79] See above, p. xx. I am grateful to Elizabeth Parkinson for help in clarifying some of these tricky areas.

The difficulties faced in administering the tax are illustrated by comments in the notebook Sir Roger Twysden kept of his activities as a J.P. In 1662 he was concerned about whether or not poor people who did not pay church or poor rates, yet lived in houses valued at anything up to £13 a year, should be charged. He thought the problem was particularly acute in the Weald, in places such as Goudhurst where rich men, including clothiers, had engrossed farms and left poor carders, weavers and spinners in the former farmhouses. In his opinion the tenants should not be charged, for by taking away their land, the landlords were making these people into cottagers and thus exempt from the tax.[80] The problem was clarified in 1664, when a new Amendment made the landlord liable,[81] but again this was not until after the return for Lady Day.

A second problem in analysing the returns is to distinguish one kind of exemption from another. In the borough of Bredgar, in the eastern division of Milton hundred, four inhabitants were charged for the hearths in their dwellings, but were specifically exempted for their brew house chimneys; and in Bobbing in the same hundred, Mrs Sanford, who was charged on twenty-two hearths, was exempted on her three brew house, wash house, and bake house chimneys. It is obviously important to establish how often such exemptions occurred without explanation before considering the distribution of exemption as an indication of poverty. In fact, random checks throughout the returns suggest this is not a major problem except in Shepway lathe, in Loningborough and Stowting hundreds, and the lower half hundred of Folkestone. In these instances the duplicate names have been omitted from Table 2 and Map 11. Elsewhere, very few names are repeated in the charged and exempt lists for a single borough or parish.

A third and more intractable problem lies in understanding what lies behind some of the entries with high numbers of exempted hearths. Some may relate to the issue discussed by Twysden. Others may reflect the condition of the houses. In Goare borough, in the eastern division of Milton hundred, 'two old empty houses ready to fall down' have seven hearths between them and are listed as exempt, while in St Augustine's borough nearby, Mr Pagett had 'a new house with six chimneys the hearths not yett layd', which appears in the chargeable section but with no charge against it since the hearths were not yet in use. It is possible, but not provable, that elsewhere some exempt properties with high hearth numbers were not charged because the building was not yet complete and the hearths were not taxable.

---

[80] CKS: U47/47 01, citing a law of 1588/9, 31 Eliz. c.7.
[81] 16 Charles II c.3, published in Arkell, 'Printed instructions', p. 58; see above, p. xix.

Finally, there is the problem of almshouses, hospitals and free schools. These were charged only if they had annual incomes of over £100. Thus Mr Broadnax was charged for fourteen hearths in the wealthy St Nicholas Hospital at Harbledown outside Canterbury, and Mr Thomas Browne was charged on thirty hearths as Warden of the College in Crane South, Greenwich.[82] On the other hand, the hospital in Harrietsham had twelve hearths which were exempt from payment. It is more appropriate for analysis to list these as thirty, fourteen or twelve one-hearth households, rather than include them in the ten-plus category, even though the warden of the larger establishments probably had more than a single hearth in his own apartment. However, many other almshouses or hospitals appear not to have been identified as such. Between 1572 and 1660 at least forty-six such establishments were endowed in Kent, which together with twelve more surviving from an earlier date provided accommodation for 492 poor people - more than was spent in most other southern counties.[83] Yet apart from the institutions mentioned above only seven almshouses for between two and six residents in Brasted, Godmersham, High Halden, Lenham, Linton, Luddenham and Tenterden, none of which was charged, are named in the returns. There must have been many more, such as those known to exist in Pudding Lane, Stone Street, Week Street, and East Lane in Maidstone town,[84] but none is readily identifiable in the hearth tax; they probably lie among the large number of exemptions, which are unfortunately not properly divided by street, and it is not clear whether each occupant was listed separately with a single hearth, or whether the almshouses are represented by some of the larger entries for three or more hearths. Without detailed work on individual parishes it is impossible to clarify this, but it is a potential problem which needs to be borne in mind when considering the extent of exemption and the large number of non-chargeable properties which had three or more hearths.

Over the county as a whole, 32 per cent of houses were exempt, the average for the five lathes ranging between 30 and 33 per cent. But this masked considerable local variations. In the Isle of Oxney on the edge of Romney Marsh, as few as 7 per cent of the inhabitants were not charged, while at the other extreme, in Downhamford to the east of Canterbury, 54 per cent were exempt. One caveat which should be borne in mind when interpreting the figures, is that around seventy boroughs in the county have no exemptions listed at all. Many are very

---

[82] This was the Trinity Hospital, founded by the Earl of Northampton in 1613.

[83] W. K. Jordan, 'Social institutions in Kent, 1480-1660', *Archaeologia Cantiana*, 75 (1961), 32-56.

[84] P. Clark and L. Murfin, *The History of Maidstone* (Stroud, 1996), p. 56; description of Maidstone in 1650 by Nicholas Wall, mapped by Allen Grove and Robert Spain, 1974-5, CKS: 17/270.

small boroughs, but it is suspicious that that there were virtually no exemptions in Oxney or in the upper half hundred of Eastry, and none at all in the whole lower half hundred of Wye. In Cambridgeshire, analysis of later returns indicated that some parishes for which there were no exempt in 1664 had sizeable numbers who were not charged in 1674, suggesting that the earlier returns are not complete.[85] The same may be the case in Kent, but the necessary comparative work on later returns has not been undertaken. The highest proportions of rural exempt, as Map 11 illustrates, lay in Downhamford in the far east, and in the Wealden hundreds of Cranbrook, Little Barnfield, Marden and Tenterden. In general, leaving aside the High Weald parishes where the declining cloth industry was causing problems, central Kent had fewer exempt households than the areas to east and west. Towns were always rather different, and the numbers for these can best be seen in Table 1. Cranbrook, with its failing cloth industry, had 57 per cent, and Maidstone and Westerham were not far behind with 50 and 53 per cent respectively.[86] Elsewhere, the inland market towns tended to have between 40 and 50 per cent exempt, while the developing coastal towns of the north had around 30 per cent or less.[87]

It is clear that unlike many other parts of England, exemption before the revised Act of 1664 did not just affect people with single hearths. It was confined to those with single hearths only in four hundreds in the eastern lathes of Shepway and St Augustine. In other hundreds in these lathes 80-90 per cent of exempt households had single hearths. Elsewhere in the countryside single-hearth households were more likely to account for only 50-80 per cent of exemptions, and in the towns of central and western Kent, as well as in Westgate hundred on the outskirts of Canterbury, they fell below 45 per cent. Where single-hearth exemptions were rare, two was the norm, although up to 10 per cent of entries might have more, the proportion rising to nearer 20 per cent in one or two urban hundreds such as Blackheath, Rochester and Westgate. Thus far more households with two or more hearths were exempted in the towns than in the countryside.

Since Twysden specifically referred to the problems encountered in Goudhurst and surrounding areas, it is worth looking at Cranbrook, Marden and Tenterden, three of the hundreds in the clothing district where exemption was highest. In all three, exemptions

---

[85] Evans, *Cambridgeshire Hearth Tax*, p. xxvi.

[86] See Appendix V for the suggestion that much of Canterbury may have had an exemption rate of around 50%.

[87] That approximately half the inhabitants of Kentish market towns were exempt was noted by P. Clark and P. Slack, *English Towns in Transition* (London, 1976), p. 21, but they thought (p. 114) that lower exemption rates were normally only found in social capitals and stagnant market towns.

formed 47 per cent of households. Of these, 69, 71 and 59 per cent had single hearths; 25, 26 and 30 per cent had two, while the rest lived in properties with three or more hearths. In Tenterden, where 10 per cent had three or more hearths, the exemption column is headed by a note that the following 'are exempted by reason of their poverty from the usuall taxes to church and poore and are not worth five pounds and soe are not chargeable by the Act'. Thus the high proportion with three or more hearths would appear to have lived in far larger houses than their wealth would warrant, and they may illustrate the situation described by Twysden. The same may also have been true in Rolvenden, where 38 per cent of households were exempt, 17 per cent of whom had three or more hearths.[88]

Empty Houses

The fact that exempt households in towns were more likely to have two or more hearths, and those in the country to have single hearths, is almost certainly not just a matter of degrees of poverty; it also reflects the type of property. But before turning to the houses themselves, there is one other category in the returns which needs to be examined because it has a bearing on the same issue. This is the number and distribution of empty houses at the time of the tax. Most of these were taxed, although a few, such as those which were falling down in Goare borough in Milton hundred, escaped. Over the whole county 497 empty houses were listed

Although isolated cases might occur anywhere, the majority of empty houses were concentrated in well-defined areas. Only ten hundreds had more than ten empty houses each, eight of them lying along the north coast, plus the town of Ashford, and Westgate hundred, which lies within and on the outskirts of Canterbury.[89] The highest numbers occurred in Blackheath hundred (191), in the towns of Deptford, Greenwich, Woolwich, Lewisham and Eltham, and in the lower, or northern, half hundred of Toltingtrough (48), which included

---

[88] Work by Anthony Poole (pers. comm., 1999) on the Churchwarden's accounts for Benenden parish in Rolvenden hundred has revealed that ten of the forty-five male exemptions were labourers (one of whom had 4 hearths), and others were poor weavers, shearmen or tradesmen. However, among their number are some who appear to have been far too wealthy for exemption in normal circumstances: e.g. Richard Sharpe, gent., who had lands valued at £40 p.a. (although he may have been charged on another property in the parish) and Richard Burden, yeoman, with lands valued at £29 p.a.

[89] The hundreds with ten or more empty houses are Blackheath (191); Little and Lesnes (19, mostly in Erith); the upper (southern) half hundred of Ruxley (15, mostly in Bexley); the lower (eastern) half hundred of Shamwell (18, mostly in Temple borough, Strood); Toltingtrough (48); Chatham and Gillingham (18); Rochester (35); Westgate (20); the eastern half hundred of Milton (21, mostly in Milton town and Bredgar) and Ashford (11).

Gravesend and Northfleet. These of course were largely the developing naval and dockyard towns and their surroundings.

Few of the empty houses were small. In the ten hundreds where the majority lay, only 11.5 per cent had single hearths, while 27 per cent had five hearths or more. In the Deptford, Greenwich, Woolwich area this is particularly noticeable, for 126 (66 per cent) had at least three hearths, twenty-two of them having ten or more. Furthermore, many of these houses were owned by gentlemen or officers. In some cases the houses may have been empty because their owners were abroad, but in other cases they were obviously intended to be let. Many of them may have been large properties aimed at the wealthy market, but others were probably meant to be subdivided. In Mottingham, Sir Anthony Batteman had twenty hearths in his own house, but also paid on six in an empty house. In Strood, Francis Wansall had eight hearths, plus two empty houses with eleven more hearths; and in Rochester Mrs Cripse, widow, seems to have lived in a house with three hearths, but had three empty houses with six hearths between them. Sir Nicholas Crispe, a wealthy royalist, overseas merchant, slave trader, and farmer of the duty on sea coal, who lived in Bread Street in the City of London and in Hammersmith,[90] had twenty-seven hearths classed together as 'tenements' in an empty property in Eltham, as well as an empty house with six hearths in Deptford. These instances could be multiplied. They seem to show the local landowning class realising the advantages of owning property to let - a common enough occurrence at all times. The fact that so many were empty at the time of the hearth tax may mean that short-term lets were normal, or since these were growing towns, that the houses were newly-built and had not yet been rented out.[91] That landowners were closely involved in the growth of the towns is clear from the case of John Evelyn, the diarist. He owned *Sayes Court*, Deptford (which had nineteen hearths) and between 1654 and 1692 provided land on the west side of what is now Deptford High Street for the erection of nine houses, although in his case he was not directly responsible for either building or leasing the properties.[92]

Many of the larger houses were probably intended for officers and gentlemen, though these formed only a small proportion of those who were moving into the area. The one or two-hearth houses were no doubt for lesser folk, but there is unlikely to have been enough

---

[90] DNB, 5 (1973 edn).

[91] The popularity of investing in property is also revealed in probate inventories, A. F. Dulley, 'People and homes in the Medway towns: 1687-1783', *Archaeologia Cantiana*, 77 (1962), 170-1.

[92] P. Guillery and B. Herman 'Deptford houses: 1650 to 1800', *Vernacular Architecture*, 30 (1999), forthcoming.

accommodation for the workforce which surged into this area in the late seventeenth century. In 1663, 238 men were employed in the Royal Naval Dockyards in Deptford; in 1664, 302 were recorded in Woolwich; and in 1665 there were 800 in Chatham, including 440 shipwrights, 129 labourers, 47 house carpenters, 41 joiners, 23 scavelmen, 18 bricklayers, 17 'ocam boyes', 15 boat makers, plus plumbers, pump makers, coopers and pitch heaters.[93] Given that there were private docks as well as official ones, and that many people in service industries will have been no wealthier than those in government employ, there must have been very large numbers of craftsmen and labouring poor in these towns. By 1686 Chatham claimed that its population had trebled in forty years, and in the 1680s and 90s both Chatham and Deptford were complaining of the excessive charges landowners had to bear to cope with poor relief. The problems were compounded by the fact that employment was irregular, with periods when the workers in the dockyards were laid off, and there were long arrears in the payment of wages.[94] Given that some of the poor of the cloth working district of the Weald, where birth rates are known to have been declining and migration was clearly in progress from the 1640s,[95] are likely to have moved to the northern towns in search of employment, one might have expected to find a high proportion of exempt and of one-hearth houses in the northern towns.

Up to a point, that is what we do see, as Table 1 shows. In Deptford, 337 households, forming 34 per cent of the total, were exempted from paying in 1664. In Chatham, 134 households, or 31 per cent were exempt. But in Woolwich the number was only 35 or 12.5 per cent. In the first two cases the percentage of single-hearth houses: 115, or 11.5 per cent of the total in Deptford, 43 or 10 per cent in Chatham, and 48 or 17 per cent in Woolwich, falls far below the percentage of exemptions. But, as discussed above, the proportions of both exemptions and single-hearth houses tend to be higher in the inland towns, notably in Maidstone and Cranbrook, but also in Westerham, Tenterden, Tonbridge, Sevenoaks and Ashford. This suggests that poverty in the older towns was worse, and the influx of labour and the problems caused by the non-payment of wages did not result in a higher proportion of exemptions in the northern towns.

In the new towns it seems likely that many of the newly arrived workforce would have been too destitute, at least on arrival, to

---

[93] Coleman, 'Naval dockyards', pp. 140-1, quoting *S.P. Dom.* Charles II, 29, no 69.
[94] Ibid., pp. 141-5; the problems and progress of the shipyards is discussed in more detail in D. C. Coleman, 'The Economy of Kent under the later Stuarts', (University of London unpublished Ph.D. thesis 1951), pp. 245-53.
[95] Dobson, 'The last hiccup', pp. 408-10; *Contours of Death*, pp. 59-65.

have been able to afford to rent the empty houses which were available. So it seems probable that a proportion of the poor were lodgers in other people's houses, and thus hidden from the hearth tax altogether.[96] Whether the sort of people who took in poor lodgers were themselves able to pay the tax is beyond the scope of this essay. Probably some were, some were not. Secondly, and most important of all, most of the houses in the northern towns will have been new houses, put up during the second half of the seventeenth century. Among the work force noted in Chatham in 1665 were forty-seven house carpenters and eighteen bricklayers, and in Deptford it is known that many of the new late-seventeenth and early eighteenth-century houses were erected by enterprising artisans, some of whom worked in the dockyards as well.[97] The contrast between the relatively small number of exemptions and single-hearth houses in Chatham and Deptford, and the larger numbers in the older towns, is almost certainly as much to do with the age of the houses and the way the poor were housed, as it was to do with absolute numbers of people in various social or occupational categories. Before this can be pursued further, it is necessary to look at the evidence of the buildings themselves, and see whether the survivors shed any light on how the figures in the hearth tax might be interpreted.

[96] This conclusion was also reached by Dulley in his analysis of slightly later probate inventories from Rochester, Chatham and Strood, 'People and homes', p. 163.
[97] RCHME unpublished survey report, 'Deptford houses: 1650 to 1800' (1998), pp. 23-4; Guillery and Herman, 'Deptford houses', forthcoming.

HEARTH TAX TABLES FOR KENT FOR LADY DAY 1664

Table 2 sets out the data included in the transcript of the Quarter Sessions Returns, as used for the percentage bands of Table 3 and the distribution maps. The data is arranged by hundred, with the numbers in physically detached boroughs included with those of the hundred in which they lie. For further information about the location of boroughs, see Appendix VII.

The column of '20 or more hearths', which forms the basis for Map 5, is a sub-set of the previous column of '10 or more hearths'.

It will be found that the figures in the columns of hearth numbers in Table 2 do not always add up to the figure in the 'total entries column'. There are a number of reasons for this:

Where the manuscript has no hearth total against a name, the entry is included in the 'total entries' column, but omitted from the detailed columns.

Where a single entry with a large number of hearths is clearly labelled as an institution, e.g. a hospital, or a grouping of tenements, a single entry has been placed in the 'total entries' column, but in the detailed columns the total has been divided into single-hearth households.

Where a person has been charged on two houses together, these are counted as a single overall entry, but are split in the detailed columns.

Where one or more names have been repeated in both the 'chargeable' and 'non-chargeable' sections, indicating that householders with ovens or furnaces in their kitchens, brew houses or wash houses have been listed twice, the entries in the 'non-chargeable' section have been omitted from the tables.

Since they could not be included on the distribution maps, the figures for the parts of Westgate hundred which lie within Canterbury City (the precincts of Christ Church and the Archbishop's Palace, St Gregory's borough and Staplegate borough) are not included in Tables 2 and 3. These figures are tabulated and discussed in Appendix V.

Table 2 KENT HEARTH TAX DATA, LADY DAY 1664, BY HUNDRED

HUNDREDS	Total entries	Total hearths	Total 1 hearth	Total 2 hearths	Total 3 hearths	Total 4 hearths	Total 5 hearths	Total 6 hearths	Total 7 hearths	Total 8 hearths	Total 9 hearths	Total 10 or more	Total 20 or more	Total exempt
ALOESBRIDGE	64	154	26	13	11	8	2	2	1	1	0	0	0	10
ASHFORD TOWN	268	685	82	96	31	22	12	12	5	2	1	3	0	115
AXTANE	619	1671	239	172	72	47	34	16	6	6	4	20	2	223
BARKLEY	322	776	150	73	33	28	11	12	3	6	3	3	1	118
BEWSBOROUGH	258	536	114	59	26	19	7	3	1	1	0	6	0	93
BIRCHOLT BARONY	95	208	41	26	10	11	3	3	0	1	0	0	0	25
BIRCHOLT FRANCHISE	129	352	47	35	17	12	6	4	4	0	2	1	1	50
BLACKBORNE	307	757	130	52	51	43	10	11	4	4	1	1	0	61
BLACKHEATH	2382	8307	394	879	409	251	159	115	43	51	20	115	14	619
BLEANGATE	515	1156	255	107	51	50	24	16	3	4	3	3	0	182
BOUGHTON UNDER BLEAN	229	558	85	70	35	10	16	7	2	0	0	4	0	57
BRENCHLEY AND HORSMONDEN	449	966	231	110	39	36	7	10	5	1	3	6	0	132
BRIDGE AND PETHAM	227	537	110	51	32	15	7	4	3	0	0	5	2	58
BROMLEY AND BECKENHAM	265	790	86	95	26	19	12	10	4	0	5	13	1	89
CALEHILL	618	1467	254	158	97	52	17	18	3	5	3	7	2	205
CHART AND LONGBRIDGE	572	1467	239	139	69	52	29	15	7	8	3	9	2	158
CHATHAM AND GILLINGHAM	607	1886	82	240	86	98	33	24	20	10	4	10	0	180
CODSHEATH	879	2398	293	314	108	61	29	28	11	11	2	22	4	341
CORNILO	206	480	102	40	29	18	4	2	2	2	3	3	1	82
CRANBROOK	766	1857	307	213	104	67	26	24	6	7	2	9	2	357
DARTFORD AND WILMINGTON	362	1056	76	146	53	35	22	10	4	2	3	11	0	87
DOWNHAMFORD	251	505	135	54	25	19	7	6	1	3	1	0	0	135
EASTRY	306	673	157	56	30	27	11	5	3	3	0	5	1	71
EYHORNE	1372	3644	527	389	177	104	60	53	23	14	10	28	5	421
FAVERSHAM	520	1442	178	134	69	62	30	25	10	4	0	10	1	170
FELBOROUGH	406	958	195	94	50	31	11	11	3	2	3	8	1	165
FOLKESTONE	230	490	119	49	36	16	8	3	3	0	0	2	0	61
GREAT BARNFIELD	182	481	72	43	19	18	13	8	3	1	1	3	1	38
HAM	58	114	28	12	13	2	3	0	0	0	0	0	0	14
HEANE	61	152	20	20	8	6	4	0	2	0	0	1	0	19
HOO	223	548	81	61	29	27	15	3	3	3	0	1	0	63
KINGHAMFORD	204	465	120	33	16	8	13	3	4	0	1	5	2	76
LARKFIELD	617	1561	223	174	94	52	32	12	10	1	2	12	3	184

	Total entries	Total hearths	Total 1 hearth	Total 2 hearths	Total 3 hearths	Total 4 hearths	Total 5 hearths	Total 6 hearths	Total 7 hearths	Total 8 hearths	Total 9 hearths	Total 10 or more	Total 20 or more	Total exempt
LITTLE AND LESNES	310	895	88	99	35	36	17	9	7	4	4	9	0	62
LITTLE BARNFIELD	79	189	44	16	8	5	0	1	0	1	0	3	1	36
LITTLEFIELD	134	356	74	30	10	7	1	3	1	1	0	7	3	41
LONINGBOROUGH	357	702	198	61	60	16	11	4	2	3	1	1	0	116
MAIDSTONE	421	1056	171	121	59	37	17	5	8	1	5	9	0	163
MAIDSTONE TOWN	802	2616	171	278	92	91	54	32	26	20	13	25	1	402
MARDEN	624	1357	283	170	65	60	17	11	6	4	4	3	0	294
MILTON	1032	2911	330	300	145	98	58	42	29	13	8	19	2	208
NEWCHURCH	39	72	19	12	4	3	1	0	0	0	0	0	0	17
OXNEY	113	268	47	21	16	23	0	3	3	0	0	0	0	8
PRESTON	70	107	47	12	6	3	0	1	0	0	0	0	0	26
RINGSLOW	304	576	190	37	24	20	11	2	8	1	0	3	0	136
ROCHESTER	712	2378	98	221	122	98	42	40	22	11	7	26	1	250
ROLVENDEN	217	527	82	57	35	27	4	7	4	1	1	1	0	81
RUXLEY	819	2256	243	304	106	62	26	21	16	10	7	23	2	241
SELBRITTENDEN	223	600	76	57	28	32	15	2	4	2	0	6	0	58
SHAMWELL	643	1974	156	194	101	72	35	43	17	13	2	10	1	156
SHEPPEY	220	597	78	50	35	24	13	13	3	1	0	3	1	39
SOMERDEN	439	1109	165	124	57	42	24	16	0	1	1	9	2	119
ST MARTIN AND LONGPORT	23	46	10	5	6	2	0	0	0	0	0	0	0	4
STOWTING	177	355	88	37	31	14	3	2	0	0	0	1	0	48
STREET	126	377	49	24	27	13	5	2	3	0	0	3	1	35
TENHAM	209	643	76	45	29	17	12	14	5	3	4	4	2	43
TENTERDEN	296	803	97	102	25	38	11	6	7	7	0	6	1	138
TOLTINGTROUGH	804	2352	208	318	79	57	40	38	20	11	11	22	3	178
LOWY OF TUNBRIDGE	515	1282	211	131	63	54	18	13	7	1	6	8	1	213
TWYFORD	457	1029	233	117	45	28	10	8	2	2	0	12	3	150
WACHLINGSTONE	400	972	170	90	67	40	10	9	5	2	0	5	3	119
WESTERHAM AND EDENBRIDGE	419	1192	120	158	50	27	26	13	6	6	1	13	2	164
WESTGATE	350	1135	94	104	54	53	18	15	8	5	4	9	2	105
WHITSTABLE	162	340	74	47	14	17	8	1	0	0	0	1	0	54
WINGHAM	317	737	145	85	40	19	14	4	2	1	0	7	2	92
WROTHAM	362	875	158	95	34	28	13	9	4	1	1	8	2	131
WYE	333	863	145	84	33	31	11	11	6	4	2	6	2	109
TOTALS	27077	72644	9636	7813	3560	2520	1222	875	433	283	162	588	84	8695

Table 3   PERCENTAGE BANDS FOR THE KENT HEARTH TAX DATA, LADY DAY 1664

HUNDREDS	% 1 hearth	% 2 hearths	% 3 and 4 hearths	% 5 - 9 hearths	% 10 or more	% exempt
ALOESBRIDGE	40.63	20.31	29.69	9.38	0.00	15.63
ASHFORD TOWN	30.60	35.82	19.78	11.94	1.12	42.91
AXTANE	38.61	27.79	19.22	10.66	3.23	36.03
BARKLEY	46.58	22.67	18.94	10.87	0.93	36.65
BEWSBOROUGH	44.19	22.87	17.44	4.65	2.33	36.05
BIRCHOLT BARONY	43.16	27.37	22.11	7.37	0.00	26.32
BIRCHOLT FRANCHISE	36.43	27.13	22.48	12.40	0.78	38.76
BLACKBORNE	42.35	16.94	30.62	9.77	0.33	19.87
BLACKHEATH	16.54	36.90	27.71	16.29	4.83	25.99
BLEANGATE	49.51	20.78	19.61	9.71	0.58	35.34
BOUGHTON UNDER BLEAN	37.12	30.57	19.65	10.92	1.75	24.89
BRENCHLEY AND HORSMONDEN	51.45	24.50	16.70	5.79	1.34	29.40
BRIDGE AND PETHAM	48.46	22.47	20.70	6.17	2.20	25.55
BROMLEY AND BECKENHAM	32.45	35.85	16.98	11.70	4.91	33.58
CALEHILL	41.10	25.57	24.11	7.44	1.13	33.17
CHART AND LONGBRIDGE	41.78	24.30	21.15	10.84	1.57	27.62
CHATHAM AND GILLINGHAM	13.51	39.54	30.31	14.99	1.65	29.65
CODSHEATH	33.33	35.72	19.23	9.22	2.50	38.79
CORNILO	49.51	19.42	22.82	6.31	1.46	39.81
CRANBROOK	40.08	27.81	22.32	8.49	1.17	46.61
DARTFORD AND WILMINGTON	20.99	40.33	24.31	11.33	3.04	24.03
DOWNHAMFORD	53.78	21.51	17.53	7.17	0.00	53.78
EASTRY	51.31	18.30	18.63	7.19	1.63	23.20
EYHORNE	38.41	28.35	20.48	11.66	2.04	30.69
FAVERSHAM	34.23	25.77	25.19	13.27	1.92	32.69
FELBOROUGH	48.03	23.15	19.95	7.39	1.97	40.64
FOLKESTONE	51.74	21.30	22.61	6.09	0.87	26.52
GREAT BARNFIELD	39.56	23.63	20.33	14.29	1.65	20.88
HAM	48.28	20.69	25.86	5.17	0.00	24.14
HEANE	32.79	32.79	22.95	9.84	1.64	31.15
HOO	36.32	27.35	25.11	10.76	0.45	28.25
KINGHAMFORD	58.82	16.18	11.76	10.29	2.45	37.25
LARKFIELD	36.14	28.20	23.66	9.24	1.94	29.82

	% 1 hearth	% 2 hearths	% 3 and 4 hearths	% 5 - 9 hearths	% 10 or more	% exempt
LITTLE AND LESNES	28.39	31.94	22.90	13.23	2.90	20.00
LITTLE BARNFIELD	55.70	20.25	16.46	2.53	3.80	45.57
LITTLEFIELD	55.22	22.39	12.69	4.48	5.22	30.60
LONINGBOROUGH	55.46	17.09	21.29	5.88	0.28	32.49
MAIDSTONE	40.62	28.74	22.80	8.55	2.14	38.72
MAIDSTONE TOWN	21.32	34.66	22.82	18.08	3.12	50.12
MARDEN	45.35	27.24	20.03	6.73	0.48	47.12
MILTON	31.98	29.07	23.55	14.53	1.84	20.16
NEWCHURCH	48.72	30.77	17.95	2.56	0.00	43.59
OXNEY	41.59	18.58	34.51	5.31	0.00	7.08
PRESTON	67.14	17.14	12.86	1.43	0.00	37.14
RINGSLOW	62.50	12.17	14.47	7.24	0.99	44.74
ROCHESTER	13.76	31.04	30.90	17.13	3.65	35.11
ROLVENDEN	37.79	26.27	28.57	7.83	0.46	37.33
RUXLEY	29.67	37.12	20.51	9.77	2.81	29.43
SELBRITTENDEN	34.08	25.56	26.91	10.31	2.69	26.01
SHAMWELL	24.26	30.17	26.91	17.11	1.56	24.26
SHEPPEY	35.45	22.73	26.82	13.64	1.36	17.73
SOMERDEN	37.59	28.25	22.55	9.57	2.05	27.11
ST MARTIN AND LONGPORT	43.48	21.74	34.78	0.00	0.00	17.39
STOWTING	49.72	20.90	25.42	2.82	0.56	27.12
STREET	38.89	19.05	31.75	7.94	2.38	27.78
TENHAM	36.36	21.53	22.01	18.18	1.91	20.57
TENTERDEN	32.77	34.46	21.28	10.47	2.03	46.62
TOLTINGTROUGH	25.87	39.55	16.92	14.93	2.74	22.14
LOWY OF TONBRIDGE	40.97	25.44	22.72	8.74	1.55	41.36
TWYFORD	50.98	25.60	15.97	4.81	2.63	32.82
WACHLINGSTONE	42.50	22.50	26.75	6.50	1.25	29.75
WESTERHAM AND EDENBRIDGE	28.64	37.71	18.38	12.41	3.10	39.14
WESTGATE	26.86	29.71	30.57	14.29	2.57	30.00
WHITSTABLE	45.68	29.01	19.14	5.56	0.62	33.33
WINGHAM	45.74	26.81	18.61	6.62	2.21	29.02
WROTHAM	43.65	26.24	17.13	7.73	2.21	36.19
WYE	43.54	25.23	19.22	10.21	1.80	32.73

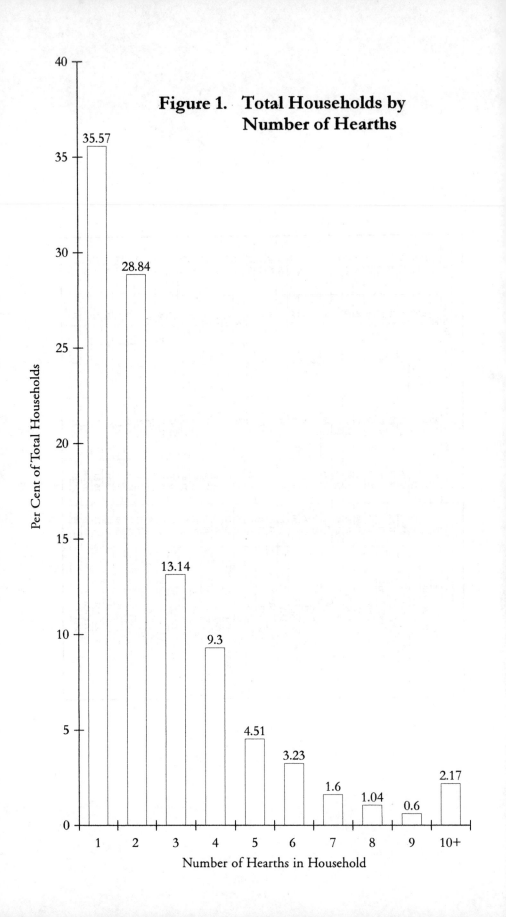

Figure 1. Total Households by Number of Hearths

THE EVIDENCE OF THE HOUSES

Rural Houses

Many of the largest houses in the county were medieval in origin, even though they had been substantially added to and rebuilt by 1664, and the families which first owned them had usually long gone. This is not the place to unravel the complicated histories of buildings like *Knole* or *Westenhanger Castle*. It is, however, worth mentioning that the hearth tax is often an extremely useful corrective when studying such buildings, for it frequently indicates that they were far better heated than can be deduced today. This is the case at *Westenhanger*, where very few of the sixty hearths on which Viscount Strangford was charged, can be identified,[98] not to mention more modest gentry residences such as *Pett Place*, Charing (Sir Robert Honywood, 20 hearths), and *Ford Place*, Wrotham (John Clerke, Esq., 15 hearths) (Plate IB).[99] Such houses vary enormously in date and plan, but by 1664 most of the polite rooms, together with many of the service rooms, would have been heated.

Sir Robert Barnham, who lived at *Boughton Monchelsea Place*, a house built in the third quarter of the sixteenth century, was charged on twenty-four hearths in 1664. The positions of fifteen of them can be identified in his probate inventory when he died in 1685; ten lie in the best rooms, such as the parlour, dining room and various chambers, including the nursery, but others are in the chambers over the wash house and the gate house, which were more likely occupied by servants.[100] At *Roydon Hall*, East Peckham, Sir Roger Twysden paid for thirty hearths. No doubt the majority lay within the house itself, but the sixteenth-century walled garden includes two little heated rooms built into the walls to either side of the main gate, and also a delightful garden house, situated on an eminence, with two heated rooms looking out over the Weald. All four fireplaces must have been included in Sir Roger's total. The question of whether all the hearths listed, particularly at this social level, lay within the main residence, or whether some were in houses on the estate, is difficult to decide. In theory, all the hearths should have been in the main house or grounds, with the tenants paying separately, but in practice it is possible that

---

[98] Information from David Martin.
[99] Information from Jayne Semple.
[100] Hasted, *History of Kent*, V, 339-40; J. Newman, *West Kent and the Weald*, 2nd edn (The Buildings of England, Harmondsworth, 1980), p. 176; PRO: PROB 4/6343.

hearths in estate cottages and the home farmhouse were sometimes included as well.

In addition to earlier houses which were up-dated, there were handsome new properties of the seventeenth century, mostly built by the new gentry out of their newly created wealth. The twenty-plus category includes houses such as *Broome Park*, Barham (20 hearths) (Plate IA), built between 1635 and 1638 by Sir Basil Dixwell, recently arrived from Warwickshire; *Hall Place*, Bexley (29 hearths) rebuilt in the 1640s and 50s by Sir Robert Austin, baronet, who had risen from obscure gentry origins to become sheriff of Kent in 1637/8; *Groombridge Place*, Speldhurst (20 hearths) built between 1652 and 1674 by Philip Packer Esq, clerk of the Privy Seal to Charles II; and *Yotes Court*, Mereworth (21 hearths), with chimneys dated 1656 and 1658, built by Mr James Masters, son of a London merchant and son-in-law of Sir Francis Walsingham of *Scadbury*.[101]

From the fifteenth century onwards brick chimneys had been incorporated into all houses of any size and status, and during the sixteenth century the stacks were often a status symbol, marked on the exterior by decorated gables and chimneys.[102] Kent was late in its adoption of brick, and never as whole-hearted as parts of East Anglia, but ornamental stacks of the sixteenth century occurred on gentry houses such as *Roydon Hall*, East Peckham, *Ford Place*, Wrotham (Plate IB), or the smaller *Wickens* in Charing (Highslade) (Plate IIA). Occasionally there were more shafts than the number of fireplaces. This was a notable East Anglian feature, but can be found in some gentry houses in Kent, e.g. *Wickens*, where the kitchen fireplace originally had two flues, so that there were six shafts for five fireplaces.[103] Although chimneys of that sort were no longer built by the 1660s, houses where this occurred might have been over-charged unless the assessors went inside to check the number of hearths. In Hertfordshire it has been suggested that this may explain instances where the number of hearths drops by one between the hearth tax assessments of 1662 and 1663.[104]

But what sort of stacks were used by the far more numerous people below the level of the gentry? In the Middle Ages almost all

---

[101] For details of all these houses see Everitt, *Community of Kent;* Hasted, *History of Kent;* Newman, *West Kent and the Weald,* and *North East and East Kent,* 3rd edn (1983), and A. Quiney, *Kent Houses* (Woodbridge, 1993).

[102] See J. A. Wight, *Brick Building in England from the Middle Ages to 1550* (London, 1972), pp. 87-102. Illustrations in Quiney, *Kent Houses,* figs 26 and 27; K. Gravett, *Timber and Brick Building in Kent* (London and Chichester, 1971), figs pp. 102-13.

[103] The kitchen fireplace rose through two flues, but another fireplace was added later, apparently before 1664 when Anthony Aucher, gent., who was probably the tenant, was charged on 6 hearths (Highslade borough, Calehill).

[104] J. T. Smith, *English Houses, 1200-1800: the Hertfordshire Evidence* (RCHME, 1992), p. 188.

houses were heated by a single hearth in the open hall, although many had a second fireplace in a detached kitchen where cooking took place. Even after 1500, when open halls were ceiled over and enclosed fireplaces were introduced, very few houses had hearths in any other room. One reason for this was the nature and construction of many of the earliest enclosed fireplaces. Although brick was not unknown, and was certainly used by some wealthy peasants for chimney stacks from around 1500, the majority of the earliest enclosed hearths were of timber construction.[105]

These took a number of forms. The crudest way of confining the open hearth was to construct a smoke bay in which a small part of the hall remained open to the roof, the rest being ceiled over, allowing space for a chamber above. At *Little Bursted Farmhouse*, Lower Hardres, the house was built this way,[106] but usually open halls were adapted to this form in the early sixteenth century, e.g. *Burgoyne's*, Chilham, or *Hever Brocas*, Hever. [107] It was also a layout used for many smaller new houses until well into the second half of the century, as at *White Cottage*, Boughton Monchelsea. Another method was to build a tapering stack of framed timbers, lined with plaster; this did not form part of the main structure, and could be removed later without leaving any trace. Only a few survive, as at *Nightingale Farmhouse*, Yalding, and *Dormer Cottage*, Petham, but it is likely that many such timber chimneys once existed.[108] Finally, there was the brick stack. All three solutions were in use from the late fifteenth century, the decision to use one or the other probably depending upon money, the kind of house involved, the sort of fireplace required, and the availability of materials. Fireplaces were chargeable in the hearth tax whether they were open hearths or were confined within a stack of timber and plaster or brick. But the timing of the transition from open hearth to smoke bay and timber stack, and from them to brick stacks is relevant to the interpretation of the tax, for normally only brick stacks had fireplaces on the upper floors. While in theory there is no reason why several smoke bays or timber chimneys could not have heated a number of ground-floor rooms, in practice it is rare to find more than the hall, and perhaps a kitchen, heated in this manner.[109]

---

[105] The details of the various kinds of enclosed fireplaces are discussed in Pearson, *Medieval Houses*, pp. 108-15 and P. S. Barnwell and A. T. Adams, *The House Within: Interpreting Medieval Houses in Kent* (RCHME, 1994), pp. 130-5.

[106] Barnwell and Adams, *House Within*, p. 130.

[107] For *Burgoyne's* see ibid., p. 131; at *Hever Brocas*, Hever, the open hall was only built in 1532, and was half-floored shortly afterwards (Pearson, *Medieval Houses*, p. 115)

[108] Barnwell and Adams, *House Within*, p. 134.

[109] No timber chimneys with upper fireplaces are known to the author in Kent and they are, in fact, extremely rare anywhere. One survives at the *Old Medicine House*, formerly from Wrinehill, Staffordshire, but now re-erected and restored at Blackden, Holmes Chapel,

It is often assumed that the change from open hearth to enclosed fireplaces and chimney stacks was well under way by 1577 when William Harrison, in *The Description of England*, refers to 'the great multitude of chimnies lately erected'.[110] However, what is meant by this statement, and what difference it might have made to the number of fireplaces within a house, is ambiguous. In the first place, although the hearth might be built in a fireplace with a chimney, this could be a timber chimney, which usually did not serve more than a single hearth. Secondly, although by and large the upper strata of society had made the change to brick stacks by then, many sizeable houses retained their open hearths well into the seventeenth century.

In exceptional cases this may have been deliberate policy on the part of high status gentry who kept their open hall for show and ceremonial. A good example in Kent is *Penshurst Place*, whose aristocratic owners never ceiled the fourteenth-century great hall, although there were plenty of other heated rooms in the house. But discounting these, it is likely that some medieval halls still remained open to the roof as late as 1664. A number of terriers indicate that the process of change from open hearth to enclosed stack was still in progress during much of the seventeenth-century. In 1630 the parsonage house at Harbledown near Canterbury is described as having a 'hall without a chimney or a loft', although there was a brick chimney in the parlour.[111] In West Malling in 1640 the mansion house had 'one old hall without a chimney, one parlour with a chimney, a back kitchen without a chimney only a flue to evaporate the smoke' (which almost certainly refers to a smoke bay), plus two chambers with chimneys.[112] In Chislet in the late 1640s 'an ancient mansion house called Chislet Court' was 'built of stone for the most part open to the roof, and the other part two storeys high with a great kitchen'.[113] Finally, as late as 1662 and 1663 the vicarage at Hadlow was described as having a 'hall without any ceiling, being open to ye top, two lower chambers within ye hall over which one high chamber. One kitchen open also to ye top, one parlour with an upper chamber over it'. This sounds like a description of an unadapted open-hall house, the two lower chambers within the hall being the service rooms lying in the

---

Wrinehill, Staffordshire, but now re-erected and restored at Blackden, Holmes Chapel, Cheshire.

[110] W. Harrison, *The Description of England* (Dover edn., Washington and New York, 1998), p. 201. For recent comments see J. Hatcher, *The History of the British Coal Industry. Vol I, before 1700: Towards the Age of Coal* (Oxford, 1993), pp. 409-18; C. Platt, *The Great Rebuilding of Tudor and Stuart England* (London, 1994), pp. 4-6

[111] CCA: Glebe Terriers, DCb/D/T H10.

[112] CKS: Terriers, Rochester Diocese, DRb/At 53.

[113] Lambeth Palace Library: XIIa/22, Parliamentary Survey of Archbishop's Lands.

classic medieval position beyond the screens passage in the hall, with a chamber above. The actual heating in this house is not described, and it has not been identified in the hearth tax; but by 1765 this same vicarage was built in brick, which implies that the medieval house had been replaced.[114] Where a vicar or rector held several properties and the house was used by a curate, the dwelling might easily become out-of-date. What happened to church livings was just as likely to occur to secular dwellings, particularly to those let to tenants. At *Hurst Farm*, Chilham, for instance, although parlour and chamber fireplaces were introduced in the seventeenth century, the hall of this large medieval manor house of *c.* 1300 seems to have remained open until the present ceiling was inserted in 1714.[115]

The upgrading of some medieval houses went through two stages. In many houses there is evidence for a sixteenth-century smoke bay which was later succeeded by a brick stack. When a smoke bay was created, the house would normally have only had a single hearth, unless a kitchen was added at the back with its own smoke bay, as occurred at *Hale Street Farmhouse*, East Peckham. Only when the smoke bay was replaced by a brick stack was it possible to heat both the hall and the chamber above it, and not until this stage did the majority of farmhouses have second fireplaces to heat the parlour. Brick stacks in a number of examples are dated in the first three decades of the seventeenth century, e.g. *The Blue House*, East Sutton, of 1610, *Lower Newlands*, Teynham, of 1611, *Swallows*, Boughton Monchelsea, of 1616, and *The Old Manor House*, Chiddingstone, of 1638. All these are large, four-bay medieval open-hall houses, the largest in their neighbourhoods and certainly attached to sizeable farms. It may be argued that, while no doubt of considerable standing in the Middle Ages, they had become nothing more than tenanted farms of no great importance by the seventeenth century, and cannot be used as evidence of a wider trend among yeoman farmers. But this seems unlikely, for the mere fact that the alterations are dated, and often include gabled oriel windows and moulded ceiling beams, is an indication of wealth and pride. Both the physical and documentary evidence suggests that the process of replacing single enclosed fireplaces by chimney stacks with multiple fireplaces was spread over a long time even at this relatively high social level.

Lower down the scale, smoke bays lasted even longer. In Boughton Monchelsea, in an area south-east of Maidstone where houses tend to be above average in size and quality, a recent survey disclosed a

---

[114] CKS: Terriers, Rochester Diocese, DRb/At 34.
[115] Pearson, *Medieval Houses*, p. 115

number of relatively small mid or late sixteenth-century houses with two main ground-floor rooms, the smaller divided into two, and two first-floor chambers. These were manifestly inferior to the larger medieval houses mentioned above, such as *Swallows* in the same parish, which were still heated by inserted smoke bays, or contemporary larger and smarter houses which by then were being erected with multiple brick fireplaces, as in the rebuilt hall range of the *Cock Inn*, dated 1568. In these smaller houses the only fireplace was in a short smoke bay at one end of the ground-floor hall. Later, brick stacks were built into the smoke bays. Most examples are undated, but one of them, *White Cottage* on the Green, seems to have acquired a stone and brick stack, with two fireplaces heating the hall and its chamber, in 1670, this date being scratched on the rear of the new stack. Dating the undated examples is not easy, but narrow chamfers to the surrounds suggest that in many smaller houses brick stacks were inserted only late in the seventeenth century. Thus a number of them, like *White Cottage*, may have had single hearths in 1664, but two or three hearths a few years later. *White Cottage* and its peers are unlikely to have been the smallest and poorest houses in Boughton Monchelsea, and their occupiers were almost certainly not among the 25 per cent in that parish who were exempt in 1664; but they probably were among the 27 per cent who were charged on single hearths. What we are looking at here is not poverty, but the slow process of updating at a modest social level.[116]

The replacement of timber chimneys often took place even later. At *Stone Hill and Old Forge Cottages*, Sellindge, the open hall of what was formerly a single house had a timber chimney inserted in the sixteenth century which was apparently not replaced by a brick stack with three fireplaces until 1657, the date carved on the gable of a contemporary oriel window (Plate IIB). At *Hoggeshaws*, Milstead, on the Downs of central Kent, the same process was only completed in 1700, the date inscribed on the brick chimney. At *Dormer Cottage*, Petham further east along the Downs, it is unlikely that the ceiling of the open hall and insertion of the timber stack took place before the mid seventeenth century. That chimney still survives, and it is possible that there was only one fireplace until the nineteenth century.[117] This is only a small house, and by the nineteenth century it had probably sunk to cottage status, but in the seventeenth century it would have been a

---

[116] S. Pearson in P. Hastings, *Upon the Quarry Hills: a History of Boughton Monchelsea Parish* (Boughton Monchelsea, 2000), pp. 163-71.

[117] The date is suggested by the seventeenth-century decoration of the small post standing on the fireplace bressumer and supporting the main beam of the inserted ceiling. Since half of this small cottage was rebuilt in the nineteenth century, it is impossible to be certain that there never was another fireplace.

house of medium quality - *retardataire*, but not necessarily an index of poverty.

The reason this discussion has concentrated on what happened to fireplaces in older houses lies in the fact that in Kent few of the surviving farmhouses or smaller dwellings were built during the middle years of the seventeenth century. In Boughton Monchelsea parish in central Kent, a survey of thirty-two listed buildings of eighteenth-century or earlier date indicated that the largest houses tend to be either medieval or early seventeenth century in origin, the smaller to be sixteenth or eighteenth century, with only one completely new late seventeenth-century house.[118] In east Kent, as we shall see later, there was a major late seventeenth-century rebuilding, but it took place after the time of the 1664 hearth tax.

Three Case Study Parishes

To put flesh on the bones of this general account of houses, isolate some of the regional differences, and discover to what extent houses below the level of farmhouse can be identified in 1664, three parishes have been examined in more detail, with the hearth tax evidence considered alongside surviving buildings and other documentation (Table 4). The parishes of Charing and East Peckham were chosen because research had already been done there, and Goodnestone-next-Wingham was added to provide evidence from east Kent. Unfortunately, it was not possible to include any of the large parishes in the clothing district of the High Weald. Three parishes are far too few to provide a general picture of the county. They must not be taken as typical of the areas in which they occur, for every parish has its individual characteristics stemming from its soil and farming, landholding patterns, and accessibility to resources such as markets, woods, and marshland grazing.[119] Despite this, the maps show that there were general differences in hearth numbers in different parts of the county, and the case studies provide a glimpse of some of the underlying detail which accompanies the figures.

---

[118] Pearson in Hastings, *Upon the Quarry Hills*, p. 165.

[119] A survey of medieval houses in sixty parishes across Kent began to identify the regional distribution and characteristics of medieval houses (Pearson, *Medieval Houses*, chapter 10), but it was not possible to undertake work on that scale for this volume.

TABLE 4

Comparison of Hearth Tax Data in Three Case Study Parishes

H	CHARING				EAST PECKHAM				GOODNESTONE			
	C	NC	Tot	%	C	NC	Tot	%	C	NC	Tot	%
1	30	29	59	35	37	46	83	62	12	18	30	46
2	38	16	54	32	34	3	37	28	12	1	13	20
3-4	37	3	40	23	10	-	10	7	16	1	17	26
5-9	14	-	14	8	2	-	2	1.5	2	-	2	3
10+	3	-	3	2	2	-	2	1.5	3	-	3	5
Tot	122	48	170		85	49	134		45	20	65	

NC	28%		37%		31%	

4681 acres[120] = 36 houses per 1000 acres	3403 acres = 39 houses per 1000 acres	1865 acres = 35 houses per 1000 acres

Charing[121]

Charing is a large parish in Calehill hundred in the lathe of Scray. It lies in the centre of the county, stretching across several topographical regions and containing 4681 acres in the nineteenth century. To the north, a small sector lies on the chalk uplands; just below the scarp of the Downs, the main village, called Charing Town in the hearth tax, is situated on the spring line, where a small market settlement had grown up outside the gates of one of the residences of the archbishop of Canterbury. By the seventeenth century the market had ceased to function, replaced by a street of shops. To either side of the village, large arable fields characterised the valley between the Downs and a line of Gault Clay; to the south, numerous small farms and a couple of commons lie on the low hills and sandy soils of the Lower Greensand.

The ecclesiastical parish of Charing was divided between five boroughs: Charing Town, which encompassed the nucleated settlement; Acton and Highslade, lying to west and east both above and below the scarp of the Downs, and Sanpett and Field on the Greensand to the south. Parts of Highslade and Field are known to stretch beyond

---

[120] Acreages taken from the VCH, III, 358-70. These are the acreages of the ecclesiastical parishes in 1844, and therefore no more than an approximate guide to the acreages in the seventeenth century.

[121] Research on the history of Charing has been undertaken by Pat Winzar, helped by the Palaeography Group of the Charing and District Local History Society. I am extremely grateful to her for identifying relevant documentation, and discussing the problems of seventeenth-century Charing with me.

the parish boundary, but the taxpayers have here been counted in total since we do not know how many lived outside the parish. In 1664 (Table 4) there were 170 households in these five boroughs, giving a density of thirty-six houses per 1000 acres. Of the 170, fifty-seven had three or more hearths, with seventeen having five or more; fifty-nine had single hearths, and forty-eight households, with between one and three hearths, were exempt from paying the tax at all. Exemptions were highest in the town (43 per cent), but there were proportionally more single-hearth households in the rural area (37 per cent) than in the nucleated settlement (30 per cent). Surviving houses and probate inventories give a general picture of the parish over time. About fifty houses of seventeenth-century date or earlier survive, and of these twenty-six have clear signs of medieval origins. Most of the rest are of sixteenth-century date, although a few were not built until the seventeenth century.[122] In the rural areas most of the medieval dwellings are large, four-bay, houses, with an open hall between two-storeyed ends, often with high quality detailing to the timberwork.[123] In the town, some fourteen late-medieval buildings survive, eleven of them lying in the High Street; some are of normal four-bay design, but at least a couple have a tiny medieval open hall and a single two-storeyed bay at one end. Two medieval shops dating from the fifteenth and the sixteenth centuries have been positively identified, and several others are suspected.

Eighty-five probate inventories with room names survive, one is dated 1495, the rest were drawn up between 1565 and 1698. Of these, seventy-five give information about hearths, listing fire implements within various rooms, from which one may deduce the presence of a fireplace. However, from the 1660s to the 1690s, when inventories of individuals who paid the hearth tax a few years before can be identified, these often fail to register the presence of every hearth, so that several people who paid tax on three or even four hearths appear to have only one from the goods in their inventories. This did not just affect Charing, but can be observed, for example, at Sevenoaks in Kent, and elsewhere in England.[124] Thus the value of probate evidence is limited.

[122] Figures taken from the survey by the RCHME and from personal observation, augmented by information from the DoE List of Buildings of Special Architectural or Historic Interest.

[123] For the details see Pearson, *Medieval Houses*, Barnwell and Adams, *House Within*, and Pearson et al., *A Gazetteer of Medieval Houses in Kent* (RCHME, London, 1994).

[124] As discussed by M. Spufford, 'The limitations of the probate inventory', in *English Rural Society, 1500-1800* , ed. by J. D. Chartres and D. Hey, (Cambridge, 1990), pp.144-5, moveable goods (among which one may include hearth furniture) were sometimes not listed in an inventory because they had either been removed before the inventory was made, or formed specific bequests in the will, or belonged to the widow rather than to the deceased. In Sevenoaks, where forty-eight inventories can be correlated with the hearth tax, 73% had fewer hearths in the inventory than were charged, and in one instance, a tailor who died in 1668

Nonetheless, one or two points can be made. Prior to 1625 not one of the twenty-one inventories with hearth information has any reference to a chamber fireplace; but between 1625 and 1664 ten out of twenty-three, or 43 per cent, refer to fireplaces in chambers, and between 1664 and 1698 fifteen out of thirty-one, or 48 per cent, have upstairs fireplaces. The increase in references to first-floor fireplaces ties in well with the fact that dated fireplaces in surviving buildings only start appearing in the first decades of the seventeenth century, for those who built brick stacks with multiple hearths during the first two decades of the seventeenth century are unlikely to have died before 1625. A second point is that the actual numbers of fireplaces also increased, although, as indicated above, the inventory figures are not very reliable. Thus no inventory prior to 1625 lists hearth furniture for more than two fireplaces, between 1625 and 1664 13 per cent seem to have had three or more, and between 1664 and 1698 the figure rises to 19 per cent.

The surviving houses range considerably in size and quality. At the top end of the scale is *Pett Place*, a major gentry house, of medieval and sixteenth-century date, with twenty hearths charged to Sir Robert Honywood, Kt. Five minor gentry had between four and twelve hearths, including the vicar, Mr Henry Ridgeway, (6), Anthony Aucher, gent., (6), and Mr Gabriel Pierce or Peirce, (8). The vicarage was formed by the amalgamation of a medieval 'wealden' house and a sixteenth-century church house; Anthony Aucher was probably leasing *Wickens* (Plate 3), a house built around 1600 with decorative chimney stacks, in which the five original fireplaces using six original shafts, had by then been augmented by the addition of a fireplace in the kitchen chamber;[125] Gabriel Pierce lived in *Peirce House*, an early fifteenth-century building in the village centre, which had been considerably extended in the early sixteenth century. Nearly all the gentry properties lie along the spring line below the Downs, but to them one might add *Brockton Manor* on the greensand, owned by George

---

declared in his will that ' the Jacke [in the hall], and the plate behind the fire thear and the furnace in the Cichen shall not be Aprized to the Executrix but bee and Remayne to the House'; not unnaturally there is no evidence for either the hall fireplace or the kitchen furnace in the probate inventory, see *Sevenoaks Wills and Inventories, in the reign of Charles II*, ed. by H. F. C. Lansberry, Kent Records, 25 (Maidstone, 1988), pp. 70-3. Possibly this sort of arrangement was common, even when not specifically mentioned in the will. In other cases the appraisers may simply not have thought it worth itemising the bellows, creepers, tongs or andirons which would indicate the presence of a parlour or chamber fireplace; or, because it was summertime (50% of the inventories in Sevenoaks), the hearth furniture may have been stored, accounted for in a service room or attic under a general and unrevealing heading.

[125] See above p. lxiv. *Wickens* belonged to a minor gentry family named Dering, but was not occupied by them at the time ('Autobiographical Memoranda by Heneage Dering' in Yorkshire Diaries and Autobiographies, *Surtees Society*, 65 (1875), pp. 334-5).

Withick, an aspiring rather than a recognised gentleman, possibly from a family of clothiers, who had six hearths in one of the few seventeenth-century houses in the parish.[126]

Twenty-three probate inventories dating between 1664 and 1700 can be correlated with the hearth tax. Among them are seven for yeomen, five from the rural part of the parish and two from Charing Town. Their inventory values range from £29 to £1489 (median £141); they had between four and eleven rooms in their houses, and paid tax on between two and four hearths. The wealthier among them are likely to have lived in the large medieval farmhouses with seven or eight rooms which are scattered across the parish.[127] However, only the home of one, Anthony Baldock, can be definitely identified, and he occupied the rather smaller than usual *Little Swan Street* in Sanpett borough. He was a modest yeoman, charged on two hearths, and when he died in 1679 his inventory goods were valued at £81.[128] His house dates to the sixteenth century. It was always two-storeyed, and when built had a hall, heated by a smoke bay, and a second room on the ground floor, with chambers over. By the mid seventeenth century the smoke bay had been replaced by a brick stack with fireplaces heating the hall and chamber above, with an unheated parlour and best chamber over. Only one fireplace can be deduced from the inventory, plus a furnace which probably lay in a lean-to at the rear.

Three husbandmen, two with three hearths and one with only one, had inventories valued at £25, £38 and £83. One of them, Robert Rayner of *Barnfield* in Field borough, with an inventory value of £38, lived in part of a large medieval open-hall house (Plate IIIA). He was only charged on one hearth in 1664, although in his inventory of 1668 goods were itemised in six rooms, and we know that the house itself had three hearths by this date. The open hall at *Barnfield* went through the classic development: i.e. a sixteenth-century smoke bay was inserted heating only the hall, followed in the early seventeenth century by a

---

[126] In the early seventeenth century George Withick bought the manor of Brockton (Hasted, *History of Kent*, VII, p. 440), and in a rent roll of the manor of Charing in 1629 George Withwick, gent., was charged 12 shillings for 'his Mannor of Brockton'(CKS: U55 M125). It is probable that this house was *Brockton Farmhouse* on the edge of what was Brockton Heath. It had hall and parlour fireplaces in a double stack, with heated chambers above; and it is likely that a heated kitchen, perhaps with a heated chamber above, was replaced when a 19th-century service wing was built at the back. The house survived until 1999, when it was demolished for construction of the Channel Tunnel Rail Link.

[127] The land attached to two surviving large medieval houses, each with three later hearths, can be identified on a map of 1639 when they formed part of the Calehill estate, owned by the Darrell family (CKS: U386 P1). Newland had just over 301 acres in 33 parcels, and Sandpett had just over 112 acres in 20 parcels.

[128] Identification from the map of the Calehill estate. Baldock was not a tenant of the Darrells, but his land adjoined theirs and his house is named and illustrated on the map. Inventory, January 1678/9 CKS: PRC 27/27/206.

central brick stack which served three fireplaces in the hall, kitchen and chamber over the hall. The reason that Robert lived in only part of the house was the result of partible inheritance. In 1626 his grandfather had divided his property between two sons, one inheriting the kitchen and six other rooms at the north end of the house, the other getting the rest, only the 'new loft' being specified as it contained a special bequest. It is likely that the brick stack had been inserted shortly before, and that the new loft, which must be the present attic room above the hall chamber, was created at the same time. This half of the house contained the hall and parlour with chambers over them, plus the loft, and thus had at least five rooms. The north end, with the kitchen, was the part which descended to Robert. It had only the kitchen fireplace, although by *c.* 1700 the extra rooms in the house mentioned in 1626 had been rebuilt as a rear wing with a new stack to heat it. When Robert died in 1668 his inventory lists six rooms: hall, milkhouse, drinkhouse and parlour, with chambers over the hall and parlour. In his will the only property he had to leave was 'the moyty and north end of the house called Barnfield', which went to his eldest son, the younger ones receiving only money.[129] Thus *Barnfield*, one large dwelling when built, and one large dwelling today, was divided for at least most of the seventeenth century. No other surviving house split by partible inheritance has so far been identified, although there is documentary evidence of properties being divided in similar fashion.

Only a few surviving rural houses may have had single hearths in the late seventeenth century. One is *Hunger Hatch Cottage*, a small medieval dwelling of three rooms with no chambers or lofts above. A smoke bay was inserted in the sixteenth century, and in the seventeenth the hall and parlour were ceiled over, creating two low upper chambers, and a brick stack was built within the smoke bay; it had only a single hearth until the nineteenth century when the service bay was also ceiled over and the house was turned into two cottages. In 1639 the house is shown on the map of the nearby Calehill estate, tenanted by one John Myles who rented just over six acres in two parcels. Thus, this five-room house seems to have been home to a smallholder.[130] Another equally unusual survival is *The Thatched Cottage*, Church Hill. This is a three-bay dwelling of late seventeenth-century date, one of several buildings which were erected on the edge of Brockton Heath. It was a purpose-built version of the type to which *Hunger Hatch Cottage* had been adapted. It too had five rooms: two of the three ground-floor rooms having lofts above, the third being open

---

[129] Robert Rayner, will, February 1626/7, CKS: PRC 32/50/91; Robert Rayner, will, October 1668, PRC 32/53/554; inventory, December 1668, PRC 27/20/126.
[130] See map reference in note 127 above.

to the roof. Again, at first only the hall was heated. Although this particular house was probably built after 1664, its somewhat earlier neighbour, *Church Hill Cottage*, of similar size but with two hearths, may be one of two shown on the 1639 map lying on the edge of a plot belonging to George Withwick, whose six-hearth house lay on the other side of the heath. The fact that two houses appear in one plot so near the edge of the heath suggests that the occupants may not have been farmers, but supported themselves by a trade or craft, or by labouring for others.

Between 1600 and 1700 a variety of sources name over a hundred craftsmen and tradesmen in Charing, including those involved in the textile industry, building trades, purveyors of food and drink, makers of wearing apparel, smiths, metalworkers and leather workers. Probate inventories show many of them to have been relatively wealthy men, and seven, who died shortly after 1664, have inventories which can be correlated with the hearth tax.[131] Three lived in the rural part of the parish. Thomas Simmons of Acton borough, was a tile maker and a man of substance with an inventory value of £186; he had eight rooms in his house, with fine furnishings and linen, even a silver bowl; and a farm with cattle, pigs and crops sown on seventeen acres, as well £20-worth of tiles and £15-worth of bricks. He was charged on three hearths in 1664 and the site of his house can be identified, although the building was rebuilt in the eighteenth century. Simon Beeching, a blacksmith, lived in Sanpett borough; his inventory was valued at £67 and he was charged on two hearths. The third man, George Burwash, a linen weaver whose inventory totalled £42, cannot be precisely identified in the hearth tax as there are two men with this name, one with a single hearth, one with two.

A lime burner, two fell mongers, a butcher and a grocer's widow lived in Charing Town. Richard Rade, butcher, had an inventory valued at only £38 in 1683, but he had eight rooms in his house and four hearths; his house is not identifiable, but was obviously among the larger in the High Street.[132] Alexander Burwash was a wealthy grocer, who died in 1662 with goods worth £308. He had a hall, kitchen and shop, all with chambers over, plus a chamber over the entry, a buttery, cellar, brewhouse and warehouse. The hall, kitchen and kitchen chamber were heated, and in 1664 his widow was charged on four hearths.[133] Richard Beeching, a fell monger who was sometimes termed 'gent', had five rooms and was charged on three hearths. He

---

[131] Thomas Simmons, May 1669, CKS: PRC 27/21/88; Symon Beeching the elder, December 1670, PRC 27/22/28; George Burwash, April 1689, PRC 27/32/3.
[132] Richard Rade, January 1682/3, CKS: PRC 27/29/273.
[133] Alexander Burwash, April 1662, CKS: PRC 17/14/10.

was seventy-six when he died in 1690, and his inventory was only valued at £26. Since only one hearth is identifiable in the inventory it is possible that he lived with younger members of his family and that his inventory does not include the whole house nor all the goods in it.[134] Francis Speede, lime burner, whose inventory was valued at £60, had nine rooms and was charged on two hearths.[135] Finally, Thomas Kilham, another fell monger, died in 1674 with an inventory value of £96, £70 of which was in wool, skins and pelts, indicating that he was still working at his death and that he did not live in great style. In fact, he almost certainly lived at *30 High Street*,[136] one of the smallest medieval houses in the street, originally with a tiny open hall, and two rooms beyond the screens passage with a single chamber over them, although by the seventeenth century the hall had been ceiled, providing an extra room upstairs. Until the early eighteenth century only the hall was heated, and Kilham was charged on only one hearth in 1664. His inventory of 1674 lists a heated hall, a buttery, a shop by implication, and chambers over the hall and shop; there was also a wash house with a furnace which probably lay at the rear.

None of the occupiers of identifiable houses in Charing parish was exempted from paying the hearth tax. But in 1670 the inventory of Mr Gabriel Peirce of *Peirce House* included various not very expensive items in the house in Ms Creswell's occupation, and 'in the outhouses where Ms Wolfe and Sarah Harte live'.[137] Unfortunately none of these women figures in the hearth tax, although men with the same surnames paid on three and four hearths in the town, suggesting the possibility that they had been among the higher status residents of the parish, and that their circumstances were greatly reduced by the death of their menfolk. Twelve of the forty-eight people who were not charged in 1664 were women. Whether some of those who were not charged lived in larger buildings which had been divided into tenements, rather than in outhouses or complete small houses, is not clear from the documentary evidence. By the end of the century divided properties in the town start to be mentioned, but the references come from the 1690s rather than earlier.[138] Analysis of the parish registers suggests there was a slight increase of births and decline in deaths in the 1680s, which

[134] Richard Beeching, born in 1613; inventory: July 1690, CKS: PRC 27/32/104.

[135] Francis Speede, August 1667, CKS: PRC 27/19/139.

[136] Thomas Kilham, September 1674, CKS: PRC 27/26/61. Certain identification, from privately owned deeds, begins with Kilham's son in 1701.

[137] Gabriel Peirce, January 1669/70, CKS: PRC 27/21/78; published by P. Winzar, 'Peirce House, Charing: the house and its owners', *Archaeologia Cantiana*, 111 (1993), 190-92.

[138] Will of Robert Weekes, August 1692, CKS: PRC 32/56/137; will of Thomas Davies, May 1690, CKS: PRC 32/56/181; inventory, December 1693, PRC 27/33/96. Will of Samuel Davies, July 1706, CKS: PRC 32/58/79, and privately owned deeds of 48 High Street.

might indicate that by the end of the seventeenth century pressure on the existing stock of houses in the town was beginning to mount, and houses which had formerly been in single occupation were starting to be split up. No evidence has been found to suggest that this had begun by the time of the hearth tax.[139]

The impression of Charing in the late seventeenth century is of a parish of large and medium-sized farms, with a bustling centre where most of the necessities of life could be obtained. It had its quota of poor, although the documentary evidence does not illuminate their circumstances. In fact, in terms of the hundred of Calehill, or even the lathe of Scray, it was a prosperous parish, for it had fewer exemptions or houses with single hearths (28 and 35 per cent as opposed to the hundred figures of 33 and 41 per cent), a higher proportion of two-hearth houses, and a few more gentry than the average. Those who lived in single-hearth houses were not necessarily poor, and their houses were often well-built with at least five rooms.

East Peckham[140]

The parish of East Peckham covers 3,403 acres in the hundreds of Littlefield and Twyford. It lies on the edge of the Low Weald, and its soil, although considered by Hasted to be 'deep and miry',[141] is largely a fine and fertile loam. Agriculture was mixed, featuring both cattle and corn, with hops and fruit becoming increasingly important from the late seventeenth century onwards. It lies outside the area covered by Zell in his study of industry in the Weald,[142] but documentary evidence suggests that textiles played an important part in the local economy in the sixteenth and early seventeenth centuries, and two new fulling mills were recorded in 1624.[143] The Medway runs through Stockenbury borough at the southern end of the parish, crossed by Brandt bridge which linked parts of the Weald to the north of the county. There is no large settlement, although many of the houses are grouped in small hamlets. For taxation purposes the parish was divided into three boroughs, with Upper and Lone boroughs to the north in Littlefield

---

[139] That towns in Kent in the later seventeenth century, including market towns, experienced less severe demographic decline than the countryside and at least maintained their population levels has been discussed by A. D. Dyer, 'The market towns of south-east England, 1500-1700', *Southern History*, 1 (1979), 123-34, and Dobson, 'The last hiccup', p. 407.

[140] I am extremely grateful to Margaret Lawrence for sharing so much of her knowledge of East Peckham with me, for giving me access to unpublished documents, and arranging for me to visit many of the houses in the parish.

[141] Hasted, *History of Kent*, V, p. 92.

[142] Zell, *Industry in the Countryside*.

[143] CKS: U838 T303.

hundred, and the larger Stockenbury borough to the south in Twyford hundred.

In 1664 the two northern boroughs had twenty-nine names between them, charged on a varying number of hearths. The church, vicarage and parsonage lay in Upper borough, as did *Roydon Hall*, home of Sir Roger Twysden, baronet, who has already figured as a J.P. administering the hearth tax: he was charged on thirty hearths. Thomas Whetnall Esq. was charged on thirteen hearths at *Hextall Court*, now *Peckham Place*. One gentleman, and the parsonage, occupied by Thomas Summers, both had six hearths, while ten other people were charged on three or four. Only fifteen had one or two hearths, six of whom were exempt. In contrast, in the southern borough of Stockenbury, where 105 names are listed, seventy had one hearth, thirty-three had two, leaving only one person charged on three. Forty-three, mostly single-hearth dwellings, were exempted. Given these striking figures, one might expect few of the Stockenbury houses to have survived. Yet this is not the case. In the whole parish, nineteen medieval houses survive in whole or in part, and forty-two houses in all would appear to date to the seventeenth century or earlier, the majority lying in Stockenbury.[144] Forty-three probate inventories for the period 1664 to 1700 have been identified for the parish, twenty-two of which can be connected with people listed in the hearth tax; several of them can also be linked to surviving houses.

Two seventeenth-century or earlier houses have been identified in the small borough of Lone (eight households in 1664), and in Upper borough nine of the twenty-one houses survive. *Roydon Hall* has a sixteenth and seventeenth-century core, and evidence for several of the eight three- and four-hearth houses remains. The rectory and its six hearths no longer survives, but when Thomas Somers [*sic*] died in 1675 he had a house of twelve rooms, and an inventory total of £325 8s.[145] In 1664, *Court Lodge*, a large medieval wealden house, was lived in by John Parkinson, charged on three hearths,[146] and *Forge Gate Farmhouse*, with a large medieval hall and cross wing, probably also had three or four hearths, although demolition of part of the building means that only one survives today. *Paris Farm* has a handsome wing, its parlour fireplace dated 1598, with a heated chamber above, and a similarly heated hall range dated 1699, which is almost certainly the rebuilding of

---

[144] Thirty-two houses have been examined in detail, either for this publication or by the RCHME in 1989 (Pearson et al., *Gazetteer*), nine more seventeenth-century or earlier houses are included in the DoE List of Buildings of Special Architectural or Historic Interest.

[145] CKS: PRS I/19/104.

[146] In 1679, Thomas Whetnall of Hextall sold *Court Lodge*, 'late in the occupation of John Parkinson', CKS: U48 E6.

a medieval hall. The house was owned by the Barton family, but was probably leased in 1664.[147]

Two surviving houses in Upper borough which are likely only to have had single hearths in 1664 are *Little Moat*, a large fourteenth-century base-cruck hall, formerly an important dwelling which had probably descended the social scale by the seventeenth century; and *Forge Gate Cottage*, a sturdy two-bay, two-storey dwelling of the late sixteenth century, probably built with four rooms, although an outshut was soon added, and heated by a timber chimney which was only replaced by a brick stack with two fireplaces around 1700. James Hunt, a blacksmith, who was charged on a single hearth, died in 1667.[148] He had a house with three rooms on the ground floor, two chambers, and a shop which was clearly a smithy. His inventory totalled £49, plus £13 in bonds and £42 in debts owing to him. It would be nice to think he lived at *Forge Gate Cottage*, but this cannot be proven. Arthur Cheeseman also lived in a house charged on a single hearth, and when he died in 1669 his goods, valued at £13 6s., were listed in a hall, milk house, buttery and backside, and a single chamber.[149] Both his house and his wealth suggest someone much poorer than Hunt.

In terms of the number of hearths, Stockenbury borough had none of the variety found in Upper borough. Only one house, possibly identified as *Little Mill*, had as many as three hearths. The rest had one or two. Despite this, not all the surviving houses are small. *Beltring Green Farmhouse* is large by any standard, with a finely detailed medieval hall of 50 sq.m., formerly with two projecting cross wings at either end. Other sizeable medieval houses were *Pinkham* (demolished in the 1970s) and *Hale Street Farmhouse*. Not only were several of the earlier houses large, but some of their seventeenth-century inhabitants were wealthy yeomen farmers. John Stanford of *Beltring Green Farmhouse* was charged on two hearths. We know little about him, but he had two brothers, Henry and Richard, who also lived in the borough and were each charged on two hearths. When Henry died in 1673 his goods were valued at £548, mostly tied up in cattle and corn, and his house contained eleven rooms. When Richard died in 1699 his inventory totalled £241, and he lived in a house of ten rooms.[150] Five other wealthy yeomen farmers were charged on two hearths, but had inventories valued between £136 and £333, and between six and

---

[147] CKS: U119 T13 1593-1746.
[148] CKS: PRS I/8/121.
[149] CKS: PRS I/3/34.
[150] CKS: PRS I/19/116; PRS I/19/117.

thirteen rooms in their houses.[151] Although one or two less wealthy individuals can also be linked to two-hearth houses, it appears that at the upper end of the scale there was little, except the small number of their hearths, to distinguish the farmers of Stockenbury from those of Charing, or the northern boroughs of East Peckham itself.

Not all the houses in Stockenbury were as large as these, and not all the inhabitants as wealthy. In the Middle Ages, East Peckham was notable for the small size of its houses, and many of the smallest lay in Stockenbury. It can be shown that the size of medieval halls is normally in proportion to the size of the rest of the house, so that comparisons of house sizes can be made across the county, using hall sizes as a guide. In some parishes in the Low and High Weald, such as Staplehurst and Benenden, the median size of open halls is over 40 sq.m. In the rural part of Charing parish, the median size is 38 sq.m., but in Stockenbury, despite the survival of a handful of larger houses, the median size of medieval open halls is only 27 sq.m.[152] Smallest of all are *23 Smithers Lane* with a hall of 17 sq.m., and *Bullen Cottage*, in which the hall is only 15 sq.m. After the Middle Ages, small houses, consisting of a hall and two little rooms on the ground floor and two chambers above, continued to be built in the borough. *Hale Street Cottage* is a sixteenth-century smoke-bay house of this kind.

What sort of people lived in these smaller houses? Only a few of those charged on single hearths in 1664 can be identified in other documents, and not all of their houses were small. Richard Hatch, who lived at *Old Well House*, a surviving medieval building which had a smoke bay built in the hall in the sixteenth century, had nine rooms and goods valued at £179 when he died in 1671. Thomas Cheeseman, who was a husbandman, had seven rooms and goods totalling £77 in 1673.[153] However, two men who left probate inventories lived in smaller houses and were exempted from payment. When John Webb, miller, died in 1671 his inventory was valued at £20 12s. and his house had five rooms, with a heated hall and a furnace in the brewhouse, plus old and little butteries, a hall chamber and a men's chamber.[154] John Day, husbandman, whose goods were only valued at £14 when he died in 1675, seems to have had a house of four rooms: a heated hall, a drink buttery, a further chamber and a chamber on the stairs. The most obvious room lacking from both inventories is a parlour.

[151] John Barnes died in 1677 with an inventory valued at £136 and six rooms in his house (CKS: PRS I/2/39), Thomas Bishop (d. 1687, £250, 10 rooms, PRS I/2/98), John Cheesman (d. 1678, £254, 10 rooms, PRS I/3/36), John Keble (d. 1686, £333, 13 rooms, PRS I/11/3), and John Stone (d. 1695, £298, 8 rooms, PRS I/19/14.

[152] Pearson, *Medieval Houses*, pp. 123-4 and Fig. 139.

[153] Richard Hatch, CKS: PRS I/8/37; Thomas Cheeseman, PRS I/3/35.

[154] William Pattenden, CKS: PRS I/16/21; John Day, PRS I/4/21; John Webb, PRS I/23/29.

Although not identifiable in probate records, Stephen Cheeseman, who was also exempted from payment on a single hearth in 1664, can almost certainly be associated with a surviving house: *23 Smithers Lane* (Plate IIIB). He appears, from the evidence of deeds, to have leased this from Thomas Whetnall Esq. of *Hextall Court* in Upper borough.[155] The original building of c.1500 had a tiny hall of 17 sq.m., with two small service rooms at one end and a parlour at the other, both with chambers over, but with upstairs partitions which did not go right up to the apex of the roof, allowing the smoke from the open hearth to drift across to either end.[156] In the sixteenth century, a timber chimney to heat the hall was constructed within the parlour, reducing that room to little more than a closet. The house was still heated by its timber stack in 1664, the present brick stack probably not replacing the timber one until the early eighteenth century. In the late seventeenth century the house had six or seven rooms, and although not large was extremely well built, so Cheeseman's poverty must have resided in his circumstances, not the quality of his dwelling. Thus it seems that some of the people who had single-hearth houses, sometimes even being exempted from the tax, may have lived in sturdy, but plain and small, medieval or sixteenth-century houses with two to four rooms downstairs and two or three chambers above. In these buildings the single fireplace was probably still set within a timber chimney, which survived into the eighteenth century, if not longer.

Some of the earlier houses in East Peckham were originally very low in height. *Little Mill*, possibly owned by John Butler who was charged on three hearths in 1664, has fragments remaining of a very low medieval building which was either wholly open to the roof or had no more than lofts above the rooms at the ends of the open hall; it was heightened and enlarged around 1600.[157] The earliest part of *123 Snoll Hatch Road*, possibly lived in by John Keble, was an equally low house, built in the first half of the sixteenth century with a loft over the ground floor, its hall probably heated by a timber stack; in the early seventeenth century a new parlour wing with a brick fireplace was added, and then around 1700 the old range was heightened. These houses may be the tip of an iceberg, with other low houses remaining

---

[155] A few years ago, a receipt for rent in 1784 was found within the house. It was possible to relate this to private deeds which took the ownership and occupation of the house back to 1691, when it was 'now or late in the occupation of Stephen Cheeseman'. The deeds have been transcribed by Margaret Lawrence.

[156] In Pearson et al., *Gazetteer*, p. 50, the house was interpreted as having a two-bay hall, its parlour end having been demolished. But recent investigation indicates that it actually had a single-bay open hall between two end bays of two storeys each, as described above.

[157] The Butler family certainly had the mill and adjacent property in the immediate vicinity, CKS: U55 T314.

in use in the late seventeenth century. When such houses came to be heightened or rebuilt, their timber chimneys were replaced by brick ones.

Change and upgrading in East Peckham took a long time, and was still taking place at the very end of the century. Thomas Bishop was charged on two hearths in 1664, but the hearth furniture for three fireplaces and a kitchen furnace were listed in his inventory of 1687; Henry and Richard Stanford were also charged on two hearths each, but their probate inventories indicate that by the time they died, in 1673 and 1699, their houses were both heated by four fireplaces. *Old Well House* in Hale Street, is a medieval house of medium size which had a smoke bay created within the hall during the sixteenth century. In 1660 a twenty-one year lease on the house and forty-three acres was granted to Richard Hatch, and in 1664 he was charged on one hearth.[158] His inventory of 1671, as discussed above, still only has evidence for a single hearth in the hall, plus a furnace in the kitchen. Yet analysis of the building shows that by 1700 at the latest the smoke bay had been superseded by a double brick stack with four fireplaces.[159] *Brook Farmhouse*, owned by the Marten family, had two hearths in 1664, but the present house has four fireplaces in a brick stack which is also unlikely to date from later than 1700. Thus it looks as if many of the smoke bays and timber chimneys of the older houses in the borough were being replaced just after the time of the 1664 tax. John Butler's house, which may be *Little Mill*, had already received new fireplaces, but in other buildings the brick stacks were inserted a few years later. The earlier houses had not reached the end of their useful lives, for many of them survive today, but by the late seventeenth century they were in need of considerable updating.

Probate inventory evidence substantiates the suggestion that the wealth of testators and size of buildings in East Peckham may have been less than in Charing. Whereas the median wealth of testators in Charing was £78, and the average number of rooms in inventories (34 examples) was 4.9 on the ground floor and 3.3 above, the median wealth of the forty-three East Peckham inventories was £54, and the average number of rooms (31 examples) was 4.9 on the ground floor and 2.9 above. In other words, testators of East Peckham tended to be poorer, their houses on average having the same number of ground-floor rooms, but fewer chambers upstairs. Stockenbury borough, with its high number of single-hearth and exempt households, is virtually unique in this part of Kent. Twyford and Littlefield hundreds, in which

---

[158] CKS: U48/T1.
[159] Barnwell and Adams, *House Within*, pp. 142-3.

East Peckham lies, have higher proportions of single-hearth housholds (51 and 55 per cent) than the 33 per cent for Aylesford lathe as a whole. But in Stockenbury borough, as many as 62 per cent had only one hearth. The 134 households in the parish in 1664 is equivalent to thirty-nine houses per 1000 acres, indicating that, despite having no nucleated settlement, houses were more densely distributed than in Charing parish. This suggests that there may have been an unusually large number of small farmers, whether called yeomen or husbandmen, who were rather different from the large-scale yeoman farmers predominating in Charing and probably in many other parishes in the centre of the county. Work on deeds reveals an extremely active land market, with a lot of property owned by people living outside the parish, often Londoners.[160] Whether this was common throughout Kent, or was unusually prevalent in East Peckham, and what effect it might have had on the housing stock, is not at present clear.

Goodnestone-next-Wingham
The small parish of Goodnestone-next-Wingham covers 1865 acres in the Downs of east Kent. It lies within the hundred of Wingham in the lathe of St Augustine. In the Middle Ages most of the parish formed part of the archbishop of Canterbury's manor of Wingham. This comprised the large parish of Ash, with fertile arable land and marsh on the levels to the north, Wingham itself, with its sizeable nucleated settlement, and three smaller southern parishes on the rolling downland where the soil, although inclined to chalk, was good and there was also extensive woodland.[161] Most of the demesne land of the manor lay around the village of Wingham and in Ash. In Goodnestone, as in other downland parishes, several resident minor gentry families became the major landowners as the archbishop's estate broke up. Much of the land in this part of Kent remained open and unenclosed as late as the late eighteenth century, although the occupiers' scattered parcels were not subject to communal regulations as in the Midlands. Throughout the area arable farming was of primary importance, although all farms had livestock as well, the larger ones with grazing for cattle on the marshes north of Ash.

In 1664 the hearth tax lists sixty households in the parish, distributed between the boroughs of Goodnestone and Rowling, plus at

---

[160] For example, Addlestead in Stockenbury was sold by a man from Hammersmith to John Cheeseman in 1659 (CKS: U47/17 T53) and Pierce Mill, formerly within the parish although now in Hadlow, was sold by several London owners in 1672 (CKS: U36 T 1832).

[161] The following brief resumé of the history of Goodnestone is largely taken from Jane Andrewes, 'Land, Family and Community in Wingham and its Environs. An Economic and Social History of Rural Society in East Kent from c.1450 - 1640', unpublished PhD thesis, University of Kent, 1991. I am grateful to her for allowing me to read and use her work.

least five in the borough of Twittham.[162] In the sixteenth and seventeenth centuries the main gentry families were the Enghams of Goodnestone, who moved into the district in the early sixteenth century from Woodchurch on the edge of Romney Marsh, and the Boys of Bonnington, the senior but minor branch of a well-known family in the county. A third estate, Rolling or Rowling, was partly owned by the hospitals of St John Northgate, Canterbury and St Nicholas, Harbledown, and was leased to various gentry and yeomen families. In the seventeenth century *Rowling Court* was held by the Richards, an aspiring yeoman family which achieved gentry status during the seventeenth century. In 1664 Sir Thomas Engham at *Goodnestone Court* had twenty hearths and Sir John Boys of Bonnington and Gabriel Richards, gent. of Rowling, both had ten. Below them, two people had five and six hearths, leaving seventeen with three or four hearths, thirteen with two, and thirty with one. Twenty people, or 31 per cent, were exempted from payment. Thus there were proportionally greater numbers of exemptions and households with single hearths than in Charing, but fewer of both than in East Peckham (see Table 4).

As will be discussed below, the hearth tax figures do not suggest that Goodnestone is necessarily typical of east Kent. The reason for choosing this particular parish for detailed study is its unique return for the Compton Census in 1676. The Census, compiled by the local clergy, was intended to list all communicants, recusants and dissenters in each parish in England. In most cases the returns are little more than lists of numbers.[163] But a few clerics put down more, and the return for Goodnestone is one of the most detailed in the country.[164] Everyone in the parish is entered by name, in families, together with the station and occupation of the head of the household. Thus married couples are followed by their children in order of birth, and servants if there were any. The list is divided into gentry, yeomen, tradesmen, labourers and poormen. Although this list was compiled twelve years after the 1664 hearth tax, a number of names occur in both sources, and when used in

---

[162] A small part of Twittham borough lay within the parish and five names listed in 1664 are identifiable in the 1676 Compton Census. The modern civil parish of Goodnestone also includes Chillenden, but in the seventeenth century this was a separate ecclesiastical parish and borough, lying in Eastry hundred, so it has been excluded from this discussion.

[163] For the Compton Census see *The Compton Census of 1676: a Critical Edition*, ed. by Anne Whiteman, British Academy, Records of Social and Economic History, NS 10 (Oxford, 1986). The Census for Kent has also been published by C. W. Chalklin, 'The Compton Census of 1676 - the dioceses of Canterbury and Rochester', in *A Seventeenth Century Miscellany*, Kent Records, 17 (1960), pp.153-74, and M. J. Dobson, 'Original Compton Census Returns - The Shoreham Deanery', *Archaeologia Cantiana*, 94 (1978), 61-73.

[164] The complete return for Goodnestone is reproduced in Whiteman, *Compton Census*, pp. 636-44, and discussed by Peter Laslett in *The World We Have Lost* (London, 1965), pp. 64-76.

conjunction with probate documents and other contemporary records, something can be inferred about the people who had particular numbers of hearths in 1664. In addition, the buildings of the parish have been briefly surveyed to give some idea about the houses themselves. In 1676 the Census lists 281 inhabitants in sixty-two households, plus four hospitallers, who lived in almshouses. Twenty-nine of the sixty-two households are almost certainly identifiable in the hearth tax, so we have information concerning just under a half of those named in 1664.

At the upper end of the social scale, all three gentlemen listed in 1664 had died or left the area, and the families of Sir Thomas Engham and Sir John Boys do not occur in the Census. The Engham's house may have been tenanted by Edward Hales Esq., who is listed with his wife, six children and fifteen servants at the head of the Census.[165] Only the last two children were baptised in the parish, in 1674 and 1675, which suggests that the Hales had only recently arrived.[166] Sir John Boys of Bonnington had died in 1664, leaving his property to three daughters, who had sold it by 1676.[167] Gabriel Richards of Rowling had died in 1672, but *Rowling Court* was occupied by Mrs Elizabeth Richards, her niece and one servant.

Twenty-seven yeomen families were listed in 1676, of whom fifteen are identifiable in the 1664 hearth tax. Laurence Neame is perhaps the son of Margaret Neame who had five hearths in 1664; he lived with his wife, two small children and eight servants, which implies that he was a farmer of substance. Six other yeomen, four of them with servants, lived in houses with three or four hearths. Probate inventories of the very late seventeenth century include four for yeomen, with goods valued between £250 and £450, living in houses of eight or nine rooms, three of them including servants' chambers. Among them was Thomas Wanstall, who died in 1701. It appears that he was too young to be included in either the hearth tax or the Census, but three Wanstalls with three and four hearths clearly belonged to the village elite in 1664. Only Edward, who died in 1680, has left an

---

[165] Laslett, *World We Have Lost*, p. 65, says that Hales rented from the Penningtons, but this is because he confused Goodnestone-next-Wingham with the north coast parish of Goodnestone-next-Faversham.

[166] Goodnestone Parish Registers, transcribed by Kenneth V. Elphinstone, 1933. I am grateful to Frances Smith for lending me a copy of the baptismal register, which indicates how very young many of the children named in the Census were.

[167] Goodnestone was alienated to Brook Bridges Esq., who rebuilt the house and died in 1717. Hasted thought this took place in the reign of Queen Anne (*History of Kent*, IX, pp. 242-3). Whenever it happened, it is clear that by 1676 the Enghams were no longer living in the parish. Boys died in 1664 leaving three daughters who sold the estate in 1666 to Thomas Brome Esq., whose son William, of Farnborough, sold it to Brook Bridges in 1710 (Hasted, *History of Kent*, IX, pp. 245-7).

inventory which survives. In 1676 he lived with his wife, four grown children and two servants in a three-hearth house, and his inventory shows that he had at least eight rooms.[168] Somewhat less well-off yeomen included David Court, also charged on three hearths, who died in February 1674/5 leaving a widow with four young children and a servant; his inventory totalled £57, and his goods were only listed in three rooms, although he must have had more in his three-hearth house - an indication of how unreliable inventory evidence may sometimes be. Five more yeomen had two hearths, among them Stephen Church who lived in Twittham borough with a wife, six under-age children, and two servants. When he died in December 1692 only four rooms were listed, although there appear to have been fireplaces in both the hall and chamber above; however, lack of service rooms in this inventory may again mean that some rooms were left out. His inventory was valued at £46.[169] Three yeomen had only a single hearth. William Pain and his wife lived with their grown-up son, and when William died in July 1689 six rooms were listed in the house, only one of these definitely being upstairs, over the heated hall. Despite this, his inventory totalled £106, of which £64 was in thirty-three acres of wheat and barley.[170] The less wealthy in this group are likely to include husbandmen, for which there is no separate category.[171]

Goodnestone is now little more than a hamlet. It was never large, overshadowed by its much larger neighbour, Wingham, only two miles away. Nonetheless, nine tradesmen were listed in 1676, and seven of these can be identified in 1664. They were a butcher, a weaver, a shoemaker, a carpenter, a grocer, a brickmaker and a 'kempster', all with only a single hearth in their houses. The butcher, John Manvell or Menvile, had a young family and a servant, and was charged on one hearth; he was the only tradesman in the parish to have a servant. The weaver, Christopher Clarke, was also charged on a single hearth. The other five were exempted from paying. James Dixon, the shoemaker, had two children who were old enough to take communion, but Richard Saffrey or Safry, the carpenter, William Selden the brickmaker and Henry Webster, the 'kempster', had under-age offspring. Margaret Tucker, widow, was a grocer and lived alone. She is the only tradesman in the parish for whom there is an inventory, made in October 1679. Three rooms were listed: a hall, chamber over the hall, and a shop, and her goods were valued at £16, those in the shop amounting to £1.[172]

---

[168] Unfortunately the inventory is not complete and has no total. CKS: PRC 27/28/251.
[169] CKS: PRC 27/33/22.
[170] CKS: PRC 27/31/259.
[171] Laslett, *World We Have Lost*, p. 65.
[172] CKS: PRC 27/28/107.

Thus the general impression is one of rural tradesmen barely able to scrape a living.[173]

The final group for which correlations can be made between the hearth tax and the Compton Census are the labourers. In 1676 there were twelve labourers in the parish. Five of them can be identified twelve years earlier. Symon Tucker was charged on a single hearth, while John Hart, William Gray, Thomas Cox and Thomas Holmes were exempted. It is easy to see them as men at, or near, the bottom of the social scale. But one could be mistaken. One of the labourers listed in 1676 is John Nash, married to Aphrey. A John Nash was exempted from paying the hearth tax in Rowling in 1664, and it is possible that this was his father.[174] Research into the Nash family of Goodnestone indicates intriguing twists to this family's fortunes. In the early seventeenth century the Nashes owned a farm of fifty-sixty acres in Rowling. By the later seventeenth century the property had passed by marriage to a Canterbury family, although it is possible that members of the Nash family continued to farm it as tenants. The John Nash who was not charged for his single hearth in 1664 is likely to have been one of this family. A second John Nash, possibly his son, married Aphrey Court in 1675 and was certainly the 'labourer' listed in 1676. His descendants apparently became relatively prosperous maltsters in Goodnestone in the eighteenth century.[175] Although a link with the hearth tax is not certain, it is clear that both earlier and later members of the family were reasonably well-off, while in the third quarter of the seventeenth century the only two known representatives in the parish were exempted from paying tax and classed as labourers. In 1676 most of those classed as labourers either had no children, or only very young ones, giving the impression that being a labourer may sometimes have been a stage in a man's life rather than the status he would retain for ever. Likewise, it is possible that a decade earlier those who were exempted from paying the hearth tax were not always poor, but were either beginning or ending lives which were more prosperous at other times.[176]

---

[173] The occupations of the exempt, including many labourers, are in line with those identified in Warwickshire, see Arkell 'Incidence of poverty', p. 37 and Table 7.

[174] David Nash Mills, *The Nash Families in Goodnestone-next-Wingham*, Faversham Papers, 55 (1997). The family also owned property in the next parish of Woodnesborough, and a John Nash is charged on a single hearth there in 1664, suggesting either that the same John was responsible for two houses, or that the family tree was somewhat more complex than Mills suggests.

[175] Mills, *Nash Families*, pp. 45-9.

[176] The possibility of social mobility and the varying stages of the life-cycle in Goodnestone is discussed by Laslett, *World We Have Lost*, pp. 66-7, and in general by Husbands, 'Hearth, wealth and occupations', in *Surveying the People*, pp. 74-5.

None of those classified as 'poormen' in 1676 can be identified in the 1664 hearth tax. There were twelve families in this category, ten of which were headed by women, at least two of whom appear to have been newly widowed with young children born in the previous few years. At the end of the list are four hospitallers who lived in almshouses endowed in 1672. As discussed below, the almshouses may have been there in 1664, and if so, this is another instance of hidden almshouses in the 1664 tax. The surnames of seven of the 'poormen', and all of the hospitallers are new to the parish in 1676, not occurring in 1664. This suggests that at the lower levels of society the population may have been extremely mobile, as those writing about the poor in Kent have noted.[177]

What kind of houses did the people of Goodnestone inhabit in the late seventeenth century? Unfortunately, we know little about the twenty-hearth house of the Enghams. The estate was bought by Brook Bridges Esq. in the early eighteenth century, and he rebuilt the house, leaving no trace of the previous one. When an earlier Sir Thomas Engham died in December 1620 his inventory listed goods in twenty rooms.[178] It is not a particularly full inventory and the only certainly heated room was the kitchen, although the house must have had a number of fireplaces. In the grounds of the present *Goodnestone Park* lies the so-called *Dower House*, illustrated in an engraving of 1719 alongside Brook Bridges' new mansion.[179] This is a late fifteenth-century wealden house, with an open hall between two-storeyed ends, all set under a single roof. The engraving shows three chimney stacks: a single one over the hall, a double one at the parlour end, and another in a rear extension. In the house itself only the hall fireplace remains from before 1664. While the house had four or five fireplaces, it clearly never had twenty, and cannot be the Engham's seventeenth-century mansion. In 1664 it is likely that it was inhabited by one of the seven yeoman farming families who had four or five hearths in Goodnestone borough.

When John Boys Esq. of Bonnington died in 1618 his inventory listed nineteen rooms,[180] and in 1664 Sir John Boys was charged on ten hearths. The mansion house they lived in is now no more than a building platform in a field, in front of which lies a large medieval open-hall house and, a few feet away, a curious narrow range of early sixteenth-century date, jettied on both long sides and originally unheated. By the 1660s the medieval house seems to have had four

---

[177] Clark, 'Migration', pp. 57-90; Dobson, *Contours of Death*, p. 65.
[178] CKS: PRC 28/8/80
[179] J. Harris, *The History of Kent*, I (London, 1719), p. 132.
[180] John Boys Esq., October 1618, CKS: PRC 28/9/80

fireplaces, but the jettied range was still not domestic.[181] Both buildings now face south-east, but formerly faced north-west towards the drive to the mansion house behind. Thus the present *Bonnington Farmhouse* may, like the *Dower House* at *Goodnestone Park*, have been the home farm, inhabited in 1664 by one of the yeoman families, while the jettied range was probably a non-domestic estate building, only later turned into cottages. The third gentry house, *Rowling Court*, was occupied by the Richards family who had ten hearths in 1664. It survives, at least in part. It is a complex house, built of brick in the sixteenth and seventeenth centuries, and seven or eight of the early fireplaces can still be identified. Elizabeth Richards, who occurs in the Census of 1676, died in 1678, and her probate inventory refers to ten rooms in the house, although it does not list all the service rooms that are likely to have existed.[182] She had two parlours and a painted chamber with no evidence of hearth furniture; but there were fireplaces in the hall, kitchen, best chamber and the chamber where she died. As so often, fewer hearths appear in the inventory than were charged in 1664.

Not many other early houses survive in the parish. There may be early remains at *Uffington Court*, an estate once owned by the Boys family,[183] and probably leased to one of the yeoman farmers. Otherwise the only other early timber-framed buildings appear to be *Rowling House*, and the *Old Post Office* in the village centre. The latter is the medieval wing of a once larger building, the open hall of which has been demolished. The hall had probably gone by 1664, the wing becoming a house in its own right, heated by four fireplaces in a back-to-back stack. The number of hearths indicates that this was again the home of a wealthy yeoman family. *Rowling House* is probably sixteenth-century in date; it was heated by a stack with two flues serving the hall and chamber above. The rest of the house has been rebuilt, but as no house in Rowling borough other than *Rowling Court* had more than three hearths, there can only have been one other at the most, and it was probably one of the three three-hearth houses which can be correlated with yeoman families in 1676.

All the other houses are built of brick. Only *Hop View* at Sadler's Hill, *Little Twitham Farm Cottage*, and the almshouses are likely to precede 1664. Both the former are of one-storey, with attics set partly in the roof. *Hop View* has three ground-floor rooms, with back-to-back fireplaces heating two of them. In 1717 this was part of the property purchased by John Nash (thought to be the son of John,

---

[181] The farmhouse had two more fireplaces, in an angled stack, added by the end of the century, and the jettied range had and end stack and a Dutch gable added at about the same time.

[182] CKS: PRC 27/27/145.

[183] Andrewes, 'Land, Family and Community', p. 80.

the labourer of 1676). Nash called himself a yeoman when he married in 1712, and later, while living here, he became a prosperous maltster.[184] *Little Twitham Farm Cottage* has only two rooms per floor, with fireplaces heating the hall and attic chamber above. Despite its small size the house has a decorative Dutch gable at the fireplace end and elaborate brick pilasters along the front, while an early barn indicates that it was an independent farm. It could have been the four-room, two-hearth dwelling of Stephen Church, yeoman, who died in 1692. The brick almshouses for four people, with two rooms down and two up, heated by four fireplaces in two projecting stacks and embellished with another fancy gable end, was endowed by Gabriel Richards when he died in 1672, ie. later than the hearth tax (Plate IVA). However, as Newman points out, the decorative brickwork is not far removed from that at *Broome Park*, Barham, of 1635-8 (Plate IA), and the monument to Richards in the church suggests the almshouses may already have been in existence when he died.[185] Apart from these last, no surviving early houses in the parish are incontrovertibly in the single-hearth category so, unlike Charing and East Peckham, we do not have direct evidence of what houses with single hearths were like.

In both Charing and East Peckham approximately 30 per cent of the houses implied by the figures in the 1664 tax returns survive today. In Goodnestone, where only nine houses have been identified as having earlier remains, the proportion of survivors is only 14 per cent. That Goodnestone is not unique is suggested by the fact that pre-1664 houses are just as rare in the large parish of Ash on the levels to the north, where about six medieval buildings and seven or eight later ones form only 13 per cent of the dwellings required by the households listed in 1664.[186] In all parishes in east Kent most of the early houses are sizeable, and only a few smaller ones survive. In Nonington, further into the Downs to the south of Goodnestone, *Southdown Cottage* is a rare medieval example with a tiny open hall and two end bays, one open to the roof, one with a loft over it. Other small houses remain in Wingham, including *113 High Street*, a low house of one storey and attic, with only two rooms on each floor and a single fireplace in the hall (Plate IVB).[187] Despite its apparent meanness, the initials and date TB 1667 are proudly inscribed in the dormers, indicating that as late as

[184] Mills, *Nash Families*, pp. 39-47.

[185] Newman, *North East and East Kent*, pp. 335-6.

[186] Pearson, *Medieval Houses*, and *Gazetteer*, and DoE List of Buildings of Special Architectural or Historic Interest

[187] David Eaves, 'Wingham: Its Vernacular Buildings pre 1700', unpublished Diploma thesis in Local History, University of Kent, 1982, believes this to be a medieval building updated, but the timbers look very late, and it may be a late seventeenth-century dwelling replacing a medieval house on the same site.

this the owner clearly thought his dwelling was worth drawing to people's attention. Throughout east Kent, and in contrast to the centre of the county, the general scarcity of pre-1664 houses and the reasonable size and quality of most which remain make it likely that they were of relatively high status, occupied by yeomen in the late seventeenth century. The few surviving smaller houses with single hearths may have been the homes of husbandmen, but for this we have no positive evidence.

After 1664, in the very late seventeenth and early eighteenth centuries, rebuilding in east Kent took place on a scale unknown elsewhere in the rural parts of the county. In Goodnestone itself, several small, low brick houses were erected, perhaps under the improving eye of the new landlord, Brook Bridges.[188] In the large parish of Ash at least thirty-six brick houses, both in the village and on the surrounding farms, were built between 1670 and 1730. Some are as small as the Goodnestone houses, others have two full storeys, sometimes with attics above, providing seven or eight rooms, heated by three or four fireplaces, set either in a large central stack, or in end stacks, the gables often being decorated in the fashionable 'Dutch gable' style. Similar brick farmhouses can be found elsewhere on the levels, in parishes such as Ickham, Sarre and Worth.

The surviving houses, both in the Downs and on the levels, suggest that on the whole only the homes of the well-to-do survive from 1664 or earlier, and that there was a massive rebuilding of smaller and poorer dwellings in the years that followed. But one must be careful not to generalise too much, for the documents show that standards of living were not uniform throughout the region. The distinction between rich and poor in the Goodnestone hearth tax, where 46 per cent had single hearths and three houses, forming 5 per cent of the total, had ten or more hearths, is even more apparent in the neighbouring parish of Nonington. There 77 per cent of households had single hearths and 60 per cent were exempt, while two houses, again forming 5 per cent, had ten or more hearths, leaving even fewer households in the middle bracket.[189] In contrast, in Ash, there was far less polarisation, for although 49 per cent had single hearths, no-one

---

[188] Three formerly low dwellings in the centre of the village have ground-floor beams and fireplaces of c. 1700, the upper parts having been rebuilt again in the nineteenth century. In one the outline of a low roof in one gable wall indicates that in c.1700 this house had only a ground floor and low attic above.

[189] Boroughs of Nonington and Easole, both in Eastry hundred. Hasted, *History of Kent*, IX, p. 251, places Nonington in Wingham hundred, but in the 1664 hearth tax it is difficult to see which borough in Wingham hundred could include householders from this parish.

had more than seven, so a far higher proportion of the population fell into the middle bracket.[190]

A general correlation between numbers of hearths and personal wealth has been remarked on in other parts of England,[191] and can be seen in Kent as well. Although the differences are not as marked as one might expect, the few inventories that relate to Goodnestone also give the impression that in the Downs of east Kent testators may have been proportionally poorer than testators in the centre of the county and those who lived on the larger farms on the lower land to the north. In Charing the median wealth of testators was £78, in East Peckham, £54, but in Goodnestone it was only £45 (16 inventories). Figures for Ash and Nonington help to put this in perspective: in Ash, on the flat, the median for fifty-five inventories between 1665 and 1685 was £117, but in Nonington, up in the Downs, fourteen inventories produced a median figure of only £25. Thus although we know there were a number of wealthy yeomen living in sizeable houses in the Downs, the inventories suggest that even people prosperous enough to have inventories were in general somewhat poorer than those who lived on the levels in east Kent or elsewhere in the county. In Goodnestone, the homes of those too poor to make wills cannot be identified in documents, and do not survive today.

Generalisations are treacherous from such small numbers, but all the forms of evidence combine to suggest that society in the Downs, whose healthier climate attracted many of the gentry, was polarised between the rich and poor. At the top were the gentry living in large houses, below them a small band of relatively prosperous farmers, and below them sizeable numbers of very much poorer folk. This polarisation had been a feature of east Kent in the Middle Ages,[192] and is perhaps characteristic of corn-growing areas, where large arable farms required a labour force, either living-in as servants, or dwelling separately in houses too small and poor to have survived. However, on the levels, over which most of the gentry estates extended, those below gentry level, many of whom were tenants of the gentry, could more easily make a living. By the time of the hearth tax some already lived in substantial houses with between five and nine hearths, but many more must have been on the verge of replacing their old ill-heated medieval dwellings with up-to-date brick ones.

As discussed above, the hearth tax evidence suggests that houses in Goodnestone were rather better heated than some in east Kent, and

---

[190] Boroughs of Chilton and Overland in Wingham hundred.
[191] H. M. Spufford, 'The significance of the Cambridgeshire hearth tax' *Proceedings Cambridgeshire Antiquarian Society*, LV (1962), 53-64, esp. table 6.
[192] Pearson, *Medieval Houses*, p. 137.

the number of people exempted is lower than elsewhere. In fact, from the Exchequer's point of view, Goodnestone did not compare unfavourably with Charing, for on average there were 2.5 hearths per household in Goodnestone, and only 2.3 hearths in Charing, a situation caused by the higher proportion of large houses and the relatively small number of two-hearth households in relation to the total. East Peckham, with its small farms, and unusually high number of single-hearth households and exemptions, had only 1.8 hearths per household, producing far less revenue than either of the others. Nonetheless, whatever the yield to the Exchequer, both the physical and documentary evidence suggests a very real disparity in wealth and housing standards between east Kent and regions further west.

Town Houses

Towns and their houses varied considerably, but for purposes of analysing the hearth tax they fall into two categories: towns which were growing rapidly in the later seventeenth century, in which most of the houses were new; and medieval towns which had a substantial quota of old buildings. In 1664 all the old centres: Canterbury, Rochester, the Cinque Ports, and the inland towns, contained large numbers of early houses, but a handful of them appear to have been more prosperous than the rest. Canterbury, Rochester and Maidstone were still flourishing. Each was strategically placed to serve a wide area of Kent; the first two were cathedral cities, Canterbury was the largest urban conglomeration in the county and the centre of east Kent, and Maidstone was the assize town for the west.[193] All had a fair number of gentry and professional residents requiring suitable accommodation. The result was that just over 20 per cent of the houses in Maidstone and Rochester had five or more hearths, and under 60 per cent had only one or two (Table 1). Unfortunately, we cannot accurately calculate the figures for Canterbury City, but the suburban parishes of St Dunstan's and Longport have very similar profiles.[194] The Cinque Ports and the smaller inland towns also retained much of their medieval fabric; but for a variety of reasons most of them were no longer prospering. In 1664 we have almost no information for the Cinque Ports, but the inland towns had few large dwellings, in most

[193] For a general discussion of towns in the seventeenth century see Chalklin, 'The towns', in Armstrong, *Economy of Kent*, pp. 205-13.
[194] See Appendices IV and V for Canterbury. Within the city as a whole, including the urban areas of Westgate hundred listed in Appendix V, 29% of those charged (the exempt in Westgate have been left out of this calculation) had 5 or more hearths, and 41% had only one or two. The similar figures for Maidstone, again excluding the exempt, are 30% and 24%. These proportions, together with the suggested total of exempt as around 50%, indicates that Canterbury probably had similar, if not greater, extremes of rich and poor than Maidstone.

cases only 7-13 per cent of houses having five or more hearths, and well over 60 per cent having one or two. In all these towns a few new houses were built in the later seventeenth century, but the timber-framed and jettied buildings which distinguish them are largely of the early seventeenth century and earlier. Where money was no object, such houses could have had as many hearths as new dwellings, but houses erected before the mid seventeenth century were built with fewer hearths than later ones, and even when updated, they were seldom as well endowed.

The following examples are largely taken from the Cinque Ports of Sandwich and Faversham, since this is where fieldwork has taken place. Neither were included in the 1664 hearth tax, but Faversham, although small, was still a prospering port, and the profile of its hearths in the 1671 tax suggests it had affinities with Maidstone and Rochester.[195] Sandwich, on the other hand, was noticeably in decline. In 1697 Celia Fiennes described it as 'a sad old town all timber building ... run so to decay that ... its just like to drop down the whole town'.[196] While the types of medieval house found there are quite unlike those in the failing broadcloth town of Cranbrook, one suspects that its hearth tax profile would not have been all that different from the latter, which had the highest number of single hearths (47 per cent), and the lowest number of houses with five or more hearths (7 per cent) of any town in the county.

The medieval houses in all these towns were originally heated by no more than a single hearth in an open hall, perhaps with detached kitchens in larger properties, although the evidence for these has usually gone.[197] By the early seventeenth century, the open halls in Faversham, which normally ran along the street frontage, had largely been replaced by storeyed ranges with fireplaces on both the ground and first floors. The stacks were either placed externally to the hall and cross wing, as at *39-40 Court Street*, so that two stacks provided four fireplaces heating key rooms, or, as at *1-4 East Street*, a single large stack was inserted to heat both the hall and adjacent wing. In these houses four or five rooms out of eight or ten were provided with fireplaces, leaving a number of unheated ground and first-floor rooms and attics. In Sandwich, where the open halls usually lay to the rear of a storeyed street range, more medieval halls survived, simply having upper storeys

[195] The 1671 hearth tax for Faversham is published in Hyde and Harrington, *Faversham Hearth Tax*, pp. 50-7.

[196] *The Illustrated Journeys of Celia Fiennes*, ed. by C. Morris (Exeter, 1982), p. 123.

[197] In some late-medieval houses there is evidence for timber smoke bays in rear wings, probably used as kitchens. Examples are *4-5 Best Lane*, Canterbury, *Archaeologia Cantiana*, 110 (1992), 378-80, and *5-6 Market Place*, Faversham, *Archaelogical Journal*, 126 (1969), 249-52.

and chimney stacks inserted in them, and in some cases only one seventeenth-century stack was introduced to heat the newly-ceiled hall and the room above. This occurred, for example, at *5 Strand Street* in 1615, and at much the same time in *3* and *41 Strand Street*. The result was houses of six or even eight rooms with only two, or at the most three, seventeenth-century hearths. At *39 Strand Street*, a rather larger medieval house with eleven or twelve rooms after the hall had been ceiled, two chimney stacks provided four fireplaces, although by the early eighteenth century another stack had been built with two more fireplaces.[198]

Early seventeenth-century houses in the older towns were often given much the same provision. *No. 25 Court Street*, Faversham, was built by a wealthy mariner, John Trowtes, in the second or third decade of the seventeenth century; in his inventory of 1635 eight rooms and a cellar are listed: a shop and a hall at the front and a kitchen and buttery at the rear, all with chambers over. It is clear that the hall, kitchen and chambers over them were heated, but the shop and buttery and their chambers were not. His successors were charged on four hearths, and the house conforms to the same pattern today.[199] By the time *28 Palace Street*, Canterbury, was built in 1647, good quality houses had begun to be rather better heated. It is two rooms deep, with three storeys, cellars and attics. The shop at the front was unheated, but the other five main rooms all had fine fireplaces within a single stack, leaving only the attics and cellars unheated.[200]

How these houses were occupied is another matter. Not much work has been done on the way earlier houses were used in later periods, and the situation is usually complicated by drastic nineteenth and twentieth-century alterations. In Sandwich the physical evidence suggests that many of the deep, narrow houses in the town centre may have remained in single occupation, and it is likely that some of the rooms were used for storage or commercial rather than domestic purposes. But in Faversham, where houses were shallower and street frontages wider, they tended to get divided, so that one original house now forms two or three separate dwellings. Both physical evidence, as at *57-8 West Street*, and rentals, suggest that this trend began during the seventeenth century, probably among rather smaller houses than those

---

[198] These comments are based upon recent fieldwork by the author in these towns. See also, S. Pearson 'Heating and houses in Faversham town' in Hyde and Harrington, *Faversham Hearth Tax*, pp. 4-7, and E.W. Parkin, 'The ancient Cinque Port of Sandwich', *Archaeologia Cantiana*, 100 (1984), 189-216.

[199] M. Laithwaite, 'A ship-master's house at Faversham, Kent', *Post-Medieval Archaeology*, 2 (1968), 150-62; Hyde and Harrington, *Faversham Hearth Tax*, pp. 128-40.

[200] Canterbury Archaeological Trust, *Archaeologia Cantiana*, 106 (1988), 185-6; 107 (1989), 366-7; 109 (1991), 323-7.

described above. At the same time purpose-built pairs, like *91-2 Abbey Street*, made their appearance. They tend to have single stacks with two fireplaces heating the main room and the chamber over, any rear service accommodation remaining unheated until the nineteenth century. In the 1671 hearth tax return for Faversham there were 107 two-hearth entries, forming 25.5 per cent of the total, and it seems likely that these included both subdivided older houses and purpose-built pairs. Identifying the eighty-three single-hearth houses which formed 20 per cent of the total is much more difficult. They may have been subdivided buildings, but if they stood alone then probably few, if any, survive.

By the second half of the seventeenth century new types of town houses were being built. Not only had the gables and jetties of the earlier buildings gone, but the internal layout was changing, and even at a low social level it seems that nearly all rooms, apart from shops, were provided with fireplaces. It is this, above all else, which led to the marked differences apparent in the hearth tax between the expanding naval and dockyard towns of the north coast, and the older towns in central and eastern Kent. London was the yardstick here. At the high end of the social scale new houses are likely to have been built in brick. In Stoke Newington, north of the City of London, two houses, two-rooms deep, built in 1658 with three storeys, cellars and attics, have been identified in the 1674 hearth tax as having ten hearths each. In 1664, six four-storey houses with two rooms on each floor were erected in Bloomsbury Square; each room was heated, and the houses were charged on eight hearths in 1672-3.[201] In appearance these were modest terrace houses, the precursors of the ubiquitous Georgian houses of London; they show that by the 1660s some of the better-built medium-sized houses in London and its suburbs were extremely well-appointed, with fireplaces expected in every room. The houses themselves were no larger in floor area than many of those in the older towns of Kent, but they were far more up-to-date in plan and in the amenities provided. Do they indicate greater wealth on the part of the occupier? It is impossible to say this on the basis of the hearth tax alone.

At a lower social level a similar distinction prevailed, and it is here that we have some evidence from Kent. Brick was available in the Deptford area, but although most of the remaining early houses in Deptford survive because they were built of brick, the majority of houses in the town continued to be built of timber until about 1750.

---

[201] A.F. Kelsall, 'The London house plan in the later 17th century', *Post-Medieval Archaeology*, 8 (1974), 80-91.

The earliest houses to have been identified are *144a-162 Deptford High Street*, a row of twelve brick houses built around 1680, at least in part by a potter, who may have had easy access to local brick. *No. 150*, an isolated survivor from this early period, has two full storeys, plus attic and cellar, with a single room on each floor, the three upper ones having fireplaces.[202] Thus a small house of this sort might have three hearths. In the 1740s the occupants of the terrace included shipwrights, a sailmaker and a house carpenter. The earliest timber houses to survive are *19-31 Tanners Hill*, not built until around 1728, but almost certainly reflecting the arrangements of earlier timber buildings in the town. They were all of two storeys with attics, some having only a single room on each floor, others two rooms deep. The smaller houses had two or three fireplaces, the larger had at least four and sometimes more. The occupants in this case are known to have included dockyard watchmen or labourers, a shipwright, a carpenter, a porter and a fisherman.[203]

New buildings of this sort were not confined to the north-western towns, although they were probably more prevalent there. In the east of the county new houses were also being built in Deal, which grew during the seventeenth century from a small fishing settlement to a town with 1,500 inhabitants in 1676.[204] In 1679 the archbishop of Canterbury leased out two tenements and a wash house at *8-10 Chapel Street*.[205] *No. 10*, which may date back to this time or may be a little later, has a two-room plan of two storeys, attic and cellar, with six fireplaces heating all but the attic rooms. *No. 4 Brewer Street* is a smaller version of the same plan, without cellars, and with four fireplaces to six rooms. At the lower end of the scale *138 Middle Street*, is a single-cell house of two storeys and an attic, both of the lower rooms being heated. These houses are probably later than 1664, but it is likely that they represent the various types which were being constructed from the 1660s onwards.[206] A final example of what might be expected at a low social level comes from Folkestone, where a number of stone and brick houses dating to the second half of the seventeenth century were

[202] RCHME, Survey Report, *Nos 144a-162 (even) Deptford High Street*, Deptford, NMR index no. 96631 (1998). The development of Deptford housing is discussed in an RCHME unpublished report, 'Deptford Houses: 1650 to 1800', 1998, and in Guillery and Herman, 'Deptford Houses', forthcoming. I am grateful to Peter Guillery for showing me this in advance of publication.

[203] RCHME, Survey Report, *Nos 1-31 (odd) Tanners Hill*, Deptford, NMR index no. 96635 (1998).

[204] For the growth of Deal, see C. W. Chalklin, 'The making of some new towns, c1600-1720', in *Rural Change and Urban Growth, 1500-1800*, ed. by C. W. Chalklin and M. A. Havinden (London, 1974), pp. 229-52. I am grateful to Charles Bain-Smith for arranging to show me some of the many seventeenth and early eighteenth-century houses surviving in the town.

[205] Lambeth Palace Library: TA 188/1-19 Chapel Street.

[206] Houses such as *19 Farrier Street* and *146 Middle Street* have external features of somewhat earlier date, and appear to have been heated by stacks with three flues.

recorded before demolition in the 1940s. They too had a single heated room on each of two floors, with an unheated attic above.[207]

These Kentish examples are in line with contemporary town houses going up elsewhere, as in Whitehaven, Cumberland, where two-storey, single-cell houses with two heated rooms were owned and built by masons and carpenters and occupied by artisans.[208] In Shadwell in East London, working only from documentary sources, Michael Power has demonstrated that the average number of rooms in the small houses of this relatively poor area was 3.7, while the average number of hearths in 1664 was 2.7. Houses in this part of London were small, and 44 per cent of households were exempt from the hearth tax, yet even so it seems that the ratio of hearths to rooms was high.[209] Thus while in the older towns, houses of all sizes tended to have had a mixture of heated and unheated rooms, it appears that by the late seventeenth century nearly all the rooms in a new house could be expected to have a fireplace: a house of eight rooms would probably have six to eight hearths, and one of two rooms and an attic would have two, or possibly even three. It is in this light that one should look at the hearth tax figures, which show Deptford and Chatham with few single-hearth houses, and over 70 per cent with two, three and four hearths. It is likely that these latter were small houses of the sort discussed above.

The provision of extra fireplaces in the houses of the coastal towns may have gone hand in hand with the availability of relatively cheap coal, shipped into the Kentish ports from the north east. It was certainly the main fuel of seventeenth-century London, and provided an alternative to the increasingly expensive coppiced firewood which was otherwise available, although whether the poor could afford coal is open to question.[210] It is likely that the northern ports followed the London trend, but at this date in Deal the fireplaces themselves were still quite large, often with rounded backs, and were probably still designed with wood in mind.[211]

If surviving small houses in the newer towns are likely to have had two or more hearths, the question arises as to what single-hearth houses were like. The evidence at present is sparse. In Deal, the outlines of one or two very low ornamental Dutch gables remain embedded in

[207] B. H. St J. O'Neill, 'North Street, Folkestone, Kent', *Antiquaries Journal*, 29 (1949), 8-12.

[208] S. Collier, *Whitehaven, 1660-1800* (RCHME, London, 1991), pp. 44-5, 85-6.

[209] M. J. Power, 'East London housing in the seventeenth century' in *Crisis and Order in English Towns, 1500 - 1700* ed. by P Clark and P. Slack, (London, 1972), pp. 237-62; idem., 'Shadwell: The development of a London suburban community in the seventeenth century', *The London Journal*, 4 (1978), 29-46.

[210] Hatcher, *Coal Industry*, pp. 40-55, maps 1.1 and 3.1.

[211] The high cost of transport almost certainly meant that coal did not penetrate far beyond the ports, while the scarcity of timber in eastern Kent by this date may partially explain the slow introduction of extra hearths into smaller houses in the countryside.

the walls of later buildings, implying the former existence of one-storey-and-attic houses, and such houses might only have had a single hearth.[212] In the inland towns, where the incidence of single-hearth houses was much higher: 47 per cent in Cranbrook, and between 25 per cent and 35 per cent in Ashford, Sevenoaks, Tenterden, Tonbridge, West Malling and Westerham, it is likely that many of the poor lived in earlier houses in which only the main room was heated, perhaps by a fireplace in a timber stack, as discussed above in the section on rural houses. However, single-hearth households in the hearth tax may not always represent houses *per se*, but divided properties, occupied by two or more families. In due course, when the documentary evidence has been examined with this sort of question in mind, it may be possible to find the answer.

---

[212] E.g. next to *13-14 Griffin Street*.

CONCLUSION

The hearth tax has frequently been used to indicate the size of houses, and this in turn has been taken as a reflection of wealth. Although it is obvious that houses with twenty hearths are likely to have had wealthier occupiers than those with under five, it was not necessarily the case, as Husbands points out, that those with three or four hearths had wealthier owners than those with one or two, so direct correlations of this sort can lead to questionable conclusions if based on too small a sample. We have seen individual cases such as Henry Stanford, yeoman, of East Peckham who lived in a house with two hearths, but died with an inventory valued at £548, and on the other hand craftsmen and labourers in Deptford who occupied houses with as many as three fireplaces. Nonetheless, both Husbands and Spufford have amply demonstrated a general correlation between hearths and wealth in different parts of the country.[213] It is hoped that the discussion of hearths and houses in Kent has likewise shown that hearths and wealth may be related, but that it is also critically important to bear in mind the type of buildings with which the hearths are associated. Husbands suggests that architectural style might have made a difference to the number of hearths a house had. In fact, at least in Kent, it was not so much style, or even plan form, as the age of a building and the form and physical structure of its hearths and chimney stacks which influenced the number of fireplaces a building might have.

It is fashionable when discussing the hearth tax to relate it to the 'Great Rebuilding', a phrase coined by W.G. Hoskins in 1953 to describe a period of major alterations to existing buildings and the erection of new houses between 1570 and 1640.[214] Regional and local research has subsequently shown that the situation was more complex than Hoskins allowed, with houses in different parts of the country being updated at different times. Machin[215] suggested that rather than one rebuilding there were cycles of rebuilding continuing into the nineteenth century - and beyond. One may, indeed, ask whether a blanket term of this sort helps to clarify what actually took place, or

---

[213] Husbands, 'Hearths, wealth and occupations', in *Surveying the People*, pp. 66-8; Spufford, 'Cambridgeshire hearth tax', table 6.

[214] W. G. Hoskins, 'The rebuilding of rural England, 1570-1640', *Past and Present*, 4 (1953), 44-59. For recent works which still use the concept, see C. Platt, *Great Rebuilding*; P. Williams, *The Later Tudors, 1547-1603* (Oxford, 1995).

[215] R. Machin, 'The great rebuilding: a reassessment', *Past and Present*, 77 (1977), 33-56.

tends to mask the real situation. In Kent, which was particularly rich in high-quality medieval houses, the best of them in all localities were retained for as long as possible, and were usually lived in by those with the greatest wealth. From the early sixteenth century onwards they were upgraded by ceiling over the hall and inserting enclosed fireplaces of increasing sophistication. Although this led to houses being used in a different way,[216] it hardly constituted rebuilding in any meaningful sense. Such adaptations took place throughout the sixteenth and seventeenth centuries, depending on the region and the status of the occupiers. Some houses obviously also had additions, and in some, particularly in the towns, the hall was rebuilt, but this was not the norm in the countryside. In rural areas a few of the best medieval buildings were completely rebuilt, particularly in the clothing district of the High Weald,[217] but elsewhere many of the new houses of the late sixteenth and early seventeenth centuries were smaller and would appear to have been new dwellings erected to accommodate a rising population. In Boughton Monchelsea, for example, they were grouped in two hamlets, probably intended to house those who came to work in the ragstone quarries. By the late seventeenth century there was a great upsurge of building in the towns around the coast, but again this was to provide homes for an entirely new urban population. Only in the rural areas of east Kent does there appear to have been a genuine and large-scale rebuilding of earlier houses, and this took place from the late seventeenth century onwards, after the time of the 1664 hearth tax.

The 1664 hearth tax reflects standards of heating at a single moment during a period of transition. It captures the situation at the point when new opportunities of employment on the London fringes and in the naval and dockyard towns were setting in motion massive changes in the fabric of those northern towns, and just before rebuilding began in rural east Kent. In all parts of the county the occupiers of older buildings were slow to upgrade them, while new ideas about what constituted an acceptable level of heating meant that newly erected buildings were far better equipped. The result was an uneven equation between hearths and wealth. A similar discrepancy occurred in the twentieth century when central heating was introduced: on the whole, old middle-class houses lagged a couple of decades behind new working-class flats in making what was ultimately an inevitable change.

---

[216] M. Johnson, *Housing Culture*, (London, 1993).

[217] Around Cranbrook the wealthiest clothiers completely rebuilt the medieval houses they inherited, or at least rebuilt the reception rooms, leaving only part of the original for services (Pearson, *Medieval Houses*, pp. 141-2). However, the situation in that area is not typical of Kent as a whole.

A question which is seldom asked is whether the tax itself inhibited the introduction of new fireplaces. On the one hand extra fireplaces may have been seen as status symbols, and their introduction subject to peer pressure, on the other the fact that it was such an unpopular tax suggests that it was seen as unfair, and may have delayed some people from upgrading their properties. This is perhaps a question of particular relevance in a county like Kent where a large proportion of the population was clearly in a financial position to introduce more hearths by this time. It is also important to understand how individual houses were occupied, particularly in towns where rented accommodation within houses must have been widespread. These are aspects which require more work before the evidence can be interpreted correctly. Nonetheless, publication of the tax for most of the county brings to the fore some striking and important contrasts in the state of housing, which has the potential to reveal a great deal about Kentish society, both at county and local level, in the third quarter of the seventeenth century.

INTRODUCTION TO THE MANUSCRIPT

By Duncan Harrington

The frontispiece to this volume is taken from the original constable's return for the Liberty of Ashford, in the lathe of Scray. Although it dates to 1662 it has been illustrated because signed constables' returns so rarely survive. The general introduction, pages xvi-xvii, details the requirement for the householders to provide signed returns. Meekings explains:

> The Petty Constables (a term including the officials of the smallest local area such as Headboroughs, Tythingmen and Borsholders) were to notify the occupiers that a statement of the number of their hearths would be required from them; the latest date for this notification was to have been, in the first instance, 31 May 1662, but as the Act was not published in time, a Proclamation ordered it to be done immediately.[218] Occupants were to supply their statement within the next six days: for a false assessment the penalty was to be a £2 fine, and where no return was made the Petty Constables were to inspect the house and assess the number of hearths, becoming liable to a £5 fine for each week they neglected to do this.[219]

He goes on to describe in detail the exemptions[220] and notes that the assessments were to be delivered to the clerk of the peace for enrolment at the next Quarter Sessions, in the first instance those of July. The majority were enrolled in a single column (of names and hearths) on the recto and verso of the membranes. Enrolled returns rarely survive from 1662 and the only one for Kent is that for Lady Day 1664, which is entered in a double column. The Kent Family History Society published transcripts of those for the lathes of St Augustine and Shepway, but before publication neither text was compared with the

---

[218] Commons Journals, pp. 383, 385.
[219] Meekings, *Surrey Hearth Tax*, pp. xii-xiii.
[220] See above, pp. xvi-xvii.

Exchequer duplicates and are thus not as accurate as the present listing.[221]

Whilst no 1662 Cinque Port enrolled Assessment has survived, the return for Faversham shows its Assessment was enrolled at the November Sessions although it was actually made in July.[222] Meekings says:

> The original Petty Constables' Assessments were not returnable to the Exchequer, but among the Particulars of the Accounts, especially for the half-year to Michaelmas 1662 or the year to Lady Day 1663, a proportion of the Petty Constables' Returns appear to be either their original Assessments, or duplicates of them, revised to show details of payments; that for part of the Prince's Liberty, in Lambeth, dated 23 July, 1662, and re-dated 23 September, 1663, for example, was used in this way; it has A placed against the names of those who paid and C against those exempted by [an adjoined] certificate, whilst against the rest is written Poor, no distress or empty, no distress.

Among the 1663 Kent returns, mostly enrolled on parchment, are many with headings written over erasures which clearly show this point. The clerk of the peace had to enrol the Assessments and make a duplicate Roll which, signed by three or more justices, was to reach the Exchequer within a month.[223]

What makes the Ashford Liberty return of 1662 unique amongst these original returns is that the entries are either signed by the householders themselves, or they have made their mark.[224] The complete transcript forms Appendix VI. At first sight some of the signatures have a very similar appearance. This may simply reflect the handwriting of the period rather than the scribe's attempt at creating an illusion of verisimilitude. Whilst the bulk of the entries are written by one scribe, almost certainly John Smallwood, other entries are completely written, as opposed to just being signed, by the householders. Sir Roger Twysden, a Kent justice of the peace,

---

[221] D. W. Harrington, 14 (1983) and 182 (1984). Both titles are now out of print and available only as microfiche.
[222] PRO: E179/262/21, see transcript of this in Hyde and Harrington *Faversham Hearth Tax*, pp. 8-13.
[223] Meekings, *Surrey Hearth Tax*, pp. xii-xiii..
[224] CKS: U1107/O1. The manuscript, amongst the Dering collection, also contains the borsholders returns from the half-hundreds of Aloesbridge, Bewsborough, Bridge & Petham, Cornillo, Newchurch, Westgate and Wingham, the hundreds of Bleangate, Eastry, Marden, Ringslow and the Borough of Longport, Canterbury. Although undated it appears, both from the archive group, and the content to pertain to the first year of the tax.

responsible for the southern half of the lathe of Aylesford, wrote that
on

> the 8th day of January 1663/4 Sir Thomas Style Captayn Dalyson
> Sir John Reyney and myself met at Town Malling as we had
> severall tymes before about hys majesties revenue arising out of
> herths of which I have spoken somwhat before, But really we
> could make small progresse in it, by reasons of the perplext
> ambiguity of the latter act, and requiring things allmost
> impossible as ... that every particular man is to give an accompt
> in writing what hearths he hath and the borsholder to engrosse
> on the backside the truth of it, which was troublesome hardly
> one beeside the minister beeing found able to write his name in
> the whole parish much less to write hys byll and this is that wee
> could not make them understand.[225]

Whilst he was primarily concerned with the region for which he was
responsible, the comments are just as valid for other areas. The Liberty
of Ashford comprised the northern part of Ashford parish including
almost all the built-up area of the town.

Arthur Ruderman points out that 104 out of 125 households in
the Ashford return were able to sign their names – a higher proportion
than might be expected from Sir Roger's pessimistic remarks. As they
were all charged, he suggests this may reflect the most prosperous
section of the community. The 1664 return (see p. 296) gives a total of
268 households, of which 115 (43 per cent) were exempt on grounds of
poverty. If the 1662 return had a similar proportion of exemptions,
then about 47 per cent of all householders were able to sign their
names. Amongst those listed are four that refused to sign, of whom at
least two are known to have been non-conformists with such extreme
views that they are unlikely to have countenanced any new taxation to
the Crown. Ashford had a core of fervent non-conformists so that it is
perhaps surprising that the constable, John Smallwood, only had only
four refusals, especially since his predecessor in office, Thomas
Cuckow, was summoned before the King's Council to answer for the
non-collection of Ship Money in the town.[226]

Ruderman has been able to identify a large number of the
premises and has come to the conclusion that the occupiers appeared
before the constable in a random order. He says:

---

[225] Twysden Notebook, CKS: U47/47 O1; p. 47 n. xj.

[226] Based upon details obtained from Arthur W. Ruderman, *A History of Ashford* (1994), p. 6; idem,
'Hearth Tax', *Journal of Kent Local History*, 13 (Sept. 1981), 2-3; Calendar of State Papers
Domestic January and May 1639.

... comparison of this original return of 1662 with that of 1664 is not easy, since only names and the number of hearths are given. However assuming that persons of the same name (including changes within a family) were in the same house, comparison is possible for 129 of the total of 141 dwellings. Of these 87 returned the same number of hearths in both years, while only eight cases had a greater number in 1664, on the other hand 24 dwellings returned fewer hearths. Whether these householders physically removed the hearths they had previously, or covered them from view, or merely made a false return (perhaps with the connivance of the constable) we do not know but this certainly supports the implications of the amending Acts that the tax was unpopular and avoided when ever possible.[227]

The Quarter Sessions copy comprises eighty-five numbered parchment membranes, measuring approximately 165mm x 760mm (6½ in. by 30 in.) to which have been added another five membranes which have been given A numbers. The explanation of these five membranes is to be found at the beginning of PRO: E179/249/37B, the Exchequer duplicate, which says:

An account of the firehearthes and stoves which were not returned at the quarter sessions of the peace holden at Maydstone for the county of Kent in the fifteenth yeare of his Majesties Reigne and in the yeare of the Lord 1664 According to an act of parliament entitled [an additionall] act for the better ordering [and collecting] the revenue ariseing by Hearth Mony.

Later binding has now incorporated these un-numbered membranes, covering Queenborough, East Farleigh, Loose and the lower half of Toltingtrough hundred, into the Quarter Sessions file, and the scribe also used some appropriate blank sections on the earlier Quarter Sessions return for some sections that form part of E179/249/37B.[228]

The return and its duplicate appear to be written by just two scribes; perhaps these were two of the signatories to the Exchequer return.[229] Their hands are demonstrated by the following sections of the same text taken from E179/249/37A,[230] folio 25v (Plate V), and CKS: Q/RTh, folio 47v (Plate VI). The two texts are remarkable for

---

[227] I am very grateful for this information from Arthur Ruderman.
[228] See Appendix II for a listing.
[229] The E179 duplicate has on folio 74v the clear finger print in ink of a scribe.
[230] Because of its physical size the PRO computer request is "EXT 6/100".

their similarity, even following the same pattern. Christopher Dering, clerk of the peace, received £60 as a reward for his expenses, assistance and making fair copies of the 'firehearthes' assessments.[231] No reliable autographed material has so far come to light to prove whether it was Christopher himself and his assistant who actually wrote the Quarter Sessions copy and the Exchequer duplicates although it seems likely. Christopher was given a further reward of £6 10s. 0d. in May 1665, possibly representing the copying of the lists that were received later.[232] As clerk of the peace he also received £7 6s. 5d. in poundage on the money received.[233]

Christopher Dering, clerk of the peace 'liveth at Pluckley' according to a notation on the accounts for Lady Day 1664.[234] However, it would appear that he may simply been staying briefly at *Surrenden* in Pluckley, the residence of his relative Edward Dering. Styled Christopher Dering of *Wickens* in Charing he was born 8 August 1625 the son of John Dering.[235] He married in 11 June 1663, Elizabeth the daughter and heiress of Thomas Spackman of Wiltshire by Joan daughter and heiress of Francis Kennerly of Lincolnshire. Elizabeth Dering died at Albury, Surrey on 19 April 1724 aged 89 and was buried in the Brent chapel in Charing church on the 27 April. Christopher had died earlier aged 69 on the 18 December 1693 at the chambers of his son Heneage Dering in the Inner Temple and was also buried in the Brent chapel.[236] Christopher had been admitted to the Inner Temple in November 1648 and called to the bar 11 February 1655/6.[237] According to Heneage, in Michaelmas 1664 his father went to live in Maidstone. In 1667 he moved to Acton in Charing, and around Michaelmas that year finally went into his own house of *Wickens* which had been inherited from the Brent family.[238]

The old DNB says that Christopher Dering 'was secretary to Heneage Finch, chancellor of England and Earl of Nottingham'. It did not say when or where this information was obtained. Heneage Finch was born 23 December 1621 probably at *Eastwell*, Kent and having been admitted to the Inner Temple on 25 November 1638 rose rapidly

[231] PRO: E360/77 and E179/330/22 m. 11 is his receipt dated 27 March 1665.

[232] PRO: E360/77 and E179/330/22 m. 2 is his receipt dated 3 May 1665.

[233] See above, p. xvii.

[234] E179/330/6 folio 46v.

[235] Baptised at Charing: *Archaeologia Cantiana*, 10 (1876), 327-52, includes pedigree.

[236] DNB under Heneage Dering LLD (1665-1750), Dean of Ripon; W. Berry, *Kent County Genealogies* (1830), p. 402.

[237] F. A. Inderwick, *Calendar of Inner Temple Records, vol. II, 1603-1660* (1898), p. 319; idem, *Inner Temple Admissions 1547-1660* (n.d. pb. 1877), p. 319. I am grateful to John Titford for this reference.

[238] 'Autobiographical Memoranda by Heneage Dering', *Surtees Society*, 65, (1875), pp. 334-5. (I am grateful to Sarah Pearson for this reference).

through various offices to become Solicitor-General on the 6 June 1660.[239] Heneage Finch did not become chancellor of England until 19 December 1675 and Earl of Nottingham until 12 May 1681. Upon joining the Inner Temple he became a distinguished student, with special proficiency in municipal law. Could this be what brought Christopher Dering to be the clerk of the peace?

The differences in spelling between the two texts would suggest that perhaps the listing was either taken down phonetically or that the scribe simply imposed his own 'correct' spelling. Such differences occur in the spelling of Christian names such as Jeffery or Geoffrey, Stephen or Steeven, Phillip or Phillipp, Gregory or Grigory to give just a few examples. Besides a smaller than expected number of Puritan and biblical first names there is an entry for Marcellus (Swanton) which Miss Withycombe says has been used very rarely in England since the sixteenth century when a good many classical names came into use as Christian names.[240] Other unusual first names are Abiezer (Boykin) and the male names Blase (White) and Saphire (Paramour). In surnames the differences often amounted to whether the i comes before e or vice versa, a constant has been doubled, y for i, e for i, ley for ly, u is substituted for o, o is substituted for r, and the name ended with er or ar. A published example of these slight differences is given for the hundred of Faversham.[241] The more worrying aspects are where the initial letter is different so that Hawkins is shown as Wankins, Mayor as Ayer and Thomas Fish as Thomas Ash. Some cross-references have been given in the index to try to eliminate these diverse variations. Readers are reminded that the index does not show where there is more than one entry for a page and are advised to scan each page carefully.

The collection of the hearth tax in Kent at Lady Day 1664 was the responsibility of three individuals, the sheriff of Kent, the sheriff of Canterbury, and the Warden of the Cinque Ports. For the county, Thomas Bigg had been appointed sheriff for 1663 and would have remained in office until November 1664.[242] He was charged with raising £2864 2s. 0d. for the half year to Lady Day 1664, which as shown on E360/77 amounted to 57,282 chargeable hearths. However, when Bigg's deputy sheriff, Valentine Hodges, declared his account on 5 May 1665, Thomas Bigg was £1084 7s. 0d. in arrears, practically all of which was owing by the constables.

---

[239] DNB under Heneage Finch, first Earl of Nottingham (1621-1682); *The Complete Peerage*, by G. E. C., ed. by H. A. Doubleday, IX (1936), pp. 790-2.

[240] E. G. Withycombe, *The Oxford Dictionary of English Christian Names* (1989), p. 205.

[241] Hyde and Harrington, *Faversham Hearth Tax*, pp. 37-48.

[242] *List of Sheriffs for England and Wales from the Earliest Times to AD 1831*, PRO Lists and Indexes, IX (1898).

The total charge of 57,282 chargeable hearths can be broken down into the five lathes: Aylesford, 16,530; St Augustines, 6544; Scray, 9951; Shepway, 6699; Sutton at Hone, 16,592; together with Rochester, 880, and a supplementary of 86. The accounts recorded in E179/330/6 ff. 36-45 list the totals of the hundreds and half-hundreds, and the totals of most of the boroughs are written on the Exchequer duplicate by columns, including the non-chargeable hearths. A random check of borough totals produced by the computer for this volume was found to agree with the Exchequer figures – a compliment to the Exchequer clerks who had to add all these entries by hand.[243]

The City and County of Canterbury was collected separately from the County of Kent. The hearth tax was made an excise duty in 1663 and a further act of 1664 removed collection from the province of the sheriffs to a specially appointed receiver.[244] Francis Clarke, knight, was made receiver for Kent and the City and County of Canterbury by his patents of 23 June 1665 and 3 May 1666.[245] He showed in his declared account of 13 December 1667 that all the Lady Day 1664 arrears had been collected, and that he had also collected the Lady Day 1664 duty for the City of Canterbury which had previously been uncollected by the sheriff of the city.[246]

John Barrett was the sheriff of the City and County of Canterbury at Lady Day 1664. Because he failed to collect the hearth tax on time the whole of his charge of £134 10s. 0d. on the citizens of Canterbury, for 2690 hearths, passed as arrears to the receiver Francis Clarke to collect. Meekings, in a summary of hearths for the city of Canterbury, notes that at Michaelmas 1662 there were 3586 hearths,[247] at Lady Day 1664, 2690 hearths, and at Michaelmas 1664, 3792 hearths.[248] What his abstracts do not explain is the considerable discrepancies in numbers, nor why Francis Clarke appears to owe £191 8s. 0d. for the 1664 Lady Day collection for Canterbury. There may be insufficient data to elucidate the matter but the explanation is probably connected to the entry for Michaelmas 1663 where John Barrett, is

---

[243] There are discrepancies between the computer and Exchequer totals which can partly be accounted for by the fact that hearths in detached portions of hundreds have, in this volume, been assigned to the hundred in which they geographically lie. Nonetheless, the high total in Shepway lathe must have some other cause. It may, for example, include the chargeable hearths in the Liberty of Romney Marsh, although this would be unlikely to account for such a lage disparity. Further work is required to clarify this.

[244] Excise Duty Act 15 Chas. II c.14, repealed in 1689. See above, p. xviii.

[245] C. A. F. Meekings, *Analysis of Hearth Tax Accounts 1662-1665,* List and Index Society, 153 (1979), p. 143 indicates Sir Samuel Starling was receiver for the County and not the City or Cinque Ports in the half year collection to Michaelmas 1665.

[246] PRO: E360/77.

[247] An Exchequer duplicate of assessment exists.

[248] PRO: E360/164 extracted from, Meekings, *Analysis,* pp. 129-43 and p. 403.

charged £196 4s. 0d. for 3924 hearths, which was the total for the city and the precincts. The computer totals for the chargeable hearths in the City and County are 2695 (Appendix IV), which with 1094 further chargeable hearths in that part of Westgate hundred which lies within the city (Appendix V), together add up to 3788. This is not far from the 3924 hearths that Barrett was required to collect, and very close to the 3792 hearths which Meekings notes for Michaelmas 1664, suggesting that the money Clarke was required to collect incorporated not only the separately administered City and County, but also the rest of the built-up area of Canterbury.

The Cinque Ports were also separately assessed. John Strode, Lieutenant of Dover Castle and Deputy Warden of the Cinque Ports in his declared account of 5 April 1666, showed that 8944 hearths in the Kentish Ports were charged with £447 4s. 0d. for the half year to Lady Day 1664.[249] Meekings does not say whether these figures are broken down, and the original documents have not been examined. However, for Michaelmas 1662 a set of figures for the Cinque Ports has survived amongst the state papers, and since this total of 8918 is very close to that for 1664, the figures are given here for reference:[250] Deal, 1073 hearths; Dover town and port, 2208; Faversham town, 1156; Folkestone, 238; Hythe (given as 4 wards), 384; Hythe parish, 16; Lydd town, 365; New Romney town, 388; Ramsgate, 247; the parish, town & port of Sandwich (given as 12 wards), 2033; Sarre, 47; Tenterden town and hundred, 688, and Walmer, 75. The figure for Fordwich town is damaged but looks like one hundred and fifty plus, bringing the total to just over 9000 hearths. In 1671 John Strode, Deputy Warden and receiver for the Cinque Ports, was still in arrears on his 1664 charge (which presumably included Lady Day 1664) 'lost in empty houses, by plague, poverty and no distress and depending on Mayors and Jurats'.[251]

When Samuel Lambe received his commission on 23 October 1671 it was for Kent, Canterbury and the Cinque Ports, and he was thus the first to collect for the whole county. An assessment exists for this year. Although now damaged and incomplete it still consists of 142 membranes, PRO E179/129/746, and contains details of the hearths for some of the Cinque Port areas for which there are no other surviving returns.

Appendix II shows the arrangement of the PRO membranes and the surviving constables' returns for Lady Day 1664. Whilst many of these last have now been transcribed, it has not been possible to

[249] op. cit., pp. 335-6.
[250] PRO: SP46/134/296 and Hyde and Harrington, Faversham Hearth Tax, p. 80.
[251] Meekings, Analysis, quoting from E360/164 and E179/265/35 folio 1.

publish these at this time. Collation of some of the returns shows that usually the scribes worked down the returns writing the entries from left to right in the two columns. Once again the Christian names and surnames are often slightly differently written, many phonetically, as was found between the fair copies. However, some spellings are rather wider of the mark. The following examples of the wild differences which occur come from the half-hundred of Chart, in Chart and Longbridge hundred. *Shelvington borough*, Edward Tourt not Tourth, Robert Massder not Maxted, William Beadle not Widow Beagle, Richard Waters not Wachers; intriguingly Mr Small and Mr Maytham have had their first names added in the enrolled copy. *Bucksford borough*, The parsonage is shown as Axton, The Court Lodge as Nevitt, 'Ninne' as Mr George Moore and 'Bucksford' as Edward Ellis, most of the other variants are relatively minor although perhaps one might not expect to find William Dason fair-copied as Dawson and Daniel Nower became Goodwife Nower and Widow Riding became Reading. *Chelvington borough* (or Chilminton in the constable's return) has Elizabeth Eems for Eeves, Thomas Seger for Sedger, John Honos for Jones and the non-chargeable entries should read Seath Moat 1, John Noble 2, George Finne 1, George Bunckly 1 and Widow Cockle 1. *Worting borough*, Richard Cashby not Caseby, *Swinford borough*, John Sandige not Savidge, John Missin not Missing and John Masters not Mercer, *Hothfield borough*, Lawrence Bissenden not Wissenden, Thomas Tuck not Toke, Alice Ridle not Kedwell. Richard Master 5 doesn't appear on the return but a note has been added at the end by the constable George Moore, 'Robert Steere borsholder of the Great Borough in Hothfield hath returned Thomas Britton 4 hearths the house not being inhabited, Thomas Wells 2 hearths and Richard Master 5 herths' in the non-chargeable section Widow Parker becomes Baker, Widow Bramfield appears as Broomfield, and Widow Gumry as Groomebridge. *Shippenden borough* (Shrippenden) has Thomas Hady not Hodge, Henry Stace not Elvy, John Moone not Man, the Non chargeable section includes Richard Wells for Willes, Widow Rolph for Roust, Peter Holmes for Holness, Peter Watches for Waters and William Shepard for Staphery, *Rumden borough*, *Street borough* and *Snoad Hill borough* had no real discrepancies although James Jarvis is shown in the last as having two hearths. Finally *Rudlow borough* Widow Barker and Thomas Barker are shown as Parker and John Mayny is shown as Mayning.

Without further research it is impossible to say how typical this half hundred is of the whole text. It seems likely that whilst there may be some variation in the number of hearths in the non-chargeable class, the chargeable list was more accurately recorded, as mistakes in the latter were likely to cause problems in collection. Some of the spelling variations may be attributed to phonetic spelling and the scribe's perception of the 'correct' spelling, but the disturbing conclusion is that most surname variations are caused by miscopying. This suggests that the 1664 Quarter Sessions assessment was compiled from the constables' returns with some reference being made to an earlier listing, and that the duplicate was then made from this, possibly by dictation. Anyone searching for particular names in the lists should be aware of these problems.

The transcription in this volume is the Quarter Sessions return for Lady Day 1664. It was undertaken over a period of time from 1982 before the general use of computers. Original spelling has been retained throughout, but capitalisation has been modernised, and contemporary contractions extended. The whole of the Quarter Sessions text was computerised and then checked against the Exchequer duplicates in PRO E179/249/37A and 37B. These Exchequer duplicates were created by the clerk of the peace as the time that he made the county copy for the sheriff and were used by the Exchequer to audit the sheriff's accounts. Occasionally when a name is omitted in the E179 duplicate the columns are slightly altered within the borough, but on the whole they followed the same pattern. The differences between the texts were then re-checked back against the original Quarter Sessions manuscript to ensure that the Quarter Sessions text had been correctly interpreted. Whilst it is hoped that transcription errors have been reduced to a minimum there has occasionally been room for doubt. For example, did a surname have two t's or an l and t? Likewise, it has often been difficult to distinguish between n, u or v. A few entries missing from the Quarter Sessions file are shown in italics. The E179 duplicates have suffered from damp and are considerably more damaged than the Quarter Sessions copy, making the latter much easier to read. Fortunately those sections not legible, even under ultra-violet light, in the Quarter Sessions copy were visible in the E179 duplicates. All the numbers of hearths originally in Roman figures have been converted to Arabic numerals here.

John patton Borsholder.
Borough of Hawccrouth

Chargeable		Chargeable	
Lady Roberts widd.	iiij	Thomas Lake Esq.	vj
Thomas Bayley	vj	Robert Gorondon	vj
John Williams	iij	John Evernden	ij
Richard Batts	ij	Widdow Ragly	iij
James Alley	iiij	Thomas Atkin	ij
Henry phillipps	iij	Richard Ballard Jun:	ij
Samuell Bridgland	ij	John Goodman	iij
Isaac Walter Son	iij	John Wildish	ij
Peter Goldman	iiij	Thomas Wimshit	ij
John Alfourne	iiij	Moses Filer	ij
Robert Jarrett	iiij	John Moore	ij
Robert Guy	ij	George Daw	ij
Samuell Neale	iij	John Whonam	j
Thomas philpott	j	John Souly	ij
Samuell Bayly Ju	ij	Richard Bassock	vj
Stephen Lawson	iiij	Richard pouter	j
Mathew pouter	ij	Ralfe Reaue	ij
Mathew Browne	ij	Richard Ballard son	iij
Stephen Langford	j	Richard Hovdden son	ij
William Marton	iij	Edward Barnden	vj
Richard Wimsett	ij	an empty house where	
Edward Lorkhorst son	ij	Hen: morriam dwell	j
John Browning	ij	Richard Vintett	
Thomas Morrill	iiij	peter Storner	
Robert Stouthopp	iiij	John Bromley	
Alexand: Lurkhurst	iij	Edward Lurkhorst	ij
Mr Lathe widd	ij	Thomas Tindall	v
and in an empty house	v	Elias Blewett	iij
Stephen White Jun	iij	Thomas offey	iij
William Hills	vj	John Rimington	ij
John Rothester	iij	John Wirkham	ij
John Wood	iij	Joseph Jggledon	ij
Christop Salttroot	ij	Jonah Hulton	iiij

Joseph Judye	ij	John Heyther	iij
Edward Beale	j	John ffowle	ij
Widdow Hoare	ij	Widdow Gardner	ij
Edmund Borrner	j	Thomas ffrone	j
Abraham Saffruck	j	Widdow Judye	j
Thomas Judye	j	Christopher Northam Jun	j
John Sannon	j	Robert Hunt	j
John Allon	j	John Richardson	ij
Joseph Murton	j	Dinah Myborne widd	j
Widdow Obones	j	Samuell Lolfden	j
John young	ij	Widdow Grinsted	j
Widdow Lumherst	j	John Hopper	ij
Elias Rolfe		Alexander Courkman	ij
John Parton Borsholder	j		

Borough of Faire Crouch.

Chargeable		Chargeable	
Lady Roberts widd	cccij	Thomas Lake esq	bij
Thomas Bayly	bij	Robert Hevenden	bij
John williams	iij	John Evenden	ij
Richard Batts	ij	Widdow Bayly	ij
James Alley	iiij	Thomas Atkin	ij
Henry ffillips	iij	Richard Ballard Jun	ij
Samuell Brodyland	ij	John Goodman	
Isaac walter sen	iij	John Weldish	iij
Peter Coleman	iiij	Thomas Wimshit	ij
John allforne	iiij	Moyses Tyler	ij
Robert Jarrett	iiij	John Moore	ij
Robert Guy	ij	George Dan	ij
Samuell Neale	iij	John Whenam	j
Thomas Philcott	j	John Sexly	ij
Samuell Bayly Jun	ij	Richard Baspork	bij
Steeven Danson	iiij	Richard Yeuter	j
Mathew Yeuter	ij	Ralfe Heave	ij
Mathew Browne	ij	Richard Ballard son	ij
Steeven Langford	j	Richard Hovelden sen	ij
William Martin	iij	Edward Barnden	bij
Richard Winslett	ij	An empty house where Henry Meriam dwelt	iij
Edward Lorkherst sen	ij	Richard Winsett	iij
John Chenning	ij		

VI Quarter Sessions return, CKS: Q/RTh folio 47v

[fol. Or]

KANT

An accompt aswell of the names of the persons and number of hearths and stoves in theire respectyve possessions that are Chargeable by virue of a late act intituled an act for the establishing an additional revenue upon his Majestie his heires and successors for the better support of his and theire crowne and dignity as alsoe of the names of the persons and number of hearths and stoves in their respective possessions which are not chargeable by the said act which accompt being transmitted by the justices of Peace unto the clarke of the peace of the said county is by him engrossed in parchment to be still kept in the said county And now this duplicate thereof being signed by two justices of the peace and the clarke of the peace of the said county of Kent is transmitted into his majesties court of Exchequer by virtue of another late act entitled an additionall act for the better ordering and collecting the revenues arising by Hearth money.

A duplicate hereof was transmitted unto the exchequer on the xvij[th] day of August 16 Charles 1664.

[PRO: E179/249/37A fol. 1:
A TRUE DUPLICATE conteyning an account etc.
{signed} Wm. Peyton
Philip   *?Packer*
Chr. Dering Clerk of the Peace.]

[fol. Ov]

Lath of	Sutton att Hone	j[f] roll
	Aylesford	xxij
	Scray	xliiij
	Shipway	lxviij
	St Augustine	lxxiiij

[fol. 1r]

In the Lath of
SUTTON AT HONE
THE HUNDRED OF BLACKHEATH

The upper part of Deptford

Chargable		Chargable	
Rob[ert] Heath Esq	15	Mr Snelling	3
Mrs Pett	6	Mr Rich[ard] Donson	6
Widdow Jobourne	6	Christo[pher] Hartover	4
Mr Jeffries	4	Mr Chamberling	6
Simon Stokes	2	Jonath[an] Jeffries	6
Thomas White	2	Thomas Ashoe	3
Anth[ony] Pim[m]e	2	Capt[ain] Tobias Sackler	4
Math[ew] Bunch	5	Joseph Haywood	4
John Bradshaw	4	Thomas Gates	3
Capt[ain] Brookes	7	Widdow Grimsted	5
John Sheldrome	4	Dr Britten	8
John Ingrom	2	Widdo[w] Goodchild	4
Capt[ain] Ruth	5	John Phillips	4
William Dod	8	Thom[as] Bristock	2
Edward Wilden	2	James Blackman	3
Edward Traffan	2	John Johnson	3
John Heakly	1	Samuell Harris	3
John Foulding	4	Thomas West	3
Thomas Moore	2	John Waight	2
John Bolding	3	Thomas Gooding	3
Roger Spauldrell	2	Michaell Bowles	2
John White	5	Robert Townesend	4
Nicholas Bennett	4	Rob[ert] Dostard	3
William Suter	4	Thomas Gates	5
Thom[as] Child	7	Thom[as] Bowles	2
Mr Rob[ert] Waith	12	Christo[pher] Grout	3
Thomas Hopley	3	Rob[ert] Johnson	3
Thom[as] Marten	2	Steph[en] Thornton	2
Mr Willi[am] Hoskins	6	Thom[as] Clements	1
James Harwing	1	Nicholas Nelcey	2
John Blewman	1	James Hopkings	2
John Biggs	2	Clem[ent] Jorden	2
William Bird	1	Trust[um] Bradshaw	2
Henry Gudridge	3	Richard Wilson	2
Richard Saxbes	6	Widdo[w] Croxford	4
Mr Thomas Raymond	5	Thomas Blizard	3

Widdow Sturt	6	Mr John Hall	3
Mr Willi[am] Collett	11	Rich[ard] Middleton	5
Robert Radley	3	Willi[am] Hewlett	4
Mr Rob[ert] Walter	5	Mr Thom[as] Readinge	6
Richard Lambe	4	Henry Allen	4
Walter Lattey	2	Widd[ow] Hoult	3
Rich[ard] Philbie	5	Thomas Farr	2
John Barrow	2	Will[iam] Valley	2
Thomas Short	4	Thom[as] Higgings	2
Walter Moss	2	Geo[rge] Felder	2
Thom[as] Pitcher	6	John Spriggins	1
Thomas Aust	3	Nicho[las] Tarrent	2
Edward Borman	2	Will[iam] Dyer	2
William Pollie	2	Henry Sturgion	1
Roger Beale	2	John Reade	2
John Billingsley	2	Nicho[las] Bleach	3
John Barnett	2	Mr Rich[ard] Edlings	5
Widd[ow] Cole	2	Thomas Rennalds	3
Thomas Hester	2	John Wallis	2
Widd[ow] Shipwright	2	Christ[opher] Coward	2
Christ[opher] Coulson	4	Mrs Muster	13
Willi[am] Wrock	3	Anth[ony] Woodriffe	3
Widd[ow] Breden	3	Sam[uel] Hammon	3
Thomas Cooke	2	Mr Will[iam] Whitly	5
Mr Rich[ard] Thomas	10	Edward Smith	4
Thomas Evans	2	Mr John Bright	8
Mr Gammon	6	Tho[mas] Crawley	2
Anth[ony] Collett	2	Nicho[las] Holman	5
Robert Phips	3	Will[iam] Woodstock	8
Nicho[las] Paine	8	Will[iam] Borbro	1
Rich[ard] Austin	2	Daniell Dunn	6
John Findeall	3	Antho[ny] Briggs	3
Rich[ard] Perkins	4	James Browne	3
James Parker	3	Mr Will[iam] Welch	5
Geo[rge] Stanford	2	Joseph Picks	3
Will[iam] Evans	2	Thomas Scivill	2
John Peters	1	John Mackerell	4
Richard Rouse	5	Joseph Gallant	8
Mr Walgrave Siday	7	John Aggs	3
Mr Rob[ert] Langidge	4	John Horsington	3
S[i]r John Cutler	8	Widd[ow] Robbins	11
James Sumner	5	Edm[ond] Young	5
John Detheck	3	Arthur Hall	4

Mr Munfort	5	Thomas Smith	2
Walter Braman	4	Stephen Smart	2
Widd[ow] Gray	1	Griffith Joanes	3
Robert Bayley	2	Jo[h]n Colewrick	2
Math[ew] Pollentine	5	Jo[h]n Halfepeny	2
Jeffery Findeall	2	Loveinge Edwards	2
Mr Thomas Carter	14	Thomas Italy	3
Will[iam] Tomkins	1	George Bowyer	3
[fol. 1v]			
Will[iam] Weeks	4	Widd[ow] Sewer	7
Mr John Buckridge	7	Will[iam] Sewer	1
Rich[ard] Brooks	2	Will[iam] Baker	2
Rich[ard] Wood	2	Robert Rennalds	2
Will[iam] Edmunds	6	Tho[mas] Smith	4
Henry Wise	4	Will[iam] Hill	2
Mr Jo[h]n Chamberling	5	Will[iam] Prest	4
Rob[ert] Haughton	5	Richard Pullinge	3
Richard Collard	3	Tho[mas] Hurlock	3
Richard Joabe	3	Tho[mas] Smith	4
Will[iam] Russell	4	Richard Bennett	2
Thomas Fox	2	Joseph Ousbourne	2
John Morgan	3	Thomas Woodson	3
Mr Lings	4	John Daniell	4
Benj[amin] Hodges	1	Robert Luse	2
Richard Lauson	2	John White	2
Tho[mas] Wilcock	2	Thomas Hart	2
Rob[ert] Harboure	2	Phill[ip] Norton	2
Will[iam] Shepheard	2	John Davis	2
Andr[ew] Baker	2	Roger Hall	2
James Bayly	2	John Fox	2
Widd[ow] Cane	4	Thom[as] Catterell	2
Widd[ow] Badnedge	3	Widd[ow] Thames	2
Will[iam] Fuller	2	Rob[ert] Evenden	1
Widd[ow] Bichen	2	Giles Ponder	2
Will[iam] Smith	2	John Robbers	3
Will[iam] Evans	2	Antho[ny] Cooke	2
Thomas Cole	3	Robert Marshall	2
John Adkinson	2		

Empty Houses

Chargable		Chargable	
Math[ew] Pollentine	2	Clement Hather	4
Mr Floud	11	Widdow Robberts	3

Mr Thom[as] Payne	3	Arth[ur] Hall	4
Widdo[w] Munfort	2	John Hall	6
Rich[ard] Flecher	3	Cap[tain] Russell	4
Mr Snelling	4	Mr Rob[ert] Waith	3
Mr Phillips	14	Rich[ard] Middleton	2
Mr Jeffries	4	Henry Loader	2
Joseph Hutley	2	John Dukes	2
John Coney	2	Mr Taylor	2
John Smith	3	Mr Sympson	7
Widdow Wild	4	Mr Primfield	5
John Haslewood	3	The Kings Slaught[er] house	4
The Kings Dogkinell	3	Mr Prittiman	3
Mrs Alderson	2	Mr Fisher	7
Mr Pem[m]ell	14	Mr Ricketts	3
S[i]r Nicho[las] Crispe	3	Gen[era]ll Goodson	2
Billington Smith	3	Eph[ram] Simmons	3
Marten Allen	2	Owen White	2
Mr Collett	2	Cap[tain] Sackler	1
Joseph Hayward	1	Tho[mas] White	1
Thomas Ashoe	1	Mr Carpenter	3
Thomas Hawtree	4		

In Surry

Chargable		Chargable	
Rowl[and] King	2	Rich[ard] Staples	2
James Abbis	3	Tho[mas] Browne	2
Goodm[an] Duck	2	Goodm[an] Carter	4
Goodm[an] Freeman	2	Goodm[an] Lamhouse	2
At the Bell at Hatcham	5	Geo[rge] Halsteed	5
Esq[uire] Pips	23	Alex[ander] Woolford	4
Goodman Ellis	4	Edward Newman	2

Upper part of Deptford [continued]

Not Chargable		Not Chargable	
John Batt	1	Thomas Mell	8
Levy Cooke	5	Widd[ow] Neale	6
Walter Pearce	4	John Fann	2
James Cording	3	Will[iam] Walker	2
Tho[mas] Fesant	1	Richard Swift	2
Widd[ow] Warren	2	John Haslewood	3
Widd[ow] Harris	1	Will[iam] Botly	2
John Walker	2	Jo[h]n Creswell	2
John Turner	2	Henry Norman	2

Widd[ow] Collins	1	Sam[uel] Batt	2
Widd[ow] Speight	6	Robert Hardinge	2
Mr Bates	2	John Watts	3
Richard Marten	2	Henry Lusher	3
Widd[ow] Minson	2	John Boyden	1
John Adkins	1	Stephen Skerrill	2
Hen[ry] Baycraft	3	John Spencer	1
Robert Bethorne	2	John Shoitboult	2
John Tayler	2	Thomas Parker	2
Henry Clarke	2	Widd[ow] Masteis	4
Widd[ow] Barrow	4	John Adkins	2
Will[iam] Elbie	2	Richard Paine	2
Geo[rge] Hickman	2	Will[iam] Penny	4
Tho[mas] Melmor	2	Widd[ow] Randall	4
Tho[mas] Champe	2	Chris[topher] Whitlock	3
[fol. 2r]			
William Birch	1	Simon Dexter	1
W[illia]m Underwood	2	Rich[ard] Linsey	2
John Walton	2	Tho[mas] Maydle	2
Richard Elbie	4	Len[nard] Twentyman	2
Will[iam] Smart	1	Rich[ard] Smart	2
Widd[ow] Randall	3	Will[iam] Fisher	3
Widd[ow] Keniston	2	Cart[er] Banks	2
Robert Chandler	2	Tho[mas] Clements	2
Rich[ard] Wigginton	2	Widd[ow] Reeve	3
Widd[ow] King	1	Widd[ow] Walton	1
Widd[ow] Hince	1	Widd[ow] Whipp	1
Isa[a]c Sharpe	2	Joseph Rine	2
Widd[ow] Bull	2	Widd[ow] Purling	1
Ralph Stansteed	2	Math[ew] Eaton	2
Tho[mas] Locking	2	Cut[h]b[ert] Smith	2
Widd[ow] Wells	3	Ben[jamin] Michell	2
Widd[ow] Willis	3	Widd[ow] Bowers	2
Richard Edlin	3	Stephen Butler	2
Widd[ow] Scivill	2	Edward Butler	2
Widd[ow] Adcock	2	John Lee	2
Widd[ow] Cole	2	Richard Dowdy	2
Will[iam] Gam[m]on	2	John Hassock	2
Joseph Moody	2	John Evans	2
John Halsteed	2	Blaze Chandler	1
Will[iam] Hayward	1	John Jefferies	2
Widd[ow] Winter	1	Richard Lock	2
Edward Carter	2	Hen[ry] White	2

John Baker	2	Edward Platt	2
Nicho[las] Burden	2	Gilford Alford	2
Widd[ow] Blewman	2	Edward Brewer	2
Andr[ew] Blewman	1	Oliver Draper	2
Will[iam] Warren	2	Thom[as] Coop[er]	2
Tho[mas] Collins	1	Tho[mas] Draper	2
Sam[uel] Hobbs	3	Jo[h]n Woodnott	2
Widd[ow] Davis	2	Robert Mile	1
Rich[ard] Story	2	Widd[ow] Wise	3
Tho[mas] Paine	3	Will[iam] Gaines	2
John Russell	3	Step[hen] Hoult	2
James Austen	2	John Brittan	1
Tho[mas] Perkinson	1	Henry Mageson	1
Griffin Joanes	2	Widd[ow] Downes	1
Widd[ow] Herrington	2	Will[iam] Russell	2
Hen[ry] Michell	2	Rich[ard] Earbie	2
Geo[rge] Drake	2	Widd[ow] Johnson	2
Fran[cis] Willis	2	Tho[mas] Ellis	2
Hen[ry] Wibourne	2	Widd[ow] Cox	2
Widd[ow] Elinor	2	Jam[es] Parmerter	3
Geo[rge] Lillie	2	Rob[ert] Thornborough	3
Joh[n] Gaine	2	Widd[ow] Feild	1

The lower parte of Deptford

Chargable		Chargable	
John Eveling Esq[uir]e	19	Arthur Slater	3
Henry Cooper	5	Widd[ow] Blackwell	6
John Fowler	6	Peter Drewett	5
Eliza[beth] Larkin	3	Edmund Rayner	7
Rich[ard] Hearte	3	Jonas Marten	3
John Sherwood	3	Will[iam] Vissard	6
John Foulden	4	John Langridge	2
Will[iam] Batt	4	Will[iam] Russell	3
Thomas Barrs	8	Thomas Hoopwell	3
John Smith	2	Will[iam] Allin	5
Owen Bagwell	5	Will[iam] Bagwell	3
Widd[ow]Westbooke	6	John Devenporte	4
John Moorehowse	3	John Gladis	4
James Barber	2	Tho[mas] Musgrave	2
Abr[aham] Barber	4	Tho[mas] Day	2
John Anderson	3	John More	2
John Russell	3	Andr[ew] Drake	3
Hugh Ayres	2	Will[iam] Rumlie	3

Phill[ip] Benbridge	2	Will[iam] Turner	3
Ryse Halbert	4	Chris[topher] Brickell	2
Will[iam] Butler	5	John Kielie	4
Capt[ain] Poole	9	Tho[mas] Crampton	4
Joseph Hore	2	Rob[ert] Graves	2
Edward Swallow	6	Widd[ow] Bailie	4
Will[iam Betts	2	Lewis Jones	4
Rich[ard] Smith	4	Math[ew] Browne	5
John Reading	2	Jo[h]n Crouch sen[io]r	2
James Foard	2	John Carrier	2
Jo[h]n Braman	4	Math[ew] Hoalt	3
John Anger	3	Edw[ard] Lay	2
John Branson	6	Tho[mas] Lewes	2
Henry Cremer	5	Rob[ert] Lyon	5
[fol. 2v]			
Tho[mas] Newton	2	Tho[mas] Adis	2
Geo[rge] Merrinton	12	Robert Callis	10
James Campenett	6	John Garrett	2
Henry Boddy	2	James Murrell	4
Will[iam] Scivill	4	Arth[ur] Hills	8
Henry Johnson	2	Ben[jamin] Fletcher	7
Nicho[las] Lancaster	8	Isa[a]c Welch	11
Peter Rowlie	3	Roger Spriggs	5
John Ruffhead	5	Hump[hrey] Cadbery	4
Eph[ram] Simmons	3	Geo[rge] Hodges	4
Geo[rge] Marten	4	W[illia]m Sherrington	2
Geo[rge] Barten	5	John Smith	2
Geo[rge] Hipton	2	John Palmer	3
Ralph Leech	4	Will[iam] Creech	4
Thomas Fox	3	Edw[ard] Pumfeild	5
John Allen	4	Rich[ard] Westbrook	3
Will[iam] Clemence	4	John Dobbs	3
Willi[iam] Remnant	3	Tho[mas] Turvill	2
John Burton	2	John Russell	7
Widd[ow] Henslie	5	Mich[ael] Sanders	5
John Pearce	3	Edward Cardin	3
Francis Strong	3	Widd[ow] Holmes	5
John Dench	4	Abr[aham] Wells	3
Richard Jackson	3	James Mathewes	5
Joseph Smith	4	W[illia]m Ashman	2
Edw[ard] Lowenes	3	Tho[mas] Davis	3
Widd[ow] Moyles	2	Edw[ard] Randell	4
James Clemence	3	Will[iam] Willebie	2

Edw[ard] Cheesman	2	Sam[uel] Bridges	3
Thomas Webb	2	Will[iam] Blabie	2
Widd[ow] Keele	-	Tho[mas] Eaton	3
Rob[ert] Wollie	2	John Miller	4
John Boyer	3	Miles Robeson	6
John Cock	3	Rich[ard] Joanes	4
Mart[in] Richards	2	Jo[h]n Coxs minor	3
John Badgnedge	3	Tho[mas] Em[m]itt	2
Rich[ard] Kerk	5	Jo[h]n Tappie	5
Widd[ow] Rumley	4	Geo[rge] Elsome	3
Tho[mas] White	3	Allen Stephenson	11
John Turpin	3	Tho[mas] Hooper	3
Widd[ow] Saxson	2	Jonas Palmer	6
Rob[ert] Grout	4	Tho[mas] Clapp	4
Tho[mas] Cranaway	2	Tho[mas] Evan	2
Step[hen] Pate	3	Rob[ert] Malcock	2
Mrs Moore	5	Math[ew] Loynes	5
Widd[ow] James	3	John Yonge	3
Jacob Cassell	3	Marmad[uke] Rayden	8
Richard Perkins	3	Joseph Waters	5
Widd[ow] Bathrem	3	Ben[jamin] Boate	6
Hen[ry] Feilder	2	Walter Griffin	1
Will[iam] Davis	4	Will[iam] Hutton	2
Tho[mas] Briant	3	Tho[mas] Greene	5
Widd[ow] Jesson	8	Will[iam] Weeks	3
Jo[h]n Crouch jun[io]r	3	Jacob Baker	3
Rob[er]t Ashworth	2	Hen[ry] Seeres	2
Rich[ard] Bushell	4	Peter Norbery	2
Will[iam] Collins	2	Gre[g]o[ry] Strader	2
Rich[ard] Haughton	2	John Rumlie	3
Anth[ony] Wiggens	2	Tho[mas] Carrier	2
Will[iam] Meacham	2	Pers[ival] Gaskin	3
Tho[mas] Baken	2	Will[iam] Game	2
Rich[ard] More	1	Geo[rge] Simons	2
Will[iam] Cranaway	2	Will[iam] Hill	4
W[illia]m Mathewes	4	Rob[er]t Venice	6
David Hore	2	Will[iam] Archer	2
Edw[ard] Cullier	2	Gilber[t] Anckcell	4
John Craftes	3	John Nelson	2
Henry Lee	2	Rob[er]t Southerne	9
Rob[er]t Warrener	3	Edw[ard] Alford	5
Edm[und] Wilmott	3	Rob[er]t Bradley	4
Rob[er]t Willis	2	Tho[mas] Ould	4

James Ansdell	7	Peter Wright	2
John Bowers	2	John Mansfeild	2
Edw[ard] Harris	3	Will[iam] Edghill	6
Will[iam] Browne	4	Rob[er]t Parsons	2
Hugh Currell	12	Math[ew] Ball	3
Will[iam] Mathews	3	Rob[ert] Seabrooke	4
James Compton	6	Will[iam] Waller	2
Andr[ew] Lankton	4	Sam[uel] Baele	2
Dan[iel] Hellin	8	Elias Clapp	6
Mart[in] Allen	1	John Lee	4
Fran[cis] Sparrow	2	Fran[cis] Riddell	3
Jo[h]n Fuzard	3	Hen[ry] Marven	2
Eliza[beth] Howard	5	Row[land] Rawlins	3
Widd[ow] Stone	3	Geo[rge] Gaskins	3
Ezek[iel] Smith	5	Tho[mas] Legg	4
Dan[iel] Kingson	2	Tho[mas] Day	4
Tho[mas] Benn	4	John Hayles	2
Tho[mas] Glasebrook	4	Sim[on] Scatliff	3
Widd[ow] Potts	3	Widd[ow] Day	4
Chri[stopher] Smith	3	Will[iam] Pidgion	4
[fol. 3r]			
Phill[ip] Hussie	6	A[a]ron Wallis	7
Rich[ard] Pitcher	5	Rich[ard] Rattliff	4
Nicho[las] Carrier	2	Hum[phrey] White	4
Rob[ert] Gray	4	Tho[mas] Snooke	3
Widd[ow] Boate	5	Widd[ow] Weathers	5
Simon Banister	2	Tho[mas] Stepney	2
Widd[ow] Baldwin	4	Step[hen] Loadem	2
Thom[as] Roberts	4	Rich[ard] Raxsell	2
Phill[ip] Kennett	2	Mich[ael] Crayton	5
John Shewers	2	John Higgins	2
John Waldoe	3	George Greene	2
Mich[ael] Norris	3	Easter Pope	8
John Barnett	2	John Rawlins	3
Henry Shales	5	Geor[rge] Blessett	3
Henry Sheeres	8	Henry Holbert	5
Nich[olas] Hill	5	Anth[ony] Younge	9
John Morgan	4	Ann Russell	2
John Monke	3	Christ[opher] Gunman	3
John Chester	4	Will[iam] Staines	4
Will[iam] Page	4	John Manning	2
Will[iam] Clowder	2	Dan[iel] Sawyer	3
Dan[iel] Chester	3	Thom[as] Robinson	3

James Leager	5	James Keelie	4
Math[ew] Cox	2	Math[ew] Frogham	5
Widd[ow] More	5	Widd[ow] Bontwell	4
Will[iam] French	4	Joseph Hukeley	3
Will[iam] Hukely	4	Widd[ow] French	2
Hen[ry] Hughes	7	Tho[mas] Followfield	3
John Hodges	2	Edm[und] Higgens	3
Edw[ard] Christians	3	John Marks	3
Daniell Fesie	3	Tho[mas] Higgens	2
Widd[ow] Tilson	4	S[i]r Geo[rge] Cartwright	26
Mr John Davis	11	Mr Jonas Fish	8
Capt[ain] W[illia]m Boddilow	6	Mr Jo[h]n Uthwatt	6
Mr Tho[mas] Cowley	11	Mr Will[iam] Casey	1
Will[iam] Grimitt	2	Rob[er]t Hacker	1
Edw[ard] Chapman sen[io]r	3	Abra[ham] Garrett	2
John Possell	2	John Poure	2
John Stoke	3	Tho[mas] Woollie	2
Widd[ow] Minson	3	Will[iam] Pippitt	1
Rob[er]t Coulie	3	Fran[cis] Sheffeild	3
Hen[ry] Carelas	4	Tho[mas] Buckmaster	2
Tho[mas] Emmett	2	Will[iam] Ansdell	1
John Arresmith	2	Hen[ry] Loader	4
Widd[ow] Huett	2	Hen[ry] Boddie	3
W[illia]m Houltbrooke	3		

Empty Houses

Mr Bramwell	10	Mr Rayner	5
John Russell	10	Tho[mas] Carrier	10
W[illia]m Craunaway	3	Capt[ain] Young	6
Thomas More	12	Thom[as] Lucas	6
Goodm[an] Lovell	3	The Kings Payhouse	2
In the Porters Lodg[e]	2	Mr Fennes	10
Mr Blackman	10	Mr Edghill Block	1
In the Masthouse	2	Jo[h]n Roper	3
Tho[mas] Lucas	3	Major Manlie	10
Widd[ow] French	2	William Waller	12
Mr Waler one stove	1	Mr Castle	8
Mrs Poward	20	Capt[ain] Kerbie	6
Jo[h]n Waldoe	4	Margarett Simson	7
Mr Margates	8	Christ[opher] Freeman	2
Mr Hen[ry] Hughes	32	Capt[ain] Rob[ert] Kerbie	3
S[i]r Nich[olas] Crispe	6	Thom[as] Bans	3
Mr Staples	5	Mr Blackman	6

Thom[as] Lucas	9	Hen[ry] Boddy jun[io]r	1
Thom[as] Fisher	1	Hen[ry] Miller	4
Jo[h]n Loynes	2	Miles Robbeson	3
Rich[ard] Joanes	3	Mr Whiting	4
Martin Richards	2	Mr Smith	5
Mr Tho[mas] Carrier	10	Mr Tho[mas] Hughs	8
James Barker	4	Mr Russell	12
Mr Jorden	4	Mr Waller	10
Rich[ard] More	2	Josep[h] Huckley	4

Lower part of Deptford

Not Chargable		Not Chargable	
Edw[ard] Chapman	1	John Bayle	3
Widd[ow] Broggenne	4	Widd[ow] Chyme	1
Tho[mas] Rumlie	2	Widd[ow] Payne	3
Rich[ard] Wise	3	Widd[ow] Russell	3
Eliza[beth] Russell	2	Tho[mas] Baxster	1
Lewis Waters	1	Widd[ow] Lee	1
Widd[ow] Moulton	1	Widd[ow] Langlie	2
[fol. 3v]			
Rich[ard] Readinge	2	Widd[ow] Poorter	2
Tho[mas] Hunt	1	Edward Spencer	1
Tho[mas] Russell	2	Widd[ow] Lappitt	2
Math[ew] Lancton	3	Widd[ow] Purser	2
Widd[ow]Murton	2	Hen[ry] Seeres	4
Jo[h]n Shurie	2	John Man	3
Tho[mas] Reade	3	Widd[ow] Johnson	2
Widd[ow] Hackman	2	Jo[h]n Ingrome	1
Marg[aret] Newell	1	Edw[ard] Nash	1
Widd[ow] Hill	1	Will[iam] Bond	2
Tho[mas] Cleeves	2	Will[iam] Winchly	4
Rich[ard] Loader	3	Rich[ard] Bowes	3
Edw[ard] Gregory	2	James Simonds	2
Tho[mas] Clarke	2	Widd[ow] Smith	1
Widd[ow] Heaths	5	Walter Michell	1
Tho[mas] Fisher	2	Tho[mas] Hare	1
Will[iam] Casie	1	Widd[ow] Sallis	5
Sam[uel] Banfier	3	Widd[ow] Trivitt	4
John Hyett	4	Widd[ow] Alderson	4
Rich[ard] Waller	4	Tho[mas] Ilcock	5
John Cox	3	Widd[ow] Hankes:Widow	2
Math[ew] Browne	3	John Evans	3
Sam[uel] Roper	3	Jo[h]n Stringer	3

W[illia]m Tarrent	2	John Hodges	2
James Burgis	3	John Clemence	2
Widd[ow] Ingold	3	Tho[mas] Downes	2
John Child	3	Tho[mas] Tillie	2
Widd[ow] Bishop	1	Widd[ow] Hacker	2
Widd[ow] Hoult	2	Widd[ow] Pescod	2
Rob[ert] Mollie	3	John Frame	2
Edw[ard] Nicols	2	Geo[rge] Bowin	2
John Harris	1	Widd[ow] Haeles	1
Widd[ow] Simons	2	Will[iam] Sharpe	2
Francis Pollicott	2	Widd[ow] Kemp	1
James Rose	1	Edw[ard] Reedes	3
Widd[ow]Smith	3	Widd[ow] Ramsie	2
Rich[ard] Huges	2	Widd[ow] Kellie	2
Gooddie Dyer	1	Widd[ow] Murton	2
Will[iam] Dutton	2	Widd[ow] Bowers	1
Tho[mas] Penny	1	Geo[rge] Randolph	4
Rob[ert] Chuny	2	Will[iam] Coates	4
Widd[ow] Browne	4	Fran[cis] Stafford	3
John Brooks	3	Tho[mas] Keyes	2
Widd[ow] Reeves	2	Widd[ow] Little	1
Widd[ow] Evans	2	Geo[rge] Newton	2
John Rubery	3	Hen[ry] Morgan	1
Henry Robbison	1	Tho[mas] Rangham	2
Widd[ow] Ellett	2	Jo[h]n Tetsell	2
Geo[rge] Willibie	2	W[illia]m Hancock	1
John Smithie	1	Roger Oliver	1
Widd[ow] Cleese	2	Widd[ow] Byworth	1
Abra[ham] Hobson	2	John Collins	2
Rich[ard] Phips	2	Tho[mas] Moyles	2
John Wilson	2	John Axson	2
Will[iam] Tayler	3	Nich[olas] Parsons	3
W[illia]m Newell	3	Widd[ow] Pierce	2
John Russell	1	Rob[ert] Reade	1
John Ireland	1	Rob[ert] Townes	3
Jacob Pen	1	Fne: Perkins	1
Widd[ow] Febridge	1	Widd[ow] Trowell	1
Nich[olas] Hartenbrook	1	Will[iam] Smith	5
Rich[ard] Baker	1	Widd[ow] Cartwright	3
Widd[ow] Cullier	2	Rob[ert] Casie	2
Will[iam] Asbie	2	James Brooks	2
David Browne	1	Widd[ow] Alford	2
Widd[ow] Bull	1	Mary Orsbon	1

Widd[ow] Govett	1	Widd[ow] Coulie	1
Rich[ard] Passie	1	Widd[ow] Osbourne	1
Will[iam] Tyler	1	Charles Evans	1
Tho[mas] White	2	Tho[mas] Sallie	2
Will[iam] Anger	1	Andr[ew] Smith	1
Tho[mas] Tregunell	1	Goodman Tyler	2
Jo[h]n Wheathers	4	Rich[ard] Spriggins	3
John Bodham	3	Widd[ow] Row	1
Roger Spry	4	Edw[ard] Sherwood	3
Dani[el] Fesey	3	Rob[ert] Hy	1
Geo[rge] Cassell	3	Nicho[las] Wilkins	3
W[illia]m Cry	2	Chris[topher] Mullett	1
Goodm[an] Rogers	1	Rich[ard] Gardner	1
Jo[h]n Croucher	7	Griffin Davis	2
Math[ew] Hill	1	Widd[ow] Axson	1
Ar[thur] Putt	3	Tho[mas] Seeres	2
Rich[ard] Lucas	2	Chris[topher] Harper	2
Will[iam] Love	2	Jo[h]n East	3
Thomas Love	3	W[illia]m Evenards	3
Dudley Harvie	2	Tho[mas] Dandie	2
Rob[ert] Winsley	3	Widd[ow] Baker	2
John Hares	3	Edward Lentall	1
William Cry	4		

John Huskins Richard Crank & John Wright Constables

[fol. 4r]

Woolwich

Chargable		Chargable	
Mr Christ[opher] Pett	10	Mr W[illia]m Acworthe	8
Mr W[illia]m Sheldon	8	Mr Jerymy Blackman	15
Mr Jo[h]n Faulkner	10	Mr Antho[ny] Deane	7
John Thornden	3	Peter Russell	7
James Bartrum	2	Dan[iel] Chrismas	3
Will[iam] Cowdre	5	Widd[ow] Sawell	2
Thomas Day	3	John Spooner	5
Francis Straton	6	Tho[mas] Swarfer	4
Sary Bowyer	6	Henry Munday	3
John Ladbroke	3	Thomas Boothe	4
Allix[ander] Alley	7	Nathan Butler	6
John Blonden	4	Abra[ham] Gollston	7
John Hutchens	4	Sam[uel] Dannes	5
Thomas Comforde	4	Rich[ard] Feindall	2
Rich[ard] Watterman	4	Henry Morgaine	2

Willi[am] Soane	2	Denes Watters	2
Eliza[beth] Giefs	2	John Leeche	1
John Wiete	1	John Lesener	3
Tho[mas] Medcafe	2	John Hankine	5
George Barkere	3	Rob[er]t Sughger	12
Geor[ge] Garrett	2	John Thomas	2
Will[iam] Newson	2	James Tinke	2
Jeremiah Mordine	3	Will[iam] Greene	3
John Welch	3	Christo[pher] Lambe	2
Edward Homes	2	John Bennett	1
Will[iam] Cooper	2	John Adams	5
John More	2	Will[iam] Pigg	2
Jane Chesman	5	John Happelford	1
Dan[iel] Henry	2	Tho[mas] Rawlins	7
John Jenman	3	Evans Henry	1
Ed[ward] Harrison	2	Tho[mas] Fell	4
Thomas Thompson	2	Noyes Floyde	1
Will[iam] Lorry	3	Eliza[beth] Clarke	2
Will[iam] Rose	2	Edw[ard] Madison	2
Will[iam] Mason	3	Rob[ert] Plare	2
John Wickker	4	Charles Ladbrooke	3
Edward Harrison	2	John Waux	2
Tho[mas] Savidge	2	Will[iam] Sherwood	2
Tho[mas] Kierby	1	Antho[ny] Lambeth	2
Math[ew] Welche	3	Tho[mas] Rambreg	2
Will[iam] Couller	2	Rich[ard] Dixson	2
Tho[mas] Russell	2	Sam[uel] Barker	2
Will[iam] Layton	2	Doro[thy] Palmer	6
Ann Terpentine	3	Will[iam] Batt	2
Ann Glover	2	Henry Streete	5
Josep[h] Maxom	1	Rich[ard] Heathe	2
Edward Smith	2	Tho[mas] Stacey	3
Simon Heuwes	5	John Knight	1
Tho[mas] Comes	2	John Fepes	1
Edward Cockes	3	Will[iam] Fainge	3
Tho[mas] Boyce	4	Stephen Daniell	2
Peter Graytricke	2	Elias Elie	2
Rich[ard] Wilcks	2	Henry Tapsell	3
W[illia]m Danggerfell	1	Tho[mas] Parsons	2
Will[iam] Stedman	2	John Kingson	3
John More	3	Edw[ard Fell	2
Ralph Clarke	2	Tho[mas] Hooke	3
Tho[mas] Heath	3	James Harden	3

Edward Hells	2	George Wattson	2
James Stakes	3	Tho[mas] Ramford	3
Edw[ard] Grinly	3	Hen[ry] Layes	2
Edw[ard] Withers	3	Rob[ert] Lamon	2
Peter Warner	4	Francis Cocker	2
Will[iam] Sters	3	Tho[mas] Bowyer	4
Tho[mas] Coke	2	Math[ew] Richardson	2
Rob[ert] Ellery	4	Rob[er]t Moster	2
Tho[mas] Wiels	2	Rodger Beeste	4
Will[iam] Wilford	3	John Longe	2
John Clothier	6	Will[iam] Bartrum	2
Geo[rge] Pickersgill	2	Will[iam] Baddouns	2
Kath[erine] Laisee	5	Joane Hall	1
James Thomas	1	Rob[ert] Blackden	4
Rob[ert] Wodden	3	Rob[ert] Ellerny	5
Tho[mas] Hatten	3	Stephen Anslee	1
Margery Hockings	4	John Duninge	1
Will[iam] Con[n]away	2	Benjamin Hanlare	2
Will[iam] Watts	1	John Robarts	2
John Haddeson	2	Elizabeth Scote	2
Kellee Williams	2	Thomas Phillipps	2
Will[iam] Mason	1	John Torline	1
Paull Limbey	7	John Jellines	6
Rob[er]t Sprin[g]er	4	John Cooke	3
John Steakes	2	Rich[ard] Smith	5
Thomas Hoocke	4	Walter Stafford	5
Rich[ard] Livinge	4	Will[iam] Tabalse	2
Joseph Goffe	4	Nicho[las] Worte	3
Joshuah Hensy	7	Rich[ard] Stinton	1
Nicho[las] Ulfe	3	Will[iam] Frances	1
Tho[mas] Williams	2	Dan[iel] Stevens	3
[fol. 4v]			
John Poole	3	Hannagh Reade	1
Tho[mas] Battell	2	Will[iam] Masone	1
Rich[ard] Audle	2	John Clarke	3
Tho[mas] Wootten	3	Henry Gyes	1
W[illia]m Kichinman	1	Rich[ard] Cornfed	1
John Crucher	1	Geo[rge] Barnett	2
James Russell	2	Henry Penny	6
Ralph Hollman	2	Tho[mas] Sparke	2
Eliza[beth] Dockett	2	Will[iam] Woddall	1
Will[iam] Day	1	Marten Lutor	1
Rich[ard] Wheller	2	Tho[mas] Nicolds	2

Will[iam] Righte	2	Geo[rge] Nuby	2
Tho[mas] Perkins	2	Paule Tetterre	3
Nicho[las] Batten	2	Tho[mas] Eatten	3
Rich[ard] Page	2	James Rowland	3
John Cortes	2	John Pancke	2
Edw[ard] Clemans	2	Jonas Newman	3
Will[iam] Cokerell	3	Tho[mas] Hooke	3
Frances Scott	3	John Marshall	2
Phillip Hewes	2	Tho[mas] Poste	2
Rob[er]t Stansbee	2	Will[iam] Odill	2
Tho[mas] Woode	3	Hen[ry] Coppett	3
Frances Holbred	1	John Hatten	2
Abraham Stanford	4	Ralph Bowers	3
Rich[ard] Dixson	2	John Collings	1
Will[iam] Flowers	2	John Wright	2
Math[ew] Ovenden	2	John Newman	3

Emptie Houses

Mr Ackden one Howse	2	The same Acden	3
The same Acden	11	The same Acden	4
Mr Pordige one howse	6	Mr Henry	3
Mr Henry one other howse	3	Rob[er]t Strugger	5
William Cleere	3	Mr Whitinge	3
Henry George	2	Mrs Kirke	2
Barbary Sheldon	2		

Not Chargable / Not Chargable

Widd[ow] Grace	2	Widd[ow] Henry	2
Widd[ow] Hicks	2	Widd[ow] Saunders	2
Widd[ow] Dickson	1	Widd[ow] Maddram	1
Joseph Maye	1	Widd[ow] Whare	1
Arthur Anderson	1	Edw[ard] Mathews	1
Richard Ham[m]an	1	Rich[ard] Curey	2
Rob[er]t Lattone	2	Tho[mas] Jennings	2
Tho[mas] Churchman	2	John Dayes	2
John Hagskins	1	Rob[er]t Barley	2
Steven Turner	1	Tho[mas] Nores	1
Widd[ow] Hubbard	2	Widd[ow] Hopper	2
Will[iam] Kiete	1	Widd[ow] Righte	2
Edw[ard] Thompson	2	Geo[rge] Tode	2
Widd[ow] Churchman	2	Widd[ow] Quitone	1
Widd[ow] Hewes	1	Widd[ow] Garrett	2
Will[iam] Grinam	1	Dan[iel] Thompson	2

| Will[iam] Tyler | 1 | Widd[ow] Massee | 1 |
| Rich[ard] Barnes | 1 | Thomas Mapsden Constable | |

Mottingham

Chargable		Chargable	
Mr Sam[uel] Mico	11	Mary Stakes	3
Tho[mas] Wiley	5	John Lucas	4
Rob[er]t Silley	3	Mich[ael] Comforte	2
John Genoway	5	Mr Stodder	5
Mr Marsh	1		

Not Chargable		Not Chargable	
Olliver Endersby	4	Geo[rge] Robinson	4
Tho[mas] Norton	2	Cesar Bridges Constable	

Charleton

Chargable		Chargable	
S[i]r W[illia]m Dewcy Barronett	40	S[i]r Anth[ony] Bateman knight	21
Mr Tho[mas] Blount Esq	23	Mr Abra[ham] Browne	6
Mr Nicho[las] Barber	6	Mrs Eliza[beth] Newton	6
John Holdin	6	Sam[uel] Harrow	4
Henry Whiffin	6	John Whiffin	5
Will[iam] Andrewes	6	Will[iam] Blake	2
Adam Hopkins	2	Thomas Stakes	1
Sam[uel] Beoman	6	Michael Altham	2
Will[iam] Barton	4	Math[ew] Blissitt	3
Rob[ert] Dowger	6	John Latter	2

Emptie Howses

S[i]r Antho[ny] Bateman	6	Mr Gulliford	6
Mr Eltoned	3		

Not Chargable		Not Chargable	
John Dalborn	2	Tho[mas] Rundall	3
Will[iam] Chapman	3	John Pett	3
Widd[ow] Chambers	1	Widd[ow] Pemberton	3
John Blake	2	Rich[ard] Thomas	1
John Marcy	2	Peter Streton	1
Widd[ow] Whiffin	2	John Hooper	3
Will[iam] Musall	6	Sam[uel] Beoman Constable	

[fol. 5r]

Lee

Chargable

John Harvy Esq	10
Geo[rge] Thomson Esq	21
Mrs Sarah Mercer	8
Mrs Eliza[beth] Snelling	8
Mr Geo[rge] Shaw	10
S[i]r John Lenthall	5
Abra[ham] Constable	7
Natha[niel] Campion	7
Rob[ert] Hepenstall	1
Tho[mas] Butler	2
John Shepstor	2
John Jessyman	5

Chargable

Morrice Thompson Esq	15
Peter Delonoy	13
Mr Ben[jamin] Collier	8
Mr Ste[phen] Watkins	6
Mr Joseph Cox	7
Will[iam] Cawstine	6
Mrs Susan Temple	10
Will[iam] Whitten	2
Thomas Burley	3
Tho[mas] Newell	11
Tho[mas] Ward	2

Not Chargable

Mr Stoddard	2
Widd[ow] Handford	1
The vestry to the church	2

Not Chargable

Martin French	2
Widd[ow] Simson	1
Tho[mas] Ward Constable	

Eltham

Chargable

Mr Fran[cis] Watters	18
Ralph Artewayes	2
Ralph Merefeild	6
Tho[mas] Merefeild	4
Walter Littlefeild	2
Henry Bynd	2
Mr Blackwell	25
Rob[ert] Brookes	2
John Gascoyne	2
Jeremiah Alridge	5
Mrs Thomazen Mercer	9
Rob[ert] Peake	4
Henry Castelman	6
Tho[mas] Castelman	4
Tho[mas] Beech	4
John Haveringe	2
Mr W[illia]m Overton	14
Mr Rich[ard] Owen	7
Mr Clem[en]t Hobson	6
Mr John Bewly	13
Mr Christ[opher] Comporte	10

Chargable

Mr Geo[rge] Grynes	6
Mr Edw[ard] Grace	5
John Gentle	5
Mr Step[hen] Pemble	8
Mr Allexander	6
Mr Nicho[las] Haley	7
Ben[jamin] Farroe	9
Jeremiah Sage	2
Henry Snow	4
Mr Dan[iel] Poyntell	6
Rob[ert] Whitehead	2
John Crooke	2
Widd[ow] Streete	5
Rich[ard] Greene	2
Mr Law[rence] Chambers	11
Rich[ard] Pollington	1
Mr Calebb Trenchfeild	11
Mr Tho[mas] Shetterden	8
Mr Fran[cis] Pecke	4
Mr John Gelibrand	5
John Locke	4

Mr Fran[cis] Soane	12	Mr Nicho[las] Smith	10
Mrs Taylor	14	Mr May	5
Mrs Phillpott	9	Peter Pettley	4
John Jesseman	4	Thomas Griffin	8
John Wingham	5	Sam[uel] Wiffin	5
John Coates	4	Will[iam] Butter	6
Nicho[las] Smith Constable		*[blank]*	
[blank]		*[blank]*	
Will[iam] Hasleopp	2	Edw[ard] Smale	11
Sam[uel] Carter	1	Gyles Barber	3
Augustin Wood	7	Nich[olas] Faulkner	5
William Barnes	4	Tho[mas] Harwood	2
Barnard Holyday	3	Hugh Bind	3
Joshua Farroe	5	James Guy	2
Edw[ard] Browne	2	Mr Tho[mas] Crispe	11
Henry Biggs	6	Rich[ard] Nun	2
Tho[mas] Birch	3	Will[iam] Smith	1
Tho[mas] Sapp	5	Tho[mas] Jenings	6
Widd[ow] Loytton	3	John Phillips	4
Nicho[las] Carpenter	4	Wilfred Thomson	2
John Hedger	2	Charles Wells	2
S[i]r John Shaw	1	Mr Gibson	1
Rob[ert] Dickeson	3	Tho[mas] Parrott	3
Ed[ward] Webb	2	Mr Langworth	11
An Bynd	4		

Emptie Howses

Mr Nicho[las] Haley	3	Mr John Soane	4
Anth[ony] Weekes	1	Baptist Swithzer	1
Sir Nicho[las] Crispe his Tenem[en]ts	27	Tho[mas] Beech	2
Mr Nicho[las] Smith	3	Jere[miah] Greene	9
Coll[onel] Tho[mas] Pantton	14	Widd[ow] Streete	2
[blank] Pococke	2	Tho[mas] Sapp	2
John Temple	2	Nicho[las] Smith Constable	

Not Chargable

Not Chargable		Not Chargable	
Rich[ard] Smelt	2	James Greene	1
Henry Footer	1	Rich[ard] Bynd	2
Tho[mas] Wheeler	2	Francis Wilcocke	2
W[illia]m Roff	2	John Sellers	3
Edw[ard] Parrott	2	And[rew] Stevens	2
Tho[mas] Eldridge	3	Phillip Locke	2

Rich[ard] Gillam	2	Rob[ert] Harvy	2
Rob[ert] Kent	2	Rob[ert] Rose	2
Widd[ow] Kent	2	Widd[ow] Hobbs	3
Widd[ow] Coman	2	Hen[ry] Stubbs	2
Zacha[riah] Price	2	Eliza[beth] Earle	1
[fol. 5v]			
Tho[mas] Page	1	Sim[on] Clafford	2
Widd[ow] Tribbett	1	Geo[rge] Jenings	1
Rich[ard] Willey	1	Rob[ert] Bushar	2
Dan[iel] Fox	1	John Williams	1
Edw[ard] Loytton	2	Jane Queene	3
John Tyndall	1	John Hills	1
Rich[ard] Beecher	1	Christopher Tyndall	1
Able Pemble	1	Rebecca Bird	2
John Chilmead	1	Jobb: Packe	2
Henry Hallerd	1	Widdow Thomas	1
James Carrington	2	Widdow Mills	1
Francis Salte	1	John Almons	1
John Kingsland	3	Willi[am] Edmuns	1
Tryman Alewood	1	Willi[am] Rowlwright sen[io]r	1
Willi[am] Rowlewright ju[nior]	3	Will[am] Cockraft	2
Willi[am] Cutton	2	Sam[uel] Hutchins	2
Willi[am] Castleman	2	Em[m]a[nuel] Locke	2
George Brayman	2	Edward Bird	2
Richard Foster	2	Richard Hobbs	2
Arthur Harwood	2	Joanne Chapman	3
William Bryant	9	Willi[am] Crosbey	1
John Lock Constable			

Lewsham

Chargable		Chargable	
Rich[ard] Moore	7	Will[iam] Rogers	1
Rich[ard] Freeman	5	Ezek[ial] Smith	3
W[illia]m Skiffe	2	Susanna Constable	4
Mr Marmaduke Millington	12	Tho[mas] Myland	3
Widd[ow] Pristman	2	Henry Eaton	4
Mr Rich[ard] Kitchell	5	Mrs Eliza[beth] Offley	6
James Trew	3	And[rew] Twentyman	2
Jeffry Morphew	4	Tho[mas] Herman	1
W[illia]m Constable	5	Mr W[illia]m Spranger	5
Bart[holomew]Stow	3	Tho[mas] Palmer	3

Widd[ow] Holloway	1	Erasmus Harlinge	4
S[i]r Will[iam] Wild	18	John Peirce	6
James Maplesden	3	John Freeman	3
Mr John Stevens	3	Mr W[illia]m Sedgwick	22
John Grumbridge [junior]	4	Tho[mas] Mattkin	1
W[illia]m Pincker	2	Hen[ry] Tyvatt	2
Geo[rge] Dawes	2	Sam[uel] Stevens	3
Abr[aham] Mylls	1	Allix[ander] Hickman	1
Tho[mas] Hodgkin	3	Rich[ard] Broockhowse	1
James Chiffins	2	John Baker	2
Mr Edw[ard] Trotter	8	Rob[ert] Fenne Esq	17
Nicho[las] Carter	4	Mr Geo[rge] Edmunds	6
Hen[ry] Dissington	2	Mr Anth[ony] Webster	12
John Coalegate	2	Charles Broockhowse	1
Timithy Clarke	1	Henry Dellver	7
W[illia]m Phillip	2	Francis Langam	4
John Chitty Jun[ior]	1	Will[iam] Bray	8
Theoder Randall	4	Will[iam] Greene	3
John Spencer	2	Jozyas Buckland	1
Mr Joseph Curtice	8	James Style	5
Mr W[illia]m Williams	3	Ste[phen] Wells	3
W[illia]m Stone	4	Rob[ert] Violet	3
Sam[uel] Drewry	2	Jo[h]n Gumbridge sen[io]r	6
John Criffins	1	Edw[ard] Right	2
James Sheares	3	John Clowder	2
Cuttberd Prettious	1	Jo[h]n Richardson	4
Rob[ert] Fisher	1	Abr[aham] Clowder	3
Mrs Ann Ridgwey	3	Tho[mas] Syzely	2
Geo[rge] Raunce	3	Tho[mas] Stroakes	1
Geo[rge] Chiffins	3	Tho[mas] Randall	5
W[illia]m Morphew	3	Abr[aham] Chiffins	3
Mr John Leygh	6	Abr[aham] Sym[m]onds	5
Francis Vallentin	5	Rob[ert] Lyne	3
Mr Rob[ert] Edmunds	5	John Chitty sen[io]r	1
Mr Geo[rge] Bladworth	2	Rich[ard] Clarke	3
W[illia]m Barrow	5	John Offall	6
John Hill	1	James Ongley	1
Widd[ow] Rundhill	1	Rob[ert] Sillvester	2
Rich[ard] Jewell	3	John Robinson	3
Mr Jo[h]n Winne	14	W[illia]m Lovett	3
W[illia]m Allingam	2	Widd[ow] Ricrafte	3
Mr Roger Langley	5	W[illia]m Raynard	3
W[illia]m Newland	4	John Willice	1

Henry Batt	1	Tho[mas] Avend	6
Edw[ard] Matthew	2	Mr W[illia]m Shermer	6
Hugh Symms	2	Rich[ard] Myles	2
Dan[iel] Right	1	Rich[ard] Clowder	3
Henry Normar	2	Rob[ert] Jackson	2
Henry Broockhowse	1	Ph[ilip] Battersbye	1
Tho[mas] Houldinge	2	Rob[ert] Wood	2
Henry Woodfall	2	John Newland	1
[fol. 6r]			
Tho[mas] Glover	3	Tho[mas] Aldersea	1
Tho[mas] Handford jun[io]r	2	Addam Allingam sen[io]r	2
Abr[aham] Grumbridge	7	James Newland	1
Christ[opher] Addams	1	Tho[mas] Handford sen[io]r	2
John Batt	1	John Hargate	1
Nicho[las] Clowder	3	Hen[ry] Foster	4
W[illia]m Pillion	1	John Hearne	2
Symon Chiffins	4	Mr James Symms	10
Chris[topher] Broockhowse	4	Rob[ert] Broockhowse	2
Widd[ow] Eager	1	Tho[mas] Browne	2

Emptie Howses

Mr Acton	2	James Treu	2
John Peirce	7	Mr W[illia]m Spranger	2
Barth[olomew] Slow	2	Mr Eyles	1
Jarmin Morphew	1	John Coalegate	2
Henry Delver	1	Mr Geo[rge] Edmunds	2
Abr[aham] Sym[m]onds	1	Widd[ow] Constable	2
W[illia]m Morphew	2	John Jessyman	1
Mr Bellthars Heyres	1	Mr Tho[mas] Burges	5
Mr Littlegroome Kittley	1	W[illia]m Newland	2
Henry Constable	3	Mr John Craine	3
Mr Lewice	1	Mr Hollow	4
Geo[rge] Chiffins	1	Henry Foster	3
Symon Chiffins	3		

Not Chargable		Not Chargable	
Widd[ow] Eaton	2	W[illia]m Harrice	2
Geo[rge] Gladman	1	W[illia]m Glimster	1
Sam[uel] Morton	2	Thomazin Willestone	1
Widd[ow] Frynabye	1	And[rew] Hill	2
Widd[ow] White	3	Widd[ow] Rayner	1
W[illia]m Vallance	2	John Hodgkine	1
Widd[ow] Ashby	2	Tho[mas] Reade	1

Widd[ow] Mathews	1	Widd[ow] Bell	1
W[illia]m White	2	John Barker	2
Geo[rge] Geale	4	John Mathews	2
Bar[tholomew] Smith	1	Symon Heath	1
John Burbidge	2	Sackfeild Baldwine	1
W[illia]m Dyer	2	Francis Barron	1
Edw[ard] Seaborne	1	Rich[ard] Wattman	1
John Barker	1	Widd[ow] Tapsall	1
John Green	3	Tobyas Mantle	1
John Haite	1	Widd[ow] Parsons	1
Moses Budgin	2	Widd[ow] Mowseall	2
Will[iam] Chiffins	2	Widd[ow] Tivatt	1
Widd[ow] Craine	3	William Tivatt	2
James Seares	1	W[illia]m Collier	1
Math[ew] Sim[m]ons	2	Widd[ow] Willecome	1
Christ[opher] Kittley	1	Widd[ow] Bolton	1
Marke George	3	Widd[ow] Carter	1
Tho[mas] Alline	1	John Abbott	1
Richard Blewitte	1	John Harte	1
Widd[ow] Rofe	1	Rob[ert] Blewitte	1
Math[ew] Kingsland	1	Widd[ow] Newland	1
Widd[ow] Batt	1	Rob[ert] Dawley	1
John Miller	1	Roger Cooke	1
Rob[ert] Batt	1	Francis Lawson	2
Rich[ard] Allingam	1	Addam Allingam jun[io]r	1
Widd[ow] Heath	1	John Blake	1
		Widd[ow] Harrice	1

John Spencer and Abraham Symonds Constables

East Greenwich
Church Wall

Chargeable		Chargeable	
Abraham Dry	3	Mr John Bright	8
Mr William Champlin	12	Mark Blessett sen[io]r	3
Mrs Elizab[eth] Stacy wid[ow]	8	Mr Henry Morris	5
Mr Richard Thomas	6	John Page	5
Jeremy George	2	William Coales	3
Mr Francis August	10	John Ellott	5
Thomas Sparkes	2	Richard Wood	2
John Black	2	John Benton	2
Thomas Baker	2	James Delton	2
Barnabus Priddeth	3	Thomas Hatree	5
Dorothy Pattington wid[ow]	2	William Hinsbey	2

Thomas Wilshire	4	John Hollyman	1
Phillipp Woodnutt	2	William Wootton	1
John Whitehead	2	Robert Buttler	2
William Lock	2	John Dawes	5
William Ogam	4	William Youngly	3
Thomas Foster	1		

Combes Hill

Chargeable		Chargeable	
Richard Fisher	3	Thomas Rowe	4
Nathanill Hilles	6	Thomas Dry	1
William Renolds	3	Mrs Judith Mason	29
Thomas Brewer gen[tleman]	9	Mr William Colson	10
William Hooker Esq.	23	Mr Mark Cottell	23
Mr Robert Jefferies	6	William Goodhew gen[tleman]	5

[fol. 6v]			
John Clifton	8	Mr Will[iam] Penning	9
Mr Christop[her] Culling	11	Judith Spencer wid[ow]	5
Mrs Mary Lanier	5	Mr Fran[cis] Primrose	12
Mrs Mildred Collier	8	Mr Thomas Lanier	8
Mr Arthur Art	7	Mr Thomas Potter	14
Mr Thomas Warden	8	Mr James Langrick	8
Mr Thomas Oswell	8	Thomas Brimington	2
Mrs Elizab[eth] Rooper	8	Stephen Boyer	5
Richard Boyer	2	Mathew Smyth	2
Ann Rushinn widd[ow]	4	Thomas Cooke	1
William Clarke	2	Edward Bence	4

London Street

Chargeable		Chargeable	
Thomas Prater	2	Capt[ain] Tho[mas] Robinson	6
Mr Joseph Hackwell	9	Francis Webb gen[tleman]	7
George Creed	2	Edward Barnett	3
Nathaniell Feild	1	Thomas Hewes	2
Robert Dry	2	Edward Hager	2
Arthur Guilliam	3	Mr Francis Purdinia	12
Mathew Blessett	3	Richard Potter	2
Mark Blessett Jun[io]r	1	George Garrett	2
Michaell Yates	6	Thomas Williams	2
Mrs Elinor Wakeman	5	Mr Francis Hayton	5
Richard Greene	10	Humphrey Taylor	2

George Marshall	2	Mr Anthony Masson	4
George Saxbey	2	Mr Thomas Plume cl[erk]	6
John Williams	5	Thomas Cotton	2
Edward Bottley	1		

Highstreet West

Chargeable		Chargeable	
Mathew Osbourne	1	William Stiff	1
Elizabeth Coult	2	Robert Rivers	1
Mr John Strange	4	Mr Tho[mas] Ramsberry	5
Richard Gill	4	William Hewes	4
Thomas Topping	2	Thomas Land	3
Francis Glidwell	2	Benjamin Davison	2
Bridgett Tufton	4	John Absolam	2
Elizabeth Rogers	1	Leonard Cooke	3
John Shalcroft	8	Luke Smyth	4
Peter Lyon	4	Francis Long	6
Humphrey Perry	4	John Lucas	1
Jane Adcock	6	Edward Puttney	5
William Stone	5	James Kempshall	5
Francis Cranaway	4	Capt[ain] Thomas Pibus	6
Judith Squibb	11	Anthony Hoane	2
John Moore	2	Richard Hoane	2
Nicholas Good	2	Robert Heaster	2
Robert Sloman	2	James Herringham	3
John Howe	3	Jane Skelton	2
John Whitney	5	Charles Taylor	3
Rose Beadberry	4	Miles Hart	2
Richard Kennett	5	James Farthing	5
Richard Budd	2	John Kelsey	2
John Blundall	4	George Wheeler	2
John Morris	3	John Rawlings	2
Jonas Sym[m]ons	2	John Williams	4
Alexander Bishopp	4	John Waite	2
William Baker	2	John Horton	2
Robert Haimes	2	Thomas Chiff	2

Highstreet East

Chargeable		Chargeable	
Robert Goding	2	Mr Thomas Franck	4
Elinor Whinnard	1	Robert Peacock	1
Mr John Rochford	6	Edward Marshall	2
George Bretian	2	William Thompson	2

William Ratford	2	Thomas Silverside	2
Andrew Robertson	3	Anthony Elton	2
William Cheese	2	Margaret Robertson	5
William Silstall	2	Thomas Fortune	2
John Fuller	6	William Ratford	3
Henry Beaman	2	Francis Sim[m]es	2
William Smyth	2	Sarah Maruin	2
Hugh Muckleston	4	Elinor Wethers	4
Mr Edward Turner	11	William Garrett	4
Henry Upchurch	6	Humphrey Swann	3
Thomas Beckley	3	John Phillipps	7
John Wood	6	John Clarriage	6
William Richardson	3	Ralph Blundall	3
Nathaniell Ryly	6	John Mow	4
John Bines	1	William Marshall	2
Robert Holland	4	Margaret Lord	6
Mr Francis Higgeson	6	Richard Phillipps	3
Edward Rickman	2	Richard Webby	7
Avary Gardner	5	John Heath	3
John Pitcher	3	Thomas Audry	3
Richard Ball	2	Thomas Nicholas	2
William Fisher	6	Roger Bates	6
Mr James Brierton	5	Mr David Fiffee	10
[fol. 7r]			
Sir James Bunce	12	Mr James Tarsell	7
Mrs Sarah Groves	5	Mr Edward Saltmarsh	3
Capt[ain] James Lambert	8	John Mow Jun[io]r	2
Margarett Chapman	4	Thomas Patteson	3
John Hart	2	Joane Barney	2
John Allen	2	Elizabeth Marten	2
John French	2	Robert Firebarne	2
		Joane Barney	2

Billingsgate

Chargeable		Chargeable	
Thomas King	4	John Watton	4
Thomas Taylor	2	Robert Penton	2
Robert Barton	2	Martin Hoult	2
Henry Taylor	6	George Rennolds	4
Thomas Hood	2	John Deane	2
John Watson	2	Mrs Judith Deane	7
Nicholas Penton	3	Mr George Baker	12
Thomas Paine	2	Richard Buskell	2

Thomas Printer	3	Thomas Charr	2
John Flaws	4	William Hanson	2
Alice Barker wid[ow]	4	Ralph Lewis	4
John Downes	2	Nowell Winch	2
Thomas Huchins	1	John Symmes	2
William Gill	1	John Gam[m]on	2
Richard Batten	2	Francis Bray	2
Joseph Plumley	2	John Hilles	2
Ralph Hodgkins	2	Richard Kindall	2

Fisher Lane

Chargeable		Chargeable	
John Pigott	7	Francis Huchins	2
William Pigeon	3	John Barker	2
Thomas Hoane	2	George Ramsey	2
John Clarke	2	Richard Frost	2
Joane Miller	2	Thomas Ewer	2
Richard Buttler	2	William Hanger	2
Walter Price	2	Charles Baker	2
Hugh Pottifer	6	Robert Welles	6
Edward Tayler	2	Richard Hunt	2
John Hodgskins	2	Anthony Bryant	2
William Miller	3	John Sym[m]ons	2
John Phillipps	2	John Jurry	1
Reuben Fryer	1	William Louridge	2
William Stoner	2	John Sackes	2
Roger Howell	2	Robert George	1
Hugh Morgan	2	John Sandy	2

Stable Street

Chargeable		Chargeable	
Elizabeth Davis	4	Mr Thomas Boone	6
Mr Francis Gunn	4	Mr Robert Smyth	8
Andrew Hobbs	2	John Rowland	2
John Marsh	2	John Mathewes	2
Robert Bates	2	William Walker	3
Richard Allen	4	Elizabeth White	3
William Culvart	3	Thomas Spurr	3
William Milles	2	Thomas Bray	2
Richard Ashworth	2	John Fisher	3
John Turner	1		

Dock and Taverne Rowe

Chargeable		Chargeable	
Henry Stevens	3	Mathew Davis	1
John Denman	2	James Broughten	2
William Bannester	6	Sarah Clarke	3
Robert Annis	5	Elizabeth Ball	12
Thomas Charlton	2	Thomas Browne	2
John Ellis	6	Mr Thomas Smyth	6
William Diskett	3	Reuben Goulding	2
William Buddell	4	Edward Castleman	5
Adam Edghill	5	Hamond Chadwick	14
Luke Ball	2	Richard Blissett	5
Benjamin Glanvill	12	Mr William Smyth	10
Mr John Worrell	14	Thomas Wray	5
Nicholas Doe	5	Edward Walker	3
Capt[ain] John Dutton	5	Nicholas Brunton	2
John Aleworth	3	John Oxmond	2
Mathew Penn	7	Henry Milles gen[tleman]	6
Mr Thomas Gladman	6	Mr Robert Bosvill	6
Mr John Everist	5		

Crane South

Chargeable		Chargeable	
Gowen Rennolds	2	Mr John Walker	2
Mrs Elinor Tucker	2	John Sandy	2
Alexander Back	5	Thomas Bartlett	5
William Cleere	5	Richard Broadbent	5
Mr Tho[mas] Browne the }	30	Capt[ain] George Cock	15
Warden of the College }		Henry Gill	4
William Hatter	2	Thomas Holmes	4
Thomas Hart	4	Thomas Dousey	2
Mr Christop[her] Musgrove	28	Capt[ain] John Goulding	9
Mrs Elinor Nutton	5	Jo[hn] Merrick	2
Samuell Sweeting	3	Nathan Bates	1
William Bankes	1	William Wilbey	3
John Wilbey	4	Richard Wilbey	2
Stephen Richards	2	James Poundy	2
Joseph Farmer	2	Phillip Hoare	4
James Lowd	8	John Huchins	2
John Wilson	2	Jacob Jacobs	2
William Sim[m]ons	2	Thomas Chapman	2
William Faceby	3	Robert Shepheard	4
John Payne	4	Capt[ain] Edward Kirby	6

| John Johnson | 4 | John Blabourne | 2 |
| Richard Clarke | 8 | Henry Reeves | 3 |

[fol. 7v]

East Lane East

Chargeable		Chargeable	
James Foord	2	William Sanders	2
Richard Davis	2	Edward Hadister	2
Stephen Hilles	4	John Turner	2
Bridgett Lutton wid[ow]	12	Edward Griffin	4
Joane Gurney	4	Edward Aderson	1
William Bracking	3	Jane Burry	3
Alice Jennings	3	Thomas Pease	4
Henry Scamwell	4	Robert Dyer	4
Elinor Avery	3	Timothy Low Esq	4
Adam Cliff	4	Mrs Anne Neale	10
Charles Broadrick	13	Capt[ain] John Terith	11
S[i]r William Boreman	11	Mr Richard Clarke	9
Mr Thomas Marr	9	Mr George Baker	9
Capt[ain] Edward Nash	9	Peter Horton	2
Richard Dunckley	2	Thomas Swift	6
Miles Fluellin	2	Thomas Hilles	4
John White	4	Thomas Puttney	2
Thomas Hall	2	Julian Bridges	8
Mrs Hannah Hide	11	Mr William Prittiman	10
Mr James Curfellow	14	John Fisher	2
Mrs Ann Cripps	7	Richard Bell	3
Mr Samuell Wilson	14	Mr Edward Cledgett	10
Mr Richard Bickford	6	Robert May	4
Edward Wooden	6	Henry White	6
John Rowland	2	John Hull	2
William Sampson	2	Thomas Willes	4
John Smyth	3	Nicholas Couch	2
Thomas Booth	2	S[i]r Theophilus Biddulph	21
George Woodnutt	2	Thomas Woodnutt	2

East Lane West

Chargeable		Chargeable	
Mr Uriah Bavington	10	Capt[ain] Will[ia]m Parker	7
Mrs Susan Bulteele	8	Mrs Alice Munteth	10
Thomas Francklin	3	William Bridges	5
Roger Pettley	2	Peirce Hodges	2
Jane Chamberline	3	Mr John Cutts	5

Mrs Mary Warner	5	Mr John Newland	5
Andrew Avery	2	Roman Price	3
Mr James Barton	3	John Tomplin	2
John Arnold	2	Susan Wattson	4
William Robinson	5	Jacob Dickinson	4
Mr Robert Ellis	8	Mr Nicholas Cooke	13
Mr Elias Davage	13	Mr John Flaxmore	5
Mr Edward Packenham	17	Mr William Sainteman	10
Edward King	3	John Dyer	3
Joane White	3	John Barker	3
Capt[ain] Richard Shairman	12	Thomas Sturly	3
William Thomas	2	John Clarke	3
Paul Due	1	William Smyth	4
Peter Bray	3	Tobias Grub	5
Phillipp Newson	2	Thomas Gosling	2
Robert Walker	3	James Foretree Esq	10

The Kings Barne

Chargeable		Chargeable	
Mr John Allin	5	Mr Richard Malum	8
Thomas Willoby	2	Capt[ain] Thomas Smyth	4
John Waterman	2	Thomas Foster	1
Mr Joseph Smyth	4	John Pitcher	2

In Empty houses [East Greenwich]

Chargeable		Chargeable	
Mr Robert Snapes	6	George Wetherall	2
William Prickman	10	Augustin Peters	3
Mr Henry Travis	3	Mr William Salter	9
John Smyth	4	Mrs Bridgett Lutton	9
John Woodall	5	Mrs Jane Rowe	5
Mr Robert Oldridge	5	John Asser	6
John Davis	3	Joanne Blessett	3
Mr Francis Pudinia	8	Mr John Strange	16
Mr James Bathurst	8	Thomas Ellis	5
George Egerton	3	Robert Hudder	2
Francis Beere	3	George Miller	4
Thomas Hatree	5	Thomas Tidder	5
John Stanbridge	4	Mrs Stilstead	6
Collonell Gravener	16	Jeremy Stoner	3
Joane Wandall	2	Thomas Holmes	4
Mr John Knowles	5	Captaine Walters	9
Mr Marke Pease	7	Mr White	4

Thomas Jordan	4	John Greene	6
Mr John Burton	7	Thomas Jawbon	5
Abell Marchant	2	In the church porch	1

In East Greenwich

Not Chargeable		Not Chargeable	
Robert Greene	2	Abraham Jerland	2
John Jones	2	Ann Miller widd[ow]	2
John Thomas	1	John Henbey	1
John Rogers	2	John Durkin	2
William Bridges	1	Elizabeth Odam	1
Richard Holliman	2	Richard Lancaster	1
Anthony Bever	2	Widdow Dyer	2
Francis Hardpenny	2	Abraham Mottington	1
William Hippingstall	2	Richard Tomling	1
Jane Wood	1	Alice Cooper	1
John Dirking	2	John Dives	2
Abell Marchant	2	Jane Hoult widd[ow]	2
Susann Wood widd[ow]	2	Ann Adcock widd[ow]	2
James Larder	2	Richard Hodges	2
John Hopkins	2	John Owin	2
Dunstane Allen	1	Henry Austen	2
[fol. 8r]			
Richard Avis	1	William Eastmore	1
Thomas Epsome	2	John Earle	3
Joane Linskin	2	Edward Mathewes	2
John Groome	2	Thomas Ward	2
John Griffen	2	John Stuck	2
Joane Russell	2	Thomas Whinard	2
William Farmer	5	Richard Bennett	2
William Bottley	3	Trustram Bivens	2
William Browneing	2	John Coggar	2
John Cooper	1	Henry Gill	2
Thomas Foster	2	Jane Hutchins	2
Ann Queeney	2	John Church	2
Thomas Venables	2	William Hood	2
James Gardiner	1	David Olliver	1
Thomas Cooke	2	Jane Carter widd[ow]	2
Jane Sim[m]ons	2	Elizabeth Aversly	2
Joane Phillipps	2	John Jury	2
Sarah Larder widd[ow]	2	Margarett Axe	2
George Williams	2	Ralph Lyon	2
Lancelott Glover	2	Henry Edwards	1

Robert Harwood	2	George Browne	6
Margarett Brooker	2	Ann Hunt widd[ow]	2
John Rennolds	2	Joane Norton	1
Thomas Allen	2	Joane Howard	1
Joane Morehouse	2	James Staples	2
Peter Towsey	2	Jane Askin	2
William Comport	2	David Maskall	2
William Major	1	Mrs Ann Linn	4
Peter Worrell	2	Anne Banes	2
Robert Tibbutt	1	William Bollow	1
William Halfpenny	2	Jane Drinkwater	2
Elizabeth Puttney	2	John George	1

John Gillibrand & Richard
Saxbie High Constables

James Farthing	}	Petty Constables
Roger Bates	}	
Nicholas Doe	}	
Richard Davers	}	

[fol. 9r]

THE HUNDRED OF LITTLE AND LESNES

The parrish of Erith

Chargable		Chargable	
Henry How	2	Thomas Waller	4
Edward Webb	2	Richard Vaux	1
Anthony Billett	1	Robert Standly	1
Tho[mas] Whitfield	2	John Taylor	2
Thomas Ferman	1	John Kendall	4
Mr John Tomlin	6	John Pryer	2
John Roe	3	Will[iam] Parry sen[io]r	1
John Streete sen[io]r	5	Richard Spillman	4
Thomas Godfrey	1	Thomas Cole	2
Tho[mas] Ham[m]ond	1	Edward White	2
John Streeteabbey	2	George Harwood	4
Mr Stephen Thomas	8	John Allen	1
Ralph Hunter	3	John Meares	1
Thomas Pratt	1	Mr Draper Esq.	6
Eliza[beth] Philpott	2	John Dixon	2
John Martin	1	George Salter	1
Margaret Staples	4	John Salter	1
Joseph Woodman	2	Mrs Jane Thomas	2

John Streete jnr	1	Geo[rge] Titcumbe	3
John Ham[m]ond	2	Will[iam] Harwood	1
Briscoe Johnson	2	Tho[mas] Browne	3
Sam[uel] Tanner	4	Stephen Phelpe	2
S[ir] Tho[mas] Thinn	10	Bartholo[mew] Brookesby	5
Ben[jamin] Reddinge	4	Tho[mas] Standly	1
John Baxter	-	Richard Farler	4
John Higinges	1	John Brookes	1
John Porch	1	Hen[ry] Griffing	1

Not Chargable   **Not Chargable**

Richard Spillman	1	Eliza[beth] Philpott	1
Tho[mas] Browne	1	John Browne	1
Alexa[nder] Feacham	1	John Leake	1
Thomas Hammond constable			

The Towne of Erith

Chargable   **Chargable**

Mr Hen[ry] Shelbey in his house	11	& in Mannings House	6
Rob[ert] Tomlinson	2	Thomas Roote	4
Arthur Kittelwell	5	Richard Skinner	8
Christo[pher] Turner	7	Will[iam] Bradley	3
Culverwell Talner	4	Joane Hene	7
Martha Reeve	4	John Massion	1
Joyles Fulcher	2	Rob[ert] Dutton	4
John Thoughts Jnr	2	Tho[mas] Tallor	2
Richard Tanner	2	Thomas Batt	5
Joseph Reddy	2	Mary Andrew	6
James Nevell	2	Joyles Nelson	1
John Cumber	3	Will[iam] Ham[m]ond	3
Francis Deacon	2	Daniell Wild	4
Emanuell Seager	3	Sam[uel] Austen	2
Tho[mas] Meakins	5	John Olliver	1
Zacha[riah] Godstone	2	Christo[pher] Thomas	5
Jonas Tracy Snr	1	Will[iam] Collings	1
Thomas Harmond	3	John Watts	2
Henry Porch	4	-	-
John Barnaby	2	John Harvill	5
John Thoughts Snr	2	John Massion	2
Thomas Billett	1	Daniell Beecher	2
Will[iam] Andrews	3	Tristum Salter	3
Jonas Tracy Jnr	2	John Crampion	1

Will[iam] Billett	1	John Neall	2
Edward Roggers	2	Tho[mas] Collman	2
Joyles Bubbs	2	Tho[mas] Crosfeild	2
Edward Gorram	3	Jeffery Sidgwicke	2
James Snow	4	Hump[hrey] Batt	3
Thomas Henderson	2	John Winifrith	1
Thomas Seager	1	Henry Greete	1

Emptie Howses

Chargable		Chargable	
Bar[tholomew] Brookesby	7	Rob[ert] Dutton	8
W[illia]m Howes	1	John Ferris	5
Henry Dixson	2	Mr Vanacker	7
John Thornton	2	Marmion Walker	1
Mr Sam[uel] Bartlett	4	Thomas Cossins	2
Will[iam] Wood	2	Bar[tholomew] Brooksby	4
Mr Hen[ry] How	1	John Herrier	1

Not Chargable		Not Chargable	
Goody Jackson	1	Goodie Whittle	2
Goody Gatlinge	1	Goody Woodinge	2
Goody Joyles	1	Robert Dutton constable	

East Wickham

Chargable		Chargable	
S[ir] Thomas Leigh Knt	18	Mr Sanderson	9
Mr Will[iam] Smith	10	Mr Weavell	4
Mr Ghost	10	Mr Thompson	4
Rob[ert] Neighbour	5	Clem[en]t Foster	5
Anth[ony] Neighbour	2	John Warner	2
Rob[ert] Scudder	3	Daniel Ward	1
Rich[ard] Hunte	4	John Gavell	2
Tho[mas] Stafford	2	John Packman	1
James Coxe	1	Richard Heynes	1
Peter Darlinge	1	Christo[pher] Forty	2
John Holdinge	2	John Bedford	1
In an empty of Clement Foster	3		

Not Chargable		Not Chargable	
John Steynes	2	Francis Dickins	1
Mathew Darling	2	Widd[ow] Carter	2
John Houlden constable			

Crayford Towne

Chargable		Chargable	
[blank]		Mr Rich[ard] Porter	7
Mr John Feanex	4	Mrs Jane Havercamp	9
John Thorndell	6	Robert Fletcher	4
Tho[mas] Feilder	3	John Keepes	3
Will[iam] Freeman	2	Tho[mas] Ewer	2
John Collings	4	Christo[pher] Marshall	5
[fol. 9v]			
Richard Webster	2	Edward Copus	1
Thomas Bassett	2	John Kettle	4
John Overy	3	John Lavender	2
Mathew Barr	2	Will[iam] Reade	5
Will[iam] Sorry	2		

Emptie Howses

The Lady Norton	2	Mrs Marloe	2
Mr Halford	3	Mr Page	2
Will[iam] Sorry constable			

The Parrish of Crayford

Chargeable		Chargeable	
Mr Yates Rector	9	Mrs Ward widd[ow]	15
Mr Berkett	10	Mr Tho[mas] Gould	6
Henry Frith	5	John Marshall	10
Thomas Lawrence	7	Henry Fearne	3
Will[iam] Chroucher	5	Tho[mas] Lawrence	3
Frances Barley	2	Tho[mas] Steevens	6
Jude Stevens widd[ow]	4	Michael Perkins	2
Rob[ert] Hardinge	3	Edw[ard] Stakes	3
Richard Michell	1	Peter Webster	2
Sam[uel] Gibbs	2	Phillip Savedge	1
John Smith	3	John Barly sen[io]r	7
Richard Hamon	1	George Hatt	3
John Barnes	3	Henry Lewson	4

Not Chargable		Not Chargable	
Blanch Avery widd[ow]	1	Sarah Williams Widd[ow]	1
Daniell Hesterson	1	Simon Booth	2
George Gooding	1	Rob[ert] Francklen	1
Richard Tokens	1	Nicho[las] Cobham	2
Katherine Hall	1	Eliza[beth] Curtice	1
Will[iam] Lithall	2	Rich[ard] Blanch	1

Tho[mas] Peader	1	Rich[ard] Smith	1
[blank] Williams widd[ow]	2	Will[iam] Francke	2
Will[iam] Parker	1	Edw[ard] Past	2
Jane Harmon	5	Peterva Overstreete	2
Geo[rge] Taylor	2	Rob[ert] Scoder	1
Henry Venner	1	William Reeve	2
John Collins	3	John Goram	1
Edw[ard] Adgoe	3	John Barloe	2
Geor[g]e Hall constable			

Plumsted Parrish

Chargable		Chargable	
Mr Thomas Denham	6	Mr John Gossadge	10
Mr John Poole	6	Mr Thomas Borton	8
Mr Pearson	9	Mr Mey	4
John Hankin	3	Henry Sanders	2
John Saxbee	2	John Browne	3
Tho[mas] Nikalls	3	Rob[ert] Proudlove	3
John Tattman	4	Rich[ard] Osborne	2
Will[iam] Piggett	2	John Godfree	2
Rob[ert] Crossingame	2	Widd[ow] Fincher	5
Rob[ert] Williams	4	James Plumer	4
Thomas Fitch	4	Tho[mas] Tarlin	4
Tho[mas] Digbee	5	Richard Poole	3
Will[iam] Wells	2	Elizabeth Wright widd[ow]	4
Christo[pher] Coalegate	2	John Cooke	2
John Ferrell	3	Richard Venables	2
Jeremiah Browne	2	Henry Goulding	4
Richard Fisher	2	George Addams	2
Tho[mas] Smith	2	Richard Biggs	1
Widd[ow] Freind	1	Widd[ow] Grineway	1
Fowks Burkes	1	Will[iam] Tinker	1
Will[iam] Moore	1	Mr Shepheard	4
Mr May	2	Mr John Lee	4
		Mr Spencer	2

Not Chargeable		Not Chargeable	
Andrew Brett	3	Widd[ow] Parratt	1
Widd[ow] Saxby	1	Widd[ow] Elves	1
Widd[ow] Thatcher	1	Widd[ow] Bayly	1
Widd[ow] Nivoll	1	Widd[ow] Whiteinge	1
Rob[ert] Salisbury	1	Widd[ow] Herridge	2
Widd[ow] Marridge	1	Rich[ard] Morgan	2

Richard Luke	1	Tho[mas] Petty	2
John Osbourne	2	Rob[ert] Wascott	1
Francis Bottell	2	Rob[ert] Collard	1
James Stamps	2	John Cooke constable	

[fol. 10r]

THE HUNDRED OF CODSHEATH
in the Lath of Sutton att Hone

Parish of Shoreham

Chargeable		Chargeable	
George Polley Esq	12	Henry Gilbourne Esq	7
Thomas Pettley Esq	5	Mr Edward Olliver	3
William Hartnupp	4	Joseph Nash	4
David Dennis	2	Roger Carpenter	1
Michael Elke	2	Edward Hilles	2
John Round	3	Robert Olliver	3
Joane Nash Widd[ow]	4	John Whitehead	8
Mr Hall	2	John Whiffen	4
Mr Hall in another house	2	Robert Hilles	4
In a house late Robert Dallin dwelt in	1	Robert Hills in another house	1
Robert Hills		in another house	1
William Gibson	4	Robert Chandler	4
Edward Everest	2	Joane Reeve	3
Henry Spillsted	3	Thomas Lewen	3
Ro[bert] Poyner	3	Thomas Chapman	2
John Fryth	3	Mary Dally widdow	2
George Deines	1	John Rowne jnr	3
Benjamin Porter	2	William Small	2
Robert Attwood	2	Leonard Tomlyn	2
John Gransden	1	Edward Polhill	2
Dorothy Eversfield wid[ow]	2	Leonard Round	2
Jo[hn] Perrett	2	George Sanders	2
Jo[hn] Russ	2	Robert Dallin	2
Edward Fuller	2	Jo[hn] Lightfoot	1
Jo[hn] Willis	1	Widdow Francis	1
George Gooden	1	William Archall	1
Thomas Senyard	1	Henry Wooden	1
Jo[hn] Small	1	Symon Chittenden	1
Alexander Hilles	1	Thomas Perch	1
William Smyth	1	Henry Perrett	1
Edward Powcy	1	John Hilles	2

John Grandsden Borsholder

Not Chargeable		Not Chargeable	
Erasmus Lake	2	William Vaughan sen[io]r	1
Rachell Lightfoote	2	Charles Parker	2
Jo[hn] Causten	2	Mathew Tasker	1
James Marchall	2	Thomas Adly	1
Benjamin Britling	1	William Vaughan jnr	1
William Hearst	1	Thomas Homwood	1
Jo[hn] Kingsland	1	Robert Tilman	2
Thomas Downes	1	Fardinando Monke	1
Jo[hn] Plumley	1	George Lightfoote	3
Richard Fletcher	2	Richard Wooden	1
Gilbert Henge	2	Widdow Maynard	1
Edward Porch	1	Widdow Marchall	1
Widdow Senyard	1	Goodman Fenn	1
Allen Senyard	1	James Booker	2
Edmund Fleete	2	John Gransden Borsholder	

Halsted Parish

Chargeable		Chargeable	
Mrs Elizabeth Ash	20	Edward Mortimer	2
John Elliot	1	Thomas Hunt	2
[blank] Elliot and }	2	John Cottingham	2
Thomas Hunt }		Widdow Clarke	2
Thomas Wakelyn	1	John Johnson	1
Thomas Write	2	Marten Goulding	1
Widdow Dew	1	Widdow Smyth	1

Not Chargeable		Not Chargeable	
Widdow Hall	1	John Aldridge	2
Widdow Cooper	1	Widdow Christopher	1
William Bookham	1	Nicholas Bookham	2
Richard Onyons	2	William Meare	1
John Hibben sen[io]r	1	Solomon Judd	1
		Alexander Durling	
		Borsholder	

Ottford Parish

Not Chargeable		Not Chargeable	
Daniell Martin	1	Widdow Wigsall	3
Jo[hn] Goudge	1	Alexander Archer	1
Richard Hinge	1	Jo[hn] Dobbs	1

Thomas Nettle	2	Nicholas Botting	4
Richard Westerman	1	Robert Browne	2
James Hibbing	2	Richard Monk	1
Widdow Baker	1	Richard Baker	1
Thomas Martin	1	Richard Maddocks	4

Ottford Parish

Chargeable		Chargeable	
John Styleman	3	Francis White	3
John Burchett	2	Richard Mathewes	1
Thomas Fawkes	2	Mrs Adams	6
John Herriot	2	Thomas Wheeler	4
William Chalkhurst	3	Roger Howell	1
Richard Hawkes	1	William Small	2
George Dennis	4	Richard Burchett	2
Jo[hn] Hackett	1	Jo[hn] Thorpe	1
Thomas Symther	4	Daniel Mackling	3
Nicholas Goldsmyth	2	William Edwards	4
Widdow Barber	4	Stephen Landen	4
Widdow Freake	4	Mr Robert Heath	6
Mr John Carpenter	6	Samuel Walker	6
Mrs Polley widd[ow]	6	Mr John Collinvill at	
Mr Callant	3	home the lodge & old ruins	16
Mr Robert Petty	10	Richard Partenger	3
Edward Pownder	3	Richard Dolling	
[fol. 10v]			
David Polley Esq[uire]	6	Thomas Lush	6
George Wedey	3	Widdow Robinson	2
		William Chalkhurst	
		Borsholder	

Parish of Sandrish

Chargeable		Chargeable	
John Hyde Esq[uire]	16	Norton Curteis Esq[uire]	15
Samuel Sharpe cler[k]	8	William Outrem gent'	6
Henry Mandy	5	Richard Smyth	8
John Hall sen[io]r	1	Nathaniell Otty	3
John Cox	3	Richard Russell	2
John Phillipps	1	Peter Hartland	4
John Wicken	3	John Waymarke	4
Thomas Lampard	2	William Lampard	2
Gervase Watts	6	Margarett Garland widd[ow]	3
John Sampson	2	more	7

George Olliver	3	Anne Nidd widd[ow]	3
Thomas Nidd	3	John Smyth	3
Edward Atherfould	5	Henry Roberts	2
Moses Carryer	2	Robert Palmer	4
Thomas Atherfould	4	William Dannett	7
John Trepe	1	William Thomas	2
Mary Mandy widd[ow]	4	Thomas Hall	2
Thomas Small	2	John Jeffrey	2
Hezekiah Brunger	2	Henry Chapman	2
Robert Brunger	2	Robert Rogers gent'	6
Peter Pemell	3	Mrs Owtrem widd[ow]	5
John Barr	2	Edward Cartwright	1
William Chapman	5	George Roberts	3
John Hawes	5	Michaell Burr	6
Thomas Foorder	3	Richard Jessopp	4
Widdow Cowlard	2	John Skinner sen[io]r	2
John Peake	1	William Peake	3
Thomas Stonham	2	William Saman	3
Richard Wayker	3	Richard Knight	2
William Styles	1	William Marshall	2
Widdow Lambert	2	James Knight	3
Richard King	2	George Calven	3
Thomas Olliver	2	Adam Medherst	3
William Rose	2	Richard Cacott	2
Sarah Overy widd[ow]	6	James Harwood	2
Elizabeth Jorden	5	John Cowlard	2
Francis Saman	3	Richard Skinner	4

Not Chargeable		**Not Chargeable**	
John Woodgate	1	Thomas Lisney	2
Edward Banester	3	Thomas Beadle	1
John Hall of Idehill	2	William Harwood	1
William Blackman	1	Thomas Bateman	1
Thomas Alchin	1	Widdow Champs	2
John Skinner Jun[io]r	1	Richard Young	1
Bartholo[mew] Hall	2	Widdow Doulton	1
Widdow Farley	1	Henry Lampard	1
Augustine Garland	2	John Rumney	1
Christoph[er] Baker sen[io]r	2	Christoph[er] Baker jnr	2
Widdow Lampard	1	Andrew Garland	3
Thomas Barr	1	William Barr	3
Abraham Small	2	Widdow Roberts	1
Widdow Cooper	1	John Plumer	1

Daniell Evernden	1	Widdow Baker	2
Henry Foord	2	Widdow Jymson	1
Robert Bromfield	1	Walter Cooper	1
Jeffery Walker	1	Widdow Swone	1
William Walker	2	William Blackman	2
Sarah Rogers widd[ow]	1	Thomas Perryer	2
John Banester	1		

Seavenokes Towne

Chargeable		Chargeable	
Earle of Dorsett	85	Thomas Lamberd Esq[uire]	14
Francis Farnaby gent'	18	Mr John Cooper	12
Mr Olliver Theobald	6	Mr Walter Smyth	8
Mrs Elizabeth Hooper	2	Mr John Bloome	10
John Cronke	3	Mr William Allen	4
Richard Aslett	2	William Cockett	6
George Johnson	3	Phillip Ridgis	2
Richard Rogers	2	John Groombridge	4
Richard Cockett	4	Timothy Stone	3
Henry Murgin	2	Joane Bostone	4
Jane Baker	2	William Everist	2
Richard Salmon	2	Edward Baker	10
Robert Bourman	2	Thomas Wood	2
William Richardson	2	Widdow Murgin	3
Edward Stringer	2	John Allen	1
Jo[hn] Gates	2	Edward Ridgis	5
Elizabeth Butterfield	2	James Porter	1
Mr Turner	11	Mr Francis Best	8
Mr Thomas Wesson	7	Thomas Allen	4
George Wood	2	John Beardsworth	3
John Thornton	8	John Staple	2
Robert Skinner	2	John Jenkins	1
Robert Tarpe	2	Mrs Dorothy Chapman	2
Richard Bantken	3	Thomas Beetchar	2
William Spilsted	2	Samuel Wellar	2
Mr Richard Boss	5	Gilbert Kipps	3
Richard Cronke	4	George Novis	2
Jo[hn] Allen	2	Percevall Smyth	2
Thomas Wheeler	2	Moses Francis	2
Mr Edmund Wesson	2	Widdow Cooke	6
[fol. 11r]			
John Wilson	2	Mrs Wesson	6
George Crafts	6	Alexander Fowle	2

Widdow Beetchar	2	Widdow Burges	7
John Walter	2	David Durtnall	2
Henry Bostock	4	Henry Swaesland	2
William Lawrence	1	Robert George	11
Truss[tram] Mantle	3	John Flood	2
Mr Thomas Charley	8	Widdow Lovelace	2
Mrs Groome	2	Giles Lawe	2
William Mantle	2	Walter Browne	2
Francis Baker	2	William Flote	1
Nicholas Masters	2	Mr Robert Newman	9
Bartholomew Wood	6	Widdow Beardsworth	4
David Woodriffe	2	Widow Sone	2
Edward Sone	1	Widow Cole	4
John Kelsey	2	Nicholas Whale	2
Henry Sisley	2	Mr Edward Courthopp	4
Richard Randall	3	William Spencer	2
Nicholas Trice	3	Thomas Wiggenden	2
Edward Wood	4	William Upstone	3
John Martin	2	Nathaniell Owin	3
Nicholas Martin	5	Thomas Greene	3
Jane Lawe	2	Richard Spilsted	2
Nicholas Kelsey	1		

Not Chargeable		**Not Chargeable**	
Thomas Lawrence	2	Goodman Ridge	1
Richard Alchin	2	Thomas Dalchin	3
William Scot	1	Luke Hammerson	1
Henry Thorpe	1	Widdow Bassett	1
Widdow Fant	2	Robert Tye	2
William Akers	2	James Munnion	1
John Clark	2	Goodwife Belchamber	1
James Browne	2	Widow Bates	1
Edmund Pattenden	1	John Medhurst	1
Thomas Marten	1	Widdow West	1
Adrian Small	1	John Crafts	2
Goodman Ring	1	Robert Phipp	3
Widdow Collyer	1	John French	2
John Fletcher	2	Goodman Still	2
William Walters	2	John Johnson	1
James Hampton &	4	Robert Martin	1
Samuel Kester		Widdow Sinklis	1
Widdow Chakelin	1	John Gates	2
John Henderson	2	John Pattenden	1

William Giles	1	William Smaile	1
Widdow Merrum	1	Richard Atkins	2
Reignald Medherst	1	Thomas Hinge	2
Robert Cole	3	William Belchar	2
Ralph Bayman	2	Widdow Muddey	1
Goodwife Hollaway	1	James Walter	1
Thomas Sone	2	Thomas Thorneton	2
John Downes	1	Thomas Lander	1
Trustram Strayner	2	James Beecher	1
John Merrum	2	William Baker	2
Goodman Olliver	2	Thomas Crafts	1
Widdow Crafts	2	Goodman Downe	1
James Browne	1	Widow Tanton	2
Peter Durance	2	Harry Colegate	1
Widdow Francis	2	John Hilles	1
Benjamin Whiffin	1	William Turner	1
Widdow Tye	1	Sidney Francis	1
Widdow Durance	1	Clim: Cockett	1
Edward Maidhouse	1	James Smyth	2
Goodwife Edwards	1	Goodman Stevens	1
Goodman Munchin	1	Robert George Borsholder	

Seavenockes Weild

Chargeable		**Chargeable**	
Mr. Olliver	6	James Hunt	6
Thomas Hilles	4	Thomas Moreland	4
John Everest	2	Mr William Wall	6
Thomas Rigsby	4	Thomas Carryer	2
Thomas Skinner	2	John Baker	3
Francis Spilsted	2	Edward Smyth	1
Richard Everist	1	Widow Nicholls	3
Edward Fletcher	2	Robert Everest	5
Stephen Hall	2	John Hall	2
William Turner	3	Thomas Rogers	7
Edward Stimson	2	Thomas Vines	2
William Fremlyn	5	Augustine Webb	1
Thomas Tayler	3	Thomas Waller	2
Richard Uridge	4	Richard Morgan	4
Widdow Hawse	1	Phillip Dennis	1
William Murgin	3	John Hawse	2
Thomas White	2	William Kenwood	2
John Cogger	3	John Beadle	2
George Wood	3	Richard Purvey	2

Daniell Everist	2	Lyonell Sutton	1
Edward Lampard	4	William Thisleton	3
Thomas Hibben	2	Richard Childrens	1

[fol. 11v]

Not Chargeable		**Not Chargeable**	
Widdow Greenehill	1	John West	2
Thomas Holloway	2	Richard Masters	2
Edmund Head	2	Robert Pickett	2
Widdow Sutton	2	John Goodshew	1
Andrew Waters	1	Joane Randall	1
Sampson Allen	1	James Skinner	2
John Clements	1	John Taylor	2
Widdow Fant	1	Richard Marten	1
Humphrey Taylor	2	John Milles	1
Nicholas Taylor	1	Robert Clifford	1
Thomas Hawse	1	Richard Woodgate	2
Widdow Garrett	1	Thomas Giles	2
William Humphrey	2	Widdow Muglett	1
Robert Clifford	1	John Clifford	2
Arthur Clifford	1	William Plastoe	2
Thomas Humphrey	2	Thomas Wells	1
Widdow Crowhurst	1	Richard Grove	1
Cris[topher] Welles	1	Anthony Thatcher	2
Widdow Wakefield	1	John Wells	1
John Driver	1	Widdow Marten	1
Thomas Brigtridge	2	Richard Morgan Borsholder	

Liberty of Riverhead

Chargeable		**Chargeable**	
The Lady Bosville	18	Mrs Culpepper	10
Richard Rigsby	4	Mr Rerisford	6
Mr Jeston	4	Mr. Clarke	7
Mrs Peirepoint	10	Simon Payne	2
John Copeland	2	Thomas Ward	1
Richard Everest	2	Robert Turke	1
Edmund Chapman	3	Thomas Stileman	7
David Jeffery	2	William Round	2
Henry Hall	4	John Banester	1
Henry Wakerell	2	Edward Hampton	2
Alexander Garland	1	John Hewes	2
William Charlewood	2	Thomas Masters	2
Widdow Jeffrey	3	Robert Russell	2

John Middleton	1	Margaret Tomlyn	1
Richard Hills	3	James Lawrence	2
John Haynes	3	Widdow Hunt	2
Robert Betts	2	Edward Porter	3
William Fuller	2	Widow Soane	1
Richard Ewridge	5	Mr Winn	5
Mr Hacksupp	5	Widdow Hope	4
John Stileman in		Widdow Hewson	2
an empty house	2	Richard Smyth	2

Not Chargeable		**Not Chargeable**	
John Swatford	2	George Canfield	2
William Clifford	2	Richard Waghorne	2
Widdow Cuss	3	William Nitingale	1
Thomas Brad	2	Allen Cryer	2
Robert Charlwood	2	Thomas Turke	2
Widdow Nitingale	2	Brian Olliver	2
Widdow Partridge	2	Simon Payne Borsholder	

Parish of Kemsing

Chargeable		**Chargeable**	
John Theobald Gent[leman]	8	William Wigsell	4
John Frembling	10	John Christopher	6
Widdow Codd	3	Widdow Rogers	5
Widdow Miller	5	William Best	3
Richard Whiffen	6	John Allen	5
Thomas Chilmead	3	Thomas Kipps	4
Grigory High	2	Nicholas Fremblin	3
Richard Fremblin	2	James Rallison	1
Widdow Slider	5	Robert Bookam	1
John Small	2	Widdow Chilmead	2
Thomas Dalton	2	Henry Stone	2
John James	2	Robert Stephens jnr	2
Benjamin Gooden	3		

Not Chargeable		**Not Chargeable**	
Widdow Chowneing	4	William French	2
Widdow Fletcher	1	John Milliams sen[io]r	2
John Milliams jun[io]r	1	Robert Thomas	1
Robert Stevens sen[io]r	2	Edward Bookham	1
Widdow Haltropp	2	Mathias Johnson	1
Widdow Watts	1	John Fowle	1
Robert Charlewood	2	Thomas Pettman	2

Edmund Cadwell	2	James Rallison Borsholder	

Parish of Seale

Chargeable		Chargeable	
S[i]r Tho[mas] Pierce Barron[e]t	13	Daniel Newman gent	18
Mrs Brett	4	Samuel Masters	6
Lawrence Fench	4	Robert Goodhue in }	
Francis Craft	4	an empty house }	4
Richard Browne	5	Timothy Maynard	3
Nicholas Madox	6	Margaret Bryant	5
[fol. 12r]			
Edward Antherfold	1	William Antherfold	2
John Wery	1	John Harmer	2
John Loveioy	3	Thomas Still	2
Thomas Browne	3	Widdow Cox	7
Henry Swaisland	9	Richard Hye	2
William Stapley	3	James Randall	2
Edward Guisling	4	Thomas Penyall	3
Widdow Adgoe	1	Mr Stowell	7
John Hanselden	3	John Porter	3
Stephen Milles jun[io]r	2	Edward Pywell	3
Richard Stone	2	John Story	4
Thomas Stringer	1	Widdow Ellis	1
William Guiesling	2	Thomas Randall	1
Thomas Strean	2	Stephen Milles sen[io]r	1
Robert Francks	2	[blank]	
John French	4	John Rogers	4
John Smyth	1	Thomas Colvill	2
Henry Munck	1	Thomas Kebble	2
John Shoebridge	3	Thomas Smyth	4
William Thompson	1	[blank] Wood	1
Henry French	1	William Love	1
Prew Weare	1	Francis French	5
Edward Cox	5	Henry Sum[m]ers	2
[blank]		[blank]	
Robert Olliver	3	John Olliver	3
George Rich	3	Rob[er]t French of Fulk	1
Robert French jun[io]r	1	Thomas French	1
William Barten	1	Richard Cullins	3
Thomas Goddin	3	Jeremiah French	2
Jeremiah Tilman }		John Porter	2
in an empty house }	1	William Gardner	1

[blank]		[blank]	
Mr Richard Olliver	8	William Banner	3
Robert Burgis	2	James Pelsett	5
Widdow Porter	3	John Ashdowne	1
George Gardner	2	Richard Olliver sen[io]r	4
Mr John Ward	2	Richard Roberts	3
Stephen Olliver	5	Robert French	3
William Huggins	3	Thomas French	4
James French	3	William Porter	3
Allen Poope	2	James Weekes of Godden	1

Not Chargeable		Not Chargeable	
John French [th]e clerk	3	John Darker sen[io]r	2
Leonard Bullen	1	Thomas Rallison	2
Widdow Carr	1	Peter French	2
Ould Carr	2	John Wood	2
James Smyth	2	William Christopher	1
John Kister	1	Widow Barten	1
Widdow Wear	1	John Wear	1
Widdow Roberts	1	Richard Cutt	1
John Wacker	1	John Bidgen	1
William Fuller	1	John Gardner	1
Robert French sen[io]r	1	Thomas Masters	1
Henry Hadswell	1	George Claggett	1
Widdow Gardner jun[io]r	1	Widdow Drainer	1
John Wheetly	3	Symon Deane	1
Widdow Lawrence	2	Edward Swaisland	3
Edward Vines	1	William Porter	6
John Bryant	1	George Wood	2
Widdow Baker	1	Richard Woly	1
Robert King	1	William Kister weaver	1
John May	1	Widdow Hubel	1
John Babb	1	Widdow Wood	1
James Weare	1	Samuel Weare	1
Edward Antherfold	1	William Antherfold	2
John Wery	1	John Rogers Borsholder	

Parish of Chevening

Chargeable		Chargeable	
Mr Polhill	26	Mr Bevan	48
Mr Wattson	8	Doctor Clarke	8
Christopher Thomas	5	Edmund Thomas	6
Anthony Fuller	7	Widdow Denham	5

Henry Gillett	2	John Herett	5
Richard Bassett	2	Thomas Ward	2
John Walker	2	John Smyth	3
John Ward	2	Nicholas Rootes	2
Thomas Stubbersfield	2	Widow Shorey	2
William Shorey	3	John Roper	3
Edward Druett	2	Thomas Ward	4
Michaell Milles	1	Widdow Palmenger	3
Widdow Sage	1	William Ward	2
Richard Boggett	2	Thomas Wackarell	3
Anthony Ward	1	Richard Stiles	3
Widdow Eagles	2	William Heatcher	2
John Bomer	1	Richard Mercer	2
Thomas Reeves	5	John Stevens	2
Thomas Stiles	2	John Tooth	1
William Keble	2	Robert Farley	2
John Lampard	1	Francis Hills	1
Thomas Hinson	1	William Sanders	1
William Stevens	1	Robert Stevens	1
Francis Stevens	1	William Ward	2

Not Chargeable

Not Chargeable

Robert Phillips	2	Walter Bath	1
Widdow Kebble	2	Widow Rogers	2
Edward Lowlis	2	Goodman Cush	2
[fol. 12v]			
Thomas Plum[m]er	3	John Cox	1
Henry Stubbersfield	2	Richard Cox	3
John Ruates	2	John Burd	2
Widdow Francis	1	Widdow Loft	1
Thomas Daly	1	William Burd	2
Anthony Francis	1	John Everest	2
Thomas Ward	2	Widdow Giles	1
Robert Cogger jnr	1	Nicholas Rootes	1
Robert Cogger	1	Elizabeth Burd	1
Thomas Stiles	2	Robert Tharp	2
Francis Foord	1	Thomas Walgett	1
Francis Buckam	1	Richard Bustar	2
Widdow Funnell	1	Thomas Baker	1
Widdow Parmenger	1	William Tooth	2
Trustram Treaner	3	Abraham Cary	1
Thomas Stevens	1	Thomas Wood	1
William Kebble	2	John Driver	1

Richard Walter	1	Robert Bearton	2
Widdow Sym[m]ons	4	Widdow Patchett	1
George Daling	1	Richard Mercer	1
Valentine Everest	2	Thomas Charwood	1
John Barkwell	1	Edward Fry	1
Jesper Fill	1	George Dalling Borsholder	

Borough of Leigh

Chargeable		Chargeable	
Earle of Lecester }	-	William Whitehead	8
in the parsonage }	5	John Marten	6
house }		Francis Skevington Esq[uire]	5
Widdow Webb	2	Henry Heaver	4
Widdow Marten	1	George Woodsell	2
Edward Wait	4	Thomas Moody	2
Joseph Cart clerk	4	Henry Rogers	3
Francis Basit	3	John Wicking	14
Nicholas Wickenden	3	John Brooker	2
Richard Dicker	3	Elizabeth Prat	4
Thomas Rich	4	Stephen Belingham	2
Henry Silcock	4	John Bauset	2
John Avis	2	William Silcock in }	
Richard Pelsett	2	an empty house }	4
Widdow Randall	2	John Welfare	2
George Basitt	2	Widdow Soane	2

Not Chargeable		Not Chargeable	
Anthony Young	1	Thomas Furrant	1
John Collins	2	Robert Bellingham	1
Widdow Young	1	Widdow Joanes	1
Thomas Steate	1	Widdow Podman	1
John Hemwood	1	Widdow Young	1
Richard Fuller	1	Widdow Engram	3
Robert Taylor	2	John Wheetly	2

John Bassett Borsholder
Thomas Wynn Constable of Codsheath hundred

THE HUNDRED OF SOMERDEN
in the lath of Sutton att Hone

Frienden Borough

Chargeable		Chargeable	
S[i]r John Seyliard Barrt	10	S[i]r Bernard Hyde Knt	25

William Trendle	6	Thomas Potter Rector }	
Richard Streatfield gent	6	of Chiddingstone }	5
Mr Thomas Seyliard	4	Mrs Powell	4
Widdow Ashdowne	4	Stephen Stretfield gent	5
John Hollamby sen[io]r	3	John Hollamby jun[ior]	5
James Beecher	2	Samuell Greene	3
Thomas Dudney	3	Thomas Wanmer	3
Widdow Medhurst	5	Richard Children	2
Thomas Sutton	11	Sarah Stretfield widd[ow]	5
Michael Bassett	5	William Woodgate	5
Thomas Wacklyn	4	Thomas Wacklyn in }	
John Dawling	4	an empty house }	2
Thomas Harrison	5	John Care	1
John Homesbey or }		Walter Edlow	2
Francis Lucksford }	4	Joane Beecher widd	3
Edward Everest	4	Robert Wanmar for }	
John Jessupp	2	Isaac Burgis's farme }	2
Edward Young sen[io]r	2	Henry Beecher	2
Edward Wickended	2	Edmund Medhurst	2
John Everest	4	John Bassett	6
Richard Stretfield for }		Samuel Crudd	2
Guildredge }	4	John Morris	4
in another empty house	1	William Wickenden	1
Jessupp Backett	4	Margery Heaver widd	1
Thomas Bateupp	3	John Hollamby of}	
John Spilsted	2	the black house }	2
Abell Poulter	2	Thomas Maynard	2
Ralph Moaze	1	Stephen Arnold	2
Thomas Webb	1	William Winter	1
Nicholas Winter	1		

Not Chargeable		**Not Chargeable**	
James Turner	1	Henry Turner	1
Robert Turner	1	Thomas Gourley	1
John Farnes	1	Reynald Meecomb	1
Thomas Stace	1	Nicholas Welch	1
George Danton	1	John Smyth	1
Edward Young jnr	1	Widdow Hoade	2
Stephen Bellingham	1	Widd[ow] Jessup &	1
		Wid[dow] Wallis	
Thomas Brookes	1	Widdow Fairebrother }	
Widdow Winchester	1	& Widdow Elliot }	1
Andrew Pope	1	George Goldsmyth	1

Beniamin Cooke		Wid[dow] Jenkins & }	
John Jessup Borsholder		Wid[dow] Hollamby }	1

[fol. 13r]

Cowden Borough

Chargeable		Chargeable	
Mr Thomas Aynscomb	6	Theophilus Marten gent	9
Symon Care	1	William Harrison	1
John Wickenden of Polfields	2	Mathew Wicking	1
Widdow Knight	1	Thomas Wickenden	1
John Wickenden	1	Robert Smyth	1
Alexander Ware	2	Henry Care	2
Thomas Pigott	3	Edward Underhill	3
Thomas Friend sen[io]r	3	Jonas Allen	2
John Everest sen[io]r	4	Thomas Bannester	1
William Terry	1	William Chapman	1
John & Will[ia]m Chapman	1	Henry Hall	5
Michaell Bassett	2	John Coulstock	2
Richard Turner	6	Henry Burgis	5
John Osbourne	4	Jonas Knight	2
Richard Wamner	1	Edward Still	5
Nicholas Turner	2	Abraham Tulley	2
John Everest jun[io]r	2	John Hards	4
Thomas Care	2	Widdow Hurst	2
William Jackson	2	Anna Saxpie	2
Richard Burgeis	4	Richard Knight	5
William Stevens	2	William Stanford	1

Not Chargeable		Not Chargeable	
John Killick	1	Peter Wicking	1
John Wickenden taylor	1	Richard Shoebridge	1
William Kemp	1	John Bennet	1
William Turner	1	John Still	2
William Willet	1	Richard Wicking	1
Francis Tapsell	1	Richard Harrison	1
James Hart	1	John Phillips	1
John Eastland jun[io]r	1	Henry Browne	1
John Gasson	1	Widdow Greenewood	1
Widdow Stevens	1	Widdow Wicking	1
Richard Burges Borsholder			

Stanford Borough

Chargeable		Chargeable	
Thomas Birsty gent	6	John Ashdowne of Hever	12
Thomas Brocket gent	6	William Vivion gent	4
Thomas Woodgate	3	Thomas Still	3
Thomas Symons or }		Henry Pigott	5
Walter Goodsall }	6	Thomas Pierce	1
William Duglas	5	Richard Ashdowne	4
William Streathfeild	3	Alexander Osbourne	4
John Leavis	1	William Overie	5
William Everest	1	William Wickenden	2
Henry Care sen[io]r	2	Henry Care jun[io]r	2
Rich[ard] Medhurst of }	3	William Merchant	2
Wootstock }		William Brooker	3
Humphrey Medhurst	1	Thomas Paige	2
William Wallis	2	William Falkenner	2
John Rootes	2	Richard Willard	2
Thomas Pigot	1	Widdow Doggett	2
John Bannester	3	John Leigh	2
Christopher Longley	1	William Ingram	2
Walter Bilborough	2	William Austen	2
Stephen Lamb	1	Richard Medhurst of }	
Henry Stanford	4	Brookestreet }	3
Susan Cronck	1	John Ashdowne jun[io]r	6
James Stanford	3	Robert Abraham	2
Thomas Medhurst	3	John Catt	2
Richard Maynard	3		

Not Chargeable		Not Chargeable	
Widdow Law	1	George Weller	3
William Tye	3	Widdow Clarke	2
John Osbourne	4	Richard Stanstreet	1
Widdow Hoare	1	John Harrison	1
Widdow Read	2	Widdow Bassett	1
Widdow Burt	3	Alexander Kingswood	2
John Friend	2	John Cary	1
Elizabeth Bridger	1	John Medhurst	1
Widdow Freeman	2	James Fathers	1
John Cooper	1	Robert Friend	1
William Embry	1	George Taylor	1
Thomas Woodgate	2	Edward Wickenden	2
Thomas Medhurst	1	William Overy jun[io]r	1
Robert Nightingall	2	Thomas Mairesbey	3

Walter Bilborough Borsholder

Kings Borough

Chargeable		Chargeable	
James Speed	3	John Sewer	3
William Wells	3	Walter Carnell	3
James Verrall	1	William Sale	1
William Chapman	1	William Rose	4
William Beawmont	1	William Greene	2
Richard Wood	2	John Kettle	4
Thomas Arnold	3	Widdow Everest	3
Walter Woodgate	2	Robert Pellen	3
John Arnold	4	Thomas Curd	2
John Chapman	2	Thomas Driver	2
John Miles	3	Richard Winter	3
[fol. 13v]			
John Medhurst	2	George Sale	2
Richard Medhurst	2	John Edmunds	1
Robert Chapman	1	William Thornton	2
Richard Ashdowne }		George Cox	2
In Clark's house }	2	Thomas Stoneham	2
Joseph Crundwell	2	George Waters	2
John Cooke	1	Thomas Saunders	1

Not Chargeable		Not Chargeable	
John Thornton	1	John Relfe	2
William Elliot	1	James Burley	1
Widdow Medhurst	2	Widdow Ellis	1
Robert Carter	1	Robert Gorridge	1
Richard Whisler	1	James Parker	1
		William Wells Borsholder	

Groombridge Borough

Chargeable		Chargeable	
Phillip Packer Esq[uire]	20	Walter Goodsall	3
Henry Hilder	6	Peter Trice	4
Richard Constable	3	John Avis	3
John Wilkins	5	Richard Marchant	2
Henry Jeffery	3	Robert Catt	2
John Crowhurst	2	Henry Jeffery Borsholder	

Penshurst Towne

Chargeable			Chargeable	
Mr Thomas Lee	11		Martin Pike	5
Anthony Combridge	4		Francis Hamms	3
Thomas Barr	6		Walter Woodgate	2
Mrs Elliot	2		John Charlton	3
John Fremlyn	5		Anthony Sym[m]ons	2
Thomas Pierson	1		Robert Clubb	2
William Budgin	2		Alexander Winnifrith	2
William Jempson	2		John Moyse	2
James Minch	2		Mrs Goldham	2
Widdow Newman	2		Thomas Browne	1
Thomas Ongley	1		Thomas Bourne	1
Richard Winifrith	1		Robert Beecher	1
John Willett	1		Thomas Curd	1

Not Chargeable			Not Chargeable	
Thomas Dubble	1		John Whitebread	2
Widdow Lockier	1		Widdow Soane	1
Widdow Beecher	1		Widdow Durtnall	1
Isaac Dane	1		Baptist Winnifrith	1
			Isaac Deane Borsholder	

Penshurst Borough

Chargeable			Chargeable	
Robert Earle of Leicester }			Thomas Seyliard Gent	10
in part of Penshurst Pallace }	21		William Beecher	6
more in Foord Pallace }	6		more in his empty house	2
Fortunatus Woodgate	4		Richard Streatfield	6
Richard Silcock	3		Richard Hamms gent:	10
Edward Luck	4		Edward Rivers	2
Christop[her] Combridge	5		Oliver Combridge	5
Francis Combridge g[en]t:	6		more in his empty house	4
Andrew Combridge	3		Robert Crudd	3
Richard Cronck	3		Alexander Merchant	2
Joel Woodgate	3		Thomas Gilberd	3
John Medhurst	4		Widdow Barr	4
John Barr	2		Thomas Munnion	2
Robert Jessupp	3		Widdow Streatfield }	
In an empty house	1		& John Wells }	5
John Rivers	3		Robert Skinner	2
Widdow Beckett	3		Widdow Hollamby	3
Thomas Rivers	2		Samuel Rivers	2

Andrew Pullen	2	George Willett	2
Richard Lockier	3	Thomas Sexton	4
Thomas Adgoe	4	Robert Arnold	3
William Welles	3	John Wallis	1
Widdow Morrant	1	Edward Deane	1
Thomas Bateupp	3	Thomas Giles	2
John Grayland	2	Henry Tye	5
Edward Hammond	1	Symon Medhurst	2
Samuel Crudd or}		John Rummens	2
Thomas Turner }	1	Jesper Jessupp	3
William Maynard	2	Stephen Barber	1
William Roberts	1	Thomas Wallis	1
Thomas Fulman sen[io]r	1	Thomas Fulman jun[io]r	1
Widdow Fulman	1	John Norwood	1
William Edwards	1	Widdow Jessupp	1

Not Chargeable		**Not Chargeable**	
Richard Turley	1	William Hollands	1
John Paise	1	John Wells	1
Fortunatus Fulman	1	Widdow Curd	1
		Edward Merchant	1
		Thomas Rivers borsholder	

[fol. 14r]

THE HUNDRED OF WESTERHAM & EADENBRIDGE
In the Lath of Sutton att Hone

Part of Edenbridge & part of Cowden

Chargeable		Chargeable	
Widdow Soane	3	Widdow Hunt	2
William Coale	2	James Coale	2
Widdow Joanes	3	Widdow Children	2
George Johnson	6	Widdow Cosham	5
Widdow Hubbard	6	Michaell Spatehurst	2
William Taylor	5	John Stanford	2
Mr Henry Duke	4	John Wood gent:	2
John Browne	2	Widdow Allen	2
William Dudney	1	Widdow Hoare	1
George Swann	2	John Streatfield	2
Thomas Bassett	4	Francis Watkins	2
Edward Staplehurst	3	James Stanford	1
Joseph Sale	3	Henry Bancock	1

Richard Pigott	1	Robert Liegh	2
Henry Huggins	1	Widdow Cronk	4
Robert Driver	1	James Cobbett	1
Thomas Foottey	2	John Brabourne	1
Edmund King	4	John Leigh of Brownes	5
Thomas Holmden	4	James Harborrough	1
Michaell Moyce	1	William Som[m]erton	1
David Powell	3	Thomas Dane	1
George Leigh	5	Richard Jem[m]ett gent	10
Widdow Children	6	Robert Brooker	4
John Holney	5	Edmund Sleach	2
John Wells	1	Francis Cartwright	1
Richard Knight gent	8	Richard Still	6
John Langford	6	Edward Knight	3

Not Chargeable

John Brooker	2	Thomas Neve	1
Henry Edsall	1	Nicholas Fidlyn	2
George Johnson	1	Robert Waller	1
Widdow Day	2	John Lupten	1
John Hoare	2	William Miles	1
John Morgan	1	Widdow Bassett	2
John Medhurst	1	Thomas Shooebridge	1
George Groomebridge	1	Richard Young	1
Richard Arnold	1	William Cronk	2
James Aylard	1	Mr Carlton in an }	
Zachariah Honar	1	empty house }	2
John Bassett	2	John Beard	1
Edward Risbrooke	2	Thomas Footey constable	

Cudham Borough & Merchgreene

Chargeable

Robert Seyliard gent:	11	John Milles	1
William Walter	2	John Milles	2
Widdow Stanford	5	John King	3
John Emes	1	Thomas King	5
Robert Saxbye	3	Robert Harvie	1
William Allen	1	John Wickenden	3
Robert Nittingale	5	John Harborow	1
Robert Hunt	3	John Paine	1

Not Chargeable

Edward Leigh	2	Widdow Milles	1

| Richard Kidder | 1 | Edward Latter | 1 |
| John Driver | 2 | | |

Westerham Towne

Chargeable		Chargeable	
S[i]r William Leich Knt	22	William Boothby Esq[ui]re	12
Thomas Maning Esq[ui]re	27	Michaell Knight gent	17
Widdow Page	4	Joseph Swann	4
Charles Brooker	3	Mrs Seyliard	7
Mr Lorkin	2	John Thorpe	8
John Dawling gent	7	John Plumley	2
Anthony Saxby jun[io]r	5	George Tyman	4
John Tidman	2	Edward Cooper	2
Thomas Watts sen[io]r	11	Anthony Saxbye sen[io]r	5
Edward Wheatley	5	John Liegh	4
John Peake	6	Thomas Deane	12
Thomas Brooker	8	Tobias Gratwick	6
William Charlwood	4	John Milles	5
Thomas Sharpe	1	Richard Wells	10
Will[ia]m Swann	5	John Steere	2
George Stapleton	2	Widdow Smyth	2
Edmund Thomas	4	John Lodge	5
John Burgis	3	John Dalton	5
Robert Heath	2	Christopher Stephens	1
Giles Everest	1	Joseph Edlow	2
Henry Marrant	3	Widow Rogers	1
Anthony Sumpter	2	Henry Tapsell	2
Edward Thornton	8	Francis Medhurst	2
William King	2	William Lane	2
John Gatland	1	Samuell Dawling gent:	7
Bryan Burton	2	John Shepheard	2
Thomas Waymarke	3	John Holmden gent:	9
George Lawrence	3	Richard Wood	4
Ownsted Styles	3	Widdow Staple	2
Robert Johnson	2	Edmund Lane	4
Edward Whitacre	3	James Allen	3
Thomas Watts jun[io]r	4	Anthony Jackson jun[io]r	5
John Dawling gent:	6	George Chart	2
Widdow Stephenson	2	Widdow Coaker	1
[fol. 14r]			
Thomas Puckle	2	Elizabeth Spencer	2
John Ward	2	Anthony Jackson sen[io]r	2
Richard Bowyer	4	Mr Porye	8

John Burgis	2	Samuell Dawling	8

Not Chargeable		**Not Chargeable**	
Thomas Eldridge	3	William Holmden	1
Widdow Foord	1	Thomas Welles	3
Widdow Edsall	2	Edward King	3
Henry Sacre	2	Wassell Spencer	3
Thomas Foord	1	Francis Smyth	1
William Mace	1	Mathew Everest	2
John Ownstead	2	Widdow Hedly	2
Thomas Wickenden	1	Widdow Marchant	2
Richard Fith	2	Thomas Pocknell	1
Peter Grimes	2	Thomas Pierce	1
William Spilstead	5	Widdow Bannester	1
Elizabeth Bannester	1	John Hayward	1
William Wilder	1	John Mead	2
Nicholas Perrin	2	John Ashton	1
Thomas Bartholomew	3	Widdow Heath	1
Ann Jarman	1	Widdow Edwards	2
William Lawrence	1	William Underhill	2
Richard Gates	2	Edward Perrior	2
Richard Wood	2	Nicholas Merchaunt	2
John Johnson	2	Thomas Merchant	3
Widdow Jeffery	2	Nicholas Deacon	2
Ralph Shawe	1	Arthur Shaw	2
Thomas Quidenton	1	Widdow Forder	1
Widdow Tunbridge	1	Widdow Johnson	1
Thomas Quidinton	1	Widdow Gates	1
John Tratt	2	John Jewell	1
Richard Cronke	1	William Dawkins	2
Thomas Harding	1	Widdow Woodhams	2
Richard Cooper	3	Richard Ward	7
Charles Smyth	1	Richard Eaton	1
Abraham Medhurst	2	Henry Hatcher	1
John Preston	2	Richard Thornton	1
Widdow Stacye	1	Widdow Kipps	1
William Locke	2	John Hollyday	2
Widdow Buckland	1	Nicholas Joanes	2
Thomas Harling	1	Henry Spilstead	2
Anthony Kittle	2	John Poole	3
Thomas Gatland	1	Thomas Plummer	3
Thomas Burton	1	Widdow Dent	1
James Cumber	2	James Allen sen[io]r	1

John Bramble	2	Edward Gasson	4
Widdow Joanes	1	John Seaman	2
George Turner	1	Edmund Lane Borsholder	

Westerham Upland

Chargeable		**Chargeable**	
George Petty gent:	18	Thomas Knight gent:	14
George Toller gent:	2	Henry Toller gent:	5
Robert Streatfield	6	Robert Godden	4
Bryan Coale	3	Widdow Chapman	1
Widdow Wells	3	Nicholas Francis	3
James Chapman	4	John Dudney	2
Henry Chapman	2	George Ward	2
Thomas Bitterdick	3	William Stacye	5
John Seares	2	Solomon Fielder	2
Michaell Holmden	6	Richard Sum[m]erton	1
John Sum[m]erton	2	Thomas Stanford	3
John Blackman	2	Michael Staley	3
Thomas Driver	2	John Driver	2
Andrew Rivers	3	Thomas Bates	2
James Harborow	2	George Medhurst	2
James Morgan	4	Thomas Milles	1
John Plumbley for }		Edward Greene	4
the windmill house }	2	& for Medhurst house	1
Thomas White	2	William King	2
Richard Francis	2	Giles Browne	4
John Frith	2	William Marten	2
Stephen Walker	2	Edward Whitaker	5
John Jewell	3	Thomas Shewbridge	2

Not Chargeable		**Not Chargeable**	
Edward Arnold	2	Henry Bryan	2
William Young	2	John Bewman	2
James Merchant	2	John Drew	1
Thomas Dudson	1	Mark Millions	2
Francis Brewhood	1	Widdow Francis	1
William Varge	2	John Wicken	1
William Baker	2	John Bartlett	2
Mathew Driver	1	Robert Streatfeild constable	

THE HUNDRED OF BROMLEY & BECKENHAM
In the Lath of Sutton att Hone.

Bromley Towne

Chargeable		Chargeable	
The Lord Bishopp of Rochester	14	The Lady Miller	16
Mr Baines	10	Mr Bruster	10
Mr Gratwick	6	Mr Acton	6
Mr Giles	9	Mr Turner	13
[fol. 15r]			
Mr Harlackenden	5	Mr Bigg	4
John Seamor	1	John Lascoe	2
Henry Smyth	2	Widdow Wood	1
Henry Chapman	4	John Piercevall	2
Richard Barr	2	Thomas Seamor	2
William Shotten	5	Widdow Besley	2
William Kempsall	2	Nicholas Gardiner	2
Widdow Titchbourne	4	John Ashworth	2
Robert King	7	James Wood	1
Goodwise Davidge	3	William Davidge	6
John Davidge sen[io]r	1	Thomas Carr	3
John Davidge jun[io]r	2	Edward Child	3
Henry Lewis	2	Timothy Brett	3
Francis Healy	2	Christopher Hall	1
John Giles	2	William Watts	1
Widdow Hubberd	2	Edward Snellin	2
Thomas Smyth	1	Richard Woolfe	4
Edward Seamor	2	Thomas Freeman	3
William Poett	1	Richard Tanner	2
Henry Staple sen[io]r	2	Henry Staple jun[io]r	2
Widdow Henger	2	William Toltwood	2
Thomas Boane	2	William Wooden	3
John Coates	1	Tobias Staple	1
Not Chargeable		**Not Chargeable**	
William Cashford	2	George Ownsted	2
Evon Roberts	1	Thomas Emant	1
John Etherton	2	John Bland	1
Robert Bland	2	John Cooper	2
Thomas Mantle	1	David Clements	2
Augustine Peters	1	John Russe	2
Percivall Hassall	1	John West	2

Nicholas Glover	2	John Joanes	1
Widdow Oxenbridge	2	Thomas Fremlin	2
Edward Oxenbridge[252]	2	Thomas Burbidge	2
Samuel Bayley	2	Old Hunt	2
Marten Hall	2	John White	1
[blank] Adams	1	Robert Clarke	2
Richard Bath	2	Richard Mullins	1
Widdow Arnold	2	[blank] Shoell	1
William Moone	2	Bartholomew Woolfe	2
Widdow Best	2	John Best	1
William Best	2	Thomas Ashman	2
Nicholas Marshall	1	Widdow Bird	2
Henry Delton	2	Richard Marshall	1
Widdow Harwood	1	Widdow Dyer	2
George Petly	2	Humphrey Curtis	2
James Curtis	1	William Phillipps	2
William Speed	2	Widdow Cock	1
John Bleese	1		
Widdow Ashworth	2		

Plasto

Chargeable		Chargeable	
S[i]r George Smyth	9	Mr King	5
Mr French	5	George French	2
Thomas French	4	William Love	6
Henry Constable	6	Widdow Bath	1
Mary Boman	2	Mr Marsh	6
Mathew Wayne	3	Thomas Sym[m]ons	2

Elmsted

Chargeable		Chargeable	
Mrs Bettenham	10	Mr Palmer	7
Thomas Earlidge	1	Adam Roberts	1
Milkstreet house	10		

Widmor

Chargeable		Chargeable	
Mr Allison	13	John Littlegroome	5
Philemon Woolfe	2	Widdow Mortimer	3
Dr Satterthwayt	13	Richard Onyon	2
Widdow Tanner	3	Widdow Beadle	4

[252] entry interlined.

Elizabeth Underhill	6	Thomas Earlidge	2
Richard Clay	2	James Shott	4
Martin Shott	3	Richard White	3
John Funiell	2	John Holloway	2
Jacob Earlidge	1		

South Borough

Chargeable		Chargeable	
Mr King	9	John Steven	5
Robert King	3	Nicholas Stevens	3
Thomas Wood	4	Daniell Giles	4
Thomas Wood cordwayner	2	Andrew Beadle sen[io]r	5
William Fuller	2	[blank] Gibbs	5

The Common

Chargeable		Chargeable	
Thomas Pagge	5	Mr Besweeke	6
Mr Hobbs	2	John Pockley	2
Mr Hall	11	Mr Miells	2
John Mills	2	John Henger	5
Jacob Glover	6	William Russ	1
William Maning	1	Thomas Wright	2
James Pettley	1	George Staple	2

Masons Hill

Chargeable		Chargeable	
Mr Webb	13	Richard Hawes	2
Harmond Hill	4	Widdow Walker	4
Richard Stubberfield	3	John Garrett	2
Richard Wattson	4	Ralph Wattson	4
John Wellard	4	Henry Ingram	3
Mr Throckmorten	4	Goodman Jurner	1
John Ashworth & John			
Funnell Borsholders			

[fol. 15v]

Parish of Beckenham

Chargeable		Chargeable	
John Scott Esq	24	William Clowder	7
Widdow Davis	4	Edward Miles	6
Nicholas Lane	3	Thomas Smyth	3
Thomas Bedford	2	Richard King of Wolssi	2
William Mondkin	2	Phillip Gilbert	2

Richard Allen	2	Mr Howes	4
William Bachelor	2	James Warren	2
Thomas Newland	1	Mr Clissold	9
Mr Bosvile	9	Mr Brogrowe	15
Mr Hilles	1	John Adgate	2
Nicholas Henge	4	Edward Pate	4
John King	2	John Purl	2
John Phillipps	3	John Pope	3
Thomas Foster	2	Roger Tapsfield	1
Edward Gulstone	1	Mrs Harrison	3
Widdow Etherton	2	Robert Slighter	2
Richard Hursum	3	John Bygrove	3
William Ellet	1	Mr Clements	1
Daniell Hill	3	George Yeomans	1
John Jackson	2	William Hammond	1
Rowland King	3	John Tanner	2
Anthony Lane	1	Mr Pyne	2
John Carpenter	2	George Carpenter	1
Gilbert Pronten	3	Robert Roberts	3
Richard King at }		Richard Kempsall	5
the signe of the George }	7	John Nyles	1
Widdow Musgreme	5		

Not Chargeable		**Not Chargeable**	
William Violett	1	John Ashbey	1
Widdow Daniell	1	Robert Musgrove	1
Widdow Newland	2	John Wood	1
Thomas Battersby	1	Giles Phillipps	1
William Musgrove	2	William Goshage	2
John Harrison	1	Thomas Egerlen	1
John Daniell	1	John Lee	1
Richard Eastland	2	Thomas Stoate	1
Widdow Lynford	1	Edward Wilkinson	1
Joseph Batterby	1	William Willicom	1
Widdow Barr	1	Alice Toultod	1
Widdow Lane	1	Ralph Boord	1
John Woodard	1	Thomas Barr	1
Richard King the taylor	1	Widdow Robbins	1
George Pace	2	James Holden sen[io]r	1
James Holden jun[io]r	1	Robert Holden	1
Ann Woodard	1	James Sanders	1
Robert Cooke	1	John Cooke	1
Widdow Hammond	1	Widdow Tomsett	1

Richard Swand	1	Thomas Newland Borsholder	
		Nicholas Stephens Constable	

Vil of Brasted in the said Lath

Chargeable		Chargeable	
John Heath Esq	17	William Pinder Rector	5
William Deane	4	James Atherfold	4
Thomas Whitaker	4	Richard Wells	4
John Mead	2	Goodwife Jewell	2
Widdow Stevens	2	Robert Saxby	2
Thomas Collinwood	1	David Dartland	2
James Bayly	6	Richard Cooper	3
Thomas Smyth	3	William Watts	2
Thomas Round	3	Thomas Rance	2
Jeffery Glover	2	Stephen Summers jun[io]r	2
Thomas Kidder	7	Widdow Holmden	3
Tobias Midleton	2	Stephen Olliver	2
William Akerst	1	James Mead	5
William Smyth	2	Edward Pywell	4
William Marten	2	Thomas Deane	2
Robert Marten	1	Richard Lambert	2
Moses Plumley	6	John Fairebrother	1
Henry Waller	3	John Dartnall	1
Widdow Blackman	2	William Lynes	2
Richard Usterson	1	Widdow Watts	1
Christopher Waymarke	2	William Newman	7
Robert Morgan	6	John Usterson	1
Joseph Wright	2	Anthony Waller	2

Not Chargeable		Not Chargeable	
Richard Gatland	2	Richard Burd	2
Thomas Swann	2	Stephen Sum[m]ers sen[io]r	2
John Martin	2	Widdow Marten	2
Widdow Price	2	John Coomes	2
George King	2	Giles Marten	2
William Smithers	2	Widdow Holmden	1
Edward Everest	1	William Dartnall	2
John Day	2	Abraham Jennings	2
Robert Deputy	3	Will[iam] Willington	1
William Dartnall	1	Sampson Bird	1
John Longhurst	2	Henry Sym[m]ons	2
In the almeshouse	5		

The upland part of Brasted

Chargeable		Chargeable	
S[i]r John Seyliard	11	Edward Walter	2
George Searles	3	Francis Kibble	2
[fol. 16r]			
Francis Jorden	1	Michaell Walter	1
John Palmer	3	Christopher Stevens	1
John Burlett	5	William Murgin	2
Thomas Palmer	3	Edward Francis	1
Tobias Cross	5	Stephen Cockett	2
William Brightrid	3	Richard Brooker	5
Widdow Knight	3	Nicholas Marten	1
Thomas Burgett	3		

Not Chargeable		Not Chargeable	
Widdow Crandall	3	Widdow Gassen	1
Thomas Searles	1	Widdow Roper	1
John Day	1	Widdow Soane	1
Goodman Cavell	2	William Pearles sen[io]r	1
William Pearles jun[io]r	2	Robert Grimes	1
Richard Nash	3	Nicholas Purdey	3
		Francis Jorden Borsholder	

THE HUNDRED OF DARTFORD & WILMINGTON
In the Lath of Sutton att Hone

Dartford Towne

Chargeable		Chargeable	
John Eaton	3	Mark Fielder jun[io]r	4
David Gaping	4	Timothy North	4
William Blabee	2	Richard Fielder	2
Mr Browne for the Braselmill	2	John Needle sen[io]r	2
Henry Draper	3	William Browne	2
John Edgett	2	Thomas Poole	2
Thomas Eve	2	Daniell Croome	5
Thomas Rogers Esq	8	Richard Willett	2
Thomas Burton	2	Francis Gatland	2
William Haslewood	2	Francis Hubbard	3
Henry Needle	3	William Lash	3
George Binney	2	Thomas Phillipps	1
Robert Franck	2	John Martine	2
Thomas Marloe	3	Mr John Starr	6
Edward Kemsley	4	John Chilobb	3

Henry Whitehead	3	William Blackwell	4
Widdow Wellard	2	John Brainedge	4
[blank] Farby Esq[uire]	7	Thomas Burford	4
Israel Round	4	Mr John Poole	5
John Killingbeck	5	Thomas Haywood	2
Marten Haslewood	3	Thomas Smyth	2
George Ashdowne	2	Richard Sherlock	2
Henry Hawkes	2	John Needle jun[io]r	2
Grace Savidge widd[ow]	2	Richard Watts	3
Widdow Gatland	2	Thomas Smalwood	2
Thomas Barny	1	Mr Garnon	3
John Ragsdell	3	John Sibley	5
John Harebottle	4	John Barnett	4
William Averell	2	Robert Harwood	1
Francis Coames	3	Wesson Pettett	6
John Ames	6	Thomas Bainbridge	6
Robert Rowed	4	Robert Russell	3
Edward Roase	6	Henry Lawrence	7
Isaac Stephens	2	Israell Round at }	
Mr Chambers	4	Phipps house }	2
Henry Pearne	4	Richard Shott	4
John Round	5	Widdow Goslin	2
Thomas Harwood	4	Mr Kelley	6
John Clare	3	George Ward	5
John Phipps	5	William Shorte	3
William Dankes	2	Robert Johnson	3
Jonathan Hugbone	2	Edmund Tooke Esq	14
Mrs Andrewes	2	Miles Baldock	2
Daniel Everden	2	Thomas Cox	2
John Jackson	6	Abraham Hilles	2
Peter Carter	3	John Hewes	4
William Dredge	2	William Huish	13
[blank] Stevens for the Charle	3	Isaac Manning	4
Phineas Reynolds	5	Widdow Manning[253]	2
Thomas Gell	3	John Clarke	3
William Wood	3	George Eldreck	19
Robert Warter	2	Widdow Noakes	2
Widdow Twisleten	4	John Parker	3
Thomas Jackson	3	James Taping	3
Jeremiah Edwards	2	Robert Burden	5
William Tasker	2	John Darker	6

[253] Interlined entry.

Thomas Walsone	2	John Arnald	2
William Scarborough	3	Symon Carryer	2
Thomas Darker	2	Daniel Wooding	8
John Shott	1	John Bachelor	1
Thomas Wackerill	2	Henry Piercey	1
James Harris	4	Christopher Webster	1
Richard Buckland	2	Widdow Spelman	2
John Twisleton Esq	14	William Holmes	1
Dr Woodcock	6	James Harris }	
Richard Leavins	2	for malthouse }	2
John Dodman	1	William Painter	5
Edward James	7	John Harvey	1
Arthur Darker	2	Widdow Smyth	2
Thomas Peircye	5	Henry Ishams }	
William Kemp	5	for Darkers }	3
Henry Isham	3	John Mock	3
Leonard Johnson	4	Richard Drinkwater	1
Mark Blackman	1	James Hind	4
William Bubes	3	William Damsell	3
		Perceval Stephens	6

[fol. 16v]

Thomas Perkinson	2		
John Fuller	4	Mr John Browne	10
Edward Southwell	3	John Sumner	2
John Beale	2	Robert Fry	2
Christopher Lurchin	2	Francis Edwards	2
Mark Fielder sen[io]r	5	Richard Barnes	3
Mr Thomas Warren	14	Mrs Fielder	9
Jeremy Grubb	2	Tho: Fielder of Stoneham	10
George Sandell	2	John Dixson	2
James Everee	3	Thomas Parker	1
Robert Austen	2	Rowland Fry	7
Widdow Summers	2	Richard Weekes	2
Thomas Fielder sen[io]r	5	Robert Glover	17
John Clarke	1	Alexander Skeath	5
William Dredge	5	Widdow Moseley	1
Sydrach Kelmsley	2	John Watford	5
Thomas Vale	2	John Orton	4
Rowland Fry for }		John Oliver	2
Watts house }	2	Richard Porter	3
Richard Lurchin	2	Allen Best	3
Roger Elsee	1	William Twist	2
Joseph Perring	2	Richard Bubes	1

Thomas Jenkins	4
Robert Pearcey	5
William Willis	4
[blank] Keck Esq	13
John Bassett	2
Luke Small	2
Richard Wesson	1
Henry Harman at Stannel	5
James Gapeing	3
Leonard Hickman	2
Richard White	2
William Milles	2
Widdow Lake	4
Thomas Feilder	2
John Piper	2
Edmund Fuller	3
John Houlding	2
Thomas Houlding[254]	2
Thomas Hubbard	2
Robert Carryer	2
George Small	2

Mr Snow	5
Emanuell Ellsee	2
William Hannings	2
John Mock	4
Thomas Loweres	4
John Milles	2
Richard Mixbury	4
George Small at the Heath	2
John Saunders	3
Jeremy Stonnard	5
Phillip Ellery	3
John Wawkins	2
John Ward	2
Widdow Johnson	4
Symon Houlding	2
John Harwood	3
Phillip Browne	4
John Quittenton	2
Thomas Hadloe	2
John Hayes	1
Sarah Summers wid[ow]	2

Not Chargeable

Morgan Teddar	1
Elizabeth Emerson	3
John Hawkes	1
Thomas Emmerson	1
Thomas Teddar	2
Henry Rudland	1
Festus Fulk	2
Francis Baldwin	2
Thomas Emmerson	3
In an empty house late }	
Thomas Barnes dwelt in }	3
Widdow Hollands	2
Widdow Harding	2
Widdow Denn	3
William Adgoe	2
George Spilman	1
Widdow Defraine	1

Not Chargeable

John Phillipps	1
Widdow Hedgcock	2
Andrew Shott	1
William Careles[255]	1
Joane Hedger	2
Widdow Tibb	1
John Williams	2
Widdow Rudland	2
Thomas Hatchman	2
Widdow Flewell	1
Sarah Hewes	1
Widdow Ware	1
Barbara Andrewes	1
Widdow Eaton	2
Thomas Rumminge	2
Robert Richards	1
Widdow Wackerell	1

[254] Interlined entry.
[255] Interlined entry.

Thomas Stansall	1	Robert Kester	1
Nathaniell Mace	1	Widdow Baker	1
Mildred Smyth	1	John Hailes	2
John Mumford	1	Welch Kate	1
William Hoble	2	John Rumney	1
John Lambert	2	Henry Harris	1
Christopher Chum[m]	1	John Flavell	1
James Stephens	2	In an empty house late }	
Widdow Em[m]erson	2	William Gaskin lived in }	1
George Due	2	Ralph Cadman	2
John Peacock	2	William Gaskin	2
John Walter	2	Jeffrey Agge	1
Stephen Pantrey	1	Edward Duffin	2
John Onsloe	1	Barthol[omew] Spencer	2
In an empty house late }		In an empty house late }	
Eliz[abeth] Mankes lived in }	1	widd[ow] Sandwell lived in}	2
John Monke	2	Widdow Harebottle	3
Widdow Glover	1	Daniell Howe	2
William Webb	1	William Kittle	1
In an empty house late }		Widdow Irons	1
James Ware lived in }	1	In an empty house late }	
Henry Draper George Small		John Warter lived in }	1
& William Tasker constables			

Wilmington

Chargeable		Chargeable	
Mr Beadle	4	Mr Francis Langwoth	10
Mr Lancelot Bathurst	9	Mr Tho[mas] Twisleton	14
Henry Harman for 2 houses	3	John Harman	1
Henry Haite	2	Daniel Wooding	3
Arnold Rowed	4	Francis Driver	2
In an empty house late }		James Harris	2
John Charles lived in }	3	Widdow Milles	2
Christopher Rance	2	Thomas Mace	5
Thomas Cox	3	Thomas Watts jun[io]r	2
Henry Kempe	1	Richard Everest	1
Daniell Toppey	2	Thomas Huggins	2
[fol. 17r]			
John Skelton	1	William Bruster	1
John Haite jun[io]r	2	William Collison	2
John Mitchell	1	Robert Alchin	2
Thomas Lenham	3	John Parker	2
John Charles	1	James Charles	1

Thomas Watts sen[io]r	3	John Haite sen[io]r	2
Richard Cowper	2	Nicholas Rawlins	2
John Hamden	4	Mr Shumett	4
Richard Harman	9	William Tayler	1
Widdow Edmunds	1	Francis Howard	1
James Harris in }		Thomas Graves in }	
an empty house }	3	an empty house }	2

Not Chargeable

Michaell Grey	2	Widdow Fielder	2
Henry Allen	2	In an empty house late }	
In an empty house late }		Edward Chapman lived in }	1
Richard Michell lived in }	1	Widdow Abbott	2
Sater & his sister	2	John Peirce	2
Henry Edmunds	2	William Lucas	1
James Haslewood	1	Andrew Chexfield	1
Widdow Huggins	1	[blank] at the Bankes	2
Francis Adgoe	1	John Gladherst	1
		William Collison Borsholder	

THE HUNDRED OF AXTON
In the Lath of Sutton at Hone

Parish of Southfleet

Chargeable

S[i]r William Swann Knt	15	Mr George Swann	11
Mr John Stacy	16	Mr Thomas Standsall	6
John Kennard	4	John Lake	8
William Fisher	5	Thomas Edmeades	5
Mary Wakelin	7	Ann Harding	4
John Russell	2	William Bronger	2
Isaac Robotham	3	John Tugnest	2
William Hall	3	Thomas Nunn	3
Richard Goding	3	William Jackson	1
Anthony Cotwell	1	Richard Tappy	1
Thomas Beets	5	Thomas Holt	5
Robert Phillips	4	Nicholas Hammond	3
John Hollandsby	3	Ralph Wooding	3
Thomas Jones	1	Widdow Clarke	1
John Wakelin	1	Richard Lomas	2
Richard Nunn	1	Edward Marshall	2
John Glover	4	Thomas Gray	1
Samuel Bulley	3	James Young	2

Thomas Smith	2	Robert Cobham	3
Anthony Mathewes	3	Widdow Lindsey	1
Richard Kettle	1	Thomas Robotham	1

Not Chargeable

		Not Chargeable	
Widdow Bing	1	Widdow Palmer	1
Edward Plastow	1	Widdow Hilles	1
Widdow Famous	1	Widdow Soane	1
Widdow Hoardly	1	John Overy	1
John Godhelpe	1	William Holt	1
In an empty house	1	Edward Kidder	1
Edward Alard	1	Edmund Pharoe	2
Thomas Bush	1	Widdow Palmer	1

Parish of Swanscombe

Chargeable

		Chargeable	
Mr Ralph Welden	19	Mr John Watts	6
Mr John Greene	3	Robert Cott	3
Mr Hamden	2	Edward Marshall	6
Stephen Witeing	2	Peter Browne & }	
John Haslewood	2	Nicholas Lampert }	5
Thomas Pike	2	John Gumins	2
John Burr	3	Sucklin Beare	2
William Baker	3	John Standley	1
Edmund Booth	1	Nicholas Middleton	4

Not Chargeable

		Not Chargeable	
John Harvey	2	John Dennis & }	
John Church	2	James Greenwood }	4
John Poplin	1	Thomas Lewis	1
John Skiff & John Parker	2	James Young	2

Greene hive

Chargeable

		Chargeable	
John Walter	3	Walter Owen	2
Henry Acourt	6	William Cally	4
Mathew Cumfitt }		William Torly	2
in an empty house }	-	Thomas Course	7
Godfrey Breck	3	Robert Waldock	5
S[i]r William Swann In }		William Hull	4
an empty house }	-	Thomas Powndy	5
Thomas Rodwell	6	Richard Smyth	3
Thomas Cooke	2	Mr Edward Brent	9

| Edward Marshall | 1 | Henry Stevens | 2 |

Not Chargeable

		Not Chargeable	
[blank] Goslin	1	Richard Gurnett	2
Daniel Nusonn	2	William Titner	2
William Austen	2	Robert Bully	1
William Hartrope	1	Edward Rosier	2
Judith Miller	1	Widdow Peirce	1
John Kennard	1	Gilbert Woodward	2
[fol. 17v]			
Widdow Gibbons	3	William Morton	3
Widdow Grace	2	Alexander Coplin	2
Widdow Edwards	1	Thomas Taylor	2
William Williams	1	John Perry	1
Arthur Ware	1	Thomasin King	1
William Corbett	1	John Stevens	3
Widdow Hopkins	2	John Berkentree	2
Robert Willis	2	George Thorne	2
Thomas Mepham	2	John Austen	2
Peter Hilles	2		

Parish of Stone

Chargeable

		Chargeable	
Mr John Chase	10	Mathew Chase	12
Mr John Manford	17	Barbara Elliot	6
William Elliott	4	William Standley	5
Francis Kettle	2	John Lamb	5
Robert Ducklin	2	Jonathan Ware	6
Francis Mellesby	3	John Rowland	4
Thomas Coulter	3		

Not Chargeable

		Not Chargeable	
Thomas Skiff	3	Edward Marrable	2
Richard Lewis	2	Robert Lightfoot	1
William Idleton	1	John Barker	1
Emanuel Belsom	1	Widdow Gray	1
Widdow Smith	1	Widdow Titner	1
Widdow Holton	2	Widdow Em[m]erson	2
Widdow Huggins	1	William Acourt	2

Parish of Darenth

Chargeable

		Chargeable	
Thomas Young gen[t]	11	Mr Waters	5

William Franckwell	4	Anthony Waller	1
Thomas Garrett	2	William Dirling	5
Henry Baker	1	Richard Spencer	1
Mathew Comfort	2	Edmund Taylor	3
Thomas Humphrey	1	William Phillipps	2
Mr Kennaston	11	John Payne	4
John White	2	William Lane	5
George Langridge	2	John Franckwell	5
John Vane	1	Thomas Middleton	2
Thomas Everest	2	Edward Polhill	2
Bernard Ellis	6	William Dunmall	3
John Humphrey	3	John Huggins	3
Richard Lake	4	John Course	2
Thomas Noakes	2	Stephen Everest & }	
Henry Hye	3	Widdow Munn }	2
John Ebbutt	3	Thomas Ebbutt	3
John Kettle	1	Arthur Noakes & }	
In an empty house	3	Thomas Lane }	3

Not Chargeable		**Not Chargeable**	
Richard Dyrling	2	Francis Shackfeild	1
George Lawrence	2	James Crowther	1
Widdow Acres	2	William Bodnam	1
William Hibbs	2	Thomas Cumber	2
Thomas Collins	2	John Smyth	2
Nicholas Dingley	1	Thomas Allen	1
Widdow Kettle	1	William Knott	2
Henry Wooden	2	William Godhelpe	1
Francis Brewster	4	Stephen Harvey & }	
John Reason	2	Richard Plum[m]er }	3
John Swayne	1	Widdow Garrett & }	
William Walker	1	Widdow Lawrence }	2

Parish of Sutton at Hone

Chargeable		**Chargeable**	
Christoph[her] Searles Esq	7	Henry Phillipps	3
William Fenn	1	Abell Abott	2
John Dingly	1	Richard Harman	5
John Rickett	1	William Ebbolt	3
John Eve	1	Mathew Hilles	2
Thomas Fletcher	1	Mr Keniston	2
Edward Chapman	2	John Stephens	8
Mathew Sexton	2	William Burr	3

James Reeve	2	John Sym[m]ons	2
John Richett	1	James Lenham	2
Henry Sexton	2	George Whiffin	1
William Rawling	2	Mr Egglesfeild	8
In the Pallace house	21	In the Stewards Chamber	1
Mr Badby	15	John Adams	5
Mr Haslewood	6	James Acketts	4
Dr Gifford	4	Edward Cobb	2
William Cakam gen[t]	4	Peter Medhurst	2
John Phillipps	2	Widdow Mason	2
John Dorman	4	William Roper	5
William Adgoe	3	Henry Northall	3
Thomas Ebbutt	9	Anthony Jones	2
Christopher Hudson	2	Lancelott Hilles	3
William Childs	7	Widdow Ludlow	1
Mathew Pope	2	William Porch	1
Edmund Stacy	3	Jeremy Baker	5

Not Chargeable		**Not Chargeable**	
John Harman	2	Thomas Pope	1
John Cooper	1	Alexander Dally	1
Edward Hackney	1	Richard Sutton	1
Edward Evens	1	Thomas Hawkins	1
George Porch	2	William Carryer	1
Robert Canckham	1	George Porch	1
William Alchin	1	Thomas Boreman	1
Thomas Porch	2	Jonathon Wickers	1
Thomas Knott	2		

[fol. 18r]

The Parish of Ash cum Ridley

Chargeable		**Chargeable**	
Reynald Peckham Esq[ui]re	13	Thomas Morrice cl[erk]	8
Richard Miller	5	William Lance	4
James Lance	5	Thomas Middleton	2
John Dalton	3	William Johnson	3
John Burges	4	Nicholas Turner	2
John Walter	2	Abraham Oliver	4
Richard Whiffin	5	Thomas Goldsmith	4
Robert French	2	Hugh Lance	1
Thomas Mugg	2	Edward Wooding	5
Richard Robinson	1	William Munn	2
Thomas Budd	1	George Whiffin	2

Thomas Webbin	5	Jeoffry Jorden	3
Leonard Ladduck	2	Mrs Stacy	5
James Wouldham	2	William Bucher	2
Widdow Fenn	9	John Standen	2
Robert Dorman	2	Richard Cronck	3
Edward Masters	2	Daniell Sach	2
Richard Whiffin	4	William Glover	1
Richard Lechford	1	George Wybourne	2
William Hodsall gen[t]	6	Richard Miller	6
Thomas Wood	2	Richard Fuller	2
George Abrill	3		

Not Chargeable		**Not Chargeable**	
Thomas Whiffen	1	Thomas Fisher	1
John Smith	2	George Middleton	2
Robert Hills	1	Robert Burr	1
Widdow Gray	1	William Kettle	1
John Mills	1	James Middleton	1
John Dalke	1	John Lenham	1
Edward Love	2	Thomas Cooper	1
William Carrier	1	John Garrett	1
John Wyburne	1	James Wouldham	1
Henry Reeve	4	Thomas Swann	2
Henry Gray	1	Richard Wallis	1
Abraham Edwards	1	William Pettman	1
William Johnson	1	Thomas Best	1
Widdow Wharton	1	Mathew Wyburne	4

Parish of Fawkham

Chargeable		**Chargeable**	
Mrs Walter	13	Mr Archbole	4
Robert Peirce	2	Nicholas Chapman	6
James Hoadly	1	Widdow Hackett	1
Thomas Feilder	3	Thomas Kackett	3
Thomas Carrier	1	Richard Kingsland	3
Robert Goodwin	2	Thomas Smyth	1
Thomas Walter	2	Richard Drakes	1
Edward Garrett	2	William Fox	1
Thomas Belcham	1	In an empty house	2

Not Chargeable		**Not Chargeable**	
Edward Carrier	1	Robert Johnson	1
Widdow Masters	1		

Parish of Farningham

Chargeable		Chargeable	
Sir John Cotton }		Mr Browne clerke	4
Knight & Barr[one]t }	13	Thomas Smyth	4
Thomas Carpenter	6	Thomas Plum[m]er	7
George Miller	4	Thomas Astwood	10
John Oliver	9	James Lance	2
John Kempe	2	Mathew Sweepe	3
John Johnson	1	John Shott	2
Robert Weston	2	Thomas Chapman & }	
Edward Goldsmith	2	William Johnson }	2
Francis Marshall	3	William Wooden	3
Oliver Everest	2	Henry Pound	2
William Milford	2	Edward Bing	1
John Pondsey	2	John Udelt	1
In and empty house	2		

Not Chargeable		Not Chargeable	
James Harris	2	William Potts	2
Nicholas Moyse	2	Edward Lawnder	2
Widdow Rennolds	1	Widdow Bing	1
Francis Miller	1	Widdow Linn	1
John Staple	1		

Parish of Longfield

Chargeable		Chargeable	
Thomas Burrow	8	James Middleton	3
John Letchford	4	Robert Ashdowne	1
William Goodwin	1	Henry Rutland	1
Thomas Whitehead	1	Widdow Gardner	1
John Longham	1		

Parish of Kingsdown

Chargeable		Chargeable	
Mr Archbole	5	John Whiffin	2
Thomas Chapman	4	Robert Richardson	2
Henry Johnson	2	Henry Acourt	5
Nicholas Middleton	2	John Johnson	2
William Johnson	2	Edward Chapman	5
Thomas Godden	2	Thomas Adgoe	4
[fol. 18v]			
Thomas Wooden	4	George Baker	2
Richard Whiffin	3	William Rowlinson	2

| Charles Johnson | 6 | John Moxly | 2 |
| George Hilles | 1 | Nicholas Richardson | 3 |

Not Chargeable		**Not Chargeable**	
Edward Baker	2	William Love	2
William Romney	1	Thomas Sticker	3
Valentine Romney	1	William Lenham	2
Henry Goodwin	1	William Baker	1
Widdow Huggins	1	Widdow Best	1

Parish of Hartley

Chargeable		**Chargeable**	
Mr Eves	3	Thomas Young	5
Henry Pigott	4	Edward Best	3
Henry Middleton	4	John Edwards	3
Widdow Reeve	5	Leonard Carryer	3
more in another house }		John Fox	3
standing empty }	2	Nicholas Wheeler	2
And in her house }		John Best	2
reserved by her landlady }	2	Edward Swann	1
Ham Canham	1	Jonas Baker	1
John Townsend	1	Widdow French	1
Robert Baker	1		

Not Chargeable		**Not Chargeable**	
Robert Kettle	1	Richard Lawrence	1
		Edward Carryer	1

Parishes of Eynsford & Lullingstone

Chargeable		**Chargeable**	
Henry Bosvile Esq	10	George Gifford Esq	10
Mr Palmer cler[k]	3	Richard Kingsland	4
Christopher Hayward	4	Henry Dunmoll	3
John Beckett	3	James Henmarch	4
James Goldsmith	2	George Knott	2
Thomas Durling	5	William Netlingham	2
John Crooke	1	Henry Everest	2
William Fisher	4	Francis Fisher	1
Arthur Boomer	1	Thomas Lander	2
John Mosier	2	John Searles	2
Abraham Dalton	2	William Hadlow	1
Hugh Lash	1	Henry Durling	1
John Scudder	1	Thomas Mosier	1

Henry Lenham	3	William Lander	1
Thomas Marrant	1	Robert ~~Thomas~~ Hockley	1
Widdow Rawlings	4	Mrs Mason	5
William Durling	2	Christoph[er] Durling	2
Edward Bankin	2	John Hart	1
William Wakelin	3	Thomas Lander	4
Mr George Kenestone	5	George Chapman	4
John Lander	2	John Fuller	2
Henry Coffin	2	William Ebbott	4
William Hadlow	5	[blank]	
William Hart Esq[ui]re	40	Henry Waller	4
Thomas Mace	2	Henry Kennalls	2

Not Chargeable		**Not Chargeable**	
Edward Terry	1	Francis Terry	1
Thomas Fisher	1	Thomas Friday	1
Widdow Ling	1	James Bankin	1
Widdow Dunmoll	1	Abraham Henman	1
Marke Burr	1	Nathaniel Burr	1
Mark Burr jun[io]r	1	Nathaniel Burr jun[io]r	1
Thomas Burr	1	Thomas Smith	1
Henry Crewer	1	William Mace	1
John Rivers	1	Widdow Harman	2
John Burr	1	Widdow Hawly	1
William Knott	1	Thomas Knott	1
John Oates	1	Thomas Everest	1
John Deane	1	Edward Lenham	2
Edward Carlie	2	Francis Walker	1
Henry Lenham	1	Edward Mumford	1
William Boomer	1	Francis Rownd	1
Robert Burr	1	Thomas Rowe	1
William Lightfoot	1	Joseph Cornford	1
Edward Lash	1		

Parish of Horton Kirby

Chargeable		**Chargeable**	
The Lady Wyat	12	Mr Buller	13
Henry Lane	5	Robert Weston	5
Richard Baycott	6	Mr Collins	3
William Buckle	8	Nathaniel Adgoe	3
Mr Justice	4	Mr Harton	3
for Kings farme	4	John Paine	6
Bullings farme	2	~~Francis Marshall~~	~~7~~

Francis Marshall	7	George Wells	2
John Northall	2	Francis Dunmow	3
Thomas Shott	2	John Burten	2
Thomas Miller	4	Henry Dye	3
Edmund Adgoe	2	William Adams	1
Arthur Sanders	2	Widdow Staples	3
John Allichin	3	John Smyth	1
[fol. 19r]			
Stephen Hare	1	Widdow Allichin	1
Richard Perkins	1	Widdow Jinks	1
Abraham Goodborow	1	Richard Clarke	1
John Cooper	1	Richard Hethcock	1
William Chester	1	Richard Plum[m]er	1

Not Chargeable		**Not Chargeable**	
Henry Knott	2	Thomas Hadlow	1
George Jorden	2	Widdow Adams	1
Widdow Acketts	1	Widdow Canham	1
Widdow Watts	1	Widdow Scodder	1
Widdow Edwards	1	Widdow Ashdowne	1
Widdow Sancock	1	Widdow Reeves	1
Widdow Aleword	1	Widdow Everest	1
Widdow Bonner	1	John Canham	1
Richard Cheverton	1	John Aleword	1
Thomas Wooding	1	Edward Wood	1
John Polhill	1	John Chester	1
Thomas Packer	1	Robert Wooding	1
Henry Allichin	1	Richard Boys	1

John Walter & Thomas Middleton constables of the hundred of
Axton

THE HUNDRED OF ROKESLY
In the Lath of Sutton att Hone

The upper part of the said hund[red]

In Nockhoult

Chargeable		**Chargeable**	
Mr Collins	3	William Waller	4
Goodman Clements	5	Thomas Stevens	3
Timothy Stevens	3	William Waller jun[io]r	2
Richard Waller	4	William Jennings	2
Widdow Hoult	2	Henry Tickner	2

Robert Darling	2	John Stow	2
Thomas Browne	2	Henry Waller	4
Widdow Godden	2	John Caren	2
Thomas Cacatt	2	Stephen Tooth	4
John Feverstone	2	Lancelett Sampson	1
Leonard Bates	1	William Banks jun[io]r	1
William Allen	1	Richard Martin	2
William Banks sen[io]r	1	John Harris	4
Henry Mundey	2		

Not Chargeable

Widdow Robinson	1	Widdow Tayler	1
William Collins	2	William Adams	1
John Waller	2	Thomas Wells	1
John Greene	2	Edward Hernden	5
William Harris	1	Widdow Know	1
Anthony May	1	Stephen Saxten	1
Goodman Grout	1	Christopher Sampson	1
		William Waller Borsholder	

Parish of Cudham

Chargeable

William Beadle	1	William Whiffin	1
Henry Glover	3	[blank] Jewell	4
[blank] Wakelyn	3	Thomas Darker	1
Hugh Wane	2	Richard Wane	1
[blank] Casing	1	Henry Whiffin	1
Henry Birkin	1	Thomas Farrant	1
[blank] Phillipps jun[io]r	1	Roger Know	2
[blank] Wright	2	John Toller	2
Hugh Birlin	1	Thomas Beadle	1
John Hayward	5	Henry Farrant	2
William Whiffin jun[io]r	1	John Ounsted	1
Thomas Hole	2	Michael Crane	3
Thomas Know	1	Francis Brasier	5
Edward Lisney	3	Joseph White	1
John Brasier	3	John Carrier	2
Alexander Broadford	1	Edward Terrey	2
Thomas Medhurst	1	Thomas Wood	2
Henry Baker	1	Richard Glover	3
William Leigh	3	Thomas Henman	2
Ma[rt]in Warren	1	William Tickner	2
James Wane	1	Thomas Durlin	1

[blank] Nitingale	1	Thomas Farrant	2
Thomas Toller	1	Jo[hn] Beadle	1
Jo[hn] Farrant	1		

Not Chargeable

Not Chargeable

George Toller	1	Henry Birkin	1
Robert Birkin	1	Thomas Rootes	1
Widdow Beadle	1	John Humphrey	1
Henry Whiffen	1	Richard Outred	1
Henry Birchwood	1	William Arnes	1
William Happy	1	John Day	1
Richard Drue	1	Thomas Ashton	1
Richard Johnson	1	Richard Clifford	1
		William Lee Borsholder	

Parish of Farmborough

Chargeable

Chargeable

Thomas Broome }		Edward Powell	3
serjt at Law?　　}	16	Henry Hall	4
John Bath	3	William Best	6
[fol. 19v]			
John Mace	4	Widdow Hall	3
[Edm]und Coale	6	Richard Masters	3
Henry Mace	2	John Smith	5
Stephen Adams	3	John Dalton	2
Christop[her] Stiles	2	William Parson	4
Nicholas Portingall	3	John Rawling	2
Widdow Delver	3	George Coale	3
Edward Geale	2		

Not Chargeable

Not Chargeable

Mary Turner	2	William Cornford	4
John Phillips	2	Alice Monke	1
Hugh Tye	1	John Owten	2
Thomas Allen	2	William Carr	1
John Twoe	2	George Brooke	1
Elizabeth Tue	1	Vincent Cornford	2
John Hartstone	2	Morgan Thomas	1
George Balden	2	George Smyth	2
John Castleton	1	John Hibbin	1
Henry Whiffin	1	John Masters	2
		Nicholas Portingale Borsholder	

Parish of West Wickham

Chargeable		Chargeable	
S[i]r Stephen Lennard Bart	14	Mr Henry Penning	8
Mr Robert Stiles	11	Mr Bunting	4
John Martin	7	Richard Whiffin	4
Stephen Cockerell	6	John May	3
James Phillipps	1	Robert Berkin	4
Arthur Else	3	William Caustin	2
John Staple	4	Thomas Bedford	2
Nicholas Mowseley	1	Edward Cowper	1
William Bennett	4	William Wicker	4
William Hindes	2	Richard Mabanck	1
Mathew Norwood	3	John Carter	5
Stephen Brasier	6	Mr Page	1
John Phillipps	2	Robert Phillipps	2
Edward Wooden	3		

Not Chargeable		Not Chargeable	
John Beadle	2	John Harris	1
John Prim	1	William Jackson	1
Daniell Cockerill	1	Samuel Wright	2
Daniell Bently	1	William Playre	1
William Wood	1	Richard Ellis	1
Widdow Peerles	1	Nicholas Monk	2
Robert Saunders	1	Jane Hearst	1
		William Wicker Borsholder	

Parish of Chelsfield

Chargeable		Chargeable	
John Brasier	3	George Wothersby	1
John Slan	1	John Cox	4
George Wakelyn	1	Richard Jewill	4
Henry Langridge	2	Richard Terry	1
Daniell Hafin	1	John Allen	2
Thomas Heath	1	William Chapman	1
Robert Barton	1	Thomas Woodly	1
Thomas Goulding	5	Thomas Ward	1
Steph[en] & J[oh]n Allen	3	Widow Smyth	2
James Spratt	3	Abraham Dalton	2
George Wakelyn	3	John Know	3
John Brasier	4	William Lock	7
Thomas Marten	2	John Eve	1
James Stiles	3	Thomas Mace	1

William Chapman sen[io]r	1	Robert Petley	4
John Brasier	1	Henry Soane	3
William Wakelin	3	William Eve	1
William Harris	1	John Woodstock	1
Robert Milles	4		

Not Chargeable		**Not Chargeable**	
John Jackson	2	William Due	2
William Kester	9	Robert White	1
Thomas Barkin	1	George Dew	1
Widdow Lye	2	William Cooke	1
Francis Wakelin	1	John Watts	1
Widdow Colegate	1	Widdow Johnson	1
Robert Dennis	2	John Trevatt	1
Richard Johnson	1	Robert Luts	2
John Hibbon	1	William Thomas	1
George Hoyes	2	Robert Aliard	1
John Ham[m]ond	2	Robert Delve	1
George Macc	2	Thomas Wakelin Borsholder	

Parish of Keston

Chargeable		**Chargeable**	
Edward Smythe cler[k]	2	George Perch	3
Thomas Whiffen	3	Mrs Dipford	2
John Raddams	2	Joseph Stiles	1
Ann Fuller widd[ow]	2	George Darling	1
Nicholas Whiffen	2	Thomas Mantle	2
William Phillipp	1	Thomas Death	3
William Lane	1	John Beadle	2
Francis Bentley	2	William Whiffen	1

Not Chargeable		**Not Chargeable**	
Widdow How	2	Widdow Bentley	1
Widdow Phillip	1	William Covell	2
Robert Delver	1	Henry Rowne	1
John Covell	2	Peter Chipper	1
George Jackson	1	Widdow Covell	1
		Francis Bentley Borsholder	

[fol. 20r]

Parish of Heys

Chargeable		**Chargeable**	
The Lady Scott	14	Mrs Bingley	7
Mr Styles	2	Robert White	7

Matthew Mumford	2	Mrs Kempsall	3
John Dorrington	3	Robert Delton	3
Thomas Edger	6	George Glover	3
John Ownsted	3	Thomas Hibben	2
Thomas Shott	3	Thomas Greene	1
Michaell Mitchell	2	Mr Wood	1
Jarman Morphew	3	Robert Ownsted	3
George Covell	2	John Delver	4
Thomas Mumford	2	John Ward	2
John Holloway	2	William Woodstock	2
William Birkin	2	James Woodley	2
Humphrey Batt	1		

Not Chargeable		**Not Chargeable**	
Mr George Pyke	4	John Slaye	1
Robert Jackson	1	John Phillipps	1
Henry Delton	2	John Hunt	2
John Surbie	1	Widdow Devonish	1
Thomas Hunt	1	John Delton	2
George Ware	1	George Penial	2
John Moyce	1	Widdow Holloway	1
Goodwife Watts	1	Thomas Best	1
Widdow Hall	1	William Howe	1
Nicholas Phillips	1	Goodman Wade	1
Widdow Gent	1		

Parish of Downe

Chargeable		**Chargeable**	
Mr Sandys	8	Mr Wood	6
Mr Glover	5	John Whiffen	5
Stephen Squire	6	Widdow Rootes	2
Richard Peake	2	Thomas Knowe	6
Henry Farrant sen[io]r	1	Thomas Farrant	3
Alexander Ham[m]ond	4	Henry Powell	3
Thomas Croocher	3	William Hammond	1
John Staple	4	John Squire	2
William Cootes	1	Thomas King	2
William King	2	Nicholas King	1
Henry Baker	2	Thomas Bradford	4
Widdow Marshall	4	Edward Rootes	1

Not Chargeable		**Not Chargeable**	
Henry Farrant jun[io]r	3	Thomas Mitchell	2

Humphrey Dennis	1	Thomas Outred	2
Thomas Crondle	2	Valentine Haylock	1
Joseph King	2	Matthew Covell	1
William Stile	1	Widdow Frith	1
		Alexander Hamond	
		Borsholder	
		Robert Ownsted constable	

The lower half h[undre]d of Rokesley

Parish of Chislehurst

Chargeable		Chargeable	
S[i]r Oliver Boteler	24	S[i]r Richard Bettenson	15
S[i]r Andrew Kneviton	9	Mr Ellis Conliffe	9
Mr Thomas Blinkhorne	15	Alderman Maynell	8
Mr Richard Edwards	12	John Harman	2
Robert Heather	3	John Tanner	1
Griffin Oburt	2	John Levice	2
Christop[her] Rogers	2	David Adams	4
John Weller	2	his tenant	2
John Martin	2	John Stevens	3
Tobias Chapman	2	John Stansmor sen[io]r	2
John Covell	1	William Winter	3
Nathaniel Potter	2	Andrew Brooke	1
William Wilmott	1	Richard Tubman	2
Richard Allen	3	Richard Haffall	2
Thomas Haffall	2	John Jackman	2
Widdow Hengar	2	Thomas Cooke	2
Thomas Marshall	2	Edward Poulter	3
Richard Rogers	3	George Cock	1
John Acourt alias Gardner	4	Thomas Farrant	2
Thomas Coates	5	Humphrey Curtis	1
Stephen Perry	1	John Delver	2
Widdow Stansmore	2	George Start	2
Richard Bush	2	John Adeane sen[io]r	1
James Engerson	1	John Adeane jun[io]r	2
Robert Palmer	1	Michaell Blissett	3
John Woodine	3	Thomas Tubman	1
William Hamden	8	Widdow Deley	3
Thomas Hebb	3	John Cox jun[io]r	1
Richard Manning	5	Robert Derlin	3
Richard Cox	3	Edward Comport	1
William Brooker	6	John Gilbert	2

Robert Wright	2	James Stakes	2
William Gibons	2	Robert Whitfield	6
Christop[her] Carter	3	William Law	2
Abraham Man	9	Richard Delver	2
Widdow Coates	3	Richard Blake	2
Thomas Hodsden	2	John Stansmor jun[io]r	1
Robert Hobbs	2	Thomas Giles	5
[fol. 20v]			
Francis Tappey	3	Nicholas Small	3
William Hall	2	Erasmer Dier	2
Thomas Trippett	2	Jeremy Coates	2
Richard Chapman	3	Robert Weekes	2

In houses at present empty

Mr John Ellis	7	Mr Hogsflesh	8
Towne Court	3	John Delber	2
Tobias Chapman	3	Widdow Stubbs	2
Mr Jellibrand	2	Richard Staple	2
John Popioy	4	Mr Stevens	1

Not Chargeable   **Not Chargeable**

Widdow Vennes	2	John Taylor	3
Richard Gladish	2	John Ratcliff	2
Richard Willey	1	Widdow Rogers	1
Widdow Packman	1	William Steed	1
John Cox sen[io]r	1	Joseph Pinke	1
Robert Childs	1	Widdow More	1
Widdow Munck	2	John Scudder	4
Nathaniel Potter & Richard			
Chapman Borsholders			

Hamlett of Linckhill

Chargeable   **Chargeable**

Mr John Petter	6	Thomas Medhurst	3
William Woodgate	4	Richard Ashdowne	4
Thomas Holmden	2	Nicholas Budgin	1
Edward Cripps	4	William Turner	2
Robert Fuller	4	Edward Stevens	3
Thomas Birsty jun[io]r	5	Thomas Holmden sen[io]r	1
Edward Wells	1	Thomas Gates	1
George Campfield	1	William Bower	1
John Arnold	2	Widdow Wallis	2
Henry Walter	1	James Friend	2

John Jessup	1	William King	3
Widdow Willard	2	Michaell Cronck	1

Not Chargeable		**Not Chargeable**	
John Duglas	1	Thomas Adsonn	2
Widdow Dunsteere	2	Robert Tye	1
Anthony Wallis	1	Thomas Embry jun[io]r	1
Thomas Embry sen[io]r	1	Thomas Aylard	1
Thomas Saxbie	1	Robert Goldfinch	1
George Vennar	1	Michaell Cronke Borsholder	

Parish of St Paul's Cray

Chargeable		**Chargeable**	
S[i]r Leonard Feerby Knt	15	John Knot	2
John Edwards	2	Elias Bagthwaite	1
Widdow Wood	3	William Church	2
Thomas Swann	2	John Botterell	4
Mr John Ashley	5	William James	3
Christop[her] Bagthwaite	2	Mr Moore	7
Richard Jeall	4	Henry Murrey[256]	7
David Polhill	1	Nathaniell Mercer	3
Richard Browne	2	Capt John Connis	2
Walter Brightered	2	Thomas Willis	1
Nicholas Oliver	2	Abraham Willis	2
		Rich[ard] Geale in a house empty	2

Not Chargeable		**Not Chargeable**	
John Bancks	2	William Limber	2
Widdow Jewell	3	Christop[her] Edwards	2
John Edwards	2	Thomas Edwards	1
Lawrence Musgrove	1	Thomas Natt	2
Widdow Jorden	2	Henry Murrey Borsholder	

Parish of St Mary Cray

Chargeable		**Chargeable**	
Mr Edward Manning	12	Mr Robert King	7
Mr John Connis	10	Mr Alexander Haddon	6
Mr Robert Manning	8	Mr Thomas Felton	11
Mr John Hansard	13	Thomas Ham[m]ond	3
Samuel Dolten	4	Richard Small	3

[256] Interlined entry.

William Murry	3	Widdow Dorman	1
William Bigg	3	Morgan Cheesman	2
John Savage	2	Jeremy Manning	3
John Start	2	Ann Manning widd[ow]	9
Ann Spurling widd[ow]	5	George Burton	3
Thomas Boreman	3	Thomas Bagthwaite	5
Matthew Sweetapple	3	James Jem[m]ett	2
Mathias Inwood	4	John Walker	4
Robert Price	4	Nathaniell Jones	1
William Partridge	2	William Jessopp	2
Widdow Hobbs	2	Timothy Garland	3
Henry Hutchins	2	Tobias Rumly	2
Henry Rumly	2	Robert Boomer	5
Thomas Savage	2	Edward Collins	4
Richard Banks	2	Thomas Edwards	5
Edward James	2	Robert Oliver	2
Arthur Bulling	1	Widdow Boomer	1
William Saxby	2	William Chucks	2
Henry Bassett	1		

Not Chargeable

Robert Cooke	2	Henry Noyte	1
Widdow Chucks	2	John Podington	2
Widdow Peirceson	2	John Mock sen[io]r	2
John Mock jun[io]r	1	Widdow Atkins	1
William Cooper	2	William Gatton	1
[fol. 21r]			
William Wray	2	Francis Whitehead	2
John Collins sen[io]r	2	John Collins jun[io]r	2
Michaell Browne	1	Thomas Gravener	1
Widdow Spilman	2	Thomas Gravener jun[io]r	2
John Craft	2	Mr Thomas Farnfould	4
Widdow Rumley	2	Thomas Seager	2
James Crafter	2	William Sanders	3
Edward Hawes	2	Abraham Wilson	2
Thomas Seabright	2	Robert Lenham	2
[blank] Gatts	2	Thomas Mislebrooke	2
Mark Fielder	2		

Parish of North Cray

Chargeable		Chargeable	
Mr Cooke	17	Mr Buggin	16

Robert Mace & }		William Harvill	6
John White }	7	Richard Woodley	7
Roger Frith	4	John Elliot	4
John Edwards	3	Daniell Hayward	3
William Chapman	2	Henry Temple	2
Henry Kickley	2	John Fuller	2
Edward Packman	2	Richard Littlefeild	2
Michaell Pickman	2	Henry Walter	2
Henry Frith in an }		John Watford in }	
empty house }	4	an empty house }	2
Richard Woodley in }		Roger Frith in an }	
an empty house }	4	empty house }	2

Not Chargeable

William James	2	William Gunter	1
Mary Glover	2	William Harvill Borsholder	

Parish of Foots Cray

Chargeable

Mr William Gill	4	Nicholas Manning	4
Thomas Bagfield	2	John Moore	6
Robert Marshall	9	John Cannan	8
John Rowland	3	Stephen Frith	2
Richard Baker	5	Anthony Ellis	3
Thomas Woodley	5	John Wouldham	4
Peter Furlonger	2	Mr Beveridge in }	
William Handen in }		an empty house }	1
an empty house }	3	Jonas Johnson }	
		in an empty house }	4

Not Chargeable

Abraham Baker	1	Barnard Ellis	1
James Ellis	1	William Phillipps	1

Parish of Orpington

Chargeable

The Lady Spencer	13	Mr Browne	15
Mr Boddenham	13	Richard Abbott	3
Mr Gilpin	6	Littlegroome Kickly	6
Henry Abbott	6	Robert Small	3
John Abbott	3	Jesper Lane	3
Henry Staple	3	John Dyer	1
John Lane	2	Ben[jamin] Powell	2

Nicholas Cross	1	Ezechiell Chandler	2
Daniell Maynard	2	Robert Greenwood	1
Mr Bland	6	Ralph West	2
James White	2	Thomas Death	2
Mr Beveridge	8	Michaell Croucher	3
Richard Milles	-	Henry Staple	7
Jesper Lane jun[io]r	2	Mr Stych for his house }	
William Jennings	2	at Croton }	7
William Mace	2	Mr Stych more for his }	
Clement Clay	2	house at [th]e Towne }	7
Henry Miller	2	Fortunatus Gouldsmyth	2

Not Chargeable

Not Chargeable

Edward Rowland	2	John Watson	2
William Colman	2	Ezechiel Chandler sen[io]r	2
George Dodd	1	Giles Wild	2
Daniel Wild	3	William Freeland	2
Robert Bancks	1	Thomas Blackman	1
George Cooke	1	Matthew Watts	2
Nicholas Jackson	1	John Lymber	2
Robert Shott	2	Edward Walker	1
Thomas Wilkenson	2	Edward Knott	2
Widdow Pann	2	George Drew sen[io]r	2
George Drew jun[io]r	2	Samuell Ward	2
Peter Hunter	2	Widdow Ashmore	2
John Coleman	2	William Bigg	1
		Edward Chapman &	
		George Phillip Borsholders	

Parish of Bexley

Chargeable

Chargeable

S[i]r Rob[er]t Austin Barr[one]t	29	Henry Carew gent	10
Henry Grimes gen[tleman]	10	Mrs Barrow	8
Mrs Giles	3	Dr Borman	8
John Harris	5	John Harris	5
Nicholas Campion	2	James Barton	3
Mathew Wood	2	John Pickett	4
Thomas Ravin	4	John Lane	3
John Brasier	2	John Arnold	2
Stephen Martin	1	Robert Middleton	1
Mrs Packwood	2	Thomas Williams	3

[fol. 21v]

Robert Vine	4	Samuell Auckland	5
Richard Fitchett	2	Godfrey Gytupp	2
Henry King	2	Nicholas Preest	3
Manesses Watford	7	Anthony Fitchett	4
Richard Dalton	1	Henry Tunbrig	2
William Bexley	9	Widdow Hatchman	3
John Clarke	2	Mrs Ockley	2
Widdow Cooke	2	Abraham Phillips	1
Frances Sawell	2	George Crucher	6
Michaell Wood	2	John Watts	2
Robert Wright	1	David Godfrey	2
William Meere	3	Robert Kittle	2
George Hayward	2	James Laince	2
Jeoffry Gyver	4	Richard Saxby	4
John Goodberry	4	Widdow Lane	2
Richard Mixbery	1	Mrs Sprigg	3
Thomas Shorter	2	John Popioy	1
Thomas Vine	1	William Shott	3
John Fairman	2	Robert Bexley	1
S[i]r John Wroth Bart	13	John Gouldwell Esq	10
Richard Staple	6	Richard Maies	2
Anthony Wools	1	Thomas Parker	2
Daniel Wyburne	3	Richard Deane	4
John Wood	4	George Wybourne	4
[blank - erased entry]		Thomas Gillibran	3
Clement Cressy	2	Joane Crucher	2
William Cooper	7	Henry Thoroughgood	2
Robert Cooper	1	Allen Wybourne	6
Heward Fitchett	4	John Cox	4
John Streetly	2	George Parry	1
Francis Moore	5	Richard Moore	5
Robert Judd	3	Widdow Gillibraine	1
Thomas Caustin	6	William Wybourne	3
William Howe	2	Henry Billio	1
Thomas Holding	1	John Pratt	2
John Lowers	2	George Street	2
Allen Wybourne	2	Thomas Austen	1
John Hewitt	2	John Hussey	2
Nicholas Kingsland	2	John Page	5
Thomas Derling	5	Ephraim Paine	4
Thomas Moore	2	John Rickett	2
Thomas Streetly	1	Henry Deane	4
James Tappy	1	Edward Welbeloved	3

John Miles	1	Robert Shott	2
John Shott	1	Robert Clavell	2
Thomas Wright	2	Mr John Lee in }	
John Goldwell Esq }		an empty house }	7
in an empty house }	2	Mrs Barrow in }	
William Bexley in }		an empty house }	1
in an empty house }	2	Mathew Wood in }	
Thomas Caustin }		an empty house }	1
in an empty house }	2	William Shott in }	
Joane Deane in }		an empty house }	2
an empty house }	2		

Not Chargeable

Timothy Merson	2	Robert Foster	1
Widdow Crecher	4	Ralph Gouldsmyth	3
John Dew	2	Nicholas Pinke	1
Thomas Burridge	2	Charles Cooper	1
Joseph Phillips	1	Daniell Eglington	2
John Burchwood	1	Thomas Laizenbey	1
Joseph Robinson	2	William Cadman	1
William King	1	John Tayler	1
Robert North	2	William Cooke	2
Joane Dean	2	John Phillips	1
Widdow Lowers	2	John Witten	2
Widdow Barker	2	William Dalton	1
Widdow Soman	1	William Hunter	1

Richard Moore & George
Croucher Borsholders

[fol. 22r]

AYLESFORD LATH
THE HUNDRED OF EYHORNE
In the Lath of Aylsford

The Upper Halfe Hundred

Borough of Lenham

Chargeable		Chargeable	
Richard Wilkinson Esq	10	William Sharly &	
Robert Baldock	4	John Goslyng in the }	
Henry Hussey	6	vicarage house }	7
Thomas Fidge in }		Robert Mason	6
an empty house }	5	Thomas Bourne	10
John Brockwell	8	Widdow Reynar	9
Robert Lake	6	Edward Wakely	9
William Stoakes	2	John Deedes	7
Thomas Ford	4	Thomas Robbins	5
Caleb Rassell	2	Richard Bezant	5
Widdow Marshall	2	John Gosling	6
John Elgarr	2	John Rogers	3
Francis Royden	2	Thomas Taply	5
Ralph Hoyden	3	Widdow Hopper	1
Abraham Parker	2	Peter Epps	2
James Hyham	2	Thomas Pierce in an }	
Robert Piercy	3	empty house }	4
Henry Stonestreet	1	Thomas Whittle	3
Edward Nutting	2	George Miller	3
Widdow Essex	3	Widdow Barling in }	
Thomas Turner	2	an empty house }	2
William Edwards	2	Griffin Smyth	2
John Chybald	1	Michaell Symons	1
Richard Razell	2	John Smyth	2
Richard Tilden	3	Allen Wenman gent	9
William Henneker	3	Thomas Fillmer	4
John Stedman	3	James Clarke	1
George Tilden	1	Thomas Bodle	1
Richard Turner	1	John Spencer	1
John Raisdowne	2	John Dowle	1
Henry Stedman	2	Robert Segar	1
John Clarke sen[io]r	3	John Henneker	1
Richard Parker	1	Richard Back	2
James Clarke jun[io]r	1	Richard Thatcher	1

John Giles	1	John Huggins	2
Widdow Filmer	2	Ellen Henneker	2
William Essex	1	John Allen	6
Henry Henman	1	Israel Court	1
Thomas Howting	1	Mark Bodle	2
Henry Adman	7	Edward Hadds	4
Edward Spillett	3	William Hayden	3
Hugh Knowlden	2	Richard Whitaker	1
Robert Fletcher	3	Richard Brattle	4
James Court	1	Frances Thomas	6
Richard Brattle	2	John Burges	4
Robert Tilbie	3	Matthew Badnor	3
Thomas Brenchley	1	John Mekins	2
Matthew Bunce gent	3	Augustinne Carr	1
Thomas Ferris	4	John Platt	3
Thomas Austen	2	William Hales	2
John Mayton	1	Edward White	1
Henry Thirstone	3	Henry Baldock	2
Richard Tritton	2	Anthony Start	2
Mr Hubbert	3	Richard Barrett	1
William Waters	1	John Miller	1
Thomas Jenkins	1	John Waters	1
Widdow Marten	3	Solomon Hope	1
Goodw[ife] Rigden	3	John Peckham	4
Thomas Anvill	6	James Fullagarth	5
John Boughten gent	7	Mr Belshar	4
Robert Fisher	3	James Earls	2
George Colegate	2	Edward Gilbert	2
Theodorus Beacon	2	Nicholas Adams	4
George Reynor	2	John Knight	3
Phillip Hunt	3	Mrs Chambers	1
Christopher Clement	1	Christopher Bonny	4
Thomas Lawrence	1	Widdow Viney	3
Timothy Miller	5	Widdow Jennings	2
Bartholom[ew] Brenchly	2	Alexander Rigden	1
Stephen Meed	3	Robert Deane	2
John Williamson	1	Christopher Stoakes	1
Thomas Hills	1	John French	3
William Waters	1	John Potter	1

Not Chargeable

John Munck	1	John Hanford	4
Susan Collard	1	George White	1

William Austry	4	Widdow Grant	2
Elizabeth Reader	2	Widdow White	4
Widdow Stedman	2	John Ferris	2
The Trustees for the }		Stephen Read	2
Almshouses }	6	John Dane	1
John Adams	1	Widdow Beagle	1
Widdow Carter	2	Widdow Hyham	1
Thomas Cooper	1	Jonah Court	1
Widdow Sare	1	Henry Henman	1
Christopher Stickard	1	John Downe	1
Widdow Downe	1	Widdow Miller	1
William Hyham	1	Widdow Comber	1
Thomas Start	1	Margaret Comber	1
Thomas Beadle	1	William Norwood	1

[fol. 22v]

William Earles	1	Thomas Morris	1
Widdow Elvy	1	Widdow Fetherstone	1
Ralph Hooker	1	Thomas Barner	1
John Milles	1	John Pett	1
George Thompson	1	Widdow Goare	1
Widdow Olliver	1	Widdow Beddington	1
Richard Plum[m]aden	1	John Thompson	1
Widdow Britt	1	Christoph[er] Morfoot	1
Widdow Ferris	1	William Farnes	1
Elizabeth Fuller	1	David Chybald	1
Widdow Hutchins	1	Widdow Holmsby	1
		Robert Fishenden	
		Borsholder	

The Borough of Shelve

Chargeable		Chargeable	
Richard Wilkinson Esq	6	Mr Curtis	20
Robert Thompson gent	12	Antho[ny] Thompson gent	3
Mr Slaughter clerke	4	Thomas Ames	4
Edward Hatch	3	Augustine Woolton	4
Robert Filmer	3	Edward Rooke	2
Adam Croft	5	Widdow Elliot	1
Thomas Elliot	2	Joshuah Clarke	3
Lebbeus Tilbie	2	Richard Baker	2
Robert Jorden	2	Thomas Wood	3
Robert Elvy	3	John Wilson	1
John Murton	1	James Thunder	3
John Ferris	5	Thomas Dix	2

Richard Pendor	2	John Bunce Esq	12
Will[ia]m Fillmer	2	Richard Packman	1

Not Chargeable		Not Chargeable	
Arnold Murton	1	John Turle	1
George Lettis	1	George Gray	1
Widdow Wilson	1	Thomas Grant	2
		Thomas Wood borsholder	

The borough of Frensted

Chargeable		Chargeable	
Thomas Thatcher	10	Mr Attkeson	4
Mrs Slaughter	4	William Pannett	4
William Finch	5	Mr Conoway	4
Thomas Fillmer	3	Nicholas Tayler	1
Lawrence Jackson	1	James Marshall	1
Michael Chittenden	2	Thomas Filmer	2
John Cooke	2	Robert Seaman	2
John Pannett	2	Thomas Burges	1
Robert Andrewes	1	Benjamin Ayerst	2
Francis Adlow	1	John Wood	5
Widdow Terry	2	Thomas Bateman	4
Richard Chittenden	5	Mr Nittingale	3
Edmund Adey	4	William Croucher	2
William Howtinge	3	Richard Chittenden	3
Robert Wood	5	William Symons	2
John Baker	2	Symon Laud	1

Not Chargeable		Not Chargeable	
Symon Sellynge	1	Symon Bennett	4
William Lord	1	George Graves	1
William Bub	1	Jonas Bachelor	1
William Paine	1	Widdow Kesfeild	1
Bartho[lomew] Walbanke	1	Edward Hind	2
		Robert Wood borsholder	

The borough of Stockbury & Bicknor

Chargeable		Chargeable	
Thomas Hooper Esq	12	Thomas Larkin	6
Thomas Gover	3	Abell Peake	3
Edward Baker	4	John Gorly	2
Richard Allen	5	Richard Symons	3
George Fisher	1	Robert Grinnell	1

John Beantly	1	Richard Tomlin	2
Thomas Hilles	2	Thomas Piper	2
Edward Brockwell	2	Thomas Clarke	1
Richard Rosen	1	Joshuah Lott	3
John Kennard	1	Edward Hadlow	1
Nicholas Tibbalds	1	John Cleveland	2
John Standly	2	Rebeccah Kennard	1
Edward Backett	4	Stephen Newman	2
William Lake	8	William Straine	2
Stephen Allen	3	Robert Sealden	4

Not Chargeable

Not Chargeable

Thomas Schoones	3	William Godfry	1
Michael Godwin	1	Steven Allen Borsholder	

Borough of Eldnodington

Chargeable

Chargeable

Thomas Cattlet gent	6	James Willes	4
Nathaniell Benson	6	Widdow Taylor	2
William Attwood	2	Robert Wilding	1
		Robert Wilden Borsholder	

Harrisham Borough

Chargeable

Chargeable

Mr Lynch	8	John Francis	4
Symon Hinckley	4	Thomas Brockwell	3
John Hope	4	Sampson Kennard	3
Sampson Kennard	3	John Webb	5
Henry Mapeston	4	George Maylim	3
James Taylor	4	Thomas Newman	2
Thomas Newman	1	Robert Hope	5
Robert Hovenden	3	William Harris	2
Nicholas Page	3	Thomas Potten	5
Thomas Sidgwick	5	Robert Bottell	1
Thomas Fillmer	3	John Carter	4
Robert Cavalee	3	George Ely	2
Widdow Steed	4	Widdow Lidden	2
[fol. 23r]			
Widdow Adams	3	William Boys	2
Mathew Nash	1	Robert Burford	1
Richard Bottell	4	Thomas Britcher	1
William Crisfield	1	William Roper	1
Christopher Short	1	Richard Rochester	3

Thomas Chouning	2	John Harris	3
Nicholas Sutton	2	Grigory Browne	1
George Wildboare	1	Richard Gibson	5
Richard Broadbery	1	John Ellis	2
Thomas Coleman	1	John Thomas	2
Francis Thomas	2	Francis Climson	2
Edmund Nicholson	1	Henry Adams	1
Richard Browne	1	Dr Graves in Steed Hill House	14

Not Chargeable

Not Chargeable

John Hodges	3	Robert Vane	2
Moses Kempe	1	Robert Moore	1
John Bunting	1	William Clarke	1
Richard Taylor	1	Widdow Wrenn	1
Widdow Tapley	1	John Cooper	2
Thomas Chrisfeild	1	Allen Marden	1
Richard Sweetlove	1	Nicholas Howting	1
Perriman Jenkins	3	Thomas Tilden	2
Thomas Wilkinson	1	Henry Elvy	1
Nicholas Elvenston	2	William Bargrow	2
Robert Bottell in } an empty house }	2	Henry Mapleton in an } empty house }	1
In the Hospitall	12		

Hawkinge & Bredhurst

Chargeable

Chargeable

Robert Staple	3	John Allen	4
Thomas Figg	3	George Allen	2
John Doe	2	Robert Woollett	1
Richard Kempsell	2	Robert Austen	2
Edward Carter	1	Thomas Wedd	2
Henry Staple	2	John Lemmon	1
Thomas Longe	6	George Nash	3
John Saywell	2	William Paine	6
Thomas Bird	1	Widdow Hodgeskin	2
Richard Weston	2	Jonathon Sawyer	2
Widdow Hudsford	2	Thomas Cox	1
Robert Knight	3	Robert Packman	2
Thomas Champion	2	Thomas Bunton	2
Emanuell Cooper	3	Richard Trey	6
John Chambers	2		

Not Chargeable

		Not Chargeable	
John Wood	2	Lawrence Fryday	1
Humphrey Dunkin	1	James Knowles	2
Widdow Goulden	1	Richard Wise	2
Nicholas Miles	1	Robert Andrewes	1
William Frowd	1	Stephen Willard	1
William Jorden	1	Stephen Cheesman	1
		Henry Staple Borsholder	

Parish of Hollingbourne

Chargeable

		Chargeable	
S[i]r William Cage	16	Mr Francis Barnham	7
Mr George Pelham	14	William Farley	6
John Bateman	10	Thomas Thatcher	8
William Reynolds	11	Nicholas Thatcher	8
John Shrawly clerk	6	Henry Poore	5
Robert Harris	2	Edward Charlton	2
John Wyborough	1	Henry Whibley	1
Henry Medhurst	1	John Usmor	2
John Hilles	2	Widdow Smyth	2
Benjamin Wood	1	Widdow Wood	2
John Stiles	1	William Spice	2
James Willard	1	Alexander Wood	1
Widdow Hart	1	Thomas Dane	1
Robert Stonehouse	5	John Bonny	6
John Willes	2	Thomas Bentley	4
William Browne	2	William Pottine	4
Edmund Attwood	2	Richard Ashbey	7
John Wise	2	William Knight	6
Thomas Filmer	2	Thomas Stiles	2
William Chambers	2	Richard Russell	6
William Lake	1	Thomas Ginings	4
William Mustard	4	Thomas Sinnings	2
John Spence	3	Thomas Brockwell	2
Edward Sum[m]ers	1	John Brockwell[257]	2
Stephen Ferall	2	Widdow Brenchley	2
Widdow Nash	2	Widdow Short	2
Thomas Davis	4	Edward Kennard	2
George Chilman	2	Widdow Thomas	3
Robert Durtnall	4	Robert Parker	2

[257] Interlined entry.

Mr Mark Wiseman }		William Carter	3
with his 2 copper hearths }	9	Widdow Foster	5
Thomas Bottle	2	Richard Murford	2
Mathew Ealy	3	Alexander Bottle	2
Joseph Peckman	4	Francis Kennett	2
Stephen Potten	1	Gamaliel Edmunds	2
Richard Giles	1	Henry Frembly	1
Henry Wissenden	2	Widdow Hilliard	2

Not Chargeable		Not Chargeable	
Widdow Wollett	1	Widdow Mourton	1
Widdow Hewson	1	Widdow Freeman	1
Widdow Peckman	2	Thomas Eagles	2
[fol. 23v]			
Widdow Harpe	1	Richard Lord	1
Robert Copland	1	Widdow Foord	2
Alexander Wilkins	1	Mathew Bingham	2
Adam Cushman	2	William Symons	1
William Medhurst	1	Thomas Bonny	2
Widdow Baldock	1	Thomas Wilson	1
Abraham Weston	2	John Horton	2
George Woodyn	2	Arthur Browne	2
Christopher Thompson	1	William Peck	1
John Potten	2	John Medhurst	2
William Ward	1	Richard Wills	4
William Sellinge	2	Nicholas Muddle	1
Thomas Medhurst	2	Nicholas Fekins	2
John Fekins	1	Margery Chapman wid[dow]	1
Widd[ow] Chapman of Eyhorne	1	Daniel Francklyn	1

Henry Staple Borsholder

Thurnham Parish

Chargeable		Chargeable	
William Sutton cler[k]	5	Thomas Reynolds gent	7
Richard Spice	5	Katherine Bettenham wid	6
Samuel Masters	1	John Bills	2
Richard Barrington gent	1	John Watts	3
Daniel Cloake gent	8	Tobias Eglestone	2
Richard Peniall	3	John Yorke	2
John Norris	6	Stephen Luck	2
James Fuller	4	William Coulter	2

Mary Robinson widd[ow]	3	Francis Godden	9
Peter Godden	4	Joane Godden widd[ow]	4
James May	2	Robert Shornden	2
Thomas Knight	2	John Underwood	3
John Farley	3	John Chambers sen[io]r	4
Robert Danes	2	John Chapman	3
Jeremiah Turner	1	William Jones	8

Not Chargeable		**Not Chargeable**	
Samuel Shornden	1	John Datson	2
Thomas Hawes	1	Richard Fairman	2
Arthur Beach and }		John Rayman	1
Widdow Hawes }	2	Joane Norris widd[ow]	1
Katherine Bettenham wid[dow]	1	Widdow Hadlow	1
Richard Richardson	1	Mary Watts widd[ow] &	
Henry Conney	2	Elizabeth Hubbard wid[dow]	2
		William Jones Borsholder	

Liberty of Allington

Chargeable		**Chargeable**	
William Sym[m]es	9	John Chrisfeild	2
William Ongley	4	Thomas Jordan	1
Thomas Oliff	1	Edward Gorham	2

Not Chargeable			
James Tunck	1	Thomas Olive Borsholder	

The lower halfe hundred of Eyhorne

Borough of Sutton Valence

Chargeable		**Chargeable**	
Edward Maplesden gent	7	Maxi[millian] Taylor gent	7
Thomas Tindall gent	10	Thomas Ware	3
John Buckhurst	4	Richard Hilles	2
Thomas Huney	3	Elizab[eth] Waller wid	2
James Lambe	6	Thomas Piper	4
William Browne	1	William Austin	1
William Satten	2	William Piggen	1
John Crompe	4	Thomas Wild	2
James Spice	2	Francis Tumber	2
Francis Tilden	2	Saphir Day	2

William Mockitt	2	Thomas Culmer	3
Robert Turner	3	Thomas Usher	1
Francis Davis	2	Thomas Watkins	3
Thomas Turner	2	James Wiggings	4
Nicholas Classon	1	John Acton	1
John Coveny	1	Nicholas Classon jun[io]r	3
Henry Finch	5	Thomas Hofood	1
Abell Bowen	3	John Busher	1
John Peters	3	William Rayner	1
John Chaxfield	1		

Not Chargeable

John Harpar	1	Widdow Smyth	2
William Bungor	2	John Fisher	2
Widdow Hines	2	Thomas Luck	1
Elizabeth Besbedge	2	John Staveny	1
Richard Norrod	1	John Norrod	1
Widdow Baker	1	Widdow Sharpe	1
William Paris	1	Thomas Kutly	2
John Grant	1	John Homesby	2
		Nicholas Classon	
		Borsholder	

The Borough of Boughton Maleherb

Chargeable   **Chargeable**

The right Hon[ora]ble }		Gabriell Hall	3
Countess of Chesterfield }	37	Chris[topher] Chambers	2
Thomas Dive	4	Robert Barling	2
Nicholas Taylor	2	John Tamkin	2
John Glover	1	Symon Clynch	1
Widdow Bucher	2	William Fleet	2
Stephen Hooker	2	Thomas Hooker	2
James Bunce	2	Peter Philpott	2
Anthony Allen	2	Anthony Dive	1
Thomas Hart	3	Daniell Sedwicks	1
John Spillett	6	Isaack Atkinson	6
Thomas Sym[m]ons	2	Mr Rob[er]t Ellis clerk	5
Henry Hall	3	John Houting	4

[fol. 24r]

Not Chargeable   **Not Chargeable**

John Tyler	1	John Page	1
Widdow Briggs	1	Thomas Banks	1

Widdow Pettet	1	John Witherden	1
Widdow Hooker	4	Widdow Homsbie	2
		John Spillett Borsholder	

Towne Borough of Hedcorne

Chargeable		Chargeable	
John Ramsden	7	John Waters	2
John Peckham	2	Avary Ramsden	5
John Harman	5	John Carter	5
Edward Brockwell	6	John Baker	3
Caleb Johnson	3	William Thunder	8
Richard Cushman	12	Christopher Fullager	1
George Butcher	1	Thomas Duke	2
William Yates & }		John Lucost	3
John Southerden }	4	Thomas Willard	1
John Packham sen[io]r	2	John Love	2
Mary Harnden widd	3	John Eigelden	2
Samuel Ely	1	Anthony Rayner	3
John Viney	2	Richard Southerden	1
John Potter	4	William Stokes	2
William Hills	2	William George	1
Widdow Burrish	3	Robert Manwaring	1

Not Chargeable		Not Chargeable	
John Brunger	1	Richard Tipett	1
Widdow Fishenden	1	John Gipson	1
Edward Judg	1	John Sell	1
Robert Powell	1	Widdow Letts	1
Widdow Williams	1	William Larkin	1
William Grayline	1	John Harper	1
Widdow Highstead	1	John Brunger jun[io]r	1
Widdow James	1	James Comes	1
Widow Giles	2	William Bryant	1
Henry Gilbert	2	William Buckman	2
Richard Kither	1	George Genbie	2
Matthew Dixon	1	William Amos	1
William Gipson	2	John Bridge	1
		Thomas Duke Borsholder	

Parish of Bromfield

Chargeable		Chargeable	
William Cage Esq[ui]re }		Thomas Dann	3
in Leeds Castle }	32	Robert Pawley	5

Grigory Odiam in }		Michael Benty	2
an empty house }	2	John Sweetlove	1
Henry Marketman	1	George Clapson	1
Thomas Willmot	1	Robert Satterden	2
George Clapson sen[io]r	2	Francis Boycott	2

Not Chargeable		Not Chargeable	
Widdow Andrewes	1	John Mills	1
William Shipster	1	Richard Andrewes	1
George Gower	1	Mathew Mills	1
George Wilson	1	Widdow Dive	1
		Henry Marketman	
		Borsholder	

Parish of Boughten Munshalsey

Chargeable		Chargeable	
S[i]r Robert Barnham	24	Mr John Alchorne	12
Bar[one]t			
William Hills	1	Widdow Hernden	1
William Joy	3	Mathias Rutton	4
Widdow Huggens	4	Christopher Spice	2
William Dayes	1	Richard Garrett	3
Thomas Wills	1	Nathaniell Turner	3
James Boad	5	James Buckhurst	4
Thomas Potter	1	James Collaway	1
Richard Nash	1	John Goodwin	2
George Snoad	2	John Brichar	2
Stephen Goodwin	2	William Claggett	2
Thomas Dray	1	Widdow Solman	3
Thomas Hulks	3	Hansor Madsor	2
Thomas Raynes	2	Hugh Barnett	4
Edward Taylor	3	George Hurt	5
Thomas May	2	George Day	5
Widdow Sedger	6	Living Iden	3
Tobias Young	2	Robert Rabbett	6
Isaac Richardson	1	Richard Iden	2
Alexander Marten	2	John Turke	1
John Tew	1	John Banks	2
Thomas Godden	4	Richard Usmer	4
James Morely	1	Edward Cudbush	1
Edward Austen	1	Valentine Knight	5
Thomas Walter	2	John Coney	1
Thomas Perren	1	Francis Brummon	1

William Okell[258]	1	Steeven Walter[259]	2
Thomas Hulks	1	Widdow Wilkins	2
Elizabeth Fisher	4	George Crowe	1
John Page	1	Thomas Barnar	2
William Honey	1	Widdow Frenchborne	3
Wyat Chune	4	John Marten	3
George Walker	1	John Hernden	3
Marten Blackburne	2	Widdow West	4
John Joy	3	William Young	1
Widdow Fetherstone	1	William Page	1
Robert Baker	2	Thomas Joy	1
Richard Longmar	2	James Brooman	2

Not Chargeable

John Rootes	2	Robert Clarke	1
Thomas Quaife	1	John Corbitt	1
Richard Quaife	1	Richard Bayly	2
Widdow Landen	2	Stephen Norwood	1
Widdow Marten	2	John Bennett	2
[fol. 24v]			
John Downe	1	William Hubbert	1
Robert Bassock	1	John Taylor	1
Richard Joy	1	Widdow Downes	1
John Haywood	2	Widdow Roberts	1
Widdow French	1	John Hollams	1
Jacob Norrington	2	Robert Bankes	1
Richard Stanford	2	Widdow Ward	1
Widdow Scultropp	1	Richard Longmar	
		Borsholder	

Langly Parish

Chargeable

S[i]r Nathan[iel] Powell Bart	16	Peter Browne	4
William Smyth	6	John Butcher	3
William Boosh	3	Nicholas Browne	2
Thomas Austen	1	Edward Boad	3
Richard Pierce	2	Thomas Joy	4
James Joy	1	Anthony Godden	4
John Pattenden	2	John Fullagat	6
Abell Beeching	9	Mary Hunt	2

[258] Interlined entry.
[259] Interlined entry.

Henry Medhurst	2	Benjamin Slainy	2
Robert Sharsted	2	Edward Adams	1
Thomas Taylor	2	Thomas Charlton	5
John Pauly	8	William Reader	4
Henry Merriam	1	William West	3
John Souten	2	Henry Wilkinson	1
Thomas Avery	2	William Perkins	5
Francis Russell	1	Widdow West	3
William Owlett borsholder	3		

Not Chargeable

James Stonehouse	1	John Sculthrop	1
William Waters	2	John Durkin	1
William Moore	1	Robert Boade	2
Widdow Fryer	1	Widdow Usher	1
Thomas Sayer	1	Nicholas Lovering	1
John Homard	1	John Buttler	1

Otham Borough

Chargeable

Alabaster Floud gent	14	John Henley	9
Edmund Ellis	9	Richard Netter	7
John Oliff	4	Robert Caviell	7
Roger Chittenden	2	James Smoothing	1
Thomas Wall	5	John Closson	5
John Nicholson	5	Attawell Woollett	2
Henry Woollett	1	William Groomebridge	1
Richard Brenchly	1	Richard Willes	2
Peter Willmott	2	Thomas Brenchley	2
Thomas Pearce	1	Daniell Colson	2
John Woollett	1	James Ward	2
Isaac Allen	2	William Sudger	3
John Crippen	2	Peter Sanders	3
Samuell Bongost	1	Richard Gorham	1
John Rouse	1	Edward Hilles	3

Not Chargeable

Henry Yeomans	1	Widdow Stamford	1
William Jeffrey	1	Elizabeth Philpott	1
Widdow Sutten	2	Ann Ralfe	1
Edward Fenner	1	John Brenchley	1
Edward Warner	2	Richard Warner	2
William Allen	1	Ellen Oldwood	1

| Ralph Oldwood | 1 | William Owlett borsholder | |

Parish of Ulcombe

Chargeable		Chargeable	
S[i]r Francis Clarke Knt	18	Doctor Cood	10
Thomas Handfield sen[io]r	6	Thomas Handfield jun[io]r	3
Peter Salmon	4	Robert Tilbey	1
Edward Coveny	2	Robert Kingsnorth	3
Richard Homsbey	2	Robert Hoope	2
Benjamin Firminger	3	James Filmer	4
more in his millhouse	3	William Mercer	4
more in his house att }		Robert Taylor	2
the wood }	4	Mr Hussey	6
Thomas Struggles	6	Thomas Figge	4
Walter Cooke	1	Edward Stace	2
Edward Hoope	3	John Pack	3
Thomas Stiles	3	Thomas Barham	3
William Hatch	3	Widdow Tregg	2
Robert Hoop [th]e miller	2	Thomas Bix	3
Edward Morfoot	1	Widdow Iddenden	2
Robert Davis	2	Isaac Carter	3
John Early	3	Peter Godfrey	7
Richard Smyth	3	Henry Luen	3
Thomas Griniell	3	Edward Cooke	5
Richard Gorham	2	Daniell Swayn	1
Thomas Struggles	2	Christop[her] Hubbard	6
Thomas Tompson	1	John Carter	1
Thomas Milles	1	Widdow Lushington	3

Not Chargeable		Not Chargeable	
Leonard Bigg	1	Daniell Haiselden	1
Anthony Lows	1	Richard Sleyney	1
Robert Plane	1	Thomas Hodges	2
Thomas Huggen	2	Widdow Moorfoot	2
Thomas Budgen	2	George Bricher	1
Thomas Carter	1	Thomas Maileham	1
Widdow Moor	1	Stephen Downe	1
Widdow Usmore	1	Edward Browne	1
John Tilman	1	Widdow Baldock	1
[fol. 25r]			
Widdow Man	1	Edward Keeping	2
Widdow Vane	1	John Hope	1

John Bunce	2	Robert Vincett	3
Widdow Nutting	1	Robert Kingsnoth Borsholder	

Chart next Sutton

Chargeable		Chargeable	
John Smyth Esq	10	In the vicarage house	3
James Lambe	2	Thomas Barber	6
Peter Steere	6	John Simcox	7
Widdow Morgan	7	Thomas Scoone	5
John Mathew	8	more for Norton house	2
Thomas Huggins	4	John Robbins	3
Richard Packham	7	Richard Miller	1
Widdow Moule	8	William Huggins	2
John Gouldring	4	Thomas Fells	3
Robert Hunt	2	Richard Masters	5
Widdow Amhurst	4	Richard Stace	4
William Boughton	2	James Rich	6
William Standly	2	Stephen Blackbourne	3
Christopher Dourtnall	1	John Owlett	1
Robert Wood	2	James Bennett	1
William Wood	2	Thomas Standly	2
Thomas Waight	4	Thomas Mepham	1
George Clarke	2	John Browne sen[io]r	3
Thomas Blackbourne	2	Walter Luck	2
Allen Turner	2	Robert Browne	2
John Hunt	1		

Not Chargeable		Not Chargeable	
Widdow Hilles	1	John Browne jun[io]r	1
George Goldwire	1	John Watkins	2
Robert Wilkinson	1	Robert Cheesman	1
Widdow Read	1	James Hoppar	1
John Smyth	2	Widdow Coulter	1
Thomas Leaver	1	Widdow Potman	2
John George	2	Thomas Masters	2
Richard Bills	2	Thomas Chapman	2
William Sponge	1	Widdow Baker	2
Nicholas Husher	1	Nicholas Pelham	1
John Tollherst	1	Edmund Frayman	1
Richard Foord	1	Francis Blackbourne	1
Thomas Hunt	1	John Cooke	3
Widdow Osmer	1	John Masters Borsholder	

Parish of Bersted

Chargeable		Chargeable	
John Mun Esq	13	Edward Naper gent	6
Edward Maplesden gent	9	Silas Johnson gent	6
James Iden	6	Thomas Brewer	5
John Lott	6	Richard Guinn	11
Joane Allen	6	Thomas Jemmett	6
John Pilcher	6	Mrs Mabb	7
Widdow Hilles	5	John Aysham	5
Widdow Packman	3	Robert Brookes	2
Robert Chilman	3	Richard Young	5
Peter Queox	1	James Burr	3
William Carman	2	John Baker	1
Widdow Brodnax	3	John Ward	2
James Wood	2	Edward Maynard	5
Widdow Smoothing	3	Thomas Carman	2
Isaac Allen	3	James Hinckley	3
Thomas Bur	3	Patrick Shuter	4
George Butler	3	Mark Stainsmore	4
William Cobb	1	Nicholas Wheate	2
John Birbidge	1	John Diamond	3
John Leaper	6	Widdow Peirce	2

Not Chargeable		Not Chargeable	
Abraham Rowse	1	Thomas Tattenden	1
Widdow Datson	1	John Fekins	2
John Fryday	2	John Young	3
Daniel Wraith	2	William Isham	2
Peter Sadbury	3	Isaac Burbidge	1
William Eagles	4	John Clapson	1
Widdow Baxster	2	William Venns	1
Widdow Field	2	Mary Baker	1
Widdow Tayler	1	Henry Wilkinson	1
Hester Baseley	1	Widdow Cobb	1
Walter Gouldsmyth	1	Thomas Isham	1
		Patrick Suter Borsholder	

Sutton Valence Innborough

Chargeable		Chargeable	
John Turner	3	George Cutbeard	7
George Maplesden	4	Ann Mooreland	4
Jeremiah Nell	3	Thomas Bishopp	4
Mr Barrington	4	John Fenner	5

IA *Broome Park*, Barton borough, Barham (Kinghamford). Built by Sir Basil Dixwell, an incomer from Warwickshire, between 1635 and 1638. He was charged on 20 hearths in 1664.

IB *Ford Place*, Neppicar borough, Wrotham (Wrotham). Home of the Clerke family. A large medieval house which was adapted and enlarged in the sixteenth and early seventeenth centuries. Only one range out of three survives today and most of the chimney stacks have been taken down. In 1664 John Clerke, Esq. was charged on 15 hearths.

IIA *Wickens*, Highslade borough, Charing (Calehill). A minor gentry house built around 1600 with six chimneys originally serving five fireplaces. By the time of the hearth tax a further fireplace had been added. The house was owned by the Dering family, but in 1664 it was probably occupied by Anthony Aucher, gent., who was charged on 6 hearths.

IIB *Stone Hill* and *Old Forge Cottage*, Sellindge (Street). A medieval open-hall house, provided with a timber chimney in the sixteenth century, which was later replaced by a central brick stack with three fireplaces. This may have occurred as late as 1657, the date carved on the gable of the oriel.

IIIA *Barnfield*, Field borough, Charing (Calehill). A large medieval open-hall house whose open hearth was first replaced by a smoke bay, and later, when the exterior was encased in brick, by a brick stack with three fireplaces. In 1664 the right half was occupied by Robert Rayner, husbandman, who was charged on one hearth.

IIIB *23 Smithers Lane*, Stockenbury borough, East Peckham (Twyford). A small medieval open-hall house, which had a timber chimney inserted in the sixteenth century. This was probably not replaced until the eighteenth century. In 1664 the house appears to have been lived in by Stephen Cheeseman, exempted from paying tax on a single hearth.

IVA *Gabriel Richards Almshouses*, Goodnestone (Wingham). The almshouses, with four fireplaces for four hospitallers, were endowed by Gabriel Richards in his will of 1672. It is likely, however, that they had been erected some years before, the architectural detail being more in keeping with a building of the 1640s. The hospitallers are not identifiable in the hearth tax, but were listed in the Compton Census of 1676.

IVB *113 High Street*, Wingham (Wingham). In east Kent many seventeenth-century houses were of one storey with an attic above, only the main room being heated by a fireplace. This example, with two rooms on each floor, is dated 1667.

William Raynes	2	John Bishopp	2
Alexander Wottle	5	Joseph Wattle	2
Mabella Barrington	2	Thomas Turner	3
John Rouse	3	Widdow Shelley	4
Thomas Walker	2	Robert Binnes	1
Widdow Binnes	2	Francis Bates	2
Edward Gillett	2	Christopher Hubbert	8
Anthony Watkins	4	James Joy	1
Richard Wood	3		

Not Chargeable		**Not Chargeable**	
John Boulton	1	John Usmer	1
Jane Culmer	1	James Hilles	1
Thomas Jorden	1	Widdow Parks	1
Widdow Bills	1	Daniel Medhurst	2
Richard Sutton sen[io]r	2	Richard Sutten jun[io]r	2
[fol. 25v]			
Thomas Trowell	1	Daniell Maytham	2
James Ashby	2	Symon Ady	1
Michael Dove	1	Thomas Bunnyer	1
Thomas Roberts	1	Widdow Foster	2
William Lawes	2	Nicholas Larke	1
Edward Davis	1	Widdow Raynes	1
		Richard Wood Borsholder	

Borough of East Sutton

Chargeable		**Chargeable**	
Dame Ann Filmer	17	Mr Thomas Backett	5
Thomas Carter	8	William Carter	5
Mrs Slaughter	7	Stephen Peene	5
John Busher	1	Robert Spillett	5
Widdow Davis	1	Thomas Hogbin	4
Edward Jenings	5	Richard James	2
John Packham	3	Stephen Crucher	5
John Benison	2	John Farnes	2
John Woollett	3	Robert Frid	4
John Frid	3	Richard Nash	1
Robert Wiborow	2	John Clapson	1
John Trowell	1	Richard Bates	1
Symon Bates	2	George Jenkins	3
John Baker	2	Widdow Virgin	4
Thomas Chalturn	2	Thomas Cladish	2
Robert Cheesman	1	Widdow Weekes	2

William Stiddall	2	Widdow Sharpe	1
William Claggett	2	Widdow Bony	1

Not Chargeable		**Not Chargeable**	
Stephen Burford	7	John French	4
Richard Weekes	1	Nicholas Lowes	2
Robert Swayne	3	Thomas Allen	1
Widdow Hall	4	Henry Collison	1
William Collison	1	Stephen Collison	1
William King	1	Matthew Hammond	2
William Cooke	1	William Richardson	1
Richard Kite	1	William Wrath	1
Widdow Frid	1	Nicholas Cooke	1
Widdow Willes	1	Lawrence Frid	1
John Bingham	1	Widdow Benison	1
		Nicholas Low Borsholder	

Parish of Leeds

Chargeable		**Chargeable**	
Sir William Meredith ba[rone]t	25	John Moore clerk	6
Ralph Freake in two houses} stand empty }	6	Grigory Odiarne	8
		Francis Freeman	4
William Halsnod	7	William Troy	5
Walter Bayden	2	Henry Davis	5
Daniel Hadlowe	1	James Lovell	2
John Shuter	1	Andrew Cox	2
Robert Collison	3	Mrs Eliz: Foord wid[ow]	6
Abraham Charlton	7	William Downe	1
George Coppar	4	William Gilbert	6
Henry Mercer	2	Isaac Wassall	2
William Rowse	2	Thomas Taylor	3
Arthur Watts	3	John Saxbie	6
William Pattenden	2	William Hill	3
John Bingham	1	John Danne	3
Elizabeth Rowse wid[dow]	2	Nicholas Skoones	2
Robert Evernden	4	John Essex	2
John Packham	2	Thomas Shewell gen[t]	6
Alexander Waterman	3	William Danne	4
Henry Watts	7	Edmund Collison	5
Henry Collison	3	Thomas Sanders	3
Richard Gillett	3	John Downe	1
Robert Hatch	4	Richard Peene	2

John Effell	3	Anthony Tourt	1
James Tapley	1	Thomas Ashbey	2
Alice Mason widd[ow] }		John Holland	3
Thomas Beckett g[en]t }	4	Ann Wood widd[ow]	1
Edmund Randall	1	Edmund Barnard	2
Elizabeth Carter	1	William Oxley	2
Alexander Durtnall	3	Henry West	1
John Goldsmith	1	Symon Price	3
John Milgate	2		

Not Chargeable		**Not Chargeable**	
Reynald Carter sen[io]r	1	Reynald Carter jun[io]r	1
Elizabeth Brason	1	Robert Hooker	2
Thomas Downe	1	Thomas Peene	1
Robert Wood	1	Robert Mercer	1
George Cooper	1	Allen Edwards	1
John Rogers	1	John Miles	1
John Fishenden	1	Widdow Miles	1
William Gaskin	2	John Plane	1
Clement Hadloe	1	Thomas Ledger	1
John Davies	1	Thomas Sparke	1
William Waters	1	Isaac Vane	1
Widdow Charles	2	George Southerden	1
Anthony Dawes	1	John Miller	2
Edward Whiting	1	John Staple	1
Widdow Adams	2	Henry Goodlad	1
Thomas Price	2	Widdow May	1
		John Milgate Borsholder	

[fol. 26r]

THE HUNDRED OF SHAMWELL
In the Lath of Aylsford

The Upper Halfe Hundred

Cobham East Borough

The Right Honble }		William Hayes	4
Duke of Richmond }	51	Mr Buck	3
Richard Briver	2	William Houlding	2
Thomas Aylard	3	Warren Almond	1
Richard Joanes	3	Daniel Pigeon	6
Thomas Hanscomb	5	Robert Fenner	4
Widdow Wood	3	John Read	4

Edward Bates	3	George Bradford	4
George Ifield	1	Edward Davis	2
John Gosney	5	Thomas Mooreley	3
Robert Boghurst	2	Widdow Davis	3

Not Chargeable   **Not Chargeable**

Widdow Wood	4	Benjamin Hayte	2
Vincent Roberts	1	Nicholas Potter	1

Cobham South Borough

Chargeable   **Chargeable**

Richard Parker	7	William Cozens	7
Mary Shrimpton	7	John Wattson	6
Edward Carryer	3	Thomas Norris	4
Rowland Hilles	3	John Jackson	2
Henry Royse	1	George Ifield	1
John Jeater	3	Charles Hunt	2
Thomas Hubbard	2	Robert Moyce	2
James Bourne	2	Nicholas Mugg	4
Richard Carryer	4	Robert Middleton	2
John Rumney	2	Thomas Plaister	2
Richard Beard	1	Christopher Ashley	5
Edward Fowlkes	3	Francis Wood	1
William Hayes	3	Robert Surbey	2

Not Chargeable   **Not Chargeable**

Thomas Caverdine	2	John Saunders	1
Thomas Carryer	2	Easter Gilesland	4
James Durrant	3		

Halling Borough

Chargeable   **Chargeable**

Sir John Marsham	8	Thomas Rich	3
William Clemence	17	Richard Hawes	5
Abell Terrey	3	Thomas Hawes	8
John Cock	2	Elizabeth Palmer	2
William Godberry	2	Mathew Marshall	1
John Lane	2	William Miller	2
William Long	1	Thomas Carryer	2
Thomas Gardner	1	John Peckman	2
Thomas Long	2	Phillip Fanne	3
Robert Mussard	1	John Brett	4
Valentine Turley	1	William Wellard	2

William Gamball	3	James Easdowne	1
Richard Rayphell	1	Augustine Fodderidge	2
Edward Wilson	2	Stephen Everton	1
William Hutson	1	George Lewis	1

Not Chargeable		**Not Chargeable**	
Jane Turley	1	Thomas Freeman	1

Chalke East Borough

Chargeable		**Chargeable**	
Jacob Parsons	5	Daniell Bingham	4
Vincent Right	3	Solomon Parris	3
William Pigeon	2	Peter Browne	7
Robert Beveridge	3	Richard Fuller	4

Chalke Westborough

Chargeable		**Chargeable**	
Mr Peter Butler	6	John Philpott	4
William Webb	3	John Hilles	3
James Peacock	2	John Curtis	1
Mr Wood	4	Reioyce Head	4
John Durling	2	John Ellit	2
Bryant Plaistow	3	Widdow Burden	1
James Bourne	1	George Senior	1

Cuxton Borough

Chargeable		**Chargeable**	
Sir John Mersham }		John Robinson clerk	5
Kn[igh]t & Barro[ne]t }	19	Reignald Rich	6
Richard Cozens	4	Phillip Beckett	2
Henry Gardner	5	Jane Cozens widd[ow]	5
Richard Best and }		James Bird	1
George Beynard }	4	William Haltropp	3
John Ketly	2	Thomas Gostling	3
Robert George	3	Humfrey Russell	1
Nicholas Grandson	1	Symon Newberry	2
William Collinson	2	William Corke	2
John Smyth	2	Nicholas Loft	2
Thomas Devenish	3	Jane Cozens widd[ow]	3

Not Chargeable		**Not Chargeable**	
William Russell	3	Edward Newberry	2
Moses Taster	2	George Brissenden	1

Richard Newberry   1
[fol. 26v]

Shorne Westborough

Chargeable		Chargeable	
Mary Baynard widd[ow]	5	Richard Pack	4
Bonham Baynard	6	William Baynard	1
William Edwards	7	Arnold Brasier	2
John Band	2		

Not Chargeable		Not Chargeable	
John Foster	1	John Hotte	1
George Valentine	1	William James	1

Shorne Northborough

Chargeable		Chargeable	
Nicholas Loft	5	Rachell Bond widd[ow]	4
Robert Hayt	4	William Head	7
Robert Wharton	4	Edward Waring	6
Thomas Ray	2	William Fletcher	2
Thomas Masters	3	William Masters	4
Richard Westmoore	3	Richard Giles	1

Shorne Southborough

Chargeable		Chargeable	
George Woodyer gent'	13	Henry Parker gent'	12
Gervase Maplesden	7	George Maplesden	7
Richard Balam cler[ke]	7	John Clay	6
William Woolfe	5	Nicholas Bundock	4
William Emmes	6	Samuell Henley	3
Katharine Loft widd[ow]	6	George Walter	2
Richard Everest	2	Thomas Wood	3
William Williams	2	John Gillett	1
Thomas Langfield	2	William Pettley	1
John Watts	1	Edward Balding	1
Henry Derrick	2	Thomas Collett	2
John Sutton	3	Elizab[eth] Gugley widd	3
William Burton	5	John Wilson	1
Thomas Blake	3	Elias Greenhill	1
Christoph[er] Hopgood	4	Elizabeth Winne	1
John Goldsmith	3	John Pidgeon	2
John Wharton	1	William Rose	2
George Mugge	2	Abraham Sparks	1

George Ifield	2	Richard Leicester	2
Francis Smyth	2		

Not Chargeable		**Not Chargeable**	
Joane Sheldrick widd[ow]	2	Elizab[eth] Mumford widd[ow]	2
Joane Grigson	1	Ellinor Verton widd	2
Elizabeth Davis wid[dow]	2	Joane Lessenden	1
Margaret Jackson	2	Mary Lock	1
Dorothy Warring	1	Ann Pinner	1
Grigory Anderson	1	Henry Ray	1
Thomas Essex	1	Robert Pearce	1
Edward Hubbard	1	John Wye	1

Denton Borough

Chargeable		**Chargeable**	
Richard Carryer	6	Richard Gipson	4
		John Wattson Constable	

The lower halfe hundred of Shamwell

The upper borough in the parish of Higham

Chargeable		**Chargeable**	
Luke Cordwell Esq	12	Daniel Emptage	4
Edward Read	2	Richard Grasham	2
Henry Cooper	2	Robert Paies	1
Francis Wakling	2	John Buffett	2
Richard Bankes	1	Isaac Burt	1
Charles Buttler	1	John Cartwright	3
Edward Haslewood	3	John Haslewood	1
William Dove	1	John Cracknayle	1
Thomas Copland	6		

Not Chargeable		**Not Chargeable**	
Robert Mason	1	William Morett	1
Nicholas Snatt	1	Edward Clout	1
William Stepkens	1	Robert Brewer	1
Henry Wooden	2	Widdow Smyth	1
Widdow Dubby	1	Joseph Skipp	1
William Beecher	1	John Joyce	1
Nathaniel Wilkins	1	Widdow Reapingale	1
Widdow Gouldock	1	Richard Grasham Borsholder	

Higham Lower Borough

Chargeable		Chargeable	
Stephen Joad	10	James Topley	3
Jeffry Platt	2	John Day in Great Oakley	4
Nicholas Cosin	4	William Gyssom	3
William Browne	2	George Pratt	2
Daniell Lampton	4	George Cartwright	3
John Smyth	4	Willyam Paine	1
John Piscott	3	John Barnes	2
William Goodall	1	Thomas Woodland	3
Thomas Copland	3	Richard Adam	1
Thomas Hornall	2		

[fol. 27r]

Not Chargeable		Not Chargeable	
Thomas Dennan	5	Thomas Dennis	1
Widdow Beane	1	Widdow Dowle	1
Richard Tossell	1	John Underdowne	1
Thomas Jones	1	John Whitehead	1
Thomas Goodman	1	Thomas Wilson	2
Robert Worley	1	Jeffery Platt Borsholder	

Oysterland Borough

Chargeable		Chargeable	
William Inman	3	Thomas Watts	1
Robert Mitchell	1	Thomas Shorneall	1
Widdow Taylor	4	John Johnson	1
David Downe	1	Richard Scott	1
Widdow Cole	3	Robert Sammon	2
Vincent Wayt	2	William Scott	2
[blank] Juce	4		

Not Chargeable		Not Chargeable	
Widdow Stock	2	William Cornelius	1
		Richard Scott Borsholder	

Frindsbury West Borough

Chargeable		Chargeable	
Henry Pannell	10	Nathaniel Bradley	10
Thomas Johnson clerk	4	John Woodgreene	6
Francis Iles	7	John Baynard	6
William Writtle	6	Thomas Clemence	5
John Blake	5	Edward Smyth	6

Henry Young	7
John Taylor	3
Richard Towers	6
Ralph Charles	2
Widdow Britten	3
Charles Butcher	4
Widdow Ivett in an }	
empty house }	5
Richard Lowne in one }	
empty house }	5
Jane Edwards	2
George Grigory	3
John Sanders	1

William Herbert	2
John Young	6
Edward Wheatly	3
[blank] Woolfe	4
Richard Daniell	3
John Woodgreene	4
Widdow Cowdwell	5
Widdow Gardner	4
John Usher	1
Fardinando Winnpress	3
Mary Elkington	3
John King	2

Not Chargeable

John Read	5
Widdow Baxster	2
John Toosland	2
Thomas Hood	2
Car [blank] Billing	2
Widdow Iles	1
Thomas Taylor	1
Nicholas Wheatly	2
Lawrence Bulard	1
Richard Pierce	2
Widdow Carryer	3
John Cockley	3
Arthur Hall	2
John Pummell	2
Valentine Iverson	2
Widdow Thompson	2

Not Chargeable

Widdow Summers	1
George Mattins	2
Francis Rogers	1
Thomas Pack	2
Widdow Granely	1
Edward Watkins	2
Widdow Toard	2
William Perin	2
Richard Dobson	1
John Hood	2
Widdow Lucy	3
John Lawson	2
Henry Arnett	2
Mathew Gilman	1
Widdow Young	2
Edward Wheatley Borsholder	

Freindsbury East Borough

Chargeable

Robert Watson gen[tleman]	8
Mrs Needler widd[ow]	8
George Crower	2
Widdow Taverner	2
Widdow Wood	2
James Tapley	4
John Nicholson	3
[blank] Whitfield	2

Chargeable

William Pennestone	6
Richard Brenchley	4
Roger Pannell	4
Richard Terrell	6
Henry Scoales	4
John Pannell	4
Widdow Moyce	6
Gunner Hudson	3

Thomas Harris	1	Henry Hammon	1
In Chattenden farme }		Benjamin Parrit	3
house which stands empty }	3	Walter Sammon	1
John Shepward	4	Thomas Conford	1
William Mead	2	George Saule	1
William Wright	2	Thomas Wright	1
Thomas Charrett	1	Joseph Scudder	1
Widdow Butler	2	Thomas Bicknall	6
Widdow Butler	2		

		Not Chargeable	
Henry Scoales Borsholder		William Greene	1

Temple Borough Strood

Chargeable		**Chargeable**	
John Whalley	2	Francis Wansall	8
Widdow Cart	3	Richard Wood	3
Elizab[eth] Bartholomew wid	4	Widdow Ponnett	4
John Warren	4	James Ashbey	4
Augustine Ponnett	6	Edward Robinson	5
Thomas Stringer	2	William Skinner	3
Stephen Grigsbey	2	Richard Andrewes	2
Robert Dunkin	2	Thomas Hayes	4
Thomas Andrewes	5	Robert Goatter	3
Thomas Rowland	2	William Hilyard	2
William Beckinsall	5	Edward Smyth	6
Robert Wood	4	Abigall Wood widd[ow]	7
John Hulkes	3	Samuell Head	5
[fol. 27v]			
William Mayor	3	James Augar	4
Samuel Hallwell	5	John Johnson	4
William Poysinn	4	Widdow Jelfe	3
Widdow Sneddall	4	Peter Gayney	2
John Norton	2	Nicholas Hall	2
John Pembrooke	2	Widdow Arkinstall	3
Thomas Berry	2	Widdow Hooke	6
Widdow Phipp	3	Joseph Cesar	6
Richard Country	6	Bartholomew Harwood	2
Henry Britten	3	Symon Murfield	6
George Hoult	3	John Chapman	2
James Barrowes	3	Richard Wood	6
John Fowler	2	John Bashford	5
Christopher Bigg	3	James Beale	2

James Wells	2	Henry Hoosier	2
William Pemble	2	John Allen	2
Phillip Damant	2	Thomas Payne	4
John Meare	2	Edward Shunkes	2
John Clipton	3	Widdow Ratherry	3
Robert Hargrove	2	John Cable	5
Ralph Scoales	3	John Figg	3
John Cooper	2	Richard Houlder	2
Anthony Bridges jun[io]r	2	Nicholas Speareman	5
William Middleton	4	William Waters	1
Widdow Philpott	1	Richard Brown	6
Anthony Bridges sen[io]r	2	Henry Figgett	4
William Child	4	Walter Gillett	2
Anthony Harrell	2	Nicholas Clarke	4
Thomas Miller	2	Isaac Blake gent[leman]	8
Sisley Brookes widd[ow]	8	Henry Smyth	3
John Shaw	4	Mrs Swann widdow In }	
Francis Wansall In }		an empty house }	8
two empty houses }	11	Henry Figgett in }	
William Wiseman gent }		an empty house }	3
In an empty house }	8	more in another empty house	2
Richard Country in }		Nicholas Speereman in }	
an empty house }	2	an empty house }	2
Henry Hoshier in }		John Lathbury In an }	
two empty houses}	6	empty house }	7
Widdow Tills In}		William Ellis in an }	
am empty house}	3	empty house }	2
Samuel French in an empty house	6		

Not Chargeable		**Not Chargeable**	
George Spangborne	2	Hugh Crewes	2
George Birch	2	Thomas Kilbey	2
Widdow Spangborne	1	Widdow Groves	2
Widdow Springfield	3	Michaell Huffam	4
Allen Figge	2	Thomas Clay	2
Thomas Garrett	2	William Parkinson	2
Thomas Parsons	5	John Stretton	2
John Terry	2	William Broomebrick	1
Nicholas Browne	1	John Parsons	1
Widdow Allington	1	Widdow Butler	2
Richard Frogley	2	Widdow Gammage	2

| Richard Cleeve | 2 | William White | 2 |
| Widdow Jessopp | 2 | Thomas Payne borsholder | |

Strood Dutchey

Chargeable		Chargeable	
James Cripps gent	7	Mrs Ann Collett widd	6
William Shanke	4	John Slade	2
William Carryer	2	Robert Gayscoyne	1
John Lathbury	3	John Adams	3
Roger Pilcher	2	John Blanchfield	5

Not Chargeable		Not Chargeable	
John Shawe	2	Ann Prince	1
Symon Jenings	2	Mary Wenman wid	1
John Hearne	4	Roger Pilcher Borsholder	

Cooling Borough

Chargeable		Chargeable	
Mr Lord clerke	6	John Taylor	4
George Franck	9	William Eason	5
David Heath	3	John Warren	3
Edward Coale	2	Widdow Beecher	1
William Lovell	1	Richard Miller	1
Henry Bourne Borsholder	2		

Strood Little Borough

Chargeable		Chargeable	
George Parker gent	9	Christopher Morland gent	8
Widdow Brantford	4	John Griffen	3
John Thompson	3	William Leffgreene	3
Isaac Carter	6	John Slade	6
Stephen Helbey	4	Thomas Lovell	8
Robert Cable	2	John Lacey	2
John Metham	2	James Adams	2
Arthur Tranah	2	John Beckett	2
Elias Putland	6	Batholomew Eason	5
William Burford	3	Richard Peirce	2
Thomas Mudge	3	John Lemine	1
Bonham Boyden	2	William Dowle	3
[fol. 28r]			
Samuell Harbour	2	Jacob Norwood	3
Augustin Parson	2	John Williams	2

Empty houses

Thomas Mudge in one	6	Jeffery Milles in one	4
The heires of Thomas }		Mr Groves in one	3
Duning in one }	6	Eliz[abeth] Laughling wid[ow] in two	5

Not Chargeable		Not Chargeable	
Edward Kennett	2	Phineas Buss	5
Elizabeth West widd	2	Thomas Wilkins	2
John Benfield	2	Thomas Stone	3
Robert Candy	1	William Gymber	2
William Phillipps	2	John Gammon	2
Thomas Crouch	2	John Daniell	1
Peter Bacus	1	William Hilles	2
Richard Bayly	2	Andrew Pattoune	2
John Midleton	1	Venus Merrels widd	1
Thomas Waters	2	John Terry	2
William Johnson	2	Nicholas Wall	2
		William Dowle Borsholder	

Cliff Church Street and Reed Street Borough

Chargeable		Chargeable	
Robert Parker	3	James Tamsett	3
Thomas Newman	4	John Browne sen[io]r	4
Widdow Thomas	5	Oliver Whitborne	2
Robert Cockerill	2	Widdow Rogers	1
Richard Fisher	1	John Feareman	2
Edward Bee	1	William Perritt	4
Robert Alexander	1	Thomas Winsor	1
Ambrose Lenham	1	William Wellard	1
John Parker	1	Robert Parker	3
William Barnes	1	William Norman	1
William Butler	1	Richard Hilles	4
George Mitchell	1	Richard Perritt	6
		Thomas Hill Borsholder	

Cliff West Borough

Chargeable		Chargeable	
Richard Perritt	8	Nicholas Perritt	8
John Browne	7	Thomas Berry	4
Thomas Napper	1	Abraham Bridges	1
Richard Overy	5	In the parsonage house	6
Richard Jeffrey	1	James Collyer	1

Jacob Sutton	4	Thomas Baverly	3
Thomas Kempton	3	Nicholas Parker	4

Not Chargeable		**Not Chargeable**	
Mary Castleton	1	*[blank]* Medcapp	1
John Easdowne	1	Thomas Kempton	
		Borsholder	

Cliff Cooling Street Borough

Chargeable		**Chargeable**	
John Boghurst	7	John Nye	6
Thomas Smyth	3	Benham Marketman	4
Jacob Sutton	7	Thomas Hott	1
John Garland	6	Thomas Mudge	2
John Tame	3	William Weekes	1
Richard Johnson	3	Grigory Stewart	1
[blank] Sellis	6		

Not Chargeable		**Not Chargeable**	
Thomas Hutson	1	Nicholas Gillett	2
Thomas Fisher	1	John Askew	1
Robert Edmunds	1	John Eleffe	1
Henry Thompson	1	William Davis	1
		Thomas Smith Borsholder	
		William Pemble Constable	

THE HUNDRED OF TWYFORD
in the Lath of Aylsford

Parish of Teston

Chargeable		**Chargeable**	
Sir Oliver Boteler Bar[one]t }		In the vicarage house	3
& George Brook jun[io]r }	18	Robert Hodges	5
William Field	2	Ann Field widd[ow]	3
John Hammond	2	Elizabeth Osbourne wid	3
Stephen Fann	3	John Panckhurst	1
George Brookes sen[io]r	3	Henry Field	3
Thomas Cryer	3	John Frencham Borsholder	1
John Stretfield	1		

Not Chargeable	
James Saxbie	1

Parish of West Farliegh

Chargeable		Chargeable	
Thomas Brewer Esq	11	Judith Brewer	4
Oliver North	4	Augustine Hodges	4
Henry Goulding	3	Henry Cattlett	4
Walter Barton	4	Robert Hodges	3
John Leeds	1	Robert Gull	2
Thomas Parker	3	William Stretfield	3
William Marten	1	John Stanley	1
William Burges	1	John Daves	8
John Cheesman	4	Widdow Craddock	2
William Hunt	2	Widdow Ware	1
Goodman Reason	1	Daniel Lampon	3
Edward Cooper Esq	13	John Kenward	3
Thomas Browne	5	Stephen Barefoote	1
Robert Barefoote	2	Thomas Stone	2

Not Chargeable		Not Chargeable	
Widdow Pange	1	John Southernden	2
[fol. 28v]			
John Sutten	2	Thomas Smyth	2
Thomas Lemy	1	John Cattlett borsholder	

Parish of Nettlested

Chargeable		Chargeable	
William Pierceson	1	Widdow Cockell	1
Widdow Sutten	1	Thomas Harden	2
Edward Wiggenden	1	John Ippenbury	2
Goodman Olliver	2	William Goulding	3
Dame Katharine Scott	22	William Chardy	5
John Cumber	2	George Browne	2
Thomas Catt	2	William Curd Borsholder	2
William King	1		

Not Chargeable		Not Chargeable	
John Launce	1	William Baker	1
John Bourne	1	John Castleden	1
Widdow Lambert	1		

Borough of Stockenbury

Chargeable		Chargeable	
John Stanford	2	Thomas Bishopp	2
Thomas Dann	2	John Cheesman jun[io]r	2

Richard Bennett	2	Thomas Cheesman	1
William Marten	1	John Cheesman sen[io]r	2
William Huggens	2	William Coe	2
Widdow Cockrell	2	Widdow Stone	2
Henry Huggens	1	Thomas Jewell	1
James Freeman	2	Henry Wakeline	2
Thomas Field	1	Richard Hilles	1
John Stone	2	Peter Beecher	1
William Freeman	1	Bartholomew Hodge	1
John Johnson	1	John Buttler	3
John Biggenden	2	John Finch	1
William Day	1	Thomas Paulie	1
William Dennis	1	Stephen Allen	1
Widdow Biggenden	1	John Checksfield	2
John Symmons	2	George Pattenden	2
Richard Freeman	1	William Pattenden	1
Widdow Thompson	1	James Freeman	1
John Judd	2	Widdow Marten	2
Thomas Best	1	Iden Plane	2
William Rofe	2	Francis Plane	1
Richard Standford	2	John Keble	2
Isaiah Symmons }		Widdow Turke	2
in two houses }	3	Henry Standford	2
Thomas Bennett	1	John Barnes	2
Henry Cheesman in }		Thomas Hatch	2
two farmhouses }	3	James Gardiner	1
Marten Gibbons	1	Thomas Symmons	2
Richard Hatch	1	Michael Cheesman	1
Robert Sandell	2	Robert Browne	1

Not Chargeable		**Not Chargeable**	
Thomas Smyth	2	John Head	1
John Dennis	1	Widdow Honie	1
Mary Spirke	1	Thomas Medherst	1
Robert Burr	1	William Luck	1
William Allingham	1	Nicholas Barefoote	1
John Day	1	John Parker	1
William Sparke	1	John Crowerst	1
Widdow Kinge	1	John Willard	1
Thomas Luck	1	Thomas Kinge	1
John Webb	1	Widdow Frummons	1
William Shawe	1	Richard Cheeseman	2
John Smyth	1	George Lucke	1

Francis Kinge	1	Thomas Stanford	1
John Childrens sen[io]r	1	John Childrens jun[io]r	1
Huggen Plane	1	Widdow Tebb	1
John Best	1	Elizabeth Barefoote	1
Richard Willard	1	Widdow Butcher	1
John Lilly	1	John Cheesman	1
Stephen Cheesman	1	Christopher Gardiner	1
William Waller	1	John Gibbons	1
Widdow Baker	1	Reynald Evans	1
John Jewell	1		

Parish of Yalding

Chargeable		Chargeable	
Stephen Pattenden	2	Henry Dennis	2
Ezekiell Fleete	6	Peter Fletcher	1
Mary Summers	4	Isaac Packe	2
Anthony Hyland	1	Widdow Seamarke	1
John Hatch	1	Richard Todman	1
Stephen Stanford	1	Henry Tayler	1
Richard Stace	2	John Marten	1
John Turner	1	Thomas Humphrey	4
Absolom Homan	2	William Stace	2
John Cooper	1	Richard Bromfield	1
Henry Dennis sen[io]r	2	Stephen Ragly	1
John Ousnam	4	Nicholas Marten	3
Thomas Langley	1	John Browne	3
Thomas Brett	6	Marten Goreham	1
Richard Carpenter	2	Stephen Willard	1
John Lingue	7	William Goreham	1
Widdow Mannering	2	Daniel Chittenden	2
[fol. 29r]			
Thomas Rings	1	Samuell Dasey	1
William Winder	1	John Bull	1
Mary Barefoote	3	Edward Elliot	1
Thomas Terrey	1	Robert Browne	1
George Mowse	2	Henry Finch	1
Mark Gardiner	2	George Penhurst gent[leman]	5
John Furner	5	Thomas Langley	5
Thomas Jeffery	4	Widdow Tapley	2
Widdow Furner	1	Thomas Stone	2
George Cumber	1	Thomas Beckett	2
George Manley	6	John Kenward	8

Richard Duddy	2	John Fyler	5

Not Chargeable

		Not Chargeable	
Richard Larkin	1	Thomas Dann	2
Richard Turner	1	Richard Groomebridge	1
Widdow Sidge	1	Widdow Harden	1
John Ember	1	Goodman Sarles	2
John Andrewes	1	Widdow Greenested	1
William Whibley	1	Henry Lawrence sen[io]r	1
Noah Stone	1	Thomas Downe	1
John Wettkins	2	Thomas Hins	2
William Harden	1	Widdow Wilkins	2
William Warnes	1	Henry Lawrence	1
John Selence	2	Edward Greenested	2
Thomas Skilton	3	Goodman Greeneaway	1
Thomas Walker	2	Thomas Chowneing	1
Thomas Whibley	1	Richard Morley	1
John Chowneing	1	Goodman Thorne	1
Widdow Burgish	1	Widdow Fleet	2
Widdow Brensted	2	Thomas Young	1
Widdow Richardson	1	John Sennocke	1
Daniell Pickett	2	Thomas Daw	2
Thomas Bannester	2	William Scott	1
John Ellis	1	John Johnson	2
William Dennis	2	Richard Duddy Borsholder	

Borough of Whetsted

Chargeable		**Chargeable**	
Widdow Soman	3	Robert Plum[m]er	1
Anthony Judd	1	John Pattenden	2
Solomon Were	4	James Jenings	3
Robert Pattenden	2	Henry Wood	2
Thomas Kippin	4	Henry Plane	2
Thomas Fowle	4	Isaac Pack	11
John Allen	1	Goodman Lawrence	1
Nicholas Fishenden	3	Edward Game	1
Thomas Stone	2	Mr Paine's Heires	11

Not Chargeable		**Not Chargeable**	
John Page	1	Edward Moreley	1
Thomas Brookes	1	Edward Giles	1
Stephen Willard	1	Goodman Dunck	1
Goodman Lewis	1	Goodman Gour	1

| In an empty cottage | 1 | In an empty cottage
Steeven Woodgate
Borsholder | 1 |

Hunton Borough

Chargeable		Chargeable	
The Lady Fane	30	Mr Bishopp	7
Mr Beeston	16	Thomas Steddall	3
John Garford	6	Henry Cattlett	2
John Jarrett	1	John Smyth	2
John Bromfield	1	Richard Wood	1
Francis Parker	1	Richard Bankes	3
Thomas Ash	3	John Wood	3
Widdow Amhurst	4	Thomas Austen	5
Richard Barham	1	Robert Pett	3
Mr Early	4	George Cumber	4
Edward Holliman	3	Thomas Elliot	2
Widdow Rich	6	Thomas Bigg	5
John Reynalds	1	Thomas Whibley	1
Mrs Snatt	10	William Heath	1
Widdow Nash	3	John Merriam	1
John Manwarning	2	Widdow Furner	2
Thomas Catt	4	Michael Carpenter	1
Thomas Warly	2		
Michael Cooper	1		

Not Chargeable		Not Chargeable	
Thomas Bazeley	1	Robert Pawly	1
Widdow Piner	1	Thomas Bromfield	1
Christopher Holloway	1	Richard Chambers	1
Widdow Allen	1	William Bingham	1
William Barling	1	Widdow Stone	2
James Mercer	1	Matthew Dowle	1
John Boulton	1	Stephen Diprose	1
Lancelott French	1	John King	1
Richard Bennett	1		

[fol. 29A] [260]

---

[260] Located in this position in E179. This parish is contained on a single small section of parchment glued to the bottom of the folio.

In the
HUNDRED OF TWYFORD
in the said Lath of Aylesford

Parish of Watringbury

Chargeable		Chargeable	
Sir Tho[mas] Stile Barro[ne]t	22	Mrs Mary Scoles widd:	12
St Leger Codd gent[leman]	6	Mrs Deborah Codd widd:	11
Robert Crofts gent[lemen]	6	Benjamin Cutter cler[k]	4
Thomas Beckett }		Lawrence Evernden	4
att Westberies }	4	David Sandell	2
more at his other house	3	Elizabeth Hoppar widd	1
Thomas Palmar	3	John Sim[m]ons	4
William Olliver	3	Henry Sandell	2
Nicholas Orpine	2	William Pett	3
William Gosling	1	William Stone	1
Thomas Medhurst	1	John Moyse	2
Stephen Dann	2	Robert Weston	1
Thomas Mitchell	2	Thomas Castleden	2
Thomas Archole	1	William Raine	3
Thomas Lawrence	1	Edward Marshall	2
John Covie	1	Francis Cobb	1

Not Chargeable		Not Chargeable	
Thomas Pike	1	Samuell King	1
Widdow Tunbridge	1	James Gates	1
Thomas Tomsett	1	Widdow Evans	1
Walter Hilles	1	John Ridley	1
John Latter	1	Richard Young	2
Thomas Crouch	1	Thomas Grinsted	1
Thomas Oben	1	Widdow Gooldsmyth	1
Richard Stevens	1	Christopher Burden	2
Richard Dankes	1	Thomas Ellett	2
Edward Edmunds	1	John Pattenden }	
Isaac Newpett	2	Borsholder }	2

[fol. 29r continued]
THE HUNDRED OF LITTLEFIELD
In the Lath of Aylsford

Mereworth Parish

Chargeable		Chargeable	
In Mereworth Castle	23	Mr James Masters	21

Mr George Love	8	In the parsonage house	5
Thomas Crope	3	John Bridger	2
[fol. 29v]			
Widdow Foster	1	John Saunders	2
John Chaxell	1	Peter Swift	2
Widdow Dorman	2	Thomas Billingherst	1
Richard Broadbridge	2	John Browne	1
William Knell	2	John Holden	1
John Stone	2	Passwater Gessoppe	3
in Cheesman's house	2	John Hartum	1
George Everden	1	John Fenn jun[io]r	1
William Billingherst	1	Thomas Lewin	1
John Covell	1	Thomas Knell	1
Robert Faireman	2	Widdow Hopper	2
Thomas Stone	3	John Gardiner	1
Richard Sutton	1	George Hope	2
George Parker	1	George Darnham	1
Robert Cumber	2		

Not Chargeable		**Not Chargeable**	
Widdow Baker	1	Thomas Eason	1
William Glidd	1	Stephen Gardiner	1
Nicholas Collins	1	William Hartum	1
John Finn	1	Widdow Saxbie	1
Thomas Conford	1	John Cuckow	1
Widdow Moore	1	Richard Dunmoll	1
Thomas Hubbard	1	George Stone	1
Nicholas Hubbard	1	Widdow Jackett	1
Nicholas Holden	1	John Hayes	1
Thomas Cockerell	1	Robert Drinker	1
Robert Saxby	1	Widdow Hubbard	1
Thomas Dawson	1	John Comber	1
William Berry	1		

East Peckham Upper Borough

Chargeable		**Chargeable**	
S[i]r Robert Twisden Kt & Bart	30	Mr Samuell Grimes	4
Mr Ralph Love	2	Thomas Sum[m]ers	6
John Perkinson	3	Henry Godfry	1
Robert Arnoll	1	Anthony Hickmott	4
Walter Brooke	4	George Sedgwick	3
Widdow Smyth	1	Robert Milles	3

Marten Startupp	3	James Hunt	1
Arthur Cheesman	1	John Johnson	1
Josias Bell	2		

Not Chargeable		**Not Chargeable**	
John Jervis	2	Stephen Walter	1
Elizabeth Bates	1	Widdow Woodgate	1

Lone Borough

Chargeable		**Chargeable**	
Sr Humphrey Miller}		Thomas Whetnall Esq[ui]re	13
in an empty house }	4	Edward Manley gent	6
Richard Summers	4	James Hayes	1
John Knell	1		

| **Not Chargeable** | | **Not Chargeable** | |
| Thomas Som[m]ers | 1 | Widdow Luck | 1 |

West Packham Upper Borough

Chargeable		**Chargeable**	
William Clampard	7	Anthony Fayreman	6
Thomas Varnon	2	Samuell Coake	2
John Goodhue	3	Widdow Miller	3
Widdow Smallman	2	John Best	2
George Baker Esq	11	Widdow Dunmoll	2
Robert Stone	1	John Snell	1
William King	2	Francis Cary	1
John Eason	2	Clement Elfick	1
Isaac Honey	1		

Not Chargeable		**Not Chargeable**	
John Sutton	1	James Hernden	1
Jeremiah Dunck	1	John Bingham	1
William Carey	1	William Broaker	1
Widdow Lander	1		

THE HUNDRED OF BRENCHLEY & HORSMANDEN
In the Lath of Aylesford

Brenchley Towne Borough

Chargeable		Chargeable	
John Monckton cler[k]	4	Mr Thomas Marten	14
John Weston	7	William Woodgate	5
Widdow Pierceson	8	George Jarrett	1
Nicholas Fuggle	2	William Weston	1
William Chittenden	1	Mathias Pierceson	2
Walter Waggon	2	Nicholas Fishenden	3
Matthew Diamond	2	Nicholas Willard	1
William Wiblie	4	James Whatman	3
Thomas Overie	3	Nicholas Welles	2
William Bassage	4	Dunstane Foreman	1
William Pattenden	1	Amos Gatland	4
John Ware	2	George Scott	1
Edward Woody	4	Henry Corke	2
Isaac Shelley	2	Thomas Dann	2
John Ferrall jun[io]r	2	Thomas Corke	2
Widdow Wells	2	George Johnson	3
Anthony Huggate	3	William Dann	1
John Bishopp	6	John Bowles alias Eldridge	6
[fol. 30r]			
Thomas Broker	1	Edward Jarrett	1
Thomas Olliver	5	Richard Winton	2
Robert Nebbs	1	Robert Halfenden	1
John Sares	2	James Skinner	3
Thomas Waggon	2	James Pierceson	2
Roger Knell	1	George Pettoe	1
Edward Welch	1	James Hunt	3
John Austen	3	Thomas Wells	2
Richard Wells	3	Nicholas Burgess	4
Robert Burges	2	John Springate	6
William Cayly	2	Edward Walker	4
Richard Wymshurst	1	Widdow Austen	2
Mr Robert Collyer	6	Mr Thomas Brett	2
William Willard	1	Nicholas Swatland	2
Mrs Dorothy Fishenden	4	Stephen Hunt	6
Edward Pierceson	3	John Ferrall sen[io]r	2
Thomas Hayward	4	Edward Buggin	1
Margaret Hartridge	2	Thomas Stone	1
John Joy	2	Thomas Seereing	1

Walter Barton	1	John Swan alias Jeffery	2
Stephen Porter	1	William Porter	1
John Stringer	1	John Hickmott	2
William Hickmott	1	John Constable	1
Richard Bond	1	Thomas Chaxell	1
Goodman Banester	2	Edward Latter	3
James Godfrey	1	George Wyatt	2
John Stone	1	John Inge	1
John Pierceson	2	Richard Bray	2
Edward Salmon	1	Mr Christopher Suddell	3
John Wybourne	1	Edward Ragly	2
Robert French	1	William Burr	1
Widdow Monckton	2	Widdow Bennett	1
Thomas Larken	4	Richard Foreman	2
William Jarrett	2	Arthur Cackett	1
Tobias Austen	1	Preserve Lufe	1
Abraham Stringer	1	Widdow Scott	1
John Corke	1	Robert Ballard	1

Not Chargeable

William Ware	1	Daniell Hope	1
Richard King	1	William Chowneing	1
James Praule	1	George Cackett	1
Daniell Winton	1	Thomas Chaxell	1
Robert Rimmington	1	Walter Price	1
Robert Wiblie	1	Goodwife Palmer	1
George Fenn	1	Widdow Vinton	1
John Cockett	1	John Hyland	1
Widdow Fousden	1	Widdow Earle	1
Widdow Jarrett	1	Richard Hunter	1
Widdow Shinkfill	1	Goodman Kerry	1
Thomas Clarke	1	Francis Broker	1
Robert Jacob	1	Widdow Crayford	1
Richard Dawson	1	Widdow Casterell & }	
Widdow Stone	1	Widdow Large }	1
William Beckett	1	Goodman Chaxell	1
Thomas Dane	1	John Baker	2
Widdow Turner	2	Widdow Tomsitt	1
Henry Gatland	1	Widdow Clout	1
Godfrey Dane	1	Widdow Praule	1
Edward Hunter	1	Edward Winton	2
John Stedman	1	Widdow Helder	1
Widdow Dawkings	1	William Mitchell	1

| Thomas Howe | 2 | Matthew Diamond Borsholder | |

The Free Borough of Horsmanden

Chargeable		Chargeable	
Thomas Chamberlaine	2	Thomas Gray	4
Widdow Monck	2	Thomas Ongley	2
Thomas Hope	3	William Hollands	1
Peter Austen	2	Thomas Moate	2
Nicholas Rickard	1	George Wilson	1
Peter Adames	2	Stephen Hodge	1
John Keene	3	Thomas Willard	1
Thomas Hywood	2	William Beacon	4
Francis Austen	18	John Mirriam	4
Richard Bray	3	John Austen	1
William Twort	2	Richard Day	4
John Wickes	7	Thomas Russell	2
Richard Tadd	2	Thomas Tworte	2
John Hope	4	James Chamberleine	1
John Osbourne	3	John Couch clerk	7
John Hickmott	4	Henry Dawson	3
Thomas Hickmott	1	William Jarrett	4
Matthew Newby	4	William Pierceson	2
Francis Nevell	3	Abraham Wagorne	2
Edward Morgan	1	Isaac Shelley	1
Thomas Pierceson	2	Thomas Giles	2
George Russell	2	William Mercer	1

Not Chargeable		Not Chargeable	
Thomas Foster	1	Robert Faryer	1
Widdow Vennar	1	John Pullene	1
John Hodge	1	Widdow Whetnall	1
Widdow Rickwater	1	Widdow Whetnall	1
John Downeard	1	Thomas Perrene	2
Richard Glide	1	Dennis Geere	1
[fol. 30v]			
Henry Summers	1	George Day	1
Widdow Wood	1	John Farnes	1
John Deprose	2	Widdow Mitchell	2
Thomas Hollands	1	Widdow Chibald	1
John Dawkin	1	Widdow Rickwater	1
John Eastland	1	Thomas Giles Borsholder	

Burram alias Brantingberry Borough

Chargeable		Chargeable	
Alexander Courthop gent	16	Joseph Wagorne	3
Widdow Perren	4	Edward Hollands	1
James Daniell borsholder	1	Thomas Baker	1

Borough of Badmanden

Chargeable		Chargeable	
William Mercen	4	Benedict Brabon	2
[blank] Brooker	3	Thomas Towrt	1
Thomas Milles	1	Thomas Kirken	2
Stephen Kirken	3	Thomas Daniell	3
John Baker	1	Widdow Hollands	2
John Cheesman	1	Widdow Avard	3
John Barnes	5	Richard Tylor	3
John Hickmott	5	John Bowles	2
John Duke	1	John Bowles in an }	
William Knell	1	other house }	2
Daniell Evenden	2	Leonard Hickmott	2
William Hartridge	5	Richard Maynard	4

Not Chargeable		Not Chargeable	
Thomas Nebbs	1	Robert Hayward	1
John Wragly	1	John Atherall	1
Richard Eastland	1	Henry Dennis	1
William Foster	1	Widdow Baker	1
Edward Packham	1	John Cundly	1
John Wilson	1	William Thornton	1
Margaret Peckham	1	Stephen Atkins	1
Richard Wilson	2	John Marten	1
Daniell Chacksell	1	Henry Otmer	1
Widdow Wilson	1	Widdow Bowles	1
Widdow Jarrett	1	Thomas Kirken	1
Anthony Milles	2	John Hickmott Borsholder	

Borough of Lamberherst

Chargeable		Chargeable	
Mrs Ann Porter	19	Thomas Offley Esq	9
Henry Houghton Esq	7	William Wykes gent	6
Mrs Ellen Ballard	6	John Warthington clerk	6
Thomas Marten gent	5	William Neale gent	9
William Hunt	2	William Dewe gent	1
Richard Rabson	4	John Russell	3

Richard Weller	2	Thomas Tamkine	2
John Andrewes	2	Allen Wenn	2
Widdow Cheesman	2	Widdow Westbourne	1
Maurice Bassett	2	Widdow Dine	1

Not Chargeable		Not Chargeable	
John Roade	2	Nicholas Gutfale }	
Stephen Hunt	1	Amos Chitchenham }	2
Walter Copping	1	John Gutfale	1
Widdow Wood	1	Thomas Gyles	1
Widdow Pattenden }		John May	2
Widdow Baker }	2	William Neale Borsholder	

Borough of Beane Crouch

Chargeable		Chargeable	
William Dyke Esq	10	John Inge	7
Robert Wakelyne	4	Richard Perine	2
Robert Weekes	2	John Harmer	2
Thomas Saxbie	4	William Franckwell	2
Robert Hoadley	1	John Ferrall sen[io]r	4
Edward Cayley	1	Alexander Roberts gent }	
		hath digged up 3 hearthes }	

Not Chargeable		Not Chargeable	
John Russell	2	Henry Cooper	1
		Richard Perrin borsholder	

Teperedge Borough

Chargeable		Chargeable	
Mr Bolney	12	James Hartredge	3
John Eversfield	1	John Balden	1
Thomas Driver	4	Mathew Cruch	2
Stephen Cheesman	1	John Martin	1
John Albourne	1	Richard Larkin	2
William Watts	1	Widdow Larkin	1
Widdow Gobons	1	Mrs Wibourne	9
John Innges	4	Widdow Bishopp	4
William Mapsden	1	John Fowle	2
Thomas Knight	2	John Waggon	3
Francis Wilkins	1	Richard Marten	2
Edward Jones	1	Widdow Albourne	1
Nicholas Lesard	1		

Not Chargeable

Widdow Perrit	1	Widow Innge	1
Roger Fann	1	Thomas Brooke	1
Stephen Innge	1	John Lesere	1
Elizabeth Fann	1	Thomas Sennocke	2
Widdow Hutten	1	Sidney Vickery	1
William Cruch	1	John Martin borsholder	

[fol. 31r]

Bayham Borough

Chargeable

Peter Boulten	1	John Pattenden	1
Humphery Milles	3	Stephen Woodgate	3
David Eagles	3	Thomas Crundall	3
Robert Ware	2	Nicholas Gutsole	1
John Woodgate	2	John Chamberlaine	2
John Drowlie	3	Nicholas Allen	2
Edward Rayly	2	William Allen	1
Nicholas Read	1	Walter Brooker	2
William Brooker	2	John Humphrey	3
Walter Read	1	John Huggett	2
George Lambert	3	John Lamb	2
Henry Crookford	1	Widdow Wood	1
John Lawrence	1	Anthony Crookford	4
John Fuggle	2	Rychard Wymshurst	5
John Weston	2	Thomas Roberts	1
Josias Jeffrey	1	Richard Dawkins	1

Not Chargeable

Widdow Love	1	Widdow Joy	1
William Clowt	1	James Gutsall	1
Robert Stone	1	Widdow Paddock	1
Widdow King	1	John Bayley	1
Widdow Towner	1	Walter Russell	1
Widdow Lambert	2	Richard Brooker	1
John King	1	William Newman	1
		William Allen borsholder	

Abbies Borough

Chargeable

Edward Caylie	6	Thomas Burch	1
John Scott	2	Henry Large	2
John Pattenden	1	John Diprose	2

John Wells	1	Thomas Hooke	1
Thomas Dann	2	Arthur Nicholls	1
William Gibbons	4	Francis Claggett	1
John Tasker	2	Thomas Day	4
John Fishenden	6	Edward Russell	4
Mary Henley	4	William Russell	4
Thomas Read	1	Thomas Kebble	1
Mary Hawkes widd[ow]	2	Robert King	4
Widdow Marten	3	John May	3
Robert Buse	1	John Colman	3
John Carpenter	2	Richard Gam[m]on	1
Richard Brookes	1	John Weakes	1
William Walker	2	Francis Bewly	1
Mathew Wells	1	Thomas Turner	3
Thomas Fishenden	2	Abraham Eightacres	1
David Praul	1	John Grombridge	4
William Larking	1	Edward Russell in } an empty house }	1

Not Chargeable		Not Chargeable	
Richard Buggen	1	Thomas Croose	1
Richard Rencham	1	John Joy	1
Stephen Dawson	1	James Worley	1
Robert Lester	1	William Lester	1
Thomas Lawrence	1	John Groombridge borshold[e]r	

THE HUNDRED OF WACHELINGSTONE
In the Lath of Aylesford

Borden Borough

Chargeable		Chargeable	
M[aster] James Peate cler[k]	3	M[aste]r Downes	16
Edward Wooden	3	Henry Bristow	2
Thomas Worsley	1	Moses Bennett	3
William Wallis	4	William Mancer	2
John Polhill	3	George Cooke	1
James Harris	3	Thomas Latter	2
Thomas Gouldsmyth	3	Robert Marshall	2
John Acock	3	John Crowherst	3
William Latter jun[io]r	3	John Webb	1
Robert Woodman	3	Henry Hubbert	5
George Cooke	2	John Bacon	2

Anthony Elliot	1	Widdow Cackett	2
Clement Elliot	3	John Worsley	1
Thomas Archer	2	William Latter sen[io]r	5
John Wilkins	4	Robert Betts	2
M[aste]r Liegh	4	John Barton	3
Thomas Carter	4	William Wash	2
George Whitfield	6	Richard Stileman	4
William Turner	4	Henry Chalklin	2
Widdow Bennett	1	William Chalklin	2
Abraham Hosemer	1	Thomas Fry	2
William Eldredge	5	John Coulman	2
Goulding Johnson	2		

Not Chargeable		**Not Chargeable**	
Mathew Caverley	1	Robert Caverley	2
George Clarke	1	John Jefferey	1
Edward Chapman	1	Widdow Marden	1
Widdow Groombridge	1	Robert Pickall	1
John Greene	1	Widdow Wells	1
Dorothy Marchant	1	Francis Norman	1
William Elliot	1	John Cheesman	1
Elizabeth Hawkes	1	Widdow Cooke	1
John Fuller	1	Widdow Ring	1
Ralph Harnupp	2	Henry Hubart Borsholder	

Hall Borough

Chargeable		**Chargeable**	
S[i]r John Rivers	20	John Lucke	6
William May	4	William Constable	4
William Lockyer	5	Richard Flemen	1
John Hollamby	1	John Roberts	2
Humphrey Boroughs	1	Edward Cackett	1
Edward Everist	3	John Silcock	5
John Crondall	4	Manasses Gissopp	4
Daniell Waghorne	1	John Goldsmyth	2
Richard Beecher	2	Alexander Goldsmyth	2
John Betts	1	William Crayford	1
Edward Fry	2	Richard Ancock	2
Edward Cheesman	3	William Car[man]	1
[fol. 31v]			
Edward Medherst	2	Robert Goldsmyth	1
Widdow Duglas	4	Anthony King	1
Robert Hollamby	2	William Treape	2

William Clifton	2	John Osbourne	2
Sarah Gouldsmyth	1	Edward Fry jun[io]r	2
John Woodham	3	Jeremiah Gilford	1
Robert Lewis	1	Widdow Skinner	3
Richard Skinner	2	Roger Rogers	2
William Peerles	2	John Woodhams	1

Not Chargeable   **Not Chargeable**

John Crayford	2	Richard Brooker	2
Thomas Uridge	1	John Sares	1
John Grove	2	John Wallis	2
Thomas Theacher	1	Thomas Fulman	1
Widow Symonds	1	Nicholas Day	1
William Theacher	1	Edward Sares	1
Nathaniell Gissupp	1	Robert Sadler	1
Robert Hollamby jun[io]r	1	Thomas Goldsmyth	2
Thomas Cetch	1	Richard Skinner Borsholder	

Rusthall Borough

Chargeable   **Chargeable**

M[aste]r Kingsmeale widd[ow]	11	George Leader	7
Thomas Hunt sen[io]r	2	Edmund Archer	4
Reuben Jefferey	5	John Bloome	3
Thomas Jefferey	3	William Cox	6
Thomas Stace	1	Thomas Saxbie	2
Widdow Turner	8	Edmund Baker	5
Robert Dann	2	Robert Bourne	2
William Symons	1	Robert Hollamby	6
Widdow Marden	3	John Waggon	3
-		*interlined* Richard Coife	2
Widdow Coife	2	Stephen Hinsley gen[tleman]	4
Henry Jeffery	3	Thomas Cheesman	3
Thomas Humphrey	1	Henry Humphrey	4
Widdow Colbran	1	James Groombridge	1
Edward Jeffery	1	John Carryer	4
Thomas Appleby	2	S[i]r Richard Chiverton	6
Edward Jeffery	4	David Austen	3
John Wibourne	4	Widdow Weller	4
Edward Mercer	2	Thomas Fry iun[ior]	7

Not Chargeable

Mary Thetcher widd[ow]	2
Walter Bourne	1
John Thetcher	2
John Fulman	2
Thomas Hunt iun[ior]	2
John Carryer borsh[older]	

Not Chargeable

John Carryer	1
Francis Groombridge	1
Richard Petts	1
George Piper	2
Widdow Beecher	1

Speldhurst Borough

Chargeable

M[aste]r Pynson clerke} & Richard Lee }	7
M[aste]r Marten Pike	7
Widdow Harrison	2
Adam Farmer	3
Richard Hollamby	3
William Stymson	1
Richard Fann	3
Stephen Collegate	3
Everest Francks	1
Widdow Croudwell	4
Robert Collgate	1
James Caverly	1
William Croudwell	1
Nicholas Russell	1
Thomas Rogers	3
Widdow Childrens	7
William Van	2
William Longly	1
John Turner	8
John Fry sen[io]r	4
Edward Fry	3
John Saxby	2
Robert Curd	3
Robert Stretfield	3
William Dann	1
Reuben Ongley	3
William Jeffrey	1
Samuell Rogers	3
John Woodham	3
Edward Lambert	5
Thomas Rivers	2

Chargeable

Nicholas Ashdowne	5
Thomas Johnson	2
Stephen Moyce	1
William Avice	3
Shiers Constable	4
Peter Tooth	1
Widdow Abraham	1
Thomas Hollamby	3
Thomas Sudes	1
Richard Weller	1
Thomas Eldredge	3
John Mercer	1
Everest Francks	1
Robert Woodgate	3
Edward Hunt	1
Samuel Farnes	3
Thomas Waghorne	4
William Goodsall	2
Solomon Van	2
Richard Jeffrey	3
John Fry iun[ior]	3
Joshuah Weekes	2
Edward Sharpe in } an empty house }	4
Richard Wood	3
Jeremiah Gilbert	2
Samuell Waghorne	3
John Turner	4
John Cronke	4
John Wickenden	3
Stephen Hodgsken	3
John Longly	1

Not Chargeable		Not Chargeable	
Mark Collgate	1	William Turner	1
William Waghorne	1	Richard Waghorne	1
Widdow Tooth	1	John Morris	1
Widdow Harden	1	Katharine Nicholas	1
Widdow Coates	3	John Torly	2
Edward Waghorne	1	Widdow Apes	1
John Hollamby	1	John Turner	1
William Lambert	2	Widdow Jeffrey	1
Goodwife Venn	1	William Colbran	2
Widdow Young	2	Robert Inkepenn	1
Robert Turner	2	Robert Fulman	2
Widdow Wilcock	1	Richard Fulman	2
William Blunt	2	Damonickell Russell	1
John Weddington	2	John Richardson	1
Richard Turner	1	Alice Tooth	1
Edward Terrey	1	Edward Jeffrey	2
Christopher Durrant	2	William Curd	1
Widdow Jeffrey	1	Robert Curd	1
Edward Lambert borsholder			

Suneingley Borough

Chargeable		Chargeable	
Richard Amherst Esq[uire]	39	William Glover	3
William Field	3	William Huggett	4
Richard Buss	1	Widdow Turner	3
James Beach	1	Thomas Harris	2
John Sacker	1	Robert Baker	3
Thomas Larkin	3	William Snashall	4
John Mercer	2	John Raggett	2
John Gibbons	1	Thomas Dane	1
Widdow Turner	3	William Johnson	3
Thomas Avard	6	Thomas Uptaine	1
[fol. 32r]			
Widdow Walker	1	Thomas Ham[m]ond	3
Thomas Bayle	3	John Osbourne	4
Richard Sisley	1	Widdow Crouch	1
Richard Beng	3	William Sisley	2
Gabriell Hartnop	2	Robert Wood	1
Widdow Henwood	2	Thomas Gibbons	1
Richard Bell	4	John Earle	1
Richard Robson	4	Thomas Crouch	2
John Tayler	1	Peter Barton	2

John May	1	William Baker	2
Isaac Hartopp	1	William Huggat	1
Thomas Weller	1	John Sisley	1
Thomas Cackett	1	Francis Manktelow	1

Not Chargeable		**Not Chargeable**	
John Chatsfield	1	Widdow Willard	1
Thomas Alcock	1	Thomas Ginner	1
Phillip Champion	1	John Rootes	1
Widdow Hartnop	1	Richard Godfrey	1
Widdow Stone	1	Widow Turner	1
Widdow Urgoe	1	Widdow Mantlelow	1
Thomas Willard	1	Richard Turner	1
William Waters	1	Widdow Turner	1
Thomas Cackett	1	Edward Turner	1
William Glover	1	William Snashall Borsholder	

Tudley Borough

Chargeable		**Chargeable**	
Samuell Vanluer	4	Richard Dann	3
John Manings	6	Robert Day	4
Edward Falkner	3	Thomas Towen	2
Robert Gibbons	4	John Symons	3
Michael Banner	2	Francis Wood	4
John Ellis	1	Robert Mercer	1
Rowland Bewly	1	Richard Banner	3
Widdow Amherst	2	Stephen Masters	4
Moses Hodges	2	Robert Watman	2
Widdow Brooke	1	Widdow Willard	4
Michael Hartridge	4	Thomas Ellis	6
William Archer	3	Edward Balden	1
Widdow Milles	4	John Swatland	4
Briant Cackett	3	John Gibbons	1
William Waters	3	William Lorken	1
Henry Copper in the parsonage house	1	William Archer [in] Trowly Farme	2
Michael Hartridge	1	John Archer	1
John Fathers	1	Richard Allen	1

Not Chargeable		**Not Chargeable**	
Thomas Hodges	1	John Smyth	1
Richard Allen	2	Thomas Clarke	1

Andrew Thromings	2	John Willard	1
William Clarke	1	Lambard Clarke	1
Samuel Vanluer	1	Richard Dann	1
Robert Day	1	Robert Gibbons	1
Widdow Miles	1	Edward Falkner	1
Michael Banner	1	Widdow Bushell	1
Widdow Hensom	1	John Chesman	1
Edward Falkner Borsholder			

THE LOWY OF TUNBRIDGE
In the Lath of Aylesford

Tunbridge Towne

Chargeable		Chargeable	
William Dyke Esq[uire]	11	Doctor Amherst	11
M[aste]r Styleman	4	M[aste]r Christop[her] Wase	7
M[aste]r Thomas Weller	5	M[aste]r Thomas Rootes	5
M[aste]r George Hooper	3	John Bannester	3
Owen Brett	5	Francis Smyth	3
John Miller	4	George Barnaby	2
William Freeman	2	Thomas Johnson	2
Richard Wood	5	Nicholas Brooksted	2
Edward Moyse	4	Robert Wallis jun[io]r	2
John Birch	1	John Rootes	2
William Pierce	3	Richard Rootes [th]e carry[er]	3
Robert Wallis sen[io]r	2	Frances Carter widd[ow]	4
Alexander Rottenbridge	4	Giles Roberts	4
William Grigg	4	Nathaniel Ratchell	2
M[istres]s Weekes	6	John Inskipp	4
Edward Whitfield	7	Richard Rootes at [th]e Crowne	9
M[aste]r John Stretfield	3	Stephen Putland	4
John Rogers	4	Mary Milles widd[ow]	2
Humphrey Baldwyn	1	William Rootes	3
James Fowle	4	John Everest	2
Robert Wybourne	2	Thomas Olliver	4
William Driver jun[io]r	4	Thomas Marten	2
{Samuell Attersoll	2	M[aste]r Leake in }	
{more in an empty house	4	an empty house }	5
William Driver sen[io]r	4	John Rixon	2
Abraham Johnson	2	Oliver Bennett	8

Frances Wall widd[ow]	4	Elizabeth Rootes widd[ow]	4
Widow Kitchinham	2	George Rumney	5
Widdow Muggridge	3	M[aste]r George Pettley	9
Thomas Sweatman	1	Richard Gabe	2
Roger Strange	2	Robert Everest	1
Thomas Johnson [th]e	2	Widdow Ewridge	1
Maltman			
William Dalton	1	Daniel Piper	1
Henry Bartlett	2	John Willard	1
Nicholas Johnson	2	Richard Gardner	3
An empty house wherein }		In an empty house late }	
John Evenden dwelt }	2	John Wilkins dwelt in }	5
		[blank] Turner widd[ow]	2

Not Chargeable

Not Chargeable

Nicholas Parkes	1	William Hasleden	1
Edward Barnard	2	Thomas Barrett	2
John Hasleden	1	Richard Chowneing	3
Widdow Greenewood	2	Widdow Bennett	2
Edward Rootes	1	Robert Johnson	2
Richard Thornton sen[io]r	2	Richard Thornton jun[io]r	1
John Leneham	1	Thomas Harbrough	2
William Howe	3	Edward Pullinger	1
Henry Bartlett	2	John Wellar	2
Alexander Richardson	2	Robert Barrett	2
[fol. 32v]			
John Ireland	2	Thomas Brigden.	2
Samuel Evenden	2	Richard Horne	1
George Burges	1	Edward Richardson	2
John Dryland	2	John Luck	1
Richard Harman	1	John Burrell	1
Francis Nevell	1	Robert Turner	1
Mary Barrett widd[ow]	1	Andrew Hedgman	1
Edward Luffe	1	Widdow Sherley	1
Thomas Dennett }		Thomas Parker	1
& William Masters }	2	William Broughton	2
John Myssam	4	John Harris	1
Widdow Clarke	1	Thomas Constable	1
Edward Richardson	1	William Thorpe	1
Walter Coife	1	Joshua Whitfield	1
Richard Baker & }		John Kettle	4
John Johnson }	1	Richard Ashdowne	2
John Johnson	2	Widdow Attersoll	1

David Sherelock	1	Clement Ring	2
William Walter	1	Prawle Prawle	1
Thomas Maser	1	Robert Hanstead	2
John Boys	1	John Pickhurst	2
Thomas Argles	1	James Sherlock	2
Thomas Webb	1	Widdow Bartlett	2
Thomas Carter	1	James Pullinger	1
James Cavye	1	Widow Shakerly	1
Robert Heale	2	Sarah Marsh	2
John Rootes constable			
& Francis Smith borsh[older]			

Hadlow Borough

Chargeable		Chargeable	
S[i]r Richard Colebrand	6	M[istres]s Clemence Rivers	10
John Kirrill gent[leman]	9	William Lea gent[leman]	9
Richard May gent[leman]	5	Thomas Long	2
John Wells	3	George Cropp	5
Richard Snatt	3	Ann Pellham	4
Edward Sharpe	4	John Wallis	3
Thomas Bray	3	James Chamberline	6
Nicholas Hayman }	3	Robert Greneaway	3
more in North Frith }	1	Thomas Barton	10
George Turner	3	Thomas Rich	4
Francis Stoneham	1	Geoffry Austen	4
Stephen Denton	2	Andrew Archer	2
Alexander Rottenbridge	1	William Terry	2
Thomas Hayes	1	Thomas Pattenden	1
John Crud	4	Henry Barton	6
John Welles	1	Thomas Biggenden	1
John Bateman	4	Thomas Barton	1
John Neale	6	Henry Kebble	4
Widdow Rimington	4	Solomon Stevenson	1
Thomas Luck	4	Widdow Peirceson	1
Richard Battes	1	Jacob Burden	1
Robert Marten	1	Thomas Evenden	2
William Pawley	1	Mary Newman	3
Widdow Chambers	4	William Norman	1
Jorden Gilbert	6	Ralph Bennet	2
George Castle	1	Richard Fuggells	2
Thomas Fuggells	3	Thomas Hartredge	3
Thomas Brigden	3	William Pierce	3
William Wells	2	John Willard	1

George Betts	2	Robert Hubbell	2
Thomas Swatland	1	William Charlton	2
William Sum[m]er	1	John Walklin	2
Vincent Ashdowne	2	John Bourne	4
John Dennis	1	Thomas Long	1
Thomas Sharebrooke	1	Henry Inge	2
Solomon Pawley	10	Thomas Carnell	3
Robert Mosely	1	John Betts	1
Samuell Grimes	4	John Dussonn	3
Widdow Pawly	3	Hugh Banes	2
Edward Wildish	6	Solomon Newman	1
George Blacher	1	Nicholas Howe	2
Roger Vinten	1	Robert Baker	1
William Sands	1		

Not Chargeable		**Not Chargeable**	
Thomas Rolfe	1	John Easonn	2
Nevill Hayes	2	Richard Codd	1
Edward Wraight	1	Solomon Stevenson	2
John Goldfinch	1	Thomas Hodge	1
John Marten	1	Walter Marten	1
William Luck	1	Widdow Kiddall	1
John Nevill	1	Thomas Chalklin	2
James Hayes	2	Francis Sym[m]ons	2
Thomas Sym[m]ons	2	John Treppe	1
John Marten	1	Ann Baker	2
Symon Read	1	John Collens	1
Richard Dubell	1	Henry Luck	1
William Naysh	2	John Hayes	1
Thomas Pitt	2	Thomas Bishopp	2
John Chalklin	2	John Grinstead	1
George Luck	1	Thomas Watson	1
John Pattenden	2	William Brattle	1
Thomas Pattenden	2	Thomas Merrit	1
Thomas Phillipps	1	William Cockoe	1
William Standford	2	John Gooding	1
John Rolfe	2	Thomas Western	2
Nicholas Faucett	1	John Pavye	1
Nicholas Sym[m]ons	2	John Wyngett	1
Francis Turrill	2	Thomas Solomom	2
William Ball	1	Widdow Manings	1
Thomas Crowherst	1	William Boan	2
Henry Newman	1	Francis Luck	1

Thomas Read	1	John Peckham	1
Nevill Hayes	1	Richard Phillipps	1
Francis Rose	2	William Howe	1
Robert Webb	1	Thomas Tyrrell	2
John Punter	1	Widdow Moss	2
Robert Cheesman	3	Alexander Soman	1
Widdow Homard	2	Widdow Manley	1
Francis Gason	1	Richard Tuner	1
William Sanders borsholder			

[fol. 33r]

The East Part of Southborough

Chargeable		Chargeable	
The Lord Muskerry	15	Mary Williamson	2
William Howe	3	William Towne	4
Robert Everedge	1	Michaell Davis	2
Henry Cruttenden	5	William Larging	2
James Burges	2	William Baker	3
John Crosfield	3	John Tusson	2
James Godden	1	John Copper	7
John Gibbons	4	Briant Durtnall	4
Isaac Laffam	2	Thomas Ware	3
Richard Larking	3	John Fathers	1
Thomas Turner	4	John Swann	4
John Hookes	1		
Arthur Amherst Borshold[er]	2		

Not Chargeable		Not Chargeable	
William Godden	1	William Smyth	1
John Mitchell	1	Walter Fathers	1
Widdow Goodden	1	Thomas Cackett	1

The West part of South Borough

Chargeable		Chargeable	
Robert Ware	4	Alexander Rottenbridge	5
Edward Harbert	7	Richard Waller	4
Ann Jeffery widd[ow]	5	Peter Mercer	1
John Curd	3	{William Waghorne	3
John Rootes of Farriersgate	3	{In his owne house	2
John Bassett	3	John Mercer	6
Thomas Coyfe	2	William Pack	3
Jane Dive	2	Elizabeth Dive	2
Edward Mercer	4	Anthony Alcock	7

John Latter	4	Andrew Goldsmyth	4
Richard Mercer	2	Samuell Jeffrey	5
Henry Savidge	7	John Sturt	2
Mathew Sharpe	1	William Turk	3
John Wybourne	6	Richard Waghorne	2
Nicholas Dennett	1	John Stubbersfield	1
Susanna Lambert	1	Edward Jeffrey	7
John Chambers	2	John Rootes of tyle house	2
Thomas Woodgate	3	Richard May	3
Nicholas Crouch	1	Anthony Chittenden	1
John Goldsmyth	4	Stephen Dennett	3
Edward Mercer of [th]e forrest	1	John Collens	1
Richard Saxbie	5	William Jeffrey	3
William Walter	9	Thomas Chambers	3
Reuben Jeffrey	5	Thomas Kennard	3
Andrew Latter	3	Edward Rum[m]ings	2
John Maynard	1	Nicholas Marten	1
Edward Fry	2	William Mercer	3
Samuell Theobald	3	Grigory Staple	3
John Jeffrey	4	Roger Vinten	1
Richard Alcock	1	John Driver	2
Robert Waters	1		

Not Chargeable

Not Chargeable

Widdow Copping	1	Andrew Latter	1
John Lewen	3	Margaret Pagden	1
Widdow Curd	1	Michaell Lusted	1
Thomas Champ	2	Peter Harvey	2
Widdow Willard	1	Widdow Gyles	1
Widdow Gibbons	1	John Gallard	1
Widdow Marten	1	Edward Mercer	1
Widow Collens	1	Widdow Bates	1
Thomas Abraham	1	William Elliot	1
Widdow Marden	1	Widdow Bourne	1
Widdow Ashbey	1	Widdow Rummings	1
Widdow Johnson	1	Richard Crowcher	1
John Crowcher	1	Widdow Seaver	1
Thomas Fry	1	Edward Harris	1
Widdow Jeffrey	1	Widdow Williams	1
William Dane	1	Nicholas Cobb	1
William Etten	1	Edward Clubb	2
John Crouch	1	Paul Fissenden	1

John Sennock	1	William Greene	1
Thomas Renalds	1	John Staple	1
Goodman Ring	1	Widd[ow] Betcher	1
Widdow Walker	1	Thomas Wyncett	1
William Dickson	1	Samuel Theobald borsholder	

Helden Borough

Chargeable		Chargeable	
[blank] Earle of Leicester	40	M[aste]r William Saxbie	5
Henry Dixon Esq[uire]	18	Thomas Brasier	4
Widdow Reames	6	Thomas Howe	4
John Barkwell	2	William Walter	4
William Cozens	6	Widdow Francks	3
Edward Hadlow	4	Giles Webb	4
George Nicholas	1	Widdow Parker	3
Humphrey Couchman	3	Thomas Fowle	2
William Bostock	3	John Curd	4
Robert Noakes	2	Gilbert Wells	2
John Childrens	6	Widdow Childrens	3
William Fuller	9	Richard Polhill	5
Robert Goodghew	4	Giles Rogers	1
Roger Wall	4	Arthur Childrens sen[io]r	5
Arthur Childrens jun[io]r	3	Samuell Evenden	3
Zacharias Olliver	2	Symon Waters	3
John Rigsby	2	John Rawe	1
John Richardson	1	Symon Medherst	3
Thomas Bassett	2	William Barr	3
Nicholas Bardsworth	3	Widdow Powlten	2
John Turner	2	Richard Sanders	3
Richard Long	2	Arthur Nicholls	6
John Walter	1	Thomas Medherst	2
Thomas Austen	1	Andrew Milkham	2
John Waters	1	Widdow Webb	3
Richard Webb	3	Nicholas Kidder	2
[fol. 33v]			
William Woodgate	4	William Waters	4
Thomas Webb	2	Michaell Dane	2
George Finch	2	Thomas Turner	4
John Milles	3	Ambrose Page	2

Not Chargeable		Not Chargeable	
William Webb	1	Richard Bennett	1

William Lomus	1	John Radwell	1
John Boulter	1	Widdow Hodley	1
John Mepham	1	Edward Coomes	1
William Lockyer	2	Henry Chowneing	1
John Chaxsfield	1	John Stevens	1
Richard Hawks	1	John Austen	1
Richard Dammar	1	William Farrant	2
George Fuller	1	John Carpenter	2
Robert Austen	1	John Collens	1
William Johnson	1	James Medherst	1
Ambrose Page Borsholder			

THE HUNDRED OF LITTLE BARNEFIELD
in the Lath of Aylesford

Bromley Borough

Chargeable		Chargeable	
Thomas Colepepper Esq[uire]	15	Anthony Fowle Esq[uire]	10
Thomas Allison	2	Thomas Standen	2
Robert Browne	1	John Barber	1
Edmund Rawlins	2	Thomas Sibley	2
Thomas Polly	1	John Balcomb	4
Moses Cackett	2	Mark Gayes	1

Not Chargeable		Not Chargeable	
Katharine Jones widd[ow]	1	Peter Mancer	1
John Robins	1	Widdow Marten	2
John Beard	2	Thomas Pickerell	1
Widdow Bradds	1	Widdow Sampton	1
Richard Barrow	1	Thomas Ward	2

Combewell Borough

Chargeable		Chargeable	
Dame [blank] Campion	20	Morgan Standen	3
Francis Pierce for } the old pillory }	3	Francis Pierce for } the new pillory }	8
Sisely Seaton widd[ow]	4	Stephen Baker	1
Thomas Taylor	2	William Gaskin	1
Thomas Gaskin	2		

Not Chargeable		Not Chargeable	
Elizabeth Fletcher widd[ow]	1	Alexander Gayes	1
[blank] Santoe	1	*[blank]* Careley	1

Chingley Borough

Chargeable		Chargeable	
William Couchman	1	Robert Seaton	2
George Needler gent[leman]	10	Thomas Olive	4
Thomas Offley gent[leman]	1	Thomas Hughes	3
John Ham[m]ond	1	William Eastland	2
Edward Hinckley	3	Thomas Gabriell	2
William Lulham	4	Thomas Ollowe	2
John Parris	3		

Not Chargeable		Not Chargeable	
George Gurr	1	Thomas Stephens	1
William Lawrence	1	John Poyle	1
John Milles	1	William Downeward	1
Margarett Foord	1	Widdow Cooke	1
Widdow Primmer	1	Widdow Gibbons	1
Nicholas Fuller	1		

Lillesden Borough

Chargeable		Chargeable	
John Springett	6	John Austen	3
Thomas Austen	1	Robert Highwood	2
Richard Derrick	3	Stephen Cackett	2
William Taster	3		

Not Chargeable		Not Chargeable	
William Browne	1	Nicholas Walker	1
Thomas Apps	1	Widdow Franklyn	1
William Austen	1	Jeremiah Austen	1
George Seaton and }		Jeffery Glidd	1
William Austen }	1	James Austen	1
John Booreman	1		

Pattenden Borough

[Chargeable]		[Chargeable]	
Richard Batherst	4	Walter Austen	1
John Russell	1		
Thomas Hughes constable			

THE HUNDRED OF WROTHAM
In th[e] lath of Aylesford

Towne and Borough of Wrotham

Chargeable		Chargeable	
S[i]r John Rayney Barr[one]t	18	Reginald Peckham Esq[uire]	9
Joseph Burchett gent[leman]	6	{William Parker cler[k] }	
John Fielder	6	{ att the great house }	17
William Terry	3	{ att [th]e Parsonage house	6
Richard Wood	5	{ att [th]e Vicarage house	2
William Willard	3	John Storey	3
George Petter	4	William Sharpey	5
John Staley	2	Isaac Tomlin	5
John Alfrey	6	John Marten	2
Stephen Marten	3	Thomas Tilden	6
Thomas Caverley	2	George West	2
John Tunbridge	1	Robert Carpenter	2
Nicholas Skinner	5	Widdow Tomlin	4
Robert Ware	2	John Styles	4
Robert Gardner	3	Widdow Hadlow	4
Rober[t] Bright	2	Widdow Lampert	1
Widdow Gransbury	2	Thomas Nevell	1
Widdow Terrey	2	Thomas Assiter sen[io]r	4
[fol. 34r]			
William Terry's widdow	1	Robert Dorman	1
John Benson	2	John Alchin	1
William Harelden	1	John Sexton	2
Samuell Hawes	2	Widdow Grigory }	2
Mathew Huchford	2	alias Chowneing }	

Not Chargeable		Not Chargeable	
Thomas Bright	2	Thomas Murgin	2
Robert Berry	3	William Fenn	2
Charles Wibourne	2	Daniell Stimson	1
Mathew Mune	2	John Baker	1
Thomas Allen	1	Bartholomew Bristow	1
Edward Gouldsmyth	1	Widdow Fuller	1
Henry Parker	1	Thomas Assitter jun[io]r	2
Thomas Larkin	3	William Swift	2
John Burr	1	William Skinner	1
Jane Murgin	1	Thomas Bretter	1
George Cornford	1	Widdow Kitchen	1

Widow Smyth	1	Reignald Terrey	2
James Allen	1	Widdow Cooke	1
George Petter borsholder			

Rofeway Borough

Chargeable		Chargeable	
William Miller	4	William Sanders	4
David Harris	4	Henry Wood	2
Widdow Beck	3	Widdow Brattle	4
Robert Baldwin	3	James Thompson	1
Thomas Fann	2	William Pattenden	4
Thomas Bates	3	Thomas Godden	4
Thomas Newman	4	Stephen Swann	3
Widdow French	4	Nicholas Saxton	1
Thomas Jarret	1	John Baldwin	1
Robert Saxton	1	John Duck	4
George Costen	1	Robert Plomley	2
William Terry	1	M[istres]s Smyth and }	
		John Brattle }	4

Not Chargeable		Not Chargeable	
Widdow Fenn	1	Leonard Hadlow	1
Thomas Baxster	1	Richard Turall	1
Robert Fenn	1	Robert Egleston	1
George Dorman	1	John Fowle	1

Parish of Iteham

Chargeable		Chargeable	
S[i]r J[oh]n Sidley kn[igh]t		M[istres]s James	11
& Barr[one]t	19	James Hickford clerk	5
George Selbey Esq[uire] }		Reignald Baxter	6
William Selbey gent[leman] }	21	John Burnett	3
Widdow Milles	3	John Skinner	1
John Sylyard	2	Widdow Sanders	3
Stephen Summers	3	Ralph Hartwell	1
William Hawkes	2	William Shipley	1
Robert Webb	1	Mathew Lenn	2
Henry Edmunds	2	Abraham Sum[m]ersole	2
Thomas Sawyer	2	Nicholas Livermoore	1
Nicholas Barnes	1	William Turner	2
Widdow Allen	4	Thomas Edmonds	1
Richard Merrit	1	Richard Albert	2
Thomas Honey jun[io]r	2	William Parker	2

William Britlin	2	Widdow Richardson	1
Thomas Hooker	2	George West	2
William Hadsall	2	Widdow Hudsall	1
John Beechen	1	John Jennings	1
Nicholas Turner	1	Francis Polley	1
William Craft sen[io]r	3	S[i]r J[oh]n Sidley in ol Cleeres	
		inserted above 'empty'	4

Not Chargeable		**Not Chargeable**	
Thomas Charye	1	John Covell	1
Beniamin Morris	2	Thomas Honey sen[io]r	1
John Hawley	1	Robert Shooebridge	1
John Leedes	1	James Avarell	1
Edward Wood	1	John Taylor	1
William Craft	3	Widdow Venner	2
Thomas Bright	1	Robert Bright	1
Thomas Godfrey	2	George Fenn	1
Reignald Perrit	2	John Standen	1
Nicholas Wootten	1	Widdow Walker	1
Widdow Cooper	1	Widdow Milles	1
Widdow Fox	1	William Jones	1
Widdow Catt	1	John Laggett	1
Daniell Bird	1	Alice Sutten	1
Thomas Clampard	1	Widdow Alcock	1
Nicholas Saxton	1	Widdow Standen	1
William Catt	1	Widdow Claggett	1
Widdow Baker	1	Thomas Startfield	4
John Skinner borsholder			

Parish of Shipbourne

Chargeable		**Chargeable**	
William Coveney	5	Thomas Knight sen[io]r	5
Henry Crump	5	Henry Allen	3
David Wamseley	3	Stephen Batchelor	1
Walter Harman	2	Solomon Jupp	4
Francis Read	3	John Hubble	2
John Parker	2	William Hubble	2
Nicholas Collins	2	Thomas Miller	2
Thomas Knight jun[io]r	5	John Barr	1
John Collins	1	Henry Collins	1
Robert Harrison	1	Andrew Waters	1

John Buss	1	Widdow Goodwin	2
Thomas Couchman	2	Robert Masters	2
Francis Robson	4	Francis Berry	1
Thomas Williams	1	William Hayes	1
Walter Baker	1		

Not Chargeable		**Not Chargeable**	
Nicholas Knight	-	Anthony Harrison	-
Widdow Huggins	-	Thomas Paltock	-
William Webb	-	John Williams	-
[fol. 34v]			
George Stubberfield	-	Thomas Denton	-
Abraham Seaton	-	William Batchelor	-
John Atherfold	-		

Wimfield Borough

Chargeable		**Chargeable**	
M[aste]r Nicholas Milles	7	William Baldwin	7
Edmund Aieles	2	Richard Lorkin	1
Nicholas Hubble	2	Henry Thorneton	1
George Aieles sen[io]r	2	George Richardson	2
Mark Hubble jun[io]r	2	Richard Easland sen[io]r	2
William Ellett	2	William Baldwin	2
Robert Hubble	2	Thomas James	2
Alexander Peene	2	William Iffield	1
Thomas Iffield	1	Mark Hubble sen[io]r	1
John Terrey	1	Henry Hubble	2
George Baker	1	Edward Costen	1
Henry Iffield	2	Mark Adames	1

Not Chargeable		**Not Chargeable**	
Nicholas Mugg	2	Thomas Smyth	1
John Greene	1	Thomas Hubble	1
Robert Berry	1	Widdow Baldwin	1
Widdow Aieles	1	Widdow Brench	1
George Aieles	1	Widdow Walter	1
Thomas Austen	1	Richard Faint	1
Richard Smyth	1	Henry Fenn	1
Richard Smyth	1	William Blank	1
William Hilles	1	Edward Moyse	1
John Eaglestone	2	William Ellett Borsholder	

Hale Borough

Chargeable		Chargeable	
Dame Frances Vane	31	Thomas Standley gent[leman]	7
Mathew Darbey clar[k]	4	William Chownedge	5
Mark Gardner	2	William Furner	4
John Gallat and }		Thomas Pywell	2
John Wheeler }	3	Widdow Kebble	3
Thomas Everfield	3	Edward Coates	1
Walter Harman	2	Henry Collen	2
Richard Stevens	2	Sarah Newman	2
William Bennett	4	John Dorman	3
Robert Gorham	2	John Sam[m]on	1
Nicholas Berry	2	Bartholomew Ashenden	1
Beniamin Austen	1	James Carter Borsholder	3

Not Chargeable		Not Chargeable	
Thomas Ashenden sen[io]r	1	William Harris	1
Thomas Ashenden jun[io]r	1	Robert Dendy	1
Widdow Coger	1	Thomas Swann	1
Widdow Warren	1	Isaac Dann	1
Thomas Moyse	1	Richard Floud	1
James Balden	1	Widdow Chambers	1
Widdow Harris	1	William Eversfield	1
Widdow Rallison	1		

Neppecar Borough

Chargeable		Chargeable	
John Clerke Esq[uire]	15	M[aste]r Parrey	6
Thomas Tomlin	6	Richard Loane	8
Henry Tapsfield	3	John Benson	4
Richard Bassett	1	Thomas Everest	6
Valentine Holemsby }		Thomas Tapsfield	2
alias Nicholas }	17	George Ivell	1
Richard Cladding	2	Nicholas Sum[m]ers	4
Thomas Marten	7	Richard Milton	2
Widdow Carrier	2	Edward Bassett	2

Not Chargeable		Not Chargeable	
James Muns	2	Thomas Hinge	1
John Hinge	2	Richard Tooth	2
John Stimson	1	Richard Milton Borsholder	

Parish of Stansted

Chargeable		Chargeable	
M[aster] Will[ia]m Hodsall	4	Thomas Scudder	4
Bakers		William Scudder	5
{Thomas Lance	5	Francis Carpenter	3
{In another house	3	Moses Hodges and }	4
{In another house	3	Robert Hodges }	
William Bowman sen[io]r	3	Henry Lane	2
George Gibson	2	Jeffery Jorling	5
George Hilles	2	William Marten	3
Thomas Hall	3	Adam Barber	1
Edward Hall	3	Oliver Whiffin	2
Nicholas Fulkes	2	Elias Beale	1
Nicholas Mun	2	Thomas Whitehead	1
John Skinner	2	George Henham	1
Thomas Kettle	2	Joseph Ongley	1
M[istres] Topping	1	Robert Brewerly	1
M[aste]r Pegler	3		
William Bowman jun[io]r	1		

Not Chargeable		Not Chargeable	
Thomas Parvin	1	Widdow Baker	1
Richard Barber	1	Richard Brand	1
Reignald Bennett	1	William Cooke	2
Thomas Miller	2	John Chart	2
M[aste]r Pegler in an old }		Widdow Henham	1
brewhouse }	1	John Miller	1
		Thomas Hall borsholder	

[fol. 35r]

THE HUNDRED OF LARKEFEILD
In the Lath of Aylesford

Parish of East Malling

Chargeable		Chargeable	
S[i]r Thomas Twysden	23	William Tomlin	4
John Burgis	3	William Vidgeon	2
Moses Watts	3	Thomas Dowle	3
John Giles	3	Edmund Gilder	2
John Marten	3	Clement Dann	3
Edmund Gipson	1	James Watts	3
M[aste]r Thomas Furner	10	M[aste]r Thomas Furner	2
George Cotton	4	Alice Meeres	1

Isaac Gostling	4	Thomas Edwards	4
Robert Whittle	7	Richard Smyth	1
John Tomlyn	4	Francis Tomlyn	3
Robert Trott	1	Thomas Pack	2
Widdow Everden	3	William Tomlyn	3
Richard Short	3	George Luxford	4
Francis Ray	3	Richard Mott	3
George Baynard	3	Robert Palmer	3
Nicholas Ashdowne	2	Thomas Beeching	2
William Burgis	3	William Smeke	1
Nicholas Gillett	4	William Bourne	2
Edward May	2	James Lushford	1
John Basden	1	John Pack	2
Marten Ray	1	Josias Wootton	4
James Fletcher	7	Abraham Ashdowne	4
Joseph Tomlyn	1	M[istres]s Worrall	5
M[istres]s Codd	6	Robert Swann	2
James Kemsley	4	Edward Stretfield	3
John Gransden	5	James Fletcher	4
Walter Sybourne	3	John Pennyall	2
Charles Read	3	Thomas Newman jun[io]r	3
James Malim	2	Henry Munn	4
Thomas Worldridge	2	Hugh Nethersole	3
John Bond	1	Richard Goldsmith	2
Richard Shepheard	3	David Moone	3
John Johnson	3	George Garfar	3
William Dann	3	John Pack	2
Edward Milles	5	Henry Burden	4
John Hind	2	John King	2
Walter Tomlyn	3	Christopher Record	2
John Clements	3	Thomas Fletcher sen[io]r	2
Thomas Fletcher jun[io]r	2	John Haysted	3
Richard Smyth	2		

Not Chargeable		**Not Chargeable**	
Widdow Plumb	2	Richard Cox	2
Arthur Willard	1	Widdow Stone	2
William Cozens	2	Robert Clements	2
James Witte	1	John Turner	1
Richard Musedar	1	John Beeles	1
John Lounes	1	William Clarke	1
Richard Baker	1	George Baker	1
Richard Kennard	1	John Beecham	1

James Elfe	1	John Bright	1
Thomas Hopper	1	William Edmunds	1
George Fowler	1	Thomas Newman	1
Robert Rensted	1	Thomas Plumb	1
Henry Bigg	1	Samuel Ray	1
Henry Fenes	1	Edward Piwell	1
Edward Hune	1	George Chouner	1

Parish of Burham

Chargeable		Chargeable	
William Chambers	5	Stephen Kemsley	3
Thomas Chambers	5	Thomas Day	2
John Webb	3	William Usher	6
Nicholas Rayfield	2	John Wilkins	1
Robert Bewley	3	Thomas Boghurst jun[io]r	1
Symon Hilles	2	William Borrowes	1
John Faggon	1	Widdow Tilden	3
John Fryar	3	William Saxton	1
Anthony Balding	1	William Richardson	2
Giles Wadeley	1	Abraham Bensted	2

Not Chargeable		Not Chargeable	
Thomas Boghurst sen[io]r	1	Nicholas Boghurst	1
Francis Stevens	1	Mary Howe widd[ow]	1
Widdow Williams	1	Richard Beard	1
Robert Beale	3	John Wyat	1
Richard Lowdwell	1	John Webb borsholder	

Parish of Berling

Chargeable		Chargeable	
Michaell Rabbett cler[k]	4	John Bolton	4
James Garfores	4	Henry Castreet sen[io]r	2
William Knowles	3	John Huggins	5
William Everest	2	William Ellis	2
John Dann	1	George Ollive	3
John Baker	1	William Attwood	2
George Dennis	2	Thomas Busbridge	3
Thomas Greene	1	John Fetherston	1
Richard Knowles	2		
[fol.35v]			
Armigill Whiteing	2	Andrew Tanner	2
Henry Castreet jun[io]r	2	Walter Ollive	1
Thomas Luffe	3	John Luffe	1

William Curles	3	John Castreet	2
George Whiteing	1	John Goldwell	1
John Eastland	2	Nevill Godden	3
William Diker	3	Edmund Crowherst	1
William Nordish	1	George Grigory	1
George Gurr	1	William Hubbert	1
Widdow Cripps	3	Thomas Chambers	1
Arthur Archer	1		

Not Chargeable		**Not Chargeable**	
John Marshall	1	Richard Marshall	3
Thomas Buttler	1	Widdow Turner	1
William Olive	1	John Harrison	1
Daniell Nuttell	1	Joseph Truelock	2
Thomas Muglett	1	William Jenkins	1
Charles Butler	1	Richard Mare	1
Thomas Cleeves sen[io]r	1	Thomas Cleeves jun[io]r	1
Widdow Kerry	1	Thomas Briggs	1
James Williams	1	Robert Lewis	1
Armigill Whiting borsholder			

Parish of Woldham

Chargeable		**Chargeable**	
M[aste]r John Larking	5	M[aste]r William Nicholson	3
M[aste]r Thomas Manley	5	Thomas Nicholls	3
Symon Partrige	4	James Kingsnoth	2
John Pell	3	Elias Kemsley	4
John Claggett	1	Richard Harvey	1
Richard Parsons	2	John Ellyot	2
Thomas Kingsnoth	2		

Not Chargeable		**Not Chargeable**	
Robert Powell	1	Thomas Natt	1
William Enge	1	Thomas Hills	1
Widdow Godden	1	Widdow Haues	1
Widdow Booth	1	Widdow Wayman	1
Widdow Stuberfield	1	William Austen	1

Addington Parish

Chargeable		**Chargeable**	
M[istres]s Watton	10	William Pollhill	5
Peter Davis	4	M[istres]s Moreland	3
William Bing	6	Thomas Godden	5

Thomas Young	1	Thomas Couchman	4
John Gosling	2	Edward Crowherst	3
Thomas Hatch	2	John Ray	2
Richard Buggs	1	William Turner	2
Nicholas Brobson	5	Thomas Phillips	2
Thomas Mosebury	4	Richard Jackson	2
Anthony Ellis	2	John Buttinger	3
Henry Cogger	1	Thomas Blackman	1
Robert Woodier	1	Richard Knight	2
John Turner	4		

Not Chargeable

John Woodyer	1	William Southgate	1
James Welles	2	Thomas Harvie	1
Thomas Marten	1	Thomas Quarrinton	1
John Fescue	1		

Parish of Ditton

Chargeable

M[aste]r Brewer	9	James Hackett	3
John Palmer	2	Mary Palmer widd[ow]	2
Thomas Wood	3	Thomas Catleden	5
Anne Attwood	3	Robert Edmunds	4
John Miller	2	John Smyth	2
William Long	4	Thomas Ward	1
David Ray	7	Jesper Boreman	5
William Ham[m]ond	2	Thomas Miller	5
William Welch	2	In the parsonage house	5
Edward Baker	2		

Not Chargeable

| William Pretty | - |

Parish of Swadland

Chargeable

Thomas Garraway cler[k]	3	Thomas Williams	3
Richard Parker	4	Eliz[abeth] Causten widd[ow]	6
John Giles	5	William Pack	2
Samuell Batt	5	John Lambe	2
Thomas Wells	5	Nicholas Payne	2
William Read	2	Thomas Ray	5
Robert Bance	3	John Curd	2

George Savidge	4	Lawrence Duck	2
Thomas Mercer	2	John Short	2
John Scarlett	2	John Mercer	4
John Vowsden	2	Thomas Cox	1
Henry Collison	2	Thomas Powne	1
William Lambert	1	Stephen Howe	2
John Flower	2	James Pack	3
John Lander	1	William Gull	2
Widdow Thurston	2	Thomas Marten	2
William Clement	2	Nicholas Staines	1
Haman Ray of Paddlesworth	3		

[fol. 36r]

Not Chargeable		**Not Chargeable**	
William Panckes	3	Widdow Palmer	1
Thomas Carryer	2	John Mathews	1
Thomas Howlett	2	Thomas Buttler	1
Richard Johnson	1	Robert Wellard	1
Humphrey Gilbert	1	Thomas Parsons	1
Richard Pierceson	1	J[oh]n Cozens empty house	2
William Goteer	1	James Grinsted	2
Widdow Mumford	1	John Lamb borsholder	

Parish of Laybourne

Chargeable		**Chargeable**	
Robert Olliver gent[leman]	10	John Lorkin clerke	7
David Dane	5	Samuel French	3
Edward Dennis	5	Thomas Ayherst	3
Thomas Alchin	2	Widdow Beckett	2
Francis Short	2	Richard Cooper	2
William Day	2	Thomas Iden	2
Thomas Pledge	2	William Welch	3
John Welch	1	Richard Cooper borsholder	

Not Chargeable		**Not Chargeable**	
Thomas Durling	2	Widdow Bewman	4
Widdow Phipps	2	Widdow Milles	1

Alington and Preston

Chargeable		**Chargeable**	
The Lady Ashley	3	The lady Colepepper	27
M[aste]r Collins	11	Richard Draby	6

James Savidge	10	William Smyth	3
Robert Fann	2	Phillip Grave	2
John Walter	2	Skyre Hart	3
James Goulding	2	Francis Marshall	1
Giles Woodley	1	William Masters	2

Not Chargeable		Not Chargeable	
Widdow Parker	1	Robert Woollett	2
Thomas Milles	2	John Mooreland	2
Richard Stanford	2	William Pretty borsholder	2
Thomas Littleale	3	William Freeman	2

Parish of Raish

Chargeable		Chargeable	
William Dean	2	Edward Walsingham	4
John Watts	3	William Vsher	3
Thomas Lokley	2	George White	1
David Rich	4	William Edwards	2
John Coger	2	John Cooper	1
George Baynard	4	William Turley	2
Thomas Marten	3	Richard Boreman	3
William Browne	5	Gabriell Turrell	2
James French	2	George Hubbard	2
John Fletcher	4	John Palmer	2
John Birch	1	Richard Munns	1
Nicholas Tyrrell	3	Robert Walter	2
Nicholas Boreman	1	Edward Swann	2
Christopher Poot	2		

Not Chargeable		Not Chargeable	
John Gates	1	Margarett Fenn	1
John Fowsden	1	Thomas Farnett	1
William Newman	1	Elizabeth Foster	1
Thomas Whiteing	1	Edward Rootes	1
William Sym[m]ons	1	John Capen	2
Thomas Stone	1	Widdow Newman	1
Robert Walter Borsholder			

Parish of Offham

Chargeable		Chargeable	
M[aste]r Sampson	7	M[istres]s Clerke	4
John Austen	6	Richard Evans	5
Thomas Tresse	3	John Adyson sen[io]r	1

John Adyson iun[ior]	3	Thomas Palmer	2
Thomas Watts	3	Thomas Johnson	4
Thomas Scott	5	John Greene	7
Nicholas Wiggenden	1	Richard Rich	4
John Carr	1	John Wiggenden	1
William Knell	1	George Tapsfield	1
Edward Welch	1	Anthony Chamberlyn	1
William Gilbert	1	M[istres]s Wells	1

Not Chargeable		Not Chargeable	
Henry Hooke	1	Robert Stone	1
John Martin	1	Henry Broad	1
Thomas King	1	Henry Farby	1
Armigill Pennyal	1	William Eaglesfield	1
William Robinson	1	Thomas Scott borsholder	

THE HUNDRED OF HOO
In the lath of Aylesford

The Upper Halfe Hundred

Deane Borough

Chargeable		Chargeable	
John Pett	7	Thomas Pett	4
M[istres]s Dirkins heires	2	M[aste]r Mapeston	2
Richard Stockwell	2	Robert Barker	4
John Lay	4	Miles Taylor	1
Thomas Bennett	1	Richard Hooker	2
[fol. 36v]			
Ann Sanders widd[ow]	2	Clement Browne	3
Joseph Hammond	2	Roger Powell	1
Thomas Dove	1	William Godfrey	3
Thomas Bearman	2	Richard Belt	1
George London	1		

Not Chargeable		Not Chargeable	
Richard Elson	1	Widdow Coffing	1
Mary Wadman widd[ow]	1	William Lewer	1
M[istres]s Dirkin	1	George London	1
Widdow Stonnard	2		

Churchstreet Borough

Chargeable		Chargeable	
M[aste]r Howard clerk	4	John Plumley	2
John Olliver	4	Thomas Rankins	7
William Wood	3	Ann Scott widd[ow]	3
Joseph Hunt	1	Edward Weekes	2
Thomas Milles	1		

Not Chargeable		Not Chargeable	
Anthony Christian	1	John Bates	1
George Church	1	Matthew Geaton	1
Thomas Burley	2	William Starr	1
James Carman	2	Edward Jervis	1
John Barnes	1		

Boxley Borough

Chargeable		Chargeable	
William Cozens	8	William Pett	2
Elizabeth Long widd[ow]	5	John Clements	3
Phillip Boghurst	2	John Ayhurst	2
James Barber	2	M[istres]s Plumley	4

Pensone Borough

Chargeable		Chargeable	
Thomas Woodall	8	John Goldsmyth	4
James Pledge	3	Joseph Miller	5
Robert Dodd	4	John Loane	2
Henry Heath	2	William Scott	2
John Overy	2	Henry Frith	2
Thomas Sharpe	1	Nicholas Pledge	1

Longdowne Borough

Chargeable		Chargeable	
Israell Miller	7	William Holt	3
Richard Sherman	2	Edward Woodall	3
James Dane	3	Alice Olliver widd[ow]	3
Thomas Heath	2	Richard Sparkes	1
John Sacks	1	Jo[h]n Cart for Ropers	4
Sarah Church widd[ow]	1	John Tresler	1
William Stoakes	1		

High Halstow Borough

Chargeable		Chargeable	
George Cripps	5	James Fletcher	5
Edward Dunning	2	John Bond	3
John Mercy	4	William Lower	2
Richard Taber	1	Thomas Brewer	2
John Sharpe	3	Thomas Massey	1
William Lecester	2	Edmund Jeffryes	2
Edward Loft	3	Richard Brewer	3
William Taylor	1	Thomas Heath	5
Richard Pegrum	2	James Gates	1
John Loane	2	Peter Wood	1
John Lee	4	John Colewright	1
Thomas Hawkins	1	Thomas Dunning	4

Not Chargeable		Not Chargeable	
Ann Turner widd[ow]	2	John Tauntington	1
Thomas Wittam	1	John Plumley	2
David Marshall	2	Mary Heath	2
Edward Thurrock	2	Alice Gatling widd[ow]	5
John Wright	2	William Holt constable	

The Lower Halfe Hundred of Hoo

Parish of St Mary Barnstreet Borough

Chargeable		Chargeable	
M[aste]r Walter Berling cl[erk]	4	Nicholas Blacke	8
John Haisell	6	Phillip Raynes	5
Daniell Parker	5	James Lash	4
Robert Scott	2	John Milles	1
John Gill	2		

Not Chargeable		Not Chargeable	
Robert Moore	1	Edward Molins	1
John Baker	1	John Duke	1
William Humphrey	3		

Hardellfield Borough

Chargeable		Chargeable	
John Rootes	6	Thomas Bartlett	4
Benham Dufty	1	Peter Dewarfe	3
Edward Grew	2	Thomas Raines	1

Thomas Browne	3	Nicholas Duftey	2
Joseph Amos	1	James Payne	4
Richard Wood	2	John Lewes	4
John Woollett	4	Samuell Cheesman	5
Thomas Osmer	4	Alexander Chelsum	3

[fol. 37r]

Not Chargeable		Not Chargeable	
George Skiff	3	Jacob Bull	1
Richard Scultupp	1	James Burbridge	1
John Browne	1	Thomas Halsted	1
Thomas Bascum	1	Stephen Belinger	1
John Parker	1		

Inn Borough

Chargeable		Chargeable	
Barbarah Hollaway	5	Ralph Wood	4
John Chapman	4	Edmund Cozens	5
Dorothy Miller	2	Edward Woodkins	4
William Sanders	5	Edward Wilkins	2
William Couchman	4	John Buttler	2

Not Chargeable		Not Chargeable	
John Milner	2	Edward Good	1

Gavell Borough

Chargeable		Chargeable	
Thomas Ousmer	2	Thomas Jeffs	4
Thomas Lasell	3	Thomas Dodd	5
Adam Hills	2	Moses Watts	4
Richard Priscod	3		

Not Chargeable		Not Chargeable	
Samuel Marbrooke	1	William Turner	2
Symon Wooldridge	1	John Flint	1
Katharine Marsh	1	John Lason	2
Thomas Weekes	1	Henry Scott	2

Alhallowes Street Borough

Chargeable		Chargeable	
Edward Colbey	12	Thomas Bennett	2
John Wells	6	John Berry	3
Thomas Loft	3	Thomas Scott	5

Thomas Gill	3	George Bennett & }	
Richard Kent	2	John Gill }	3
George Bennett	2	Robert Cellock	2

Not Chargeable		**Not Chargeable**	
Mary Bishopp	1	Amos Gatland	1
John Day	1	James Westbrooke	2
John Packenden	1	Margery Rose	1
Elizabeth Downes	1	John Mortlock	1
Robert Throwley	1		

Slowe Borough

Chargeable		**Chargeable**	
Richard Michell	3	Thomas Burley	1
Henry Brewer	2	Michaell Andrewes	5
John Smyth	1	Jeremiah Rumbell	1
Thomas James	1	Richard Hayes	1
Robert Marsh	2		

Not Chargeable		**Not Chargeable**	
Eleanor Munson	1	Thomas Lewes	1
Jane Mitchell	3		
Samuel Cheesman constable			

Parish of Aylesford

Chargeable		**Chargeable**	
Sir John Banks	25	George Duke Esq.	15
Peter Philcott	5	John Taylor	10
Robert Kemsley	2	John Palmer	7
Stephen Roberts	1	John Godfrey	2
Robert Wayman	2	Thomas Dawson	2
Nicholas Rayfield	4	George Chowneing	4
Thomas Madgin	2	Robert Joy	2
William Godfrey	3	Thomas Edwards	2
Edward Clarke	7	Richard Wright	1
John French	1	Jeremiah Woodham	5
Edward Soman	1	Thomas Young	1
Widow Bunting	1	James Payne	2
Thomas Fryer	3	George Baldock	4
Nicholas Taylor	2	Edward Haynes	2
Thomas Smyth	2	William Swann	2
William Swinborne	3	Thomas Ward	5
Stephen Bligh	2	George Skinner	1

Not Chargeable

Thomas Jennings	1
Henry Milles	2
Henry Hollandsbey	1
Thomas Kennett	2
Widdow Ward	2
William Lilen	2
John Maynard	1
George Bird	1
William Chapman	1
Stephen Burley	1
Widdow Lott	1

Not Chargeable

John Jennings	1
Widdow Cox	2
John Greenwell	1
John Burchall	2
Robert Gillett	2
Edward Smyth	3
Robert Winton	2
Nicholas Wall	2
George Luck	1
John Marten	1
Nicholas Tayler	1

Rugmer Hill Borough

Chargeable

James Hollyman	4
Thomas Wilkins	3
Henry Dennis	1
William Richardson	1
Joseph Lasey	2
Widdow Coveney	2
Elizabeth Thetchers	1
John Welsh	3
Thomas Daw	1
Thomas Outred	1
Henry Trew	5
Thomas Smyth	3
Robert Cox	2
Christopher Hobert	3
Edward Chowne	3
John Eastland	1
[fol. 37v]	
Symon Hodges	2
George Eastland	1
Widdow Day	2
Thomas Booker	1
William Pierceson	3
Thomas Woodgate	2
John Bowles	4

Chargeable

William Wood	3
Widdow Marten	4
Peter Prane	2
William Stacey	1
William Fryman	1
James Hernden	1
Marten Richards	1
William Coveney	4
William Sherlock	2
Wal[t]er Outred	1
John Blackbourne	6
Nicholas Figg	4
Francis Parker	3
Maston Fleet	2
William Ramsden	1
Richard Tyler	2
Peter Everest	4
John Barton	1
Edward Downeard	2
William Diprose	1
Roger Pierceson	4
Thomas Boorne	3
Henry Golding	1

Not Chargeable

Edward Turner	1
Samuell Norman	1

Not Chargeable

William Garaman	2
William Polley	1

George Stoke	1	William Irinseede	1
Thomas Smith Borsholder			

Towne Malling
in the lath of Aylesford

Chargeable		Chargeable	
Mr Buffeild	6	John Stone	2
Mr Brewer	6	Thomas Jemmett in }	
Richard Turner	4	an empty house }	4
Mr Nicholas Geales	11	Henry Girdler	-
Richard Smyth	2	Mr Hodges	5
		Richard Chambers[261]	4
Thomas Lake	4	William Robins	4
Wyat Burden	3	Joseph Knock	1
Edward Sandall	6	Thomas Plane	1
Goodman Mills	1	Widdow Segar	2
James Smyth	4	William Jorden	4
Thomas Marten	3	Richard Groves	1
Thomas Whiteing	2	Samuel French	9
George Smyth	5	Nicholas Newsted	3
Joshuah Allen	1	Richard Smyth	4
Dorothy Chambers	6	William Wood	2
Dorothy Chambers in}		Moses Helby	3
an empty house }	4	John Weller	6
William Chambers	2	Thomas Davis	2
Richard Rogers	4	Thomas Baldwin	3
Widdow Bulfinch	2	Stephen Carpenter	2
John Collins	2	Mrs Hall in an empty house	7
Daniel Haltropp	3	Mr Weekly	3
John Turner	2	Edward Blackman	2
Samuel Elwood	4	Mr Chapman in }	
Mrs Terrey	2	an empty house }	7
Peter Boureman	4	William Waghorne	2
[blank] Edwards in }		Thomas Kedwell	4
an empty house }	2	Mathew Harvey	2
Widow Hunt	2	Samuell Hewett	
James Hartrum	1	Solomon Blackman in }	
John Clipwell	3	an empty house }	1
Mr Tress	8	Philipp Howlett	3
James Stinson	3	Mary Maynard	4
John Carpenter	1	Henry Cockerell	2

[261] Interlined entry.

Widdow Oben	2	Widdow Fuson	2
Edward Driver	2	Henry Gowers	2
Thomas Godden	5	Phillip Broadwater	1
Richard Wood	3	Francis Foreman	3
George Carter	2	Thomas Sigherst	2
Widdow Mouse	2	John Coulter	1
Walter Crouch	2	Thomas Baker	1
Thomas Watts	1	Thomas Looke	6
John Phipps	3	Edward Sedgwick	3
Henry Ady gent	5	Robert Coulter	2
Elizabeth Stanners	-	Mr Selby	10
Goodman Butler	1	John Pattenden	1
Edward Sedgwick in } an empty house }	2	Mr Ady in an } empty house }	2

Not Chargeable   **Not Chargeable**

Edward Miller	1	Widdow Hatch	1
Widdow Lewen	1	Widdow Fowler	1
John Terry	1	Robert Rose	1
Widdow Sculthorp	1	Robert Chambers	1
John Axom	1	Thomas Oben	1
Widow Powel	1	Widow Fereles	1
John Hewett	1	Widdow Gramplett	5
Nicholas Claggett	1	Thomas Sum[m]ers	2
Widdow Cape	1	Widdow Stanton	2
Anthony Gipson	3	Widdow Gosling	1
Widdow Turner	2	Valentine Stinson	1
Jonathan Stone	1	Widdow Chambers	1
Thomas Wybourne	1	Hercules Lake	1
Thomas Muzell	1	Widdow Larkin	2
Thomas Gray	1	Thomas Whiting	1
Thomas Smyth	1	Robert Word	1
[blank] Harris	1	Widdow Small	1
John Miller	2	[blank] Ewen	1
Phillip Allen	2	Thomas Smyth	1
Richard Brewer & James Hodges constables			

[fol. 37A]

HUNDRED OF HOO
in the Aylesford lath

The Borough of Oxinoth

Chargeable		Chargeable	
Sir Humphery Miller	18	Max[milian] Dalyson Esquire	10
Mr Dallender	4	Henry Wood	4
Robert Clampard	2	Stephen Chilman	2
William Stone	2	William Bassett	3
George Fenn	1	Thomas Pigeon	1
John Oliver	2	John Sifleet	2
William Terry	2	Geoffry Honny	2
Nicholas Luck	1	Widdow Godfrey	1
John Barker	2	William Henley	1

Not Chargeable		Not Chargeable	
William Dann	1	John James	1
Richard Gorger	1		

[fol. 38r]

THE HUNDRED OF MAIDSTONE
in the lath of Aylesford

Parish of Dettling

Chargeable		Chargeable	
Mr Nettler	11	Mr Fryday	3
John Rich sen[io]r	3	James Dabbs	5
John Rich jun[io]r	5	Robert Loudwell	1
John Rogers	1	Richard Wise	2
William Shornden	1	John Shornden	1
William Wellard	2	John Fryer	1
James Daines	2	Nicholas Browne	1
William Harvie	4	William Smyth	1
William Shawe	1	William Kemsley	1
John Hooker	1	Robert Philpott	1
John Hassell	2	Thomas Turner	4
Edward Kemsly	1	Samuel Staple	2
James May	2	Henry Hadlow	2
Marmaduke Weekes	2	Thomas Venner	2
George Chilman	4	Thomas Penny	2
Walter Crisfeild	4	Ralph Rayner	1

Not Chargeable

Robert Shornden	1
Hamond Hadlow	2
John Walter	2
Arthur Browne	1
Thomas Smyth	1
Thomas Shornden	2
Widdow Kemsley	1
Widdow Shawe	1
Widdow Fletcher	2
Widdow Peirceson	1
John Beesam Borsholder	

Not Chargeable

Peter Hassell	1
Richard Pollhill	1
Thomas Miles	1
John Roades	1
William Drew	3
John Lorkin	3
Widdow Vickhurst	1
Widdow Poplar	1
Widdow Crafford	1

Part of Stapleherst in the Borough of Dettling

Chargeable

William Cage Esq	17
John Beesam	2
James Baxter	1
William Fusonn	1
John Rooper	3
William Hilles	2
John Champes	4
William Page	3
Mrs Lusher widd	3
Francis Crompe widd	3

Chargeable

Francis Piper	1
Thomas Barnes	1
John Lorkin	1
John Spice	4
John Chambers	3
James Welles	1
John London	3
Jacob Scoone	4
Elizabeth Reeve widd	3
William Conny	1

Not Chargeable

Liveing Chilman	3
William Wodden	2

Not Chargeable

Widdow Curtis	1
John Beesam borsholder	

Parish of Boxley

Chargeable

Mr Haymes	4
Mr Bourne	12
Mr Higford	12
Mr Roope	11
John Wise	4
William Wallatt	3
Robert Hartrupp	9
Cosmon Lea	1
John Smyth	4
William Spice	3
William Godfrey	3

Chargeable

Mr Charlton	4
Mr Knatchbull	9
Mr Parker	7
Mrs Wyatt	5
The company of } Vintners }	10
Abraham Beckett	4
Thomas Mitchell	5
James Newman	1
Nicholas Gouldsmith	3
Walter Muddell	2

Nicholas Gouldsmyth	3	Richard Brooke	2
Thomas Jekin	2	William Porter	4
Widdow Gosling	1	William Austen	1
John Hinman	3	Jeffry Baker	2
Widdow Tollis	3	Richard Watts	1
Thomas Hall	2	Robert Paine	3
Robert Weekes	2	Robert Willard	1
Richard Betch	2	Thomas Powell	3
John Gouldsmyth	2	Thomas Turd	2
William Platt	3	George Wyatt	3
Thomas Taylor	7	Widow Hutchfur	2
Richard Marten	2	Ralph Covell	1
Thomas Burbidge	5	John Edmunds	2
Edward Hilles	2	Thomas Parker	2
John Smyth	2	George Champion	1
John Thorpe	1	Widdow Tilby	1
William Hartrupp	6	Robert Hine	1
John Beale	5	John Dabbs	3
John Charlton	3	John Milles	5
Nicholas Gouldsmyth	2	Francis Fryer	2
John Edmunds	2	William Mathewes	2
Widdow Heath	1	George Greenhood	3:
John Curb	1	Robert Langly	1
Thomas Bedham	1	Mrs Fryer	5
William Allard	4	Henry Fenner	3

Not Chargeable		**Not Chargeable**	
Thomas Well	1	John Muddell	1
Robert Rowe	1	Grigory Fuson	1
James Hadd	1	Daniell Baldock	2
Robert Swetser	1	Widdow Coven	1
Robert Platt	2	John Sanders	1
Richard Wilson	2	Widdow Knott	1
George Dann	4	Zachary Johnson	1
John Pryer	2	Peter Tayler	2
[fol. 38v]			
Richard Lewis	1	Widdow Bryant	1
John Drew	1	Thomas Kemp	2
Edmund Botting	1	Thomas Stueny	1
John Payne	1	James Ridge	1
John Baker	1	George Langly	1
James Betch	2	Henry Turner	1
Robert Jafarr	2	Phillipp Rowe	2

Richard Middows	1	Thomas Nicholas	1
Abraham Harpe	1	Thomas Bridge	2
Thomas Radge	1	Thomas Batler	2
Thomas Ward	2	Arthur Greenwood	1
John Hilles	1	Edmund Kidney	1
William Dadd	3	William Matthewes	4
John Browne	1	William Mallindell	2
Thomas Messey	6	James Hubbard	1
Widdow Harpe	2	Henry Pettendell	1
Widdow Knitt	1	George Crabbell	2
Thomas Ridge	1	Richard Masters	1
John Luce	1	John Partridge	1
Widdow Gouldsmyth	1	Henry Gilbert	1
Widdow Moore	2	Thomas Brenchley	1
Richard Chack	1	William Hacking	1
William Rowles	1	John Hiland	1
		Thomas Bedum borsholder	

Linton & Crockhurst

Chargeable		Chargeable	
Francis Barnham gent	6	Archibald Clinkard gentleman	14
Mrs Toke widd	5	Mrs Maplesden widd	2
Widdow Iden	2	John Charlton	5
Robert Goulding	3	Mr Thomas Maddox	2
James Iden	3	{Richard Rich	7
Edward Rich	3	{& in an empty house	1
Stephen Cheesman	2	Richard Mercer	3
Widdow Gull	7	Francis Startout	5
Thomas Chalker	3	David Steere	4
John Dine	3	Stephen Bassock	4
James Hadlow	2	Anthony Hearne	2
Roger Startout	3	Francis Godden	2
Edward Masters	1	John Burford	3
Jeremy Fleet	2	John Mason	1
Thomas Fowle	4	Thomas Masters	1
Thomas Durkin	3	William Buss	2
George Packs	2	Walter Marsh	2
Liveing French	1	George Charlton	3
Widdow Davis	2	{Christopher Hobert gent	8
Henry Webb	4	{More in an empty house	2
John Holliman	4	William Bishopp	3
{John Hunt	4	Nicholas Bishopp	6

{in his house at Savage	3	Nicholas Burford	2
John Noakes	1	William Gutsall	1
Richard Sum[m]erton	2	Henry Mannering	2
John Holland	1	Anthony Herne	3

Not Chargeable		**Not Chargeable**	
Henry Wood	2	Edward Buttler	2
Widdow Smyth	1	Richard Waters	1
William Miskin	1	John Waters	1
Widdow Holland	1	James Usmer	2
Edward Walker	2	James Wise	1
Widdow Masters	1	Mathew Medcalfe	1
Richard Stace	1	John Hearne	1
John Rennolls	1	John Munn	2
Widdow Knowlden	2	Giles Cutbush	4
William Munn	2	John Munion	1
Widdow Hearne	3	Thomas Lamb	2
Henry Soane	2	Widdow Frencham	4
Stephen Stockwell sen[io]r	2	Richard Embers	1
In the almes houses	4	John Dine Borsholder	

Barming

Chargeable		**Chargeable**	
Richard Webb Rector	9	Henry Goulding	4
John Webb	5	William Beckett	11
Thomas Penven	4	Anthony Holman	2
Francis Tomlin	2	Richard Coord	2
John Prebble	2	Elizabeth Fletcher widd	4
Widdow Peirce	1	Daniell Ashpoole	2
John French	3	Richard Bassuck	2
Richard Coale	1	Widdow Lanes	1
John Curtis	1		

Not Chargeable		**Not Chargeable**	
Isaac Beale	1	Edward Sacre	1
William Tupper	2	John Rennolds	1
Richard Beale	1	Richard Hyland	1
Widdow Barnett	1	Ambrose Seamarke	1
John Beckett	2	Widdow Beale	1
Richard Fearby	1	John Pett	1
George Overy	1	Daniel Ashpoole Borsholder	

East Farleigh

Chargeable		Chargeable	
Mrs Ward widdow	7	John Fuller	4
William Turke	2	Nicholas Amherst	9
Andrew Gull	3	Edward Feild	2
Francis Greene vicar	4	John Wood gent	7
Mris Lanes widdow	3	William Wesson	2
[blank] Preble widdow	2	William Godden gent	9
Robert Dennis	5	Steeven Crowe	1
[fol. 38Ar]			
[blank] Startout widdow	3	William Gouldsmith	2
Isaac Mitchell	1	[blank] Saxby widd	2
John Charleton	2	Thomas Comber	5
[blank] Iddenden widd	4	Robert Stubbersfeild	2
George Bigg	3	John Bigg	2
Frognall Fitch	3	John Cheeseman	4
Iden Allard	5	[blank] Dorman widd[ow]	5
Thomas Beale	2	Christopher Beale	1
Alexander Browne	3	James Groombridge	1
John Stubbersfeild	2	Edward Bedwell	2
Miles Whale	2	William Comber	3
John Goulding	3	Thomas Osborne	4
Edward Jarvis	3	John Everden	2
James Martin	5	Thomas Sculthrope	3
John Hinnes	2		

Not Chargeable		Not Chargeable	
William Mitchell	2	Gabriell Turner	1
John Ashpoole	1	Peter Scot	1
Joseph Lassey	1	William Taster	2
Thomas Sharpe	1	John Coveney	1
John Seamarke	1	Thomas Lownes	1
Henry Coveney	1	Nicholas Turner	1
William Crow	1	After Budds	2
James Kither	1	[blank] Cheene widdow	1
Nicholas Taster	1	Christopher Bigg	1
Francis Shepaster	1	Richard Southerden	1
Robert Groombridge sen[io]r	1	James Broman	1

Parish of Looze

Chargeable		Chargeable	
Mrs [blank] Beale	14	Thomas Medley	3

Lucius Seymer	4	Josias Nicholls	6
[fol. 38Av]			
William Charleton	4	William Gilbert	4
Walter Jones	2	John Peene	12
Henry Austen	7	James Tayler	3
[blank] Godden widbow	3	William Charleton junior	3
Abraham Page	2	Abell Crispe	7
John Charleton senior	4	John Charleton junior	3
Richard Parson	3	Richard Greene	3
Phillip Bassock	2	Thomas Springat	2
Thomas Eversden	3	William Masters	3
Thomas Martin	2	James Crownage	2
Henry Brooman junior	3	William Peene	4
William Browne	4	Jervas Coppen	2
William Swan	2	James Dednam	3
Steeven Cheesman	2	Robert Story	1
Thomas Crispe	2	[blank] Fisher widbow	2
John Rouse	3	Isaac Ware	2
Robert Pett	3	Thomas Crispe	3
William Mason	2	Abraham King	4
John Edmed	2	James Attwood	3
Anthony Chamberlin	1		

Not Chargeable		Not Chargeable	
[blank] Wells widbow	2	[blank] Brooman widbow	1
[blank] Haynes widbow	1	[blank] Wedd widbow	2
Edward Law	1	John Heymes	1
William Peke	1	[blank] Baker widbow	1
John Ware	2	[blank] Potter widbow	2
Phillippia Hoad	1	[blank] Willson widbow	1
William Young	1	John Wood	1
George Smith	1	Robert Wilkins	1
William Baker	2	Richard Jervis	2
Joane Hawkes	1	[blank] Hills widbow	1

[fol. 39r]

THE TOWNE OF MAIDSTONE
In the lath of Aylesford

The High Towne

Chargeable		Chargeable	
Dame Ann Asteley	18	John Merriam	2

Edward Jury	7	Mrs Elizabeth Romney widdow	5
John Tonge	4	James Newton	4
Lawrence Newton	5	William Sharparrow	3
Mrs Alice Cross widdow	2	Robert Joy	4
Mr George Ongley	7	Jeremy Smyth	4
Thomas Jetter	2	William Charlton	7
Thomas Blist	3	*[hole in parchment]*	
Walter Giles	13	*[hole in parchment]*	
John Carter	5	Margery Joy widdow	2
Thomas Benson	5	John Callant junior	8
Mr John Callant senior	8	Robert Ham[m]ond	2
James Longly	2	Mr Gervase Maplesden junior	3
Francis Tress	2	Robert Goare	4
John Goare	7	Henry Woollett	6
Stephen Weekes	7	Thomas Moore	4
Nicholas Roberts	5	Richard Duke Esquire	8
Dudly St Leager	7	Mrs Margaret Richardson	4
John Kitchingham	5	Frances Wall widdow	6
William Russell	3	Thomas Wall	3
Daniel Clarke	2	John Chandler	7
Samuell Wilson	3	Mr Alexander Hewes	6
Mr John Viney	4	Mr Edward Maplisden	8
Robert Padnar	1	Mr Thomas Gravett	4
Humphrey Boone	2	Mrs Mary Bestbeech widdow	6
Barnabus French	3	William Pelham	5
John Moyce	3	Ralph Mitchell	2
John Willard	2	Richard Roberts	4
William Gofford	6	Thomas Booker	2
Thomas Rowland	5	William Barefoote	2
Samuell Fletcher	5	Thomas Howting	9
John Gosling	3	Thomas Wood	9
James Lake	2	Gervase Scott	2
Thomas Marshall	7	Mr Gervase Heely	3
Mrs Dixon widdow	13	Thomas Hope	2
Augustine Hall	5	Mr George Tomlyn	7
Mr William Polhill	9	Jane Seager	2
Richard Walker	6	Mr Gervase Maplisden	8
Edmund Colvill	9	Robert James	5
Thomas Merriam	8	William Blackman	5
Mr Francis Lambe	5	Mrs Mary Golding	5

Mr William Bickford	17	Isaac Kilbourne	4
Robert Hayler	5	Richard Usborne	5
Thomas Walter jun[io]r	4	Thomas Walter sen[io]r	7
Mr Daniel Collins	7	John Lutwick	2
John Guardland	3	Mr Robert Brooke	10
John Barwick	5	Jonathan Sheppar	4
Mrs Margaret Boad	5	Richard Wick gent'	5
William Wildish	4	Robert Callant	8
Mr John Collins	6	Robert Brooke	3
Dr Shevan	5	Robert West	2
Mr James Ruse	8	Elizabeth Browne	2
Richard Feild	4	Christopher Lee	5
Thomas Tirrell	2	Nicholas Bodiam	3
Thomas Cowper	4	John Wilkes	6
James Woolball	5	William Acton	3
William Willard	7	John Downes	9
John Peirce	3	Samuell Wood	3
Mrs Elizabeth Webb	5		

Not Chargeable		**Not Chargeable**	
George Bensun	4	Sarah Browne	3
Solomon Gravett	1	James Dadson	1
John Bayford	2	William Smyth	1
Gabriell Beale	1	Thomas Whitebread	1
Thomas Cripps	2	William Tanner	1
Joseph Tyhurst	1	William Gooding	1
James Paine	1	John Hall	2
Thomas Scultupp	2	John Greeman	2
John Videon	2	John Beane jun[io]r	1
Henry Goff	5	Robert Gosford	1
Henry Wilson	3	Elizabeth Chambers	1
George Longly	1	Thomas Hammond	1
Thomas Butcher	1	Robert Lake	1
James Mason	2	Widdow Tonkerrell	2
Widdow Gosling	1	John Hills	1
Thomas Goffe	4		
[fol. 39v]			
Richard Hilles	1	Zachary Barrett	2
Robert Beane sen[io]r	2	Edward Boswell	2
Stephen House	1	John Percivall	2
Elizabeth Baldwin	1	William Cosford junior	2
Walter Jackson	3	Thomas Eason	2
Edward Barnett jun[io]r	2	Widdow Jones	1

William Wall	3	John Saywell	3
John Halsnod	3	John Woodgate	3
John Attoway	1	Dorothy Kipps	1
John Hills	1	James Sarys	6

Pudding Lane

Chargeable		Chargeable	
Mr John Thatcher	7	George Greene	5
Christopher Dawson	2	Bryan Holmes	3
Henry Hunt	2	Robert Cripps	2
William Maddox	2	Robert Pangborne	4

Mill Lane

Chargeable		Chargeable	
Thomas Hoad	3	Nicholas Rawling	2
Robert Cutbush	1	George Walker sen[io]r	4
Mathew Taylor	2	Henry Ayerst	4
Mrs Margarett Mors	2	John Carey	4
Robert Lake	5	Robert Bigg	5
John Paul	3	Abraham Whetland	2

Not Chargeable		Not Chargeable	
Elizabeth Moore	2	John Rewben	2
Alexander Gooding	4	Robert Sorry	2
James Medhurst	2	Deborah Branch	3
Clement Whiteing	2	Thomas Perriman	2
Alicia Reeve	2	Stephen Fowle	1
John Deacons	1	Mary Jackson in tenements	4
Mary Jackson	7	Richard Chambers	3
Robert Packnam	1	Edward Bourman	1
Robert Allard	2	John Watchers	2
Widow Post	1	Jane Palmer	2
Thomas Buttres	2	Edward Daniell	2
Edward Allen	1	Stephen Buttres	1
John Brumley	1	Henry Smyth	1
John Rogers	2	Phillipp Gilbert	1
Boney Wyden	2	[blank] Dawson	1
Abraham Beard jun[io]r	1	William Dann	2
Thomas English jun[io]r	2	John Dawson	2
Thomas Smyth	1	William Cully	1
Abraham Bensted	2	William Benge	2
William Buttres	2	James Newman	2
Thomas Rolfe	2	Richard Rummager	1

John Cleeve	2	Edward Atkins	4
Ellen Goseling	4	Henry Browne	2
Ann Maynard	2	John Richardson	1
John Hodges	2	William Cattlett sen[io]r	1
Matthew Brooke	3	Widow Marten	2
George Watts	2	Elizabeth Barret	1
Daniell Hilles	1	John Stonestreet	1
Abraham Eagles	1	James Wells	7
Widow Hoofer	3	Thomas Dodge	2
Jane Barrington	1	Thomas Acton	1
Christopher Baldwin	3	Widdow Jackson	2
Christopher Wilson	1	Richard Wassell	1
Mary Young	2	Edward Wilcock junior	2
Robert Leppar	3	William Sudgwick	1
George Willard	2	Widdow Pepper	1
John Younge	1	Thomas Burham	1
Richard Maylim	1	William Olliver	1
Robert Spice	1	Thomas Burbridge	1
Henry Smyth	1	Thomas Friend	1
John Bowden	1		
John Brooke	2	*[hole]*	
Mary Brooke	3		

Bullock Lane the Greene and the Waterside

Chargeable		Chargeable	
Mr Thomas Fletcher sen[io]r	10	Thomas Harlackenden Esq	15
William Maddox Esq.	8	Mr Caleb Banks	10
Thomas Fletcher jun[io]r	4	Dr Tartareene	8
Mr Michaell Altham	5	Michaell Whiteacre	3
Mrs Dorothy Biven widd	2	Mrs Elizabeth Aucher wid	6
Jo. Mortymer sen[io]r	2	James Hurt	3
Roger Comber	4	John Smalvill	5
Sir John Beale Barronet	19	Dr Levin Floud	7
Mrs Katherine Thomas widd	4	Richard Hill	4
[fol. 40r]			
William Weaver	4	Nicholas Masters	2
Richard Britcher	2	Thomas Swinnock	4
Mr Thomas Furner	3	John Wilmott	2
Widdow Godden	2	Edward Jackson	3

Not Chargeable		Not Chargeable	
Thomas Wickhouse	2	Francis Haimes	2
Widdow Wall	2	Robert Duxberry	4

Edward Knight	1	Francis Tonkerell	2
Richard Ternden	2	George Elfie	1
William Sharpe	3	William Tayler	1
John Haines	2	Samuel Bloudshew	1
George Conell	2	Elizabeth Jones	1
Elizabeth Carr widdow	3	Susan Weston widdow	1
Abraham Beard	1	Widdow Masters	1
Elizabeth Cresswell	2	Ann Beard	1
Elizabeth Longly	1	Samuell Wall	2
Susan Hayward	2	Thomas Buswell	2
Peter Marten	2	Thomas Cutbush	2
Thomas Smyth	2	Morgan Hall	1
Widdow Hawkins	2	John Cheesman	1
Francis Page	1	John Henman	1
Widdow Cox	1	Widdow Rolfe	1
James Medly	1	Richard Ebbs	2
Robert Mitchell	2	Peter Bay	2
Humphrey Porter	2	Thomas Singer senior	2
Ann Binfield	2	William Larkin	1
John Botten	1	Jane Miles Widdow	1
William Bromfeild	1	William Sparrow	1
Thomas English senior	1	Widdow Burham	1
Henry Greene	1	Richard Peirce	1
John Burbridge	2	John Larryman	2
Thomas Tapsell	2	John Ward	2
John Shimmings	2	Richard Ward	1
Richard Percival	1	Milmay Maplisden	2
Henry Backett	2	Francis Jones	2
Richard Ward senior	4	Richard Marsh	2
Anthony Parker	2	Ann Curles	4
Nicholas Munns	1	Thomas Syfleete	5
Daniell Collens	1	Cuthbert Collens	2
Mary Page	2	Cornelius Pollard	2
Robert Foster	2	George Tayler	3
Richard Eastry	2	William Muzzard	2
Thomas Allen	2	Widdow Sharpe	1
Elizabeth White	1	George Comber	2
David Bodiam	5	Thomas Wills	3
Robert Godden junior	2		

Wickstreet or the Borough of Wick

Chargeable		**Chargeable**	
Thomas Saxbey	10	Thomas Smyth	5

John Grinnell	4	Elizabeth Case widow	8
Mrs Pope widdow	7	Edward Maddox	3
Thomas Ellis	3	Henry Roberts	5
Henry Cobb	3	William Cox	6
Barnabas French	3	Thomas Willard	3
Thomas King	4	John Willard	3
Widdow Whiteman	4	Thomas Whiteman	2
Arthur Francis	3	William Hoad	4
William Mitchell	2	William Gooteer	7
Mr Robert Sanders	6	William Barrett	4
John Hayman	7	Henry Bentley	4
William Cattlett	4	Alexander Warren	3
Christopher Gorham	3	Mr John Godden	10
Arthur Harris	6	George Peirce	4
John Padner	3	Nicholas Hunt	2
Thomas Wattle	2	Mr Edward Barrington	10
George Tupper	12	John Buckhurst	4
Richard Hodges	6	Thomas Goatley	2
Henry Ruse	8	Mrs Hedgcock	16
Mrs Alice Cripps	10	Jane Boone widdow	3
Robert Barrett	4	Mrs Weekes widdow	7
Mr Caleb Bankes	6	Richard Farrance	2
John Hammond	2	John Blyth	6
William Turner	3	Mr John Cripps junior	6
Mr Nicholas Bennett	2	Mr Thomas Pett	7
Mr John Cripps senior	8	Robert Stiles	2
Walter Kingsnoth	4	Christopher Hernden	2
William Rutter	3	Widdow Platt	3
Thomas Skilton	4	John Mortymer	6
David Jones	15	Peter Harrison	4
Jonathan Troughton	2	Mrs Mary Smyth	12
John Tarry	12	John Woodfeild	5
Thomas Kipps	3	John Dennis in }	2
John Dennis	4	an empty house }	
[fol. 40v]			
Joane Ward widdow	2	Thomas Bond	4
William Startout	2	Robert Joy	2
Ellin Taylor	2	John Troughton	4
Rowland Lawrence	5	Widdow Hindes	3
William Clarke	4	Thomas Hoad	3
James Roach	5	Richard Huntly	2
Mr Griffith Hatley	9	Mr Thomas Woodward	4
Mrs Alicia Sanders	5	Thomas Venman	8

John Lanes	5	The Lady Culpeper	13
Mr Richard Billes	8	Thomas Rowland in }	3
John Austen	4	an empty house }	
John Godden	5	Caleb Woollett	6
Mr Jonathan Troughton	6	Gabriel Beckman	9
John Haines	3	Thomas Deane	4
John Osborne Esquire	12	Mrs Elizabeth Elmestone	6
Mr Richard Cripps	9	Peter Phipps	5
John Wharfe	4	Robert Godden	6
Mrs Luce Swinnock widdow	8	Dr Robert Stapeley	9
Henry Woods	1	William Broad	4
Repent Nicholls	5	Ann Bass	4
Henry Robins	6	John Redgway	3
Thomas Smoothing	7	Symon Goldwell	3
Thomas Whetstone	2	William Hoad	4
James Howe	3	Richard Symonson	2
John Banks	2	Robert Hurt	3
Francis Warren	2	Richard Marsh Esquire	8
Walter Francklyn Esquire	11	George Climpson	2
Mr John Crompe	9	Daniell Beekman	7
James Everstitch	3	John Dunning	8
Edward Wilcock	4	Samuell Ball	3
Mr Michael Beaver	9	Mr John Beale	6
Mr George Dennis	4	William Brett	3
Thomas Coppin	2	Mrs Ann Hunt widdow	2
John Mason	3	Mrs Sharpey widdow	2
Albion Bradshaw	6	Mr Lambert Godfrey	6
Mr Farnham Aldersey	8	Thomas Post	6
John Lanes junior	4		

Not Chargeable		**Not Chargeable**	
Abraham Double	2	George Taylor	3
Richard Peirce	2	Elizabeth Huggens	2
William Large	2	Mathew Tapley	2
Thomas Lake	2	Thomas Norman	1
Robert Parker	2	Abraham Goff	2
Thomas Farrance	2	Richard Chowneinge	2
John Kingsnod	3	Jacob Kipps	2
Nicholas Hixson	2	Thomas Hayman	1
Moses Tyhurst	2	Henry Rigden	2
Samuell Double	2	Richard Blunden	2
John Hoad junior	2	John Fry	2
James Beard	2	Paul Burges	1

Widdow Wickenden	2	Thomas Smyth	2
James Wanden	4	William Woollett	2
Elizabeth Bayford	1	Caleb Salmon	2
Mary Bush	1	Edward Cooke	2
Dennis Baker	2	James Boate	2
Thomas Lemmon	1	Christopher Mitchell	1
William Wood	1	Susann Fuller	1
Jane Hearne	2	Anne Leake	1
Robert Beckett	2	Richard Masters	1
Thomas Salmon	3	Deborah Broad	2
Ann Wood widdow	2	Samuell Moone	2
Sarah Chowning widdow	2	John Wraight	2
William Varnell	2	Francis Maylim	3
William Hoad junior	2	Nicholas Thomas	2
Edward Pollingham	6	Robert Moone	4
John Sutton	2	John Cheesman	2
Edward Tolhurst	1	Ralph Wilmott	1
Robert Pollard	2	John Fancombe	2
Thomas Mason	2	Israel Baker	2
Thomas Brice	2	Thomas Collison	1
Richard Burrish	2	Clement Savage	2
Edward Goff	2	Francis Marshall	2
John Brumfeild	2	Thomas Savage	2
John Tayler	1	Robert Savage	1
Henry Critwell	2	Robert Couchman	1
Edward Glover	1	John Sym[m]ons	2
Walter Tabor	2	Edward Pagett	2
Robert Brodnax	2	Thomas Barrett	1
John Young	2	Edward Brimsted	2
Samuel Poyle	1	Isaac Kilborne &	
		Francis Tresse borsholders	

East Lane

Chargeable		**Chargeable**	
Mr John Deerum	5	Mr James Allen	5
[fol. 41r]			
John Best	5	Richard Wattle	4
Richard Blaker	2	Gyles Clark	5
Joyce Merriam	2	George Baker Esquire	7
Mrs Codd widdow	4	Mr Warham Horsmanden	7
John Hoad senior	4	Mrs Mustred	6
Robert Bance	2	Edmund Goldwell	4
Mr Richard Harward	4	John Warren	2

Walter Woollett	2	William Wall	2
Robert Marsh	3	John Boone	3

Harbor Land

Chargeable		Chargeable	
Mrs Elizabeth Hall widdow	11	Margaret Stonestreet	7
George Stiles	3	Robert Hartridge	5
William Kitham	2	Edward Howting	2
John Howting	3		

West Tree

Chargeable		Chargeable	
Thomas English Esquire	12	John Savage senior	3
Richard Hubbard	4	John Wells	3
Mr Ambrose Melway	6	William Sorry	2
John Savage junior	4	John Champe	3
William Darby	4	Stephen Reinolds	4
Mr Alexander Roberts	9	Thomas Read	3
Robert Tubberd	2	Richard Pettingale	4
Robert Tilden	4	Thomas Goble	2
Thomas Videan	2	Thomas Sanders	4
William Baker	2		

Not Chargeable		Not Chargeable	
John Bishopp	1	John Ellis	2
Stephen Austen	1	James Brooke	1
Stephen Helbie	1	Edward Helbie	1
Phillip Darby	2	William Ilett	1
Edward Huggett	2	Robert Gilford	2
Nicholas Simmons	1	Edward Kempe	1
George Jeffrey	2	Daniell Lanes	2
William Masse	2	Edward Cripps	2
John Evans	2	Augustine Osborne	1
Henry Tubbert	1	Henry Brice	1
William Wilkins	1	David Carryer	1
Margaret Cowper	1	Hester Baker	1
Elizabeth Danzey	2	Mary Barret	1
Susan Brizleden	1	Widdow Smyth	1
Widdow Cleeve	1	Mary Fowle	2
Ann Shimmings	1	Edward Barnett senior	2
Richard Pany	2	Clement Savage borsholder	

Stone Borough

Chargeable		Chargeable	
Sir John Tufton knight		John Gray	4
and barronet	24	William Crispe	3
Edward Peirce	3	William Dynes	1
Clement Jones	3	George Marten	2
John Couchman	2	Widdow Hills	1
William Palmer	2	Augustine Pennial	2
John Dawes	1	Arthur May	5
Thomas Landen	2	Mathew Hailes	3
Richard Brenchley	2	Henry Course	5
Robert Shasted	2	Edward Souten	2
Henry Venner	1	Richard Rayman	4
Thomas Comber	5	Abraham Reeve	4
John Burbridge	4	Richard Harris	4
David Foard	6	Thomas Catlett	3
George Walker	4	Roger Eastry	1
Mrs Mary Harris	3	John Cage Esquire	8
Isaac Beard	3	John Dorman	2
Thomas Harris	9	Henry Course	5
Robert Shasted	2	Edward Souten	2
Henry Venner	1	John Dorman	2
Abaraham Reeve	4	Richard Rayman	4
John Bedwell	2	Thomas Walter	2
Mr Thomas Turner	13	John Tilden	5
John Wachers	5	Thomas Walker	5
John Stedman	4	Elizabeth Fowle	5
Symon Peene	3	Samuell Mercer	6
William Evernden	3	Robert Baseden	3
William Lanes	4	Stephen Bassock	2

Not Chargeable		Not Chargeable	
Robert Cheese	2	Robert Vane	1
Edward Ward	1	Stephen Lightfoot	1
Christopher Hill	2	Widdow Tayler	1
[fol. 41v]			
Widdow Hope	1	Richard Jenkins	1
Thomas Norman	2	Widdow Broadbrookes	1
John Champe	1	Widdow Greene	1
Thomas Pattison	1	John Hilles	2
John Rogers	1	Thomas Evans	1
Widdow Browne	2	John Allen	1
Daniell Stanyard	2	Robert Foster junior	1

Nicholas Clapson	1	James Allison	1
Christopher Tilman	4	Edward Post	2
Walter Bensted	2	Widdow Austen	2
Richard Nash	1	Thomas Wickner	2
Phillis Hilles widdow	2	Richard Mayne	1
Robert Hayse	2	George Bowman	1
John Gover	2	John Banes	2
Benjamin Archer	4	Augustine Parker	2
Thomas Burges	2	John Cockley	2
William Heeley	4	William Stone	1
John Cleeve	2	John Grinsted	2
George Bills	2	John Gull	2
Thomas Clapson	1	George Peene	2
Robert Barham	2	Arthur Bunyard	1
John Jeakins	1	Richard Haies	2
Samuell Argent	1	Nicholas Stephenson	4
Robert Gyles	2	John Giles	2
Thomas Turner	2	William Fowle	2
Edward Grinsted	4	Henry Cutbush	2
James Fowle	1	Widdow Aves	1
Robert Fenner	2	George Fenner	1
John Stockwell	1	Guy Willmott	3
George Masters	1	Widdow Hunt	2
Richard May	2	Alexander Breecher	3
John Chousman borsholder			
John Gore constable			

THE HUNDRED OF CHETHAM AND GILLINGHAM
In the lath of Aylesford

The Half Hundred of Chetham

Chargeable		Chargeable	
Peter Pett Esquire	12	Mr Phillipp Barrow	9
Mr Edward Grigory	9	Mr Phineas Pett	9
Captain John Crux	10	Mr William Bostock	7
Mr William Harman	4	Captain John Brock	11
Mr Daniell Bordwell	4	John Horting	2
William Ricketts	4	Robert Fitzhugh	7
Thomas Evens	4	Francis Marten	4
Robert Hogbin	4	John Salter	6
Richard Borten	2	Walter Warrinton	3
Stephen Lee	3	Margaret Bradford	2
In ye King's pay house	14	Capt. Phineas Pett	8

Capt. John Allen	8	Mr Joseph Fenn	5
Henry South	4	Mr John Browne	4
Henry Hartly	4	Thomas Wise	5
Thomas Stretton	7	John Smyth	3
John Rans	2	John Ross	2
David Hope	2	Sarah Feild	2
Thomas Eason	4	John Clinton	2
Robert Monke	1	John Williams	3
Roger Benson	4	Martin Aldridg	5
George Warner	2	Robert Tayler	4
John Gise	2	Stephen Wall	2
William Bedam	2	John Boyer	2
John Shepheard	2	Richard Yarwood	2
William Woodcott	4	William Tweny	2
William Marshall	2	Nicholas Fuller	2
John Cheesman	4	William Safford	6
John Spradberry	2	Jonas Hartropp	3
Robert Giles	4	Edward Springfeild	2
Richard Turner	2	William Linton	2
Richard Basset	2	Mr Henry Sheafe	12
Robert Eason	4	William Farrington	3
Thomas Denn	2	John Beckett	2
Thomas George	1	Thomas Badbey	4
Edward Rowden	5	Mr William Hempson	12
William Bright	3	Mr William Jenman	13
Isabell Larkin wid	3	Stephen Webb	3
Francis Britt	3	George Adams	2
John Weyett	3	John Jeffrey	3
James Marsh	6	Henry Adams	6
Thomas Browne	5	Savage Bott	2
[fol. 42r]			
Robert Clothier	5	Ambrose Louell	2
George Westerby	3	John Knight	8
Edward Vinckell	6	Samuell Maborne	4
Francis Sanders	3	Nicholas Grant	2
Thomas Smith	3	William Olliver	2
Susanna Walker	4	William Ammeare	3
John Misley	4	John Booke	4
John Roberts	3	Richard Gin	3
Elizabeth Rolf	7	Peter Bland	6
George Henis	4	Robert Abbott	2
Andrew Rogers	6	John Charles	3
John Charlton	4	Thomas Bulfinch	4

John Hereford	2	John Ferman	1
Richard Jones	3	Michael Ranells	2
Luke Abbott	1	Thomas Bray	4
Bennett Garrett	7	Lawrence Hadlow	7
Thomas Stock	2	John Short	4
Richard Jenman	7	John Handcraft	7
William Ataway	3	Mary Polman widd	4
John Ataway	5	Elizabeth Lowdell widd	3
Anthony Adsley	2	John Hunt	3
Sarah Long widd	3	Francis Miller	3
John Godfrey	2	John Cooper	2
Mathew Hacker	2	Thomas Stockwell	2
Henry Hartnapp	1	Thomas Best	3
George Everden	2	Edward Mumford	2
Thomas Swift	2	Phillip Leversuch	1
Mary Nordish widd	1	Thomas Foreman	5
William Godfry	2	William Marten	1
John Kemsley	2	Sisly Burly	2
John Hollaway	2	Peter Stevens	2
Abraham Lewes	3	Isaac Woodcott	2
William Wybourne	4	William Beast	2
Thomas Drye	3	John Holding	1
Caleb Herbert	3	Mary Stronge widd	6
Thomas Rivers	3	Thomas Hamly	2
William Kent	2	David Boldin	3
Reynald Carrier	1	John Marchant	6
Ambrose Evans	5	Thomas Leveret	1
Thomas Rose	2	Daniell Watson	2
Gilbert Favor	4	Thomas Yeates	3
Daniell Taynter	2	James Purett	3
James Almond	6	Thomas Swan	6
Walter Fletcher	3	Luke Rogers	3
John Jefferies	2	Robert Mathewes	2
John Hopkins	1	Nicholas Ramsden	2
Anthony Paul	3	Alexander Hubbard	2
Richard Penny	2	Thomas King	3
John Brooke	3	Edward Adds	3
Thomas Spragg	2	Edward Allen	3
John Eason	5	Symon Brinsden	2
John Fuller	6	Samuell Starlin	5
John Davis	4	Christopher Coward	3
David Heath	2	Mr John Lason	4
Humphrey Tunbridge	2	Elisha Dann	2

Henry Lee	3	Robert Mixson	4
Peter Williams	2	Mr Charles Boules	13
Richard Fereg	1	John Warham	1
Thomas Tunbridge	8	Grigory Jarman	4
Abigail Powell	6	William Marles	4
Nathaniel Holt	10	Joseph Lawrence	5
James Bens	7	William Skinner	3
John Morecock	4	Gabriel Walters	5
John Anger	4	Phillip Latly	6
John Marvell	5	Richard Begford	2
Edward Shering	7	Charles Smyth	8
Robert Dyer	4	Thomas Bensonn	8
Mary Perins widdow	4	Timothy Allin	4
Henry Young	7	Mr Robert Yardley	6
Thomas Simmons	4	Richard Faler	4
Rebecca Moxley	4	Robert Cottam	4
John Wood	8	James Hilton	3
Robert Sliter	4	Thomas Fletcher	7
William Pett	6	William Harding	4
John Phillipps	5	Roger Davis	5
Elizabeth Rabnett	2	Walter Dyer	7
Thomas Woodcock	2	Martin Symmons	6
Richard Cooke	7	Joseph Holland	5
John Cony	6	Thomas Hevysides	3
Mr William Gilbourne	6	Beniamin Slany	3
Thomas Arkinstall	5	Garrett Christmas	4
Michael Dodridge	3	Phillip Hix	5
Thomas Fuller	6	George Mablestone	2
Thomas Ford	3	John Haycraft	3
Thomas Downes	4	William Hose	2
John Bainard	6	Margaret Dixon	4
Robert Browne	3	Thomas Simmons	2
James Dankes	2	William Rigden	2
John Brice	1	Edward Smyth	3
John Garner	2	John Mathews	2
William Cassingall	2	Samuel Haddock	2
Thomas Rogers	4	Henry Brice	1
Thomas Godfrey	3	John Bowers	2
[fol. 42v]			
William Marles	4	Mathew Hanch	4
Thomas Wiggens	4	Robert Fitzhugh	2
Augustin Aldridge	5	Robert Morecock	8
Thomas Jemsenn	5	James Dixon	2

Elizabeth James	2	Thomas Browne	5
Richard Hilles	2	Dr Hardy Deane of Rochester	4
Sir Oliver Boteler	4	Phineas Pett	4
James Ansell	10	Mr Haward in 4 tenements	11
George Blingsly	5	John Morecock	5
Robert Castle	8	Thomas Hevysides	4
William Woodcott	2	Thomas Adames	4
Thomas Weggens	4	Samuel Starlin	3
Richard Hilles	4	John Devenish	4
Phineas Pett	5	Edward Vinckell	4
Thomas Smyth	8	Anthony Paul	3
John Charles	3	William Amneare	2
Thomas Browne miller	4		

Not Chargeable		Not Chargeable	
Joane Hoase	2	John Davis	2
Elinor Atresly	2	John Curtis	2
John Lambard	2	William Downeing	2
Thomas Halen	1	Edward Deane	2
William Bowers	1	Christopher Bland	2
Nathaniel Hookham	2	Henry Labourne	2
James Thomas	2	Ann Attaway	2
Nicholas Farnes	2	Richard Meriday	2
Jonathan Crimborne	2	John Curtis	2
Richard Comton	2	Stephen Rogers	2
Edward Young	2	Bennett Salbey	2
Mary Glover	2	John Hobkins	1
Jeremiah Salter	2	Richard Farvis	2
Thomas Allin	2	James Toms	2
Ann Eason widdow	2	Jennett Leverett	2
Mary Fletcher	2	Thomas Skipper	2
William Revett	2	William Cottam	2
Richard Whitedowne	2	John Sparrow	2
William Bensonn	3	Thomas Johnson	2
John Armitage	2	William Crowe	2
William Thomas	2	Francis Slawter	2
Thomas Hickman	2	Hugh Cox	2
Richard Flune	2	William Greenwood	2
Lawrence Keplin	1	James Woodcott	2
John Gore	3	Thomas Hover	2
William Holloway	1	Thomas Meares	1
Ralph Kelam	3	Henry Curle	2

John Huster	2	Thomas Adsly	2
Nehemiah Warden	2	William Boules	2
John Harnett	2	Richard Culton	2
John Browne	2	John Browne	2
Ann Osbee	2	Thomasin Allen	2
Francis Tomes	2	Thomas Burgis	2
William Rogers	2	John Cock	3
William Batly	2	Abigall Warden	3
Elizabeth Harding	4	Elizabeth Gosbey	4
William Tomson	1	Francis Read	2
William Hive	2	William Whatman	2
Mathew Joanes	2	Thomas George	4
Mary Price	4	Arthur Nalder	2
Robert Richman	3	Thomas Ransom	1
Henry Kepin	1	Mary Nors widdow	4
Elizabeth Easden	2	James Jolley	2
Thomas Wilkins	2	Ann Lester widdow	2
Robert Adsly	2	William Flavill	1
William Mares	1	Ann Man	2
Thomas Raynar	1	George Poly	2
Robert Lely	1	Henry Viner	2
Martha Leopard	2	John Buck	2
Gervase Muns	2	George Bond	3
James Day	2	Rebecca Skin	4
Edward Aldridge	2	John Boreman	2
John Davis	3	Robert Podd	2
Thomas Besbridge	2	Elizabeth Hall	2
John Tuckfield	4	John Johnson	1
Edward Pallintine	1	Edward Coveney	1
John Austen	1	Jeffry Adsly	1
John Eles	1	Widdow Smyth	2
William Farman	2	Edward Mount	1
James Lester	2	Nicholas Carden	1
Humphrey Bray	2	John Long	2
George Skidder	2	Thomas Fowler	2
Thomas Dennis	2	Peter Carter	3
Jesper Bretten	1	Richard Greenstreet	1
Thomas Freeman	1	Elizabeth Sanders	2
Nicholas Meares	1	John Humphrey	1
John Wickham	2	Widdow Toms	1
Robert Fitzhugh constable			

[fol. 43r]

The Half Hundred of Gillingham
In the said Lath of Aylesford

Chargeable		Chargeable	
Edmund Edridge	5	John White	2
John Goldupp	3	William Milles	3
William White	2	Robert Greenstreet	2
Widdow Wood	4	William Jennings	1
Sim[on] Hadlowe	2	Robert Coveny	4
Robert Jennings	2	Thomas Drew	3
Simion Peters	4	Richard Brissenden	3
Widdow Andrewes	1	William Lawrence	1
Richard Doe	1	Richard Midleton	2
Michael Floud	4	James Packenham	7
Henry Davis	4	Francis Toms	2
John Downes	3	Thomas Dodd	7
Edward Carpenter	7	Robert Cowper	3
John Gosley	1	Lewis Verchell	4
John Cosens	4	John Wilds	2
Richard Vaughhan	2	Adam Lorimor	4
John Siboon	2	William Aby	3
Henry Pett	2	John Noble	3
John Pollen	1	Joseph Ripton	1
John Plomley	2	Richard Buloe	2
Widdow Jackson	4	Jeremy Read	1
John Gooreley	2	Thomas Heyhoe	2
Silvester Wilmott	2	Thomas Johnson	2
Richard Rayner	3	Thomas Finey	3
Widdow Rainbow	2	John Batchelor	4
Robert Burden	7	Thomas May	2
John Jus	2	Edward Redman	2
Cornelius Paine	6	Thomas Maddison	1
Robert Moore	4	John Chapman	4
John Meadman	4	Richard Davis	4
Isaac Harish	1	John Buck	1
William Watkins	3	William Harish	1
William Barkley	7	Richard Hunt	1
William Fulk	2	John Sanders	3
John French	4	Thomas French	4
Samuell Tayler	4	Stephen Certein	5
Mathew Ball	4	William Sherbrook	2
Richard Williams	2	John Clements	3
George Warden	1	John Davis	2
Phillipp Fisher	5	Daniell Edridge	5

Thomas Carpenter	5	Thomas Freed	5
John Peirson	2	John Stewart	5
Edward Freed	2	William Reive	4
Richard London	2	Richard Cooper	2
John Godfrey	4	John Miller	4
Widdow Clarke	2	Richard Rich	4
Christopher Licence	1	John Carter	3
William Leich	3	Robert Pannell	3
Thomas Owens	3	Sim[on] Goodin	2
Richard Hart	3	Henry Davis	2
Robert Pidgeon	1	Edward Kilbee	1
Peter Osbourne	1	[blank] Dinis	1
John Hadloe	1	Christopher Cooke	2
John Leafgreene	4	Mr John Bayly	4
Alenton Painter gentleman	7		

In houses at present empty

William White	2	William Staden	2
Mr William Hutsford	2	Widdow Bradshaw	1
John Cosens	2	Edward Allen	3
Matthew Ball	2	Sim[on] Brice	4
Alington Painter	4	George Brice	2
Robert Moore	2	[blank] Lorimor's heirs	4
Robert Burden	9	where John Chapman lived	2
Edward Gooding	2	where John Siburne lived	2
John Clements	2	one house in Grain	5

Not Chargeable		Not Chargeable	
William Tresse	1	Widdow Wavell	2
Gilbert Hayward	2	Richard Burch	3
John Hubbert	1	Mathew Otway	3
William Jarvis	1	Thomas Mordige	1
Jerom Lambert	1	Widdow Buckland	2
Thomas Kettle	2	Thomas Langford	2
John Nevill	1	Thomas Flenn	4
Andrew Carpenter	4	Lewis Cheesman	2
Widdow Watchers	2	Thomas Mascall	2
George Pannell	6	Peter Dodson	2
Joseph Bockham	2	William Spratling	2
Nicholas Mitchell	2	Richard Hartrupp	2
Richard Swann	2	William Houting	2
Thomas Goures	2	John Gasell	2
Thomas Coveny	1	Ralph Triss	6

Widdow Jenings	1	Nicholas Neal	1
John Pidgeon	1	John Ramken	1
William Woodland	1	Thomas Gell	2
John Faircloth	2	Thomas Rainbow	1
William Duck	2	Robert Smith	1
John Barloe	2	Widdow Stacy	1
[fol. 43v]			
Widdow Suton	1	Widdow Cripps	1
Widdow Yeomans	3	John Fisher	1
John Steward Constable			

THE HUNDRED OF TOLTINGTROUGH
in the lath of Aylesford

The Upper Half Hundred

Mepham

Chargeable		Chargeable	
Mr William Gibson clarke	4	William Taylor senior	4
William Swift	10	Nicholas Butcher	5
Richard Haslyn	3	Nicholas Pigott	6
Richard Whiffin	5	John Child	4
Nicholas Edmeads	4	William Spreever	2
Robert Gunning	3	Richard Durling	2
Nicholas Mugg	2	Thomas Bogherst	2
Thomas Johnson	2	Widdow Everest	1
William Lawrence	1	William Bogherst	2
Henry Lofis	3	George Masters	3
Thomas French	1	John French	2
John Johnson	2	Henry Facer	2
Robert Warren	2	John Swift	2
Thomas Skermer junior	3	Henry Bell	2
Anthony Campe	2	Widdow Hasell	2
John Bright	1	Thomas Haies	1
Thomas Wouldham	4	Robert Tayler	5
John Lechford	3	Thomas Budd	2
Abraham Accus	2	William Lechford	2
Henry Kerby	1	John Bennett	2
John Henfold	2	Thomas Gransden	1
Edward Best	1	William Higgens	1
Thomas Skermer senior	1	Robert Cooke	3

East Borough

Chargeable		Chargeable	
Thomas Watts	2	William Bogherst	2
Widdow Edmeades	3	William Terry	2
Oliff Whiffen	4	John Boys	3
Thomas Hassee	2	Henry Masters	3
Edward Avarill	1	John Easdowne	2
William Johnson	1	Thomas Cooke	2
Richard Bright	2	William Gamball	1
William Nordash	2	Arthur Gunning	3
John Buttlee	2	Mathew Lofts	1
David Whiffin	2	William Fryer	1
John Hills	2	John Scudder	1
Jonah Pilcher	1	George Wellard	1
Richard Whiffin	5	Edward Lofts	2
Nicholas Haies	1	Thomas Burles	1
Robert Rutland	2	John Round	2
Widdow Welles	2	Thomas Smyth	1

In Mepham and Eastborough

Not Chargeable		Not Chargeable	
George Vane	2	Widdow Latter	1
[blank] Edwards	1	Robert Higgins	1
Thomas Richardson	1	Widdow Scudder	1
Abraham Kittle	2	Edward Gray	1
Nicholas Pullen	2	Gabraell Reeve	1
Henry Reeve	2	William Turner	1
Thomas Munn	2	John Reader	2
Christopher Downes	1	Martin Kittle	1
William Fookes	1	Henry Homan	1

East Borough [262]

John Wellard	2	Thomas Dunck	1
John Greene	1	John Munn	2
Richard Harwood	1	Henry Henfold	1
Edward Aylard	1	In 2 small tenements empty	3

Ludsdowne Parish

Chargeable		Chargeable	
William Whittle Rector	5	George Savage	4
Thomas Burgis	3	James Warren	6

---

[262] E179 given as Not Chargeable.

John Lane	3	Henry Stevens	2
Thomas Greenwell	1	William Greenwell	1
James Bogherst	2	Richard French	1
Widdow Sancock	2	Thomas Gillett	2
James Warren for }	3	Widdow Wellard	1
Hatchhouse }		Marten Godberry senior	2
Marten Godbury junior	3	William Thompson	2
Robert Cooke of Mepham }		Arnold Brasier	2
in two houses }	2	James Edmeades	1
George Easdowne	1	*[blank]* Waite	1

Not Chargeable

		Not Chargeable	
Widdow Edmeades	1	Widdow Brasier	1
John Finch	1	Henry Goodies	1
Thomas Bennet	1	Widdow Harwood	1
Sibine Rolfe	3	John Daniell	5

Nursted

Chargeable

		Chargeable	
Robert Edmeades	6	Thomas Slaughter	6
Hackett Batt	2	William Gransden	2
Moses Scudder	1		

Not Chargeable

Widdow Fox	1	Nicholas Pigott constable etc.	

[fol. 44Ar]
The Lower Half Hundred of Toltingtrough

Gravesend Towne

Chargeable

		Chargeable	
Thomas Murfeild	2	Thomas Clarke	7
Richard Street	1	John Reddall	15
Phillip Freeman	1	James Guildford	8
Thomas Bonn	11	Edward Fisher	8
Phineas Riggs	2	Richard Carpenter	2
Richard Eades	2	Richard Dunn	2
[blank] Cambey widdow	2	John Bassum	2
Edward Ockenden	1	William Naylor	9
Robert Cole	3	Laurence Holcar	4
Mr Edward Pelling	5	Thomas Greene	1
Thomas Harrison	1	Thomas Thames	1
Thomas Hudson	1	Edward Eglintine	1

William Hall	1	Andrew Hudson	1
[blank] Brafferton widdow	2	Mr Samuel Harwar	12
Thomas Windman	2	John Hanson	5
William Scarr	4	Nicholas Nelson	4
[blank] Feild widdow	2	George Rogers	2
John Adamson	2	Robert Tilley	1
Thomas Thackes	2	William Carden	1
[blank] Winn widdow	1	William Spenall	2
William Packe	2	*[blank]* Starr widdow	2
Mrs Irish	2	John Hall	2
[blank] Edmunds	2	Henry Gayly	4
Mr John Morris	8	Daniell Bowell	7
Nicholas Brooke	4	Robert Birkett	5
Thomas Ford	4	Michaell Butter	2
Thomas Dove	3	Mr William Lister	7
William Kempsall	5	William Curtis	1
John Tomlin	1	George Kirby	2
[blank] Ridley widdow	1	*[blank]* Rugg widdow	2
John Duffield	2	John Munns	2
John Mandy	2	*[blank]* Holmes	2
[blank] Rippon widdow	2	John Smith	1
James Littlewood	1	Thomas Moulton	3
Richard Brittaine	2	James Collett	4
Barnard Gilbert	2	Roger Gilbert	2
William Stevens	1	John Foach	1
George Carpenter	2	Thomas Mears	2
Thomas Collett	2	Thomas Archpoll	2
Robert Flowers	2	Thomas Lake	1
Henry Fenn	2	John Wheatley	3
[blank] Woodfield widdow	2	John Dawes	2
John Rich	2	Mathew Arnold	2

West Streete South Side

Chargeable		Chargeable	
Samuel Hall	5	Robert Day	2
George Ball	2	Henry Hughes	3
[blank] Stainer widdow	2	Richard Gilbert	2
Edward Webb	3	*[blank]* Watson widdow	2
Henry Kirby	2	Henry Harris	2
William Mathewes	2	Edward Read	2
Richard Read	4	Thomas White	3
William Riggs	2	Nicholas Suckley	4
[blank] Rogers widdow	4	John Gramsden	2

James Lambe	1	Thomas Goodman	2
Thomas Wellard	3	William Scarr	5
John Symons	2	John Triggs	2
John Codwell	2	John Preston	5
Thomas Nash	3	Samuel Bayly	3
Thomas Hamond	2	Christopher Saxby	3
John Eagle	2	John Harris	2
Peter Goodman	2	Thomas Sayer	1
James Lambe	2	John Hills	2
John Fettyplace	5	Edward Fusty	2
Nicholas Osbourne	5	Thomas Woodgate	3
Thomas Wilkinson	3	Robert Webb	5
Richard Rockwell	2	Mr Thomas Woodcot	9
Mary Batt	9	William Dove	12
John Castleton	5	John Cheesman	10
John Ryder	9	Steven Allinson	2
Mr John Watson	4	Mr Richard Beane	6
John Watkins	6	Henry Harris	5
Robert Masters	3	William Crouch	9
William Noble	12	George Tickle	8
Mr Samuel Barlett	4	Henry Lance	9
Thomas Bromfield	11	Mr John May	6
William Read	4	Benjamin Brooke	7
Robert Stacy	2	John Hoadley	3
John Leeds	2	John Edwards	3
[blank] Henson widdow	7	James Smith	2
Richard Parker	2	Edward Hares	1
William Yeomans	3	Thomas Hills	3
William Biddle	5	Henry Pease	1
John Hawkins	1	John Gadge	2
John Cheesman	4	Thomas Wood	5
William Pride	3	John Clarke	3
Thomas Watkins	2	Robert Ricketts	2
Nicholas Webb	4	John Jones	4
Gilbert Haselby	4	Simon Osborne	2
Christopher Luther	2	Richard Acy	2
[fol. 44Av]			
Simon Hickes	7	Marke White	2
Elias Grigson	4	William Gattlett	5
Francis Lance	1	Thomas Sawyer	2
Henry Rugg	1	[blank] Ninne widdow	3
Thomas Worley	2	John Fox	1
Thomas Webb	1	Thomas Bowden	3

[blank] Hartford widdow	5	Robert Stacy	4
[blank] Hills widdow	1	Richard Brigham	2
[blank] Butcher widdow	2	Mathew Robinson	1
John Mitchell	1	Nicholas Wright	1
James Kempe	1	Richard Bild	1
James Kadwell	1	Thomas Poore	1
James Holdstoke	2	John Langford	2
[blank] Laun widdow	1	Thomas Sluce	2
Richard Rye	2	George Gibbons	1
Thomas Darnell	1	Richard Silverwood	1
Richard Hartley	1	*[blank]* Burges widdow	1
John Gray	1	Richard Coston	1
Giles Lawrence	1	Richard Stammer	4
Jone Mann	4	William West	4
Henry Clarke	2	*[blank]* Nowell widdow	3

Empty houses in Gravesend

Phillip Freeman	1	*[blank]* Cumber widdow	2
William Scarr	4	Thomas Thornes	1
William Packe	2	*[blank]* Ninn widdow	2
Thomas Dove	4	William Kempsall	5
Katherine Ridley	1	Luce Parker	1
Elizabeth Rippon	2	James Lambe	1
Thomas Goodman	2	Richard Collins sen[io]r	2
John Grainsden	2	William Birde	4
Widdow Wheatland	1	Thomas Wood	5
Alice Durnall	2	Simon Hicks	7
Samuell Hall	2	Henry Austin	2
William Dove	1	John Wharfe	2
Richard Clarke	6	John Jackson	4
Francis Lane	2	Henry Payne	2
Henry Boone	2	Giles Lawrence	1
John Duffield	2	George Collins	1

Not Chargeable		Not Chargeable	
Richard Reade	4	Henry Hughes	3
Martha Rogers	3	William West	4
Samuell Bayly	3	Phineas Riggs	2
Richard Eades	2	*[blank]* Hockes widdow	2
Edward Eglantine	2	*[blank]* Hall widdow	1
William Hall	1	Thomas Harrison	1
Thomas Steevens	1	Ellen Brafferton	2
Nicholas Hayward	2	Edward Ockenden	2

William Carden	1	*[blank]* Winn widdow	1
Dorothy Scarr	2	Richard Mathewes	2
[blank] Booth widdow	2	Elizabeth Woodfield	2
Joseph Smith	1	Mathew Holmes	2
George Carpenter	2	John Triggs	2
Richard Acy	2	Edward Hards	1
John Heath	1	Thomas Meares	2
Thomas Lake	1	Richard Gilbert	2
Bartholomew Thames	2	John Holland	2
John Codwell	2	John Siffin	1
Margery Watson	1	John Symons	2
[blank] Hayward widdow	2	Richard Clarke	1
Henry Prass	1	Alice Luther	2
Richard Brigham	2	Mathew Robinson	1
Nicholas Wright	1	Thomas Archpoll	2
William Pye	1	Simon Paylin	1
James Cadman	1	Richard Fort	2
Robert Ricketts	2	Richard Benchkin	2
Mary Hills	1	*[blank]* Butcher widdow	2
William Mitchell	1	James Kempe	1
James Buds	1	John Evans	2
Thomas Poore	2	John Langford	2
Robert Page	2	John Parminter	2
James Holdstocke	2	*[blank]* Lane widdow	1
Thomas Sluce	2	Joane Mann	2
[blank] Ingham widdow	2	Nathaniell Smith	1
Richard Salter	2	Mathew Arnold	2
John Dawes	2	John Gray	1
Richard Collins	1	Thomas Darnall	1
Richard Carpenter	2	Richard Coston	1
John Farnley	2	Richard Nelson	2
John Munnes	2	George Kirby	2
John Withers	2	*[blank]* Wilson widdow	2

Northfleete

Chargeable		Chargeable	
Robert Parker	6	William Garrett	1
John Brookes	2	James Plaister	2
James Boghurst	4	William Weller	2
Edward Darlin	6	Thomas Jones	3
John Batt	1	John Adams	2
Elizabeth Childes	9	William Lowers	3
James West	2	Robert Warren	6

Edward Clarke	6	William Webb gent[leman]	9
Martin Wollard	2	Mary Pallmer	3
[fol. 44Br]			
William Cotterell	3	Nicholas Middleton	2
William Wyatt	6	John Ellis	2
John Ellis	3	Samuel Andrewes	2
William May	6	William Boghurst	4
Joane Compton	2	John Elsey	4
Henry Cunningham	5	Ralph Jolfe	3
John Smith	2	Luke Welbeloved	6
John Howlett	1	Andrew Taylor	2
John Ellis	1	Randolph Poulson sen[io]r	2
Richard Bird	1	John Holt	2
John Iddleton	1	Francis Steevens	1
John Linxted	2	Thomas Harman	4
George Garrett	2	Nicholas Cousins	4
Dorothy Drury	1	William Childes	8
Thomas Summers	1	Richard Salter	1
James Fortree Esq[uire]	10	Amy Chubbs	2
John Evans	2	Robert Partridge	3
Ellin Collins	2	Thomas Slaughter	4
Thomas Humfrey	2	John Carnell	6
Robert Peacocke	9	Nicholas Gallup	3
Mary Hunt	2	Richard Wooders	3
Clement Rand	5	John Gilbert	3
Randolph Poulson jun[io]r	7	Elizabeth Milford	4
John Bennett	1	Thomas Smith	1
William Border	3	Anne Parker	1
James Pindar	3	John Smith	3
Robert Hadlow	1	Richard Betts	1
William Plaistow	2	Joseph Brett	2
Elizabeth Pryor	1	Judith Carlile	4
John Chapman	8	Richard Wyatt	8
John Chandler	2	Abraham Hauksley	2
Elizabeth Boulton	1		

Empty houses in Northfleete

Randolph Poulson senior	2	Francis Steevens	1
Richard Salter	2	Ellen Collins	2
Thomas Slaughter	4	Clement Rand	5
James Pindar	3		

Not Chargeable

John Brookes	2	John Eagle	2
John Adams	2	Joane Compton	2
John Smith	2	John Howlett	1
John Elsey	1	John Adleton	1
John Linxsted	2	Dorothy Drury	1
Amy Chubbs	2	John Evans	2
Mary Hunt	2	Richard Woodiers	3
Widdow Gilbert	4	Thomas Smith	1
Anne Parker	1	Richard Betts	1
Robert Hadlow	1	Joseph Brett	2
John Chapman	1	John Chaundler	2
Abraham Hawksley	2		

Milton next Gravesend

Chargeable

Mr John Smith	5	William Fell	8
John Winkle	6	George Sherman	7
John Sussan	9	George Archbey	12
[blank] Merrimouth widdow	5	William Leeds	2
Mr John Fackley	5	Mr Jacob Parsons	6
[blank] Frye widdow	12	John Lion	12
Thomas Johnson	2	Thomas Baldocke	2
Thomas Busfield	7	Edward Ratcliffe	22
Thomas Saffery	3	Mr John Marlow	20
Mr Dunning	21	Robert Bayley	4
Mr Arthur White	14	Mr William Antrobus	4
[blank] Bayley widdow	4	James Bent	2
Samuel Allison	2	William Stodwell	2
Mrs Davies	7	Henry Russell	3
Henry Paine	3	John Cripse	11
[blank] Sale widdow	4	William Coote	10
[blank] Creavest widdow	6	William Read	4
Simon Mockett	2	John Norman	1
Mr Anthony Sifflett	6	Mr Edward Mason	8
Thomas Martin	2	Thomas Cusse	2
John Garrett	2	[blank] Browne widdow	2
Clement Rand	5	William Hutton	2
John Bowell	1	Edward Meares	1
John Parminter	1	Benjamin Taylor	2
Thomas Mortimer	1	Parker George	1
James Houldstocke	2	John Foach	5
James Man	2	[blank] Tilley widdow	2

[fol. 44Bv]

Henry Mason	1	Powell Phillips	1
James Wanden	5	John Newman	1
Thomas Hull	1	Ralph Lowett	1
John Copland	4	Thomas Hayes	7
Robert Thurlow	2	Lazarus Cocker	2
John Allen	3	Edward Gibson	2
[blank] Peckworth widdow	7	John Dyar	3
Richard Kempe	2	[blank] Baldocke widdow	1
James Lister	1	John Kowes	1
Thomas Johnson	1	Robert Trippoll	2
Walter Baynard	4	Thomas Fewby	4
[blank] Effard widdow	2	Joseph Rasher	2
Humfry Mills	2	Francis Phillips	2
George Johnson	1	Mrs Elizabeth Browning	7
Mrs Anne Smith	5	Mrs Hills	6
Mrs Butcher	3	Mrs Bishop	5
Mr William Rand	7	Mr Thomas Fettiplace	5
Mr John Philpott	15	John Browne	3
Mr George Etkins	7	Richard Leake	3
Richard Evans	2	Mr Richard Bartlett	9
John Seager	2	John Sussan	8
[blank] Whitehead widdow	2	John Prior	2
Thomas Welch	2	Peeter Love	2
[blank] Turner widdow	2	Thomas Frie	4
William Trewitt	4	Thomas Waglin	6
[blank] Ninn widdow	2	Andrew Floud	1
Solomon Clarke	5	Jonas Claxon	1
Thomas Randall	2	[blank] Dunstan widdow	2
John Davies	1	John Butters	2
[blank] Ratcliffe widdow	2	George Clarke	1
Thomas Webb	2	Jacob Ellett	2
[blank] Benton widdow	1	Thomas Slanye	1
Thomas Hockley	1	Thomas Smith	1
John Pearne	2	Thomas Carwarden	3
[blank] Turner widdow	2	Robert Maydstone	3
Steven Meares	4	Abraham Lee	3
Mr George Terrick	6	Richard Johnson	3
Mrs Musgrove	6	Samuell Handy	5
[blank] Pecke widdow	1	Robert Martin	2
William Eady	2	Thomas Pearne	3
Richard Hodges	6	Roger Yeomans	2
Robert Keyes	6	Mr Michaell Farlow	6

William Olliver	6	*[blank]* Harris widdow	4
John Thackes	6	William Harden	2
Christopher Duckett	2	William Billington	1
Mr William Tringe	6	John Rider	2
Mrs Thompson	2	*[blank]* Head widdow	2
Thomas Morris	7	John Jones	10
Mr Steven Allen	6	Mr Seamer	6
William Beale	14	Josuah Walton	6
John Tomlin	3	Mr Christopher Adams	6
George Highland	3	John Best	2
John Grigson	3	Thomas Frankwell	3
Valentine Walker	2	*[blank]* Alchin widdow	2
Abraham Baker	6	Henry Hills	7
Humfry Smith	2	William Raifes	6
Thomas Strood	2		

Empty Houses in Milton

William Coot	7	*[blank]* Crowest widdow	6
Parker George	1	James Holdstocke	2
[blank] Pickworth widdow	7	Mr Thomas Fettyplace	5
John Browne	2	John Susan	8
Mr William Allen	6		

Not Chargeable   Not Chargeable

George Ashby	12	Henry Payne	3
John Foach	5	John Allen	3
Thomas Pearne	3	Thomas Frankwell	3
Rowland Allen	1	Thomas Cusse	2
Widdow Browne	2	John Bowell	1
Phillip Whaley	1	Widdow Tilley	2
Powell Phillips	2	John Newman	1
Thomas Hull	1	Ralph Lowett	1
Thomas Jackson	2	Lazarus Cocker	2
Edward Gibson	2	Lydia Moore	2
Richard Wickes	1	James Lister	1
John Keyes	1	William Hadlow	1
Francis Phillips	2	Thomas Welch	2
Peter Lowe	2	Widdow Turner	2
Widdow Ninn	2	Thomas Randall	2
Widdow Ratcliffe	2	Jacob Elliott	2
Widdow Benton	1	Thomas Slaine	1
Thomas Hockley	1	Thomas Smith	1
Widdow Turner	2	Widdow Pecke	1

Robert Martin	2	William Harden	2
William Billington	1	Valentine Walker	2
Widdow Alchin	2	Humfry Smith	2
Widdow Browne	2		
Beniamine Brooke constable			

[fol. 44Cr]

The precinct of the Cathedral Church of Rochester

Chargeable		Chargeable	
Richard Allen Esquire	7	Dr John Cod	10
Mr John Larkin in 2 houses	12	Mr John Crumpe	8
Mr Robert Dixson	9	Dr Augustine Cesar	15
Francis Barrell Esq	10	Mr Edwards	5
John Steevens	7	William Sweet	3
Richard Mathewes	9	John Hog junior	7
William Keamer	8	John Brookes	4
[blank] Hads widdow	6	Thomas Gamon	7
Edward Brimton	4	Mrs Short widdow	14
Thomas Ward	7	Mr Christopher Petty	7
William Rothwell	3	Mr George Maplisden	5
Mr John Howgrave	1	Thomas Joye	2
Edward Whitton junior	4	Mr Maplisden	3
John Heath senior	2	John Lee	6
Steeven Woollgate	5	Mr Lines	10
Samuell Moore	6	Sarah Browne	6
[blank] Coby widdow	6	Mr William Head	4
John Tyherst	7	[blank] Baker	6
Richard Say	6	James Ousmer	1
Henry Smith	2	Edward Burges	2
Mrs Cobham widdow	4	John Heath junior	2
Richard Tibballs	2	Mrs Ward widdow	6
The Bishop of Rochester	7		
Samuell Moore verger			

The City of Rochester
Middle Borough

Chargeable		Chargeable	
George Woodyer gent[leman]	18	Robert Fowler Esq	11
Mr Edward Booth	9	Mrs Short widdow	5
Mr Edward Whitton	5	Mr Henry Wriothsley	11
Mrs May widdow	6	Mr Phillip Bartholomew	12
John Hogg senior	6	Mathew Parker	6
Mr John Marlow	8	Thomas Williams	6

Henry Dunning	7	Mathew Hawkins	5
Anthony Lovell	3	Richard Cobham	4
Hearne Thurston	6	Francis Rowlandson	6
Clement Brewer	3	William Campen	4
Richard Courthrop	4	Thomas Crosley	2
George Allington	13	Jane Ward widdow	2
George Roper	4	John Cadman	1
William Chatborne	4	William Cleggett	3
Bartholomew Bridgman	3	Henry Nicholls	3
William Knowles	6		

Not Chargeable

[blank] Saxby widdow	1	William Burges	3
Thomas Joy	3	Frances Dunning	1
Anthony Hales	1	John Ivesson	1
Judith Mathews	2	Joane Crachley	3
Frances Davys	3	Thomas Williams Borsholder	

St Clement Borough

Chargeable

Thomas Sharpe	3	Henry Head	5
John Gadge	16	[blank] Kennett widdow	2
Gilbert Young	5	John Bullen	3
Joseph Travis	5	Thomas Copsay	7
John Gilter	3	William Head	5
Robert Pratt	5	Richard Hewes	3
Mr William Pass	4	Dorothy Keyes	7
Richard Greene	7	Christopher Wadd	7
Christopher Writte	2	Allen Combes	4
Edward Bourne	3	James Rolfe	4
Richard Marshall	4	John Cart	9
James Rolfe	6	George Batt	3
Edward Batten	7	Nicholas Tong	3
John Dunning	6	Bartholomew Bridgman	5
Cutbert Dunking	2	Deveraux Watson	2

Not Chargeable

Lawrence Gascoigne	4	John Nellis	4
John Pumfire	1	Thomas Joy	2
Thomas Seanes	2	John Keene	2
[blank] Bradley widdow	4	[blank] Mayer widdow	2
Thomas Dunkin	2	John Greene	1

Henry Moore	2	Steeven Carryer		1
Anthony Hales	4	[blank] Reed widow		2
		Henry Head Borsholder		

South Borough

Chargeable		Chargeable	
Walter Fisher	5	Edward Attoway	3
Edward Andrewes	4	John Bull	3
William Ellison	3	Mr William Lawton	5
James Baker	3	Bridgett Chambers	2
Mrs Gouldwell widd[ow]	4	Roger Tatenclarke	4
John Tredway	1	Thomas Hammon	4
Edward Whitton in an } empty house　　　}	1		

[fol. 44Cv]

John Battey	6	George Ayhurst	2
Thomas Vallence	3	John Penny	6
Arthur Brooker	5	Thomas Mott	19
Christopher Hodd	5	Emory Wright	4
Henry Wright	5	John Plastow	8
William Bennett	13	William Dawling	6
John Fenner	7	Robert Heath	3
Robert Leake	6	John Bates	6
Mr John Mabb	8	William Cooke	6
Thomas Staynes	4	Robert Wallison	5
Richard Hutchinson	3	Robert Maw	6

Not Chargeable		Not Chargeable	
[blank] Barlow widow	6	[blank]Browne widow	2
Barnett Tanner	2	[blank] Chadocke widow	1
Richard Varnham	1	Mary Waker	1
Susannah Dunning widow	1	[blank] Post widow	1
Joseph Crane	2		

Northgate Borough

Chargeable		Chargeable	
Richard Glover	3	Roger Smith	2
Thomas Arthur	2	Robert Shaw	7
Fulke Harold	3	Mrs [blank] Juett widow	10
Thomas Blunt	3	John Carman	2
William Hutt	2	William Turner	3
Henry Morris	3	John Laughton	2
Richard Sturgis	4	John Norewood	2

[blank] Browne widdow	2	Jeremiah Wallenger	7
John Sammon	3	Robert Sampson	2
Edward Norwood	5	Thomas Stacy	2
[blank] King widdow	4	Henry Tong	2
Henry Platt	2	Ambrose Reed	3
James Dunkin	3	Thomas Lydall	3
John Chambers	2	Robert Preston	5
James Stacy	2	Roger Russell	4
Thomas Mills	1	John Play	2

Not Chargeable   **Not Chargeable**

Elizabeth Chambers widdow	-	Anne King widdow	-
Robert Harris	-	Margaret Allen Widdow	-
Hugh Drinkall	-	Edward Ladbury	-
Francis Lane	-	Nathaniell Alt	-
Richard Mason	-	William Greenfeild	-
John Woodgate	-	Job Mathewes	-
John Wilkins	-	John Benfeild	-
John Carter	-	John Gooden	-
Henry Goffe	-	John Startup	-
Richard Warren	-		

Southgate Borough

Chargeable   **Chargeable**

Sir Francis Clarke knight	15	George May Esquire	5
Thomas Manly gentleman	12	William Wiseman gentleman	6
Thomas Gostry	2	William Sanders	2
Simon Dixon	2	Thomas Spillman	3
Thomas Flight	3	John Gamball	3
Persivall Wiborne	2	[blank] Jones widdow	3
Thomas Trippett	4	Richard Wood	3
Robert Childry	4	William Olliver	4
William Ballard	6	John Franke	4
William Summers	6	John Greenwell	3
George Newman Esquire	10	Richard Manly gentleman	9
Robert Faunce gentleman	9	Steeven Pine	8
Mathew Inwood	3	William Nickson	7
Mrs [blank] Ower widdow	3	Mrs [blank] Skovell widdow	2
Mrs Anne Griffin	4	Mr William Coade	4
Mrs Mary Constable	5	John Woolgate	3
Mathew Collins	2	Thomas Rivers	4

Thomas Bennett	8	Samuell Kennet	5
John Rabson	4	Elias Mitchell	4
John Sargeant	2	Thomas Patten	2
Edward Place	5	William Inett	5
John Turner	3	Francis Olliver	2
Thomas Burbridge	3	Peter Gray	2
Edward Booth	1	Thomas Cleves	2
Thomas Killman	2	Thomas Burnett	2
John Bunn	2	Thomas Francis	1
Thomas Bilson	2	John Wade	2
Thomas Collett	2	William Crampe	2
Mrs Inett in an }		Mrs [blank] Wood in a }	
empty house }	5	empty house }	6
Thomas Blach in an }			
empty house }	3		

Not Chargeable		**Not Chargeable**	
[blank] Sherman widdow	2	Robert May	1
Henry Ludgole	1	Thomas Smyth	2
John Lane	2	Michaell King	2
John Jones	2	James Peirson	2
Edward Perkins	2	William Hills	2
John Tayler	2	Anne Griffin empty	3
Widdow Crips empty	3	Richard Manly empty	2
Thomas Rumney empty	2	Thomas Champion	-
Phillip Cleave	-	Francis Swan	-
James Gambrill	-	Mary Nash widdow	-
		John Greenill	
		& Thomas Rivers Borsholders	

[fol. 44Dr]

Bostall Borough

Chargeable		**Chargeable**	
Thomas Nicholls	8	John Day	3
William Staynes	3	William Curd	2
James Day	4	Thomas Willson	2
William Boghurst	1	Daniell Huggins	1

Not Chargeable		**Not Chargeable**	
John Pavely	1	John Kipps	1
John Watts	1	Richard Jones	1
Thomas Tompkin	1	John Goodall	1
John Williams	1	Thomas Godfrey	1

Isaac Marshall   1   *Daniell Huggins Borsholder*

East Borough

Chargeable		Chargeable	
Mr Richard Head mayor	8	Kendricke Lake	6
Richard Hunt	2	Robert Paule	6
John Huggens	3	John Wilde	4
Robert Churchwell	4	Edward Shelley	2
Christopher Cockerell	3	George Oswell	4
George Phips	2	Thomas Dabson	2
Christopher Swiffenden	4	James Wilkinson	4
Sarah Baldwyn widdow	4	Steven Bunnett	4
William Smith	3	John Brimton	2
John Clunn	4	Robert Dove	5
Christopher Yew	4	Thomas Chadburne	2
Elizabeth Jobson widdow	4	John Willmott	4
John Dundy	6	Anne Bradford	2
Edward Tayler	2	Thomas Palmer	7
William Bird	4	Thomas Scudder	4
Thomas Walter	2	Henry Skeere	4
Richard Croswell	4	Mr Francis Tompson	10
Christian Phillips widdow	9	Henry Cleggett	3
Samuell Stow	2	William Nicholson	3
Richard Newman	3	James Furner	2
James Barker	5	Adrian Ebsworth	2
John Tayler	3	Robert Popley	4
Elizabeth Austen	5	Richard Saywell	2
John Moore	4	Thomas Stone	2
Henry White	4	David Baker	4

Not Chargeable		Not Chargeable	
Katherine Derry	2	Ann Tayler	2
Simon Hackmore	2	Mathew White	2
Mary Ansley	2	Thomas Childrey	1
Alice Jones widdow	3	Elizabeth Ashberry	3
Clement Tayler	2	Thomas Drover	2
John Martin	2	Edward Pilgrime	1
Richard Bayly	2	Henry Martin	1
John Silvester	1	Thomas Latt	1
Henry Feild	2	[*blank*] Richardson widdow	1
Anthony Tayler	1	George Browne	1
[*blank*] Hill widdow	3	[*blank*] Maule widdow	1

[*blank*] Martin widdow	1	Hugh Bush	2
Henry Blewett	3	Jonah Woodford	2
Roger Baker	2		

Eastgate Borough

Chargeable		Chargeable	
Samuel Barlow	2	John Story	2
Simon Prior	4	Tobias Battell	6
Edward Price	2	William Boone	3
John Cooke	4	William Salisbury	3
Henry Lewis	3	Richard Eason	3
Edward Goard	3	Thomas Goodwyn	3
Robert Rosse	2	John Edwards	2
Ambrose Babs	1	Edward Baker	2
Thomas Jones	3	Henry Bagnall	2
Nicholas Bartlett	3	John Sturton	1
Henry Backett	1	William Burroughes	2
Steven Freind	2	John Ward	7
Hugh Jones	2	Thomas Michell	3
Robert Hollard	2	Edward Hurtis	2
John Barrowes	3	William Harding	1
Elizabeth Lawghlen	2	Mary Spencer widdow	5
Thomas Gooding	2	Richard Burley	4
James Sheppard	2	Thomas Tayler	2
William Burnett	1	William Butler	1
Thomas Upton	3	John Stanford	2
John Cousins	2	William Clarke	2
George Murrin	4	John Adams	2
Richard Peate	2	Samuell Hubbard	1
Humfrey Heyward	1	Richard King	2
Simon Peirce	4	Christopher Bendey	3
Henry Allard	3	Thomas Smith	2
George Best	3	William Gilven	4
Nathaniell Rumney	4	Christopher Sinament	3
Joane Say	3	John Moore	5
Mr [*blank*] Denne junior	5	William Allchurch	2
John Farwell	2	Mr Denn senior	6
George Plummer	5	Edward Bearblocke	5
[fol. 44Dv]			
Anthony Norris	2	Robert Browing	4
Thomas Jacob	3	Hercules Hills	2
William Simons	3	Edward Edwards	3
Thomas Naylor	4	Thomas Jorden	3

Nicholas May	3	Samuell Walsall	6
Richard Langley	2	Anthony Brufett	2
Samuel Uxon	2	Thomas Walton	3
John Pickerell	3	Stephen Alcock Esquir senior	11
John Hudson	4	Katherine Seavorne	4
William Barker	1	Steeven Alcocke junior gent:	11
Nicholas Boghurst	10	Edward May	4
Daniell Barloe	3	John Cobham	5
Walter Duke	4	Thomas Ridgway	5
Edward Gunton	7	John Kingsnorth	3
Nicholas Doswell	2	Ralph Strange	2
Mary Atwaters	2	William Mortomy	1
John Ripingale	3	Thomas Chambers	3
Richard Wayles	2	Thomas Griffen	2
William Merriman	4	William Foster	4
Robert Graves	2	Mrs Ann Paxford	8
Mrs Bucke	10	John Becke	4
Thomas Owsby	4	Giles Cullum	2
Thomas Milson	4	Mr Henry Venman	12
Robert Carte	6	John Askew	2
Thomas Benson	4	William Barker	6
Walter Waggon	2	John Cox	3
Thomas Tayler	8	Mathew Burrowes	6
John Country	4	[blank] Harthrop widdow	4
Ann Embleton	3	Richard Grigsby	2
Richard Gooding	3	Augustine Robinson	3
John Waterman	5	Mr Henry Gowles	10
Thomas Horwood	5	Francis Skinner	7
Peter Gee	2	John Staines	2
John Sihurst	3	Steeven Simons	4
William Rumson	4	George Ogle	2
Hugh Clements	4	Nicholas Bunnett	2
Mr John Tyhurst	5	Richard Lee Esquire	20
Nicholas Bungurst	4	David Rogers	5
Elizabeth Ballard	2	Thomas Jemson	4
Thomas Milton	4	Mrs Ellett widdow	5

Empty Houses

Mrs Cripse in 3 houses	6	Thomas Mitchell	4
Elias Rolfe	3	John Kingsnorth	1
Francis Line	2	Thomas Wyatt	3

Steeven Carver	2	William Davison	2
Mrs Quesenborough	4	Thomas Holloway	3
Samuell May	3	Thomas Gooding	2
Anne Post	4	Robert Moorcocke	5
Captain John Foskew	4	Thomas Hull	3
Peter Wildes	2	*[blank]* Campleshon	3
John Country	4	William Wilkinson	3
Robert Morecocke junior	2	Daniel Startes	2
Joane Currall widdow	4	Thomas Belowine	6
Simon Dunning	4		

Eastgate Borough

Not Chargeable

Not Chargeable

John Howell	1	Mary Jeffery	2
Henry Bagnall	3	Thomas Merritt	3
Edward Mills	3	Joseph Webb	4
Edmund Rolfe	3	John Dober	3
Richard Thomas	3	Thomas Wyatt	3
Andrew Arner	3	Henry Jorden	3
William Burges	3	Richard Thompson	3
Nicholas Wilde	3	Robert Pomroy	4
Lydia Johnson	4	Daniell Hills	3
William Martion	4	Anne Plastoe	3
William Cembett	4	Francis Duke	3
John Preston	3	Thomas Rumney	3
John Babbs	3	Christopher Bendey	4
John Bradridge	3	Andrew Elecke	4
Thomas Melson	4	Thomas Lewes	3
John King[263]	2	*Leonard Marsh*	2
[Ja]ne Boone	1	*Anne Jones*	1
Mary Roswell	2	*Mary Tayler*	1
Thomas Larkin	2	*John Knight*	1
John Hixson	2	*Mary Millman*	1
Joane Smith	1	*John Johnson*	2
John Brewes	2	*Thomas Holt*	1
James George	2	*Edward Read*	2
Ann Johnson	1	*Joane Barker*	1
Joane Cryer	2	*William Stimson*	1
Edward Popley	2	*Mary Saxby*	2
Edward Muddell	2	*Joane Andrewes*	1
Edward George	1	*Charles Jones*	2

[263] Entries in italics taken from E179 series, see introduction page cxii.

Richard Warman	2	Steeven Stimon	1
Joane Greene	1	George Hennis	2
Margaret Phillips	1	Joane Williams	1
George Marlton	2	Arthur Pitman	2
Susan Netter	2	Edward Ongle	2
Steeven Rosse	2	George Baynard	1
Mary Burnett	1	Mary Colegate	2
Thomas Wareham	1	William Garrett	2
Nathaniell Richardson	1	Daniell Holmes	2
George Johnson	2	John Keene	2
Robert Newell	2	Thomas Woodgroome	2
Anne Rogers	1	Isaac Salmon	1
Joane Mounty	1	John Brandridge	2
Thomas Munns	2	Robert Mitchell	2
Robert Boone	1	William Hixson	2
William Greene	2	Thomas Hewis	2
Thomas Maskall	2	Elizabeth Tanner	2
James Smith	2	Henry Coates	2
John Hillyard	2	William Crossley	1
John Weinsley	2	Samuell Brookes	1
Robert Usher	1	Josias Pridgeon	2
			204

PRO:E179/249/37B mem 3

Ralph Grant	2	Robert Lomas	2
John Tayler	1	Elizabeth Henniker	1
Thomas Randall	1	Nicholas Laywich	1
George Mongomery	2	John Nicholson	2
Rachell Jones	2	Anthony Tomes	1
Susannah Betts	2	Peter Tanner	1
Mary Withan	1	Samuell Cox	2
Elizabeth Tapper	1	Henry Browne	1
Frances Heneker widdow	1	Francis London widdow	2
Henry Bonny	2	Ann Phillips	1
Nicholas Parker	2	Alexander Arnold	2
Stephen Constable	1	William Plumer	2
Stephen Godard	2	John Perfite	1
John Olliver	2	Edward Warlocke	2
William Muddle	1	Nicholas Bunker	1
George Waters	2	Charles Cole	2
Mary Heneker	2	Lewis Bevin	1
Austen Blackwell	2	Christopher Thaxton	2
Befenge Wyatt	2	Francis Grip	2
William Burnett	2	Gilbert Slincam	2

John Bayes	2	*Thomas Hoxley*	2
Christopher Laffling	2	*Richard Thompson*	2
Daniel Senderley	2	*Edward Edwards Borsholder*	

Hearne Thurston and Edward Gunton Constables of the City of
Rochester

Heere Endeth the Lath of Aylesford

[fol. 44r]

THE LATH OF SCRAY

The township of Newenden
in the lath of Scray

Chargeable		Chargeable	
William Hoy	1	Henry Tayler	1
Ann Hether widd	1	Thomas Dennett	1
Thomas Coler	1	Edward Seisley	1
Peter Vinton	2	John White	1
George Godden	3	Thomas Cutbush	2
James Nash	5	Edward Lomas	5
Thomas Browne Rector	1	Roger Nash	2
John Pellate refuseth to make any account of his fire hearthes	3	Thomas Welsted refuseth to make any account of his fire hearthes	3

Not Chargeable		Not Chargeable	
Rebeccah Reeve widd	1	Katharine Hams	1
[blank] Seisly widdow	1	Roger Nash Bayliffe	

HUNDRED OF GREAT BARNEFEILD
in the Lath of Scray

Chargeable		Chargeable	
William Boys Esquire	21	George Pix gentleman	7
Nathaniel Pix gent	10	John Read	12
William Boreman of Gillsgreen	3	Richard Catt	1
John Piper	2	Anthony Gibbon	5
John Brett	6	John Robins	9
John Sloman	5	John Rose	2
Thomas Chittenden of Highgate	4	John Martin	2
William Boreman	2	Widdow Fowle widd	1
James Poyle	-	Alexander Poyle	1
Edward Falkner	1	Richard Rutley	3
Richard Worsley	1	John Hucksted	4
Sidrack Bennett	2	John Allen	2
Edward Love	1	Thomas Fuller	3
James Pott	2	[blank] Mitchell widd	1
Thomas Standen	1	John Hinkley sen[io]r	2

Richard Freebody	2	William Hosmer	6
Edward Plum	3	Thomas Mitten	1
John Graunt	3	Thomas Chittenden of	3
John Chittenden	4	Sherman	
Edward Roades	2	John Neeves	4
Edward Austin	4	Mrs Grove	4
John Glasier	3	Walter Quaife	1
John Dale }	4	[blank] Robins widd	4
and in an empty house }	1	John Cray	1
Timothy Weller	1	George Springett	2
William Cullens	1	William Cooke	2
Richard Austen	8	Richard Turley	6
John Mercer	3	Edward Cushman	1
William Chittenden	3	Robert Barham	2
Henry Batchelor	4	William Whatman	5
Richard Radford	3	John Turley	4
Ephraim Bothell	2	John Maule	5
Edward Tayler	5	Robert Hunt	3
John Grant	2	Richard Sisley	3
John Hinkley junior	3	Richard Worsley	1
James Weller	2	William Divers	1
Thomas Brett	2	William Quaiffe	1
Bartholomew Fuller	2	John Holden	2
Samuel Streeter	1	Thomas Barnes	2
John Batchellor	6	John Hollands	1
Jeremy Gibbon	1	Thomas Page	4
Thomas Archer	1	The heire of Henry Robins	5
William Archer	4	James Tamsett	1
John Adams	1	William Devell	2
[blank] Tharpe widd	2	James Giles	1
Thomas Cooper	3	[blank] Gibbon widd	6
John Sharpey	3	John Kemsley	2
William Randoll	4	Henry Thatcher	5
John Payne	5	Thomas Chittenden &	6
William Hoadley	5	in an empty house	4
Thomas Sanders	2	Alexander Sharpy	6
Richard Reynolds	2	Thomas Reynolds	1
Thomas Boreman	1	John Ven	2
John Seisley	2	Edward Mussery	2
Francis Stace	1	Daniel Butcher	2
Arthur Gibbon	5	Benjamin Mott	2
Josias Charleton	6	Henry Lasher	5
Thomas Coale	7	William Moyse	2

Charles Hodge	3	Thomas Goldsmith	2
Thomas Evans	2	[blank] Spice widd	1
Richard Webb	1	James Russell	1
John Goble	4	[blank] Pray widd	1
Richard Hawkins	1	[blank] Pankhurst widd	1
Joseph Paul	5	Thomas Thornton	4
Jonas Botting	2	Henry Courthop gent	3
John Springett	3	Humfrey Kettle	4
Samuel Newman	1	Arthur Standen	2
Mathew Robins	2	The heire of Henry Robins	4
Thomas Sharpe	3	Nathaniel Pix gent	7
Richard Worsley	4	Edmund Allen	1
Thomas Andrewes	1	Thomas Spice	1
Anthony Stoneham	2	William Boreman	1
		Richard Rowland	1

[fol. 44v]

Hundred of Great Barnefeild

Not Chargeable		Not Chargeable	
Henry Springett	1	[blank] Bigg widdow	1
Nicholas Hunt	1	Henry Safferon	2
Thomas Gibson	1	[blank] Glasyer widd	1
Robert Walter	1	John Exeter	1
[blank] Bourder widd	1	Thomas Soane	1
John Ford	1	John Bennett	1
George Smith	1	[blank] Jobson widd	2
William Adams	1	[blank] Gibbon widd	2
John Cushman	1	William Fill	2
John Brooke	1	Thomas Bishop	2
Richard Cruttenden	2	Thomas Cowper	1
John Batchelor	1	[blank] Pattenden widd	1
John Reynolds	1	[blank] Safferon widd	1
[blank] Ardlowes widd	1	John Allen	1
Anthony Whatman	1	Robert Baker	1
[blank] Reynolds widd	1	John Blist	1
Richard Wildish	1	William Hovenden	1
Christopher Sedres	1	John Adson	1
Richard Harley	1	John Evernden	1
		Thomas Spice constable	

HUNDRED OF ROLVENDEN
in the Lath of Scray

Beneden Borough

Chargeable		Chargeable	
Alexander Reades	5	Abraham Winder	1
Andrew Waters	4	John Dunke	4
William Bigg	1	Lawrence Evernden	2
Richard Bigg	2	James Turner	4
Henry Morris	2	Thomas Idden	2
Mr Biggs farme	2	Robert Morris	4
Richard Hope	2	William Austen	2
Robert Holmes	2	Steeven Springett	1
William Fawlkener	3	Richard Fawkner	3
Richard Illenden	2	Simon Evernden	2
John Lander	3	George Chittenden	2
Thomas Austen	1	Thomas Alay	4
Thomas Williams	1	Thomas Hodges	2
Reader Wats	7	Walter Jones	4
William Hewson	4	John Pye	3
Richard Grant	3	James Botting	2
Richard Burden	1	Steeven Leedes	5
William Moyse	4	William Burden	3
William Olliver	3	Robert Apps	6
Roger Goldstone	5	Christopher Walter	2
Thomas Smith	2	Alexander Reades jun[io]r	4
William Moyse for the house where Laycocke did live	2		

Not Chargeable		Not Chargeable	
Elizabeth Jewherst	1	Joane Newenden widd	2
Edward Body	3	Robert Bishop	1
Samuell Harvey	4	Ann Atkin widd	2
William Beeching	3	Phebe Hills	1
Mary Hyam & Margaret Boys	1	Richard Sharpe	6
John Kent	1	Steeven Atkin	4
Thomas Tayler	2	George Appesley	1
The Vicaridge	6	Richard Foord	1
Richard Pallmer	1	Joseph Knight	2
William Jarvis	2	David Potwell	2
Phill: Turner widd	1	John Greensted	1
Bennett James widd	2	Isaac Pratt	2
Elizabeth Jegoe	1	Abraham Campany	1

Richard Tollherst	2	George Baker	2
Mary Ballard	1	Widdow Mathewes	1
John Wood	2	Widdow Evernden	1
Arthur Benson	1	Richard Woodman	3
John Munn	1	Thomas Cretholl	1
Mathew Robins his heires	6		

Maytham Borough

Chargeable		Chargeable	
George Kadwell Esq	11	John Sheafe gent	9
Alexander Weller	7	Steeven Milsted sen[io]r	3
John Penvall	3	John Fishenden	4
Francis Norwood	3	Joseph Russell	1
John Foord	2	Thomas Barber	1
Thomas Radwell	2	Mrs Sheafe widdow	2
Robert Tate	3	Henry Poute	4
Thomas Honnsett	1	John Sheafe gent	2
Mary Dering	3	John Clifton	1
Tho[mas] & Nathaniel Stretton	3	John Langley	4
Daniell Breecher	3	Nicholas Peniall	3
Phillip Atwater	3	George Preston	2
Daniel Verser	2	Richard Perles	1
Richard Netter	1	Thomas Turner	2
Richard Steed	2	Cephas Bright	1
Richard Winder	2	John Budds	3
Steeven Chittenden	6	John Atwater	3
Moyses Christopher	3	Elizabeth Lamper	1
Roger Tree	1	Allen Sims	2
William Love	3	Robert Gibbon of Beckley	6
Jonas Rolfe	2	Thomas Penvall	1
John Hodeley	5	John Batchelor	1

Not Chargeable		Not Chargeable	
Widdow Sharpe	1	Richard Mallow	1
Richard Leedes	2	Widdow Sutton	1

[fol. 45r]

Not Chargeable[264]		Not Chargeable	
Widdow Sharpe	1	Richard Mallow	1

[264] Note first four entries are repeated.

Richard Leedes	2	Widdow Sutton	1
William Foster	1	Thomas Higgison	1
Richard Penny	1	Benjamin Cary	1
Thomas Cooper	2	John Abell	1
John Dubins	1	Widdow Jones	1
Thomas Ward	4	Richard Pearles	1
Widdow Lanes	1	William Oldmayd	2
Thomas Yeomans	1	John Jeffery	3
Thomas Meere	2	William Windsor	3
Widdow Robinson	1	Thomas Pellen	3
Widdow Bennett	2		

These persons here after named are **Chargeable** but refuse to give any account of their fire hearthes viz: William Burden William Quinby Thomas Budds Thomas Honnesett Thomas Kadwell Thomas Turner Richard Steed Allen Simms & John Roberts

Halden Borough

Chargeable		Chargeable	
Richard Foster	4	Mrs Cruttenden widd	6
[blank] Adams widdow	7	John Gibbon Gent	8
Harbar Burden	7	William Quinby	1
William Jeffery	4	Thomas Upton	4
Thomas Osborne	4	Steeven Milsted jun[io]r	3
Edward Windy	4	William & Gyles Kadwell	4
John Sloman	1	Richard Merlin	3
Richard Jarrett	2	John Roberts	2
Richard Boreman	3	Roger Golstone	3
Richard Norwood	2		

Not Chargeable		Not Chargeable	
Nicholas During	1	Henry Metherst	2
Thomas Windsor	2	Thomas Sanders	4
James Tanner	1	William Vigen	1
Anne Hamman	1	Samuel Winder	2
[blank] Boys widd	1	Steeven Meere	2
William Willshire	1	Christopher Corbett	2
William Nockes	1	[blank] Windser widd	2
Henry Austen	4		

Devernden Borough

Chargeable		Chargeable	
John Weller	4	Thomas Tolherst sen[io]r	3
William Quinby	1	Edward Jones	-
Thomas Bennett	2	Widdow Baker	1

[*blank*] Smith widd	3	George Petter	4
Joseph Cruttenden	4	John Cooke	2
Thomas Tolhurst jun[io]r	1	James Chittenden	3
Thomas Budds	1	Giles Kadwell	3
[*blank*] Willes widd	4	Thomas Venus	2
William Drury	1	George Kadwell Esq[ui]re }	
John Williams	1	in two empty houses }	3
Thomas Day	1	Edward Body	2

Not Chargeable		**Not Chargeable**	
Widdow Colly	1	Widdow Curteis	1
Widdow Mockett	1	Widdow Scrimes	1
John Curtis	1	Steeven Kadwell	1

Simon Evernden constable of the said hundred of Rolvenden

THE HUNDRED OF SELBRITTENDEN
in the lath of Scray

North Borough

Chargeable		**Chargeable**	
Richard Downton Esq	8	Andrew Tucker gent	11
Giles Cooke	3	Henry Radford	3
Robert Sharpe	3	John Holland	4
John Owen	4	John Fryland	3
George Hartsole	1	Richard Murford	2
[*blank*] Bates widdow	4	Steeven Gynner	2
Constance Hamond widdow	4	John Cogger	2
James Reynolds	5	Richard Fayreway	3
Richard Baker	2	Abraham Stone	2
John Hynes	1	John Watts junior	7
Samuel Petter	4	Richard Watts	5
Samuel Hunt	13	Thomas Foord	3
William Waller	2	Thomas Lander	1
Joseph Illenden	2	Richard Simms	1
Oliver Harris	2	John Branford	5
Thomas Sharpe of Lesden	4	Thomas Sayer	4
Richard Martin	2	Robert Muddle	2
Thomas Sharpe gent	6	Walter Springett	5
Thomas Sharpe senior	2	Henry Sharpe	2
Thomas Brett	3	William Steed	4
Thomas Wills	4	George Munn	2
Richard Curd	4	John Newman	2

Joseph Pettit	4	Helena Girdler	2
Steeven Marshall	1	*[blank]* Mouse widdow	1
John Basden	4	Adam Remington	2
John Fuller	1	*[blank]* Wilding widdow	2
Steeven Gynder gentleman	10	Richard Sharpe	4
Richard Igleden	5	Steeven Webb	3
Richard Cryer senior	5	Richard Cryer junior	3
Elias Billing	1	Edward Jones	4
Thomas Mercer	4	Benjamin Cowye	1

Not Chargeable		**Not Chargeable**	
Thomas Waller	1	Robert Hillary	1
Robert Jervall	1	Thomas Thames	1
Richard Ammett	2	John Jolley	2
[fol. 45v]			
Robert Blacke	1	John Cary	1
[blank] Winchley widdow	1	William Rucke	3
John Lucke	1	Nicholas Waller	1
Nicholas Payne	2	John Hodges his widdow	1
Richard Hodges his widdow	1	Lawrence Illenden	1
Widdow Duker	1	Edmund Hodges	2
Edward Drury	2	John Curd	1
Simon White	1	William Hiron Clerke	4
Thomas Dunke	2	William Ward	1

East Borough

Chargeable		**Chargeable**	
Thomas Bryan clerke	5	Robert Kennard	4
George Petter	5	John Reed	5
John Longley senior	7	John Longley junior	2
John Cogger	2	Edward Cutbush	2
Edward Bachelor	3	Giles Cooke	3
John Peckham	2	John Bachelor	2
[blank] Sherman widdow	2	Andrew Tucker gentleman	2
John Petter	4	Elizabeth Cruttenden widdow	4
John Sumers	5	Thomas Fowle	4
Robert Ballard	1	Roger Banks	2
John Merrett	1	John Upton	4
John Cooke	2	John Boreman	2
John Fishenden	2	William Sharpe	7
Edward Chittenden	2	Roger Stoneham	3
Richard Sharpie	4	John Watts senior	4

Not Chargeable

John Binskin	2	George Moore	1
William Worsley	3	[blank] Stoneham widdow	1
William Stapely	2		

West Borough

Chargeable

Richard Kilburne gentleman	12	Allen Foster	10
George Pix gentleman	1	William Dunke junior	5
William Baker	3	James Standen	1
James Holden	3	Thomas Dennett	1
John Hyder	3	John Walter	4
Richard Campany	2	John Springett	3
Thomas Weller	4	Peter Cruthall	6
Walter Jones	1	Edward Ummanden	3
Peter Sysly	2	Thankefull Tharpe junior	4
Thankfull Tharpe senior	1	George Gibbon	4
Quintine Husher	2	William Dunke junior	1
Margaret Foster	2	John Devall	5
Richard Sloman	4	Robert Bachelor	3
Martha Sloman widdow	2	John Sloman	2
John Willard	3	George Sloman	2
Margaret Haffenden	2	William Sloman	1
John Brett	1	Anthony Walter	1
William Round	2	Robert Nower	1
John Leeds	5	Edward Nicholas	2
William Dunke of Boorne	3	William Reed	4
Robert Boorne	2	William Cooke	3
Martha Wood	3	Thomas Norley	3
Anthony Wells	2	William Moore	1
Susan Watts widdow	7	Thomas Cooper	1
Andrew Ward gentleman	4	Mrs Elizabeth Fowle	11
William Ward gentleman	8	John Lamkin	1
Thomas Dunke	2	Peter Larke	4
William Dunke senior	2	William Dunke senior for } an empty house }	4

Not Chargeable

James Holden	1	Susan Wills	1
John Tyler	1	John Davys	1
Joane Fowle widdow	1	George Glasyer	1
John Springett	1	Mary Bell	1

John Hubbard	1	John Dennett	1
John Axbie	1	William Uderdowne	1
Thomas Forman	2	Elizabeth Johnson	1
George Catt	2	George Sloman	1
Richard Collins	1	Susan Davis	1
Sarah Buck widd[ow]	1	Richard Venice	1
Boorne House	2	John Beale	1
Richard Beeching	1	Ellen Lea	1
Ann Tutt	1	William Cooke	1

Robert Lennard constable of the hundred of Selbrittenden

HUNDRED OF CRANBROOKE
in the lath of Scray

Cruthole Borough

Chargeable		Chargeable	
Edward Gouldford Esquire	17	Robert Tayler	11
John Sharpye	5	John Boreman	2
Peter Sharpe junior	4	John Bennett	4
Robert Delton	3	Thomas Roboate	1
William Love	5	Robert Bowles	1
John Courthop Esquire	3	Richard Goulding	2
Elizabeth Willy widd[ow]	6	Robert Swifte	1
John Dunkin	2	Edward Bankes	1
William Kipping	3	William Moore	2
Edward Walter	4	Richard Alphee	2
Thomas Dunke	6	Thomas Rade	3
Henry Hatch	2	William Dunke	8
[fol. 46r]			
John Goldsmith	5	George Gibbon	6
John Courthop	4	Thomas Pankhurst	3
John Bullocke	4	Richard Rabson	5
Isaac Walter	4	George Lansdell	3
Luke Willford	4	Peter Sharpe senior	10
William Coulstocke	5	John Burre	2
Thomas Skinner	2	Elias Blewet	2
John Jewhurst	1	George Myles	2
Alexander Cushman	2	Thomas Ellis	3
Thomas Parkes	1	Nathaniel Frylan	1
Daniel Wenham	3	Ann Hamwell widdow	1
George Johnson	2	Edward Saxby	2
Thomas Sharpe	2	Richard Robins	2
William Pallmer	2	John Johnson	5

Roger Beale	2	Thomas Weston	3
John Cryer	4	Christopher Dine	3
John Tolherst	3	William Hunt	1
Steeven Catt	1		

Not Chargeable		**Not Chargeable**	
Richard Witherden	1	John Munn	1
William Gore	1	John Bullocke	2
Widdow Sutton	1	William Hunt	1
Thomas Allen	1	Widdow Aston	2
John Hayward	2	Widdow Osborne	1
William Hallowes	1	Goodwife Gilbert	2
Widdow Sampson	1	Widdow Skilton	4
Thomas Fishenden	1	Alexander Drury	1
Richard Martin	1	William Jarrett	1
Richard Oxenbridge	1	Ann Newman	1
Alexander Boreman	1	Richard Burcham	2
Thomas Binham	1	John Chesen	4
John Williams	4	John Lamkin	2
Widdow Apps	2	George Iler	1
Luke Gilbert	2	Richard Pankherst	1
Widdow Morris	1		

Kings Franchise Borough

Chargeable		**Chargeable**	
Robert Holden gent	10	Richard Newball	2
Richard Petter	2	John Colvill	7
Harman Sheafe	8	Abraham Bassocke	3
Samuel Austen	6	Josias Colvill	5
[blank] Rucke widd	1	Edward Davys	5
William Relfe	2	Thomas Brooke	1
William Woodwin	4	Richard Acton	6
Richard Bridgland	3	John Daynes	3
Richard Russell	3	Thomas Amos	2
Andrew Hills	5	John Keale	2
Widdow Knatchbull	2		

Not Chargeable		**Not Chargeable**	
Robert Judd	1	John French	1
Ezechiell Morris	2	Thomas Foster	1
Widdow Bassocke	2	Thomas Cheyney	1
John Fuller	1	William Gorredge	1

John Wilding	1	Joseph Burges	1
Thomas Hunt	1		

North Borough

Chargeable		Chargeable	
Thomas Hughes	4	Robert Balden	2
Thomas Beale	3	Simon Drayner	2
Robert Whitwicke	6	Ann Bassocke	2
Thomas Drayner	4	Henry Fowle	3
John Polant	5	Thomas Bayley	3
Robert Jeffery	1	Mr Robert Draner	2
Richard Bayly in a house he}		Richard Bayly	1
left at Micha[elma]s last }	5	Richard Bayly	4
Richard Knight	4	Alexander Whacer	1
John Kingsnoth and	8	John Buckland	8
Richard Kingsnoth		James Hofford	3
John Christian	2	Mary Grove	4
John Munn	5	Francis Poute	2
Richard Webb	9	John Payne	3
John Homsby	3	Samuel Fuller	6
Robert Marchant	10	Haslen Batherst	4
Thomas Allen	3	Goulden Skinner	3
Mr Robert Clarke	5	Thomas Wesson	3
Thomas Kingshood	2	Francis Cornwell	6
Richard Tayler	3	John Water	3
Mary Pullen	1	John Slayney	3
John Bennett	3	Nicholas Wilcher	3
Thomas Harman	2	Christopher Seares	2
William Marlian	4	William Fulleger	3
John Waters	3	Steeven Gooden	3
John Fulleger	4	Henry Buckwell	2
Thomas Buren	5	William Simons	3
John Love	4	Thomas Amery	4
Robert Tamsett	3	John Baker	2
Edward Osborne	3	George Shinkfeild	3
Elizabeth Wyborne	1	Alexander Grayling	3
William Brissenden	3	William Millgate	2
William Foster	3	Thomas Fowle	4
Mr Steeven Sutton	7		
Christopher Cooper	4		
[fol. 46v]			
John Russell	1	Alice Lawrence	2
Robert Leper	1	Mary Casselden	1

Mr John Buckherst	6	Richard Newball	1
John Sherlocke	1		

Not Chargeable		**Not Chargeable**	
George Gilbert	1	Henry Jennings	1
Isbell Whachers	2	Michael Hunney	1
John Marten	1	Robert Goore	1
William Garrett	1	Widdow Gore	3
John Willard	1	John Burden	1
Thomas Wollett	1	Thomas Wood	1
John Bassucke	1	Widow Gillham	1
Widdow Dockings	1	Widdow Nichols	1
George Strood	2	Thomas Jennings	1
John Webb	2	Peter Burton jun[io]r	2
Walter Jennings	2	Richard Smith &	3
Widdow Faireall	3	Rob[er]t Bassocke	
Widdow Polley	1	Roger Brooker	4
Robert Pilbeame	1	Joseph Brunger	1
Robert Smith	1	Roger Jones	1
William Waterhouse	2	Peter Burton sen[io]r	1
Richard Hadman	1	Richard Wood	1
Widdow Daynes jun[io]r	1	John Gomerell	1
Martin Burden	1	Thomas Drayner	1
Robert Stinnings	2	Widdow Daynes sen[io]r	1
Thomas Chittenden	4	John Fryland	1
John Buckwell	1	Thomas Gullen	1

Towne Borough

Chargeable		**Chargeable**	
William March	2	Tho[mas] Nash & Peter White	4
Richard Hope	3	Jeremy Botting	4
William Silke	5	Martha Bayley widd	5
Samuel Kencham	4	George Worseley	2
Mary Weller widd	1	Nathaniel Fosten	4
Nathaniell Fosten	2	Thomas Smith	2
John Relfe gent	7	Thomas Osborne	2
Robert Robotham	3	Christopher Peckham	2
William Austen gent	5	Thomas Punnett	2
Henry Carew	4	Thomas Munn jun[io]r	2
Thomas Weller	6	Henry Crittenden	2
Alexander Reminngton	5	John Cooper clerke	4

Peter Masters	3	Robert Hawes	7
Gervas Jeffery	4	Mary Norden	6
William Vincombe sen[io]r	2	Samuell Sharpey	3
William Kilburne gent	5	John Avery	4
John Benbrigge	2	Thomas Buttery	3
Richard Frankwell	10	Mary Willis widd	3
Thomas Botting	3	John Reade	1
Aaron Bowyer	1	John Rose	3
Samuel Butler	2	Simon Uredge	2
William Goodrich	2	Andrew Godfrey	1
Thomas Dunke	1	William Wacher	3
Richard Dodge	2	Mary Hunt widd	2
John French	2	Robert Osborne	6
Steeven Smith	2	Edward Bills	3
Edmund Baker	1	Robert Wood barber	3
Elizabeth Rickard	4	Thomas Mandy	3
John Weller	3	John Hinksell	3
Richard Hughes	3	David Russell	2
Robert Foord	2	Francis March	2
Alexander Osborne	7	Thomas Ferrall	4
Thomas Ferrall	2	Thomas Ferrall	5
Thomas Booreman	2	Walter Barton	2
Steven Reynolds	2	John Wood	2
Richard Birch	2	Thomas Munn sen[io]r	6
Peter Couchman	4	Anne Wood widow	4
Anne Wood widdow	1	William Greene	4
Robert King	8	Steven Weller	3
William Birch	2	Richard Vincombe	1
John Evernden	3	John Lowell	1
Richard Lane	2	Edward Newell	1
John Parton	1	Valentine Browne	2
Margaret Crampton wid	3	William Wood	3
Robert Hartley	3	Robert Robotham	5
Richard Robotham	2	Robert Fow	1
William Osborne	2	Thomas Roe sen[io]r	1
Richard Harvey sen[io]r	1	William Cruttenden	1
Richard Crothall	2	Dorothy Weller widd	1
John Weller sen[io]r	1	John Leigh gent	4
Walter Streator	2	Thomas Daniell	3
George Humfrey	4	Richard Norwood	3
Samuel Yorkton	3	Edward Bills	2
Nicholas Beach	6	Thomas Daniell	2
John Rabson	2	Francis Pembrooke	1

Francis Lee	1	Francis Lee more	1
Thomas Harvey	2	Edward Couchman	6
John Austen	6	James Scochford	1
Samuell Crampton	1	Samuell Crampton more	1
Robert Wood butcher	3	Christopher Hutton	2
Christopher Hutton	1	Mrs Lake widdow	2
Widdow Hickmott	5		

[fol. 47r]

Not Chargeable		**Not Chargeable**	
Michael Miller	1	Elizabeth Spilsted	1
Henry Steevenson	4	Joseph Moore	1
Andrew Simons	1	Widdow Lambe	1
Thomas Scott	1	William Wake jun[io]r	2
John Spencer	2	Thomas Cheeseman	1
William Browne	2	Sarah Piper widd	1
James Crampton	1	Joane Vigean widd	2
John Boorman	3	Walter Woollett	1
John Miller	2	Joane Tredcraft	2
Margery Batherst	1	Thomas Mackley	2
Ellenore Butcher	1	Elizabeth Goodman	2
Anthony Hope	1	William Wenman	1
Phebe Tilly widd	1	John Hope	2
Widdow Chantler	1	Widdow Crothall	1
Samuell Tolherst	1	Anne Dane widd	1
William Hollands	1	Richard Warren	1
Francis Harris	1	Richard Gunn	2
Thomas Hobard	1	Widdow Peters	1
John Lurkin	1	John Roe	1
William Wake sen[io]r	1	Mary Fowle	1
Thomas Dowle	1	Richard Knowles	2
Thomas Marten	2	Thomas Hickmott	1
James Webb	2	John Fillmer	1
Elizabeth Cooke widd	1	William Vincombe jun[io]r	1
William Wenman	1	William Allchin	2
Mathew Busse	1	Thomas Whitton	1
Katherine Brignoll	1	Elizabeth Roe widd	1
John Roes widdow	2	Mary Emiott widd	1
William Young	1	Richard Harvey sen[io]r	1
Dorothy Scotchford widd	1	Francis Sheere	1
Thomas Ballcombe	1	Thomas Scotchford	1
Thomas Champes	2	Richard Roe	1

Robert Boreman	3	George Weller	2
Richard Fosten	1	Alice Allen	1
John Butcher	2	Simon Deane	2
Richard Offen	1	Richard Parkes	1
John Roe	2	Richard Sheafe	1
Simon Beland	2	Widdow Munn	2
Nathaniell Medherst	1	Thomas Jenner	2
Robert Couchman	2	William Jenner	2
John Nowell	1	Thomas Norrington	1
Thomas Skilton	1	Thomas Harris	2
Widdow Birch	1	Thomas Freeman	1
Susan Weller widd	1	Robert Judds widdow	1
Mercy Vann	1	Ellenor Hope widd	1
Thomas Poyle	1	John Greene	2
Thomas Creed	1	John Sloman	2
Steeven Tyler	1	Roger Hovenden	2
Katherine Freeman	2	Ralph Binskin	2
Ann May widd	2	Jonah Botting	2
Joane Moter widd	1	William Munn	1
Widdow Crampton	1	Thomas Parson	1
Widdow Burges	2	David Branford	2
Lawrence Judd	1	Richard Botting	1
John Cooke	1	Widdow Thornton	2
Joseph Bennett	2	Herbert Snip	1
Nicholas Harris	1	John Godfrey	1
Widdow Levett	1	Widdow Dapp	1
Edward Harris	1	John Herne	1
Thomas Austen	2	Alexander Chamberlaine	2
Widdow Boreman	1	Widdow Reynolds	1
Richard Martin	1	John Willard	1
Widdow Hamman	1	Stephen Lye	1
Widdow Marden	2	Samuell Stuard	3
Widdow Roberts	1	Peter Marten	1
Thomas Nicholson	1	Widdow Welch	1
Widdow Catt	2	William Fernes	1
John Hubbard	1	Steeven Tharpe	1
George Catt	3	Edward Savage	2
Andrew Skelton	2	William Woollett	2
John Little	1	Anne Wright widd[ow]	1
Widdow of Isaac Wood	1	Thomas Fryland	1
Edward Wachers	1	Thomas Weller sen[io]r	1
Anthony Pullen	2	Thomas Swainsland	1
William Lamsden	1	John Burden	4

John Fosten	2	John Harris	1
Steeven Morris	2	Richard Beeland sen[io]r	1
Richard Clements	1	Thomas Pankherst	1
James Crampton	1	Widdow Griffy	1
John Fryman	1	David Springett	1
James Glasbrooke	1	Thomas Poyle	1
Steeven Chittenden	1	Widdow Moore	1

Abbots Franchise Borough

Chargeable		Chargeable	
Alexander Groombridge	16	Richard Fowle	4
John Weston	7	John Ellis	4
James Parton	6	John Potter	3
Michaell Harper	4	Samuell Crampton	4
[fol. 47v]			
Alexander Courthop	4	John Botting	3
James Bredgland	8	Alexander Jeffery	2
William Jenner	3	John Knell	2
John Baker	3	John Moorebread	5
Edward Wells	2	John Miller	4
John Hayward	2	[blank] Coulgate widd	4
John Day	2	William Ballard	1
James Morris	1	Samuell Potter	2

Not Chargeable		Not Chargeable	
Thomas Berry	1	John Tolherst	1
Nicholas Hart	1	Peter Courthop	1
Thomas Bathurst	4	Joseph Orris	3
Widdow Marrian	1	Thomas Peters	1
Robert Poyle	1	Thomas Wright	2
Richard Collyer	2	John Weller	1
Widdow Earle	1	Widdow Garrett	2
John Collier	1	[blank]	

Borough of Smithsditch

Chargeable		Chargeable	
Thomas Plummer	8	Walter Double	2
William Bates	1	Anne Hovenden	4
Thomas Basden	9	Thomas Muncke	2
John Heyward	2	Dency Weller	4
Richard Holden jun[io]r	6	Richard Dibley	1
James Standing	4	John Mantle	3

John Chadwick	1	John Chantler	3
Elizabeth Underhill	1	Susannah Sharpe	2
William Day	1	Partridge Russell	2
William Brissenden	2	Ezechiell Morris	3
Richard Spice	2	Richard Newball sen[io]r	3
William Foster	4	Nathaniell Tayler	3
William Cafinch	2	Humfry Briant	2
John Gorage	4	Joseph March	2
Richard Russell	3	John Austen	3
Mildred Graylen widd	2	Mary Tolherst	3
Robert Huglin	2	Martha Tree widd	2
Thomas Cheese	1	John Webb	4
James Cruttall	3	Richard Newball jun[io]r	2
Thomas Smith	3	Allen Bryant	1
Thomas Foster	1	Hannah Parton widd	3
Lady Baker widd	38	Mr Upton of Throwley in an empty house	-

Not Chargeable		**Not Chargeable**	
Richard Sillis	1	Mary Austen widd	1
Richard Cliffe	1	Thomas Gray	2
Widdow Brunger	1	Thomas Varball	1
Thomas Markettman	1	Matthew Hattnup	1
John Wilding	1	Edward Missingham	1
Thomas Caffinch	1	Thomas Beale	2
Steeven Goodley	1	Widdow Reader	2
Joseph Judge	2	John Heyther	3
Edward Beale	1	John Fowle	2
Widdow Hoare	2	Widdow Gardner	2
Edmund Boorner	1	Thomas Frowe	1
Abraham Caffinch	1	Widdow Judge	1
Thomas Judge	1	Christopher Peckham jun[io]r	1
John Cannon	1	Robert Hunt	1
John Allen	1	John Richardson	2
Joseph Murten	1	Dinah Wyborne widd	1
Widdow Obenes	1	Samuell Kelsden	1
John Young	2	Widdow Grinsted	1
Widdow Luckherst	1	John Hopper	2
Elias Rolfe	1	Alexander Couchman	2
John Patton borsholder			

Borough of Faire Crouch

Chargeable		Chargeable	
Lady Roberts widd	32	Thomas Lake Esq	6
Thomas Bayly	6	Robert Hovenden	6
John Williams	3	John Evernden	2
Richard Batts	2	Widdow Ragly	3
James Alley	4	Thomas Atkin	2
Henry Fillips	3	Richard Ballard junior	2
Samuell Bridgland	2	John Goodman	3
Isaac Walter sen[io]r	3	John Wildish	2
Peter Coleman	4	Thomas Wimshit	2
John Allforne	4	Moyses Tyler	2
Robert Jarrett	4	John Woore	2
Robert Guy	2	George Daw	2
Samuell Neale	3	John Whenam	1
Thomas Philpott	1	John Serly	2
Samuell Bayly jun[io]r	2	Richard Bassock	6
Steeven Dawson	4	Richard Porter	1
Mathew Porter	2	Ralfe Neave	2
Mathew Browne	2	Richard Ballard sen[io]r	3
Steeven Langford	1	Richard Hovelden sen[io]r	2
William Martin	3	Edward Barnden	6
Richard Wimsett	2	An empty house where}	
Edward Lockherst sen[io]r	2	Henry Merriam dwelt }	4
John Chewning	2	Richard Vinsett	3
[fol. 48r]			
Thomas Merriell	4	Peter Combes	4
Robert Courthop	4	John Bromley	2
Alexander Luckherst	3	Edward Luckherst	2
Mrs [blank] Lacke widd	2	and in an empty house	5
Thomas Tindall	5	Elias Blewet	3
Steeven White jun[io]r	3	Thomas Offry	3
William Hilles	6	John Rimington	2
John Rochester	3	John Wickham	2
John Wood	3	Joseph Iggleden	2
Christopher Catstreet	2	Jonah Fuller	4

Not Chargeable		Not Chargeable	
John Hartnap	1	Widdow Bankes	1
Widdow Webb	1	Richard Barrow	1
Widdow Conly	1	George Jervas	1
Widdow Collier	2	Thomas Reed	1

William Forminger	2	Samuel Morgan	1
Peter Walter	1	Thomas Collens	1
Widdow Hickmott	1	Thomas Morgan	1
John Morgen	1	John Pousden	1
Peter West	1	Widdow Backett	1
James Beckhing	1	Andrew Minge	1
Widdow Morris	1	Widdow Matres	1
Widdow Baker	1	Widdow Coleman	2
Widdow Chatten	2	Jarvis Tampkin	3
Widdow Morgan	1	Widdow Atkin	3
Thomas Tolherst	1	Christopher Tolherst	1
William Peene	1	William Harvye	1
Nicholas Parkes	2	Thomas Oyler	2
William Scotchford	2	Thomas Haffenden	1
Widdow Earle	1	John Grove	1
Richard Oore	1	Thomas Miller	1
		Thomas Hunt [265]	1
Thomas Young	1	Alexander Shakerly	5
John Willson	1	Widdow Mattocke	1
Thomas Johnson	2	John Dove	2
William Crapwell	2	Steeven Wemset	1
Thomas Bacham	1	Thomas Brumley	2
John Rayson	2	Thomas Brett	1
		Peter Combes borsholder	

THE HUNDRED OF BERKLEY
in the lath of Scray

Hevenden Borough

Chargeable		Chargeable	
Sir John Henden Kt	25	Thomas Curtis	2
William Rippon	4	Robert Drayner gent	8
Jervis Morlen	6	James Blackmore	5
Ralph Neave	2	Samuell Morlen	4
William Cottingham	2	William Bennett	2
Widdow Skeere	6	William Playford	2
Steeven Wimsherst	4	John Whitfield	7
John Tayler	8	Robert Usmer	4
John Chapman	2	John Chapman more	4
Charles Leedes	5	James Oliver	1

---

[265] Interlined entry.

William Hopper	1	John Willard	1
Mathew Sampson	1		

Not Chargeable		Not Chargeable	
James Sloman	1	William Rippon	1
John Sherwood	1	Widdow Steevens	1
Widdow Binskin	1	Mary Blist	1
James Blackman	1	[blank] Butcher	1
John Hills	2	Samuell Morlen	1
John Ingram	2	John Kadwell	1
John Shelley	1	Widdow Syms	1
Thomas Heyter	1	Bernard Lamb	1
Richard Jewherst	1	Robert Fuller	2
Widdow Playford	1	John Chapman	1
John Maynard	2	Edward Wenn	1
Thomas Dunster	1	William Judd	1
Mary Bristow	1	Thomas Grinsted	1
John Bueden	1	Thomas Little	1
Richard Greene	1	William Harper	1
Mr Robert Drayner	1	Mr Edmund Steed	1

Iborden Borough

Chargeable		Chargeable	
Freegift Boorne	3	James Busse	2
Edward Ownsloe	2	William Boreman	3
Leonard Hickmott	5	Richard Mills	6
William Hunt	1	Anthony Pigott	3
John Illenden	2	Henry Osmer	4
Richard Debley	6	William Whitney	4
Edmund Cratwell	4	Richard Bateman	3
Mr Edmund Steed	9	Alexander Homsby	5
Richard Brissenden	1	Thomas Mount	3
Richard Foster	7	Thomas Irons	2
Widdow Salter	2	Alexander Lucas	2
Mr John Mills	4	James Harding	6
Robert Stedman	2	John Jennings	3
Thomas Reynolds	4	Robert Burton	3
Thomas Caffinch	2	Richard Theobald	8
James Osborne	6	Simon Reyner	1
Isaac Skinner	5	Simon Faulkner	4
Thomas Standen	2	Elias Standen	1
James Standen	1	Robert Samson	1

James Harding jun[io]r	3	Richard Harding	2
George Haffenden	3	Mrs Freebody	4
[fol. 48v]			
Richard Woolball	5	John Furner	1
Moses Lee clerke	9	and more in the }	
Richard Kenchewood	2	parsonage house }	8
Henry Wyde	2	Thomas Nower	3
Richard Backwell	2	Robert Tusenode	1
William Crittenden	1	William Clarke	4
Thomas Windsor	2	Christopher Clarke	3
Thomas Post	4	Anthony Poyle	3
Terry Aldersea gent	11	Alexander Birchley	9
Edward Couchman	1	Sir John Mayney Knight	1
Michaell Harper	1	John Earle of Thanett	1
Mr Thomas Bigg	4	Solomon Faulkner	1
Mr Terrey Aldersey	4	Mr William Randolph	4
Sir John Henden	6	In the free schoole in	6
Leonard Hickmott	2	Biddenden	
		Mr William Seyliard	2

Not Chargeable		**Not Chargeable**	
Robert Stedman	1	James Godfrey	1
Thomas Hermon	1	Robert Post	1
Widdow Hamwood	1	John Henman	1
William Shoosmith	2	Thomas Shatterden	1
Judith Bluett	1	John Hopper	2
John Franklyn	2	Thomas Borough	1
Widdow Masters	1	Adam Syms	1
Edward Wilkins	1	Edward Stone	1
John Wilkins	1	Widdow Munn	2
Richard Lucas	2	Widdow Downe	1
Widdow Wimble	1	Mary Pope	1
Widdow Evans	1	Joane Stringer	1
Henry Avery	2	John Barre	1
Henry Turner	3	Peter Jewherst	1
George Evernden	1	Henry Rootes	1
John Syms	1	William Bankes	1
Widdow Double	1	Widdow Wachers	1
William May	2	James Harding junior	1
John Walker	2	Richard Heytoe	1
Thomas Humfrey	1	Richard Venice	1
Goddard Harper	1	Widdow Harper	1
William Lambe	1	William Willard	1

William Springett	1	Widdow Syms	1
Widdow Bristow	1	James Samson	1
James Willard	1	Widdow Clarke	1
David Barre	1	John Heytoe	1
Widdow Pankherst	2		

Wachenden Borough

Chargeable		Chargeable	
Edward Leedes	1	John Chalker	2
Austin Tayler	2	Robert Swift	3
John Beale	4	Thomas Abdy	7
John Clarke	2	Widdow Kennet	2
Edward Apsley	5	Thomas Date	2
John Bishopenden	1	John Bateman	6
Widdow Birkett	1		

Not Chargeable		Not Chargeable	
Joseph Large	1	Richard Baker	1
Phillis Gaskins	1		

Worchenden Borough

Chargeable		Chargeable	
Thomas Rogers	10	Widdow Boone	3
James Bunce	6	John Morlen	2
Vincent Quilter	6	Thomas Skeales	6
John Ramsden	8	Thomas Moore	2
Robert Elficke	2	John Wilkins junior	2
Richard Collins	3	John Iggleden	3
John Weekes	1	Edward Pattison	6
Simon Rayner	2	James Harding junior	2

Not Chargeable		Not Chargeable	
Robert Little	1	John Moore	1
Widdow Vorsley	1	Jeremiah Cattman	1
Thomas Illenden	1	Thomas Springett	1
Thomas Wood	3	Simon Coltman	2
Arthur Poynett	1	John Mills	1
Widdow Chauntler	2		

Omenden Borough

Chargeable		Chargeable	
Richard Willard	3	William Buckhurst	2

John Franke	4	Christopher Fullager	5
Widdow Pattinson	5	Peter Gardner	3
Andrew Hills	2	Richard Beale	4
Robert Knight	5	Richard Turner	1
Thomas Joanes	3	John Austen	2
Nicholas Raith	4	John Cooke	3
Walter Guillham	4	Walter Guillham more	3
William Woollett	2	John Haffenden	5
Thomas Haffenden	4	Widdow Bennett	3
Widdow Edmett	4	William Varroll	2
Jervas Ramsden	1	Francis Little	1
John Mungeham	1	Widdow Tilden	4
Widdow Gadsby	1	Abraham Batt	1
Richard Newman	2	Francis Saxby	1
Nicholas Mayham	1	Jeremiah Baker	2
Steeven Robins	1	Thomas Austin	1
Thomas Price alias Hakins	2	John Glover	1
William Hubbert	2	Mr Edmund Steed	8
[fol. 49r]			
Elias Gomery	1	Robert Borne	1
Widdow Atkins	1	Reginold Clegate	1
Richard Allard	1	Christopher Clerke	1
John Knight	1	John Tilman	1
John Clerke	1	Widdow Turner	1
Thomas Bridge	2	Mr Richard Champneys	4
Widdow Bishop	1	Andrew Hills	2
William Varroll	2	John Newenden's heire	1
John Mungeham	1	Thomas Milsted	2

Not Chargeable		**Not Chargeable**	
Phillip Homewood	2	Robert Pout	1
John Gyles	1	Richard Branger	1
John Butcher	1	Richard Borne	1
Thomas Scarsland	1	William Harvey	1
Nicholas Butcher	1	Thomas Earle	2
Widdow Humfrey	2	Widdow Shooesmith	1
Richard Newman	1	Richard Champneys	1

Stephurst Borough

Chargeable		**Chargeable**	
James Besbeech	3	William Gilbert	2
William Greenhill	2	George Clerke	3
John Little	2	Thomas Dann	2

Widdow Parkes	4	William Baker	2
Henry Hider	4	Alexander Fortune	1
William Bridge	2	Thomas Milsted	3
Richard Waterman	3	James Waters	3
John Dabbs	3	William Viney	1
John Hermon	2	John Waters	1
Henry Kingsnode	3	William Reynolds	1
Thomas Kingsnode	3	William Smith	1
Gervis Goodwyn	2	William Fortune	2
Widdow Upton	1	Richard Waterman	3

Not Chargeable		**Not Chargeable**	
Richard Goodwyn	1	Widdow Masters	1
Widdow Mockett	1	Joseph Igleden	1
Allen French	1		

THE HUNDRED OF BLACKBOURNE
in the lath of Scray

Novenden Borough

Chargeable		**Chargeable**	
John Cranford Clerke	3	Robert Jorden	5
John Jorden	6	Samuell Pope	3
John Cooke	4	Robert Jorden junior	4
Jeremiah Smalefeild	2	William Edmonds	1
Steeven Powne	2	Robert Woollett	2
Arthur Baker	1	John Price	4
Sir Edward Hales bart	6	Sir John Maney Kt	7
Robert Waterman	7	Reginald Pickenden	4
George Harwood	3	Thomas Morlin	4
John Poune	1	John Wallford	4
William Tilden	6	William Tourt	9
Richard Beeching	4	George Holland	1
Edward Jorden	4	Richard Poune	2
William Cooke	8	Richard Clerke	3
John Pickenden	2	James Hubberd	1
James Lott	4	Jeremiah Woodgate	4
Richard Heneker	2	Robert Wrenn	4
Robert Goodwell	1	Christopher Edwards	2
Thomas Browne	2	Thomas Hyland	1
James Powne	3	William Harlow	1

Not Chargeable

Edward Honey	2
Allmeshouses	3
Widdow Brad	1

Not Chargeable

Thomas Martin	1
John Tanner	1

Povenden Borough

Chargeable

Michaell Peirce	5
Steeven Chapman	3
Jeremiah Sherlocke	3
Thomas Igleden	1
Robert Turley	1
William Burford	6
Thomas Cheeseman	4
John Woollett	4
Thomas Gilbert	3
William Lilly	2
John Cheeseman	2
Thomas Filly	1
Widdow Carde	2
Jonas Bayliffe	1
Thomas Barton	1
Steeven Butcher	1

Chargeable

John Paule	6
Widdow Bishop	4
George Stace	1
Thomas Igleden more	1
Thomas Gorham	1
John Waterman	4
Edward Bassett	2
John Waterman	4
Francis Austen	2
Peter Went	2
William Parker	4
Robert Rich	2
Thomas Bankes	2
Thomas Lawes	3
Widdow Adams	1
Thomas Barton junior	1

Ridgeway Borough

Chargeable

Thomas Harlakenden Esquire	13
Mathew Goble	6
Widdow Harding	4
Thomas Ramsden	3
Henry Pantry	1
Joseph Stanley	5
John Merriall	2
Edward Ferost	2
Thomas Attoway	3

[fol. 49v]

Richard Ramsden	4
John Mount	1
William Austin	3
William Hills	1
Beniamin Roblow	3
Robert Cheeseman	1

Chargeable

Steeven Munn clerke	7
John Ditton	4
John Crittenden	2
Thomas Staple	8
Richard Chittenden	4
John Burton	3
Widdow Willis	2
William Rickard	2
John Willmersherst	1
John Ditton	1
Mr Sheafe	2
John Austin	3
Walter Fox	3
William Brisley	2
Widdow Fagge	1
Robert Pemble	1

Daniell Bathop	6	Mathew Austen	2
George Scott	1	Simon Baker	1
Thomas Brissenden	4	Thomas Russell	4
Thomas Doudy	1	Mrs Joane King	4

Not Chargeable		**Not Chargeable**	
Thomas Woodgate	1	William Henley	1
Richard Boren	1	William Beech	1
Francis Daniell	1	Moses Cheeseman	1
John Dufty	1	Simon Dawson	1
John Clarke	1	John Weekes	1
Nathaniell Ely	1	Thomas Hedgcocke	1
Widdow Newman	1	Jarman King	1
Widdow Cheeseman	1	Widdow Stermy	1

Old Harlakenden Borough

Chargeable		**Chargeable**	
Richard Curd	4	Henry Firminger	5
William Lakendenar	5	Richard Browning	1
James Bankes	3	Edward Masters Esquire	3
Thomas Carpenter	3	Nathaniell Mannering	1
Thomas Harlakenden Esq	5	Thomas Yates	1
John Foreman	1	Edward Finsherst	1
Richard Milles	2	William Chittenden	4
Widdow Smithson	1	John Milsted	3
Robert Cole clerke	2	John Hooke	3
Thomas Webb	1	Widdow Webb	4
John Larkin	1		

Not Chargeable		**Not Chargeable**	
Steeven Humfry	1	John Bunkley	1
Thomas Bunkley	1	Richard Milles	1
Widdow Smithson	1	Richard Martin	1
John Hunt	2	Widdow Giles	2

Ingham Borough

Chargeable		**Chargeable**	
William Brissenden	4	Robert Smith	4
Henry Hills	1	John Honnon	1
Steven Tilden	1	Thomas Yates	3
Henry Spillett	1	John Hilby	1
Thomas Allen	3	William Binn	2

John Ashley	4	Matthew Goble	3
Richard Ditton	1		

Not Chargeable		Not Chargeable	
John Palmer	1	Robert Smith	1
John Norwood	1	Widdow Pollard	2

Great Kenardington Borough

Chargeable		Chargeable	
Widdow Croftes	1	Thomas Hones	6
John Southen	4	George May	6
William May	1	Goodman Meeke	1
Thomas Leadnor	1	Thomas Rasell	3
Widdow Sanbourne	1	John Simons	1
Widdow Stocke	1	John Hubord	1
Robert Wilverden	1	Henry Moone	1
William Packham	6	Richard Payne	4
Abraham Fuller	2	John Honas	1
Widow Wide	1	James Adkins	1
Henry Gill	1	John Vane	2
John Cheeseman	2	Richard Stanley	1
Thomas Packham	5	Richard Shoosmith	6
William Tampkins	4	Richard Horne	4
Robert Allen	3	William Mercer	2
Richard Gatland	1	William Gamon	1

Not Chargeable		Not Chargeable	
William Battham	1	John Ellis	1
William Barrett	1	Richard Stacy	1

Appledore Heath Borough

Chargeable		Chargeable	
John Columbine	3	George Adams	4
Thomas Hudson	3	James Baker	1
Samuell Parker	1	John Russell	1
Richard Swayland	1	William Easterfeild	8
George Perkins	3	Steeven Pell	3
William Farmer	2	William Walter	1
Thomas Perkins	2	Michaell Stone	4
Edward Colenbine	3		

Not Chargeable		Not Chargeable	
Nicholas Pollington	1	George Ryler	1

Steven Riller	2	William Button	1
Christopher Shrubsole	1	Widdow Bremmil	1

Little Kenardington Borough

Chargeable		Chargeable	
The parsonage house	3	John Rolfe	1
Thomas Hounes	2	Widdow Wood	3
John Fane	3	William Hadlow	2
Edward Finch	4	Nathaniell Feild	2

Not Chargeable		Not Chargeable	
Edward Finch	1	Widow George	1
Widdow May	1		

[fol. 50r]

Appledore Towne Borough

Chargeable		Chargeable	
William Esterfeild	5	Richard Fouterell	8
Thomas Tand	3	George Martin	5
Samuel Tilden	3	John Waters	5
Thomas Downe	3	Mr Bates	3
William Tripland	3	Mr Drayton	2
Thomas Page	2	John Oxenbridge	3
John Bensted	3	George Farmer	2
Thomas Fuller	2	Thomas Fuller junior	2
Thomas Fagg	2	Thomas Haward	4
John Bourne	4	Richard Fusse	1
Daniell Reynolds	3	Mr Gilliard	3
George Austen	1		

Not Chargeable		Not Chargeable	
Widdow Wheeler	1	Widdow Pope	3
Edward Watson	1	Widdow Reynolds	2
Widdow Adams	1	John Harris	1
Widdow Beane	2	Henry Coebourne	1

Hailes Bridge Borough

Chargeable		Chargeable	
William Linkherst	4	Thomas Willmershurst	3
Daniell George	7	Robert Cheeseman	2
Thomas Badnor	4	Roger Pay	1
John Staple	1	John Vinale	2

John Vinale	1	Avery Cheesman	2
Edward Vinale	3	Widdow Martin	4
Widdow Mathom	3	Nicholas Lapham	1
William Hemsley	3	Richard Davis	1
Edward Butcher	1	Josias Cheeseman	1
John Haysell	1	Thomas Wagon	4
Richard Phillips	1	William Godfrey	1
Richard Wood	3		

Not Chargeable		Not Chargeable	
Daniell George	1	Widdow Whitehead	1
John Vinall	1	Widdow Cheeseman	1
Thomas Willmott	3	Widdow May	1
Richard Phillips	1		

HUNDRED OF MARDEN
In the Lath of Scray

The Great Borough of Gowtherst

Chargeable		Chargeable	
Widdow Rochester	1	William Perrin	2
Robert Pickrell	1	Thomas Brattle	4
Widdow West	1	Henry Faulkner	1
Richard Gower	1	John Springett	3
Thomas Phillips at the Goare	4	Thomas Waters	3
Widdow Musgrave	1	John Walter	3
Henry Crispe	3	Richard Roades	2
Edward Scott	5	Edward Roades	4
Thomas Meere	4	William Waters	4
William Steevens	7	Richard Hover	3
Thomas Tate	8	William Butcher	2
James Browne weaver	1	Thomas Roe	1
Robert Kingsmell	4	James Burch	3
Richard Bonnicke	2	Thomas Buckland	1
Alexander Mantellow	1	John Lamkin	3
George Golding	1	Thomas Perrin	2
Alexander Lindredge	2	Francis Kent	3
John Beale	4	Richard Brattle	1
Thomas Hills	5	William Hilles	6
Widdow Fayreway	1	John Young	2
William Leight	2	Thomas Sibly junior	2
William Vincome	1	Jeffery Austen	2
Steeven Pilcher	3	William Hartredge	1

John Russell tyler	1	John Diamond	2
Thomas Holmes	4	Thomas Earle	2
Widdow Tomlin	2	Jacob Bridge	4
Steeven White	1	John Austen	1
Henry Bowles	2	Peter Courthop	4
Samuell Coleman	5	Thomas Welden gent	6
Robert Bathurst	5	Richard Jarvis	5
John Standen	3	Robert Steevens	2
Thomas Gatland	1	Thomas Golding	1
Robert Bennett	4	Mrs Bathurst	10
John Russell miller	2	George Moore	2
Steeven Ferrall	1	James Besbeech	6
William Coggar	2	Steeven Stringer	2
James Hembry	1	Samuell Turke	3
William Hills grinder	1	Mr Sanders	5
Steeven Hooker	3	Thomas Phillips	5
Mr Edward Thurman	6	Thomas Stringer	5
Henry Steevens	4	James Browne	2
Steeven White	2	Thomas Bridgland	1
Gregory Oakey	1	Alexander White	7
Daniell Willson	3	Abraham Beale	1
Edward Walter	6	Thomas Leight	5
John Horsemonden Esq	9	John Groomebridge	4
John Streater	4	Robert Russell	1
George Streater	2	Robert Morris	1
[fol. 50v]			
Richard Everest	3	Widdow Ockenden	2
Thomas Haffenden	2	George Weldish	2
Thomas Sibly	7	Francis Hamond	2
Mrs Day	2	Thomas Barrowes	4
Richard Thong	2	Gabriell Tomkin	3
Attayne Smith senior	4	Abraham King	4
Widdow Whatman	2	John Austen	9
Jacob Bridge for Rimington	4	[blank] Beech	4
John Horsmonden Esq	2		

Not Chargeable

Walter Coyfe	1	Samuell Potter	1
Walter Saywell	1	Thomas Lindredge	1
John Symonds	1	Widdow Smith	1
Anthony Horsmonden	1	William Dawson	1
Widdow Remington	1	Richard Hodge	1

Not Chargeable

Widdow Scott	1	William Alborne	1
Widdow Collins	1	James Whatman	2
Robert Clarke	1	John Drawbridge	1
Steeven Baker	1	Widdow Collyer	2
Abraham Luffe	3	Steeven Bennett	2
Robert Dudly	2	Roger French	1
Widdow Usban	1	William Merchant	1
Mathew Merritt	1	Thomas Steby	2
Thomas Pettman	1	James Beeching	1
Widdow Smith	1	Widdow Lamkin	1
Widdow Austen	1	Widdow Walter	1
Nicholas Burden	1	Jeremiah Stedman	1
John Baker	1	William May	1
Thomas Farmer	1	Widdow Way	1
Phillip Hadds	1	Henry Musgrave	1
Robert Larkin	1	Alexander Brett	1
Widdow Brattle	1	James Hunt	1
John Greenfeild	1	Widdow Gaskoyne	1
John Roberts	1	Widdow Fillmer	1
Lambert Goulding	1	Richard Watts	1
Widdow Remington	1	Edward Hyland	1
David Freeman	2	John Justagin	2
John Braborne	1	John Stephens	1
William Austin	2	Thomas Chapman	1
Widdow Towne	1	Thomas Usband	1
Robert Weller	1	Widdow Collier	1
George Gascoine	1	Walter Reynolds	1
William Waters	2	James Reynolds	1
[blank] Egrimony	1	Widdow Barber	1
Robert Gatland	2	Richard Harmond	1
Widdow Sones	1	Thomas Hickley	1
John Golding	2	Widdow Parker	1
Widdow Reynolds	1	William Dyer	1
William Olley	1	Widdow Golding	1
Nicholas Golding	2	Widdow Nash	1
William Trendle	2	John Carroway	2
John Hawkins	1	Mathew Dodson	2
William Munn	2	Widdow Brookes	1
Thomas Allen	2	Thomas Collins	1
Widdow Botting	2	Ambrose Bigg	2
Thomas Bigg	1	Mary Morgan	1
John Morgan	1	William Austen	1
Widdow Buckland	1	Widdow Evernden	2

William Balcombe	2	Widdow Hembry	2
Thomas Reeve	2	Widdow Beeching	1
[blank] Wenn	1	[blank] Hayward	1
Thomas Harty	1	John Austen	1
Thomas Postlewaite	2	Thomas Clarke	2
Leonard Francis	2	John Howlett	1
John Rogers	2	Alexander Remington	2
Thomas Steevens	3	Richard Atkins	1
Widdow Atkins	1	Widdow Baldocke	1
John Brightridge	1	Vincent Rugg	1
Daniell Crooch	1	Widdow Buggs	2
John Turner	1	John Garrett	2
Widdow Polley	1	Thomas Lambe	1
Richard Hodge	1	William Marchant	1
Thomas Death	1	John Cradocke	1
Widdow Hope	2	John Deane	1
Samuel Oakell	2	Thomas Rogers	2
Widdow Haynes	1	John Robinson	2
Francis Browne	2	Widdow Newcombe	2
Henry Sibly	1	Edward Goaler	1
Edward Hills	1	Daniell Crouch	1
James Besbeech	1	Widdow Hunt	1
Richard Deward	1	Widdow Cliffe	1
John Bayly	1	Richard Hampton	1
William Sadler	1	Simon Morris	1
Thomas Gurr	1	Beniamin Hembry	1
John Lye	2	Steeven Streate	3
Widdow Peirce	2	Edward Dodge	2
Edward Leafe	2	Widdow Baker	1
James Kadwell	1	Widdow Vant	1
Francis Austen	1	John Russell	2
Robert Tompkin	1	Widdow [blank]	2

[fol. 51r]

Elhurst Borough

Chargeable		Chargeable	
Samuell Cole	3	George Maplisden	8
Edward Maplisden	6	Francis Cornwell	3
Mary Jewell	2	Thomas Walter	2
William Chittenden	3	William Peters	1
John Goldsmith	1	James Cornwell senior	5
Thomas Wood	2	Attained Burr	3

Thomas Gulven	2	William Masters	4
James Cornwell junior	3	Henry Bromeman	1
William Allen	5	William Gibbons	4
James Reader	3	John Roberts	6
Herbert Goldsmith	1	Daniell Goore	2
George Afford	1	Thomas Bevetbeard	2
Enoch Hollman	4	Thomas Willward	3
David Hills	2	Richard Johnson	2
Francis Steevens	2	John Hovenden	4
John Budds	1	Robert Wiffenden	1
Thomas Law	3	Richard Larkin	2
Elizabeth Steevens junior	2	[blank] Russell widdow	1
John Evernden	1	John Allen	2
Richard Hoare	1	Robert Drust	3
[blank] Maplesden widd	2	John Musgrove	2
Thomas Bassock	2	[blank] Grigsby widd	1
William Summers	1	James Bestbeech	4
John Steevens sen[io]r	4	Susan Roberts	2
Thomas Stephens	2	[blank] Cornwell widd	3
William Maynard	3	William Whatman	2
Robert Garford	4	Isaac Willard	1
Thomas Barton	1	Nicholas Bunnett	-
John Stephens junior	5		

Not Chargeable		**Not Chargeable**	
Thomas Kingswood	3	John Thorneton	2
Thomas Miskin	1	[blank] Sabb widd	1
Robert Hall	2	John Pickenden	1
Thomas Tayler	1	[blank] Parker widd	1
[blank] Forman widd	1	Mary Sharpey	1
Thomas Lee	1	John Thorne	1
John Matcham	2	John Collens jun[io]r	2
John Day	1	Richard Numm	1
[blank] Haffleden widd	1	John Masters	1
Richard Chapman	1	James Reynolds	1
Christopher Stirings	2	[blank] Parker widd	2
Richard Burwash	2	John Conye	1
John Collens senior	1	[blank] Bridger widd	1
John Remington	1	[blank] Dewly widd	1
William Dowle	1	Thomas Conny	1
Peter Hollans	1	Thomas Reynolds	2
Elizabeth Longly	1	John Macklen	1
John Walter	1	[blank] Snelling widd	1

[blank] Stonnard widd	1	[blank] Vousden widd	1
John Peake	1	Thomas Walter	1
Michaell Griffin	2	[blank] Conny widd	1
Richard Willson	1	William Weldish	1
George Keene	1	[blank] Mills widd	1
John Harden	1	Richard Gatland	1

Laudenden Borough

Chargeable		Chargeable	
Henry Woolball	4	John Grinsted	4
John Crofts	3	Thomas Usband	6
Mathew Medhurst	2	Richard Walter	4
Walter Viney	2	Richard Blackbourne	4
William Yorkton	9	Jeremiah Jennings	2
Richard Stider	4	Ralph Ely	1
Abraham Scoone	3	Constant Kent	4
Thomas Housegoe	4	Arthur Hart	4
William Scott	4	Peter Burren	8
Robert Kett	6	Thomas Skoone	2
John Standen	4	John Weston	9
William Tollherst	3	John Burren	3
Mr John Butcher	4	Thomas Wood	7
William Scott	2		

Not Chargeable		Not Chargeable	
Thomas Lambe	2	George Amery	1
Mary Scoone widd	1	James Kingsnorth	2
Henry Caffinch	2	John Busse	2
James Wimble	2	John Medhurst	2
John Wilks	1	Richard Moore	1
Widdow Huggins	2	Widdow Cheeseman	1
Richard Lamkin	2	Thomas Scoones	2
Thomas Bingham	2	Daniell Bates	2
Widdow Strood	2	Mathew Ashdowne	2
Mary Grove	2	Robert Tucker	1
John Pye	2	Thomas Chapman	2
Thomas Bayly	1	Thomas Strood	1
Rowland Williams	1	Henry Collier	2
George Holt	1	Thomas Wood	1
Widdow Norwood	1	one empty Cottage	1
Jacob Skinner	2	Robert Manser	1
Widdow Cooper	1	William Warwicke	1

[fol. 51v]

Pattenden Borough

Chargeable		Chargeable	
Mr Edward Simonds	8	Richard Barton	3
Henry Webb	1	William Barham	1
Henry Manwaring	3	John Gamon	3
Moses Evernden	2	Widdow Roberts	4
Robert Bold	4	John Austen	3
William Steevens	1	Richard Nash	3
Widdow Payle	2	Widdow Merriam	1
John French	1	John Burch	2
Steeven Nash	3	John Nash	4
James Dann	1	John Warke	2
Francis Wyman	2	John Willson	3
Samuell Crittenden	2	Nathaniell Harnden	2
Edward Austen	2	William Iden	2
Edward Underhill	1	William Higham	1
Beniamin Chambers	1	Edward Vowsden	1
James Skinner	1	Richard Walker	1
James French	2	John Vousden	1
Thomas Austen	1	Isaac Prawle	2
Thomas Browne	2	John Ginnings	2
Widow Austen	2		

Not Chargeable		Not Chargeable	
Henry Hines	1	James Best	1
John Martin	4	Giles Summers	1
Widdow Cheesemen	1	Widdow Bell	1
John Theobald	1	Widdow Dann	1
Abraham Matcham	1	Henry Martin	2
Widdow Daniell	1	[blank] Larkin	2
Thomas Smith	1	Widdow Budgen	1
James Wood	2	Widdow Spackman	1

Dagswell Borough

Chargeable		Chargeable	
[blank] Jarvis widdow	2	[blank] Cripps widdow	4
Solomon Rolfe	2	Brian Lassells	4
Thomas Yorkton	3	Thomas Crumpe	3
Edward Honey	1	Richard Boxer	4
[blank] Crumpe widdow	4	[blank] Goodwin	2
Joseph Dann	2	Francis Gooding	4
John Mason	2	John Piper	2

Thomas Posse	4	Thomas Meere	3
John Jewell	3	James Allen	5
John Dunstan	1	William Spice	3
John Usban	2	William Mayhoe	5
John Longly	3	George Weldish	1
Edward Bathurst gent	1	John Bayly	3

Not Chargeable		**Not Chargeable**	
[blank] Chittenden widd	1	Thomas Harris	1
James Dann	2	John Walter	3
Edward Piner	1	Widdow Walker	1
Thomas Peerles	1	John Reader	1
Widdow Collyer	1	Widdow Hart	1
William Rich	1	Thomas Manser	1
Widdow Ferrall	1	Andrew Coney	1
William Harden	1	William Honey	1
Arthur Fetherston	1	John Winton	2

Sutton Borough

Chargeable		**Chargeable**	
Thomas Butcher gent	6	Thomas Lambe gent	4
Anne Lamb widdow	2	Thomas Tayler	3
Robert Tamsett	2	Thomas Milburne	2
William Bodkin	3	John Ledger	3
Henry Snoath	2	John Watchers	3
Goddard Foster	4	Ann Housley	3
Thomas Cord	4	William Mayhoe	7
Thomas Butler	2	David Austen	4
Thomas Young	5	Thomas Pottwell	1
John Butcher gent	5	Edward Usband	2
George Maplisden	4		

Not Chargeable		**Not Chargeable**	
Thomas Stedman	1	Robert Bassett	2
Thomas Grinhill	1	Thomas Gullen	2

Frenches Liberty

Chargeable		**Chargeable**	
John Butcher gent	11	John Stephens	6
Sarah Rolfe	2	Christopher Castreet	2
Thomas Everis	1	Thomas Castleden	2
Jeremiah Poyle	2	Edward Hodge	4

Christopher Weekes	3	John Smith	1
William Austen	1	Lawrence Eyler	1
Thomas Ledger	3	Abraham Chapman	4

Ruckherst Borough

Chargeable		Chargeable	
Thomas Sibly	3	Attained Smith	7
Capt[aine] Alcone	5	Thomas Willard	2
John Tickner	4	Thomas Beckett	4
Steeven Minsett	2	William Budds	2
Robert Marchant	4	Mr [blank] Bunce	2
William Wilson	1	Robert Wilson	1
Thomas Weldish	2		

Not Chargeable		Not Chargeable	
Rebeccah Page	1	Widdow Willard	1
Mathew Willard	1	Thomas Young	1
Thomas Rickwater	1	Widdow Reeve	1
John Gale	1	Thomas Davys	3
Bernard Martin	1	Robert Phillips	1
Thomas Noakes	2		

John Stephens Constable of the hundred of Marden

[fol. 52r]

THE HUNDRED OF MILTON
in the Lath of Scray

The East Division of the said Hundred

The Borough of Milton

Chargeable		Chargeable	
John Hurt vicar	3	John Daniell	7
John Witherden	4	John Knowler	4
John Bassett	3	John Tolpott	6
John Hinxell	4	John Marshall	4
James Colley	4	John Butler	2
John Scott	4	James Richman	4
James Mercer	2	John Burcher	2
John Watterer	3	Isaac Cooper	2
Zacheus Ivett	4	John Rose	5
John Spratt	2	John Taply	2
John Rumney	3	Joshuah Pix	5

John Packer	2	John Finch	2
John Cutbush	1	John Buck	1
James Ally	2	William Godwinn	2
William Simpson	6	Valentine Vahan	1
William Elgatt	2	William Covell	6
William Grant	4	William Watterer	2
William Griffin	3	William Marlow	2
William Russell	3	William Ember	2
Widdow Bissie	5	Widdow Webb	7
Widdow Leedes	8	Widdow Wellard	4
Widdow Crux	4	Widdow Anvill	1
William Cooper	6	Thomas Cooper	5
Thomas Knott	3	Thomas Violett	6
Thomas Michell senior	3	Thomas Ireene	6
Thomas Elvin	1	Alexander Fletcher	3
Alexander Covell	6	Edward Ore	5
Edward Fishenden	4	Edward Smyth	2
Edward Buckmer	4	Edward Tayler	3
Richard Smyth	4	Richard Smyth more }	
Richard Barrow	3	in the Court Lodge}	5
Richard Hearne	3	Richard Tappenden	2
Richard Longly	2	Robert Cooke	3
Thomas Barton gent	6	Thomas Hammon	4
Thomas Bassett	4	Thomas Meade	4
Thomas Kempe	2	Thomas Dillett	2
Thomas Robinson	4	Thomas Daniell	1
Thomas Tomlin gent	10	Barnard Clarke	4
William Allen	3	William Hilles	3
William Burnham	4	Stephen Carryer	3
Stephen Baker Junior	2	Thomas Readmans	2
Thomas Strayne	2	Beniamin Readmans	4
Andrew Abbett	2	Charles Simpson	4
Christopher Gore	2	Christopher Nottage	3
George Amis	3	Henry Rose	2
Henry Cockin sen	2	Henry Cockin jun	2
Henry Bunce	4	Henry West	1
Henry Corke	3	Francis Meade	2
Henry Flagden	3	Thomas Harker	-
Richard Benchkin	3	Widdow Lanes	4
Widdow Rumney	4	Marke Smart	2
Marke Elfery	2	Robert Johnson	3
Phillip Lane gent	4	Thomas Terry	2

Pierce Turner	2	James West	1
George West	2	Mary Roath	4
Thomas Scownes	2	George Mason	3
William Acurst	1	Robert Hambleton	1
Thomas Rich	2	Edward Fryday	4
Abraham Wessenden	5	Robert Fuller	4
Jo[hn] Corke	1	Thomas Winn junior	2
Richard Readmans	2	Jo[hn] Smyth	3
William Allen	1	Thomas Garrett	2
Richard Anderson	2	Stephen Bartlett	1
Cheyney Bourne	7	Arthur Reynolds	5
Jo[hn] Battell	3	Robert Mullins	6

Houses empty

Mr Deale in 3 houses	6	Arthur Whatman gentleman	2
William Cadman	4	Thomas Crus	3
Bartholomew May gent	3	Josuah Pix	3
William Allen	2	[blank] Horsnaile gent	2
Thomas Huggens	2	Widdow Leedes	1
Thomas Tomlin gent	4	Thomas Beale	3

The Borough of Milton

Not Chargeable		Not Chargeable	
Thomas Winn senior	2	Richard Potter	2
Richard Page	1	Edward Page	2
Walter [blank]	2	Henry Dyer	1
Widdow Partridge	2	William Saxby	1
Edward Countes	1	Jo[hn] Allen	1
William Pepper	2	William Champe	1
Widdow Wyett	1	Widdow Bowles	1
Widdow Knowler	1	Nicholas Edmans	1
Widdow Fathers	1	Jo[hn] Ashpoll	1
Thomas Herne	2	Jo[hn] Philpott	2
Thomas Dawson	3	William Young	2
Jo[hn] Pix	2	Jo[hn] Elgatt	5
[fol. 52v]			
Jo[hn] Cuch	2	Henry Nethersole	1
Thomas Turly	1	William Cary	2
Widdow Stonard	2	William Beadle	2
Jo[hn] Phillipps	2	Samuell Weekes	1
Widdow Jeffery	1	Widdow Allen	2
Richard Harris	1	Jo[hn] Chapman	1
Henry Heycock	2	Henry Batherst	1

Widdow Pix	1	Widdow Turner	1
Jeffry Harding	2	Richard Burten	3
Widdow Brockwell	1	William Pickett	1
Jo[hn] Field	1	Ed[ward] Hearst	1
Widdow Rickett	1	Jo[hn] Thornton	1
Stephen Watchers	1	Widdow Drew	1
Jo[hn] Sparway	2	William Molloyne	1
William Goose	1	William Tilden	1
Abraham Bond	1	Jo[hn] Branford	1
Thomas Lott	2	Jo[hn] Eastgreege	2
Anthony Barker	2	Anthony Gollyhoake	2
Thomas Giner	2	Jo[hn] Curtis	1
Jo[hn] Eaton	2	Jo[hn] Eaton	2
Judy Lockin	3		

The Borough of Milsted

Chargeable		Chargeable	
Sir Edward Hales Bart	8	James Tonge gent	11
William Tilden gent	5	John Tooke clerke	3
John Finch gent	5	Jo[hn] Chalcraft	6
William Finch	3	Jo[hn] Davis	4
Jo[hn] Land	1	Ralph Jervis	2
Richard Goodchild	3	Richard Chambers	2
[blank] Garrett	1	[blank] Rooke	2
Thomas Moore	2	John Allen	2
Widdow Floud	4	William Violett	2
Thomas Howlett	2	Richard Cheesman	4
Thomas Field	2	Richard Skeere	2
Thomas Titus	1	[blank] Dane	5
Thomas Weldish	2	Jo[hn] Popler	1

Not Chargeable		Not Chargeable	
James Goldfich	1	Widdow Parker	2
Widdow Wyart	1	Widdow Haslewood	1
Widdow Homan	1	Thomas Deane	1
Thomas Mason	1	Richard White	1
Widdow Hadlow	1	Stephen Reader	1
Widdow Birch	1		

Rodmersham Borough

Chargeable		Chargeable	
Thomas Pordage Esquire	13	Symon Greenstreet gent	4

Bartholomew May gent	7	Henry Filmer	3
Richard Chambers	6	William Law	2
Jo[hn] Garner	2	Henry Bateman	2
Robert Garrett	4	Henry Rayner	3
John White	2	Jo[hn] Munns	3
Thomas Owlett	1	Jo[hn] Doe	2
William Confert	1	Richard Wildish	2
Jo[hn] Milton	1	Henry Thomas	2
Jo[hn] Dowle	2	William Diamond	2
Jo[hn] Hilles	3	Bridgett Sead widow	2
Francis Pidgeon	5	Thomas Roper	3
Richard Axby	2	George Praule	1
Stephen Spencer	3	Edmund Fludd	1
Thomas Allen	1	Thomas Milner	1
George Violett	3		

Not Chargeable   **Not Chargeable**

Anthony Weldish	2	Bartholomew Newman	1
Widdow Cooke	1	William Harris	1
Elizabeth Brenner widdow	1	Widdow Bance	1
Widdow Ramkin	1	Widdow Baldin	2
Henry Cooper	1		

Ringsdowne Borough

Chargeable   **Chargeable**

Mrs Ady widdow	3	Richard Giles gentleman	7
Richard Finch	2	James Allen	1
Edward Smyth	2	David Dorne	4
Thomas Wise	5	William Allen	3

Not Chargeable

Richard Sersfield	2

Bredgar Borough

Chargeable   **Chargeable**

Terry Aldersey gent	8	Terry Aldersey gent}	
Terry Aldersey gent }		in an empty house }	9
in 2 other empty houses }	3	Nathaniel Winsmore clerke	1
Stephen Brockwell	5	Edward Medherst	1
John Wheatland	2	James Brennard	4
Henry Tayler	1	Abraham Hunt	1
George Gray	1	Symon Wheatland	2
Christopher Brenchly	1	Nicholas Nell	2

Richard Elliott	2	James Smyth		1
Thomas Beale	4	Thomas Standley		2
Jo[hn] Olliver	2	Jo[hn] Burwash		1
Edward Ady in an empty house	2	William Thatcher		2
		William Tirkill		7
[fol. 53r]				
Widdow Reader	3	Mrs Ann Halsnod		4
Thomas Bowell	3	William Marshall		3
Thomas Smyth	2	Thomas Cooper		5
Isaac Child	3	Edward Doe		6
Sir Edward Hales Bart		John Grove gent		7
in an empty house	2	Richard Kempshall		2
William Downe	4	Jo[hn] Goodchild		3
Not Chargeable		**Not Chargeable**		
William Land	1	Edward Haslewood		1
James Tooke	1	Widdow Barrow		1
Widdow Winter	1	Robert Seare		1
John Possingsham	2	Edward Carrier		1
Reynold Bunting	1	Terry Aldersey gent }		
John Grove gent }		one brewhouse chimney }		1
one brewhouse chimney }	1	Nathaniel Winsmore }		
William Downe }		one brewhouse chimney }		1
in a brewhouse chimney }	1	Widdow Standly		1

Bapchild Borough

Chargeable		**Chargeable**	
Samuell Leese	9	Widdow Philpott	7
Solomon Keene	5	Symon Larkin	4
Edward Gladwell	2	Richard Lake	6
Edward Elvy	5	Lewis Harris	1
John Keene	2	Jane Moore widdow	2
Henry Possingham	2	John Fordred	1
David Bissie	2	William Wachers	3
John Cox	2	John Wenbourne	4
Michaell Roper	3	Edward Ellis	1
John Masters	2	Henry Forward	4
Not Chargeable		**Not Chargeable**	
Widdow March	1	James Cooper	1
Henry Possingham	1	John Bishopp	3

Borough of Tong

Chargeable		Chargeable	
James Cleve gent	7	William Pell clerke	3
Mrs Worley widdow	6	Thomas Elvy	6
James Tong	2	John Pimm	3
William Pimm	2	Henry Bateman	4
Solomon Bishopp	3	John March	1
Samuell Humfrey	4	William Smyth	2

Not Chargeable

Thomas Smyth	2

Muston Borough

Chargeable		Chargeable	
Mr Richard Trey clerk	6	John Maxstead	7
Widdow Henman	4	Thomas Amis	5
William Bennett	3	John Gathers	2
Thomas Haszard	3	John Woollar	2
Thomas Calle	1	Edward Fry	3
Jacob Brockwell	3	William Wrenn	5
Samuell Wildish	2	Robert Hercy	2
John Coles	1	Nathaniel Dennard	2
John Bachelor	2	Henry Marshall	2
Lawrence Does	2		

Not Chargeable		Not Chargeable	
James Wood	3	Jesper Downes	2
Widdow Cheyney	1	In a small empty cottage	2
Thomas Tilby	2		

Tunstall Court Borough

Chargeable		Chargeable	
Sir Edward Hales Baronet	31	Mrs Elizabeth Fearn widdow	7
Andrew Palmer	7	John Bachelor	4
Peter Chrisfield	3	Thomas Ockenfold	2
Richard Taylor	2	Robert Boys	2
Henry Knowler	2	John Standley	1
Henry Lord	1		

Borough of Sittingbourne

Chargeable		Chargeable	
Increased Collins Esq	7	Paul Grant	8

Lawrence Bateman	6	William Allen gent	6
Thomas Causden	2	John Pagden	3
Edward Brace	2	John Farly	3
Edward Turner	2	Robert Ducksull	2
Francis Wells	1	Benjamin Brockwell	3
Thomas Jury	2	Walter Goldsmyth	2
Walter Mantle	2	Thomas Ives	4
Thomas Foord	1	William Smeed	2
Joseph Luce	2	John Gibbs	6
William Jarman	7	Thomas Bayly	7
[blank] Marlin	1	Richard Howell	1
Peter Newell	1	Mr Fer[dinand] Webb	4
[blank] Barton widd	2	Thomas Possingham	3
Edward Savidge	2	Elizabeth Barham	11
[blank] Pawson	4	[blank] Jarvis	3
John Bragg	3	William Peters	7
Elizabeth Filmer widd	5	Thomas Lushington sen[io]r	8
William Bowell	4	Thomas Allen	2
Jeremiah Netter	5	Ralph Thurston	9
Mary Millaway widd	6	Alice Effeild widd	2
John Hulsted	3	[blank] Sharp widd	3
Jonathan Loader	4	Henry Vousden	4
Richard Sturgeon	3	Isaac Wastall	5
Christopher Ellis gent	2	George Gillpinn	14
[fol. 53v]			
Silvester Harlackenden gent	6	John Waterer	4
Mr Jones clerke	4	Thomas Lushington junior	4
Henry Rowse	11	Henry Buttler	7
Richard Cox	8	Johnson widdow	3
Nicholas Pagden	2	William White	5
John Dade gent	12	Robert Hodsull	5
John Hunt	5	William Jackson	4
George Freeman	5	Trustram Bell	7
Richard Dawling	2	Thomas Skeere	1
Thomas Browne	2	James Dunell	7
		Walter Trice [266]	2
Richard Hyder	1	Widdow Tert	5
Ambrose Aldridge	3	Giles Ray	3
John Muns	2	George Pound	8
[blank] Crane widdow	2	Richard Rayner	2

[266] Interlined entry.

John Bounds	1	John Bassett	1
William Gillman	4	William Bell	1
Edward Hilles	2	Edward Drinkwater	2
John Grant	6	Thomas Pierce	4
William Walker	6	John Chapman	5
Joseph Knight	5	Thomas Bartlett	2
Joseph Scurge	2	Richard Bayly	2

Empty houses

Thomas Brotherton	2	James Allen	2
John Pagden	3	In the house where Mrs }	
William Goodwin	2	Harlackenden lived }	4

Not Chargeable

Not Chargeable

Abraham Wood	2	John Ludsum	1
[blank] Newman widow	1	Thomas Coueney	1
William Hewett	2	Alexander Hunt	1
[blank] Poole widdow	3	[blank] Frierson widdow	2
Caleb Judd	2	[blank] Scurge widdow	3
[blank] Baker widdow	1	Andrew Freeman	4
[blank] Bennett	1	William Oxley	2
John Rowe	2	Thomas Gunvill	2
Thomas Low	2	Richard Smith constable	

The West Division of the said hundred of Milton

The Borough of Borden

Chargeable

Chargeable

John Allen gent	6	Silvester Harlackenden gent	6
Anthony Spacthurst gent	4	James Rayner gent	7
Ralph Hayward gent	8	Ralph Hayward gent	4
Robert Plott gent	8	James Brenchly	3
Robert Beane	2	Christopher Brockwell	2
Nicholas Doe	6	William Wells	5
Mrs Frances Tong widd	10	William Cadman	2
Widdow Vahan	3	Widdow Johncock	2
William Hatch	2	Richard Foord	2
Thomas Foord	2	Daniel Cooke	4
William Hansnod	1	Nicholas Philpott	1
John Allen senior	5	Michael Goodlad	2
William Drewry	4	Stephen Wiborow	6
Thomas Greenstreet	2	Jacob Brockwell	3

Hamond Tomlin	4	Walter Crisfield	3
Anthony Boys	5	Mathew Watson	2
William Barnes	2	William Sceere	2
John Sedger	2	Thomas Turner	2
Henry Cooper	3	William Perin	1
James Bunce	6	Hugh Gilman	1
Arthur Willard	1	Edward Risby	2
Thomas Tonge gent	8	Henry Carter	4
John Joy	1	Widdow Tonge	3
Mrs Stringer widdow	3	George Rayner	3
Thomas Rasull	2	John Champ	1
James Robinson	1	Henry Burch	3
James Medhurst	3	William Barrow	3
James Osborne	2	Thomas Griffin clerk	7
William Bromfield	5	Timothy Garner	3
Samuel Nash	5	[blank] Hollecke	1
John Napleton	6	David Quinnell	2
Mr William Burrowes } in an empty house }[267]	2		

Not Chargeable

Widdow Backett	2	Widdow Hayward	3
Widdow Turner	1	Richard Goodwin	1
Widdow Gilman	1	Widdow Eaton	1
Widdow Nash	2	Widdow Cattlett	1
Widdow Lavender	1	Mr William Barrows in } an empty house }	2

Borough of Bobbing

Chargeable

Sir John Tufton bart	12	Mrs Elizabeth Sanford	22
George Tomlin gent	5	Francis Cobb gent	6
John Gadd	4	John Terry	4
John Miller	4	Arthur Homan	4
Abraham Amis	4	John Fawly	2
John Reigway	4	Robert Dodd	1
John Homan	1	Thomas Rofe	2
Edward Cresey	2	Francis Bennett	2
Abraham Amis one stove	1		

[fol. 54r]

---

[267] Entry interlined and similar entry under Barrowes in Not Chargeable does not appear in E179.

Stephen Stonehouse	2	Thomas Watler	3
Widdow Pannell	1	Ralph Brockwell	4
Edward Elvin	2	Thomas Featherstone	2
George Osmer	1	Gyles Wills	2
Elizabeth Booth widdow	5	William Wheatland	1
John Drewry	4	Sarah Woollett	2
Richard Shoveler	2	Clement Collins	2
Nicholas Finch	3	Robert Head	3
William Scarlett clerk	2	In the parsonage house	6
Phillipp Lane and }		James Browneing	2
Thomas Tomlin }	2	Cornelius Harfleet gent	10
John Upton	7	Thomas Harvey	3
Stephen Tapley	4	Arthur Homan junior	4
Robert Hills	2	William Pound	4
Edward Lance	1	Leonard Stacy	1
Thomas Smyth	3	Edward Nash	6
Robert Long	3	Robert Long	3
John Roberts	2	Hugh Norris	2
Walter Henneker	3	William Dowle	5
Thomas Lake & }		James Browne	2
John Turner }	2	Thomas Wootton	3
[blank] Stonard	2	Thomas Alexander	2
Ralph Marshall	4	John Martin	3
Thomas Luke	2	Thomas Milner	3
Thomas Rowe	2	Peircevall Turner	3
John Ford	2	William Norris	4
Thomas Pett gent	3		

Not Chargeable		**Not Chargeable**	
Mrs Elizabeth Sanford in }		Widdow Frost	1
her brewhouse wash }		Two widdows in a cottage	1
-house & bakehouse }	3	*[blank]* Quested	1
		William Immett	2

Houltstreet Borough

Chargeable		**Chargeable**	
Mr Crump clerk	4	Thomas Gibbon gent	7
Thomas Fanshaw gent	11	Mr Hawkins	5
Mr Rooke	9	John Osbourne Esq	12
Thomas Hills gent	6	William Fagg gent	11
Reynald Tayler gent	2	Edward Pilcher	1
Thomas Morgan	5	George Brooke	1
William Schrubsole	1	Samuell Smyth	1

Thomas Lott	2	Thomas Surgood	3
Mathew Sturgeon	1	Widdow Willard	1
Edward Bance	1	Widdow Royton	1
John Godwin	1	Daniell Hope	1
Paul Eaton	1	Henry Lawrence	1
Jeremiah Lewes	1	William Crippen	2
Richard Stevenson	1	John Nethersole	1
William Dann	1	William Adams	1
Widdow Pilcher	1	William Greenell	3
Ellis Rayner	1	Daniell Beard	1
Stephen Terry	1	Widdow King	2
James Higham	2	William Wood in an }	
John Cheesman	2	empty house }	1
Thomas Buttler	1	Widdow Bacon	1
Widdow Surgood	1	Robert Walker	3

Ham Borough

Chargeable

Chargeable		**Chargeable**	
Joshuah Coppin gent	5	John Hartly	3
John Adcock	3	Henry Frere gent	3
Thomas Wilson	2	Henry Bleshenden	2
Jeffry Riggs	2	George Baker	1
Parnella Bell widdow	2	Valentine Manuch	1
Thomas Law	1	William Fulkes	1
John Pamer	1	Grigory Ady	1
Thomas Larkin	1	Henry Roberts	2
Robert Minge	1	Widdow Hoult	2
Richard Rest	1	Richard Barnet	1
Thomas Meadman	3	Widdow Knight	4
Mathias Sweverton	2	Edward Miller	1
Alice Smyth widdow	1	John Michell	1
Ann Straite widdow	2	Abraham Lefegreene	2
Mathias Fulliger	3	John Baule	1
Widdow Minge	2	*[space]*	
George Carryer in }		Widdow Pierige in an }	
an empty house }	5	empty house }	1
Widdow Turner in }		John Evans in an }	
an empty house }	2	empty house }	2

These three are
Not Chargeable

Thomas Beane	1	Ann Wachers	1

Nicholas Robins   1

[fol. 54v]

Otteram Borough

Chargeable		Chargeable	
James Bradly	4	Thomas Bradly	2
Thomas Thatcher	5	Jane Bing widdow	5
Arthur Pordage	3	Richard Emerton	3
Thomas Woodyer	1	Walter Cooper	1
John Hudson	1		

[Not Chargeable -erased]		Not Chargeable	
Mr Wall in an }		William Browne	1
empty house }[268]	4	Widdow Brewer	1
~~Widdow Usmer~~	1	Richard Hubbard	1
		Widdow Usmer	1

Goare Borough

Chargeable		Chargeable	
John Sibly	2	Edmund Lariman	2
Robert Higgins	1	Edward Hadlow	2
Richard Gardner	2	John Evans	3
Thomas Hunt	2	Thomas Ward	5
Thomas Paine	1	Thomas Blacke	2
John Lilly	3	John Milford	5
Richard Whiffin	3	Thomas French	1
John Wide	1		

Not Chargeable		Not Chargeable	
Widdow Mason	1	Ambrose Buttler	1
Isaac Egles	1	William Forby	1
Susanna Wood widdow	1	In the vicarage house }	
In two old empty houses }		part of it being fallen down }	3
ready to fall downe }	7		

Lucis Borough

Chargeable		Chargeable	
Henry Dering clerk	4	Richard Stace	6
Mrs Thomas Widdow	5	John Startupp	6
Thomas Black	4	John Willard	3
Thomas Bourne	1	Thomas Acerly	2

[268] Entry given as chargeable in E179.

Henry King	1	William George	1
Richard Allen	1	John Bix	1
Nicholas Murton	1	John Ruffin gent	1
William Doe	1	John Cramner	1
Thomas Hadlow	1	George Carrier	2
George Tomlin	2	Thomas Ellis	1
Arthur Barnes	1		

Not Chargeable

Thomas Osbourne	1	Joane Ferne widdow	1
John Eason	1	Widdow Scodder	2
Daniel Huchins	2	Thomas Bance	1
Richard Williams	1	James Picknall	1
Robert Baker	1	*[blank]* Fathely	1
Widdow Wilson	1		

Elmsted Borough

Chargeable

Mathew Woollett	4	Henry Goulders	2
Thomas Sedge	1	George Huggens	1
William Hartupp	4	Robert Thatcher gent	10
John Nethersole	3	Elizabeth Martin widdow	1
Gabriell Fuller	1	William Browne	1
Richard Knight gent	3	John Lyford gent	11
Thomas Chapman	9		

St Augustines Borough

Chargeable

Andrew Usher	2	James Gammon	2
William Powell	1	William Talhurst	2
Thomas Iles	3	Thomas Pettitt	3
Augustine Bates	3	Henry Bayly	5
Richard Goatly	3	William Pettett	2
Phillip Parker	2	John Fox	2
Clement Browne	2	Thomas Sandwich	4
Stephen Ramsden	5	John Barnwell	7
Giles Hindes } and one not layd }	1	Jeremiah Giles	2
		Mr Pagett a new house } with six chimneys the } hearths not yett layd }	-

Wormedale Borough

Chargeable		Chargeable	
John Ruffin gent[leman]	9	Richard Edborow	6
William Humphrey	6	John Illes	2
Edward Garland	5	Thomas Dadd	3
Henry Forby	3	Mathew Stanino	7
Thomas Coulchester	1	Christopher Pannell	1
Daniell Paramour	3	Giles Swayland	1
Stephen Collett	1	Andrew Eason	1
William Lord	1	George Cooper	3
[fol. 55r]			
John Wood	1	William Surgood	1
Thomas Dadd	4	William Lott	5

Not Chargeable		Not Chargeable	
[blank] Partridge	2	*[blank]* Lance	1
Widdow Crowde	1	William Pilcher	2
In an empty house	2		

Yelsted Borough

Chargeable		Chargeable	
Christopher Petty gent	9	Joshuah Lott	9
John Pierce	1	Thomas Rayner	1
John Brockwell	1	Richard Tattenton	1
Thomas Knight	3	William Knight	3
Widdow Cooper	5	Nicholas Humphrey	1
Richard Larkin	1	Edward Clemans	1
Hugh Taylor	2	*[blank]* Carby	2
James Goulding	2	Ambrose Barrow	2
William Pattison	1	Christopher Browne	2
William Clemans	1	Reynald Bunting	2

Not Chargeable		Not Chargeable	
Widdow Gilman	1	Widdow Pollar	1
Widdow Shones	1	Thomas Lott	2

Empty houses

William Knight	1	James Goulding	1
William Shally	1	Thomas Knight	1
Reynald Bunting	2		

Deane Borough

Chargeable		Chargeable	
Thomas Reader	2	William Allen	4
William Reader	1	Robert Sellinge	1
Richard Lord	2	William Anvill	2
John Coleman	2	Richard Black	1
Joseph Black	2	James Greenstreet	1
Thomas Baker	1	John Holland	3
Thomas Reason	2	Robert Knight	1
Robert Dansey	1	Henry Brockwell	1
William Buckherst	1	John Baker	3
Christopher Jackson	2	Joseph Redmans	1
Adam Wood	1	Thomas Rootes	1
Stephen Gamon	1	John Salt	1

Not Chargeable		Not Chargeable	
Widdow Reader	1	John Symons	2
[blank] Plegger	2	Thomas Kennard	3

West Reynham Borough

Chargeable		Chargeable	
Henry Higford gent	13	John Taylor	4
William Roche	5	[blank] Amis	6
[blank] Baker	3	John Bax	4
William Man	3	[blank] Messenger	2
James Heyman	3	James Roper	2
Thomas Floud	1	Anthony White	1
Thomas Godfrey	1	William Baghurst	1
John Baghurst	1	William Field	1

Not Chargeable		Not Chargeable	
John Clarke	1	John Sharpe	1
Robert Barnes	4	William Scuther	1
Widdow Kemsley	4	Edward Hilles	1
Widdow Colly	2	Richard Longman	1
Richard Smyth	1	Robert Beates	1
Charles Butler	2	[blank] Harris	1
Thomas Smyth	3	Widdow Bing in an empty	
Widdow Roche in an empty		house	1
house	1	Mr Higford in an empty	1
		house	

Mackland Borough

Chargeable		Chargeable	
Henry Frere gent	8	Edward Barling	4
Widdow Cooke	1	John Campleshon clerke	4
Overinton Wood	7	{Henry Whitaker	7
Michaell Hodges	6	{more in another house	1
John Adams	2	Richard Adcock	1
Robert Pratten	1	Thomas Wade	3
Widdow Osbourne	5	Thomas Jenkin	8
Thomas Dankes	2	Richard Moore	8
Anthony Smyth	2	Mrs Kennard Widdow	2
John Piper	2	Peter Crittall	3
James Hunt	1	John Mountioy	2
Walter Tayler	1		

Not Chargeable		Not Chargeable	
Abraham Norris	1	Thomas Duck	1
Widdow Simons	1	William Champen	1
William Bigg	1	Widdow Reeve	1
Widdow Head	2	Thomas Olliver	1

Tufton Borough

Chargeable		Chargeable	
Mrs Loin widdow	5	Mrs Willard Widdow	6
Daniell Lee	6	Grigory Collard	2
Andrew Carpenter	2	Widdow Pancase	1
Walter Hunt	2	James Picknald	1
Thomas Ely	5	Edward Milles	1
Richard Adams	1	Daniell Lewes	1
Richard Michell	2	William Straine	1
Thomas Coe	1	Widdow Catlett	5
Widdow Platt	1	Nicholas Wood	3
James Milleon	7	James Foster	1
Widdow Simmons	2	John Derrick	1

Meare Borough

Chargeable		Chargeable	
John Earle of Thanett }		Richard Tilden	5
& Thomas Smyth gent}	19	Edward Kirby	1
William Stonnard	2	Thomas Lawrence	1
Thomas Allen	3		

<table>
<tr><td></td><td>Not Chargeable</td><td></td></tr>
<tr><td></td><td>John Garner</td><td>2</td></tr>
<tr><td>John Napleton Constable</td><td>Sutherick Ball</td><td>1</td></tr>
</table>

[fol. 55v]

THE HUNDRED OF TENHAM
in the lath of Scray

Upper halfe hundred

Borough of Bedmangore

Chargeable		Chargeable	
[blank] Lord Tenham	43	William Delawne Esq	9
John Collins gent	7	John Todd gent	4
John Streets	5	Thomas Burgis	1
James Belchambers	2	Clement Rofe	1
Nicholas Tonge	2	Widdow Geale	1
Thomas Daniell	3	Thomas Winter	4
Widdow Crampe	1	Robert Staples	1
Richard Ellis	2	John Foster	6
Nicholas Davis	1	Joseph Bates	3
Edward Marshall	3	William Fowley	1
Mary Allen	1	Thomas Fox	1
Richard Ninn	3	John Jewest	2
William Dunbar clerk	5	Hugh Barnes	6
John Ely	3	Richard Carr	1
William Allen	5	John Holmden	3
Nicholas Nicholson	9	Mrs Ady	10
Mrs Swalman	6	Jeffery Skeere	3
William Mollenger	2	James Hinckley	4
John Belchambers	2	Robert Packman	7
[blank] Cesfield	3	John Chittenden	1

Not Chargeable		Not Chargeable	
John Williams	1	Thomas Newell	2
Richard Lord	1	Thomas Philpott	1
John Brenard	2	Joseph Hart	1
George Court	1	William Pettenden	1
Lewis Stredupp	2	Thomas Strart	2
Widdow Turner	1	John Weldish	1
Robert Ellis	1	John Briggs	1

Ockenfale Borough

Chargeable		Chargeable	
Edward Gurney	6	Richard Rooke	3
William Wraith	1	Thomas Small	4
Thomas Cooke	2	Thomas Tompson	3
John Bricher	1	Robert Lever	2
William Filmer	1	Stephen Croucher	1
Thomas Ewens	2	Henry Ellet	3

Not Chargeable		Not Chargeable	
John Briggs	1	William Allen	1

Headcorne Borough

Chargeable		Chargeable	
Alexander Bridge	3	Nicholas Reader	3
Henry Start	2	Anthony Carterling	2
Thomas Burfoot	5	John Branford	2
Christopher Fullager	3	Daniell Richard	1
John Crooch	2	Richard Wood	1

Iwade Borough

Chargeable		Chargeable	
John Goateley	3	William Merryweather	1
John Milles	2		

Not Chargeable		Not Chargeable	
John Ceeling	1	Widdow Hollaway	1
Widdow Weekes	1	Richard Skeere constable	

Lower half hundred of Tenham

Borough of Bonepett

Chargeable		Chargeable	
Sir William Hugessen Knt	20	Dr Eve	6
Doctor Parkhurst	6	[blank] Wackerlin Esq	9
William Bourne gent	7	Mr John Greenstreet	8
Mr Walscot Bristoe	9	Mr William Thomas	5
Mr James Clarke	6	Mr Aylett	6
James Eley	3	Mr John Eley	8
Mr Ellis	6	Mrs Newland	4
Widdow Barnes	5	John Bigg	3
Thomas Bettingfield	3	William Webb	6

Edward Philpott [269]	6	Henry Elwin	5
Robert Brockwell	4	Widdow Peniall	3
Thomas Pluff	4	George Ward	3
Widdow Hornett	3	Thomas Cramner	5
Thomas Pigeon	3	Peter Umerden	2
Widdow Harrison	2	Anthony Bettingfield	3
William Cattlett	3	Widdow Hayth	4
Thomas Turner	3	Christopher Clarke	5
Robert Pigott	2	Edward Downe	4
Richard Giles	2	Edward Platt	6
William Hoystead	5	John Ellis	2
Robert May	2	Widdow Pisinge	2
Thomas Bennett	1	Widdow Terry	2
James Hope	2	Thomas Sutton	4
John Parker	1	Henry Brewster	1
John Bissey	1		

Not Chargeable

John Thomas	1	Richard Lock	1
Thomas Jones	1	Thomas Brooke	1
William Rayner	1	Richard Baldock	1
James Turner	2	Peter Cooper	1
Thomas Saxbie	2	William Boykett	1
John Dodson	1	Widdow Pryer	1
Martha Merser	1	Widdow Love	1
Jone Thompson	1	Widdow Lees	1
Widdow Wood	1		

Borough of Lewson

Chargeable

Thomas Brooke	5	William Tomlin	1
John Sockling	1	Richard Silkwood	2
Robert Gates	3	John Haskin	2
[fol. 56r]			
Richard Bayly	5	{Richard Broad	4
William Hilles	2	{Richard Broad more	6
Richard Keeley	1	Richard Budds	2
Thomas Turner	1	James Wanstall	1
Samuell Budds	3	Henry Weldish	1
John Dawson	7	Richard Brockwell	3

[269] The text appears to have a very badly formed vj resembling oj; given as j in E179.

Christopher Philcock	3	Nicholas Power	1
John Minge	10	Andrew Dane	4

Not Chargeable		**Not Chargeable**	
Adam Whittington	1	Thomas Gouldsmyth	1
Widdow Whittall	2	Widdow Cattlett	2

Borough of Tenham

Chargeable		**Chargeable**	
Stephen Jessey	4	James Curtis	7
Thomas Scott	1	Francis Adrian	2
William Bullen	3	Richard Keeley	1
Widdow Neames	2	Good[wife] Rose	1
Good: Beereling	1	Richard Nitingale	4
James Tonge	4	Paul Sackett	6
John Hilles	1	John Banker	2
George Philcock	2	Bezaliel Creke	2
Widdow Jenkin	1	Richard Reeve	1
Good: Landen	4	John Grimsell & }	
Robert Fox	4	Thomas Hall }	5
John Grimsell	8	Thomas Scarvill	2
Daniell Harris	2	Robert Downe	1
Richard Steed	2	William Steed	3
Isaac Davis	1	Thomas Whittington	2
Widdow Clifford	3	Michaell Turner	2
John Grimsell and Paul Sackett	1		

Not Chargeable		**Not Chargeable**	
Widdow Wootten and }		Goodman Linsey	1
Widdow Daniell }	1	[blank] Martin	1
Thomas Wildish	1	Henry Devison	1
John Gates	2		

Borough of Downewell

Chargeable		**Chargeable**	
Isaac Wildish	2	Christopher Wildish	3
Symon Acres	2	Ely Dicher	1
Thomas Maxted	2	Nicholas Tayler	1
Edward Ellis	1	Edward Vennard	1
Widdow Martin	1	Widdow Norrington	1
Edward Drury	2	William Thomas Constable	

THE HUNDRED OF FEVERSHAM
in the lath of Scray

The Upper Halfe Hundred

Stalfield Borough

Chargeable		Chargeable	
Symon Rucke gent[leman]	7	Richard Packe	2
Jo[hn] Allonson	4	Jo[hn] Dane	4
Edward Moore	2	Henry Cadman	2
Stephen Bayly	1	Henry Henneker	3
George Attkins	1	William Jeffery	1
William Brisley	1	John Miller or }	
Edward Norman	3	Francis Parker }	3
Thomas Dorne	1	Jo[hn] Terry	1
Alice Barman widd[ow]	3	William Tritton or }	
Henry Jackson	3	Mr Paine }	4
Edward Nepacar	2	Thomas Andrewes	4
Thomas Andrewes	2	Thomas Backe	1
Robert Croucher	2	William Cooke	1
Richard Whatman	2	Henry Andrewes	3
William Weldish	1	Jo[hn] Crofts	3
Ro[bert] Spice	2	Barthol[omew] Lawe	4
Edmund Elvey	4	Walter Tyler	2

Not Chargeable		Not Chargeable	
Stephen Hayward	2	Stephen Brooker	1
Matthew Whitehead	2	Ed[ward] Hursfeild	2
Alexander March	2	William Gates	1
Abraham Shilling	1	Jo[hn] Howting	1
Thomas Greene	1	Ro[bert] Nye	1
Henry Farly	2	William Farly	1
James Hames	1	Jonas Dane	1
Ro[bert] Sare	2	Jo[hn] Huchins	1

Throwledge South Borough

Chargeable		Chargeable	
{Sir George Sondes of [th]e Bath		Matthew Bunce gent[leman]	12
{ In the keepers house	4	Mr George Robinson cler[k]	4
{ more in a stable	2	James Thurston	3
{ more in 2 other houses	6	Thomas Chapman	8

Christopher Clarke	6	Mark Wanstall	4
Henry Munds	2	Abraham Marborow	1
John Allen	5	Jo[hn] Ottaway	2
Alexander Cadman	2	Thomas Wise	2
Thomas Philpott	2	Symon Tanner	2
Thomas Barnes	5	Widdow Snoath	2
Henry Mose	1	Matthew Larriman	2
Ro[bert] Thurston	2	Francis Wibourne	2
George Howting	2	James Whitehead	2
William Kempe	2	Thomas Kempe	2
William Burton	4	Richard Brett	2
William Clarke	1	Thomas Amis	2
William Danne	5	Jo[hn] Rigden	4
Moses Shrubsole	2	Andrew Vidgeon	10
William Snoath	3		

[fol. 56v]

Not Chargeable

Not Chargeable

Widdow Silver	1	Widdow Pall	1
Widdow Rigglefoot	1	Thomas Norham	1
Jeffry Pye	1	Edward Arbistone	1
Thomas Lavington	1	William Layton	3
Edward Cadman	2	[blank] Reynalds	1
Peter Rand	1	Henry Ralfe	2

Wilgate Borough

Chargeable

Chargeable

William Woodward g[entleman]	4	Thomas Weldish	3
Richard Kingsland	2	Hamond Rofe	7
Widow Rofe	3	Thomas Upton sen[io]r	1
Ro[bert] Kingsland	1	Arnold Terry	4
Symon Lilly	2	Ro[bert] Danne	4
Widdow Harris	1	Tho[mas] Upton jun[io]r	1
Edward Terrey	4		

Not Chargeable

Not Chargeable

Widdow Baker sen[io]r	1	Widdow Baker jun[io]r	1
Susanna Rasell	1	Widdow Shilling	1
Widdow Fills	1		

Borough of Kingsnorth

Chargeable		Chargeable	
Edward Bigg	3	Mr Elmestone	3
Richard Sharp	6	George Day	2
George Rayner	2	Jo[hn] Fillmer	1
William Saxbie	2	Thomas Hillen	2
Stephen Hilles	3	William Brann	3
Henry Kingsnorth	1	Ro[bert] Davis	1
Richard Bigg	6	Jo[hn] Wellman	2
Widdow Overy	5	William Bigg	1
Peter Godfrey	5	Mathew Homsby	3

Not Chargeable		Not Chargeable	
John Saxbie	3	Widdow Hawkes	1
Edward Highdowne	2	Symon Gooden	1
Jo[hn] Bull	1	George Vincent	2
Jo[hn] Witherden	2		

Sillgrove Borough

Chargeable		Chargeable	
Michael Belke Esq[uire]	6	Henry Southouse	6
Jo[hn] Bunce	5	James Bunce	3
Edward Nethersole	5	John Biggs	2
John Ginnings	3		

Not Chargeable		Not Chargeable	
Widdow Doulle	2	Thomas Gilman	1
Edward Straine	1		

Borough of Argusthill

Chargeable		Chargeable	
S[ir] George Sondes knight of [th]e Bath	32	Gabriel Giles gent[leman]	2
John Upton gent[leman]	6	Thomas Tayler	7
Francis Maxted	2	Robert Giles sen[io]r	7
Henry Tapley	3	George Leese gent[leman]	6
Thomas Harwood	5	Charles Faireway	2
Richard Hawkes	4	Arnold Leese gent[leman]	8
Symon Ruck sen[io]r	6	Thomas Knowlden	4
William Hilles	3	Mrs Bromedge	2
Jo[hn] Rivett	3	Richard Odiham	2
Thomas Bosley	6	Thomas Hawkins	2
		James Harris	2

Thomas Mase	2	Jo[hn] Broadbridge	5
Ro[bert] Marborow	1	Thomas Page	1
Henry Lilly	2	William Hooker	2
Thomas Danford	1	John Wood	1
Moses Milles	1	Tho[mas] Drury	1
Ro[bert] Whitehead	2	Thomas Chapman	2
John Crux gent[leman]	6		
Ro[bert] Giles gent[leman]	5		

Not Chargeable		**Not Chargeable**	
John Giles	4	Ro[bert] Pimbe	1
Widdow Ducksole	1	Edward Cooke	1
John Tayler	1	John Yates	1
John Woolton	3	William Harris	2
Thomas Rand	2	Richard Shrubsole	1
Jo[hn] Huchins	1	Widdow Bayly	3
Thomas Ninn	1	Thomas Goodwin	1
Michaell Scott	1	Richard Goodwin	1
Richard Milles	1	William Younge	1
William Publicke	4	Widdow Chittum	1

Leaveland Borough

Chargeable		**Chargeable**	
James Bunce	5	Francis Rayner	1
Henry Upton	4	William Rayner	1
Daniell Upton	3	James Wise	2
John Chapman	5	John Sondes Esq[uire]	7

Not Chargeable		**Not Chargeable**	
Christopher Holloway	2	William Burkett	1
Widdow Dowles	1	Richard Baker	1
James Bunce in his house 2	-		
chimneys but noe hearths layd			

Eastling Borough

Chargeable		**Chargeable**	
Mr Jemmett clerk	6	William Clinch	4
Jo[hn] Greenstreet	3	James Hubbert	4
Tho[mas] Greenstreet sen[io]r	4	Henry Bond	4
Thomas Wootton	4	Henry Jones	4
John Terry	4	William Davis	4
Thomas Peniall	1	Ro[bert] Milles	2
Alexander Thompson	3	Phillip Paine	3

[blank] Newland	2	Thomas Rayner	3
Edward Greenstreet	4	Thomas Greenstreet	1
Henry Greenstreet	3	Edward Clinch	1
[fol. 57r]			
Jo[hn] Blackbourne	3	Jo[hn] Plaine	1
James Peniall	1	Anthony Fines	2
Bartholomew Swan	1	James Chilman	1
James Browne	2	Richard Gettley	2
Thomas Raisson	1	Thomas Leese	1
Richard Gillman	2	Thomas Spratt	1
Henry Turner	1	Jo[hn] Grimson	1
Jo[hn] Weldish	1	Moses Rasell	1
Christopher Allen	1	Henry Burton	3
Matthew Greenstreet	3		

Not Chargeable		**Not Chargeable**	
Thomas Ellis	1	Geoffry Briggs	1
Richard Rachell	1	Widdow Ottaway	1
Widdow Hooke	1	Widdow Ansley	1
Widdow Whinder	1	Widdow Tayler	1
Widdow Adren	1		

Badlesmeare Borough

Chargeable		**Chargeable**	
William Bagnall gent[leman]	4	Arthur Francklin	6
Thomas Harvey	6	Henry Pemble	6
William Lamb	5	James Vidgeon	2
William Snoath	2	Jo[hn] Sills	1
George Pood	1	Richard Seath	2
Symon Harris	2	John Lamb	4
Thomas Wood	2	Jo[hn] Adams	2
William Young	1	Edward Lilly	3
Widdow Woodland	3	Widdow Hilles	3

Not Chargeable		**Not Chargeable**	
John Spaine	1	Edward Clifford	1
[blank] Harlow	1	Jo[hn] Willson	1
Widdow Batchelor	1	Thomas Rayner	1
Widdow Smyth	2	Widdow Benewell	1

Stupenton Borough

Chargeable		Chargeable	
Mrs Hulks widd[ow]	7	Stephen Grimsell	6
Jo[hn] Cobb	4	Thomas Knowlden	5
Richard Skeere	5	Nicholas Peacke	6
Ro[bert] Tayler sen[io]r	2	Ro[bert] Tayler jun[io]r	2
James Colgatt	3	Thomas Gardner	2
Thomas Spence	1	Thomas Moore	1
William Burges	1	Ezechiell Bates	4
Jo[hn] Hilles	3	Jo[hn] Chillman	3
William Bax	2	Jo[hn] Parker	4
Thomas Streets	4		

Norton Borough

[Chargeable]		[Chargeable]	
John Hugesson Esq[uire]	10	John Smyth	12
Richard Tassell	4	Thomas Tong	6
James Ely	5	William Bennett	4
Robert Downe gent[leman]	4	John Downe	4
Thomas Wildish	2	Widdow Knock	2
Walter Gudsull	2	Jo[hn] Ockenfall	1
Peter Ellis	2	Mr Roger Paine gentle[man]	7
Christopher Harlock	5	Edward Clinch	1
Francis Parker	2	Gervase Cooke	2
William Thompson	2	Thomas Highstead	1
Jo[hn] Brenchley	2	William Wood	3
Symon Hills	1	Richard Fillmer	3
Peter Attkins	4	Godfry Wise	3
Ro[bert] Coverle	5	George Mason	3

Not Chargeable		Not Chargeable	
Jo[hn] Tamkelson	1	Joseph Allen	2
Jo[hn] Were	2	Jo[hn] Robinson	3
Jo[hn] Hooker	1	Jo[hn] Corke	1
William [blank]	2	Jo[hn] Taylor	1
Anthony Lilly	2	Widdow Spratt	1
Nicholas Nash	1	Nicholas Alchin	1
Jo[hn] Lee	1	Ralph Bound	1
Thomas Michelbourne	3	Thomas Gooden	3
Jo[hn] Hart	1	Thomas Stubbs	1
Widdow Whoffen	1	William Downe	1
William Mason	1	William Rigden	1
Jo[hn] Steward	1	Allen Tayler	1

John Crux constable

The Lower Halfe Hundred of Feversham

Buckland Borough

Chargeable
Robert Plott   5

Not Chargeable
Two small cottages with   2

Luddenham Borough

Chargeable		**Chargeable**	
Isaac Terry	4	Mr Cowes at [th]e parsonage	3
Samuell Weddingham	3	John Crafts	1
Thomas Foate	3	Henry Greenstreet	3
Thomas Hillman	3	Edward Brockwell	3

Not Chargeable		**Not Chargeable**	
Henry Rayner	1	Widdow Fryday	1
George Bradfeild	1	Edward Brockwell	1
Jo[hn] Widger	1	Widdow James	2
Ro[bert] Thurgood	2	Mathew Oakeshott	1
William Howell	1	In the Almshouses	2

Chattam Borough

Chargeable		**Chargeable**	
Elias Adle	5	Edward Davis	1
Jo[hn] Beareman	1		

Brimstone Borough

Chargeable		**Chargeable**	
Mr Barham	4	Edward Head	3
Isaiah Frith	10		

[fol. 57v]

Ewell Borough

Chargeable		**Chargeable**	
William Smyth	5	Edward Knowler	8
William Turner	2	Jo[hn] Brithred	2
Jo[hn] Duckesbery	3	Ro[bert] Knowler	2
Jo[hn] Bradford	2		

Not Chargeable
[blank] Smyth   1

Goodnestone Borough

Chargeable		Chargeable	
James Love	4	Edward Chambers	5
Henry Wallard	4	Grigory Broadbridge	4

Not Chargeable		Not Chargeable	
Richard Wells	1	Edward Ellis	2
William Roson	2	Symon Saffery	1

Roade Borough

Chargeable		Chargeable	
Thomas Carter	6	Widdow Swift	2
Lewis Leese	6	Ro[bert] Streeting	2
Jo[hn] Giles	1	Alexander Godden	1
Widd[ow] Spratt	2	Widdow Collier	2
Widdow Shrubsole	2	Edward Collier	1
Joseph Heth	1	William Corke	5
Stephen Sotherden	1	Ro[bert] Care	2
Edward Maxted	5	Jo[hn] Kirke	2
James Phillipps	2	George Broadstreet	3
Henry Shrubsole	1	William Shrubsole	3
Mark Wallard	1		

Davington Borough

Chargeable		Chargeable	
Stephen Barnes	6	Francis Jeffrey gent[leman]	13
Augustine Terry in }		Thomas Reynalds	6
the great house }	12	Jo[hn] Brithreed	2
And more in [th]e farm house	5	William Amis	2
Richard Smyth	3	Edward Brissenden	3
Jo[hn] Staples	2	Ro[bert] Summersett	2
Jo[hn] Buttler	1	Nicholas Anderson	3
Thomas Seare	2	Timothy Seare	2

Not Chargeable		Not Chargeable	
Jo[hn] Edmunds	2	[blank] Folkes	3
William Lingfield	2	Andrew Smyth	1

Oare Borough

Chargeable		Chargeable	
Jo[hn] Heeler	4	Abraham Chambers	5
John Tomlin	4	William Luson	1
Thomas Damon	2	John Harding	4
William Slade	4	Jo[hn] Merritt	4
Jo[hn] Egerden	3	Richard Parker	2
Joshuah Masters	5	Nicholas Clutting	4
Thomas Callis	5		

Not Chargeable		Not Chargeable	
Widdow Field	1	Widdow Brayten	1
Widdow Pach	1	Widdow Callis	1
Widdow Thomas	1	James Harris	3
Symon Brice	2	Jo[hn] Quested	2
James Reynolds	2	Richard Slade	2
Jo[hn] Dickeson	2	Francis Verrier	3
Widdow Smyth	1	Jo[hn] Squire	1

Island of Hartey

Chargeable		Chargeable	
Leonard Smyth	6	Stephen Jeffrey	5
Jo[hn] Beale	1	Giles Pye	6
Abraham Greengrass	2	Henry Andrewes	2
Thomas Possingham	3	Henry Martin	1
James Reade	1		

Not Chargeable		Not Chargeable	
Jo[hn] George	2	Jo[hn] Aldersey	2
Ralph Pierson	2		

Preston Borough

Chargeable		Chargeable	
John Bowyer	5	Henry Jones	4
Henry Rayner	1	Samuell Weddingham	3
Thomas Minge	2	Jo[hn] Greenestreet	6
Thomas Pordage	5	Thomas Fagg	4
Jo[hn] Finch gent[leman]	6	Ro[bert] Dane	1
Edward Baker	2	William Saffrey	2
Henry Dane	3	Jo[hn] Yorke	1
Thomas Olliver	3	John Tritton	5
James Heath	6		

		Not Chargeable	
William Smith constable		Widdow Waters	1

THE ISLAND OF SHEPWAY
in the lath of Scray

Borough of Seden

Chargeable		**Chargeable**	
Nicholas Ruffin gent[leman]	11	Thomas Morris	6
Henry Elvin	3	Samuell Symonds clerk	3
Richard Harding	3	Frances Saxbie widd[ow]	2
John Possingham	2	Elizabeth Sampson wid[dow]	6
Edward Vidgen	4	Nicholas Miller	5
Richard Bullen	3	William Sharpe	6
William Day	2	John Adams	1
Humphrey Molins	3	Edward Champe	2
William Swift	4	Thomas Wood	1
James Bowes	2	Richard Champe	1
[fol. 58r]			
Richard Sammey	1	William Widdower	1
John Warrener	3	George Carter	1
Thomas Challon	1		

Not Chargeable		**Not Chargeable**	
Elizab[eth] Kettlestring	1	Richard Barrowe	1
Robert Wood	2	Elizabeth Barber	1
John Gaylor	1	William Merch	1
Sarah Hudson	1	Thomas Pointer	1
Thomas Weight	2	George Yorke	1
Widdow Flisher	1	William Tapley	1
John Tod	1	Nathan Hunt	2
William Winter	1	Stephen Osmer	1
Robert Sturfe	2	Thomas Smith	1
Thomas Codd	2	Margery Hammond	1
Arnold Turtle	2	William Rickard	1
Jonas Smyth	1		
Thomas Challon Borsholder			

Ossenden alias Oxenden Borough

Chargeable		**Chargeable**	
Thomas Durrant	6	William Hitchcock	7
John Booreman	2	Richard Wood	4

Edward Broadstreet	5	George Flisher	3
John Hunt	3	Adam Seager	2
Edward Hersey	2	John Childrich	4
William Turner	4	William Darby	8
Edward Best	2	Samuell Frost	1
Robert Hyat	3	Richard Easden	2
Richard Francis	6	John Risby	2
Nicholas Hunt	2		
William Hitchcocke Borsholder			

Warden Borough

Chargeable		Chargeable	
James Herbert Esq[uire]	24	Vincent Ladd	4
The vicarage of Warden	3	Thomas White	1
James Bunce	2	Thomas Brotherton	4
William Lewes	3	John Swan gent[leman]	3
Francis Marsh	5	Solomon Swift	2
Matthew Holmes	1	Stephen Holmes	1
Robert Dilley	1	Christopher Nitingale	3
Thomas Wyde	2	Solomon Harris	1
James Muddle	1	Hugh Fugar	4
William Burgess	1	William Holmes	1

Not Chargeable		Not Chargeable	
Thomas Pomey	1	Widdow Thompson	3
Widdow Stannard	1	John Varnett	1
Edward Dufty	1	Gregory Bayley	1
Richard Alderson	1		
Hugh Fugar Borsholder			

Borough of Rydes

Chargeable		Chargeable	
The Duke of York's highness	11	Dr Robert Wilkinson	6
George Swann gent[leman]	1	Edward Owre and }	
Katharine Osbourne wid[dow]	6	William Reynolds } gen[tlemen]	3
William Ryder	4	John Fleete	2
John Salman	3	Robert White	5
Thomas Smyth	4	Richard Hayward	4
Elizabeth Frost	6	Thomas Milsted	2
Thomas Vidgen	4	Richard Michell	2

Thomas Huggens   3
Thomas Milsted Borsholder

Borough of Holt

Chargeable		Chargeable	
William Sheild	4	William Manwaring	4
Thomas Huggens	4	Richard Eglestone	2
William Smith	4	Joseph Templeman	3
Michaell Baldwin	3	Christopher Hills	2
John Allen	3	Felix Pancas	1
William Goare	1	William Smyth [th]e wheeler	2
Richard Hooke	1	John Swift	1
Stephen Aslat	1	Nicholas Jones	1
Bryan Hope	1	Widdow Bachelor	1
Widdow Jones	1	Thomas Smyth	1
Mary Whitlock widd[ow]	1	Nicholas Bourne	1
Christopher Hobert	5	Henry Freere gent[leman]	3
William Salmon	4	Humphrey Miller	2
Ralph Rigsby	3	Robert Molins	1
Thomas Braddock	2	Randall Whitehead	1
Peter Milgate	1	Stephen Salmon	5
Henry Maxsted	1	Henry Harrison	2
Thomas Widdower	3	Andrew Robins	3
John Ayhurst	1	Widdow Smyth	2
Samuell Durrant	3	William Day	3
John Pierce	1		

Not Chargeable		Not Chargeable	
Widdow Fugar	1	John James	1
Stephen Mum[m]ery	1	George Hilles	1
Clement West	1	Richard Reeve	1
		Christopher Hills Borsholder	

Borough of Laisdon

Chargeable		Chargeable	
John Mitchell	7	James Swift	2
Edward Shrubsole	1	Chedwick Silver	1
[fol. 58v]			
Edward Bassett	1	Stephen Lidham	2
John Crux gent[leman]	3	Mary Ayling widd[ow]	1
George Holman	5	Alice Lydham	2
		Chedwick Silver Borsholder	
		Thomas Morris Constable	

The Liberty of Ospringe
in the lath of Scray

Chargeable		Chargeable	
Robert Master Esq[uire]	15	Arthur Whatman	7
{Henry Greenstreet	7	Robert Knowler	4
{Henry Greenstreet more	3	Mark Collins	6
Abraham Whatman	6	John Lucas	5
Thomas Roberts	5	Robert Giles	4
Richard Parkes	2	John Clements	2
Robert Austen	2	George Hickes	7
Arnold Terrey	3	Ann Hickes widd[ow]	2
James Hobdey	1	Widdow Southouse	4
Henry Staples	4	John Platt	6
John Goodchild	3	William Dingly	1
Symon Dorne	4	Widdow Boys	1
Peter Chapman	1	Alexander Black	2
Richard Corke	1	William Kenn	2
John Hall	4	Thomas Hall	5
William Wise	2	Thomas Greenstreet	6
Edward Croyden	1	Henry Chilman	4
Daniell Judd	15	Isaiah Frite	3
Thomas Hodges	4	Peter Tibballs	2
Thomas Bridges	2	Thomas Cathar	8
George Pollen	2	Robert Watson	2
John Hilles	3	William Chapman	1

Not Chargeable		Not Chargeable	
Thomas Arnolls	4	Jeremiah Cooper	1
Richard Russell	1	In an empty house	2
Thomas Barman	2	John Harris	1
John Fieldcooke	2	Francis Yates	1
John Dabige	1	Widdow Lilly	1
Widdow Pickerell	1	William Waters	1
Henry Giles	3	John Tayler	2
Christopher Blacklock	1	Mathew Burten	1
John Okenfould	1	In an empty house	1
James Cooper	2	Edmund Wootton	3
Walter Skilton	3	Thomas Boltun	2
John Evans	2	John Malback empty	1
Henry Lucast	1	Alexander Furly	1
Edward Atheren	2	In an empty house	1
Widdow Cooper	3	James Thompson	3

| William Philcock | 2 | Edward Wemstur | 2 |
| Widdow Outfield | 1 | Simon Doorne constable | |

THE HUNDRED OF BOUGHTON UNDER THE BLEANE
in the lath of Scray

The Upper Halfe Hundred

Borough of Harvill

Chargeable		Chargeable	
Mr Sondes	6	John Tilbie	2
Robert Tanton	2	Robert Streeting	2
Edward Giles	1	Gabriell Ruck	2
Nicholas Hilles	2	Widdow Hilles	2
Mr Davis	4	Widdow Watkins	3
John Marsh	2	John Bing	6
Mr Theobalds	5	Lewis Lees	2
Thomas Berrie	2	William Tyler	2
Ham[m]ond Ruck	2	Robert Sherstead	4
John Tilbie	3	Thomas Gibson	1
William Branford	3		

Not Chargeable		Not Chargeable	
John Martin	3	Thomas Reader	2
Edward Berrie	2	John Cobeland	2
Edward Ambrose	3	Edward Cobeland	1
George Hayward	1	Widd[ow] Simms	1
Widdow Martin	1	John Poore	1
Widdow Baldock	1	Widdow Birch	1
		Thomas Gibson borsholder	

Borough of Meneham

Chargeable		Chargeable	
Mrs Hawkins	5	Richard Burling	4

Not Chargeable		Not Chargeable	
Nicholas Lorryman	1	John Nower	1
		Nicholas Lorryman borsholder	

Borough of Wastell

Chargeable		Chargeable	
John Rynge	5	Henry Waller	2

Jonas Moss	7	Widdow Southouse	4
Thomas Giles	6	Mrs Hawkins	2

Not Chargeable

Thomas Lillie Borsholder	1
William Branford Constable	

The Lower Halfe Hundred of Boughten under [th]e Bleane

Borough of Setton

Chargeable		Chargeable	
In the vicarage house	4	Thomas Hunt	2
Reignald Harris	2	Luke Langford sen[io]r	5
[fol. 59r]			
John Packer	3	Robert Odden	3
George Wallance	3	James Mathewes	2
Robert Clinton	2	William Baker	3
Samuell Shepheard	1	Thomas Godfrey	2
Moses Law	2	John Shrubsole	1
Goodman Bates	3	Robert Dane	3
Mathew Ambrose	2	Richard Barton	2
Thomas Loyton	2	John Clinton	4
Richard Barley	3	Widdow Jones	2
Jos[eph] Heiler	3	Math[ew] Cullen	2
William Pembery	1	William Spencer	5
Luke Langford	1		

Not Chargeable		Not Chargeable	
John Larkins	1	Mercy Hanley	2
Peter Horsley	1	[blank] Beale	1
William Maxted	1	Thomas Young	1
Jos[eph] Leger	1	Widdow Carter	2
Good[man] Sanders	1	Robert Moorecroft	1
Sam[uel] Doos	1	Phillip Churchman	1
Henry Hawkes	1	Moses Law borsholder	

Staple Borough

Chargeable		Chargeable	
Robert London	1	Leonard Meire	6
Henry Good	5	Thomas Trebell	3
Robert Scott	1	Thomas Porter	3
Stephen Spencer	4	Robert Spencer	

John Barre	2	Edward Cornish	1
John Baker	1	William Palmer	1
Sid: [blank] Wise	2	Richard Peirce	2
William Hammond	3	William Saffrey	1
William Forman	2	John Edmunds	1
Mary Spaine	1	John Midleton	2
William Champion	1	William Burch	2
Samuell Chambers	3	John Spencer	2
John Napleton	2		

Not Chargeable		Not Chargeable	
Robert Legett	1	Widdow Browneing	1
Widdow Foreman	2	Widdow Wise	1
Christopher Anderson	1	Widdow Frenchborne	2
William Baker	1	Widdow Widdy	1
William Parker	1	Thomas Grimes	1
[blank] Oakeshott	1	Widdow Pett	1
		Robert London borsholder	

Borough of Graveney

Chargeable		Chargeable	
John Rogers	1	Mr Henry Hougham	5
in [th]e vicarage house	5	Thomas Taylor	3
Luke Langford	3	John Rogers	3
William Pysing	2	Nicholas Burrell	3
John Bradford	3	John Dunnings	6
Thomas Barrett	2	Henry Wallard	1
John Vicars	1		

Not Chargeable		Not Chargeable	
Daniell Cooke	2	Jo[hn] Phillipps	3
[blank] Michell	1	Thomas Godfrey	2
Henry Bond	1	Widdow Barrett	1
Walter Allen	1	Nicholas Burrell borsholder	

Borough of Waterham

Chargeable		Chargeable	
Thomas Taylor	3	Edward Clifford	4
Robert Crump	1	John Quested	2
Stephen Collins	1	Richard Fox	2
Christopher Buck	2	Edward Collins	1
Robert Jull	5	Jos[eph] Cullen	2
Widdow Jones	3		

Edward Collins Borsholder

Not Chargeable

William Risbie	1

Borough of Nash

Chargeable		Chargeable	
John Hawkins Esq[uire]	13	William Pettet gent[leman]	14
William Kenwrick	12	William Kenrick in }	
Dame [blank] Routh	13	an empty house }	5
Thomas Roberts	4	Robert Riting	2
Edward Giles	1	Christopher Shrubsole	2
Samuel Bradford	3	John Nedham	5
John Godfrey	3	John Wallard	5
William Bing	2	Gab[riel] Ruck	2
Gab[riel] Ruck	2	Ga[briel] Ruck in an empty }	
John Norrington	3	house }	1
Samuell Bradford borsholder		In the vicarage house	5

Borough of Milstreet

Chargeable		Chargeable	
Mathew Jacob	4	John Packer	7
John Ruck	2	John Chillenden	3
Edward Norwood	2	Walter Leger	3
William Slaughter	2	John Lasey	3
Ran[dolph] Shrubsole	2	Widdow Price	1
Widdow Shrubsole	2	William Franck	3
Stephen Shrubsole	1	William Allen	1
Edward Watson	1	John Masson	2
Widdow Hilles	2	Richard Scott	2
Sim[on] Odden	1	Henry Davis	1
Edward Cornish sen[io]r	1	[blank] Meere	3
Richard Nitingall	1	Stephen Harris	1
Michaell Shawe	2	Stephen Lasey	1
Robert Wamsley	5		

Not Chargeable		Not Chargeable	
John Baker	1	William Dovers	1
Nicholas Fright	1	James Tunbridge	1
[fol. 59v]			
Widdow Palmer	1	Widdow Norwood	1
Widdow Lowd	1	Gilbert Fairecloth	1

Henry Bates	1

Steeven Harris borsholder
John Clinton constable

The towne of Ashford
in the Lath of Scray

Chargeable		Chargeable	
Mr John Nowell	8	Isaac Norton	2
Thomas Fitch in an empty house	4	Mr Coply in an empty house	5
Mr James Bate	7	Mr Symon Howe	6
Mr Thomas Flint	5	John Wanstall	1
William Tharpe	2	Joy Starr	7
Thomas Fox	2	Mr Edward Woodward	7
Thomas Terry	2	John Tritton in }	
Mr Edward Line	5	an empty house }	4
Robert Gibbs	8	Mrs Ann Bettingham }	
Robert Pullen	2	in an empty house }	6
Henry Wallis	5	Ralph Dayton	7
Thomas Waterman	4	Mr John Stringer	6
Thomas Gould	1	Thomas Moore	3
Richard Grinnell	4	Edward Haylock	2
John Reeve	2	John Stider	2
Henry Allen	4	William Roberts	2
George Springer	4	Grigory Barrett	1
John Foord	3	Thomas Champion	1
Thomas Murton	2	Robert Clarke	2
Richard Smalwood	2	Lawrence Pinhuck	-
John Miller	2	John Tuckey	2
Edward Tatty	1	Francis Cowton	6
Mary Tritton	2	Richard Philpott	2
Jane Fox widdow	1	Mr Henry Viall	3
Edward Adams	2	Edward Adams in }	
John Scott	3	an empty house }	2
Widdow Philpott	3	Robert Davis	1
Mr John Hawtry	4	Thomas Redfeild	6
Henry Wise	5	John Nower gent	9
Francis Bayleif jun[io]r	4	Thomas Robinson	6
Thomas Fenner	4	Ralph Clare	14
Henry Ringham	2	William Botten	4
Mr Hilkiah Reader	7	Thomas Taylor	4
Isaac Brissenden	3	Symon Gilbert	6
Mr John Sturton in}		Leonard Armson	3
an empty house}	5	Richard Lyne	2

John Pope	5	Thomas Elvey	5
Thomas Bigg	2	Edward Goddard	4
Richard Godfrey	5	Richard Fisher	2
John Denn	2	John Spratt	2
Daniell Murton	5	Thomas Jemmett	2
Mr John Sturton jun[io]r	6	Mr Edward Boys	6
Thomas Hyder	3	John Sherwood	4
Lydia Caffinch widdow	4	Henry Master	3
Robert Day	4	William Lee	2
Sarah Sineier	4	Thomas Brattle	3
John Ring	2	Aquila Hunt	2
John Barton	1	Thomas Philpott	4
John Steed	2	Henry Landes	3
John Knowlden	2	Thomas Tatty	1
John Horton	3	Robert Lott	2
Robert Tritton	2	William Carter	3
Ann Downe	1	Roger Austen	3
William Barrett	1	Thomas Cuckow	2
John Adcock	3	Widdow Bassett	2
Daniell Langden }		Widdow Philcott	3
in an empty house }	1	Thomas Jemmett	1
Walter Brooke	2	Francis Bayliff	3
Margery Waters	3	Susanna Cobb	3
Richard Whitlock	6	Samuel Rester	3
Robert Badner	4	Nicholas Gibbon	3
Thomas Clarke	2	Thomas Blunckett	2
Thomas Hunt	3	William Osbourne	3
Widdow Franck	4	Christopher Harluck	2
George Loueday	5	John Smalwood	3
John Powell	2	Mary Jacob widdow	4
Henry Clarke	2	Edward Brissenden	6
Edward Austen	1	Samuel Wood	13
Deborah Swayne	6	Thomas Olliver	2
John Harris	2	Stephen Ridding	1
Thomas Pysing	1	Thomas Colman	2
Robert Watsby	3	Hilkiah Sherwood	2
Edward Bigg	1	Richard Barman	1
Francis Wraight	3	Robert Radford	2
Thomas Miller	2	George Winterton	2
James Young	5	Mr Osmanton in }	
John Earne	2	[an] empty house }	11
William Pope	2	Stephen Taylor	2

Richard Rersby in }			John Barrow in}	
an empty house }	2		an empty house}	4
Richard Whitlock }				
in an empty house }	2			

[fol. 61r] [270]

Not Chargeable			**Not Chargeable**	
Edward Lee	1		Robert Elfeck	1
John Swann	2		William Browning	1
Thomas Waller	2		George Smyth	1
Henry Scott	1		Samuell Sarjant	1
Widdow Quested	2		Sarah Philcott	1
Widdow Effeild	2		Joane Page	2
Samuell Rimber	2		Widdow Harluck	2
Stephen Huse	2		Widdow Kennett	1
Robert Hall	2		Widdow Hall	1
John Edmunds	1		Thomas Tidam	2
Widdow Austen	2		Thomas Austen	2
Widdow Hills	2		Roger Bentley	3
Widdow Goodwin	2		Samuel Payne	2
Richard Ansell	2		Widdow Philcott	1
Widdow Adams	2		Thomas Watsby	2
Widdow Horton	3		Richard Stuttupp	1
Widdow Master	2		Ann Coombes	1
Susanna Atkins	1		Widdow Huens	1
Alexander Rogers	1		Ralph Dowle	1
Margery Eeedes	1		Margery Pickenden	1
Mary Sharpe	1		Walter Sympson	1
Widdow Smyth	1		Peter Page	1
John Buckhurst	1		Walter Burston	2
John Keatly	1		John Ashby	1
Michaell Fisher	1		Peter Churchman	2
William French	2		Edward Bus	2
George Lott	3		Henry Francklyn	2
Mary Ellis	1		Widdow Norton	1
John Colbourne	1		John Popioy	2
Thomas Beniamin	2		Susanna Smyth	1
Mary Ashman	1		Widdow Kingsland	1
William Edwards	1		Abraham Ashenden	2
Peter Attwood	2		Gilbert Norton	1
Richard Harluck	1		Widdow Andrewes	1

[270] this misplaced section is confirmed from E179.

Widdow Philcot	1	Katherine Fagg	1
Widdow Waller	2	Christopher Harluck	-
Robert Philpott	1	Andrew Raynes	2
John Carden	2	Robert Stonehouse	2
Richard Pope	1	Edward Webb	2
Widdow Strood	4	Edward Knowler	1
Thomasin Nevill	2	Widdow Ring	1
Peter Parris	3	Arthur Hubbert	1
Mary Vas widdow	1	Widdow Coppen	1
John Peirceson	2	Edward Tilman	3
Mary Stonehouse	2	Nicholas Knowlden	1
Widdow Batcheler	1	Hester Philpott	2
John Browneing	1	John Ansell	1
William Pullen	2	John Miles	1
John Asby	1	Mary Cox widdow	1
John Pinn	1	Robert Henman	1
Moses Sydwicks	1	Robert Kingsford	2
Valentine Ashby	1	Robert Ynckpen	2
Joane Nower	2	Richard Luckett	2
William Drawson	1	Mary Linckhorne	1
Margaret Bus widow	1	Edward Pope	1
Widdow Austen	2	Allen Cox	1
John Beeching	2	Edward Hidgcock	1
John Mortimer	1	Henry Wise Constable of Ashford	

[fol. 60r]

THE HUNDRED OF CHART AND LONGBRIDGE
In the lath of Scray

The Halfe Hundred of Chart

Shelvington Borough in Great Chart

Chargeable		Chargeable	
Mr William Small	6	Henry Smyth	3
Mr George Andrewes	3	Nicholas Toke Esquire	3
Stephen Maytham	4	Edward Tourth	5
Robert Maxted	3	Edward Harrison	7
Thomas Snoad	4	John Plaine	2
Stephen Fright	1	James Barman	3
Grigory Henham	2	Richard Larryman	3
Thomas Horton	1	Edmund Spicer	3

George Hunt	2	Edward Mackney	1
William Furner	1	Robert Wide	1
Richard Pinckaman	5	John Ferne	7
William Carpenter	2	Nicholas Chapman	1
William Elvie	2	John Merrick	1
Richard Trice	1	Peter Tilman	4
Robert Waller	3	Richard Tilbie	3
Anthony Chapman	1	Richard Snoad	2
Thomas Hubbard	1	Thomas Wills	1
Edward Head	1	Widdow Smart	2
Michaell Fowler	5	Robert Fowler	1
John Chittenden	2	Widdow Norrington	2
John Chapman	3	Mrs Browne in an empt house	-
John Earle of Thannet } in an empty house }	-	In an *other* empty house } in Cuckow Street }	-
		In another house in New Street	-

Not Chargeable

Ephraim Punnett	2	Sarah Bishopp	1
Thomas Hasell	1	Susan Glover	1
Widdow Gilham	1	Widdow Beagle	1
Alice Glover	1	Widdow Mace	2
Richard Watchers	1	George Michaell	1
Thomas Burges	1		

Bucksford Borough

Chargeable   **Chargeable**

Mr William Axton	5	Mr Richard Nevitt	10
Mr George Moore	9	Edward Ellis	8
Henry Tilby	3	Nicholas Barman	2
Joseph Gilham	1	George Philpott	5
William Dawson	1	Thomas Johnson	2
Richard Drewry	2	John Botten	2
Thomas Fright	1	Henry Wilminton	3
Richard Vincerst	2	Thomas Kempe	1
Thomas Partis	1	Widdow Lucas	2
William Tilman	3	John Jackson	1
John Maytham	1	Richard Heslegrove	1

Not Chargeable   **Not Chargeable**

Gilbert Hoppar	1	Widdow Farleigh	1

Goodwife Nower	1	Widdow Chittenden	1
Thomas Reades	1	John Edmunds	1
Widdow Reading	1	Old Fright	1
Thomas Bonham	1	John Kempe	1

Chelvington Borough

Chargeable		Chargeable	
Thomas Brett	5	Thomas Stevens	9
Thomas Law	3	Thomas Sedger	3
Richard Punnior	2	John Chittenden	1
David Hubbard	2	John Lawson	3
Robert Fox	1	John Rennolds	2
Elizabeth Eeves	2	John Foreman	1
William Cheesman	2	John Jones	4
James Watts	5	John May	2
Thomas Bishopp	1	Thomas Bankes	1

Not Chargeable		Not Chargeable	
George Bunckley	1	Thomas Finn	1
Seafe Moat	1		

Worting Borough

Chargeable		Chargeable	
Nicholas Toke Esq	15	Richard Caseby	5
Peter Tassell	3	John Tippett	1

Swinford Borough in Hothfield

Chargeable		Chargeable	
John Chapman	3	Stephen Attkins	4
Walter Munns	3	Richard Snoad	4
John Weekes	8	John Savidge	3
Daniell Lilly	2	Richard Steere	2
George Finn	2	Richard Ellis	3
Samuell Print	1	John Missing	1
Richard Bourne	1	John Diamond	1
Not Chargeable		Not Chargeable	
Thomas Fairebeard	1	John Mercer	2

The Great Borough of Hothfeild

Chargeable		Chargeable	
John Earl of Thannett	51	Thomas Maylam	2
Edward Wary	1	Edward Luxford	4

Richard Norman	2	Lawrence Wissenden	2
Elizabeth Hall widdow	2	Thomas Godfrey	2
Christopher Missing	2	Thomas Mascall	1
Edward Ellis	1	Andrew Fearne	6
John Rowse	1	John Harris	5
Thomas Toke gent	6	George Mathewes	1
Peter Glover	2	John Williams	4
Katharine Rasell widdow	1	Henry Cooke	5
Henry Pantry	2	Daniel Bourne	5
Robert Willmott	5	John Hunt	4
John Hasell	1	Richard Masters	5
Thomas Sim[m]s	1	Thomas Spratt	6
[fol. 60v]			
Robert Hewes	1	Alice Kedwell	2
Robert Gadsby	5	Richard Paris	3
Richard Parks	1	Robert Steere	1
William Viney and }		John Fowle gent	4
George Shorter }	4	John Shorter	2
William Neeve	4	Thomas Britten in }	
Thomas Willes in }		an empty house }	1
an empty house }	1	Jacob Turner in }	
		an empty house }	1

Not Chargeable		**Not Chargeable**	
Widdow Miller	1	Widdow Broomfeild	1
John Shepheard	1	Stephen Jupp	2
Widdow Baker	1	Stephen Chapman	1
Widdow Drason	1	Richard Madox	1
Widdow Groomebridge	1	Hope Parke widdow	1
Widdow Parkes	1	James Sharpe	1

Shippenden Borough in Bethresden

Chargeable		**Chargeable**	
Mr Andrew Lidall	11	Thomas Parker	2
Thomas Hodge	2	Peter Lawe	1
William Norton	2	Widdow Page	1
Isaac Whitacre	2	John Hilles	3
Ralph Oxley	3	Widdow Norrington	1
Widdow Horton	3	John Lukin	2
Widdow Tysehurst	2	Thomas Tucker	2
Richard Bancks	6	Michaell Norrington	5
John Norrington	1	Edward Gadsbey	4
Edward Milsted	2	Widdow Butcher	3

Bavister Barman	4	Francis Whitfeild	4
Henry Elvy	1	Anthony Medhurst	3
William Browne	1	Richard Ward	2
William James	1	John Man	2
John Stephens	1	Thomas Wilmott	2
Widdow Norrington	2	Stephen Greene	4
John Moone	2	Itchden, The Earl of Thanets	-

Not Chargeable		Not Chargeable	
Widdow Barman	2	Mary Greenstreet	1
Widdow Tuesnode	1	Thomas Tuesnode	1
Richard Willes	2	Nicholas Richard	2
Widdow Roust	1	Daniell Wood	1
John Wood	1	Thomas Tilman	1
Peter Holness	1	Peter Waters	1
Mary Godwin	1	William Bassett	1
Widdow Bull	2	William Staphery	4
William Turner in an } empty house }	1		

Rumden Borough in Bethresden

Chargeable		Chargeable	
Lawrence Smyth	2	Samuell Sharpey	2
William Pollard	2	William Bright	2
John Rich	1	Stephen Chapman	3
John Balduck	4	Thomas Usher	5
Nicholas Rich	3	William Usher	2
Richard Walker	2	William Farrance	3

Not Chargeable		Not Chargeable	
Stephen Large	1	John Sheafe	1
Walter Leedes	1		

The Street Borough of Bethresden

Chargeable		Chargeable	
Richard Hulse gent	11	Robert Coale clerk	4
James Bateman	3	Elizabeth Hunt	5
Robert Cobb	4	James Munn	2
William Foord	4	Anthony Edwards	3
John Hawkes	2	Joseph Gilham	2
John Chester	3	Timothy Buttler	2

Timothy Wellard	1	Edward Leedes	2
James Paye	1	John Scott	1

Not Chargeable		**Not Chargeable**	
Richard Cutbeard	1	John Clarke	1
William Underwood	1	Elizabeth Moone	1
Richard Hukins	1	William Goodwin	1
Widdow Fox	1	Widdow Tilbey	1
Susann May	1		

Snoad Hill Borough in Bethresden

Chargeable		**Chargeable**	
Daniell Kingsnoad	3	Solomon Oxley	4
Thomas Holnes	4	Stephen Tonge	2
William Marks	1	John Sharpey	8
Thomas Beeching	2	John Dyer	4
James Jarvis in an empty house	-		

		Not Chargeable	
		In one cottage where a poore man dwelt	1

Rudlow Borough in Ashford

Chargeable		**Chargeable**	
George Homesby	5	Amos Jacob	5
Robert Hunt	2	John Hewes	1
Henry Tritton	3	Widdow Parker	2
Thomas Parker	2	Mr Cuffin	4
Anthony Brett	4	Richard Topliff	1
Robert Gouldhatch	1	Thomas Norrington	2
Thomas Godfrey	3	John Tidham	3
John Coult	2	Thomas Sladden	4
[blank] Hamond	3	Mr Asherst in an }	
Widdow Pully empty	1	empty house }	1
John Crouch empty	1	Ralph Frembly empty	1

Not Chargeable			
John Mayning	3	George Moore Constable	

[fol. 61r] [271]

---

[271] Note first section of this was the Ashford 'non chargeable' return.

THE HUNDRED OF CHART AND LONGBRIDGE
In the Lath of Scray

The Halfe Hundred of Longbridge

Mersham Borough

Chargeable		Chargeable	
Sir Norton Knatchbull }			
knight & baronett }	25	Mr George May clerk	5
Mr William Gipps	6	Thomas Homesby	7
George Whitting	5	John Stookes	2
John Sharpe	1	Thomas Crouch	2
Thomas Blackbourn	2	Francis Morton	2
William Mount	3	Widdow Peirce	2
John Austen	2	Reignald Videon	2
Gregory Brett	1	George Lancefeild	3
Thomas Watson	1	John Smyth	6
Thomas Blunckett	2	Edward Chiselbery	2
Henry Nicholls	4	Thomas Gosby	2
Richard Thomas	2	John Wood	2
Robert Sprat	1	Isaac Browne	2
George Topley	3	William Jimmett	1
William Egerton	2	William Jacob	2
Thomas Fairebeard	2	William Hawkins	4
Robert Edgerton	3	Thomas Hatton	6
John Miller	2	Richard Webb	1
Edward Finch	1	Robert Lott	2
Thomas Virgin	2	William Hills	1
Thomas Topliff	2	John Virgin	1
Thomas Bayle in the }			
Lady Scots house empty }	16		

Not Chargeable		Not Chargeable	
Widdow Hodgman	1	Widdow Smyth	1
Widdow Glover	4	Thomas Blackbourne	1
[fol. 61v]			
Richard Francis	1	Thomas Taylor	2
Widdow Pantrey	1	Widdow Quested	1
Widdow Heyham	2	Widdow Salmon	2
Anthony Meede	1	Henry Squire	2
Widdow Videon	1	John Eaton	1

Kingsnorth Borough

Chargeable		Chargeable	
Mr Humphrey Withwick	8	Mr Nathaniel Wilson	5
John Springett	2	Robert Elme	2
John Buttorick	2	John Godden	4
John Seeley	1	Nathaniel Mannering	8
James Philpott	2	William Hills	2
Stephen Lynck	1	Samuell Jennings	3
Richard Jenings	1	John Lawson	3
Edward Hall	1	James Ottaway	1
Edward Smyth	1	Christopher Stonehouse	1
William Gimmett	2	Stephen Allen	2
Symon Hills	1	George Seely	1
Thomas Brooke	1	Widdow Taylor	5
Edward Withwick	3	Thomas Hilles	2
John Seares	1	Edward Hall	1

Not Chargeable		Not Chargeable	
John Tibball	1	Widdow Ottaway	2
Widdow Rooke	1	William Boulden	1
Widdow Watts	1	George Tilball	1

Kenington Borough

Chargeable		Chargeable	
Mr Nevill Hall junior	11	Mr Thomas Brett	5
Mr William Hayes	7	Thomas Allen	5
John Barrow	6	John Tritton	4
Hugh Badnor	4	William Lewes	4
Epaphroditus Sadlington	2	John Lilly	2
William Gill	3	Francis Wood	4
John Rayner	3	Richard Brett	3
Thomas Carr	2	Thomas Turner	2
Michaell Cock	1	Daniell Jemmett	4
George Hunt	1	John Crouch	7
Widdow Chapman	4	Widdow Barton	1
Daniell Taylor	2	Bartholomew Thurston	2
John Woodland	3	John Spice	1
John Woodland	2	William Luckett	5
Stephen Miller	3	Thomas Hasell	4
Widdow Smyth	3	Mr Harris	2
John Brooke	2	Widdow Stonestreet	3
Richard Luckett	1	Stephen Cobb	2
Thomas Titterden	2	Widdow Swayne	1

John Terry 1

Not Chargeable		Not Chargeable	
Widdow Stockes	1	Elizabeth Hasnot	1
Ann White	1	Edward Johnson	1
Nathaniel Coste	1	Robert Olefe	1
John Ruff	1	John Rogers	2
John Adoe	2	Richard Eldridge	2
Robert Burges	2	Robert Young	1
Thomas Carr junior	2	Augustine Paine	1
Michaell Paine	2	Widdow Bathon	1
Martha Paine	2	Aquilla Howlett	2
Widdow Eyerland	1	William Feres	1
Nicholas Clifford	1	John Humphrey	3
Widdow Hodge	1	Richard Butcher	1
John Churchman	2	William Eaton	1
Widdow Hodge	2	Robert Eyorns	2
Widdow Cost	3	John Bayle	1
Robert Austin	1	George Waters	1
Widdow Cox	3	Moses Churchman	3
Thomas Blyth	1	John Kennard	1
George Wakefield	1	William Clerkfield	1
Abell Frith	1		

Lacton Borough

Chargeable		Chargeable	
Anthony Aucher gent	7	John Boice gent	8
Edward Masters gent	9	George May gent	4
Nicholas Sawkings gent	6	Edward Andrew	4
Clement Court	6	Elizabeth Flinstone	4
Margaret Carter	3	Joane Goble	5
Margarett Mose	4	Thomas Smyth	2
Ambrose Smyth	2	George Winter	3
Giles Bartlett	3	John Jeffery	1
Margaret Stace	1	Mary Lance	1
Edward Topcliff	1	Peter Mount	1
Henry Hall gent	5	Thomas Hancock	1
Godwin Bushell	4	Edward Masters	2
William Kingsford	3	Widdow Waters	1
James Granesden	1	Abraham Jenkin	2
Robert Bushell	6	Henry Farbrace	3
Roger Waters	3	Robert Williams	4

Edmund Johncock	4	Stephen Dodd	3
Michaell King	1	Martha Cadman	1
Samuell Philpott	6		

[fol. 62r]

Not Chargeable   **Not Chargeable**

Abraham Bodkin	1	Widdow Young	1
John Lennard	1	Thomas Cloake	1
John Cooper	1	Widdow Teeller	1
Thomas Cooke	1	John Sherwood	1
Symon Boulden	1	Henry Barnes	1
William Akers	1	Robert Thornton	2
Thomas Doulden	1	Widdow Arger	1
Robert Bushell	2	Widdow Edmundes	1
John Seeley	1		

Hewett Borough

Chargeable   **Chargeable**

| John Knight | 4 | William Effeild | 4 |
| John Pilcher | 7 | Thomas Pay | 4 |

Hennard Borough

Chargeable

| John Backett | 1 |

Not Chargeable

Thomas Watson	1
Samuell Young	1
Humphrey Philpot	1

Sevington Borough

Chargeable   **Chargeable**

William Andrew	8	Samuell Alcock	3
Edward Elvie	1	Valentine Pollen	1
Widdow Bushell	1	John Dodd	3
Thomas Cobb	5	Steeven Dodd [272]	2
		Isaac Sampson	1

Not Chargeable   **Not Chargeable**

| William Morris | 1 | Thomas Wright | 1 |
| Widdow Horne | 1 | | |

[272] Interlined entry.

Hinxell Borough

Chargeable		Chargeable	
Thomas Edolph Esq	4	William Randolph gent	11
James Wilkinson clerk	3	Robert Edolph gent	3
Thomas Back gent	8	Thomas Coveney	4
Edward Andrew	3	Thomas Carter	4
Mrs Meritricks	6	John Goldsmyth	6
William Freed	1	William Snoad	2
John Harrison	4	Reignald Smyth	2
John Sutton	2	Richard Wannam	2
Edward Hayward	1		

Not Chargeable		Not Chargeable	
Robert Diamond	1	Daniell Hall	1
Thomas Branor	1	Thomas Sherwood	1
John Godfrey	1	Hercules Philpott	1
Thomas Hall	1		
William Gipps Constable		The other halfe hundred is [to] be sowed on here	

THE HUNDRED OF CALEHILL
In the lath of Scray

The Upper Halfe Hundred

Sanpett Borough

Chargeable		Chargeable	
Charles Wheeler Esquire	8	James Wise	3
Anthony Baldock	2	William Barrett	3
Symon Beeching	2	Symon Millen	3
Isaac Jones	1	Nicholas Taply	5
Timothy Millen	2	Thomas Howland	3
Stephen Scott	1	Thomas Andrew	3
Robert Allingham	2	George Burwash	2
Thomas Battum	3	William Swann	3
Symon Hodges	2	Robert Moore	2
Robert Payne	2	Widdow May	4
Henry Wilmott	2	Samuell Riddinge	2

Not Chargeable		Not Chargeable	
Abraham Chisman	2	John Buttler	1
Widdow Joanes	2	Thomas Hilles	1

Nicholas Hilles	3	Widdow Vant	2
Margaret Vant	1	George Hodge borsholder	1

East Lenham Borough

Chargeable		Chargeable	
Joseph Hoysted	1	William Sherley	14
William Essex	1	William Cooper	1
Edward Wise	3	James Parker	1
Grigory Sares	2	Nicholas Parker	1
Thomas Hoysted	5	Widdow Steed	1

Not Chargeable			
John Clarke	2	Joseph Highsted Borsholder	

Well Borough

Chargeable		Chargeable	
Thomas Rasell	5	Widdow Monds	1
Abraham Smyth	3	Widdow Whitfield	1
Paul Trewell	1	William Norrington	1

Not Chargeable		Not Chargeable	
Robert Houndes	1	George Creed	1
John Bunyard	1	Robert Butler	1
Michaell Tassell	1	Thomas Swan	1
William Boykett	1	Richard Hobbs	1
[fol. 62v]			
Thomas Gray	1	Widdow Moyce	1
Widdow Smithson	1	Richard Hoobbs borsholder	

Borough of Acton

Chargeable		Chargeable	
James Clements	3	John Cloake	3
George Burwash	1	Robert Tritton	1
George Cuckow	2	John Spice	1
Robert Chittenden	1	Samuel Burchley	3
John Wilson	2	Thomas Symmons	3
Anthony Millian	3	Richard Wood	3
John Crofts	5	Thomas Thunder	4
Edward Harpe	1	Gabriel Pierce	9

Not Chargeable		Not Chargeable	
John Essex	2	Edward Vant	1
		Edward Harpe borsholder	

Borough of Sandhatch

Chargeable		Chargeable	
Daniel Taylor	6	Robert Farne	2
John Jackson	1	William Beane	1
Robert Gadsby	1	Beniamin Hopkin	4
William Gravett	1	Nicholas Scott	2
Walter Pemble	3	Thomas Davis	1
William Philpott	2	George Ansell	1
Nicholas Harlock	1	James Waters	3
Robert Parker	3	Thomas Sharpe	7
Stephen Hilles	5	John Barrington	6
Robert Chittenden	2		

Not Chargeable		Not Chargeable	
John Wootton	1	George Hall	1
Widdow Parkes	1	Henry Danford	1
Widdow Carter	1	Thomas Parkes	1
Elizabeth Davis	1	William Ansell	1
Thomas Hedgcock	1	Francis Winchester	1
John Bell	1	Widdow Johnson	2
Robert Croocher	2	Thomas Browne	3
Thomas Hame	1	Thomas Cullen	1
		John Barrington borsholder	

Feild Borough

Chargeable		Chargeable	
Edward Hales Esquire	12	William Pope	6
John Fisher	3	Mr Belcher	3
George Withwick	6	Thomas Millen	3
Francis Marsh	3	Henry Napleton	4
John Thurston	3	Stephen Gardner	2
John Tilden	2	Robert Hooker	2
Thomas Hilles	2	Henry Batcheler	2
Robert Rayner	1	Edmund Burwash	1
Widdow Tilby	2	John Chapman	2
John Wackham	1	Thomas Glover	1
William Partridge	1	Alexander Dune	2
William Burbridge	2	John Odiarne	1

Not Chargeable		Not Chargeable	
Widdow Steed	1	Widdow Hills	1
Alexander Burford	2	Richard Ward	1

Alexander Dune borsholder

Burrough of Highslade

Chargeable		Chargeable	
Sir Robert Honywood knt	20	Anthony Aucher gent	6
Daniell Bourne	3	John Aby senior	2
John Baldock	2	John Jones	2
Edward Hart	2	Nathaniell Burr	6
Gervase Jervis	4	Henry Marsh	3
Richard Such	2	Thomas Jervis	1
Nicholas Gill	1	Thomas Cooke	1
Thomas Ansell	1	Richard Sills	1
Henry Parker	1	Abraham Smyth	1
John Abdie junior	2		

Not Chargeable		Not Chargeable	
Daniell Dowle	1	Robert Elvie	1
Paul Grewell	1	Ezechiell Black	1
Thomas Greene	1	Henry Cooke	1
John Croucher	1	Widdow Cooke	1
		John Jones borsholder	

Nash Borough

Chargeable		Chargeable	
Samuell Walsall clerk	3	Stephen Hulse gent	5
James Sharpe gent	9	Bethulia Bourne	4
John Gorham	3	William Berrick	3
William Millen	4	Thomas Millen	4
Edmund Cullen	3	George Snoad	2
John Wells	2	Thomas Hilles	1
John Coveney	2		

Not Chargeable		Not Chargeable	
Widdow Ferris	3	Samuel Gibbs	3
Richard March	1	John Croocher	1
John Terry	1	James Hodges	1
Peter Johnson	1	John Coveney Borsholder	

Charing Towne Borough

Chargeable		Chargeable	
Mr Gabriell Pierce	8	Mr Henry Ridgway	6
Mr John Creswell	4	Richard Rade	4
[fol. 63r]			

John Weekes	4	John Hart	4
William Woolf	3	Richard Fidge	2
Edward Craft	2	Thomas Giles	5
Margaret Elmston	7	Richard Beeching	3
Stephen Hooker	1	Nicholas Wraith	3
William Spillett	3	Henry Woster	2
William Brisle	3	Christopher Creed	4
William Ashby	1	Francis Speed	2
Walter Abdey	2	Thomas Kilham	1
John Willard	2	John Webb	3
Edward Tayler	3	James Ledger	5
Richard Knock	2	Widdow Payne	2
Widdow Burwish	6	Richard Iddenden	1
John Hatcher	2	Symon Beeching	2

Not Chargeable		Not Chargeable	
Brent Brizle	1	Thomas Hills	2
John Elvey	1	Widdow Hunt	1
Widdow Ball	1	Thomas Carter	2
Arthur Large	2	Widdow Hooker	1
Widdow Dering	1	Widdow Morgan	2
Richard Benskyn	1	George Stamford	1
Joseph Davis	2	Widdow Hodge	1
Alexander Jennings	3	Arthur Wood	1
Ralph Scott	2	Henry White	2
Widdow Moone	1	John Bridge	3
William Luckhurst	2	John Huthum	2
Widdow Gradduck	1	Henry Wood	1
		Richard Eddenden borsholder	

Borough of Little Chart

Chargeable		Chargeable	
[erased entry]		Sir John Darell knight	17
Francis Drayton clerk	6	Thomas Taylor	3
Thomas Pemble	4	Francis Swift	4
Edward Ager	2	John Langford	3
Henry Jenings	2	Edward Manuch	2
Abraham Landen	1	William Tomkins	3
George Missing	3	William Duker	2
Richard Symonson	2	Henry Browne	1
Richard Maplesden	1	Richard Law	2

John Bently	2	Francis Raines	3
Robert Bishopp	1	Samuell Milsted	1
John Bishopp	1	Mary Burtenshaw widow	1
Mary Harris widdow	1	Lawrence Attwater	3
Robert Knock	4		

Not Chargeable		Not Chargeable	
Thomas Blunder	1	James Tilman	1
Tabitha Browne	1	Henry Deward	1
Widdow Jennings	1	Widdow Neale	1
Widdow Browne	1	Daniell Wood	1
Robert Waters	2	Richard Parson	1
James Maplesden	2	Robert Elvye	1
John Fisher constable		John Bishop Borsholder	

The Lower Half Hundred of Calehill

Borough of Hollingherst

Chargeable		Chargeable	
Thomas Tovart	5	Ann Trey widdow	3
Robert Jewarst	2	Richard George	1
Richard Barker	1	Robert Greene	1
Robert Adman	5	Sarah Gates widdow	4
George Hilles	3	Thomas Pell	2
Mathew Hasnut	3	John Carey	2
Mary Eglesden widdow	2	John Goldwell	3
Robert Pell	3	John Dawson	1
James Newenden	3	John Newenden	3
Josias Maud	3	Nicholas Suthernden	2
Stephen Rich	5	Henry Kemp	3
Stephen Cheesman	2	Stephen Rich	1
John Toumber	1	Abell Bowens	2
Peter Amis	2	John Tilden	2
Elizabeth Care widow	2	Dorothy Pope	3
Edward Isted	2	George Southerden	1
Thomas Thurston	4	Nicholas Jewherst	1
Widdow Summer	1	Thomas Swift	3
Alexander Drayner	1	George Milles	1
William Turner	3	John Mathewes	2
John Reader	3	Thomas Besbeech	3
James Knight	2	William Sherlock	1
James Clinch	3	Richard Baker	2
James Bishopp	2	Thomas Elscum	2

James Fullagar	4
Robert Bennison	2
Henry Hidder	4
Thomas Hawkes	1

Peter Whitcomb	4
William Yates	4
John Sedwicks	4

Not Chargeable

Samuell Betting	1
Elizabeth Hawkes widdow	1
Thomas Mercer	1
Elizabeth Anvill	1
William Cooke	1
John Hilles	1
Thomas Stort	1
Francis Wilbore	1
[fol. 63v]	
Stephen Taylor	1
John Parrent	1
Widdow Gates	1
Thomas Pell	1
John Gouldwell	1
Richard Baker	1
Thomas Elscomb	1
Henry Hidder	1
John Sedwicks	1

Not Chargeable

Marian Bishopenden	1
Widdow Evens	1
Widdow Browne	1
William Coppins	1
Ann Lambe widdow	1
Thomas Brings	1
John Gilbert	1
Thomas Barton	1
Widdow Easman	1
Robert Adman	1
George Hilles	1
Widdow Iggleden	1
John Newenden	1
James Bishopp	1
James Fullager	1
William Yates	1
Steeven Cheesman borsholder	

Holynes Borough

Chargeable

[blank] James Esq	10
Robert Combes	3
John Payne	5
John Raynes	4
Peter Greene	3
John Man	4
John Bigg	3
Anthony Watts	2
Symon Chittenden	1
William Wellard	1
George Dakens	1
Edward Briggs	1
John Roberts	2
Thomas Basock	1

Chargeable

Jacob Turner	6
Thomas Hoppar	3
Moses Hoppar	2
Henry Crittall	6
Joseph Wacklyn	3
John Linck	1
John Tarpe	2
Abraham Smyth	2
Joseph Fenner	1
Nicholas Taylor	2
John Butcher	1
Henry Butcher	1
Thomas Claggett	1
John Williams	1

Stephen Lott	4	William Byham	3
Thomas Jell	3	William Archer }	1
Nicholas Lilly	1	and 3 he hath digged upp }	

Not Chargeable

John Drayner	1	John Coppens	1
Thomas Roberts	1	Widdow Tantum junior	2
Widdow Tantum senior	2	Widdow Whitehead	3
Richard Pantry	1	Thomas Hoppar	1
James Rich	1	Widdow Broome	1
Widdow Adams	2	John Tapnes	1
William Miles	2	Mrs Vaugham	2
John Bridges	3	Widdow Draner	1
		Thomas Gell borsholder	

Pluckly Borough

Chargeable

Sir Edward Dering Baronet at Surrenden [273]   34

Mr Francis Bettenham	8	Widdow Hart	4
Widdow Smilson	2	John Couchman	3
Joshua Lambin	3	William Poss	4
Gilbert Norton	3	John King	4
Michael Lee	2	Thomas Hilles	2
Anthony Nower	5	Ann Fitch	6
George Deeds	5	Richard Giles	3
Nicholas Beeching	1	Thomas Roffe	3
James Matell	2	Elias Tonge	2
Edward Gooding	8	John Spice	1
Richard Finn	1	Robert Knock	1
George May	1	Robert Boughten	1
Sampson Larryman	2	Henry Branford	2
Richard Simmonson	7	John Barten	3
John Nepaker	2	John Henniker	4
John Pinkeman	2		

Not Chargeable

Thomas Couchman	2	John Anny	2
Robert Boughten	1	Widdow Argar	2
Thomas Rachell	2	John Hunt	2
George Selles	2	Michaell Sanars	1
Henry Kingsnorth	2	John Parker	3

[273] Entry interlined.

George Esselles	1	Thomas Benskyn	1
John Rose	1	Thomas Gore	1
John Godfrey	2	Edward Smyth	1
Richard Argar	2	John Henniker Borsholder	

Sednor Borough

Chargeable		Chargeable	
John Andrewes	2	Abell Pemble	2
John Marden	3	Anthony Rayner	3
Richard Kingsnod	5	Mary Rayner widdow	5
John Elliot	2	Robert Baker	3
Joseph Mune	3	William Hope	2
Richard Austen	3	Margaret Pemble	6
Robert Tilden	4	Stace Horton	9
Bell Coufney	3	Mrs: Godfrey	8
Nicholas Mors	2	Henry Saffrey	4
Edward Apsley	4	Mary Steed	4
John Garnar	4	Widdow Glover	2
John Austen	6	Edward Fenner	4
Not Chargeable		**Not Chargeable**	
John Hoppar	2	Ann Grinnell	2
John Roberts	2	Robert Checksfeild	1
John Chambers	1	Richard Sudwicks	2
John Gray	1	William Sudwicks	1
Joane Maplesten	2	Stephen Back	1
Widdow Tilbey	1	John Cary	2
Gilbert Whitshead	1	Mary White	1
Widdow Payne	1	Widdow Toscood	1
John Knock	1	Elizabeth Kingsnod	1
		Edward Fenner Borsholder	

[fol. 64r]

St John's Borough

Chargeable		Chargeable	
George Wood	1	William Wilson	3
Thomas Burton	2	Henry Knock	4
Thomas Wall	2	Daniell Kingsnoth	2
Richard Stedman	1	Thomas Winter	3
Widdow Brenchley	3	Thomas Turner borsholder	2

Not Chargeable
Widdow Hoppar

Greenehill Borough

[Chargeable]		[Chargeable]	
Mr Henry Dering	10	Richard Glover	3
Henry Wells	2	Henry Phenice	1
Edmund Barnar	5	Widdow Pemble and }	
William Norton	1	James Spicer }	4
Richard Hues	2	Edmund Bishopp	3
George Bryar	2		

Not Chargeable		Not Chargeable	
James Payne	1	George Broadbridge	1
John Wilmot	1	Henry Wells Borsholder	

Borough of West Kingsnorth

Chargeable		Chargeable	
Edward Nepakar	4	Elias Tong	2
Thomas Terry	2	Edward Else	2
William Watkins	2	Phillip Usher	3
Edward Cheesman	3	Jarman Welles	4
Richard Batham	2	Richard Butcher	1
Thomas Wood	1		

Not Chargeable		Not Chargeable	
Thomas Kingsnoth	1	Anthony Harris	1
William Hennicar	1	William Watkins Borsholder	

Standford Borough

Chargeable		Chargeable	
George Witherden	6	Thomas Hilles	1
John Chittenden	3	John Skeere	1
Edward Eastland	1	Thomas Else	2
Thomas Smyth	2	John Pell	4
Widdow Milsted	1	Henry Huney	2
George Hammond	4	Widdow Jennings	1
Richard Baker	1	Robert Rich	1
Nicholas Rich	2	Thomas Scott	2
Thomas Sellings	2	Richard Else	2

Not Chargeable		Not Chargeable	
William Boys	1	John Ransom	1
John Brookes	1	John Bishopp	-
Richard Butcher	-	Thomas Milstead	-
		Nicholas Rich borsholder	

Edgley Borough

Chargeable		Chargeable	
Stephen Hopkins	4	Thomas Iden	4
George Barling	4	Judith Martin	4
Richard Barling	4	Alice Lamb widdow	6
Francis Turner widdow	6	James Barling	4
Walter Peirce	4	Thomas Parker	2
Thomas Tassell	4	John Gladdish	3
Henry Pemble	3	John Norton	1
Edward Peirce	2	Alice Barling widow	2
Stephen Bennett	1	William Bennett	1
Warham Hales	1	James Williams	1
Robert Stickhard	2	Martha Barling widdow	2
Samuell Parker	2	Richard Sudwicks	1
Stephen Cottingham	1	Peirce Roberts	4
John Woolton	2	Nicholas Morris	4
Richard Hatchin	6	Daniell Gipson	3
Christopher Kempe	2	Henry Fetherston	3
Mary Spice widdow	1	John Hickmott	2

Not Chargeable		Not Chargeable	
Thomas Woolwich	2	John Norton	1
Henry Batchelor	1	John Gardner	1
Tomasin Austen	1	Widdow Haffenden	1
William Bigg	1	Widdow Haies	1
Widdow Pranton	1	John Evering	1
Widdow Boulden	1	Katharine Telden	1
Robert Butcher	1	George Cottingam	1
Widdow Addams	2	John Hickmott borsholder	
		William Yates Constable	

THE HUNDRED OF BIRCHHOLT BARRONY
In the lath of Scray

Borough of West Brabourne

Chargeable		Chargeable	
Clement Woodland	2	James Quested	2
Edward Young	4	Widdow Harrison	2
Symon Spratt	4	Peter Waddell	2
Mrs Bull	3	Mr Bull	6
[fol. 64v]			
John Friend	1	William Beane	6

Godfry Cheesman	4	John Howling	1
Widdow Widower	1	George Waters	1
William Norton	3	Widdow Sladden	1
John Epps	3	Thomas Cheesman	3
Widdow Godden	2	William Kingsford	1
John Spaine	3		

Not Chargeable   **Not Chargeable**

Widdow Webb	1	Goodman Simmons	1
Symon Thorne	1	Goodwife Curd	1
John Popioy	1	Peter Ledner	1
Henry Danck	1	Thomas Dowle	1
William Morris	1		

Bockham Borough

Chargeable   **Chargeable**

Mr Handfeild	6	Edward Horne	3
Thomas Smeed	3	Michaell Walstall	4
John Wood	2	William Virgin	1
Widdow Rust	1	Widdow Effeild	1
Daniell Woodland	2	Thomas Norman	1
John Bayly	1		

Not Chargeable

Widdow Edwards	1

Hastingly Borough

Chargeable   **Chargeable**

Mr Pibus	8	Thomas Crux	5
James Wood	4	Widdow Page	2
William Tayler	1	John Carden	2
Michaell Philpott	2	Alexander Vrey	4
Henry Staynes	2	Richard Hawlke	2
John Mount	1	Thomas Skilton	1

Not Chargeable   **Not Chargeable**

Symon Carden	1	Leonard Grimston	1
Thomas Philpott	1	Thomas Jacob	1

East Brabourne Borough

Chargeable   **Chargeable**

Mr Rosse	4	Henry Impett	5
John Greene	3	Robert Austen	4

Mr Thomas Jenkin	3	John Vray	4
John Elvie	2	Nicholas Hatton	3
Thomas Webb	2	Stephen Turner	2
Robert Austen	2	John Coveney	1
William Fagg	2	Edward Rigden	4
Henry Miller	1	John Stace	1
Richard Gifford	1	John Barnes	2
Edward Hilles	2	John Gifford	2
Edward Popioy	1	Thomas Stediman	1
Widdow Woodland	1	Goodman Stokes	5
Phillip Mount	4	Solomon Waddall	2

Not Chargeable		Not Chargeable	
Goodman Tayler	2	Goodman Carby	1
William Woodland	1	Henry Stockwell	2
Thomas Jarman	2	Widdow Strood	1
Thomas Barnsdell	2	Robert Ashdowne	1
Henry Johnson	1	Peter London	2
Widdow Morris	1	John Bull constable	

THE HUNDRED OF FILBOROUGH
In the lath of Scray

The Upper Halfe Hundred

Markett Borough

Chargeable		Chargeable	
Thomas Diggs Esq	26	Mr Whittingham Fogg	9
Mr Cumberland	5	Mrs Nayler	6
John Knight	4	William Farley	1
John Coleman	2	Robert Packnam	3
James Odden	3	John Goodlade	4
Henry Knowler	2	John Gilbert	4
Widdow Hummersham	5	John Strood	2
Henry Pilcher	2		

Not Chargeable		Not Chargeable	
Widdow Bolden	4	Henry Mockett	1
Nicholas Pope	1	Widdow May	1
Nicholas Lago	1	William Bayly	1
Widdow Aldrey	1	Widdow Whittall	1
Widdow Cherlock	2	John Sparkes	2

Widdow Beer	3	William Fittall	2
Widdow Meares	1	Thomas Osmer	2
Widdow Coppar	2	Richard Jennings	2
Widdow Nasey	2	Widdow Farley	1
Widdow Hayward	1	John Sturges	2
[fol. 65r]			
George Finn	1	Widdow Reyner	1
John Irons	1	Mary Best	1
William Johnson	1	Robert Acres	1
Jane Dally	2	Henry Packnam	2

Eaststeward Borough

Chargeable		**Chargeable**	
The Lady Finch	16	Stephen Milles	2
Widdow Pound	1	Robert Jull	2
Widdow Tayler	3	Henry Renalds	3
Stephen Cullen	1	Robert Pack	1
John Luckett	1	Daniell Chapman	1
John Meeres	1		

Not Chargeable		**Not Chargeable**	
James Pashley	1	William Huggins	1
		[blank] Pollard	1

Shottenton Borough

Chargeable		**Chargeable**	
Henry Bing	2	Anthony Pim senior	1
Anthony Pim junior	3	Richard Ellin	4
Widdow Dixson	2	Robert Betts	-
John Collier	2	George Thompson	1
Edward Howis	1	Cooke Clarke	1
John Gill	1	William Blake	1
Henry Harris	2	Richard Scott	1
Francis Nicholas	1	Richard Howell	1
Peter Silles	1		

Not Chargeable		**Not Chargeable**	
Thomas Pye	1	Henry Hart	1
Widdow Lagget	2	Widdow Betts	1
Paul Gill	2	John Mayner	1
John Smyth	1		

Boreland Borough

Chargeable		Chargeable	
Thomas Austen	3	John Lowd	2
Thomas Basse	3	Thomas Shipwash	4
John Willes	2	William Cleere	1

Not Chargeable		Not Chargeable	
Thomas Marborow	1	Thomas Pope	1
		Edward Friend	1

Northearne Borough

Chargeable		Chargeable	
Mr Riseley and his }		Thomas Henneker	4
tenant Thomas Bottle }	-	William Luckett	2
John Marsh	2	Edward Mount	2
William Watson	4	Thomas Plummer	2
John Kennett	1		

Not Chargeable		Not Chargeable	
Moses Pysing	2	Widdow Grigory	1
John Clarke	1	Gabriel Foreman	1

Dane Borough

Chargeable		Chargeable	
Robert Sprackling	8	Nicholas Topley	4
Christopher Maxted	5	Kennett Loud	5

Not Chargeable		Not Chargeable	
Richard Harris	1	John Hames	1
Kennet Loud	1	William Streeting	1
		Thomas Palmer	2

Moldash

Chargeable		Chargeable	
Mr Henry Chapman	8	Mr Franklin	3
Mr Robert Mercer	1	Mr Thatcher	6
Christopher Goateley	3	William Deane	5
John Amis	3	Thomas Amis	1
Thomas Clement	3	Sampson Wanstall	3
Thomas Harrison	1	Thomas Wanstall	2
{Thomas Northfleet	2	Hugh Wood	3
{in another house	1	Sampson Peirce	1

Andrew Vidgeon	1	James Vidgeon	3
Christopher Hammond	2	Thomas Rogers	1
James Warren	1	Thomas Thurston	3
Edward Scott	1	Searles Goatley	4
Richard Epps	3	Richard Amis	2
Widdow Snoad	1	James Essex	2
George Homes	1	Widdow Essex	2
John Appleton	1	Joseph Dourne	4
Thomas Young	1	John Hicks	3
Thomas Peirce	2	Walter Homes	2
James Broadbridge	2		

Not Chargeable		**Not Chargeable**	
Edward Bisley	1	Thomas Gourley	3
George Homes senior	1	John Harrison	1
John Grimson	1	Widdow Francis	1
Widdow Terry	1	Fortunatus Grey	1
George Terry	1	Richard Terry	3
Stephen Hasell	1	Widdow Macer	1
John Simmerson	1	Rebeccah Clare	1
Thomas Packnam	1	Richard Vidgeon	1
John Mathewes	1	William Raith	1
Thomas Ditcher	1	Margaret Searles	1
Widdow Tappington	1		
		Robert Sprackling	
		Constable	

[fol. 65v]

Lower halfe hundred of Philborough

The Bororough of Shamford

Chargeable		**Chargeable**	
Sir John Fagg	14	Mr Lukin	6
John Shipwash	4	Thomas Page	4
John Gilbert	3	Edward Mitchell	3
George Greenstreet	1	John Slantor	2
Robert Greenstreet	3	John Greenstreet	1
Edward Maxted	7	Widdow Carr	2
James Dadd	1	Arthur Ruck	1
Thomas Benford	4	Thomas Farbrass	3
Arthur Hammond	1	Richard Perry	2
Mr Redding	7	Mr Kent	12
Hercules Hills	6	Edward Slautor	4

Charles Strong	6	Francis Gammon	15
Henry Elvie	3	George Dunkin	3
Ottawell Shrubsole	4	Thomas Elsted	3
Abraham Griggs	3	John Taylor	3
Edward Shrubsole	1	James Mantle	9
Gabriell Lent	2	Charles Hodgman	2
Symon Paramour	1	Edward Hawker	3
John Sanders	3	Richard Stedey	1

Not Chargeable

Not Chargeable

Widdow Wood	1	Widdow Pollard	1
Thomas Burchett	1	Francis Cheesman	1
Thomas Amis	1	Widdow Tilman	1
Edward Stonehorse	2	Thomas Swayne	2
Luke Colley	2	Stephen Ansell	1
Roger Eason	1	Thomas Pagge	4
John Ladd	3	John Duncke	1
Widdow Silkwood	2	John Maxted	2
John Terry	2	Richard Betts	1
Thomas Gimman	1	Widdow Fox	1
Widdow Howell	1	Widdow Dorrell	2
Edward Mutton	2	Widdow Osborne	1
Henry Ansell	1	William Howell	1
Isaac Wood	1	William Leggett	1
Henry See	2	Widdow Adams	1
Ann Baker	1	William Rutten	2
Widdow Wood	1	Clement Elice	2

Borough of Ruttenton

Chargeable

Chargeable

Mrs Lovelace	7	Mr Hulse	5
Thomas Knowler	5	Richard Hornsby	2
William Hilton	3	George Dunkin	2
Thomas Philpott	2	Beniamin Tilman	1
William Sladding	5		

Not Chargeable

Not Chargeable

Widdow Sussin	1	Widdow Fox	2
John Burgatt	2	John Boughten	2

Borough of Godmersham

Chargeable		Chargeable	
Mr Thomas Pilcher	6	Ediff Bigg widdow	5
Christopher Viney	1	William Pilcher	2
Thomas Hodgman	1	Thomas Bolding	1
George Pilcher	1	William Carter	2
Thomas Downe	1	John Slaughter	4
John Jull	2	George Backett	2
Widdow Tayler	3	Widdow Clarke	2
Richard Epsley	4	Widdow Viney	1

Not Chargeable		Not Chargeable	
Mrs Cornish	1	Mary Chapman widdow	2
In an almeshouse	4	Widdow Chapman	1
Widdow Scourge	1	John Pantry	1
[blank] Tillett	1	Michaell Dunkin	1
Robert Smyth	1	Widdow Turley	1
Christopher Foad	1	Widdow Packman	2

Borough of Hinxhill

Chargeable		Chargeable	
Mr William Brodnax	15	Mr Nicholas Knight	9
Mr William Carter	2	Mr Thomas Smyth	4
John Fearne	3	Michaell Wanstall	4
Symon Chapman	3	John Scourge	1
Robert Renolds	1	John Carter	1
Henry Maxted	4	Thomas Cooke	3
Jacob Symmons	2	William Kennett	3
John Claggett	2	Charles London	2
John Smyth	3	Michaell Epps	3
Michaell Hills	6	Thomas Wanstall	2
Robert Wanstall	3	Widdow Coaly	1
Francis Cash	4	William Godfrey	1

Not Chargeable		Not Chargeable	
Nicholas Cock	1	Christopher Harrison	3
Widdow Grinsted	3	Richard Titman	1
John Harrison	1	John Maplesden	1
James Duving	1	William Maplesden	2
John Smyth	1	Thomas White	1
William Read	1	Thomas Pysing	2
William Batchelor	1	John Finn	1
Robert Hedgcock	1	John Norman	1

Widdow Wanstall 2

[fol. 66r]

Borough of Dorne

Chargeable		Chargeable	
Mr Daniell Gutterson	12	Robert Daley	5
Robert Juce	1	Henry Strood	1
Henry Williams	2	Robert Wood	2
Thomas Birch	1	Edward Daley	1
Miles Foade	1	Widdow Keeler	1
Widdow Pysing	2		

Not Chargeable		Not Chargeable	
John Epps	1	Richard Turnley	1
Richard Cleaveland	1	Augustine Turnley	2
James Turnley	1	Robert Hart	1
Widdow Epps	1	Ingram Castle	1
Walter Benford	1	Richard Epps	1
John Swaine	3	Christopher Harris	1
Abraham Harris	1	Ingram Hagbin	1

Borough of Challock

Chargeable		Chargeable	
John Giles Gent	10	Sampson Ovenden	6
John Bing	6	Andrew Hawker	6
Henry Farbrace	4	Richard Peirce	4
John Peirce senior	4	Avarie Giles	5
Alexander Hawker	3	John Stanford	4
Thomas Carter	4	{Henry Kingsnoth	6
George Walker	4	{Henry Kingsnoth more	3
Thomas Cooke	2	John Peirce junior	3
Thomas Godfrey	2	Watkins heire	2
Thomas Chambers	1	Henry Clarke	1
William Andrew	1	Stephen Whitehead	2
James Barker	2	Lawrence Andrew	1
John Elvie	2	William Drury	1
Margaret Farbrace	1	Alexander Andrew	1

Not Chargeable		Not Chargeable	
John Andrew junior	1	Robert Nynn	1
Thomazin Fuller widdow	1	Thomas Parson	1
William Stone	1	George Boykett	1

Alexander Andrew	1	Widdow Pollen	1
Robert Love	1		

Borough of Persted

Chargeable		Chargeable	
John Wanstall	3	William Wanstall	4
Andrew Peirce	3	Mark Wanstall	1
John Spencer	2	Robert Tayler	2
Thomas Dane	2	William Atkins	2
Gilbert Dodd	3	William March	2
Richard Crickman	2	Peter Attkin	1
Edward Cooke	2	Thomas Clement	1
George Pent	1	Henry Perrin	1
Thomas Epps	1		

Not Chargeable		Not Chargeable	
George Pollen	1	Widdow Jordan	2
Jane Bayly	1	Widdow Hawkes	1
		William Lewkin constable	

THE HUNDRED OF WYE
in the lath of Scray

The Upper Halfe Hundred

Bewbridge Borough

Chargeable		Chargeable	
John Moyle gent	10	Mr Dodson	13
Thomas Wivill Esq	10	Henry Thornhill Esq	20
William Pantrey	5	John Marsh gent	8
George Finch gent	7	John File	6
Thomas Hall gent	4	John Martin	2
Thomas Moyle gent	3	Richard Jarman	5
Robert Dann	3	Thomas Rutton gent	6
Thomas Boulding	2	Richard Wraith	2
Valentine Belk gent	5	John Amis	2
Richard Audly	2	Timothy Tetherton	3
John Jarman senior	1	Thomas Sutten	1
John Lewis	2	Lawrence Gibbs	6
Thomas Austen	2	Richard Dryland	3
Samuell Gutteridge	2	William Fenby	2
William Lyon	2	Thomas Brissenden	7
Thomas Booth	3	Richard Warham	7

Thomas Slaughter	1	Francis Baker	2
Norton Munden	1	John Kennett	2
William Austen	1	John Horne	2
Thomas Glover	1	Robert Downe	4
John Coulter	3	Alice Tilman	1
John Tong	1	Lawrence Ruck	5
Mathew Austen	4	Giles Sampson	2
Thomas Stephens	4	Edward Brett	5
John Hollands	2	John Tappenden	1
Thomas Mundey	1	Martha Back widdow	3
Andrew Raynes	4	Thomas Back gent	9
Thomas Brett	6	Dorothy Eve widdow	5
Andrew Owsnam	2	John Fisher	2
John Argar	4	John Titherton	2
John Jarman junior	2	Thomas Dann senior	1
Thomas Dann jun[io]r	2	John Bourne	2
Robert Hart	6	Grigory Vidgeon	2
Valentine Austen	4	Ann Lyon	1
Widdow Smeeths	2	Henry Fox	1

[fol. 66v]

Not Chargeable		**Not Chargeable**	
Mathew Homan	2	Katharine Spratt widdow	2
Widdow Lilly	3	Isaac Hodgman	2
Widdow Whitehead	1	Widdow Dodd	1
Widdow Jimmett	1	Widdow Long	1
Widdow Laker	1	John Barnes	1
George Whitehead	1	James Bayley	1
Marke Finn	1	Widdow Quested	1
Mary Luckett	1	Widdow Goldsmyth	1
Richard Groomes	1	Widdow Dunke	1
James Huntington	1	Widdow Terry	1
John Berry	2	Thomas Jones	1
John Lands	1	Robert Bassett	1
William Merriday	2	Richard Cooke	1
William Driver	2	William Tayler	1
Widdow Martin	1	Widdow Bodkin	1
Mary Hart widdow	1	Reynald Williams	1
Widdow Sampson	1	Widdow Blundell	1
Widdow Jinman	1	Michaell Moone	2
Timothy Coveny	2	Thomas Herington	1
Isaac Whitnall	2	Jane Spencer widdow	2

Widdow Lewis	1	George Collyer	1
Widdow Slaughter	2	Widdow Howell	2
Tabitha Simmons widow	2	Thomas Simpson	1
William Whitehead	3	Widdow Austen	1
Widdow Norten	1	John Blundell	1
Rosamond Allen	4	William Spaine	1
Thomas Bodkin	2	Richard Staines	2
William Joy	1	Widdow Brickenden	2
Widdow Marten of	1	Richard Howell	1
Withersden			
Joseph Tayler	1	Widdow Twinley	1
John Payne	2	Widdow Foster	1
Thomas Lilly	1	John Carter	1
Robert Adman	1	Peter Kent	1
John Pettett	3	Widdow Clarke	1
Widdow Mongeham	1	Widdow Dryland	2
John Sampson	2	Joane Marten widdow	3
Avis Spaine	1		

Cuckoldscombe Borough

Chargeable		Chargeable	
John Jarman	4	John Dodd	2
John Miller	2	John Egerden	1
Thomas Fisher	2	Edward Willes	2
William Waddell	3	Thomas Sharpe	2
Nicholas Searles	2	John Whitewood	1
James Butcher	1	Edward Godfrey	3
Anthony Barnsdell	1	Thomas Sutten	3
Roger Coveney	1	Thomas Butcher	2
Richard Whitewood	1	Stephen Howland	5
Robert Howland	3	James King	2
Richard Giles	3	Stephen Dodd	2
Elizabeth Dodd widow	2	James Vidgeon	4
John Gouldsmyth	2	John Waddall	2
Henry Austen	4	Richard Goodwin	4

Not Chargeable		Not Chargeable	
Thomas Brightred	1	William Gates	1
Widdow Waddell	1	Edward Smyth	1
Widdow Huggins	2	Widdow White	1
Widdow Downe	2	Widdow Pay	2
Henry Greenstreet	3	Joane Jarman widdow	1
John Payne	1	Widdow Page	2

Widdow Kennett 1

Borough of Trimworth

Chargeable		Chargeable	
George Carter gent	8	William Ruck	7
Geoffry Graunt	9	William Juce	6
Stephen Gibbs	4	Mr Allen Clarke	4
Thomas May	4	William Chapman	3
Stephen Lansfeild	3	George Lansfeild	3
Thomas Reynolds	1	Stephen Quested	1
Widdow Boulding	1	William Smyth	1

Not Chargeable		Not Chargeable	
Widdow Mason	1	John Adman	1
Thomas Rigden	1	John Adley	1
Nicholas Adman	1	Edward Birch	1
Edward Epps	1	Thomas Baker	1

Borough of Brensford

Chargeable		Chargeable	
Thomas Coomes	2	Michaell Woollett	1
Daniell Parker	2	John Webb	1
Anthony Wraith	1	Moses Simmons senior	1
Moses Simmons junior	1	Michaell Hadlow	1
John Searles	1	James Court	1
John Watson senior	1	John Watson junior	1
Edward Titherton	1	John White	1
Robert Back	4	Thomas Lawe	1
John Whitehead	2	Widdow Turner	2
William Long	1	John Terry	2
William Honyman	1	John Johnson	1

Not Chargeable		Not Chargeable	
Robert Eaton	1	William Fukes	1
Robert Williams	1	Stephen Luxford	1
Thomas Jarman	1	Thomas Hooke	1
Widdow Sparkes	1	John Coombes	1
Widdow Spratt	4		

Borough of Towne

Chargeable		Chargeable	
John Coveney gent	5	John Philpott	1

John Pilcher	1	William Smyth	1
John Philpott	1	John Philpott	1
Daniell Godden	3	John Burch	2
John Pilcher	1	George Fagg	1
John Lilly	1	William Trice	1
Robert Fagg	3		

Not Chargeable		Not Chargeable	
Widdow Burch	1	Widdow Crickman	1
Widdow Browne	1	Henry Terrall	1
John Leggat	1	John Plummer	1
William Juce Constable			

[fol. 67r]
The Lower Half Hundred of Wye

Borough of Lennacar

Chargeable		Chargeable	
Heneage Earle of}		William Spragg gent	4
Winchelsea }	47	John Perrin	2
John Mason	3	James Deale	4
Isaac Ottaway	1	Thomas Lilly	2
Humphry Cowland	4	Isaac Ottaway Borsholder	

Borough of Febing

Chargeable		Chargeable	
Tobias Quested	2	William Marchall	2
Lawrence Mount	2	Stephen Garten	1
Alice Wright widdow	3	Joane Solomon	4
		William Marshall borsholder	

Borough of Deane

Chargeable		Chargeable	
Paul Lofty	4	John Millen of Deane	4
John Millen of Warne	1	William Sharpe gent	4
		William Sharpe borsholder	

Borough of Socombe

Chargeable		Chargeable	
Thomas Godfrey Esq	14	Henry Nicholls clarke	6
Thomas Godfrey Esq }		Ralph Frembly	6

in an empty house }	4	Peter Amis	5
Edward Sladen	6	John Austen	1
Thomas Watson	4	William Boulding	1
Richard Marshall	2	Thomas Rasell	1
[space]		Richard Harrison	7
Thomas Tayler	3	Thomas Gipson	1
John Kennett	5	Lawrence Laggett	3
Edward Hodgman	1	William Dodd	1
Stephen Ellen	2	Stephen Ellen borsholder	

Borough of Gotly

Chargeable		Chargeable	
Mr Thomas Mascall	8	John Dodd	7
John Mount	3	Roger Caper	2
James Harrison	3	James Warren	2
William Kennett	3	William Godfrey	2
John Deale	3	Robert Rasell	4
John Minidge	4	Robert Dadd	1
William Hobbs	1	Robert Admans	4
William Pinkaman	1	Robert Admans borsholder	

Borough of Wilmunton

Chargeable		Chargeable	
Edward Kempe	5	Anthony Slading	3
Robert Barrow	1	Daniell Saffery	6
Widdow Tayler	1	Widdow Godfrey	1
Thomas Deale	2	Richard Watts	2
William Wells	1	William Welles borsholder	

Borough of Shottenden

Chargeable		Chargeable	
Nicholas Tooke Clerk	4	Samuell Harfleet gent	8
William Dason	2	George Pettman	3
John Tayler	6	John Gofinch	4
Widdow Whitland	2	Stephen Millen	2
John Sanders	2	John Allen	2
Thomas Hubbard	2	Richard Ladd	2
Richard Ward	3	John Elvie	1
John Kennett	1	Thomas Gawthard	2
William Spratt Constable		Richard Ladd borsholder	

The Towne of Queenborough

Chargeable		Chargeable	
Peter Ken gent Major	5	Abraham Parke gent	4
Henry Seagar gent	6	Nicholas Taylor gent	5
Richard Tompson gent	5	Henry Monger &	
Daniel Baker	5	Thomas Hall gent	4
Richard Man	3	Thomas Hinton	4
Robert Throckley	4	Richard Polley	4
Thomas Howting	2	Richard Evans	4
Thomas Branson	3	Thomas Norrington	6
Allen James	6	Robert Sturgeon	3
John Cheeseman	4	John Goaler	2
John Wrest	1	Steeven Morris	3
Thomas Lee	1	John Jorden	1
James Man	3	William Clinton	3
Henry Mugwell	2	Ralph Cooper	1
Andrew Vigeon	2	Richard Shoebridge	2
Robert Hope	2	Michaell Razell	1
John Mummery	2	William Title	2
Widdow Askew	2	William Hardyman	1
Henry Knight	5	Thomas Huggins	2
Richard Evans	3	Thomas Huggins	7
Abraham Parke gent	1	Henry Seager gent	2

Richard Evans constable

Comparison with the Constable's return for 28 November 1664 (PRO: E179/249/35/1, published in *Kent Records*, NS Vol. 3, pt. 3 (2000), pp. 132-4), shows that at least five entries towards the bottom of the list should have been marked 'non-chargeable', and that the duplicate entries - probably for washing, baking or brewing hearths - for Richard Evans, Abraham Parke and Henry Seagar also should not have been charged. This information was obtained too late to be incorporated in the text, maps or tables in this volume.

LATH OF SHEPWAY

THE HUNDRED OF BIRCHOLT FRANCHESS
in the said Lath of Shepway

Borough of Lushington

Chargeable		Chargeable	
Sir Tho. Scott knt. And Bar't	36	William Gilbert	4
Robert Parnell	4	William Elvy	5
Henry Hart	9	Henry Cavill	5
Thomas Short	1	John Thompson	1
William Parnell	2	Thomas Spicer	5
Thomas Kayes	1	Peter Beddingfeild	5
William Rigden	4	Bazill Terry	3
Richard Finch	2		

Not chargeable		Not chargeable	
William Collier	2	John Joyce	2
William Browne	1	Richard Wicks	2
Thomas Franckwell	1	Peter Quested	2
Widdow Judge	1	George Quested	4

The Southward Borough

Chargeable		Chargeable	
John Tritton	7	Widdow Lushington	5
Mrs. Austen	3	Robert Tyler	2
John Whitfield	3	Widdow Pantrey	1

Not chargeable		Not chargeable	
Widdow Thompson	1	John Hills	2
Widdow Downe	2	William Hodgman	2

Coate Borough

Chargeable		Chargeable	
Mr. Juxon	6	Henry Hammond	4
Thomas Carter	4	Thomas Hogbeane	3
John Stroud	3	John Crouch	2
Richard Cosins	2	John Ashdowne	1
Abraham Simpson	1	Edward Dowle	2

Not chargeable

Thomas Glover	1	Widdow Hudson	1
Widdow Seely	1		

Borough of Hearst

Chargeable

Mr. William Fagg	5	Thomas Glover	7
William Renolls	2	John Kesbie	2
John Netter	2	Samuell Grewell	3
Edward Waters	2	Edward Grewell	1
Samuell Alcock	3	Stephen Pilcher	3
John Seeley	3	William Webb	1
Nicholas Kesby & }	4	Bartholomew Hernden	1
his tenant }		Henry Thomas	2
Richard Prebble	1	John Walsbie	1
George Haffenden	4	John Dupper	1
John Beane	3	James Cullen	3
John Johncock	1	Widdow Griffin	2
Thomas Beane [274]	3		

Not chargeable

Widdow Gates	1	Widow Nusam	1
Hugh Davis	1	Henry Oliver	1
Nicholas Bushell	1	Widdow Essex	1
Thomas Nusam	1		

Stock Borough

Chargeable

Thomas Loftie	6	Augustine Terry	7
Gilbert Dodd	1	Widdow Wharell	1
Richard Smart	2	Richard Wood	1
Mathew Newnham	4	Thomas Worger	2
William Hills	3	Thomas Gosbie	4
Thomas Pelham	4	Timothy Beddingfeild	9
Thomas Milsher	2	Richard Ines	1
Peter Suckling	1	Edward Horne	7
Henry Clarke	2		

Not chargeable

Richard Cheesman	1	Thomas Dennis	1
Robert Kingsford	2	Stephen Bromley	1

[274] Entry interlined.

Henry Suckling	2	James Kingsford	2
Widdow Wood	1	Widdow Pelham	1
Nicholas Jell	1	Leonard Francis	2
William Cosbie	2	Widdow Smithson	1
Widdow Tayler	1	John Ellis	3
Robert Giles	2	Thomas Brett	1
Thomas Newnham	2	Richard Fagg	2
Richard Suckling	1	Vincent Miller	3
Widdow Purt	1		

Stonested Borough

Chargeable		Chargeable	
Henry Brightred	6	Richard Wicks	6
William Hogbeane	4	Thomas Kennard	3
John Foard	3	Robert Hope	2
Jeremy Minnis	2	John Hedgcock	1

Not chargeable		Not chargeable	
Haman White	2	John Beale	1
Stephen Miller	1	Richard Dandie	2
Richard Robinson	1	Widow Elvy	-

[fol. 68v]

THE HUNDRED OF STOWTING
in the Lath of Shepway

The Upper Halfe Hundred

Chargeable		Chargeable	
Sir Edward Honywood Bar't	17	Humphrey Beddingfeild gt.	4
Henry Lushington	2	Thomas Court	4
Stephen Laggett	2	John Holman	1
Henry Akers	1	Thomas Swaine	1
Humphrey Philpott	3	Thomas Hobday	1
John Bush	2	Richard Cloake	2
George Chapman	3	Widdow Court	2
Stephen Sawyer	2	John Gizard	3
Widdow Downe	1	Stephen Dyeper	1
Robert Pott	1	Mathew Browne	2
Clement Rolfe	1	John Pilcher	1
Thomas Turnley	3		

Not chargeable		Not chargeable	
John Mount	1	Widdow Pott	1
Valentine Fryer	1		

North Borough

Chargeable		Chargeable	
Benjamin Peere gt.	5	Robert Meggott	3
Mathew Court	3	Thomas Roome	4
John Kennett	2	John Belcey	3
Henry Spaine	2	Symon Bolden	3
Sampson Court	3	Robert Bolden	2
Stephen Scott	3	Widdow Pilcher	1
Widdow Rigden	1	Widdow Cloake	1
James Jorden	1	William Pilcher	1
Robert Gardner	3	John Pissing	2
Valentine Laker	1	Thomas Blacklock	3
John Athorne	1	Widdow Gibson	3
William Lucas	3	Thomas Spaine	2
John White	3	John Hambroke	1
John Hambroke for }		Edward Munns	1
Whites house }	-	Richard Huntmill	1
Thomas March	1	William Mantle	2
John Bolden	1	James Browneing	4
Steven Brice	1	John Horton	2
Sampson Horton	4	Edward Muns jun'r	2
Phillipp Grigg	1	William Uden	1
Richard Devins	2	William Howlett	4
John Shrubsole	3	Robert White	3
John Somes	4	John Nethersole	1
Widdow Gardner	1	Widdow Rolfe	1

Not chargeable		Not chargeable	
John Bolden jun'r	1	Mathew Munns	1
Michaell Wellington	1	John Worryer	1
John Hambrook in an			
empty house	1	Thomas Blacklocke	
		Constable	

The Lower Halfe Hundred of Stowting

Borough of South Horton

Chargeable		Chargeable	
Samuell Smyth cler[k]	4	Thomas Lancefeild	2

Robert Simpson	5	John Strood	1
Richard Andrew	3	Stephen Woodland senior	1
John Rolfe senior	3	John Walk	2
Thomas Gifford	1	John Bell	3
Richard Bird junior	3	Mary Kinsmell widdow	3
William Chittenden	2	John Rolfe junior	1
Symeon Spry	1	Thomas Pysing	4
Benjamin Keet	1	Phillip Best	1
Samuell Hardman	1	Walter Mantle gent	6
Charity Brice widdow	1	John Mantle	2
William Smith gent	6	George Leggat	5
Sarah Wood widdow	4	Richard Shatwater	3
Thomas Blowne	1	John Hoyle	2
James Jones	4	Susanna Pellett widdow	2
John Nash	2		

Not chargeable

Ann Lednor	1	Deborah Smith widdow	1
Jeffry Wanstall	1	Henry Spicer	1
James Miller	1	John Rann	1
Joane Sanders widdow	1	William Pilcher	2
John Whitering	1	Elizabeth Scivell widow	1
John Kennett	2	John Spooner	2
Thomas Andrew	1		

Borough of East Horton

Chargeable		Chargeable	
Henry Morris gent	3	Thomas Morris gent	3
Thomas Marsh	3	Hercules Gifford	2

Borough of Stowting

Chargeable		Chargeable	
Reginald Ansell cl[erk]	4	Thomas Jenkin gent	2
Richard Allen cler[k]	3	William Court	4
William Emptage	3	John Browne	2
William Reynolds	1	Thomas Hogben	1
Henry Coleman	1	Thomas Quested	1
Ann Cooper widdow	3	Thomas Matcham	2
Robert Parnell	4	John Pope	2
William Horne	1	Henry Miller	1
[fol. 69r]			
Thomas Mount	2	Phillip Mount senior	2

Thomas Keete	2	Richard Cheesman senior	1
Richard Cheesman junior	1	Henry Maxted	3
Robert Medman	1	John Bousar	1

Not chargeable		Not chargeable	
Reginald Ansell Cl[erk]	1	Thomas Jenkin gent	1
William Court	1	William Emptage	1
William Reynolds	1	John Pope	1
Edward Epps	1	Abraham Pope	1
John Lukins	1	William Rigden	1
John Maborne	3	John Impett	1
Peter Lednor	1	Widdow Impett	2
Henry Maxted	1	John Somes	2
Widdow Gouldsith	1	Widdow Somes	1
Widdow Coleman	1	William Fisher junior	1
Robert Brooman	1	John Bousar	1
William Fisher senior	2	Richard Brooman	1
John Wells	2	John Young	1
Augustine Spaine	1	Thomas Morris gent	1
Henry Morris gent	1	Thomas Gifford	1
John Nash	1	John Walke	1
James Jones	1	Henry Maxted Constable	

THE HUNDRED OF LONINGBOROUGH
in the Lath of Shepway

The Upper Halfe Hundred

Carterwood Borough

Chargeable		Chargeable	
Mr. Robert Lewknor	12	Mr. Floate	5
Mr. Robert Foster	5	Richard Lawrence	3
Richard Monger	5	William Monger	3
Robert Rolfe	4	John Wrake	1
Edward Hogben senior	4	William Oldfeild	3
Thomas Rigden	1	Thomas Rigden	1
David Rigden	1	Richard Baker's heirs	1
Lawrence Sturdy	2	Thomas Garnay	3
Widdow Hogben	1	Edward Hogben junior	3
Edward Pritchers	2	Thomas Homes	1
Widdow Castle	1	Alexander Nethersole	1
John Nethersole	3	William Nethersole	2

Edward Marks	4	Robert Humphrey	1
Widdow Gardner	3	Nicholas Nethersole	3

Not chargeable		**Not chargeable**	
Stephen Thomas	1	Noah Hobday	1
Gilbert Walbanck	1	Amy Wells	1

Towne Borough

Chargeable		**Chargeable**	
John Hubbert gent	6	Henry Hanington cler[k]	5
Thomas Ginder junior	5	Augustine Spayne	3
Thomas Ginder senior	1	George Corke	5
John White	3	John Hogben gent	8
John Stokes gent	3	Robert Preble	1
John Beane	6	Widdow Nevett	3
William Bell	3	John Philpott	2
William Partrige	3	Widdow Beane	1
Robert Bush	1	John Norton	1
Clement Rogers	1	George Christian	2
John Foreman	2	Daniell Ruck	8
John Stroud	4	Richard Baldock	1
Widdow Godwin	1	Moses Sharpe	4
Henry Hogben	3	John Heyman	5
Henry Boughten	4	Thomas Ladd	4
Thomas Day	3	Widdow Sladden	2
John Warly	7	Richard Knowler	1
John Gilbert	5	Richard Herbert	3
Widdow Moore	1	Thomas Wood	2
Thomas Nevett	1	Richard Hawkins	3
John Aelst gent	1	Thomas Ruck	2
John Odden	1	Michael Middlemas	2
Thomas Norton	1	William Stroud	1
Thomas Baker	3	Josias Swaffer	2
Thomas Ham[m]ond	4	Thomas Hawking	1
William Hogben	3	Widdow Sladden	2
James Nevett	1	William Gibbon	1
William Gill	1	John Sturdey	3
Edward Heyes	1	Hugh Johncock	1
Widdow Stace	1	Robert Page	1
Thomas Hobday	1	Thomas Bonham	1
John Allen	1		

Not chargeable

John Knott	1
[blank] Gardner	1
Widdow Johncock	1
Widdow Griffen	1
Stephen Benham	1
Widdow Underdowne	1
James Stroud	1
James Freind	1
Widdow Stroud	1
Widdow Mabourne	1

[fol. 69v]

James Bird	1
Edward Hayes	1
Symon Chambers	1
William Webb	1
John Penfold	1
Widdow Harrison	1
David Pilcher	1
Thomas Wood	1
John Oynes	1
Widdow Pope	2
Widdow Lucas	1
Henry Marsh	1
Roger Betts	1
Robert Marsh	1
Michaell Page	1
John Bridges	2
Mathew Horsfeild	1
Augustine Spaine	1
Robert Hawking	1

Not chargeable

John Lyon	1
Michaell Hudson	1
Widdow Somes	1
[blank] Betts	1
William Russell	1
John Woodower	1
Abraham Wall	1
John Codham	1
Thomas Bird	1
Robert Denton	1
William Jancocke	1
John Cooper	1
John Goulder	1
Widdow Hubbard	1
Michaell Norcock	1
John Warry	1
James Johncock	1
Martha Johncock	1
Moses Sharp	1
Richard Preble	2
Widdow Browne	1
Widdow Hunt	1
Nicholas Adcock	1
John Williams	1
Elizabeth Fagg	1
Thomas Johncock	1
Widdow Reeve	1
Widdow Page	1
Thomas Hawking	1
Widdow Cooke	1

Bladben Borough

Chargeable

Daniell Woollett gent	4
Robert Miles	3
Giles Brett	2
Joceline Gates gent	2
Peter Pout	2
Thomas Baker	2
James Foard	2
Richard Carden	1

Chargeable

William Woollett gent	5
Stephen Goldfinch	1
Edmund Pay	6
Edward Soale	2
John Allen	4
John Gibbons	4
Margaret Denn	3
Richard Rigden	1

Widdow Rigden	3	John Vile	1
Henry Burch	2	John Dunkin	1
Thomas Court	1	John Beere	3
James Lowe	1	Richard Mirsh	2
James Stace	2	Thomas Young	2
John Marsh	1	Joseph Horton	2
Isaac Pay	2	Richard Pay	1
Robert Jacob	2	Avary Spratt	2
Thomas Harnett	3	William Polbard	2
John Grigory	1	Stephen Hambrooke	1
John Griggs	1	Henry Bridges	1
John Pitcher	1	James Hart	2
William Wood	1	William Frierson	1
William Denn	3	John Saddleton	1
Thomas Fox	1	Alexander Gammon	1
Robert Kite	3	Widdow Pitcher	1
Widdow Andrew	1	Giles Brett senior	3
Henry Everden	1	Isaac Pitcher	1
William Bingham	1	William Epps	2
Nicholas Cooke	1	Richard Carter	1
John Revell	3		

Not chargeable		Not chargeable	
Daniell Woollett	1	Widdow Stace	1
Henry Hilton	1	William Heselbey	1
John Cooke	1	William Moore	1
Henry Finch	1	Thomas Ovenden	1
Widdow Maxted	1	Widdow Silkwood	1
Widdow Horne	1	William Terrall	1
Widdow Preble	1	Nicholas Gammon	1
Edward Johncock	1	Symon Churchman	1
Henry Maxted	2	Widdow Rigden in an }	3
Henry Kitchen in an }	1	empty house }	
empty house }			

Boyke Borough

Chargeable		Chargeable	
John & Henry Sanders	5	William Sym[m]ons	6
Thomas Oldfeild	7	William Waddall	3
Widdow Oldfeild	3	Richard Rolfe	1
Richard Oldfeild	3	Henry Hogben	5
John Pilcher	2	John Hammond	3

John Beane	3	John Sladden	2
David Wood	2	Nicholas Marks	1
John Austen	3	Thomas Page	3
Thomas Hile	3	Thomas Redwood	2
John Goldfinch	1		

Not chargeable		Not chargeable	
John Browneing	2	Michaell Page	1
Thomas Lyon	2	Robert Wood	1
Richard Wood	1	David Fox	2
James Dunn	1	John Hile	2
Alexander Somes	1	James Boykin	1
John Rogers	1	Widdow Blowne	1
Widdow Hogben	1	Joseph Horton Constable	

The Lower Halfe Hundred of Loningborough

Borough of Lyminge

Chargeable		Chargeable	
Benjamin Sladden	3	Abraham Tunbridge	2
Nicholas Peene	1	Thomas Phillipps	1
Thomas Bedgeant	1	John Kerwin	4
Richard Terrall	1	George Everden	2
Widdow Ireland	1	Adam Ham[m]ond	3
[fol. 70r]			
Nicholas Deale	1	Roger Pilcher	2
John Marsh	1	William Marks	1
Thomas Robus	1	John Penfold	3
Phillip Jenkin	1	Stephen Serjant	1
Widdow Cloake	1	William Rake	1
Robert Hogbin	2	William Wood	1
William Terrall	2	James Penfold	3
David Penfold	2	David Hogbin	1
John Wood	2	John Terrall	1
John Wills	3	George Browne	3
William Cooke	1	Edward Proud	1

Not chargeable		Not chargeable	
Benjamin Sladden	4	William Cooke	1
Nicholas Peene	1	Thomas Bedgeant	1
John Carwin	1	Richard Terrall	1
George Everden	1	Adam Hammond	1
William Marks	1	Thomas Robus	1

Richard Jenkin	4	Phillip Jenkin	1
Stephen Serjant	1	William Wrake	1
Robert Hogben	1	Henry Page	1
William Terrall	1	James Penfold	1
David Penfold	1	John Wood	1
John Wills	1	George Browne	1
Thomas Carpenter	3	William Cooke	1
Thomas Jenkin	3	Edward Proud	1
Widdow Saunders	3	Widdow Rolfe	2
Widdow Crouch	2	John Neames	2
John Penfold	1	David Hogbin	1

Eachinghill Borough

Chargeable		Chargeable	
Robert Symmons	3	Richard Hogbin	1
Nicholas Homewood	3	Thomas Marshall	2
Thomas Rigden	4	Thomas Terrall	3
Widdow Elgar	2	James Penfold junior	4
William Cooke	3	Widdow Spicer	2
Edward Hogben	2	David Hogbin	2
Thomas Spicer	2	Widdow Roome	3
Widdow Wraight	1	William Buttrice	1
Thomas Allen	3	John Stokes	1
William Hedgcock	2	Richard Rigden	2

Not chargeable		Not chargeable	
Robert Simmons	1	Richard Hogben	1
Nicholas Homewood	1	Widdow Roome	1
Thomas Fagg	1	Edward Hogben	1
David Hogben	1	Thomas Spicer	1
Widdow Spicer	1	James Penfold	1
Thomas Rigden	1	Thomas Marshall	1
Henry Streeting	1	William Beane	1
Arnold Canaby	1		

Sipton Borough

Chargeable		Chargeable	
Edward Scott gent.	8	Mr. William Strouts	9
Mr. Henry Han[n]ington	1	Mr. Jacob	4
Mr. William Sawkins	3	John Impett	2
Peter White	1	Richard Silke	2
William Prior	1	Beniamin Pilcher	3

William Marsh	1	Peter Goulder	1
William Crouch	3	Thomas Clarke	2
Richard Jenkin	3	Widdow Browne	1
John Pilcher	1	Robert Stannard	1
Thomas Walbanke	1	William Miller	1
William Marks	1	John Gillett	3
Thomas Hunt	3		

Not chargeable		Not chargeable	
Edward Scott gent.	1	Mr. William Strouts	1
Mr. Henry Jacob	1	Mr. William Sawkins	1
John Impett	1	Paul White	1
Beniamin Pilcher	1	William Jancock	1
John Stevens	1	William Crouch	1
Thomas Clarke	1	Richard Jenkin	1
William Miller	1	John Gillett	1
Thomas Hunt	1	Thomas Tilbie	1
John Chaplaine	1	Edward Hogben Constable	

THE HUNDRED OF STREAT
In the Lath of Shepway

The Upper Half Hundred

Giminge Borough

Chargeable		Chargeable	
Philipp Viscount Strangford	60	Mr. Peter Penny	7
George Foard	4	Michaell Westborne	5
Thomas Sanders	4	Richard White	2
Richard Warden	2	Henry Hilles	2
Richard Bird	3	Thomas Hunt	2

Not chargeable		Not chargeable	
Robert Hartrupp	2	Thomas Brooke	1
Richard Wanstall	1	Stephen Jaram	1
Anthony Smith	1		

[fol. 70v]

Willopp Borough

Chargeable		Chargeable	
Mr. John Dawson	7	Thomas Greenland	4
Phillipp Gibbons	4	Anthony Spaine	3
John Greenland	3	William Warden	3
Thomas Godden	2	William Foard	1

Thomas Johnson	1	Edward Wake	1
Thomas Poyne	1	Richard Shatwater	1
Francis Rose	2	In ye vicarage house	3

Not chargeable   **Not chargeable**

John Dennis	1	John Swayne	1
William Nore	3	Henry Beere	1

Stonestreet Borough

Chargeable   **Chargeable**

Mr. Cason	5	John Philpott	5
Richard Reader	6	Henry Archurst	3
Jeremy Warner	2	Robert Lodge	2
Richard Large	4	James Simmons	3
Robert Lawes	3	John Baker	1
Edward Heritage	1		

Not chargeable   **Not chargeable**

John Smyth	3	Richard Huntman	1

Summersfeild Borough

Chargeable   **Chargeable**

Sir Peter Hayman	16	Thomas Godfrey Esq.	13
John Morris	2	John Hilles	5
Peter Waddall	6	Nicholas Hunt	2
James Fisher	1	Thomas Colder	1
Thomas Thompson	4	Richard Smart	1
Robert Quested	1	Paul White	2
Thomas Poole	1	Thomas Bunce	1
Henry Eyens	4	Henry Hart	3
Nicholas Clarington	1	Phillip Gibbons Constable	

The Lower Halfe Hundred of Streat

Borough of Selling

Chargeable   **Chargeable**

Richard Burton Clerk	5	Richard Jacob	3
Richard Wolven	3	Henry Strood	3
William Fagg	2	Stephen Hogben	2
John Wraith	1	John Hotten	1
Thomas Kennett	3	Richard Cosin	3
Samuell Goldfinch	4	William Cavell	3

Elizabeth Pysing	1	Thomas Robus	2
George Clarke	2	Widdow Homes	2

Not chargeable		**Not chargeable**	
Peter Cole	3	William Cavell	1
Thomas Mantle	1	Widdow Cox	1
Widdow Fenn	1	Mary Cobourne	1
William Stone	3	Henry Jenken	4
John Hilles	3		

The Borough of Bellery Key

Chargeable		**Chargeable**	
Thomas Sprie	7	John Spicer	3
Richard Sanders	1	Widdow Hogben	3
Nicholas Brock	3	Edward Elvie	2
Thomas Gibbs	4	Widdow Hambrooke	2
John Wills	3	William Sprie	2

Not chargeable		**Not chargeable**	
Thomas Blackbourne	1	William Tapp	1

Borough of Hast

Chargeable		**Chargeable**	
Henry Prickett	3	Thomas Admitt	4
John Kenn	2		

Borough of Bonington

Chargeable		**Chargeable**	
Mr. Joyner Brook	4	Richard Adnett	3
John Hawkes	2	John Bretts	4
John Juse	2	Henry Hayward	3
Thomas Hodgmas	1	John Johncock	1
Thomas Horton	1	William Cock	1

Not chargeable		**Not chargeable**	
Richard Adnitt	1	Andrew Archley	1
Samuell Nicholls	1	Andrew Amis	1
Thomas Wisdom	1	Joane Castle	1
Hanna Longley	1	Henry Francks	1
John Wells	2	Edward Palmer	1
John Sanders	1	John Jurey	1
William Cooper	1	Thomas Robus Constable	

THE HUNDRED OF OXNEY
in the Lath of Shepway

Church Borough

Chargeable		Chargeable	
Mr Samuell Croswell	7	Edmund Wisherden	4
William Tufton	4	Richard Fowle	3
[fol. 71r]			
Widdow Fowle	4	Richard Lashenden	3
Widdow Fann	2	Thomas Goodale	1
Thomas Walker	2	William Kine	1
Richard Hall	3	John Hunt	3
John Price	1	Miles Cressingham	2
Anthony Smyth	1	John Jarves	3
Thomas Gosling	1	Levy Lingham	1
Daniell Pencroft	4	Richard Dason	2
Widdow George	2		

Not chargeable		Not chargeable	
Widdow Fuller	1	Widdow Nicholls	1
Widdow Broady	1	Widdow Walker	1
John Hoult	1	Richard Baker	1

Chrissenden Borough

Chargeable		Chargeable	
Mary George	3	William Vann	6
Widdow Turney	4	Richard Wells	4
Richard Elsick	3	Beniamin Harris	3
Robert Wood	2	Thomas Godfrey	1
Widdow Peckham heires	2	William Fann	1
Phillip Starkey	1	Morgan Bricknall	1
Giles Dany	2	John Hunt	1
William Hoy	1		

Palster Borough

Chargeable		Chargeable	
Giles Davie	4	John Springett	2
Giles Davie more	2	William Seer	4
Thomas Davie	4	John Tucknes	3
Thomas Davie more	3	Thomas Russell	1
Robert Followay	4	William Hoy	2
James Rooke	4	Thomas Sheafe	2

Widdow Hammond	1	Thomas Ward	1
Peter Waters	1	Henry Peene	4
Henry Peene and }	4	Henry Peene more	2
John Fowle }			

Not chargeable   **Not chargeable**

John Peckham	1	Widdow Seaman	1

Knock Barnett Borough

Chargeable   **Chargeable**

William Baker	6	John Hart	7
John Tompsett	1	Thomas Patteson	1
William Snipp	1	Robert Eely	4
John Oxenbridge	4	Widdow Springett	6
Richard Greenland	7		

Ownam Borough

Chargeable   **Chargeable**

John Benden	4	Thomas Paine	4
Thomas Paine	4	Thomas Waters	4
		Thomas Waters more	4

Oxney Stone

Chargeable   **Chargeable**

Sir John Henden	4	David Austin	3
Thomas East	1	John Hall	4
Richard Burchatt	1	Richard Broker	2
Digere Small	3	Jeremy Odiarne	3
William Dennett	1	Thomas Diker	4
John Beeching	2	Edward Whode	1
Thomas Jeff	1	Richard Corde	1
Widdow Marten	1	John Packham	1
John Hart	1	Thomas Hall	1
Edward Atwaters	1	Widdow Baker	1
James Blackamore	1	Thomas Dicker	1
Widdow Lidden	2	Thomas Cogar	2
Thomas Cogar	1	John Birchett	2
Widdow Dicker	2	Thomas Gooden	1
John Court	2	Robert French	3
Thomas Sharnall	2	John Lonly	3
John Shooesmith	1	Abraham Harris	3
Richard Harnett	1	Richard Buttler	1
John Webb	1	John Hall Constable	

THE HUNDRED OF HEANE
in the Lath of Shepway

The Upper Halfe Hundred

Chargeable		Chargeable	
Sarles March	5	Joseph Norwood	5
John Woodland	2	Thomas Jones	3
Thomas Marshall	2	William Lee	2
John Hogbin	3	John Pilcher	1
William Tayler	1	John Robus	1
Thomas Stace	1	David Lampard	2
John Archer	2	John Smyth	3
Thomas Harvie	2	William Baker	2
William Wilding	2		

Not chargeable		Not chargeable	
John Striting	1	Stephen Miller	1
Widdow Dorne	2	Widdow Colley	1
William Hammond	1	John Newland	1
		Joseph Norwood Constable	

[fol. 71v]
The Lower Halfe Hundred of Heane

Borough of Castle

Chargeable		Chargeable	
Thomas Carter Cler[k]	5	Thomas Chedwick	7
John Greenland	7	John Robus	4
Thomas Holmes	4	John Greenland	4
John Rose	4	Thomas Giles	3
John Johnson	3	William Thurban	2
Edward Johnson	1	John Baker	1
Phillip Eastland	2	Phillipp Hill	2
Osmond Huett	1	Widdow Sanders	1
William Lednor	3	William Sladden	1

Not chargeable		Not chargeable	
John Turney	10	John Boykin	2
William Harris	1	Thomas Rootes	1
John Marten	1	Henry Hart	1
Nicholas Jackson	1	James Bassett	2
William Stone	2	Widdow Lednar	4

Thorne Borough

Chargeable			Chargeable	
Richard Beane	3		David Oldfeild	4
Thomas Ireland	3		Aquila Johncock	2
William Turner	2		Peter Whitlock	5
Richard Wraight	1			

Not chargeable			Not chargeable	
William Humphrey	2		John Vaughan	2
John Hales	2			
			John Robus Constable	

THE HUNDRED OF FOLKESTONE
in the Lath of Shepway

The Upper Half Hundred

Evering Borough

Chargeable			Chargeable	
Mr. Robert Evering	4		Andrew Smyth	3
Thomas Stockes	4		Robert Prickett	4

Alkham Borough

Chargeable			Chargeable	
Mr. Samuell Pownall	3		Henry Peirce	2
Mathew Marsh	2		Mr. Alban Spencer	7
John Browne	2		John Baker	2
Edward Ward	2		John Pownall	3
Thomas Collard	1		William Sutton	1
Edward Collard	1		Symon Hatton	2
Richard Collard	1		John Sutton	2
William Knott	2		John Thomas	1
John Hammond	1		Thomas Claddingbould	2

Chilton Borough

Chargeable			Chargeable	
Joseph Marsh	4		Ambrose Collard	3
Thomas Sharpe	2		Richard Belsey	1
George Collard	1		John Dorne	1

Standing Borough

Chargeable			Chargeable	
Henry Fox	2		John Marsh	3

Henry Murry	1	Richard Monger	1
William Matson	2	John Stroud	1
Henry Knott	3	Thomas Castle	1
Robert Geyner	1	Robert Webb	1

Foxhall Borough

Chargeable		Chargeable	
Nicholas Cooley	4	Daniell Hobdey	3
Richard Foster	2	Widdow Wise	2
William Carter	1	John Smyth	2
Richard Marsh	5	John Dorne	2
John Simmons sen[io]r	5	Henry Warden	1
Thomas Smith	1	Nicholas Ladd sen[io]r	3
Nicholas Ladd	2	Stephen Stokes	1
Leonard Sutton	2	Mr. Narne	3
Richard Tames	3	John Simmons	2

Lidden Borough

Chargeable		Chargeable	
John Philpott	4	Gabriell Adams	4
Clement Rolfe	1	Daniell Sutton	3

Hawking Borough

Chargeable		Chargeable	
Henry Rolfe	4	Daniell Solley	2
Stephen Fagg	3	Stephen Knott	1
George Lasse	1	John Hammond	1
James Ferry	4	William Monger	1
Thomas Shepey	4	John Kember	3
Nicholas Ladd	1	William Robus	1
John Burvell	1		

Coldam Borough

Chargeable		Chargeable	
John Lushington	3	George Andrew	3
William Robinson	2	George Kember	2
Thomas Sheppey	2	John Homesbey	3
Widow Wood	1	Peter Marsh	1
Henry Lushington	3		

[fol. 72r]

In the said Half Hundred

Not chargeable		Not chargeable	
Thomas Tomlin	1	John Horton	1
Richard Jull	2	Thomas Jenken	1
Widdow Oldfeild	1	John Parker	2
Henry Bush	2	Ralph Rogers	1
Richard Bushell	1	Widdow Sutton	1
Francis Sharp	1	Nicholas Ratly	1
John Noble	1	Richard Hodgbeen	1
Widdow Gareling	1	Thomas Edwards	1
Widdow Hammond	1	William Jones	1
Stephen Simmes	1	John Carter	1
George Pilcher	1	Ellis Browneing	1
George Browneing	1	John Hambrooke	1
William Baker	1	John Watson	1
Robert Browneing	1	Ingram Tayler	1
Thomas Burges	1	Widdow Hodgbeen	1
John Bird	1	Richard Colman	1
Lawrence Harvey	1	Robert Jull	1
		George Ham[m]on Constable	

The Lower Half Hundred of Folkstone

Borough of West Brook

Chargeable		Chargeable	
James Brockman Esq.	16	Sir Edward Honywood	12
Gabriell Hall	2	William Sanders sen[io]r	2
Mr. Henry Barnes	3	Robert Fukes	1
Widdow Hammond	1	Henry Casselden	2
Stephen Horne	1	John Chapman	2
Widdow March	1	William Sanders Jun'r	1
George Smeed	1	Robert Miller	1

Not chargeable		Not chargeable	
James Brockman Esq.	3	Sir Edward Honywood	1
William Sanders	1	Mr. Henry Barnes	1
John Chapman	1	John Stockwell	1
Richard Writtell	6	Nicholas Homwood	1
John Hunt	1	Gabriel Hall Borsholder	

Borough of East Brooke

Chargeable		Chargeable	
Mr. Charles Harflett	3	Mr. Thomas Turny	6

Thomas Hammond	3	Thomas Harrison	5
Thomas Barber	5	Anthony Prickett	3
William Harris	3	Henry Clement	2
Thomas Young	2	Richard Moocks	1
Daniell Church	2	George Elger	1
John Nash	1	John Odden	2

Not chargeable		**Not chargeable**	
Mr Thomas Torny	1	Thomas Hammon	1
Thomas Barber	1	William Harris	1
Anthony Prickett	1	Widdow Gather	1
Clement Hogben	1	Widdow Badcock	1
Widdow Ashby	1	Widdow Pysing	1
Richard Robinson	1	Mary Ashby	1
		Richard Markes Borsholder	

Orping Borough

Chargeable		**Chargeable**	
John Chisman	2	Thomas Rayner	3
Widdow Rofe	1	Ingram Marshall	2
William Fagg	1	William Marshall	1
Widdow Marshall	1	William Clement	3
Joseph Marshall	1	Robert Clously	2

Not chargeable		**Not chargeable**	
John Cheesman	1	Thomas Rayner	1
Widdow Rolfe	1	Ingram Marshall	1
William Fagg	1	William Clement	1
Ingram Marshall	1	Joseph Marshall Borsholder	

Argrow Borough

Chargeable		**Chargeable**	
Robert Emptage	4	William Manger	4
Thomas Marshall	1	Henry Stokes	2
Francis Wraith	1		

Not chargeable		**Not chargeable**	
Robert Emptage	1	William Manger	1
Thomas Marshall	1	Henry Stokes	1
William Wreafe	1	Godden Godden	1
Richard Philpott	1	William Hedgcock	1
Henry Walbank	1	William Ellenden Borsholder	1

Ashell Borough

Chargeable			Chargeable	
John Hilles	7		Andrew Warman	3
Widdow Wood	3		Widdow Sladden	4
Basill Clock	5		John Adams	3
Thomas Inmeth	4		Thomas Hackeng	1
Daniell Hunt	1			

Not chargeable			Not chargeable	
John Hills	1		Andrew Warman	1
Widdow Sladden	1		Basill Cloke	1
John Adams	1		Thomas Inmith	1
Jane Pope	1		Ann Cloke	1
			Thomas Inmeth Borsholder	

Broadmead Borough

Chargeable			Chargeable	
David Hogbin	2		Thomas Ben	3
Stephen Chapman	3		Robert Woodland	1
[fol. 72v]				
Inmeth Rayner	1		Vincent Sharp	3
Thomas Chapman	1		William Clarke	2
Widdow Burten	1			

Not chargeable			Not chargeable	
David Hogben	1		Thomas Ben	1
Stephen Chapman	1		Inmeth Rayner	1
Vincent Sharp	1		William Clarke	1
Edward Phillis	4		John Burten	1
			Inmeth Rayner Borsholder	

Upingwell Borough

Chargeable			Chargeable	
Robert Hobday	7		Thomas Cullen	2
Richard Fagg	5		Richard Hunt	3
Thomas Wack	1		William Coller	1
Stephen Chapman	1			

Not chargeable			Not chargeable	
Robert Hobday	1		Thomas Cullen	1
Richard Fagg	1		Richard Hunt	1
Stephen Chapman	1		John Dadd	4
William Marsh	2		Robert Luckes	2

Steeven Chapman Borsholder

Cheriton Borough

Chargeable			Chargeable	
Mr. Zouch Brockman	6		Richard Writtell	5
Henry Mitten	5		Mr. William Reading	3
Richard Oddens	3		Robert Fagg	3
Richard Mantle	3		Thomas Hedgcock	3
Richard Grewell	2		John Smyth	2
John Hunt	2		Widdow Philpott	2
Edward Cavell	1		John Clement	1
Richard Cather	1		Henry Johncock	2
Edward Chaplin	1		William Writtell	1
George Roose	2			

Not chargeable			Not chargeable	
Mr. Zouch Brockman	1		Richard Mantle	1
Thomas Hedgcock	1		Robert Fagg	1
Richard Writtell	1		Mr. William Reading	1
Henry Mitten	1		Thomas Partridge	1
Francis Wraith Constable			Thomas Hedgcock Borsholder	

THE UPPER HALF HUNDRED OF HAM
In the Lath of Shepway

Rooad Borough

Chargeable			Chargeable	
Nicholas Baker	3		Peter Horne	2
Robert Gill	1		John Knowles borsholder	1

Not chargeable	
Richard Cow	1

Burrough of Warhorne

Chargeable			Chargeable	
Mr. John Arsherst	3		Samuell Head borsholder	5
Robert Gill	5		Richard Thoptif	3
Thomas Hodg	2		John Jennings	1
Widdow Austen	3			

East Ham Borough

Chargeable			Chargeable	
Thomas Heed	2		Isaac Abraham	2
			John Wright borsholder	2

Not chargeable			Not chargeable	
George Ellis	1		Widdow Beatman	1

Orlestone Borough

Chargeable			Chargeable	
Mr. Sherman	3		Michaell Allen	3
William Hodges	4		John Wreight	3
Henry Gill	5		Richard Portman	3
Thomas Hodges	3		John Wells	1
Thomas Perry	1		Richard Palmer	1
Abraham Clover	1		Thomas Glover	1
Edward Johnson	1			

Not chargeable			Not chargeable	
William Field	1		Roger Hunt	1
Thomas Roberts	1		Edward Johnson Borsholder	

Super Snoad Borough

Chargeable			Chargeable	
Mr. Harflett	2		George Sherman	2
William Foord	2		Thomas Wesson	2
Abraham Moone	1		John Barker	2
Widdow Clarke	1		William Chittenden	3
Nicholas Standly	3		Thomas Marten	1
Richard Glover	4		Andrew Amis	3
Daniell Fox	1		John May	1
Richard May	2		Widdow Robus	2
John Brickenden	3			

Not chargeable			Not chargeable	
Thomas Pettock	1		John Patchin	1
Widdow Reades	1		Beniamin Freeman	1
Widdow London	1		John Moone	1
Thomazin Furnager	1		John Peerce	1
George Sherman Constable			John Brickenden Borsholder	

[fol. 73r]

HUNDRED OF ST. MARTINE AND LONGPORT
In the Lath of Shepway

The Upper Halfe

Borough of Doddington

Chargeable		Chargeable	
John Stonnard	4	Richard Atton	2
Thomas Shamall	2	John Cutburt	4
Thomas Morris	3	John Lording	3
Peter Tomsett	1	Nicholas Davis	3
Edward Umphrey	1	Timothy Hart	1
John Tilley	1		

Not chargeable

John Downe	1

Borough of Southreeve

Chargeable		Chargeable	
John Wright	2	Francis Eaton	2
Samuell Crednet	3	William Joanes	3
Thomas Grayling	1	James Jagger	3
John Romnant	1		

Not chargeable		Not chargeable	
Robert Whorrall	1	Daniell Justice	1
		Henry Ingleton	1

Orleston Borough

Chargeable			
Robert Spice	2	William Jones Constable	

HUNDRED OF NEWCHURCH
in the Lath of Shepway

The Upper Halfe

Huningherst Borough

Chargeable		Chargeable	
Richard Brooke	2	John Parker	2
Stephen Head	1	William Miller	2

William Browne	1	Widdow Cocke	2
Walter Freeman	1	[blank] Amthur	2
William Cooper	1	George Jones	3
John Spice	2	John Loucas	1

Not chargeable		Not chargeable	
Widdow Page	1	Widdow Goffe	1

Church Borough

Chargeable		Chargeable	
Mr. Richard Marsh cl[erk]	3	William Chalcroft	3
Richard Morrell	2		

Not chargeable		Not chargeable	
William Hutson	2	John Smith	1
		William Wilde	1

Church Borough of Bilsington

Chargeable		Chargeable	
Richard Cock	4	Henry Payne	2
Thomas Mackney	3	John Barnsden	4
Mary Aurchley widdow	4	Francis Taylor widdow	2
John Gales	5		

Not chargeable		Not chargeable	
John Fagg	1	William Bracey	1
Isaac Newnam	2	George Knowles	1
Adam Lullam	1	Widdow Ewens	1
Mary Dandy widdow	1	John Bracey	1
Thomas Stokes	1	Andrew Hinxell	1
John Buskell	2	Mary Rescue	1
		John Gales Constable	

HUNDRED OF ALLOWESBRIDGE
in the lath of Shepway

The Upper Halfe

Brook Borough

Chargeable		Chargeable	
Mr Thomas Marsh	8	William Hoare	3
John Eve	4	Richard Foshier	1

Godfrey Sole	2	Thomas Tookey	2
Edward Evens	1	Stephen Breckenberry	2
Simon Breckenbury	4	Phillip Woodland	5
John Bur	6	Thomas Grist	1
Walter Berling	5	John Taylor	2
Francis Levey	2	John Mabb	1
Joane Wright	3	John Collar	2
John Fowle	1	John Heasell	4
Thomas Wells	2		
Robert Taylor	2		

Not chargeable		Not chargeable	
John Pannit	1	Widdow Smyth	2
Widdow Adams	1	Widdow Brett	1
Widdow Cutbert	1	John Turner	1
Widdow Shatter	1		

Missell Ham Borough

Chargeable		Chargeable	
William Hogben	3	Henry Eades	2
Captaine May	7	more in another house	3
Thomas Archley	3	Edward Watson	2
John Hoad	4	John Marsh	3
William Bewman	2	Thomas Norris	1
Widdow Dine	1	John Burwash	3

[fol. 73v]

Borough of Little Chapham

Chargeable		Chargeable	
Edmund Streter	4	Thomas Burr	6
Thomas Russell	4	Bartholom[ew] Preble	3
Robert Ellis	1	James Neckles	1

Not chargeable		Not chargeable	
Robert White	1	Widdow Sole	1
John Snoad	1		

Flotham Borough

Chargeable		Chargeable	
Thomas Earstfeild	4	John Hamshire	1
Thomas Patteson	3	Richard Hall	4
Thomas Coley	1	Thomas Hiland	1

Richard Marsh	1	James Drason	1
Thomas Smyth	1	Nicholas Elscomb	1
John Chittenden	2	John Clovar	1
Peter Hornes	3	John Parker	3
		Richard Hall Constable	

[fol. 74r]

THE LATH OF ST. AUGUSTINE

THE HUNDRED OF BLEANGATE
in the said Lath

The Upper Halfe Hundred

Stroud Borough

Chargeable		Chargeable	
Edward Warham Esq.	9	Mr. Robert Knowler of Stroud	10
Mr. Robert Knowler of Norads	8	Richard Stevens	4
Thomas Love	4	John Kettle	2
Robert Rugley	4	Stephen Chiddock	2
Edward Gateman	2	John Mummery	3
George Skinner	2	William Hugett	2
Jonas Epsly	1	Thomas Tanner	1
John Muzered	2	Jeremy Fanting	3
Richard Coleman	3	Beniamin Jervis	2
Daniell Goodwinn	3	John Skinner	2
George Beane	3	John Goare	1
George Goatham	4	Henry Hilles	1
John Coale	1	Bartholomew Buckhurst	1

Not chargeable		Not chargeable	
John Hollet	1	Elias Rowe	1
John Pickenden	1	Robert Overy	1
Luke Parrett	1	Richard Williamson	1
Thomas Bourne	2	Nicholas Bennett	2
Nicholas Builting	1	James Stapleton	1
Richard Redgway	3	Widdow Harmon	1
Widdow Emptage	1	Widdow Elven	1
Widdow Sackett	1	Widdow Baker	1
Widdow Marley	1	Widdow Percivall	3
		John Cole Borsholder	

Hampton Borough

Chargeable		Chargeable	
Edward Milles gent	2	James Bulman	8
Richard Sturges	4	William Prall	5

Richard Constant	6	John Pett	3
Richard Staines	4	Thomas Browne	1
George Howson	1	John Barber	2
Henry Sea	3	John Henman	3
John Staines	5	Henry Cockman	2
John Wallis	2	Widdow Sea	1
Adam Harris	5	John Seath	1

Not chargeable		Not chargeable	
Thomas Luke	2	Thomas Richardson	1
William Baker	1	John Young	1
Thomas Young	3	Thomas Byse	1
John Luke	1	John Henman Borsholder	

Thornden Borough

Chargeable		Chargeable	
Walter Wilsford Esq.	4	Allen Coleman	4
Christopher Kemp	1	Robert Mathewes	3
William Cock	3	John Dove	3
Daniel Downes	4	William Reamish	3
Goodman Wesson	2	Goodman Snelling	2
Thomas Jarvis	6	Goodman Aldridge sen[io]r	6
Goodman Aldridge jun'r	2	Gabriell French	2
Robert Browne	1	George Beech	3

Not chargeable		Not chargeable	
Bartholomew Tuckness	1	William Beech	1
Widdow Smyth	1	William Spaine	1
George Coleman	1		
		John Dower Borsholder	

Haw Borough

Chargeable		Chargeable	
Phillip Viscount Strangford	9	John Webb gent	4
Robert Knowler gent at [th]e Maypole	6	Stephen Knowler gent	8
		Christopher Baker	1
Thomas Knowler gent	6	William Cockman	2
Mr. Edward Warham	8	Elias Cheesman	1
Richard Morris	6	John Vanderpiere	5
John Peirce	1	William Sandum	1
Richard Long	3	Lawrence Ellis	2
Elizabeth Hayward	2	John Lovewell	4
Robert Abbott	1	John Darby	4

John Hutchins	2	Edward Coaleman	2
William Renolds	3	William Cornish	1
Francis Pilcher	4	John Morris	2
Robert Mills	6	George Goatham	1
Thomas Gateman	1		
Richard Mount	4		

Not chargeable

Not chargeable

Thomas Skinner	1	John Furminger	1
Robert Ewell	2	Robert Preston	1
Widdow Smyth	1	Gilbert Stringer	1
Widdow Wood	1	Roger Fisher	3
Robert Taylor	1	Widdow Jeffery	1
Widdow Smyth	1	Widdow Hurt	2
Edward Chambers	1	Nicholas Builting	1
John Seath	2	Widdow Addams	1
Widdow Edwards	1	Widdow Towlson	1
Elias Rowe	1	John Pope	1
Edward Pope	1	Christopher Abbott	1
William Goare	1	Widdow Symmons	2
Elizabeth Foord	1	Widdow Singleton	1
[fol. 74v]			
Henry Quested	3	John Addams	2
Francis Cobb	1	John Wellis	2
Richard Read	1	Edward Milles	1
Margary Preston	1	Sylvester Payne	1
John Randall	1	Henry Hilles	1
		Richard Long Borsholder	

Belting Borough

Chargeable

Chargeable

Edward Ewell gent	3	William Harrison	4
Isaac Terry	4	John Tall	4
John Goare	3	John Cullen	3
James Morris	1	Richard Seath	1
Robert Lovewell	1	Thomas Parker	2
Alexander Sayer	1	Thomas Turner	1
Thomas Maxted	1	Walter Briggs	1
Thomas Belsey	3	Edward Goatham	5
Christopher Abbott	4	John Abbott	5
Edward Wigmore	1	Samuell Foate	2
Joseph Quested	1	John Kemp	1

John Luke	1	Mary Cock	1
Not chargeable		Not chargeable	
John Knock	1	Robert Barnard	1
Thomas Barnard	1	William Percivall	1
Mary Badcock	1	Mildred Christian	1

East Stower Mouth Borough

Chargeable		Chargeable	
George Culmer	3	James Wood	2
Edward Browne	1	Thomas Wilkinson	1
Lawrence Stadder	4	William Smithson	4
Thomas Hogben	2	William Dead	1
John Chandler	1	Richard Norwood	2
Joseph Clarke	1		

Not chargeable		Not chargeable	
Michaell Harris	1	Henry Cladis	1
Thomas Pointer	1	Thomas Foreman	1
Thomas Lukecock	1	Edward Smyth	2
		Joseph Clerke Borsholder	

Brookgate Borough in Reculver

Chargeable		Chargeable	
Robert Cobb gent	6	Paul Sackett	4
Henry Hilles	5	John Mount	2
Thomas Bix	5	William Bicker	1
Richard Mount	2	Mary Court	5
Nicholas Scott	5		

Not chargeable		Not chargeable	
Thomas Turner	1	Widdow Eason	1
Widdow Greene	1	Widdow Ladd	1
		Nicholas Scott Borsholder	

Reculver Street Borough

Chargeable		Chargeable	
Robert Goodwin Clerk	2	Thomas Keet	2
John Pierceson	4	Thomas Heath	2
Edward Keet	5	Robert Welbey	3

Not chargeable		Not chargeable	
Hugh Webster	1	William Cock	1
William Sutherfield	1	Christopher Tanner	1

Widdow Dunkin 1 Robert Welby Borsholder

Hoath Borough

Chargeable		Chargeable	
Stephen Knowler gent	6	Edward Taddie	4
Nicholas Hammond	5	William Sinnock	2
William Rider	3	Thomas Lacy	4
John Sea jun[io]r	4	Steven Mathews	2
Henry Clark	1	Thomas Clarke	1
Widdow Chambers	1	William Mace	2
Widdow Wilkes	2	Robert Wilkes	1
Edward Maxted	1	Robert Browne	1
John Hilles	1	Widdow Sinnock	1
Widdow Staines	3	Joseph Page	1
John Steanes	2	Thomas Rellison	3
John Randall	1	Christopher Dunn	
Henry Hills	1	Christopher Winter	1
Richard Soale	2	Thomas Hollams	1
Robert Faireman	2	William Chilton	2
William Mummery	2		

Not chargeable		Not chargeable	
Thomas Friend	1	Thomas Pett	1
Thomas Giddens	1	Roger Giddens	1
John Kedman	1	Thomas Browne	1
William Westbeech	1	Thomas Chambers	1
John Sea sen[io]r	1	Ann Poulter	1
Widdow Butten	2	Christopher Dunn Borsholder	

West Stowermouth Borough

Chargeable		Chargeable	
Thomas Spaine	5	Henry Jenkin	4
Dr Parkhurst	7	Widdow Harrison	4
John Penny	2	John Reader	6
James Kennett	1	Richard Harlow	2

Not chargeable		Not chargeable	
Widdow May	2	Thomas Knowler	1
David Halams	1	Richard Horlow Borsholder	
		Robert Knowler Constable	

[fol. 75r]
The Lower Halfe Hundred of Bleangate

Borough of Earnbough

Chargeable		Chargeable	
Mr Ellis	7	George Solley	5
William Watson	1	John Mount	5
Thomas Honist	5	John Hall	2
Thomas Ellis	1	John Dodd	2
William Dodd	2	Henry Rose	3
Henry Austen	2	Ambrose Huit	2
Thomas Ewell	4	Nicholas Fostall	1
Robert Newman	4	John Richardson	2
Gervase Boykin	1		

Not chargeable		Not chargeable	
William Hoghman	1	Richard Outridge	2
Henry Oman	1	Peter Spratling	1
Mark Nash	1	Ambrose Huitt Borsholder	

Bleangate Borough

Chargeable		Chargeable	
William Keame	2	William Baker	3
John Baker	2	Paul Harris	2
Richard Cullen	2	Richard Maplested	1
Richard Homes	1	Valentine Harris	1
Thomas Pope	1	Francis Tyler	1

Not chargeable		Not chargeable	
Lawrence Huntsmell	1	Valentine Dufty	1
Widdow Symons	1	Widdow Skinner	1
Thomas Lenott	1	Widdow Lam[m]ing	1
John Morton	1	Richard Stuple	1
Adam Harris in an empty house	1		

The Borough of Westbeech & Ore

Chargeable		Chargeable	
Richard Whiteing	6	Widdow Marsh	2
Edward Maxted	4	Andrew Joad	3
John Fanting	2	John Hogben	4
George Goulder	2	Richard Rose	5
Anthony May	1	Richard Barrett	2

Thomas Wood	1	Adam Christian	1
Roger Fanting	2		

Not chargeable

Widdow Mount	1	Widdow Smart	1
Widdow Rowe	1	Widdow Tayler	1
Robert Cooper	2	Thomas Russell	1
		Adam Christian Borsholder	

The Borough of Hatch

Chargeable   **Chargeable**

Mr Alexander Cooke Cl[erk]	3	Mr Edward Rose	6
Mr Gervase Rose	7	Ambrose Rose	5
Ralph Mount	2	Thomas Norwood	4
Henry Mott	2	Ambrose Knowler	6
John Christian	3	Richard Mummery	3
Richard Steed	1	Jonathan Friend	1
David Amberton	4	Ed: Paramour	4
Moses Tipper	3	John Terry	2

Not chargeable   **Not chargeable**

Widdow Randall	4	Robert May	1
Stephen Gray	1	William Constant	1
Zachary Saxson	1	John Marbrooke	1
John Cooke	1	John Claringbould	1
William Friend	1	Edward Hayioy	1

The Borough of Craft

Chargeable   **Chargeable**

Edward Balden	3	David Friend	2
George Keele	2	Edward Soale	2
Thomas Ewell	1	John Soale	2
John Goulder	1	John Russell	1
Henry Frost	2	Thomas Balden	2
Richard Nutting	2	John Nutting sen[io]r	2

Not chargeable   **Not chargeable**

Robert Bullock	1	Cornelius Scott	1
William Browne	1	Widow Piper	1
Vincent Smyth	1	Symon Carden	1
John Nutting jun'r	1	Thomas Russell	1
James Mount	2	William Dodd	1

David Freind Borsholder

The Parish & Boroug[h] of Westbeere

Chargeable			Chargeable	
Mr. Edward Milles	10		Mr. Hincton Clerk	4
Robert Austen	6		Richard Allen	5
John King	3		Widdow Culling	1
Thomas Walker	1		Roger Sayer	1
John Gibson	1		Widdow Ewell	1
John Paramour	1		Thomas Argar	2
Valentine Cock	3			

Not chargeable			Not chargeable	
John Finch	1		Richard Phariss	1
John Hawkes	1		Joane Gipson	1
			Richard Farris Borsholder	

[fol. 75v]

The Borough of Buckwell in Sturry

Chargeable			Chargeable	
Andrew Wootten	3		Stephen Wood	3
Abraham Baker	1		Francis Eares	1
Stephen Abbett	4		William Allen Borsholder	1

Not chargeable			Not chargeable	
Thomas Couchman	4		Widdow Paye	2

The Borough of Blaxland in Sturry

Chargeable			Chargeable	
Henry Wood	4		Nicholas Allen	3
William Phillipps	1		John Best	1
Stephen Pott	1		Richard Fox Borsholder	2

Not chargeable			Not chargeable	
Stephen Holloway	1		Roger Richardson	1
Widdow Mullett	1		Widdow Craven	1
John Medew	1			

The Borough of Sturry Street

Chargeable			Chargeable	
Phillip Viscount Strangford	20		Mr. Joanes Clerk	5
Thomas Johnson	5		John Young	6
Henry Smyth	5		Robert Bax	4

Widdow Badcock	4	James Grant	4
Mathew Price	4	John Petman	4
Mathew Gray	3	John Baker	3
William Johncock	3	Ed: Tittiman	2
William South	2	William Knott	2
Widdow Cock	2	William Jeddar	2
Widdow Boycott	1	Widdow Read	1
John Austen	3	Augustine Lothes	1
Tymothy Lothes	2	Noah Lothes	1
Alexander Barrett	1	Thomas Harrison	4

Not chargeable

Not chargeable

Widdow Price	2	Widdow Threed	2
Widdow Harrison	1	Thomas Arnold	2
William Jeking	2	John Rumney	1
Ed: Duker	2	Isaac Fairman	1
Clement Gouldfinch	1	Widdow Browne	1
Ann Allen	1	Richard Onion	1
John Smyth	1	Widdow Witheat	1
Widdow Tanner	1	Goodwife Pettet	1
Leonard Browne	1	In an empty house	1
		William Knott Borsholder	

The Borough of Buckland in Sturry

Chargeable

Chargeable

Edward Young	4	John Moyce	2
Thomas Clifford	6	Thomas Spratbury	4
Robert Pharise	1	Thomas Nobbs	1
Samuell Tayler	1	Edmund Pott	2

Not chargeable

Not chargeable

John Titty	1	Widdow Emptage	1
Widdow Jeffery	1	Widdow Feles	1
Widdow Page	1	John Moyse Borsholder	

The Borough of Hoath in Sturry

Chargeable

Chargeable

Mr John Lee	4	John Cheeseman	1
William Allen	1	Nicholas George	3
John Best	2	Robert Hart	1
Widdow Glover	1	Thomas Johncock	1
James Wood	2	William Shepheard	1

| David Downes | 1 | John Pott | 1 |

Not chargeable | | **Not chargeable** | |
| William Hemaway | 1 | Widdow Hemsted | 1 |
| Richard Dominee | 1 | Thomas Jancocke Borsholder | |

The Borough of Coakett in Sturry

Chargeable | | **Chargeable** | |
Michaell Terry gent	5	John Okenfold	4
Widdow Rigden	3	Thomas Wootten	1
Roger Adams	1	William Wodwell	3
John Bevell	1	Mr. William Wellen	5
Henry Ewell	2	Vincent Adams Borsholder	1
Daniell Allen	3		

Not chargeable
| John Adams | 1 |

The Parish and Borough of Swackliff

Chargeable | | **Chargeable** | |
| Christopher Streeting | 3 | Henry Fox | 2 |
| William Pembrooke | 4 | | |

Not chargeable | | **Not chargeable** | |
| Edward Russell | 1 | Stephen Goulder | 1 |
| In one empty house | 2 | Henry Rose Constable | |

[fol. 76r]

THE HUNDRED OF WHITSTAPLE
in the lath of St Augustine

The Upper Halfe Hundred

Borough of Whitstaple

Chargeable | | **Chargeable** | |
Thomas Juice	5	Israell Ewell	3
Edward Roper Esq.	5	William Downe	3
Edward Gray	3	William Bedford	1
Anthony Jervis	2	William Flatcher	3
Abraham Upton	4	Richard Jones	1
Richard Lanes	2	Widdow Lanes	1
William Spaine	1	Widdow Lampard	2

William Weekes	2	Abraham Upton	1

Not chargeable   **Not chargeable**

Widdow Christian	1	Alexander Vallence	2
John Fox	1	Thomas Homes	1

Grimgill Borough

Chargeable   **Chargeable**

Thomas Whiteing	6	Thomas Whitfield	3
Henry Wynfield	2	Robert Hooker	1
John Smyth	1	William Foate	2
Robert Sainte	2	Michaell Eason	1
Stephen Jeddery	2		

Not chargeable

Widdow Rayly	1

Bullinge Borough

Chargeable   **Chargeable**

George Giles	4	Edward Court	4
Widdow Kite	4	Thomas Reynolds	2
William Darling	1	John Wells	2
Widdow Huggett	1		

Not chargeable   **Not chargeable**

William Barrett	2	William Gilmor	2

Bourne Borough

Chargeable   **Chargeable**

Mr Smyth Clerke	4	Widdow Laminge	3
John French	1	Jonas Short	2
Joseph Jarman	2	Henry Davis	1
Henry Musgrove	2	William Gilven	2
Elizabeth Hooker	2		

Not chargeable   **Not chargeable**

Stephen Milstead	1	Thomas Hoames	1
John Simpson	1	John Hooker	1
Christopher Pierce	2	William Hooke	1
		Israell Ewell Constable	

The Lower Halfe Hundred of Whitstaple

Chargeable		Chargeable	
Henry Jarman	4	Michaell Child	2
Nicholas Swaine	5	Christopher Pay	1
John Hall	1	Andrew Goldfinch	2
Stephen Hall	1	John Warner	1
Mr John Best	2	John Dunstall	2
George Chilmer	2	Widdow Carr	2
William Collin	1	Widdow Bridge	3
Mr Sympson	5	Mrs Francklyn	4
Mr Sackett	4	Thomas Cosby	2
John Boys Esq	16	James Bayly	3
Michaell Lott	2	Mrs Pierce	2
Thomas Young	1	John Strood	5
Edward Beane	1	John Widdick	1
Thomas Ventiman	1	John Pettett	3
William Fleet	2	John Fleet	2
Stephen Filcock	1	Henry Fleet	2
Stephen Fisher	1	Richard Bayly	5
John Clarke	5	Robert Avery	1
John Tadhunter	4	Michaell Hopkins	4
Richard Rose	1	Henry Keler	1
John Horsly	1		

Not chargeable		Not chargeable	
Widdow Smyth	1	Stephen Jarman	1
John Stone	1	Widdow Brett	1
Widdow File	1	George Beane	1
Widdow Filcock	1	Widdow Badcock	1
Thomas Albery	1	Widdow Patten	1
Widdow Firsom	1	Widdow Jacob	1
Ezechiell Smeed	1	John Mapeston	1
Richard Attwell	1	Mathew Attwell	1
		Thomas Cosby Constable	

The Borough of Sessalter In the said Lath

Chargeable		Chargeable	
Widdow Handly	3	Stephen Brockman	1
William Longe	1	Robert Dadd	1
Thomas Saint	2	Silvester Stepin	2
Mary Walker	2	Henry Marlow	4
John Fule	3	Richard Stock	1
Thomas Giles	1		

Not chargeable		Not chargeable	
Silvester Ray	1	Thomas Hollaway	1
John Marshall	1	John Williams	1
Widdow Waters	2	Anthony Parks	1
Widdow Abraham and	2	Edward Crayden	2
Witpaine		Widdow Smyth	1
Anthony Parkes &			
William Long Borsholders			

[fol. 76v]

THE HUNDRED OF WESTGATE
in the Lath of St. Augustine

Borough of Hackington

Chargeable		Chargeable	
The Lady Harfleet	14	Coll[onel] Thomas	4
		Colepeper	0
Dr William King	7	Richard Jarman	6
Mr Robert Beake	4	Richard Crookes	3
Thomas Bondler	5	George Harrison	4
Michaell Pollen	4	Widdow Claringbould	4
Thomas Cullen	4	Reignald Abraham	9
William Wickham	4	Widdow Wells	4
John Boniard	2	Symon Summersole	5
John Fordred	5	Thomas Castle	5
Charles Kingsnorth	4	Thomas Fleet	5
John Wacher	3	Thomas Pettet junior.	2
Norton Hilles	2	Widdow Menvill	2
Henry Rowe	2	James Hilles	3
John Edmunds	1	Thomas Pettet sen[io]r	1
Norton Hills	1	John Coife	3

Not chargeable		Not chargeable	
Thomas Stone	2	Widdow March	2
Widdow Evans	4	George Harrison Borsholder	

Parish of St. Dunstane

Chargeable		Chargeable	
Hudson Spencer	3	William Bayly	2
Isaac Milles	2	Jonah Cooke	2
Robert Baker	3	Mrs. Gibbon	1
Thomas Hogben	3	Joseph Falwell	5

John Bird	4	William Allen	2	
Mr. John Farnaby	7	John Lazon	2	
Widdow Darley	4	William Lott	3	
Edward Mount	2	Mrs Scranton	12	
James Penny in an empty house	4	John Sayward	3	
John Ellis	1	William Wootton	1	
Richard Gallant	2	James Evans	7	
John Allen	4	Robert Budgin in an empty }		
Collonoll Sackfield }		house }	4	
in part of a house empty }	13	Mr Durham in an empty	9	
Mr Johnson in an empty house	3	house		
Widdow Baldock in an empty house	6	Beniamin Jacklin	6	
		Widdow Flagden	3	
Mr Joseph Roberts	9	John Gilbert	6	
John Welbey	4	Richard Jarman in an empty	8	
George Olliver	2	house		
Thomas Gary	2	Thomas Carbey	3	
Daniell Jarman	2	Widdow Marsh	3	
		James Wood	4	

Not chargeable

Widdow Grant	3	Edward Saint	3
Robert Maxted	4	Richard Rolfe	1
Nicholas Bingham	1	Margaret Clarke	1
Richard Claringbould	2	Richard Hall	1
John Clunn	1	Israell Jarmin Borsholder	

Parish & Borough of Holy Cross Westgate

Chargeable   **Chargeable**

Mr Richard Redwood	10	John Friend	1
Thomas Gomm	2	Edward Fowler	2
Cornelius Detree	3	Peter Bame	3
George Hartell	4	Robert Rogers	1
John Besson	4	Robert Stubbs	1
Mr Baker in an empty house	4	Mrs Detree	3
Mrs Denn	5	Robert Welles	2
Mrs Calfe in an empty house	7	Richard Barber	7
Zachary Conyers	4	Beniamin Willers	2
Andrew Churchman	5	James Delaroh in an empty	7
Nicholas Wattson	2	house	

Henry Spaine	2	Mr Standly in an empty house	6
William Terrey	3	James Proud	4
James Meed	3	Richard Chandler	3
John Wraith	2	Widdow Hammond	2
John Morgan	2	George Jarman	3
Widdow Hacker	2	Richard Jarman in an empty	2
Elias Taylor	3	house	
John Weebow	2	Peter Spaine	3
Thomas Young	4	James Peeke	1
John Dury	1	Richard Prickett	5
John Mens	1	Elias Marshman	2
John Cock	3	Mr Whatson in an empty	3
Widdow Dunkin	2	house	
Phillipp Busher	4	Alexander Tritten	2
Peter Mohew	1	John Hickes	3
Widdow Spaine	2	Peter Apsley	2
John Marshman	5	Peter Lew	2
Richard Hill	2	Widdow Spencer	2
Widdow Bateman }	2	Israell Jarman jun[io]r	3
in an empty house}		Thomas Gill	2
[fol. 77r]			
Phineas Barate	2	Israell Jarman sen[io]r	4
Michaell Hussey	2	John Marsh	4
James Corrone	3	Richard Hacker	1
Anthony Decroe	3	John Godly	4
Widdow Chandler	1	George Baker	3
John Smyth	2	Luke Butler	5

Not chargeable		**Not chargeable**	
Roger Taylor	2	John Pollard	2
Peter Beane	1	Abraham Clarke	1
Daniell Tetter	1	Robert Duninge	2
Widdow Fowle	6	John Davis	3
John Ashes	3	Widdow Meade	1
John Price	1	Robert Haffell	2
Susan Bridge	1	Richard Robinson	2
[blank] Norlee	1	John Rayner	1
Cornelius Ferry	1	John Banks	1
Thomas Redgway	2	Isaac Rickey	2
Lancelot Kennestone	2	Widdow Read	2
Ralph Huett	3	John Gillingham	3

Zachery Conniers Borsholder

Borough of St. Michael Harbledowne

Chargeable		Chargeable	
Dr. Bargrave	3	Thomas Gookin Esq	9
John Kent gent	8	Mr. Wood	2
John Shottwater	2	William Holstock	4
John Hampton	3	Beniamin Dove	3
John Birch	1	John Spillett	2
Theophilus Hayes	3	John Wood	2
Thomas Holdstock	1	John Houldstock	1
Richard Cramp	2	Henry Clarke	5
John Bridges	3	James Sharelock	1
William Craft	2	Henry Bachelour	1
Joseph Batchelor	3	Thomas Odium	2
Thomas Sainty	2	Richard Gateman	2
Widdow Thomas	2	William Brainford	3
Thomas Woster	4	Thomas Shotwater	4
Henry Luckett	4	William Godfery	4
Widdow Court	3	Henry Pilcher	1
Mr. Robert Broadnax in St. Nicholas Hospitall	14	Mr Ratly in an empty house	4

Not chargeable		Not chargeable	
Robert Sussen	1	Richard Adcock	1
Henry Wickes	1	James Tayler	1
William Renolds	4	Elizabeth Lattimer	1
John Renolds	1	Amy Smyth	1
John Burford	1	Widdow Shrubsole	1
John Packman	4	Edward Rooke	1
Good[man] Greenstreet	2	Thomas Palmer	4
		John Spillett Borsholder	

Borough of Tunford

Chargeable		Chargeable	
Thomas George	7	Henry Tiddiman	6
James Friend Borsholder	2	John Osbourne	1

Not chargeable		Not chargeable	
William Ward	1	Symon Wood	1
James Forman	1	Widdow Mitchelbourne	1

Borough of Harwich

Chargeable		Chargeable	
James Evernden	4	Edward Hayward	3
Adam Henman	3	William Ewell	4
Edward Evans	2	Widdow Golding	2
Robert Harlow	3	John Elenden	2
Lawrence Batlemore	2	John Taylor	4
Widdow White	5	Edward Foshier	2
Edward Lawrence	4	Robert Clarke	2
Mr Peter Evans	1	Adam Henman Borsholder	

Not chargeable		Not chargeable	
Richard Carleton	1	Christopher Spice	4
Widdow Compton	4	Christopher Stonehouse	2
Robert Lucock	2	Henry Turby	1
John Milsted	1	Thomas Homes	1
Edward Baddars	2	John Corkman	2
Stephen Blackberry	1	Edward Langrave	1
Widdow Tredsoft	1	Widdow Bathmer	1
John Maple	1	Stephen Merrett	1

Borough of Rushborne

Chargeable		Chargeable	
Valentine Ewell	9	James Newman gent	2

Borough of Staplegate

Chargeable		Chargeable	
Mr. John Knott	6	Daine Turner	1
Edward Landman	1	Phillip Mannoke	2
Thomas Piper	3	William Lee	2
Robert Allen	2	Mr. Alexander Osbourne	1
Thomas Mathers	2	Susanna Share	2
William Allen	2	Peter Lambert	2
Michaell Terry	2	Jacob Spring	2
John Morrilon	3	Katherine Roda	4
John James	4	Edmund Harris	4
Mathew Renshaw	3		

Not chargeable		Not chargeable	
John Russell	1	Thomas Hall	2
[fol. 77v]			
Thomas Tattnall	3	Widdow Feakes	2

Thomas Adams	1	Henry Chedwick	1
Haman Cozens	2	Phineas Corner	2
Michaell Honore	2	John Bame	2
Widdow Collier	1	Widdow Provo	1
Robert Friend	1	Isaac Friend	1
Daniell Morrilon	1	Alexander Osbourne }	
Mathew Ranshew borsholder	1	in an empty house }	3

The Borough of St. Grigoryes

Chargeable		Chargeable	
John Denew	2	Goodman Nicholls	2
John Crippen	2	Zachary Moore	2
Moses Moore	2	James Goreeke	2
Elizabeth Briggs	3	Thomas Wilkinson	7

Not chargeable		Not chargeable	
Anthony Surdeane	4	Peter Parvoe	2
Widdow Biggins	1	Widdow Pearce	2
Grigory Vidgeon	3	Richard Grace	1
Christopher Ansley	1		

The Precincts of the Archibishops Pallace

Chargeable		Chargeable	
Sir George Juckson	12	Mr. Masterson	8
Mr Henry Foach	8	Thomas Gilham	3
Mr Ager	10	Dr. Wilsford	7
Mr White	8	James Hudson	3
James Weekes	2	Mr. Thomas March	3
Mrs. Hardes	4		

		Not chargeable	
		Thomas Wootton	2

The Borough of Cockering

Chargeable		Chargeable	
Isaac Terry	8	Mr. Nicholas Sympson	8
Edmund Young	6	William Seath	4
Thomas Wraight	2	Thomas Milles	6
Robert Seamer	2	Thomas Harris	2
Thomas Mace	4	Hugh Bore	4
John Brumly	2	William Hilles	2
Michaell Gratnall	2	John Eaton	2
John Penn jun[io]r	1	John Penn sen[io]r	1

John Blith	2	Thomas Stronge	2

Not chargeable		**Not chargeable**	
Katherine Penn widd.	2	Edward Cobb	4
Whittingham Fogg	4	John Muggell	2
Widdow Tossell	3	John Trimm	2
John Browne	1	Edward Kitchen	2
James Arnold	2	Nicholas Old	1
Widdow Cransote	2	Robert Carter	2
John Atherton	2	Edward Kitchen Borsholder	
Richard Barber &			
Thomas Harris Constables			

The Borough of Longport in the said Lath

Chargeable		**Chargeable**	
Mr. John Best	10	Thomas Abbott	3
John Barber	5	John Ledger	4
Goodman Young	4	Mr. James Stredwick	6
Goodman May	2	William Wood	3
Mr. Parker	7	Mr. George Young	5
William Seake	4	Thomas Wells	2
William Kenn	3	William Lussenden }	
Mr Paul Barrett }		in an empty house }	4
in an empty house }	5	John Franck jun[io]r	2
Edward Johnson	4	John Marden	1
William Admans	2	Mr. Bing	10
Henry Great	4	In an empty house	3
Judah Hope	6	John Atkinson	4
Thomas Aldridge	3	John Franck sen[io]r	1
Adlard Wells	6	John Easdey	4
William Beat	2	Edward Fendall	4
Katherine Denn	5	Peter Surree	5
Good[man] Pysing	1	Mathew Razell	2
William Shaw	2	Katherine Conyers }	
Goodman Jarman	5	in St. Augustine's Abbey }	38
Mrs. Mary Knowler	6	Ann Pilcher and Jacob	4
		Rayner	
John Williams jun[io]r	6	Thomas Roust	3
Henry Rust	2	Frederick Hope	3
John Bareel	6	*[blank]* Beechum	4
John Williams sen[io]r	8		

Not chargeable

Good[man] Browne	3	Good[man] Moone	2
Widdow Graysberry	2	Good[man] Stone	2
Good[man] Glover	2	Good[man] Turley	1
Good[man] Lawes	1	Good[man] Wilsden	1
Good[man] Chichen	1	Good[man] Fisher	1
Good[man] Gray	1	Good[man] Boodell	1
Good[man] Manley	2	Good[man] Mathewes	1
Good[man] Parker	2	Good[man] Anslowe	1
John Williams	2	John Welberry	1
Thomas Waterman	2	John Harris	1
Richard Fastall	2	Widdow Twisden	1
Good[man] Mason	1	Goodwife Jull	1
Goodwife Stredwick	2	Good[man] Aldridge sen[io]r	2
Thomas Aldridge	2	Widdow Porter	3
Good[man] Dalle	1	Good[man] Pysing	2
Good[man] Lamine	2	Thomas Woodruff	1
Elizabeth Harris	1	Mary Shartnell	1
Widdow Cripps	1	John Barber Borsholder	

[fol. 77Ar]

THE PRECINCT OF CHRISTCHURCH CANTERBURY
Within the Lath of St. Augustine

Chargeable

Dr. Thomas Turner Deane	27	Mrs. Mary Drayton widd[ow]	4
Mr. Robert Howell	6	Mrs. Jane Parker widd[ow]	7
Mr. Robert Sprackling	8	Dr. Peter Du Moulin	7
Mr. John Carter	3	Dr. Meric Casaubon	11
Mrs. Ann Engeham widd[ow]	4	Mr. John Smyth	3
Mr. Daniell Cuckow	7	Mr. John Culling	5
In an empty house late Mr.}		Mr. John Paris	6
John Vincent liv'd in }	2	James Russell	3
Daniell Chilton and }		Dr. Peter Hardres	11
Peter Frampton }	4	Thomas Peke Esq.	11
Mrs. Ruth Palmer widd[ow]	5	Mr. Richard Spaine	10
Richard Seabrooke	1	Mr. William Pysing	3
In an empty house next him	2	Dr. William Barker	12
Mr. William Jordan	4	Mr. Richard Langham	4
Mr Blase White	3	Mrs. Ann Fellowes widd[ow]	3
Mr. William Somner	7	Dr. John Castillion	10
Dr. Peter Gunning	9	Dr. John Aucher	11
Dr. John Bargrave	12	Mr. Edward Aldey	14

Mr. Francis Butcher	10	Dr. William Belke	10
Mr. Thomas Fotherby	14	Mr. John Reading	6
Mrs. Ann Sabinn widd[ow]	4	Mr. James Burvill	4
Mrs. Damaris Kingsley wid[dow]	10	Joseph Nicholls Dr. of physick	4
Richard Harrison	3	Isaac Jordan	1
William Davies	2	William Nayer	2
Henry Harrison in } an empty house }	2	Francis Conder	3
Jonathan Best	4	Mr. Miles Barnes in an } empty house }	2
Mrs. Frances Eddisforth wid[dow]	3	Andrew Ware	2
		Mr. Thomas Gibbs	6
Robert Cumberland	2	Thomas Barnfeild	4
John Kirke and } John Ward }	2	William Plomer	5
		In ye Glassiers office	1
Mrs. Elizabeth Turner widd[ow]	10	In ye Audit house	1
Elianor Cooke	2		
In the Church plum[m]ery	1		

Not chargeable
John Batham   1
per William Somner Audit[ou]r and Chapter Clerke

THE HUNDRED OF DOWNHAMFORD
In the Lath of St. Augustine

The Upper Halfe Hundred

The Borough of Seton in Ickham Parish

Chargeable		Chargeable	
Dr Causabon	6	John Short	4
Stephen Gilloe	6	William Gorly	3
Richard Holnes	3	Robert Beacke	3
Stephen Gissard	1	Anthony Skidmore	2
		Thomas Smyth Borsholder	4

Not chargeable		Not chargeable	
Widdow Budds	1	Paul Brooker	1
Thomas Wreacke	3	Sephriam Kempe	1
David Greenstreet	1		

Bromling Borough in Ickham Parish

Chargeable		Chargeable	
Mrs Southland	8	John Word	3
Widdow Steed	4	Michaell Solley	4
Thomas Fuller	2	Widdow Faireman	3
Edward Holnes	2	Widdow Sim[m]ons	3
William Luckett	4	Edward Miller	1
John Swanton	2		

Not chargeable		Not chargeable	
Thomas Johnson	2	Stephen Tucker	1
Paul Mesday	1	James Pattison	1
Richard Jervis	1	James Foord	1
Stephen Steed Borsholder	1	William Hunt	1

Cottnam Borough in Ickham Parish

Chargeable		Chargeable	
Widdow Terry	3	Gilbert Tattenden	1
William Godder Borsholder	2	William Wybourne	2
Robert Pettman	4	John Sladden	3
Henry Godder Borsholder	1	Widdow Dane	2

Not chargeable		Not chargeable	
Thomas Pilcher	1	Abraham Jarvis	1
Thomas Marten	1	Widdow Thorne	1
Henry Sanderson	1	Widdow Lilly	1
William Bowl	1	John Dewell	1
Richard Rogers	1	Richard Ladd	1
John Southen	1	Andrew Broadbrich	2

Borough of Staple

Chargeable		Chargeable	
Dr Du-Molin	5	Mr Lynch	6
Alexander Devison	5	Richard Terry	5
Stephen Hatcher	5	John Cartwright	2
Edward Rigden	2	William Towne	1
Thomas Kingsmell	3	John Dalle	3
Henry Stoakes	3	Richard Glover	2
John Brice	2	William Briggs	3
John Hogges	1	Stephen Fille	3
John Gibbs	1	John Hopkins	3
William Rogers	1	Richard Andrew	1
Richard Gardner	3	John Staples	1

Stephen Solley	3	John Fille	1
Daniell Bing Borsholder	1	Widdow Bax	1

Not chargeable		**Not chargeable**	
Widdow Tattnall	1	John Vinton	1
John Marten	1	Robert Sutton	1
Edward Barrow	1	George Hayward	1
Richard Woodware	1	Edward Cozens	1
John Powell	1	Widdow Gibbs	1
Francis Hoult	1		

Borough of Adsham

Chargeable		**Chargeable**	
Dr Du-Molin	8	Thomas Payne	5
John Renolds	3	Thomas Austen	4
Richard Peckden	4	John Hobdey	2
John Reynolds	2	William Cullen	1
Marke Turner	2	Charles Nicholls	6
William Silke	3	Henry Browne	2
William Savidge	3	Richard Smyth	1
Anthony Cullen	1	Richard Austen	8
Richard Austen	2	John Ladd	5
John Ladd	4	John Parker	1
John Phypott	6	Edward Epps	1

Not chargeable		**Not chargeable**	
Robert Cullen	1	George Outrige	1
Edward Hammond	2	John Stone	1
Henry Austen	2	Richard Austen	1
Thomas Clift	1	Thomas Cullen	1
Henry Knott	1	Widdow Bullock	1
Widdow Heely	1	Widdow Greene	1
Robert Davye	1	Liveing Taunton	1
Stephen Greene	1	John Ladd Borsholder	
		John Word Constable	

The Lower Halfe Hundred of Downhamford

Borough of Shourt

Chargeable		**Chargeable**	
Thomas Bayley	4	John Pembroke	2
William Hobson	3		

Not chargeable

John Kempe	1
Charles Wood Borsholder	1

Not chargeable

John Bosard	1

Borough of Stadmarsh

Chargeable

William Courthopp	9
[fol. 78v]	
Stephen Mott	3
Robert Tritton	1
John Hollum	3

Chargeable

Thomas Mantle	3
John Rayner	5
Thomas Tritton	2
Widdow Rigden	1

Not chargeable

John Sythers	2
William Steed	1
Henry Paramour	2
Henry Bartlett	2
Thomas Harlow	1
John Bradly	1
Widdow Freeland	1

Not chargeable

William Sythers	1
Hermon Tench	1
Michael Lucock	1
John Gifford	1
Thomas Woodruffe	2
Widdow Cobb	1
John Bradly Borsholder	

The North Borough of Wickhambrucks

Chargeable

Francis Larkin	3
William Ewell	2
Edward Solley	2
Robert Hall	2
William Smyth	2
John Luckett	2
William Hinde	4

Chargeable

William Trupes	4
Leonard Goldfinch	3
Robert Hall	4
Henry Read	2
John Lyham	2
William Joad	4

Not chargeable

Philemon Bachelor	1
Daniell Cooper	1
Edward Everett	1
Francis Larkin	1
John Wells	2
Augustine Wraigth	1

Not chargeable

Widdow Marbrooke	1
Francis Baker	1
Richard Dades	1
Daniell Cock	1
William Chilman	1
Edward Everett Borsholder	

The South Borough of Wickhambrucks

Chargeable

Dr Belke	7
Vincent Brice	5

Chargeable

Thomas Evernden	4
Thomas Proud	2

Robert Tritton	1	Richard Rainer	5
Mr John Smyth	5	Thomas Austen	3
John Anker	1		

Not chargeable		**Not chargeable**	
Miles Walker	1	Widdow Bushell	1
William Cobb	1	Phillipp Stace	1
Thomas Barling	1	Thomas Shery	1
Widdow Parker	1	William Blaxland	1
[blank] Hall	1	Stephen Milles	1
Thomas Sythers	1	Widdow Smyth	1
William Steddy	1	Thomas Thorne	1
William Smyth for an ould	3	Richard Grey	1
cottage		Thomas Dowdey	2
Stephen Norrington	2	Edward Milles	1
Reynold Short	2	John Browne	1
Henry Jusard	1	in an empty cottage	1
		Henry Jusard Borsholder	

Borough of Littlebourne

Chargeable		**Chargeable**	
Mr George Huffam	6	John Gouldfinch	4
Gervase Dodd	4	John Steed	1
William Standen	2	Daniell Beane	2
Michaell Denn	2	William Sanders	3
Lancelot Davis	4	David Denn jun[io]r	4
Thomas Miles	1	Robert Dewell sen[io]r	2
Robert Dewell jun[io]r	2	William Cobb	2
John Bax	5	Michaell Impett	1
Arthur Wreacke	1	Thomas Holness	2
Henry Rigden	3	Richard Impett	2
Richard Bredly	1	Henry Jacob	2
Stephen Miles	2	John Wanstall	3
Richard Overy	2	John Cockerton	6
William Read	2	William Ladd	2
David Denn sen[io]r	4	Henry Hogben	3
Jonathen Denne	3	Widdow Friend	3
Thomas Impett	1	Widdow Steed	1
Vincent Billinghurst	1	Richard Glover	1

Not chargeable		**Not chargeable**	
Robert Norton	1	Robert Johnson jun[io]r	1

John Walker	2	Stephen Overy	2
Widdow Rigden	2	Francis Marshall	1
Robert Hobdey	1	Henry Strong	1
John Stringer	1	William Pagg	1
Robert Johnson snr	1	Thomas Wraith	2
William Woollet	1	Widdow Spratt	1
Richard Strong	2	Widdow Clement	1
Robert Billinghurst	1	Richard Twyman	1
Thomas Maxted	1	Thomas Wildsden	1
Henry Cobb	1	Widdow Downes	1
Widdow Walker	1	Widdow Blackman	1
Solomon Shipton	1	Widdow Hogman	1
Widdow Austen	1	Stephen Cheesman	2
William Bates	1	Widdow Overy	2
Matthew Price	1	John Miles	1
Robert Impett	1	Thomas Friend	1
John Chamking	1	Richard Glover	1
William Whitfield	1	David Denn	1
Widdow Gage	1	William Impett	1
John Hawkins	1	Samuell Steed	1
John Dennis	1	Susann Small	1
Widdow Browneing	2	Widdow Woodman	1
Thomas Savinn	1	Widdow Best	1

William Whitfield Borsholder   David Denn Constable

[fol. 79r]

THE HUNDRED OF WINGHAM
In the Lath of St Augustine

The Upper Halfe Hundred

Borough of Wingham Street

Chargeable		Chargeable	
Sir Henry Palmer Bart	28	Mr Stephen Solley	3
Robert Beane	3	Stephen Southen	2
Richard Nearle	2	George Nearle	2
Widdow Reynolds	4	Mrs Oxenden	1
Thomas Denn	4	Henry Beard	2
William Spratt	4	David Ovell	2
Stephen Benn	3	Widdow Benn	2
John Duker	3	Widdow Widditt	2
Edward Baker	2	John Jeffery	3

Gilbert Tattenden	1	Henry Burchett	2
William Ouldfield	2	Henry Buttry	2
Isaac Lilly	1	Widdow Harrison	2
Samuell Elbery	2	William Curlin	1
Stephen Huffam	1	Thomas Port	3
Richard Read	3	William Bahell	2
John East	2	William Browneing	2

Not chargeable

Not chargeable

Widdow Packer	2	James Stone	1
Widdow Joanes	5	John Buckes	1
Widdow Buttry	4	Robert Hubbard	2
John Lamm	1	William Price	1
John Arnold	2	Edward Foreman	1
William Trice	2	Valentine Mockett	1
Abraham Lilly	1	Michaell Beale	1
Robert Parker	1	Thomas Ladd	1
Michaell Hogben	1	Robert Buttry	2
Thomas Reake	2	Widdow Castle	3
Richard Meeke	1		

Borough of Winghamwell

Chargeable

Chargeable

Sir Henry Oxenden	17	Mrs Harfleet widd[ow]	14
Thomas Attwell	2	Thomas Attwell	2
Nicholas Easts	2	Widdow Selden	2
Thomas Winter	2	George Dadd	2
Thomas Beard	2	Clement Fawcle	2
John Towne	5	Mr Boys	7
Theophilus Pattison	3	Francis Steff	2
Thomas Kingsmell	1		

Not chargeable

Not chargeable

William Bayle	1	John Clarke	1
George Cooke	1	Robert Philpott	1
William Darne	1	Michaell Browne	1

Rowling Borough

Chargeable

Chargeable

Gabriell Richards gent	10	John Pett	3
Thomas Neame	2	Hoseah Solley	1
Edward Hayes	3	Robert Fearne	3

Bartholomew Hayward	2	Lawrence Tucker	2

Not chargeable		Not chargeable	
Edward Miles	1	John Tunley	1
John Nash	1	Henry Webster	1
William Gray	1		

Borough of Goodnestone

Chargeable		Chargeable	
Sir John Boys	10	Sir Thomas Engham	20
David Rigden	2	William Wanstall	4
Edward Wanstall	3	David Court	3
Henry Norris	4	William Clowes	2
Thomas Prickett	4	John Wanstall	4
John Menvell	1	Christopher Clarke	1
Nicholas Knott	1	Thomas Grant	2
William Payne	1	Nicholas Blowne	3
Symon Tucker	1	Edward Rammell	1
John Wary	1	John Hart sen[io]r	1
John Boys Esq	2	Basill Harrison	6
David Austen	3	Francis Browne	1
George Andrew	2	Margarett Neame wid[dow]	5
Robert Goare	2	Richard Maytom	4
Richard Goldfinch	3	Mary Hopkins widd[ow]	2
Robert Homan	3	John Deane	3
William Howson	4	John Giles	1

Not chargeable		Not chargeable	
Clement Hawkins	1	David Bell	3
Thomas Cox	1	James Dixson	1
John Hart jun[io]r	1	Margarett Tucker	1
Richard Saffrey	1	George Marsh	1
Robert Buckwell	1	Richard Tanton	1
Thomas Browne	1	Thomas Moore	1
Vincent Reeste	2		

Wimblingswould Borough

Chargeable		Chargeable	
Thomas Sharpe	2	William Tucker	5
William Read	2	John Monday	2
Francis Stoppell	2	Oliver Sparepoint	1
Lawrence Morris	2	John Morris	1
Henry Morris	1	Widdow Coppar	1

Samuell Amis	1	Widdow Woodroffe	1

Not chargeable		**Not chargeable**	
John Rose	1	William Eightacres	1
William Tucker	1	Nicholas Osborne	1
[fol. 79v]			
George Sharpe	1	Roger Sharpe	1
Beniamin Pilcher	1		

Eythorne Borough

Chargeable		**Chargeable**	
Mr Walton	6	John Austen	5
John Marsh	4	Thomas Austen	1
Edward Maxted	2	Richard Sampson	1
John Gurner	4		

Not chargeable		**Not chargeable**	
James Baker	1	James Marsh	1
Widdow Rooke	1		

Twittham Borough

Chargeable		**Chargeable**	
Henry Oxenden gent	11	Richard Fuller	1
Mathew Hilles	1	Stephen Church	2
John Cartwright	2	Daniell Meed	3
Alexander Smythson	1	Edward Porridge	2
Christopher Rattliffe	2	J[blank] Lilly	2

Not chargeable		**Not chargeable**	
William Selden	1	Thomas Holmes	1
		Thomas Neame Constable	

The Lower Half Hundred of Wingham

Borough of Chilton

Chargeable		**Chargeable**	
Mr Henry Harfleet	5	Stephen Stringer	3
Steven Cleveland	6	Widdow Packer	1
Widdow Venetian	1	Peter Lubert	1
Widdow Legneale	1	John Mattson	1
John Carr	3	Francis Wood	2
John Mockett	2	Osmond Saffrey	1

John Beane	2	Mr John Gibbon	3
Solomon Jeffard	2	John Pettley	4
Mrs Solley widdow	4	Robert Jefford	4
Augustine Knight	1	William Bax	1
Stephen Carter	1	Robert Saunders	1
Stephen Stonard	1	Valentine Dillnat	2
Thomas Redman	2	Richard Saunders	1
Mr John Proud	5	Stephen Bax	5
Symon Brice	1	Thomas Saunders	1
Robert Wood	1	Michaell Wood	2
Thomas Sackett	2	Thomas Bax	3
John Durrant	3	Adam Jull	2
Joseph Wells	5	William Taylor	3
Stephen Bing	1	Stephen Goldfinch	1
Thomas Hughes	2	William Hughes	1
Humphrey Bedoe	1	John Bedoe	1
John Horne	2	Richard Solley	5

Not chargeable		**Not chargeable**	
Daniell Ralph	3	Richard Price	2
William Walteridge	1	James Kingsland	1
William Fox	1	Charles Wyld	2
John Leggatt	3	Stephen Goare	1
Widdow Raggat	1	William Holliday	1
Thomas Stredwick	2	Widdow Munns	2
Abraham Pryer	1	Edward Wellward	1
Widdow Solley	2	Widdow Clifford	1
Edward Clifford	1		

Overland Borough

Chargeable			
Widdow Underdowne	2	John Sturges	1
John Solley	1	Robert Foate	1
Abiezer Boykin	2	Richard Marbrooke	2
Thomas St Nicholas Esq	7	George Baldock	1
Widdow May	1	Thomas Browne gent	4
Thomas Brice	1	Richard Morton	4
John Richardson	2	Richard Wells	1
Stephen Chambers	1	Edward Baker	1
Thomas Rowe	2	Henry Ridgden	1
Stephen Solley	2	Daniell Saffrey	3
David Denn	3	Thomas Baldock	1
John Bax	6	Thomas Younger	5

Richard Crambrooke	1	John and Peter Legneale	2
John Musdred	2	James White	2
Bartholomew Peirce	2	Richard Johnson	2
Widdow Foate	4	John Addams	1
Andrew Holness	2	Widdow Cooper	1
Ralph Leggatt	4		

Not chargeable		Not chargeable	
Thomas Sayer	1	William Verrier	1
John Taylor	1	Marke Nethersole	1
Thomas Goodbin	1	Widdow Moyne	1
Henry Fennell	1	Richard Gibbs	1

Borough of Wenderton

Chargeable		Chargeable	
Robert Morris	2	Richard Andrew	8
Bartholomew Boykin	4	John Andrew	1
Mathew Browning	4	William Mason	1
Arthur Milles	1	Henry Reeley	1

		Not chargeable	
Richard Solley Constable		Paul Richardson	3

[fol. 80r]

THE HUNDRED OF PRESTON
in the Lath of St Augustine

Borough of Elmeston

Chargeable		Chargeable	
Robert Jaquist gent	4	Daniell Jarvis	3
Alexander Broadly Cl[erk]	3	Robert Minter	2
William Buttry	1	Thomas Gibbs	1
Nicholas Gibbs	1	Gabriell Drayson	1

Not chargeable		Not chargeable	
Widdow Craley	1	George Thomas	1
Widdow Boult	1	Reman Huttson	1

Dureson Borough

Chargeable		Chargeable	
William Jarvis	2	John Johnson	1

Thomas Andrew	1	John Reader	1
Robert Joy	2		

Blackin Borough

Chargeable		Chargeable	
Isaac Sawyer	2	John Really	2
Richard Gilles	2	Stephen Castle	2
Henry Thrum	2	Widdow Breadley	1
William Mott	1	William Amis	1

Not chargeable		Not chargeable	
Vincent Andrew	1	Joseph Bax	1
Richard Huffam	1	Richard Litherry	1
Widdow Rune	1	Widdow Moarton	1

Inn Borough

Chargeable		Chargeable	
Michaell Huffam	4	William Harrison	6
Augustin Rattly	4	Samuell Clement	3
Thomas Westbeech	1	Henry Minter	1
Henry Beard	1	Samuell Hilles	3
Thomas Terry	2	Thomas Solley	2
William Shrubsole	1	Joseph Cleveland	2
Thomas Downe	1	Mrs Wybourne widd[ow]	3
John Hammond	1	John Crisp	1
Widdow Hatcher	2	Andrew Hilles	1
John Browne	1	Thomas Coulson	1
John Whitton	1	David Murrillian	3
Stephen Thompson	1		

Not chargeable		Not chargeable	
Thomas Marten	1	Widdow Lee	1
Henry Knowler	1	Widdow Howling	1
Thomas Buckland	1	Alexander Cuke	1
John Joanes	1	Widdow Reader	1
William Harnett	1	Richard Collins	1
Widdow Nookes	1	Widdow Inne	1
Widdow Gouldfinch	1	John Browne	1
Widdow Downe	1	Widdow Paramour	
		Thomas Gibbs Constable	

THE HUNDRED OF RINGSLOW
in the Island of Thannett
In the Lath of St Augustine

St Nicholas at Wade

Chargeable		Chargeable	
Doctor Cheveney	6	Mr Napleton	7
Mr Cullen	10	John Bridges	5
Thomas Bridges	4	Ezechiell Bridges	5
Edward Philpott	5	Richard Goare	3
William Goatley sen[io]r	3	William Goatley jun[io]r	3
William Sayer	4	George Pett	4
Widdow Watts	3	John Davis	2
Paul Parker	2	Thomas Turvie	3
John May	3	Edward Cooter	1
Solomon Friend	2	Edward Adgoe	2
Robert Smyth	1	Abraham Searse	1
John Snilven	1	William Dason	1
Richard Elbury	1	Symon Aiele	1
John Swinford	1	Phillip Burchett	1

Moncton Parish

Chargeable		Chargeable	
William Rooke Esq	7	Henry Paramour gt.	10
Thomas Parker	4	Roger Toddy	5
Mr Noakes	5	Valentine Cantis	5
Mathias Cantis	5	Leiuetenant Harty	7
John Allen Clerke	4	Widdow Giles	4
Henry Mallis	2	Edward Smyth	2
John Hadlow	1	Thomas Chambers	2
John Boshell	2	John Read	1
Absolom Hinchway	1	William Mellwood	1
Widdow Carter	1	John Mallis	1
William Goldfinch	1	Edward Staines	1
Thomas Clunn	1	Edward Toms	1
Widdow Boshell	1	Richard Sharp	1

Not chargeable		Not chargeable	
Rober[t] Fence	-	William Watson	-
William Newman	-	John Carpenter	-
Widdow Nash	-	John Salter	-
Henry Adams	-	Thomas Packer Constable	

St. Lawrence East Borough

Chargeable		Chargeable	
Thomas Gillow	5	John Maxted	4
Thomas Tanner	1	Thomas Abbott	1
Widdow Lamming	1	William Sanders	2
Robert Foate	1	Thomas Woodware	1
William Curling	1	Edward Stanner	1
[fol. 80v]			
Thomas Skinner	4	Elizabeth Sampson wid[ow]	3
Widdow Scranton	1	Vincent Rickard	1
Nicholas Muckins	1	John Skinner	1
John Paramour	1	Edward Affrey	2
John Cooper	2	William Clarke	1
John Sackett	1	Luke Philpott	1
William Laming	1	John Bennett	1
Robert Curling	1	Henry Grant	1
Edward Philpott	1	Widdow Dyer	1
William Hilles	1	John Joad	2
Thomas Garrett	2	George Kite	1
Roger Curling	1	Richard Cebball	3
Thomas New	2	Richard Fowler	3
Widdow Barbitt	2	David Street	1
Widdow Tickner	3	Isaac Goger	2
Edward Pannell	1	Widdow Curling	1
John Sanders	4	Mr Peter Johnson	2
Not chargeable		Not chargeable	
Edward Pannell	1	John Curling	1
Christopher Buttris	1	John Preston	1
William Lull	1	John Bing	1
John Williams	1	William Fagg	1
Stephen Joad	1	William Langredge	1
Silvester Brooke	1	Thomas Hogben	1
Nicholas Muckins	1	William Jorden	1
Thomas Dowty	1	William Tharp	1
John Cooke	1	Alexander Pepper	1
John Googer	1	Thomas Gray	1
Bartholomew Dowty	1	John Alderston	1
Richard Ayers	1	Andrew Epsley	1
Richard Mayor	1	John Holland	1
Jeremy Maserly	1	Widdow Maxted	1
Widdow Garrett	1	Thomas Paine	1
William Dowty	1	John West	1

Haman Kennard	1	Landy Mommery	1
George Sumner	1	Widdow Fagg	1
Widdow Emberson	1	William Emberson	1
John Alderston jun[io]r	1	Henry Marten	1
John Foster	1	Thomas White	1
William Springett	1	James Muzered	1
John Kennard	1	Thomas Terry	1
Adam Knowler	1	Thomas Francis	1
John Epsley	1		

Borough of Minster Street

Chargeable		Chargeable	
John Proud	4	James Creed	4
Edward Sutterey	1	John Sharpe	7
John Fuller	3	Isaac Christian	2
Stephen Twyman	2	Thomas Dunston	1
John Dyer	4	Robert Hubberden	2
Boys Ower	3	William Ambrose	4
John Graunt	2	Prosper Gidney	2
Thomas Fuller	5	John Churchman	4
Nicholas Wraith	3	Peter Vanderslate	7
Thomas Emptage	1	Edward Harnett	2
Robert Johnson	1	John Filcock	1
John Robins	1	Peter Ambrose	4

Not chargeable		Not chargeable	
John Mounsteed	3	John Marten	2
Thomas Skilton	3	Joseph Twyman	2
Henry Terry	2	Robert Gristy	1
Robert Bristo	1	John Hayward	1
Edward Meekin	1	Richard Terry	1
Allworth Turner	1	Robert Hayward	1
Peter Davis	1	John Barber	1
William Wilmott	1	Symon Parkes	1
John Taylor	1	John Wooton	4
Thomas Hayward	1	Robert Silvester	1
Robert Woodruff	1	William Johnson	1
Richard Hedgcock	1	George Abraham	1
William Bullare	1	William Humphrey	1
Widdow Clifford	1	Stephen Downden	1
Thomas Write	1	Edward Canterton	1
Widdow Hayward	1	Selves Brooke	1

James Joanes	1	Elizabeth Bishopp	1
Widdow Churchman	1	Widdow Bristow	1
Widdow Willes	1	Widdow Biggell	1
Widdow Bennett	1	John Johncock	2
John Newen	1	William Turner	1
Robert Hayward	1	John Wraight	2
John Carpenter	1		

Way Borough

Chargeable		Chargeable	
Thomas Jenkin	8	John Pamflett	7
John Franckling	4	Edward Harnett	5
Edward Gooreley	4	John Twyman	2
Thomas Russell	3	Stephen Sanders	1
Thomas Andrewes	1	Widdow Goldfinch	2
Richard Emptage	1	Thomas Harrison	3
Beniamin Batho	3	John Huett	1
Andrew Appleton	1	Robert Fatham	1
Robert Murgin	1	Tho[mas] Jeikin }	
		John Pamflet and }	
		Stephen Blaxland }	10

Not chargeable		Not chargeable	
Widdow Emptage	1	Andrew Churchman	1
Thomas Butter	1	John Burch	1
John Granger	1	Wells Churchman	1
John Marten	1	Nicholas Twyman	1
John Sturges	2	Mathias Tomling	1
[fol. 81r]			
Edward Skilton	1	George Hollett	1
Widdow Andrewes	1	Lawrence Weekes	1
Widdow Silvester	1	Isaac Wildboare	1
Widdow Ingleton	1	Widdow Twyman	1

West Borough

Chargeable		Chargeable	
Henry Harnett	5	William Bing	3
William Rowse	1	Daniell Peke	4
Thomas Gouldsmyth	4	Robert Troward	2
Alexander Chiles	2	John Homan	2
William Head	1	John Smyth	1
Thomas Holland	3	Richard Mockett	3
John Parker	1	Henry Denn	1

Henry Pannell	1	Edward Alfrey	1
Vincent Michell	1	John Underdowne	3
John Culling	3	Thomas Cramp	6
Thomas Crambrook	7	John Johnson gent	7
William Soale	2	Paul Parker	2
Robert Maxted	1	John Cooper	3
Francis Horne	2	Thomas Giles	1

Not chargeable		Not chargeable	
Vincent Terry	1	Thomas Curly	1
Henry Parker	1	Richard Parker	1
William Dowstey	1	William Marten	1
Edward Rutter	1	Andrew Joad	1
Edward May	1	Roger Streven	1
Michaell Roberts	1	John Field	1
John Roberts	1	Vincent Pett	1
Henry Smyth	1	Richard Norwood	1
Gilbert Epsley	1		

Henry Pannell - Constable

THE HUNDRED OF CORNILLO
In the Lath of St Augustine

The Upper Halfe Hundred

Borough of Northbourne

Chargeable		Chargeable	
Sir Richard Sandys	28	Daniell Wybourne	5
John Pettett	2	James Pettett	7
James Burvill Clar[k]	4	Richard Lanes	4
Henry Soames	2	John Stannard	3
Mathew Hamond	1	Thomas Hudson	1

Not chargeable		Not chargeable	
William Bodkin	1	James Harlow	1
Daniell Allen	1	Silvester Gale	1
William Palmer	1	John Carter	1
William Palmer	1	Widdow Amis	1
Widdow Huett	1	Richard Sawyer	1
William Bushell	1		

Borough of Great Mongeham

Chargeable		Chargeable	
Mr Crayford	12	Mr Sackett	6
Samuell Pittock	4	William Sladden	2
William Troward	2	John Kingsford	3
Thomas Ralfe	1	Leonard Cooke	2
David Crowd	2	Richard Hull	3
Henry Joanes	3	John Friend	1
Robert Tuckney	2	Stephen Bradley	1
Henry Gardner	3	Daniell Kingsford	1
William Sackett	2	William Andrew	1
John Lacey	2		

Not chargeable		Not chargeable	
Widdow Brimstone	1	Samuell Brimstone	1
Abraham Norton	1	William Hobgood	1
Ingram Walker	1	Edward Clement	1
Edward Moore	1	William Friend	2
Alexander Makney	2	John Sprackeng	1
Sarah Jeffery	2	Widdow Jeffery	1
Widdow Inge sen[io]r	1	Widdow Inge jun[io]r	1
Henry Hudson	1	Widdow Sharpe	1
James Croyden	1	Sarah Smyth	1
William Beane	1	Mr Sackett in an empty cott[age]	-

Finglesham Borough

Chargeable		Chargeable	
John Sim[m]ons	4	Thomas Sym[m]ons	4
Thomas Grant	1	Joshuah Paramour	5
William Ferne	2	Richard Verryer	2
James Golder	7	William Kingsford	3
John Fearne	3	Thomas Hill	3
Isaac Slaughter	4	William Rickwood	3
Gilbert Stannard	1		

Not chargeable		Not chargeable	
Andrew Kingsford	1	Christopher Kingsford	2
Samuell Theyr	2	Widdow Parker	2
James Burton	1	John Underdowne	1
Widdow Joanes	1	Widdow Smyth	1
Stephen Homan	1	William Scott	2
William Austen	1	Robert Bartlett	2

Shoulden Borough

Chargeable		Chargeable	
Thomas Hatcher	4	John Troward	2
William Sutton	2	John Griffin	3
Mary Makeney	1	James Marsh	3
William Allen	4	Stephen Goodson	2
Richard Pettett	3	Joane Callis	2
John Pettett	3	Bennett Emptidge	2
Henry Davis	1	John Allen	1
Abraham Mum[m]ery	1	William Nash	4
[fol. 81v]			
Henry Dixson	2	Katharine Jacob	1
Henry Bird	2	David Whittitt	2
Thomas Langworthy	2	Walter Noakes	2
John Rumney	2		

Not chargeable		Not chargeable	
John Bushell	1	John Darbers	1
Henry Bing	1	Henry Soames Constable	

The Lower Halfe Hundred of Cornillo

Ashley Borough

Chargeable		Chargeable	
Mr Richard Harvey	3	Mr Ralph Philpott	3
Richard Burvill	3	Richard Marsh	3
Nicholas Burvill	3	William Smyth	1
Thomas Wildbore	3	William Horne	1
Robert Claringboule	1	Abraham Upton	2
Thomas Friend	1	William Friend	4
Edward Harnett	1	William Silkwood	3
George Beere	2	David Sayer	1
William Brockman	1		

Not chargeable		Not chargeable	
Jo[hn] Lynter	1	Richard Barber	1
James Sayer	1	Roger Marcham	1
Thomas Eastes	1	Jo[hn] Pilcher	1
Robert Burvill	1	Thomas Tyler	1
Ezechiell Pierce	1	Thomas Harvey	1
Richard Horne	1	Robert Fagg	1
Thomas Sym[m]ons	1		

In Ticknes

Chargeable		Chargeable	
Beniamin Gibbon	3	Stephen Stoakes	2
Nicholas Pittock	1		
		Not chargeable	
		John Allen	1

In Sutton

Chargeable		Chargeable	
Beniamin Sladden	2	Mr Seylyard	8
Mr Hussey	2	Thomas Brett	4
Mrs Smyth	4	Michaell Ladd	3
John Dilnott	3	Alexander Atkins	1
John Barbar	5	Henry Wilson	1
William Burch	3		

Not chargeable		Not chargeable	
William Wilson	1	William Blowne	1
Jo[hn] Pirkins	1	Jo[hn] Blowne	1
Mark Redman	1	William Knott	1
Jo[hn] Gespes	1	Jeremy Hayward	1
Jo[hn] Amis	1	Nicholas Hodgman	1
Richard Heaslebey	1		

In Ripple

Chargeable		Chargeable	
Mr John Gokin	9	Mr John Cashire	9
Mr William Standley	3	Mr Andrew Rand	8
Mr Nicholas Brett	4	Sidrach Mackney	3
John Standly	3	Mathew Ray	2
Richard Pettett	2	John Mackny	4
Thomas Cock	1		

Not chargeable		Not chargeable	
William Bett	1	Anthony Houldman	1
Thomas Redman	1	Edward Staple	1

In Marten & East Langden

Chargeable		Chargeable	
Mr Jo[hn] Casier	10	Anthony Wastall	5
Widdow Oyne	4	Jo[hn] Parker	1
Henry Sradett	1	Edmund Finnis	1
Mr William Osbourne	3	Thomas Marsh	6

Robert Austen	9	Ambo: Starke	4
Jo[hn] Rugley	2	Richard Wraight	3
Thomas Munden	1		

Not Chargeable		**Not Chargeable**	
Widdow Vile	1	Thomas Cornelius	1
Edward Chidwick	1	William Ansell	1
Widdow Brooke	1	Henry Luse	1
Stephen Crambrooke	1	William Smith Constable	

THE HUNDRED OF EASTRY
in the Lath of St Augustine

The Upper Halfe Hundred

Eastry & Street

Chargeable		**Chargeable**	
Sir George Sondes Knt. of ye}		Mr John Whiston for the }	
Bath for ye parsonage }	7	vicarage }	3
Joseph Roberts gent }		John Austen	4
for the Court lodge }	14	Mrs Susan Paramour	1
Thomas Friend	4	Roger Goulder	5
Ralph Smyth	4	Michaell Austen	3
Andrew Sole	5	Samuell Terry	1
Christopher Denn	2	Robert Wood	4
Samuell Churchman	4	John Pettett	4
John Wood	1	and in another house	2
Bartholomew Goulder	2	Thomas Horsfeild	2
William Drayton	1	Ingram Durban	1
Roger Whitehead	2	Thomas Pittock	2
William Friend miller	1	Robert Thompson	2
Samuell Pittock	1	John Ansell	5
Leonard Woodware	2	Hezechias Stacy	1
John Adams	1	Nicholas Stokes	1
John Ham[m]ond	1	John Horne	2
Robert Sackett	1	Widdow Richardson	1
Richard Thompson	2	Anthony Watts	1
Abraham Stuppell	1		

[fol. 82r]

In Eastry

Not chargeable		Not chargeable	
Robert Gibson	1	Robert Hawkins	1
Mark Hawkes	1	William Hall	1
Abraham Printer	1	Richard Neame	1
Ambrose Thompson	1	Thomas Naman	1

Hacklings

Chargeable		Chargeable	
Mr Peter Peke	3	William Browne	2
Andrew Mum[m]ery	1	Edward Noakes	1
Francis Marsh	1	Henry Bedwell	1
Roger Reeve	1		

Hamden & Selson

Chargeable		Chargeable	
Richard Hawy	3	Lawrence Tucker	2
William Hatcher	3	Mrs Boteler	1
Daniell Knott	3	James Bunce	6
John Baker	3	John Pett	2
Nicholas Pitcher	1	Grigory Baker	1

Felderland

Chargeable		Chargeable	
Ralph Philpott	4	Joseph Philpott	3
William Danton	1	John Hild	3
Edward Sympson	2		

Word Street

Chargeable		Chargeable	
John Paramour	4	John May	2
John Westbeech	4	more in his own house	2
Anthony Harrison	1	Peter Wymarke	3
John Harrison	3	William Giles	1
George Forwood	1	Edward Noakes	3
Widdow Ellis	1	William Mabourne	1
John Pope	3	John Howlen	2
James Wickes	1	Widdow Paramour	1
Richard Cumber	1	Samuell Hawke	1

Craythorn Borough

Chargeable		Chargeable	
John Rogers	3	John Pattson	2

William Belsey	1	Valentine Austen	2
Thomas Wood	2	Mathew Woodware	1
Henry Elgar	1	John Hogben	1
Thomas Elgar	1		

Socken Langden

Chargeable		Chargeable	
John Chapman gent }		Thomas Jenkin	6
five hearths & one stove}	6	Henry Peirce	3
Henry Parker	2	James Gumian	1
Thomas Knott	1	Richard Baylie	1
Henry Elgarr	1	John Knott	2
Christian Sim[m]ons	3	Jeremy Lam[m]ing	1
James Henry	2		

Barnsole

Chargeable		Chargeable	
Isaac Mum[m]ery	3	Edward Rigden	1
Symon Devison	1	Richard Nunam	1
William Beard	1	Henry Pettett	1
John Devison	1		

Geddings

Chargeable		Chargeable	
Bartholomew Spaine	4	John Saffrey	2
William Pilcher	1	George Pilcher	1
Jeremy Bird	1	John White	1

Tilmanstone Street Borough

Chargeable		Chargeable	
Richard Fogg Esq	8	Humphrey Dicus Cler[k]	6
Mr Saphire Paramour	5	Leonard Smyth	4
Richard Hammond	3	John Wood	4
Henry Harvy	2	George Falkner	2
Widdow Gurner	1	Widdow Payne	2
George Fagg	2	Anthony Hull	2
Daniell Downe	2	John Ryers	1
John Stuppell	1	Goodman Mum[m]ery	1
Goodman Brice	1	Thomas Wildboare	1
John Thorpe	1	John White	1
		In an empty house that Goodwife Hull lived in	1

Not chargeable		Not chargeable	
Goodwife Manless	1	William Sutten	2
Richard Wraith	1	Henry Huett	2
Christian Proke	1	John Baker Constable	

The Lower Halfe Hundred of Eastry

Coldfryday Borough

Chargeable		Chargeable	
Mr Thomas Blechynden	8	Mr Jackson	4
Henry Neame	1	Thomas Baker	1
Richard Pordage	3	James Baker	2
William Maitam	1	Francis Ballew	1
Widdow Harrison	3		

Not chargeable		Not chargeable	
William Webster	4	Margaret Ray	2
James Baker	1	Francis Johncock	2
Jeremy Bishopp	1	William Inge	1
Widdow Rest	1	Widdow West	1
		Jeremy Bishop Borsholder	

[fol. 82v]

Chillenden Borough

Chargeable		Chargeable	
Mr Culling	2	Stephen Sayer	3
Sylvester Neame	3	more in an empty house	2
Daniell Wood	2	Richard Hoocke	1
Thomas Bennett	1	George Baker	2
James Hunt	2	Joseph Catchpoole	1
Edward Kingsmell	1	Widdow Saffrey	1
James Sayer	2	Abraham Fride	1
Marke Gorden	1		

Not chargeable		Not chargeable	
Richard Beare	-	John Godfrey	-
William Huttson	-	Thomas Wellard	-
Widdow Philpott	-	Samuell Anchor	-

Borough of Barfreston

Chargeable		Chargeable	
Mr Edwards	4	John Smyth	4
Michaell Godfrey	2	William Wraith	1

Henry Willman	1	John Allen	2
Robert Chittick	3		

Not chargeable		**Not chargeable**	
Robert Hall	1	John Jorden	1
Abraham Philpott	1	Edward Wellard	2
William Elgar Borsholder	1		

Each Borough

Chargeable		**Chargeable**	
Francis Blann	4	Samuell Pordage	5
William Stoakes	5	Mrs Harrison	4
John Piles	1	John Harloe	1
William Carr	5	Thomas Neame	3
Widdow Hatcher	3	Widdow Read	1

Not chargeable		**Not chargeable**	
Remond Brooke	1	Widdow Pordage	1
Henry Hogman	1		

Easole Borough

Chargeable		**Chargeable**	
James Nash	13	Thomas Rogers	2
Robert Rye	1	Thomas Harrison	2
Edward Rum[m]ell	2	Thomas Dunning	2
Mathew Cooper	1	William Knott	1

Not chargeable		**Not chargeable**	
Coleman Saffrey	1	John Bird	1
Richard Filler	1	John Fennell	1
William Beech	1	Widdow Hubbard	1
Widdow Bayle	1	William Fagg	1
Widdow Claringbould	1		

Nonington

Chargeable		**Chargeable**	
John Boys Esq	18	Jeremy Gay gen[t]	8
Nicholas Creake	3	John Packden	1
William Beane	1	Richard Wilson	1
Thomas Henneker	1	Thomas Hayward	1

Not chargeable

[blank] Rooke	1
Jeremy Bartlett	1
Henry Miller	1
George Belsie	1
George Toms	1
Widdow Boycon	1
Widdow Holmes	1
Thomas Pickle	2

Not chargeable

Edward Sym[m]ons	1
John Cosins	1
Thomas Osbourne	1
Anthony Packden	1
Robert Bayley	1
Widdow Dale	1
Goodman Hobday	1

Borough of Hamwell

Chargeable

S[i]r Thomas Peyton	21
Thomas Pettett	4
James Robbins	4
Mr James Benchkyn	7
Thomas Burton	1
Richard Neame	5
Daniell Wraith	2
Amos Solley	4
Isaac Long	1
Richard Read	1
John Nash	1
Thomas Swayne	1
Richard Dastone	1
Henry Meakins	2
Thomas Baker	4
John Stockwell	1
Richard Gibson	1

Chargeable

Mr Peter Pury	4
Samuell Austen	4
Mr Vincent Benchkyn	7
Edward Dall	3
William Gibbs	3
John Morris	3
Augustine Knight	1
John Baker	1
Widdow Pordage	2
Richard Solley	2
Robert Chidwick	2
Widdow Barrowe	1
William Ayres	2
Edward Knight	1
Richard Godfrey	1
John Goldfinch	1

Not chargeable

John Richards	-
John Woollett	-
John Harrison	-
Thomas Hilles	-

Not chargeable

Roger Noakes	-
Stephen Ansell	-
Thomas Read	-

Parish of Denton

Chargeable

John Andrewes gent	19
Mr William Lunn at the } parsonage house }	5
Thomas Baker	4
John Baker	3

Chargeable

Thomas Marsh	7
Henry Oxenden gt.	5
Francis Gammon	3
William Falconer	5
William Jull thatcher	2

[fol. 83r]

William Joanes	1	Richard Dixson	2
Thomas Cullen	1	William Jull maltman	1
Widdow Graves	1	Thomas Rose	1
Nicholas Soale	1	John Brasyer	2
Henry Pickell	1	Henry Sanders	1
Roger Hammond	1	Robert Lowe	1
John Fox	1		

Not chargeable

Widdow Dadd	1	Widdow Bourne	1
Francis Hussey	1	Nathaniell Smyth	1
Ursula Beniamin	1	John Woddall	1
Robert Jull	1	Henry Sanders Borsholder	

Waldershare

Chargeable   Chargeable

Valentine Upton	4	William Smyth	2
John Silkwood deputy	4	John Beane	2

Borough of Ham & Bettshanger

Chargeable   Chargeable

{John Boys Esq.	11	John Morris	5
{And more in a house now]		Elizabeth Bunce wid[dow]	4
{empty neere adioyning]	5	Humphrey Harloe	3

Not chargeable   **Not chargeable**

William Hoppar borsholder	1	John Davis	1
		Thomas Baker Constable	

THE HUNDRED OF KINGHAMFORD
In the Lath of St. Augustine

In Giddens

Chargeable   Chargeable

Vincent Ladd	7	William Culling	6
William Adams	5	John Spaine	2
Richard Craft	1	Thomas Dickson	1

Barham

Chargeable   Chargeable

John Nethersole	5	Thomas Ginder	10

Thomas Canbourne	3	Widdow Ladd	4
Thomas Blix	3	Thomas Miller	2
Thomas Gilpin	3	Robert Godwin	2
John Dixson	1	William Vittell	1
Robert Ladd Esq	5	John Hayward	3
John Johnson	2	Christopher Dally	2
Henry Friend	3	Stephen Lawrence	1
William Marsh	1	Christopher Parker	1
Thomas Lawrence	1	Richard Baker	3
Henry Bridges	1	Richard Hopkin	4
Nicholas Fox	2	Richard Lawrence	2
Richard Claringbould	1	Thomas Epps	1

Not chargeable

William Mihill	1	Widdow Blackabey	1
Richard Budds	1	Thomas Fukes	1
Thomas Gilpin jun[io]r	1	Thomas Budds	1
Widdow Culling	1	Widdow Coller	1
James Marsh	1	Widdow Grig	1

Borough of Bishopsbourne

Chargeable

S[i]r Anthony Aucher	20	Thomas Denn	3
S[i]r Richard Hatton	5	John Burton	5
Peter Denn	5	Richard Burton	-
Mr Edward Peiton	9	John Hopkins	4
James Wood	5	Dr. Lee	6
John Goldfinch	2	John Saunders	1
Thomas Fowle	2	Anthony Culling	3
William Thompson	1	Edward Shrubsole	2
Edward Rigden	2	Samuell Brensett	2
Widdow West	1	John Midelmes	2
William Quekett	1		

Not chargeable

Robert Rayner	1	Edward Kerby	1
Richard Mose	1	Nicholas Soale	1
Robert Monday	1	John Pearce	1
Thomas Mihill	1	William Mihill	1
William Munday	1		

Borough of Out Elmested

Chargeable		Chargeable	
William Denward	5	Thomas Nash	1
John Giles	1	William Marsh	1
Humphrey Epps	4	Thomas Baker	1
Thomas Pittock	2	Edward Baker	1
William Baker	1	Francis Baker	1

Not chargeable		Not chargeable	
George Tallis	1	Edward Garling	1
John Friend	1	Robert Whidbey	1
John Rose	1	Edward May	1
William Copper	1	Edward Curd	1
Edward Culmer	1	John Stone	1
Nicholas Smyth	1	Widd[ow] White	1

Shelvinge Borough

Chargeable		Chargeable	
Thomas Belsey	7	Henry Mullett	2
Mathew Hobdey	2	Thomas Smyth	1
[fol. 83v]			
Thomas Jonas	2	John Tose	1
Thomas Rolfe	1	John Mullett	1

Not chargeable		Not chargeable	
Widdow Skarlett	1	Thomas Philpott	1
John Impett	1	John Mullett	1
Edward Hart	1	Daniell Coller	1
Widdow Fox	1	Richard Miller	2
Widdow Beddingfield }		Widdow Young	1
and Widd[ow] Gardiner }	1	Widdow Smyth	1
John Miller	1	John Mullett	1
Thomas Friend	1		

Barton Borough

Chargeable		Chargeable	
S[i]r Bazell Dixwell	20	John Rammell	3
Henry Howell	4	Christopher Stredwick	5

Not chargeable		Not chargeable	
William Streeting	1	Richard Satterton	1
Henry Tapper	1	William Williams	1

James Mullett	2	Widdow Dillnott	2
George Wright	1	Widdow Smeath	1

Parish of Kingston

Chargeable   **Chargeable**

Sir James Wilsford	10	Mr. Marsh	7
Mr. Denne	6	Mr. Barnes	3
Mr. Dingley	5	Richard Wood	3
William Friend	1	Henry Foord	4
John Cocklinn	2	Thomas Rye	3
Elias Gammon	2	Robert Boys	2
William Strood	3	Edward Sturges	3
Thomas Attwood	1	Widdow Attwood	1
Thomas Bushell	2	Stephen Mapple	2
James Dunn	1	James Sayer	1
William Brice	1	William Hopkin	1
Edward Hopkin	2	Francis Hobdey	1
Thomas Woodland	1	Robert Sankey	1
Arthur Hayward	1	William Moone	4
Richard Foord	2	Thomas Maytham	1
William Townes	2		

Not chargeable   **Not chargeable**

Mr Richard Gibbon	2	Widdow Winter	1
Ralph Adams	1	Richard Mihill	1
John Hedgcock	1	Thomas Sim[m]ons	1
Widdow Cavell	1	John Muggall	1
Charles Quested	2	John Browne	1
Augustine Brenchley	1	Richard Turner	1
John Holliday	1	Widdow Goddar	1
William Canbourne	1	Thomas Jorden	1
		Henry Foord & Thomas Broadnax Constables	

THE HUNDRED OF BEAUXBOROUGH
In the Lath of St. Augustine

The Upper Halfe Hundred

Shepperdswell Borough

Chargeable   **Chargeable**

William Mereweather g[entleman]	8	Henry Huffam gen[t].	7
		Swanton Woolgate	1

Thomas Ramwell	1	Stephen Mathewes	1
William Finn	1	Thomas Birch	1
William Owen	5	Henry Birch	1
William Knott	2	John Birch	3
Henry Belsey	2	George Gibbon	3
John Gibbon	4	William Philpott	4
James Mattson	4	Henry Lawrence	1
John Ashley	1	William Parker	1
John Hubbert	1	Stephen Hobdey	1
Francis Watson	1		

Not chargeable		**Not chargeable**	
James Burvill	1	Widdow Ashley	1
Stephen Hobdey	1	Abraham Stuppell	1
Widdow Hewson	1	Edward Browne	1

Gustone Borough

Chargeable		**Chargeable**	
Thomas Stokes	4	Edward Pruscott	4
Thomas Harrison	3	Richard Barrowes	1
Thomas Partridge	1	David Gibbs	1
Symon Lowles	1		

Not chargeable		**Not chargeable**	
Thomas Kingsnod	2	Samuell Denn	1
John Kingsnod	1	Widdow Hoply	1
Thomas Pricherd	1	Thomas Bennett	1
John Epps	1	Widdow Gibbens	2
Richard Eastes	2	Widdow Marsh	1
Gabriell Mercer	1		

Westcliff Borough

Chargeable		**Chargeable**	
Charles Tuck Esq.	10	Thomas Gibbons gen[t]	12
Edward Randall gen[t]	5		

St. Margaretts Atcliff Borough

Chargeable		**Chargeable**	
William Allen	5	Robert Upton	4
Richard Allen	3	Robert Phineas	3
[fol. 84r]			
Mathew Burkett	2	Jeremy Chitty	2

Henry Wellard	2	Michaell Allen	2
Richard Christian	1	Richard Curling	1
Henry Payne	1	Henry Tarly	1
Henry Allen	1	Thomas Philpott	1

Not chargeable		Not chargeable	
William Lawless	-	Thomas Hellman	-
John Phineas	-	George Charnell	-
Valentine Jell	-	John Hawkin	-
Thomas Boule	-	Thomas Hill	-
Henry Phineas	-	William Hoppar	-
William Olliver	-	Edward Hutton	-
Henry Hewben	-	Henry Wellar	-
William Weller	-	Richard Pricher	-
Anthony Roose	-	John Reeve	-
Edward Keene	-	James Denn	-
Joseph Ladd	-	John Kelsey	-

Whitfield Borough

Chargeable		Chargeable	
Richard Brockman	4	Richard Trapps	3
Andrew Mantle	1	Thomas Cullen	2
William Pruscoad	2	John Does	1
George Stuppell	3	William Mann	3

Waldersheire Borough

Chargeable		Chargeable	
S[i]r Edward Monins Bart.	19	John Birch	2
William Smyth	2	Robert Eastes	2
John Marsh	2	Robert Willmott	2

Not chargeable		Not chargeable	
Jeo: Cooke	1	Goodman Browning	1

West Langdon Borough

Chargeable		Chargeable	
Richard Masters Esq.	13	John Emptage sen[io]r	3
John Emptage jun[io]r	1	Nicholas Creeke	5
Valentine Jekin	4	James Whitfield gen[t]	6
Henry Barrowes	2	Richard Castle	1
John Read	3	John Moss	1
James Prichards	1	John Fox	1
Richard Innever	3	Thomas Innever	2

Thomas Taylor	1	William Tucker	1
Stephen Fryer	2	John Paye	2
Thomas Butteris	3	Widdow Marsh	1

Coldred Borough

Chargeable		Chargeable	
Roger Tiedsdell	4	George Pettett	3
George Pilcher	2	Stephen Pilcher	3
William Knott	3	Henry Huffham Constable	

The Lower Halfe Hundred of Beauxborough

Hougham Parish

Chargeable		Chargeable	
Symon Edolph Esq	16	Mr. Fineux	6
Mr. Nepewe	12	Mr. Eding	4
Mr Richards	6	Valentine Harvie	4
Richard Hambrooke	2	William Fagg	2
William Boyman	1	Thomas Valier	2
Mr. Swan[n] of Poulton	2	Thomas Tucker	1
Thomas Hogbin	4	George Pilcher	3
William Valyer	2	John Fagg	2
Phineas Gardner	1	John Dixson	3
William Pantry	1	Henry Partridge	1
William Hall	1	William Peirce	1
Thomas Cussen	1	William Wood	1
John Fagg of ye Ghost	2	William Long	1

Not chargeable		Not chargeable	
John Sim[m]es	1	Robert Sim[m]es	1
Robert Livermore	1	William Spaine	1
Nicholas Hobdey	1	William Pepper	1
Henry Baker	1	John Palmer	1
In ye vicarage house empty	2	Rich[ard] Hambrooke empty	1

Buckland And Charlton

Chargeable		Chargeable	
Robert Bosley	4	Edward Hutton	2
Humphrey Page	4	Thomas Eason	3
Thomas Hammond	3	Andrew Smithett	2
Stephen Baker	4	John Randolph	1

William Lee	1	William Wood	2
Michaell Page	1	Maurice Peirce	3
Ingram Sutton	2	Edward Lampard	3
Thomas Hobdey	2		

Not chargeable		Not chargeable	
John Croud	1	Widdow Gilman	2
Henry Gilman	2	Thomas Beere	1
Christop[her] Brockman	1	John Bance	2
Thomas Everitt	2	William Pilcher	1
James Buddle	1		

River Parish

Chargeable		Chargeable	
Marcellas Swanton	5	Richard Hobdey	4
Edward Harris	4	John Kingsmell	2
Robert Randolph	2	William Knight	5
Robert Eminy	1	Thomas Fagg	3
[fol. 84v]			
Widdow Parkes	2	Thomas Hatton	3
John Southous sen.	1	Stephen Bennett	1
William Parker	2	Thomas Marsh	4
William Pellum	2	Clement Falkconer	5
Stephen Kember	1	James Deacon	2
Henry Winter	1	John Colly	1
Alexander Hogbin	2	John Croud	1

Not chargeable		Not chargeable	
Widdow Fagg	2	Symon Lingham	1
William Buddle	1	Widdow Crowde	2
Grigory Marsh	2	Widdow Marsh	1
Widdow Wilson	1	William Perkin	2
Widdow Carr	1	William Baxter	1
John Stone	1	Widdow Lingham	2
Widdow Tomlyn	1	Widdow Kelsey	1

Ewell Parish

Chargeable		Chargeable	
Mr. Temple	4	Thomas Pilcher	3
Phillip Beere	2	William Baker	1
Francis Bryant	2	William Milles	2
Francis Pilcher	2	Robert Wigmore	1
Thomas Scott	1	Robert Hatton	2

William Russell Cler[k]	1	Stephen Rolfe	2
John Moore	1		

Not chargeable		**Not chargeable**	
Henry Collar	3	Lawrence Scott	1
Grigory Jull	1	Widdow Coulter	1
John Jull	1	Daniell Howell	1
Stephen Mum[m]ery	1	Thomas Harrison	1
Samuell Houlden	1	William Beecham	1
Henry Elgar	1	Thomas Culver	1
William Raysson	1		

Lidden Parish

Chargeable		**Chargeable**	
Thomas Hopkins	2	Nicholas Pilcher	3
Thomas Eaton	2	Thomas Sutton	2

Not chargeable		**Not chargeable**	
Stephen Pilcher	1	Stephen Watson	1
Thomas Sutton	1	John Castle	1
Richard Stace	1	William Hobdey	1
		George Pilcher Constable	

THE HUNDRED OF BRIDGE AND PETHAM
In the Lath of St. Augustine

The Upper Halfe Hundred

Borough of Blackmansbury

Chargeable		**Chargeable**	
S[i]r Arnold Braems Knt.	24	Alexander Silke	3
John Castle	1	Daniell Ovenden	1
Thomas Phillpott	2	John Phillpott	2
Widdow Anslowe	3	Robert Fryer	1
Robert Taylor	1	Symon Boulden	1

Borough of Bridge

Chargeable		**Chargeable**	
Mrs Dancye	6	William Foord	3
Robert Bargrave	2	John Herring	7
William Philpott	3	Richard Gilman	2
John Cooley	2	Richard Stroud	4

Thomas Castle	5	Richard Castle	2
Robert Packman	2	James Jorden	1
John Buly	1	William Gilman	2
Widdow Buly	5		

Not chargeable		Not chargeable	
Widdow Stronge	1	John Brett	1
Henry Coppin	1	John Eldridge	2
Richard West	1	Francis Marsh	2
Mrs. Everard	2	Francis Clement	2
Anthony Cheston	1	Thomas Hardin	2
Christop[her] Stokes	1	Widdow Ladd	1
William Taylor	4	Widdow Cheston	1
Morgan Rogers	1	Andrew Beane	1

Borough of Cheyney

Chargeable		Chargeable	
William Cheston	3	Thomas May	4
Thomas Mundey	2	John Johnson	4
William Dray	1	Nicholas Baker	1

Patrixbourne Borough

Chargeable		Chargeable	
S[i]r Arthur Slingsby	15	Mr. Baker	4
Daniell Young	4	Thomas Badcock	1
Valentine Staynes	2	Thomas Taylor	1
Stephen Savin	3	Anthony Culling	3
John Denn	6	Christop[her] Simpson	1
John Rayner	2	William Wanstall	3
Widdow Taylor	2		

Not chargeable			
Robert Boys	1		

Nackington

Chargeable		Chargeable	
S[i]r Thomas Godfrey	16	John Pilcher	2
Richard Newman	1	John Dunkin	3
William Maicock	1		

[fol. 85r]

Lower Hardres

Chargeable		Chargeable	
Mr Pulford cler[k]	4	Harmond Sole	4
Christop[her] Wood	2	William Rigden	2
Robert Austen	3	James Chadbourne	1
Robert Stace	1	Thomas Terry	2
Edward Denwood	1	John Swayne	1

Not chargeable		Not chargeable	
Nicholas Daniell	1	George Wraith	1
Widdow Culver	1	Widdow Tayler	1

Upper Hardres

Chargeable		Chargeable	
S[i]r Richard Hardres Bart	22	Mr. Christop[her] Hardres	7
William Denn	4	Henry Gray	1
John Silke	2	John West	1
John Whitnall	1	William Muzred	3
William Bingham	1	Henry Marsh	1
George Barrett	1	Richard Burch	2
John Cock	3	William Selbey	3
Thomas Attwood	1	Phillip Ovenden	1
Christop[her] Bell	1	Widdow Giles	1
Thomas Sole	1	Richard Dunn	1
Richard Baker	1	Thomas Shoveller	1
William Fox	2	Edward Mantle	2
Richard Stroud	1	William White	1
Beniamin Coleman	2	John Finn	1
George Hayward	1		

Not chargeable		Not chargeable	
Widdow Hewes	1	Thomas Constable	1
William Hollitt	1	William Adams	1
		Alexander Silke Constable	

The Lower Halfe Hundred of Bridge & Petham

Shipcourt Borough in Waltham

Chargeable		Chargeable	
Mary Court widd[ow]	5	Thomas Court	2
Thomas Fox	1	John Hobdey	1
		John Hobdey Borsholder	

Savintoune Borough

Chargeable		Chargeable	
John Thompson gen[t]	12	John Halke	3
Henry Amis	3	George Coleman	1
Robert White	3	Henry Birch	5
William Burch	4	Richard Ventiman	1
Thomas Ventiman	3	William Parker	5
Valentine Austine	6	Thomas Manger	1
Richard Page	4	George Thompson	4
		Richard Page Borsholder	

Not chargeable		Not chargeable	
Thomas Foreman	1	Whittingham Grigg	1
Robert Browneing	1	Thomas Churchman	1
Thomas Churchman jun[io]r	2	Widdow Sharlock	1
Anthony Ovenden	1	John Marsh	1
William Olfoort	1	William Ham[m]ond	2

Borough of Granaker

Chargeable		Chargeable	
John Tucker	6	Thomas Beacon	4
Thomas Gorham	2	Stephen Hilton	1
John Fox	2	Widdow Gorham	1
William Grigory	3	Stephen Pilcher	1
Widdow White	3	Walter Parke	2
Christop[her] Freind	2	Stephen Mihill	3
Stephen Clarke	2		

Not chargeable		Not chargeable	
Widdow Morris	1	Robert Cooke	1
		Stephen Mihill Borsholder	

Temple Borough

Chargeable		Chargeable	
Augustine Hobdey	2	Samuell Stroud	1
Richard Borthin	2	Richard Chrisan	2
Richard Austen	2	William Cosbie	1
John Johncock	2	Henry Turnly	1
Stephen Howland	1	John Smyth	1
		Richard Austen Borsholder	

Borough of Cotterell

Chargeable			Chargeable	
Mr. Coleman	7		Goodman Ovenden	3
Henry Johncock	1		John Coleman	5
Edward Dodson	1		William Parker in ye }	3
			parsonage house }	
Not chargeable			**Not chargeable**	
[blank] Bayly	1		[blank] Mercer	1
Widdow Spaine	1		John Coleman Borsholder	

Hanvelle Borough

Chargeable			Chargeable	
Stephen Court	3		Richard Patch	3
Mathew Cullen	1		Richard Cooke	1
Richard Dell	2		William Newport	1
[fol. 85v]				
William Fagg	3		Richard Browneing	3
John Browning	1		John Lushington	3
Richard Wisdom	1		Robert Coleman	2
Henry Marsh	3		Robert Keeler	1
Not chargeable			**Not chargeable**	
Thomas Pay	2		George Heaslewood	1
Thomas Friend	2		Thomas Coveney	2
David Hill	1		Henry Marsh Borsholder	

Borough of Broadway

Chargeable			Chargeable	
Thomas Payne	1		John Pilcher	5
Richard Jacob	2		[blank] Burden	1
Widdow Shoveller	2		Widdow Upton	2
John Coleman in }			Mathew Horsfeild	1
an empty house }	1		Goodman Grigory	3
Thomas Page	2		Thomas Stilles	2
In ye vicarage house	3		Goodman Tapley	1
Goodwife Adman	1		John Spayne	3
Not chargeable			**Not chargeable**	
Goodman Foreman	1		William Moore	1
Goodman Ferminger	1		Thomas Bacheler	1
Goodwife Woodburne	1		John Greenstreet	1
Jeremy Steed	1		Christop[her] Johncock	1

Widdow Harfleet	1
Widdow Gizard	1

Henry Rich	1
Goodwife Pashley	1
[blank] Tapley Borsholder	

Stonestreet Borough

Chargeable

Henry Franckling	4
John Ovenden	3
William White	2

Chargeable

Henry Gilbert	4
John Marsh	2

Not chargeable

James Harrison	1

Henry Gilbert Borsholder
William Ham[m]ond
Constable

APPENDIX I

Areas not returned in CKS Assessment

The Lady Day 1664 Assessment does not include the following areas listed below. The bold type denotes the Lathe in which these are located. Many of the 'omitted' areas are to be found in E179/129/746. This assessment of the county of Kent is associated with the hearth tax payments due for the year 1671 but is dated 22 July 1673. The document consists of 143 rotulets and has suffered through damp with the result that some sections are very difficult to read and it may have lost one or two rotulets. Certainly the recent cataloguing appears not to have identified the parishes in the Liberty of Romney Marsh.

When Ellen Lambe, widow and executrix of Samuel Lambe, Receiver of the Hearth tax for the county of Kent, the county of the City of Canterbury and liberty of the Cinque Ports for the year ending Ladyday 1674 submitted her particulars of account she included 90 exemption certificates; E179/129/747.[275] The certificates recorded that the people lived in houses which 'are not of greater value then twenty shillings per annum upon the full improved rent', that they neither used or occupied lands or tenements of their own or others of the yearly value of 20s. per annum, nor had any lands, tenements, goods or chattels of the value of £10 in their own posession or of anyone else in trust for them and that the houses had not above two chimneys, firehearths and stoves. And finally 'by reason of their poverty or smallness of estate are exempted from the usual taxes, payments and contributions towards the church and poor.'[276]

Appendices III and IV provide details of assessments for Tenterden and the City of Canterbury not recorded in the 1664 Quarter Sessions assessment. For Faversham, another Cinque Port, all the available returns have been published.[277]

---

[275] Complete list in Hyde and Harrington, *Faversham Hearth Tax*, pp. 70-71.
[276] ibid. p. 69 illustrates one such certificate for Marden dated 16 September 1674.
[277] ibid. The differences between the quarter sessions copy and the PRO duplicate were shown as footnotes on pages 37-48, but such differences have not been shown in this publication.

Lathe	Reason for not being included at LD 1664.	Some returns that are available. The references should be prefaced by E179/
Sutton at Hone		
Everything included		-
Aylesford		
Chatham & Gillingham small part	Belonged to Cinque Port of Hastings (Sussex)	129/705; 129/746; 129/747; 249/22; 330/14; 330/15.
Scray		
Faversham Town	Cinque Port	All transcribed.[278]
Tenterden Hundred	ditto	129/747; 330/6; 375/21[279]
Shepway		
Worth Hundred	Liberty of Romney Marsh	?[280]
Ham Hundred lower half	ditto	?
Newchurch Hundred lower half	ditto	?
Aloesbridge Hundred lower half	ditto	?
St Martin & Longport Hundred lower half	ditto	?
New Romney and Old Romney	Liberty of the Port of Romney	129/746; 129/747; 262/20; 330/6, 7, 11.
Lydd	Cinque Port	305/11.
Hythe	ditto	129/747; 262/19; 330/6, 11
Folkestone	ditto	129/747; 330/14, 15.

[278] Transcripts in Hyde and Harrington, *Faversham Hearth Tax*.

[279] This assessment is expressly associated with the levy in Kent of the three payments of the hearth tax due at Ladyday 1672, Michaelmas 1672 and Ladyday 1673. It states that it was delivered to the justices and clerk of the peace at the sessions held at Maidstone on 28 April 1674 and presumably this enrolment was made at this time. See also below in Appendix III for transcript of a 1664 return.

[280] Not clear whether the following auditors records contain details of the Liberty of Romney Marsh or merely the hundreds: E179/330/6-8, 14-16, 21; E179/375/8.

St Augustine		
City of Canterbury		129/712; 129/746; 249/21; 249/32; 330/4, 8, 14, 15, 17, 19, 20; 375/11, 42.
Bekesbourne	Belonged to Cinque Port of Hastings	129/746
Fordwich	Cinque Port	129/746; 249/21
Sarre	associated with ditto	129/746; 249/26
Birchington	ditto	129/746
Margate (St John Thanet)	ditto	129/746
Ramsgate (St Lawrence Thanet)	ditto	129/746
Broadstairs (St Peter Thanet)	ditto	129/746
Woodchurch, Ville of Wood, Acol	ditto	None found[281]
Sandwich	Cinque Port	129/746
Stonar	associated with ditto	?
Deal and Walmer	associated with ditto	129/746
Ringwould	ditto	129/747
Dover	Cinque Port	129/747

[281] Possibly included with Birchington.

APPENDIX II

1664 Documents in the PRO

PRO: E179/249/37A

The following list gives the contents of the enrolled return made by the Clerk of the Peace for Kent and returned into the Exchequer. The listing is arranged by hundreds and other administrative units and shows the folio in the Public Record Office return. Where constables' returns for the collection at 1664 Lady Day survive, their reference numbers are given. Where no returns survive, the surviving auditor's abstracts of the 1664 Lady Day assessment and returns [E179/330/6 ff. 36-46] makes it possible to say whether no return was submitted, in which case the note '[nil]' is given, or whether a return was sent in but is now wanting, in which case the note '[wanting]' is given.[282]

The assessments for some places reached the clerk of the peace too late for enrolment in this document and were therefore enrolled in a small supplementary assessment [E179/249/37B], a list of whose contents are given at the end.

folio	**Sutton at Hone Lathe ms 1-21**
1	Blackheath hundred [nil]
9	Little and Lesnes hundred [E179/249/36/8]
10	Codsheath hundred [E179/249/36/2, upper; E179/249/36/3, lower]
12d	Somerden hundred [E179/249/36/6]
14	Westerham and Edenbridge hundred [wanting]
14d	Bromley and Beckenham hundred [nil]
15d	Brasted town [nil]
16	Dartford and Wilmington hundred [E179/249/36/7]
17	Axton hundred [E179/249/36/1, upper only]
19	Ruxley hundred upper [E179/249/36/4]
20	Ruxley hundred lower [E179/249/36/5]

Scray Lathe ms 22-44

---

[282] In 1938 it was discovered that the filing of this document had broken in the past and that several membranes were filed in the wrong order. This wrong order was:-1, 2, or 3, 4, 2 or 3, 5 to 12, 14, 13, 15, 16 to 36, 39, 37, 38, 40 to 49, 51, 50, 53, 52, 54, 55, 57, 56, 58 to 84. On 2 October 1958, Mr C. A. F. Meekings re-filed the membranes, save that there was a justifiable doubt about the sequence of 2 and 3 the true order of which is now shown in the Quarter Sessions copy.

22	Newenden town [nil]
22	Great Barnfield hundred [E179/249/35/1, ff. 1-2]
22d	Rolvenden hundred [E179/249/35/1, m.8]
23	Selbrittenden hundred [E179/249/35/7]
23d	Cranbrook hundred [E179/249/35/1. ff. 17-27]
26	Barkley hundred [E179/249/35/1, m. 5, ff. 6-7]
27	Blackburn hundred [E179/249/35/1, ms. 9-12]
28	Marden hundred [E179/249/35/3]
30	Milton hundred East [E179/129/722]
31	Milton hundred West [nil]
33	Tenham hundred upper [E179/249/35/1, m.4]
33d	Tenham hundred lower [wanting]
34	Faversham hundred upper [wanting]
35	Faversham hundred lower [wanting]
35d	Isle of Sheppey [wanting]
36	Ospringe liberty [E179/249/35/6]
36d	Boughton under Blean hundred upper [E179/249/35/5]
36d	Boughton under Blean hundred lower [E179/129/757]
37	Ashford town [wanting]
38	Chart half hundred [E179/249/35/2]
39	Longbridge half hundred [E179/129/736]
40	Calehill hundred upper [E179/129/732]
41	Calehill hundred lower [E179/129/731]
42	Bircholt barony hundred [E179/249/30]
42	Felborough hundred upper [E179/129/735]
43	Felborough hundred lower [E179/249/35/1, ff. 13-16]
43d	Wye hundred upper [wanting]
44d	Wye hundred lower [nil]

Aylesford Lathe ms 45-66

45	Eyhorne hundred upper [nil]
46d	Eyhorne hundred Lower [E179/249/34/2]
49	Shamwell hundred upper [E179/249/34/12]
49d	Shamwell hundred lower [E179/249/34/13]
51	Twyford hundred [nil]
52d	Littlefield hundred [nil]
53	Brenchley and Horsemonden hundred [nil]
54	Washlingstone hundred [E179/249/34/15, west half only]
55d	Tonbridge Lowry [E179/249/34/14]
56d	Little Barnfield hundred [nil]
57	Wrotham hundred [E179/249/34/16-17, upper half; E179/249/34/18-19 lower half]

58	Larkfield hundred [E179/249/34/4, upper half only]
59d	Hoo hundred upper [E179/249/34/20]
59d	Hoo hundred lower [E179/249/34/21]
60	Aylesford Town [?]
60d	Rugmer Hill borough [?]
60d	Town Malling [nil]
61	Maidstone hundred (omits E. Farleigh & Loose) [E179/249/34/6-8: Barming, Boxley, Detling only]
62	Maidstone town [E179/249/34/9-10]
64	Chatham half hundred [E179/249/34/1]
65	Gillingham half hundred [E179/249/34/3]
66	Toltingtrough hundred upper [nil]

Shepway Lathe ms 67-72

67	Bircholt Franchise [wanting]
67d	Stowting hundred upper [wanting]
67d	Stowting hundred lower [wanting]
68	Loningborough hundred upper [E179/129/734/2, incomplete]
68d	Loningborough hundred lower [wanting]
69	Street hundred upper [wanting]
69d	Street hundred lower [E179/129/734/3]
69d	Oxney hundred [nil]
70	Heane hundred upper [nil]
70d	Heane hundred lower [nil]
70d	Folkestone hundred upper [E179/129/734/1]
71	Folkestone hundred lower [E179/249/42]
71d	Ham hundred upper [nil]
72	St Martin Longport hundred upper [nil]
72	Newchurch hundred upper [nil]
72	Aloesbridge hundred upper [nil]
	[NB There are no assessments for the lower half hundreds of Aloesbridge, Ham, and Newchurch nor for Worth hundred and no returns]

St Augustine's lathe ms 73-83

73	Bleangate hundred upper [E179/249/33/2]
73d	Bleangate hundred lower [E179/249/33/3]
74d	Whitstable hundred upper [nil]
75	Whitstable hundred lower [nil]
75	Seasalter borough [nil]
75	Westgate hundred [nil]
76d	Longport borough [nil]

77	Downhamford hundred upper [E179/249/33/6]
77d	Downhamford hundred lower [E179/249/33/7]
78	Wingham hundred upper [nil]
78d	Wingham hundred lower [nil]
79	Preston hundred [wanting]
79	Ringslow hundred [E179/249/33/10, upper only]
80	Cornilo hundred upper [wanting]
80d	Cornilo hundred lower [wanting]
80d	Eastry hundred upper [nil]
81d	Eastry hundred lower [E179/249/33/8]
82	Kinghamford hundred [E179/249/33/9, lower only]
82d	Bewsborough hundred lower [E179/249/33/1]
83d	Bridge and Petham hundred upper [E179/249/33/4]
84	Bridge and Petham hundred lower [E179/249/33/5]

E179/E179/249/37B

1	Rochester city [E179/249/34/11]
4	East Farleigh and Loose (Maidstone hundred) [E179/249/34/5]
5	Toltingtrough hundred lower [E179/249/35/1, ff13-16]
7	Queenborough [E179/249/35/1]

APPENDIX III

The Tenterden Returns

CKS:Te/JQad6

[fol. 1]

Towne and hundred of Tenterden in the county of Kent

These severall papers doe containe an accompt of the severall and respective firehearths in the severall boroughs within the towne and hundred of Tenterden aforesaid as they were taken upon the view of the severall borsholders of the respective boroughs within the said towne and hundred and by them delivered unto me upon their respective oaths and under their respective hands {in pursuance of the late Act of Parliament in that behalfe made} for the halfe yeare ending att Lady Day 1664.

Att Lady day one thousand six hundred sixty fower {videlicet}

Persons names and numbers of hearths chargeable by the said Act etc.		Persons names and numbers of hearths not chargeable by the said Act etc.	
The persons chargeable	The hearths [283]	The persons ~~not~~ ~~chargeable~~ hereafter named for one halfe yeare ended at Lady Day 1664 are exempted by reason of their poverty from the usuall taxes to church and poore and are not worth five pounds and soe not chargeable by the Act etc.	The hearths
Towne Borough		Thomas Goodgrome	2
Mr George Wightwick	23	John Cullenbine void	1
Mr William Stretton	8	John Barham	1
Richard Kyte junior	4	Hugh Gilbert	1
Joseph Clements	2	Widdow Robbinson	2
Giles Yeates	2	Widdow Dence	1
John Reader	2	Thomas Siggens	2
Samuel Reader	1	Widdow Evernden	4
John Church	4	Peter Kadwell	1

---

[283] These were spelt out but have been changed to arabic numerals.

John Bimskin	2	William Sharpe	2
Anthony Knowlden	2	Richard Ball	1
Daniel Dunck	3	Edward Osmer	2
John Caffinch	2	Thomas Wattle	2
Widdow Huckstepp	1	John Bunce	2
Thomas Searles	2	John Harpe	2
Mrs King widdow	2	Widdow Bennett	2
Roger Head	10	Richard Rolfe	4
John Adanes	4	Thomas Humfrey	2
Mrs Tilden widdow	2	Richard Voutrell void	2
Mathew Greenland	8	John Markettman	4
Mrs Butler widdow	4	Samuell Beeching	2
Mr Bodle	7	Richard Burdon	5
Robert Brooke	2		47
	97		

[fol. 2]

Stephen Brattle	6	John Tarre an almeshouse	4
George Meede	1	Thomas Gillom	3
		John ?Chaser interlined	2
James Meede	5	Mary Bradfoote	1
William Furby	2	Thomas Hayward	1
Mrs Mary Sharpe widdow	4	William Gunn	1
John Cumber	6	Edward Barnes	2
John Johnson	2	Widdow Butler	1
Mrs Emyott widdow	3	John Grigsby	1
Paul Holmes	2	John Honey	2
Thomas Bunce	1	Richard Barrett	2
Thomas Caister	3	Samuel Fuller	2
John Vallence	2	Widdow Hofer	4
Mr William Curties	6	Thomas Hills	2
Mr Robert Tighe	4	Richard Barrow	1
Francis Vause	2	Mathew Greenland void	1
Mr William Aldcroft	6	John Drew	2
Robert Austen	2	Where John Grigsby did lately live	2
Mr Edward Curties	6		
Richard Kyte	10	Samuell Fuller	2
John Huckstepp	3	Widdow Russell void	2
Thomas Witherden	4		36
John Jeffry	2		
Richard Weekes	2		
Captaine John Plum[m]er	7		

William Dunck	3
George Girdler	4
Mr Edward Shorte	13
Richard Russell	6
William Cloake	2
William Muggredge	3
	122

[fol. 3]

Castweasle Borough

Mr Nathaniell Collington viccar	3	John Daw	2
Richard Beeching	2	Jane Tulley	2
Thomas Page	2	Elizabeth Ball	1
John Vaughan	1	Anne Hendy widdow	1
John Wheeler	2	Susan Humfrey	1
Samuell Tilden	1	John Woodgate	2
Henry Girdler	4	Nehemiah Ockenfold	2
William Ockenden	5	Thomas Smalwood	3
John Woodcock	2	Thomas Thorpe	1
James Skeetes	4	Abraham Best	1
William Shorte gent	7	Thomas Kyte	2
William Strange	1	Anne Knowles widdowe	1
Sir John Maynard	4	Thomas Huckstepp	1
Paul Holmes	4	Anne White widdow	1
Thomas Harding	2	Lidia Newman widdow	1
Jervice Wide	2	John Scamberlaine	1
Thomas Weller	2	Thomas George	1
John Cruttall	1	Edward George	1
Thomas Berridge	2	Margarett Jenning widdow	1
Elizabeth Osmer widd[ow]	1	Margarett Bills widdow	1
Robert Tilby	5	John Denham	1
Robert Cruttall	2	Reynold Sampson	1
Edmund Ismunger	3	John Hopper	1
Thomas Wingfield	2	Stephen Evernden	1
John Young	2	Edward Bills	4
Richard Russell	1	Elizabeth Pattiso widdow	1
Lawrence Judd	1		36
	68		

[fol. 4]

Boresyle Borough

Thomas Stace juratt	7	Widdow Seath	1
Arthur Honey	2	Widdow Kencham	1
Mr Drayton	8	Thomas Tilden	1
Samuell Kyte	7	Thomas Cleeve	1
William Goatly	2	Thomas Knight	1
Mr Horner	7	Widdow Trowell	1
Edward Yonge	2	Edward Chittocke	1
Thomas Huckstepp juratt	4	Thomas Byshopp	1
Mr William Furby	7	Jervice Sparke	1
Thomas Iggulden	2	Widdow Hooke	1
Henry Beeching	4	Nicholas Stephenson	1
Thomas Harris	1	John Holman	1
Robert Pope juratt	4	Leonard Stephenson	1
Mrs Anne Curteis widdow	8	Widdow Lott	1
Elizabeth Birchly widdow	2	Widdow Kyte	1
John Edwards juratt	10	Widdow Jervice	1
Henry Ginnings	2	William Trowell	1
John Barber	4	William Drewe	1
Mr Codds house	3	John Homan	1
Richard Ramsden	3	Richard Gabriell	1
John Upton	1	John Sutherden	1
James Chittenden	2	John Smith	1
Augustine Rayner	1	Thomas Thorpe	1
Jeremy Dunsteere	1	Mathew Pelham	1
Thomas Ramsden	4	Samuel Whibly	1
Thomas Haffenden	5	Francis Cheesman	1
John Bridge	3	Francis Wenn	1
	106	Widdow Smith	1
		Widdow Williams where she dwelt	2
		Widdow Haffenden	2
		Richard Gabriell	1
			33

[fol. 5]

Richard Haffenden	3	Thomas Grinstead	1
Widdow Gilbert	1	Widdow Gabriell	1
William Gilbert	3	John Parris	1
Robert Goodall	2	Widdow Gibbons	1
Jervice Wide	2	Widdow Woodnott	4
John Winder	4	George Atkins	2
Stephen Neate	2	Walter Judin	2

James Cheesman	4	Richard Knight	2
	21	William May	2
		Widdow Williams	2
		John Cleeve	1

Hearths in that Borough pulled up, *videlicet*

		Arthur Honey	1
		Henry Ginings	2
		John Upton	1
		James Chittenden	1
		Widdow Gilbert	2
		Jervice Wide	2
			~~27~~

Shrubcoate Borough

Edward Finch Esq	17	The house late inhabited
William Silcocke	8	by Robert Candy being
Widdow Bodle	5	empty and noe distresse
Mrs Curteis widdow	8	etc	8
John Stonnard	1		35
Mr George Tilden	5
John Tamkin	3
Edward Croyden	3
John Boarne	4
Thomas Gilbert	3
Stephen Huckstepp	5
	83

[fol. 6]

Thomas Smith	4
Richard Hickmott	2
Thomas Wright	1
James Jervice	4
Widdow Elmestone	4
William Berry	2
Robert Wickens	2
Edward Maisters	4

Dumborne Borough

William Pattison	4	William Staple	2
Walter Woodgate	3	Joseph Phillpott	2
John Kyte	2	James Kenward	3
Edward Philcoate	2	John Bredge	2

William Huckstepp	4	Richard Austen	1
Robert Franklin	5	John Drewe	2
Robert Harding	3	Richard Brett	2
Thomas Kennard	2	Richard Scamberlaine	2
John Baseden	2	John Farme	3
Francis Lingard	4	Richard Fowle	2
Humfry Woodland	2	Richard Lynsey	2
William Goodall	4	Stephen Austeed	3
Widdow Birchett	4	Jeremy Hunt	2
William Hobbs	2	Widdow Philcoat	1
Henry Ginner	2	Robert Pike	2
Robert Worly	1		31
John Philcoate	1		
Edward Wraith	4		
Richard Farmer	2		
John Gateland	1		
	77		

Reading Borough

Walter Pemble	5	Thomas Pratt	3
Thomas Ollive	4	William Gurre	2
Simon Drayner	5	Goody Haffenden	2
Henry Pemble	4	Widdow Methurst	2
Edward Long	3	Widdow Marten	2
	21	Richard Kyte	1
			12

Robert Stace maior		Totall for the half yeare	230
John Caffinch			
churchwarden			
Firehearths chargable	574		
Totall [284]			

---

[284] Taken from JQad9ar.

APPENDIX IV

Canterbury City and County Assessment

PRO: E179/249/32
[fol. 1r.]
An account of the chimneys in the severall houses within the præcinct of
Christschurch Canterbury.   Michaelmas 1663.

Mr Deane	26	Mris Sabyn	4
Mris Drayton	4	Mr Jordan	4
Mris Nichols	6	Mris Kingsley	10
Mris Parker	7	Dr Nichols	4
Dr du Moulin	7	Ri[chard] Harrison	3
Mr Ro[bert] Sprakeling	8	W[illia]m Davis	2
Mr Carter	3	Ch[ristophe]r Stonehouse	2
Dr Casaubon	11	Hen[ry] Harrison	2
Mris Engham	4	Will[ia]m Nayr	2
Mr Cuckoe	7	Fra[ncis] Conder	2
Mr Culling	5	Jonath[an] Best	5
Mr Vincent	2	Mr Edgford	3
Mr Paris	6	Ro[bert] Cumberland	2
Dan[iel] Chilton &	4	Andr[ew] Ware	2
Pet[er] Frampton		Ro[bert] Kirk & Jo[hn] Ward	2
Dr Hardres	11	Mris Boteler	6
Mr Peake	15	Tho[mas] Bamfield	4
Mr Spaine	10	Mris Turner	9
William Pising	3	W[illia]m Plomer	5
The house where the organ is	2	Elianor Cook	2
making		----	
Dr Barker	11	Mr Baker due at Lady day	5
Mr Langham	4		344
Mr Gibbs	3	Mr Baker removed about	
Mris Fellow	3	Lady day, refused then to pay	
Mr W[illia]m Somner	7	and left nothing to be	
Dr Castillion	9	distreyned, but I have lately	
Dr Gunning	9	received of him for that half	
Dr Aucher	11	yeer 5s	
Dr Bargrave	12	B[isho]p Burnet had 3	
Mr Aldey	14	chimneys, but removed his	
Mr Butcher	10	family about Michaelmas last,	
Dr Belke	10	and noe distress was to be	
Mr Fotherby	14	found	
Mr Reading	6	So[mme] 17£-4s-0d	
		William Belke treasurer	

[fol. 1v, 2r & 2v is blank] except 'Canterbury Cathedrall Mich[aelmas] 1663'
The following are written in a neat hand but carry no dates. Meekings says,

"This served as the charge not for Michaelmas 1663 but only for Lady Day 1664 but although prepared under the second hearth tax revising Act it includes only those chargeable." [285] The scribe has started writing on the left hand column and then filled that on the right and then on the next page continued on the left. To avoid any confusion the data has been re-arranged.

[fol. 3r.]
NORTHGATE WARDE The Cittie of Canterbury The names of all the owners and occupiers of houses within the ward of Northgate of the same citty with the number of their respective hearths and stoves delivered by the constable of the said ward according to a warrant to him in that behalf directed from his majesties justices of the peace of the said city at the generall quarter sessions of the peace and goale delivery of our soveraigne Lord the King holden in the Guildhall of the said citty upon Tuesday the first day of October in the fifteenth yeare of the raigne of our soveraigne Lord Charles the second now King of England &c. being the first quarter sessions of the peace holden in and for the county of the said city next after the feast of St Michaell the Archangell in the yeare aforesaid in pursuance of an act of parliament intituled an additional act for the better ordering and collecting the revenue ariseing by hearth money.

In the parish of St Alphage	[28]	Samuell Fremo	1
Mr John Somner	6	William Browning	3
Thomas Ockman alderman	4	John Marcee	4
Mr Richard Foster	4	Michaell Morall	1
Nicholas Oxenbridge	3	Samuell Sacke	4
Richard Peirson	4	William Mesman	1
John Halsnod	3	John Cove	2
Joseph Phillipps	11	James Lessee	4
Richard Ginder	2	John Mannake	6
John Denn	2	John Macaree	1
John Godfrey gent	9	Michaell Pettit	1
Robert Munday	3	Samuel Ferree baker	1
Jeremy Rumfield	2	Nicholas Desane	1
Alice Archard	2	Richard Drayton	1
Anne Coutchman	9	Elizabeth Nicholls	1

[285] *List & Index Society*, vol. 54 (1970), p. 206.
[286] This column and others are headed hearths. There is another column marked stoves but since there are no entries in this it has been omitted to save space. The figures are written out but have been converted to arabic numbers.

Lawrence Rooke gent	10	Daniell Rigsbey	3
John Moore gent	7	Jeremy Gay gent	6
John Carby	1	Margarett Crayford widd	5
John Canderlier	1	Katherine Robertes	4
Thomas Abbott	6	Peter Hayman	7
Abraham Wantier	3	Elizabeth Platt	2
William Marrable	2	Peter Delapier	10
Elizabeth Young	2	Peter Visage	2
Thomas Barham	6	Samuell Denew	1
Anthony Denis	8	Peter Le Hooke	2
John Bix	3	Phillip Lepere	2
Thomas Barnsdell	3	Gideon Despaine	7
John Morton	5	James Le Noble	1
James Wills	4	Anthony Millone	2
Jane Gumbere	2	John Wybare	1
Margaret Hawkins	2	William Birchin	1
John Ockley	3	Nathanaell Jovenew	2
William Gill	5	John Perley	1
Ambrose Goatley	2	John Burgoe	3
Robert Spillett	1	Peter Delabew	4
John Vanren	2	John Lessee	2
Robert Titterton	2	Dunstan Higgens	4
Edward Lecahe	4	William Browne	4
Daniell Morlow	1	William Facone	7
Elizabeth Mann widd	2	Thomas Best	3
Elizabeth Hinde widd	6	John Oudarte	5
Sanford Branker	6	Richard Gray	3
Susan Le Paine	8	Abraham Didier	8
Alexander Usborne	6	John Farran	2
John Musred	7		157

[fol. 3r & 3v]

In the parish of the Blessed Mary of Northgate

Anne Fowler	4	William Denn	2
Peter Waite	8	Edward Lekeux	3
John Bird	4	Abraham Cassell	3
Henry Spicer	6	Margarett Tall	2
John Edwardes	4	John Webber	2
William Terry	2	William Oxburrough	3
Edward Hales	2	John Legash	3
William Ferrer	2	John Denew	2
William Crippen	2	George Woster	3
Thomas Goldsmith	3	William Newland	3

James Gilmore	5	James Miller	2
Thomas Crippen senr	4	James Roda	2
John Giles	6	Isaac Poter	2
William Crippen senr	2	Bartholomew Rossee	3
Edward Hollenden	2	Henry Howseere	2
Richard Mascall	5	William Fromon	2
Nicholas Fowle	3	Anthony Rosgere	2
Richard Hart	2	Robert Cockett	3
Nicholas Waters	2	Isaac Provas	5
Edward Burges	2	Francis Mose	2
John Gill	3	Phillip Detree	2
Abraham Jeffery	5	Peter Fenne	1
Paul Gilmore	4	James Browne	2
John Clarke	2	John Courton	4
Jeremy Paine	1	Peter Wood	1
Thomas Browne	1	John Mershew	3
John Ledger	4	Peter Deborbene	1
Thomas Lotter	1	Abraham Cottew	2
John Crippen	2	John Rosee	2
Michaell Hawkes	2	Jacob Wood	2
Thomas Wilkes	4		37 +133

[fol. 3v & fol. 4r]
BURGATE WARDE The Cittie of Canterbury The names of all the owners and occupiers of houses within the ward of Burgate of the same citty with the number of their respective hearths and stoves delivered by the constable of the said ward according to a warrant to him in that behalf directed from his majesties justices of the peace of the said citty at the generall quarter sessions of the peace and goale delivery of our soveraigne Lord the King holden in the Guildhall of the said citty upon Tuesday the first day of October in the fifteenth yeare of the raigne of our soveraigne Lord Charles the second now King of England &c. being the first quarter sessions of the peace holden in and for the county of the said city next after the feast of St Michaell the Archangell in the yeare aforesaid in pursuance of an act of parliament intituled an additional act for the better ordering and collecting the revenue ariseing by hearth money.

John Newman	2	John Walker	1
John Spencer	2	Thomas Chandler	1
Thomas Swaffer	4	William Sanders	1
James Cheever	2	Richard Harrison	1

John Tresser	6	Thomas Burnley	1
Richard Pysing junr	2	John Lunn	1
John Lewkner	2	John Shipton	2
Peter Johnson junr	2	Elizabeth Allen widd	2
John Kingsford	2	Thomas Jenkin	5
Edmund Chambers	4	John Pilkenton	1
Henry Hales	2	Henry Rogers	2
Jeremy Smith	2	John Hampton	2
Thomas Endfield	3	Joseph Colfe	3
Roger Newman	3	Walter Grant	4
William Turner	6	Thomas Nicholls	1
William Beane	3	James Halsnod	4
[blank] Heines	2	Jarman Little	1
Thomas Hamage	3	George Vandepiere	1
Samuell Coller	1	Edward Barrett	1
John Richardson	2	Edward Justice	3
Zachary Lee	5	John Skillett	2
Nicholas Johnson	2	John Studdam	2
Thomas Kingsford	2	Edward Betts	2
John Garland	2	Symon Oldfeild	2
John Ladd	2	Francis Collins	3
Thomas Fidge alderman	6	Henry Wigmore	2
Thomas Harris	3	John Flatman	2
Samuell Chandler	1	Peter Annott	3
Thomas Knowler	3	Richard Hornsbey	3
Daniell Ellis	2	Elizabeth Covett	2
Thomas Oxenbridge	2	Anthony Coale	2
Nathanaell Ladd	3	Isaac Churcher	3
Nicholas Williams	2	William Brome	2
James Hunt	1	James Bix	6
William Radley	1	Margarett Knott widd	4
Christopher Shrubsole	2	Elizabeth Reeve widd	5
William Allen	1	Margarett Thompson widd	7
Thomas Archley	1	Mary Stredwicke widd	2
Thomas Powell	1	Ursula Peirce widd	4
James Lilliard	2	Thomas Pollard	2
Thomas Chambers	3	Thomas Whitfield	2
Joshua Knight	2	John Johncock	3
John Whittingham	2	Mary[287] Giles widd	3
Peter Rogee	2	Richard Pembrooke	1
Gilbert Leparr	1	Bartholomew Bewshee	3

[287] Written over an erasure.

Richard Lovell	1	Richard Hudson	2
Matthew Slaughter	1	Thomas Galliard	2
Richard Kennard	3	Nicholas Fowle	2
Richard Finn	2	Dame Jane Roberts	9
John Durant	4	Edward Bullocke	2
William Reynolls	5	Symon Bodree	2
Edward Vann	2	Francis Bannicke	3
Sir Edward Master knight	9	John Pettman	2
Henry Roberts	2	97 + 141 + 36	
Richard Pisinge the elder	2		

[fol. 4r]
BURROUGH OF SAINT MARTINE The Cittie of Canterbury The names of all the owners and occupiers of houses within the Burrough of St Martine of the same citty with the number of their respective hearths and stoves delivered by the constable of the said ward according to a warrant to him in that behalf directed from his majesties justices of the peace of the said citty at the generall quarter sessions of the peace and goale delivery of our soveraigne Lord the King holden in the Guildhall of the said citty upon Tuesday the first day of October in the fifteenth yeare of the raigne of our soveraigne Lord Charles the second now King of England &c. being the first quarter sessions of the peace holden in and for the county of the said city next after the feast of St Michaell the Archangell in the yeare aforesaid in pursuance of an act of parliament intituled an additional act for the better ordering and collecting the revenue ariseing by hearth money.

The Right Hon[ora]ble Lady }		Clement Fisher	3
Mabella Finch }	23	John Knell	1
The Lady Ann Palmer	11	Thomas Simpson the elder	2
George Bingham gent	7	Thomas Hasell	2
John Baker gent	6	Thomas Outlaw	1
William Holnes	3	John Finch	2
James Knell	2	Thomas Cobb	2
John Burton	4	Robert Bewsted	1
Thomas Simpson the younger	2		72

[fol. 4r, fol. 4v & fol. 5r]
NEWINGATE WARDE The Cittie of Canterbury The names of all the owners and occupiers of houses within the Ward of Newingate of the same citty with the number of their respective hearths and stoves delivered by the constable of the said ward according to a warrant to him in that behalf directed from his majesties justices of the peace of

the said citty at the generall quarter sessions of the peace and goale delivery of our soveraigne Lord the King holden in the Guildhall of the said citty upon Tuesday the first day of October in the fifteenth yeare of the raigne of our soveraigne Lord Charles the second now King of England &c. being the first quarter sessions of the peace holden in and for the county of the said city next after the feast of St Michaell the Archangell in the yeare aforesaid in pursuance of an act of parliament intituled an additional act for the better ordering and collecting the revenue ariseing by hearth money.

[blank] Tayler clerke	6	Edward Master Esq	5
James Casle	2	John Jacob	5
John Lervew	2	Peter Delapier Doctor in	5
John Tippin	2	Physicke	
Peter Cassele	2	Anne Abbott widd	6
Liddia Robus widd	1	William Jeffery	2
John Crane gent	10	Daniell Wakeley	3
Cleare Carr widd	8	Edward Hirst gent	7
Nicholas Rufford	2	Thomas Turner Esq[ui]re	9
Thomas Burden	3	George Church	5
Elizabeth Harvey widd	4	Lancelott Ladd gent	4
William Gibbon	2	Richard Fowle	2
William Kitchell gent	5	John Whitfield gent	6
Deborah Fidge	3	Elizabeth Moore widd	5
Edward Dale	2	Vincent Denne Esq[uir]re	9
Ralph Alstone	5	Thomas Dunkin	6
John Hawkes	8	Susan Marshall widd	5
Thomas Read	2	Francis Inward	2
Peter Marshman	2	Marke Nicholls	2
Elias Young	4	James Church	2
Henry Rogers	2	Mary Denne widd	1
John Rawlins	2	Richard Bemester	5
Titus Rufford	2	John Chilman	5
John Ward	4	Mary Tassell widd	6
Edward Landman	6	John Parkinson	2
Robert Fidge	2	Arno Delilier	1
Thomas Abbott	2	Robert Mills	2
John Duboys	6	Mary Beeson widd	2
Edward Crayford gent	5	Stephen Strong	6
Thomas Bate	4	John James	1
Joane Cobb widd	4	John Felton	1
Nicholas Burges Alderman	20	John Stone	3
Thomas Lunn	4	William Hudman	1

Francis Maplisden alderman	7	William Buckhurst sen[io]r	3
Thomas Everden	2	William Buckhurst jun[io]r	1
Thomas Simpson	3	Joseph Tangett	7
Samuell Kennon	1	John Spicer	3
William Gilbert	4	Thomas Williams	4
Daniell Ellis	1	James Chittenden	3
Mary Barrett widd	3	Robert Baldwin	3
John Garrett	2	John Bridges	4
Walter Maplisden	5	James Crumpe	2
Jonathan Stiles	3	Samuell Williams	5
John Milner	2	Jane Tayler widd	4
Israell Jacob	10	Nicholas Dilnutt	5
Thomas Oughton	6	Rest Fenner	2
Randolph Ludd	3	Edward Bullocke	1
George Mills alderman	9	Thomas Denne	2
Avory Hills alderman	6	William Doleman	2
William Allen	2	Stephen Dale	12
John Cheever	3	Thomas Mayne	5
Vincent Nethersole	6	Thomas Hardres Esq[ui]re	16
William Welton	6	John Berrey	8
Richard Howland	1	Richard May gent	7
Anthony Cooley	13	Francis Collins	2
James Duthoite	5	Deborah Randolph	7
John Drayton	4	Peter Pyard	6
Samuell Despaine	5	John Dickenson	6
Thomas Kidder	5	Richard Ginder	7
Thomas Jennings	4	Katherine Jackmaine widd	1
Jonathan Dunkin	5	William Kingsley Esq[ui]re	8
Peter Boraine	7	Henry Gibbs gent	4
Richard Bucke	1	Elizabeth Bryan widd	4
George Younge	7	Stephen Edmunds	4
John Parkhurst	2	Anne Coppin widd	5
Robert Knowles	2	Thomas Young	2

261 + 244 + 59

[fol. 5r]

RIDINGATE WARDE The Cittie of Canterbury The names of all the owners and occupiers of houses within the ward of Ridingate of the same citty with the number of their respective hearths and stoves delivered by the constable of the said ward according to a warrant to him in that behalf directed from his majesties justices of the peace of the said citty at the generall quarter sessions of the peace and goale delivery of our soveraigne Lord the King holden in the Guildhall of the said citty upon Tuesday the first day of October in the fifteenth yeare of the raigne of our soveraigne Lord Charles the second now King of England &c. being the first quarter sessions of the peace holden in and for the county of the said city next after the feast of St Michaell the Archangell in the yeare aforesaid in pursuance of an act of parliament intituled an additional act for the better ordering and collecting the revenue ariseing by hearth money.

Sir William Man knight	20	Elizabeth Pettitt	6
Sir James Hales knight	18	William Wall	2
John Nutt Esq[ui]re	12	Robert Hudson	2
John Bettenham gent	6	Thomas Everden	5
William Lovelace clerke	2	Andrew Fanting	2
John Toker	4	Thomas Francis	3
Matthew Peake	11	Edward Rolph	2
Vespatian Harris	4	William Tayler	2
Thomas Young	4	Katherine Joyce widd	4
Richard Mount	5	Walter Sabin	7
Thomas Bunce	5	Francis Plomer	5
Margarett Decoates widd	2	William Sandford	6
Christopher Beechin	2	John Plomer	3
Thomas Wraight	5	Katherine Bankes widd	4
Edward Gibbon	2	Samuell Bucke	3
		131 + 32	

[fol. 5r & fol. 5v]
WORGATE WARDE The Cittie of Canterbury The names of all the owners and occupiers of houses within the ward of Worgate of the same citty with the number of their respective hearths and stoves delivered by the constable of the said ward according to a warrant to him in that behalf directed from his majesties justices of the peace of the said citty at the generall quarter sessions of the peace and goale delivery of our soveraigne Lord the King holden in the Guildhall of the said citty upon Tuesday the first day of October in the fifteenth yeare of the raigne of our soveraigne Lord Charles the second now King of England &c. being the first quarter sessions of the peace holden in and for the county of the said city next after the feast of St Michaell the Archangell in the yeare aforesaid in pursuance of an act of parliament intituled an additional act for the better ordering and collecting the revenue ariseing by hearth money.

William Smith	6	*[blank]* Harrison widd	5

Thomas Mockett	2	John Roberts Esq[ui]re	10
James Wood	2	John Rawling	4
Bartholomew Hart	2	Roger Broadnax	3
Richard Duke	4	Paul Hubberd	4
Robert Beake gent	8	Paul Wiggens	4
Thomas Francke	4	Thomas Shindler gent	6
John Dunkin	4	Mary Terry widd	4
Afra Stredwicke	3	William Elvery	6
Lawrance Read	4	Joseph Ewell	2
John Goldhatch	3	Stephen Page	2
Henry Chapman	4	John Munn	3
Thomas Bayly	2	Mary Barham widd	9
Henry Wiggens	2	Harbart Randolph gent	10
Bennett Tapley widd	5	Giles Watmer gent	7
Phillip Warrener	2	Thomas Everden	4
George Kenn	1	Edward Dunn	2
William Lissenden	3	Martin Hirst gent	8
Nicholas Stredwicke	3	Anne Richardson widd	6
Thomas Coveney gent	4	John Dodd	4
John Batchellor	4	Ralph Addams	4
Hayday Addams	6	John Strout gent	9
John Wickham jun[io]r	2	John Best Esq[ui]re	10
George Elsey	2	Edward Andrewes alderman	6
Thomas Mugwell	5	Walter Wilford gent	8
Thomas Bligh	7	Thomas Violett	5
John Hubberd	3	Nicholas Knight gent	10
John Twyman	2	Daniell Richardson	10
William Jones	3	Michaell Allen	6
Richard Steed	1	John Fry gent	10
Margarett Phinis widd	4	Robert Hughes	3
Henry Jenkin gent	5	Henry Oxenbridge	1
Thomas Worwell	2	Richard Lukin gent	8
James Alexander widd	6	Edward Elvy gent	7
Walter Mond	5	Elizabeth Cooper widd	6
John Hawkes	6	William Prichard	1
Thomas Tucke	5	Francis Lovelace recorder	10
John Foad	5	Francis Calver	10
Nich[ol]as de Farvaques	6	Rebecca Scott widd	3
John Shoulder	4	William Laurance	3
John Meere	4	William Noble	1
Paul de Farvaques	5	Thomas Burwash	5
Daniell de Farvaques	1	William Rawlinge	4

James Lekeux	3	Thomas Borne	3
James See	6	Richard Hards	4
John See	6	George Beecham	6
Abraham See	3	Robert Knocke	2
John Bount	3	Richard Goldsbury	2
John Codrane	2	John Fagg	2
Peter Shoulder	2	Thomas Elwyn gent	6
Peter Lessee	4	Richard Burney clerke	6
Henry Mockery	2	Richard Marshall	2
John Shoulder	7	Thomas Foster	6
Martin Rove	4	William Stanley mayor	7
John Molier	4	George Stanley gent	9
Samuell Coney	2	Henry Joy	2
John Roo	2	Thomas Spaine	2
Timothy Bame	1	Paul Country gent	5
Abraham Sneller	2	John Scrimshaw	3
Abraham Deswarte	2	Clement Hedgcock	2
John Quaile	1	George Young	4
David Shoulder widd	4	Abraham Clarke	2
William Noble	3	Nicholas Stantaine	6
Phillip Le Arnold	3	Mary Cornar	4
Simon Dupier	2	Anthony Pattoo	2
Mary Lamb widd	2	Peter Meshee	2
James Cassle		Bartholomew Johncocke	1
James Horsfeild	4	120 + 315 +142	
John Nevell	2		

[fol. 6r]
WESTGATE WARDE The Cittie of Canterbury The names of all the owners and occupiers of houses within the ward of Westgate of the same citty with the number of their respective hearths and stoves delivered by the constable of the said ward according to a warrant to him in that behalf directed from his majesties justices of the peace of the said citty at the generall quarter sessions of the peace and goale delivery of our soveraigne Lord the King holden in the Guildhall of the said citty upon Tuesday the first day of October in the fifteenth yeare of the raigne of our soveraigne Lord Charles the second now King of England &c. being the first quarter sessions of the peace holden in and for the county of the said city next after the feast of St Michaell the Archangell in the yeare aforesaid in pursuance of an act of parliament intituled an additional act for the better ordering and collecting the revenue ariseing by hearth money.

In the parish of Saint Andrew

John Crux alderman	4	John Barrett	6
William Wood	3	Leonard Ashenden	2
Thomas Field	12	Matthew Woodfall	1
Thomas Andrewes	2	Richard Munings gent	1
John Nutt	2		32 [288]

In the parish of Saint Mary Bredman

John Simpson alderman	5	Robert Page	8
Edward Fray	6	James Packten	3
Laurence Holeman	10	William Nuttbrowne	2
Nathanaell Sackett gent	7	Edward Johnson	2
Robert Gilbert	7	Henry Landman	5
Michaell Kite	8	Miller Barles	6
Henry Knight gent	13	John Fowle	5
Peter Evans gent	8	Richard Hogben	1
Paul Barrett Esq[ui]re	9		
Richard Iddenden	10		123
John Sawkins	5		
John Bellenger	3		

In the parish of All Saints

John Peeke	12	John Gilmore	2
George Wright	1	John Lee	5
James Fowler	6	Richard Hawkes	4
Ralph Jenkenson	11	Christopher Vaudan	2
Matthias Gray	5	James Lefroy	4
William Tayler	3	John Gillam	2
Richard Foord	7	Thomas Dixon	3
Samuel Bright	5	John Loft	2
Edward Whetstone	14	Thomasine Hills	3
Thomas Atwell	4	Peter Sedt	4
John Wrenn	4	Nicholas Ferry	2
Thomas Parker	7	Phillip Barte	2
Michaell Terry gent	6	Joseph Crow	3
William Looke	2	Francis Butteris	4
John George	3	Lewis Tibergen	2
John Hearne	2	Thomas Halsnod	2
Richard Sharpe	4	James Deringe	5
Peter Deway	4	James Mott	2

[288] Actual total 33.

James Cornewell	1	Leonard Sprackling gent	5
Stephen Besewer	4		163

[fol. 6r & fol. 6v]
In the parish of Saint Peter

John Bissett	2	John Lott	4
Thomas Richardson	2	Ambrose Sturgis	2
William Richardson	2	Henry Groves	6
George Ladd	2	Peter Cornwell	2
Simon Hatt	3	John Camber	12
John Tangett	2	John Barton	3
Robert Sutton gent	4	Robert Churcher	2
Jarvis Willmott	2	Julian Deray	2
Robert Dale	5	John Clarke	5
James Parker	2	Lester Cordelier	1
Thomas Gorham	4	John Saunders	5
Peter Le Hooke	3	John Dehamell	3
Abraham Le Hooke	1	Andrew Potto	2
Stephen Deloe	/ 5	Cornelius Sacke	2
William Gearey	2	Stephen Ladd	3
William Baldocke	2	Henry Fowler	4
Henry Carpenter	5	Jerman Claris	2
Edward Parker	3	Peter St John	2
Moses Hasted	2	James Dering	2
Henry Joanes	5	Nathaniell Riqueburow	7
John Peerce	5	Henry Cox	1
William King	4	Richard Smith	4
Anthony Moree	3	John Le Hooke	2
Arthur Tayler	2	Jacob Demow	2
Thomas Baker	3	Thomas Spragg	4
Peter Breach	3	Jacob Sacke	3
Jonas Tuckwell	4	James Provo	2
Valentine Seare	2	James Le Rosh	3
James Marrable	2	Robert Fuller	3
Jaspar Forsea	1	John Bing	3
Francis Mutton	4	James Mannake	4
John Le Roy	2	Denis Jesten	2
Thomas Leitchfield	2	John Loshare	2
		Peter Loshare	2
			82 + 121

[fol. 6v]
In the parish of Holy Crosse Westgate

Squire Beverton jun[io]r	4
George Jenings	4
Abraham Goldsburrow	2
William Pembrey	1
Roger Peale	2
David Mollier	2
Isaac Puthoo	4
Nicholas St John	2
Thomas Roberts	7
Peter Deloe	4
Jonas Deering	2
	34

Libertam per manu et super sacrum Daniel Chilton de ci[vita]te Cantuar[iensis]

Recipienti xij die Februarij anno regni regis Caroli secundi xvj^{to}
[12 February 1664]

schedula arreragia in compotum John Barrett per festum Annunciatio 1664
totall[is] MM vj^{C} iiij^{C} x^{289}
Cxxxiiij^{li} x^{s} [134£ 10s]

[signatures] William Stanley maior, Squier Beverton, Le Lovelace clerk prior com[itatu] civitat[is] Cantuar[ensis]

[289] This is very poorly written and should be MMvj^{C} iiij^{XX}x that is 2690 to equal £134-10s. Using their totals the actual number of hearths is 2695

APPENDIX V

Analysis of the Hearth Tax in Canterbury

The built-up area of Canterbury had its core in the City and County of Canterbury, which lay outside Kent county jurisdiction and was therefore not included in the Quarter Sessions returns for the hearth tax of 1664. However, other parts of the built-up area were accounted in Westgate hundred. This included parishes and boroughs both within and outside the walls, for which returns survive along with the rest of Kent. For the City and County, an assessment was made at Michaelmas 1663, which was used as the basis for the tax of Lady Day 1664, printed here as Appendix IV. Unfortunately, no figures for exemptions are given in this document, and the figures cannot therefore be included in the general tables.

The City consisted of six wards and thirteen parishes which are identified on Map 12. This also shows those areas, i.e. the precincts of the archbishop's palace and Christ Church, and the boroughs of Staplegate and St Gregory, which were accounted in Westgate hundred. To the south-east, still within the city's bounds but in the detached portion of Westgate hundred, lay the parish of St Paul, here accounted for under Longport borough. To the north-west, the parish of St Dunstan, and that part of Holy Cross parish which was situated in Westgate hundred, lay outside the city bounds. Despite this, they formed part of the built-up area, and were included in the city for some purposes, such as the Compton Census of 1676. They have therefore been listed in the table below.[290]

Table 5 identifies from both sources (CKS: Q/RTh and PRO: E179/249/32) the numbers of households in the wards, parishes and boroughs which together make up the city area. This is followed by a discussion of the probable number of those exempted from the hearth tax.[291]

The number of households in Westgate hundred, including those exempt from payment, is 334. Excluding the unique and atypical areas of the palace and Christ Church precincts, exemptions account

---

[290] Chalklin, 'Compton Census', pp. 160, 167, 168.

[291] I am grateful to Dr F. H. Panton for help in sorting out the various jurisdictions in the city. For the wards and their parishes in the seventeenth century see Alderman C. R. Bunce 'Ancient Canterbury Records, 1800-1801' republished from the Kentish Gazette.

for 35 per cent of the total, a figure in line with overall exemption in the county, but very low for an urban area. It seems likely, however, that exemption was higher within the rest of the City. The number of households in the rest of the City, which excludes exemptions, is 715.

In 1676, the Compton Census lists 5054 inhabitants over the age of sixteen in Canterbury parishes. The returns were collected by parish, but covered all the jurisdictions listed above.[292] Three multipliers have been used to turn the numbers listed in the Compton Census into population figures: 1.4[293], 1.5[294] and 1.67.[295] These multipliers suggest the population in 1676 was between 7076 and 8440.

The figures normally used to turn population totals into numbers of households also vary between 4.25 and 4.5 persons per household,[296] which give total numbers of households in Canterbury of between 1572 and 1986.

Using the 1676 estimates and the 1664 hearth tax figures, and removing the 334 households listed in Westgate hundred, the number of households in the rest of the City was probably between 1238 and 1652. Since 715 of these were charged in the hearth tax, the number of exempt households may be calculated as between 523 (42 per cent) and 937 (57 per cent). Obviously, these are rough figures, and anyway the population of Canterbury in 1664 and 1676 may not have been the same, the likelihood being that numbers increased slightly during the intervening years, thus giving rather too high an estimate of exemption in 1664. Indeed, comparison of the Michaelmas 1663 and Lady Day 1664 assessments of hearths in Christ Church precinct, indicates that in the intervening six months, names had changed, there were extra entries, and a few more hearths listed overall. Nonetheless, the Compton Census of 1676 provides the closest indication we can get to the population of Canterbury twelve years earlier, and suggests that exemption in much of Canterbury may have been in line with other inland towns, particularly Maidstone where 50 per cent of households were exempted from payment.

[292] Chalklin, 'Compton Census', pp. 160, 167, 168.
[293] E. A. Wrigley and R. S. Schofield, *The Population History of England, 1540-1871* (London, 1981), p. 35, where it is suggested as a 'crude calculation' that 30% of the population was under sixteen in 1676.
[294] The multiplier used in Armstrong, *Economy of Kent*, Appendix IIIA, where the overall population of Canterbury is given as 7431.
[295] The multiplier used in Chalklin, 'Compton Census', p.172
[296] Armstrong, ibid.

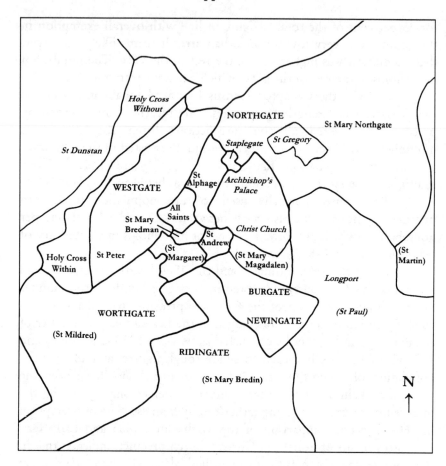

Holy Cross
Without

NORTHGATE

St Mary Northgate

St Dunstan

Staplegate   St Gregory

WESTGATE

St
Alphage   Archbishop's
Palace

All
Saints

St Mary
Bredman

St
Andrew

Christ Church

Holy Cross
Within

St Peter

(St
Margaret)

(St Mary
Magadalen)

(St
Martin)

Longport

BURGATE

WORTHGATE

NEWINGATE

(St Paul)

(St Mildred)

RIDINGATE

(St Mary Bredin)

N
↑

MAP 12 CANTERBURY PARISHES AND WARDS

Ward names, in capitals, are placed near the gates around which the administrative divisions lay. The ward boundaries are not shown.

Most parish boundaries are mapped, although some of the inner city ones which do not occur in the hearth tax have been omitted. Parish, borough and precinct names in lower case italics lie in Westgate hundred in the County of Kent. Parish names which are not italicised lie in the City and County of Canterbury. Those in brackets do not occur in the hearth tax.

Wards and parishes in the late seventeenth century were as follows:

Burgate	St Martin	Westgate	All Saints
	St Mary Magadalen		Holy Cross Westgate
	St Paul		St Mary Bredman
Newingate	St Andrew		St Peters
	St George		St Andrew (detached)
Northgate	St Alphage	Worthgate	St Margaret
	St Mary Northgate		St Mildred
Ridingate	St Mary Bredin		

TABLE 5

Parishes and boroughs in the built-up area of Westgate hundred (CKS Q/RTh), including empty properties.

Parish, borough	NC	1	2	3-4	5-9	10+	Tot
St Dunstan par	9	3	10	16	9	1	48
Holy Cross (w'out) par & bor	24	7	22	20	8	1	82
Staplegate bor	17	3	9	7			36
St Gregory bor	7		6	1	1		15
Archbishop's Palace precinct	1		1	4	4	2	12
Longport bor	35	3	8	18	14	3	81
Christ Church precinct[297]	1	2	10	19	13	15	60
	94	18	66	85	49	22	334
	(28%)	*(5%)*	*(20%)*	*(25%)*	*(15%)*	*(7%)*	

[297] The precinct of Christ Church is included in both documents, but the version in CKS Q/RTh not only includes the not charged, but is fuller than the PRO one, suggesting that changes had occurred between Michaelmas 1663 and Lady Day 1664. It has therefore been used in this table and all other calculations.

Wards, parishes and boroughs in the City and County of Canterbury (PRO E179/249/32), including empty properties. No figures for the 'not charged' are available.

Ward, parish, borough	1	2	3-4	5-9	10+	Tot
Northgate ward						
St Alphage par	18	21	24	22	3	88
St Mary Northgate par	6	28	20	7		61
Burgate ward	22	49	26	11		108
St Martin bor	3	6	3	2	2	16
Newingate ward	13	34	29	49	6	131
Ridingate ward		9	8	9	4	30
Worgate (Worthgate) ward	9	33	45	41	7	135
Westgate ward						
St Andrew par[298]	2	3	2	1	1	9
St Mary Bredman par	1	2	2	12	3	20
All Saints par	2	11	14	9	3	39
St Peter par	4	30	23	9	1	67
Holy Cross (within) par	1	5	4	1		11
	81	231	200	173	30	715
	(11%)	*(32%)*	*(28%)*	*(24%)*	*(4%)*	

[298] The parish of St Andrew is in Newingate ward, and contained nearly 400 people over the age of 16 in the Compton Census of 1676. Thus it is likely that this small entry simply represents a detached portion of the parish lying within Westgate ward.

APPENDIX VI

Ashford Hearth Tax 1662

CKS: U1107/O1
[fol. 2r] [299]
Aftar notice given to the inhabitants inhabiting within the township of Ashford and libbartie of the same by the borsholdar this is the account of the hearths and stoves within the severall respective houses dwellings lodgings and chambers of the aforsaid inhabitants inhabiting within the aforsaid township and libbarty of Ashford in the cownty of Kent
In the nowe dwelling house of Mr John Sturton thelder five hearths
In the now dwelling hous of Henry Viall theris three hearths
In the now dwellinge house of Tho[mas] Pysinge there is one hearth
Theare is in the now dwelling house ~~two~~ three hearths of me by my marke Jane 'P' Philpott
Theare is ~~three~~ two hearths in the now dwelling house of mee by my marke Thomas X Gowll
There is in the now dwellin house eight ~~hafts~~ hearths of me John[n] Stringer
Thear is in my dwelling house two hearths by my marke John 'A' Arrowe
Theare is in my dwelling house ~~five~~ six hearths by my marke Mathe[w] 'M' Copplee
Thear is in my dwelling house two hearths by mee Daniel Reat
There is in my dwelling house three hearths per me Francis Wreight
Thear is in the dwelling house one hearth of mee Thomas Champion
There is in the dwelling house one hath hearth and one hearth with privett ovend in it Henry Kingham

[fol. 3r]
Thear is three hearths in the dwelling house of mee by my marke heru[n]der Lennard Armson
Thear is two hearths in the dwelling house of mee Thomas Jem[m]ett
Theare is two hearths in the dwelling house of mee John Knowlden
Theare is fowre hearths in the dwelling house of mee by my marke

[299] Folio 1r & v, & 2v blank.

Rodgar X Bently

Theare is three hearths in the dwelling house of mee Elizabeth Phillcott

Thear is two hearths in the dwelling house of mee John Tookey

Thear is two hearths in the dwelling house of mee by my marke John X Keene

Thear is six hearths in the dwelling house of mee Francis Cowton

Thear is fower hearths in the dwelling house of mee Robert Badnor

There is three hearths in the dwelling house of mee Thomas Hunt

There is ~~fouer~~ fowre harts in the dwelling house of me Thomas Taylor

Thear is three hearth in the dwelling house of mee Francis Balyf se[nio]r

There are in the vicarage house of ashford sixe hearths Nicolas Prigg

Thear is fowre hearths in the dwelling house of mee John Foord

Theare is in the dwelling house of Mr Watars three hearths

Thear is in the dwelling house of mee John Horton fower hearths

Thear is two hearths in the dwelling hous of mee Robart Tritton

[fol. 3v]

Theare is fourteene hearths in the dwelling house of mee Ralph Clare

Theare is six hearths in the dwelling house of mee Frances Franck

Theare is fowre hearths in the dwelling house of mee John Morris

Theare is six hearths in the dwelling house of mee Richard Codsrey

Thear is three hearths in the dwelling house of mee Richard Lyne[300]

Theare is two hearths in the dwelling house of mee Robert Wal[s]bee

Theare is six hearths in the dwelling house of mee Tho[mas] 'R' Redfild his marke

Theare is two hearths in the dwelling house of mee William Poope

Thear is two hearths in the dwelling house of mee John X Earne his marke

Thear is fowre hearths in the dwelling house of mee Daniell Murton

Theare is two hearths in the dwelling house of mee Isaak 'T' Norton his marke

Thear is three hearths in the dwelling house of mee William Cartar

Thear is fowre hearths in the dwelling house of mee Thomas Moore[301]

Thear is two hearths in the dwelling house of mee Thomas Waterman

Thear is fowre hearths in the dwelling house of mee Georg X Springett

---

[300] For this and other difficult signatures, noted below, the scribe has re-written out the surname. 'Line'.

[301] Moore.

his mark
Thear is fowr hearths in the dwelling house of mee Henry 'O' Allen his
marke

[fol. 4r]
Thear is seven hearths in the dwelling house of meē Ralph Dayton
Thear is three hearths in the dwelling house of mee George Wintortone
Thear is five hearths in the dwelling house of mee Thomas Elvye
Thear is three hearths in the dwelling house of mee Isaac Brisenden
Thear is two hearths in the dwelling house of mee Edward 'E' Hailock
his mark
Thear is two hearths in the dwelling house of mee John Sprat
Theare is three hearths in the dwelling house of mee Thomas Olivere
Theare is fowre hearths in the dwelling house of mee John Scott
There is sixe hearths in the dwelling house whereof one has to furnaces
and one oven per me Tho[mas] Robisson
Theare is fowre hearths in the dwelling house of mee Steven Cobb
Theare is three hearths in the now dwelling house of mee Thomas
Hidar
Theare is three hearths in the dwelling house of mee Robert Pullen
whearof one is in the shop
Theare is five hearths in the dwelling house of mee Henry Wallis
Theare is in the dwelling house of mee three hearths William Lee

[fol. 4v]
Theare is three hearths in the dwelling house of mee the marke of
Alexandar 'A' Philpot
Theare is fowre hearths in the dwelling house of mee John Sherwood
Theare is two hearths in the dwelling house of mee John Stiver[302]
Theare is two hearths in the dwelling house of mee the marke of
Thomas 'B' Bigg.
Theare is six hearths in the dwelling house of mee Deborah Swaine.
Theare is two hearth in the dwelling house of mee the marke of John
'X' King
Theare is one hearth in the dwelling house of mee my marke Robart
'O' Davis
Theare ods fowre hearths in the dwelling house of mee Elizabeth
Brattle

[302] Stiver.

Theare is two hearths in the dwelling house of mee Robert Evenes
Theare is two hearths in the dwelling house of mee Robert Lott
Theare is one hearth in the shop of mee Edmund Austen
Theare is three hearths in the dwelling house of mee Will[iam] Osborne
Theare is one hearth in the dwelling house of mee Nicholas Angell
Theare is three hearths in the shop and dwelling of mee Robert Tomlinson
Theare is two hearths in the dwelling house of Henry Clarke and Thomas Typp

[fol. 5r]
Theare is three hearths in the dwelling house of mee William Robarts
Theare is three hearths in the dwelling house of me Robert Clark
Theare is fowre hearths in the dwelling house of mee the marke of Mary 'O' Jacobb
Theare is two hearths in the dwelling house of mee Thomas Murton
Theare is two hearths in the dwelling house of mee by the marke of Samuell 'T' Tillman
Theare is two hearths in the dwelling house of mee by the marke of Thomas 'Q' Mellar
Theare is three hearths in the dwelling house of mee Rogar Austen
Theare is two hearths in the dwelling house of mee by my marke Richard 'X' Fishar
Theare is three hearths in the dwelling house of Mary Gibbs
Theare is five hearths in the dwelling house of mee John Pope
There is nine hearths in the dwelling of mee John Nower
Theare is two hearths in the dwelling house of mee Richard Smallwood
Theare is two hearths in the dwelling house of mee John Denne
Theare is two hearths in the dwelling house of mee William Tharpe

[fol. 5v]
Theare is three hearths in the dwelling house of mee by my marke Tho[mas] 'F' Fox

[fol. 6r]
Theare is six hearthes in the occupation of mee Edmun[d] Brisenden
Theare is six hearths in the dwelling house of mee Simon Gilbert
Theare is fouer hearths in the dwelling house of me Richard Grennell

Theare is two hearths in the dwelling house of mee Aquilla Hunt
Theare is thirteen hearths in the dwelling house of mee Tho[mas Colbrand]
Theare is five hearths in the dwelling house of mee Mary Cornish
Theare is fowre hearths in the dwelling house of mee Jo[hn] Hawtrey
Theare is three hearths in the dwelling house of mee Thomas Giles
Theare is fowre hearths in the dwelling house of Thomas ~~Siviour~~ Siver
Theare is seven hearths in the dwelling house of mee Hilkiah Reader
Theare is two hearths in the dwelling house of mee Richard Philpot
Theare is six hearths in the dwelling house of me Geo[rge] Younge
Theare is fowre hearths in the dwelling house of me Francis Bayleife jun[ior]
Theare is eight hearth in the dwelling house of Mr John Nowell

[fol. 6v]
Theare is three hearths in the dwelling house of mee Fra[ncis] Boys
Theare is three hearths in the dwelling house of mee William Barrett
Theare is three hearths in the dwelling house of mee John Adcock
Theare is in the house of George Colt and John Pope occupied by Robert Gibbs eight hearths whereof three have ovens one for a furnase and for litle other use Rob[er]t Gibbs
There is in my dwelling howse six fire hearthes whereof two have private ovens belonging to them Geo[rge] Loveday tenant
Theare are three hearths in the dwelling house of mee Henry Master
Theare are six hearths in one house att Borow hill in the occupation of Amos Jacob
Theare are eight hearths in the dwelling house Mr Edw[ar]d Woodward
Theare are two hearths in the dwelling house of John Powell
Theare are three hearths in the dwelling house of mee John Smallwood: whearof one is with an oven and a furnis
Theare are six hearths in the dwelling house of Mr Simon Howe
John Smallwood borsholder

[fol. 8r & 8v blank]
This is the acount of the hearths of thos inhabitants whoe doe refuse to give them undar their hands
Theare is in the dwelling house of Robart Radford two hearths
Theare is in the dwelling house of Thomas Flint fowr hearths
Theare is eight hearthes in the dwelling house of Joy Starr whearof one

hath a furnis and a privatt oven thearin

Theare is fowre hearths in the now dwelling house of ~~mee~~ John Taillar

fol 9r

This is an acount of the hearths where no occupiar are

Theare are three hearths in one house of John Tritton which is unoccupied

Thear is two other small tenements of John Tritton which have two hearths

Theare is two hearths in a house of Thomas Cookow not occupied

~~Theare is two hearths in and house of Thomas Cookow wichnot occupied~~

Theare is six hearths in one house of Thomas Bigg not occupied

~~Theare is five hearths in one house of Jo Hatris John Hatries not occupied~~

Theare is fowre hearths in one house of Moses Maslye

Theare is one hearth in one house of ~~mee~~ Simon Gillbart

Theare is three hearth in one house of Thomas Redfilds not occupied

Theare is five hearths in one house which is in the occupation of John Earme

Theare is six hearths in one house of Mr Robert Pincett which is unocupied in the Northlane

Theare are fowre hearth in one house in the churchyard not occupied Tho[mas] Fidg of Plukly beeing landlord

Theare are two hearths in one house in New rense not occuped William Berreke of Great Chart beeing landlord

[fol. 9v, 10r & 10v blank], except on the last
'Ashford liberty Roll No. 62.'

APPENDIX VII

Kent, Hearth Tax, Lady Day 1664:
Hundred, Parish and Borough Names

This index identifies, as far as possible, the hundred and parish in which each unit used in the hearth tax lies. It only includes those places for which transcripts are found in this volume, and therefore does not cover those parts of the county for which there are no 1664 returns. Canterbury, which lay partly in Westgate hundred and partly in the City and County of Canterbury, is discussed separately in Appendix V. The table below is set out in the order of the document itself, with the page numbers of the transcript printed in this volume in the left hand column. The second column gives the total number of entries in each borough, and the fourth column gives the name of the borough or parish as used in the hearth tax, followed where appropriate by alternative spellings, either taken from Hasted, or as in modern usage. The large number of detached portions of both hundreds and parishes, and the fact that many borough names are obsolete, means that some boroughs cannot be assigned securely to parishes, and some parishes cannot be identified in the hearth tax. Where Kilburne and Hasted note that part of a parish lies in a particular hundred, but it has proved impossible to identify the relevant borough, the parish name has been included in square brackets. Between the seventeenth and mid nineteenth centuries it appears that the outlines of some hundreds, and possibly some parishes, changed. This means that the hundred and parish maps in this volume are not wholly consistent with each other, and that some boroughs or parishes (or parts thereof) in the hearth tax lie in different hundreds to those shown on the nineteenth-century Ordnance Survey map. Some instances have been noted, but it has not been possible to undertake the detailed research necessary to identify and trace the history of each change. In fact, the administration of the county was so complex that some omissions and mistakes will certainly have been made, so the following list should be taken as a guide, rather than as definitive.

The principal sources used are W. Lambarde, *A Perambulation of Kent, 1570* (Bath, 1970); R. Kilburne, *A Topographie or Survey of the County of Kent* (London, 1659); E. Hasted, *The History and Topographical Survey of the County of Kent*, 12 vols (1797-1801, 2nd edn reprint, 1972); J. K. Wallenberg, *The Place-Names of Kent* (Uppsala, 1934), and the typescript parish-borough list in CKS, compiled by E. Melling. Map evidence is based on the Ordnance Survey, 1st edn 6 inch (1/10560) map, surveyed 1863-70, and the *Kent Parishes* map, Institute of Heraldic and Genealogical Studies (Canterbury, 1999), which attempts to identify ecclesiastical parishes before 1832.

Pge	No of Entries	Hundred or other division	Hearth Tax Unit = Parish/Borough	Ecclesiastical Parishes prior to 1832
		SUTTON AT HONE		
2		Blackheath		Charlton, Deptford, Eltham, Greenwich, Lee, Lewisham, Woolwich, and part of Chislehurst
	420		Deptford, upper part	Deptford
5	4		In Surry	Surrey. Physically in Surrey & not included in maps & tables
			Deptford, upper part, cont.	Deptford
7	579		Deptford, lower part	Deptford
14	280		Woolwich	Woolwich
18	12		Mottingham	Eltham
	36		Charleton	Charlton
19	28		Lee	Lee
	164		Eltham	Eltham, Chislehurst
21	233		Lewsham	Lewisham
24			East Greenwich	
	33		Church Wall	Greenwich
25	34		Combes Hill	Greenwich
	29		London Street	Greenwich
26	58		Highstreet West	Greenwich
	69		Highstreet East	Greenwich
27	34		Billingsgate	Greenwich
28	32		Fisher Lane	Greenwich
	19		Stable Street	Greenwich
29	35		Dock & Tavern Rowe	Greenwich
	43		Crane South	Greenwich
30	58		East Lane East	Greenwich
	42		East Lane West	Greenwich
31	8		The Kings Barne	Greenwich
	40		East Greenwich, empty	Greenwich
32	96		East Greenwich, not charged	Greenwich
33		Little and Lesnes		Crayford, East Wickham, Erith, Plumstead
	60		Erith par	Erith
34	80		Erith Towne	Erith
35	27		East Wickham	East Wickham
36	24		Crayford Towne	Crayford
	54		Crayford par	Crayford
37	64		Plumsted par	Plumstead

Pge	No of Entries	Hundred or other division	Hearth Tax Unit = Parish/Borough	Ecclesiastical Parishes prior to 1832
38		Codsheath		Halsted, Kemsing, Otford, Seale, Sevenoaks, Shoreham, Sundridge, and part of Chevening, [Kingsdown], Leigh and [Speldhurst]
	90		Shoreham par	Shoreham
39	23		Halsted par	Halsted
	52		Ottford par	Otford
40	115		Sandrish par	Sundridge
42	185		Seavenokes Towne	Sevenoaks
44	85		Seavenockes Weild	Sevenoaks
45	56		Liberty of Riverhead	Sevenoaks
46	40		Kemsing par	Kemsing
47	134		Seale par	Seale
48	99		Chevening par	Chevening
50	43		Leigh bor	Leigh. Detached and physically in Somerden
50		Somerden		Chiddingstone, Hever and part of [Chevening], Cowden, Edenbridge, Leigh, Penshurst, Speldhurst
	76		Frienden bor	Chiddingstone, Penshurst
52	62		Cowden bor	Cowden.
53	74		Stanford bor	? Hever, ? Edenbridge
54	45		Kings bor	Penshurst
	11		Groombridge bor	Speldhurst. Detached and physically in Wachlingstone
55	34		Penshurst Towne	Penshurst
	70		Penshurst bor	? Leigh, Penshurst
56		Westerham & Edenbridge		Westerham and part of Cowden and Edenbridge
	78		Edenbridge/Cowden	Edenbridge, Cowden
57	21		Cudham bor & Merchgreene	Edenbridge
58	161		Westerham Towne	Westerham
60	59		Westerham upland	Westerham
61		Bromley and Beckenham		Beckenham, Bromley
	104		Bromley Towne	Bromley
62	12		Plasto	Bromley
	5		Elmsted	Bromley
	17		Widmor	Bromley
63	10		South Borough	Bromley
	14		The Common	Bromley
	12		Masons Hill	Bromley
	91		Beckenham par	Beckenham
65		Brasted Vil		Brasted.

Pge	No of Entries	Hundred or other division	Hearth Tax Unit = Parish/Borough	Ecclesiastical Parishes prior to 1832
65	69		Brasted vil	Brasted. Adjacent to and counted with Westerham and Edenbridge hundred
66	31		Brasted upland	Brasted. Physically in Westerham and Edenbridge hundred
66		**Dartford and Wilmington**		**Dartford, Wilmington**
	303		Dartford Towne	Dartford
70	59		Wilmington	Wilmington
71		**Axtane**		**Ash, Darenth, Eynsford, Farningham, Fawkham, Hartley, Horton Kirby, Longfield, Lullingstone, Ridley, Southfleet, Stone, Sutton-at-Hone, Swanscombe, and part of Kingsdown**
	58		Southfleet par	Southfleet
72	24		Swanscombe par	Swanscombe
	49		Greenehive	Swanscombe
73	27		Stone par	Stone
	58		Darenth par	Darenth
74	67		Sutton at Hone par	Sutton-at-Hone
75	71		Ash-cum-Ridley par	Ash, Ridley
76	21		Fawkham par	Fawkham
77	34		Farningham par	Farningham
	9		Longfield par	Longfield
	30		Kingsdown par	Kingsdown
78	22		Hartley par	Hartley
	86		Eynsford & Lullingstone pars	Eynsford, Lullingstone
79	63		Horton Kirby par	Horton Kirby
80		**Ruxley**		**Bexley, Chelsfield, Cudham, Downe, Farnborough, Foots Cray, Hayes, Keston, Knockholt, North Cray, Orpington, St Mary Cray, St Paul's Cray West Wickham, and part of Chislehurst, Chiddingstone and Hever**
	41	Ruxley, Upper	Nockhoult	Knockholt
81	63		Cudham par	Cudham
82	40		Farmborough par	Farnborough
83	41		West Wickham par	West Wickham
	60		Chelsfield par	Chelsfield
84	26		Keston par	Keston
	48		Heys par	Hayes

Pge	No of Entries	Hundred or other division	Hearth Tax Unit = Parish/Borough	Ecclesiastical Parishes prior to 1832
85	34		Downe par	Downe
86	108	Ruxley, Lower	Chislehurst par	Chislehurst
87	35		Linckhill hamlett	Chiddingstone, Hever. Physically in Somerden hundred.
88	32		St Paul's Cray par	St Paul's Cray
	78		St Mary Cray par	St Mary Cray
89	24		North Cray par	North Cray
90	20		Foots Cray par	Foots Cray
	60		Orpington par	Orpington
91	144		Bexley par	Bexley
		AYLESFORD		
94		Eyhorne		Boughton Monchelsea, Bredhurst, Broomfield, Chart Sutton, East Sutton, Frinsted, Harrietsham, Hollingbourne, Hucking, Langley, Leeds, Otham, Sutton Valence, Thurnham, Wichling, and part of Bearsted, Bicknor, Boughton Malherbe, Headcorn, Lenham, Marden, Otterden, Stockbury, Staplehurst, Ulcombe, Wormshill
	194	Eyhorne, Upper	Lenham bor	Lenham
96	34		Shelve bor	Lenham, Otterden
97	42		Frensted bor	Frinsted, Wichling, Wormshill
	33		Stockbury & Bicknor bor	Stockbury, Bicknor
98	6		Eldnodington bor	Hollingbourne
	75		Harrisham bor	Harrietsham
99	41		Hawkinge & Bredhurst	Bredhurst[303], Hucking
100	109		Hollingbourne par	Hollingbourne
101	42		Thurnham par	Thurnham
102	7		Liberty of Allington	? Aldington hamlet in Thurnham,
	55	Eyhorne, Lower	Sutton Valence bor	Sutton Valence
103	33		Boughton Maleherb bor	Boughton Malherbe
104	57		Hedcorne Towne bor	Headcorn
	20		Bromfield par	Broomfield
105	101		Boughten Munshalsey par	Boughton Monchelsea, ?

[303] The maps show that Bredhurst parish is in Maidstone hundred, but it has always been accounted part of Eyhorne. Since the hearth tax unit includes figures for Hucking, which is certainly in Eyhorne, it has not been treated as a detached portion.

Pge	No of Entries	Hundred or other division	Hearth Tax Unit = Parish/Borough	Ecclesiastical Parishes prior to 1832
106	45		Langly par	Langley
107	43		Otham bor	Otham
108	72		Ulcombe par	Ulcombe
109	68		Chart next Sutton	Chart Sutton, ? Staplehurst
110	62		Bersted par	Bearsted
	47		Sutton Valence Innborough	Sutton Valence
111	58		East Sutton bor	East Sutton
112	93		Leeds par	Leeds
113		**Shamwell**		Chalk, Cliffe, Cooling, Cuxton, Denton, Frindsbury, Halling, Higham, Shorne, Strood, and part of Cobham, Stoke
	25	Shamwell, Upper	Cobham East bor	Cobham
114	31		Cobham South bor	Cobham
	32		Halling bor	Halling
115	8		Chalke East bor	Chalk
	14		Chalke Westborough	Chalk
	27		Cuxton bor	Cuxton
116	11		Shorne Westborough	Shorne
	12		Shorne Northborough	Shorne
	55		Shorne Southborough	Shorne
117	2		Denton bor	? Chalk, Denton
	32	Shamwell, Lower	Higham upper bor	Higham
118	30		Higham lower bor	Higham
	5		Oysterland bor	Stoke. Detached and physically in Hoo, but cannot be mapped.
	64		Frindsbury West bor	Frindsbury
119	33		Freindsbury East bor	Frindsbury
120	125		Temple Strood bor	Strood
122	15		Strood Dutchey	Strood
	11		Cooling bor	Cooling
	55		Strood Little bor	Strood
123	24		Cliff Church St & Reed St bor	Cliffe
	17		Cliff West bor	Cliffe
124	21		Cliff Cooling St bor	Cliffe
124		**Twyford**		Nettlestead, Teston, Wateringbury, West Farleigh, and part of Brenchley, Capel, East Peckham, Hunton, Marden, [Pembury], Tudeley, Yalding
	15		Teston par	Teston
125	33		West Farliegh	West Farleigh

Pge	No of Entries	Hundred or other division	Hearth Tax Unit = Parish/Borough	Ecclesiastical Parishes prior to 1832
125	20		Nettlested par	Nettlestead
	103		Stockenbury bor	East Peckham, Brenchley
127	101		Yalding par	Yalding, Brenchley
128	28		Whetsted bor	Capel, Tudeley
129	53		Hunton bor	Hunton, Marden, Yalding
130	52		Watringbury par	Wateringbury
130		Littlefield		**Mereworth, and part of East Peckham, Hadlow and West Peckham**
	60		Mereworth par	Mereworth
131	21		East Peckham Upper bor	East Peckham
132	8		Lone bor	East Peckham
	24		West Packham Upper bor	West Peckham, ? Hadlow
133		**Brenchley & Horsmonden**		**Horsmonden, Lamberhurst and part of Brenchley, Pembury and Yalding**[304]
	156		Brenchley Towne bor	Brenchley
135	67		Horsmanden Free bor	Horsmonden
136	6		Burram alias Brantingberry bor, Brandenbury	Yalding
	46		Badmanden bor, Badmonden	Horsmonden
	29		Lamberherst bor	Lamberhurst
137	14		Beane Crouch bor	Pembury
	36		Teperedge bor, ? Tipperidge	? Pembury
138	46		Bayham bor	Lamberhurst
	49		Abbies bor	? Lamberhurst
139		**Wachlingstone**		**Ashurst, Bidborough, and part of Capel, Frant, Leigh, Pembury, Penshurst, Speldhurst and Tudeley**
	64		Borden bor	? Bidborough, ? Leigh
140	59		Hall bor	? Ashurst, Penshurst
141	47		Rusthall bor	Speldhurst
142	98		Speldhurst bor	Speldhurst
143	65		Suneingley bor	Pembury, ? Frant
144	56		Tudley bor	Tudeley, Capel
145		**Lowy of Tunbridge**		**Tonbridge**[305] **and part of [Capel] and Hadlow**
	142		Tunbridge Towne	Tonbridge
147	155		Hadlow bor	Hadlow

[304] Beane Crouch and Teperedge boroughs appear to lie in Pembury, and Brantingberry in Yalding, but neither Kilburne nor Hasted recognise Pembury or Yalding in Brenchley and Horsmonden hundred

[305] The map shows that part of Tonbridge parish lies in Wachlingstone, but this is not noted in Kilburne or Hasted and the borough which refers to it cannot be identified for certain.

Pge	No of Entries	Hundred or other division	Hearth Tax Unit = Parish/Borough	Ecclesiastical Parishes prior to 1832
149	30		Southborough, east	Tonbridge
	106		Southborough, west	Tonbridge
151	82		Helden bor, Hildenborough	Tonbridge
152		Little Barnfield		part of Goudhurst
	22		Bromley bor	Goudhurst
	13		Combewell bor	Goudhurst
153	24		Chingley bor	Goudhurst
	17		Lillesden bor	Goudhurst
	3		Pattenden bor	Goudhurst
154		Wrotham		Ightham, Shipbourne, Stansted, Wrotham
	70		Wrotham Towne and bor	Wrotham
155	32		Rofeway bor	Wrotham
	76		Iteham par	Ightham
156	40		Shipbourne par	Shipbourne
157	43			Wrotham
			Wimfield bor, Winfield	
158	38		Hale bor	Wrotham
	22		Neppecar bor, Nepicar	Wrotham
159	41		Stansted par	Stansted
159		Larkfield		Addington, Allington, Birling, Burham, Ditton, East Malling, Leybourne, Offham, Ryarsh, Paddlesworth, Snodland, Trottiscliffe, Wouldham, and part of Aylesford, [Horsmonden], [Hunton] and [West Malling],
	111		East Malling par	East Malling
161	29		Burham par	Burham
	56		Berling par	Birling
162	23		Woldham par	Wouldham
	32		Addington par	Addington, ? Trottiscliffe
163	19		Ditton par	Ditton
	50		Swadland par	Snodland, Paddlesworth
164	19		Laybourne par	Leybourne
	22		Alington and Preston	Allington, Aylesford
165	39		Raish par	Ryarsh
	31		Offham par	Offham
166		Hoo		Allhallows, High Halstow, Hoo St Werburgh, St Mary's Hoo and part of [Cobham], Stoke and West Peckham
	26	Hoo, Upper	Deane bor	Hoo St Werburgh
167	18		Churchstreet bor	Hoo St Werburgh
	8		Boxley bor	Hoo St Werburgh

Pge	No of Entries	Hundred or other division	Hearth Tax Unit = Parish/Borough	Ecclesiastical Parishes prior to 1832
167	12		Pensone bor	?
	13		Longdowne bor	?
168	33		High Halstow bor	High Halstow
	14	Hoo, Lower	St Mary Barnstreet par/bor	St Mary's Hoo
	25		Hardellfield bor	Hoo St Werburgh
169	12		Inn bor	?
	15		Gavell bor	?
	20		Alhallowes Street bor	Allhallows
170	12		Slowe bor	Allhallows
170	56	Aylesford, (Ancient Demesne)	Aylesford par	Aylesford. Physically in Larkfield
171	52	Aylesford	Rugmer Hill bor	Yalding, [Brenchley, Horsmonden]. Detached and physically in Twyford, but cannot be mapped
172	128	Liberty of West Malling	Towne Malling	West Malling. Adjacent to and counted with Larkfield
174	21	Hoo	Oxinoth bor, Oxenhoath	West Peckham. Detached and physically in Littlefield
174		Maidstone		Barming, Boxley, Detling, East Farleigh, Linton, Loose, Maidstone and part of [Bearsted], Hunton, Marden and Staplehurst
	51		Dettling par	Detling
175	23		Part of Stapleherst in Dettling bor	Staplehurst. Detached and physically in Marden
	133		Boxley par	Boxley
177	79		Linton and Crockhurst	Linton, Hunton, Marden
178	29		Barming	Barming
179	65		East Farleigh	East Farleigh
	63		Looze par	Loose
180		Maidstone Towne		Maidstone
	166		High Towne	Maidstone
183	8		Pudding Lane	Maidstone
	95		Mill Lane	Maidstone
184	107		Bullock Lane, the Green, the Waterside	Maidstone
185	224		Wickstreet/Wick bor	Maidstone
188	20		East Lane	Maidstone
189	7		Harbor Land	Maidstone
	52		West Tree	Maidstone
190	123		Stone bor	Maidstone

Pge	No of Entries	Hundred or other division	Hearth Tax Unit = Parish/Borough	Ecclesiastical Parishes prior to 1832
191		Chatham & Gillingham		Chatham, Gillingham, St James's in the Isle of Grain
	434		Chetham half hundred	Chatham
197	173		Gillingham half hundred	Gillingham, St James's
199		Toltingtrough		Gravesend, Ifield, Luddesdown, Meopham, Milton, Northfleet and Nurstead,
	62	Toltingtrough, Upper	Mepham, Meopham	Meopham
200	42		East bor	Meopham
	30		Ludsdowne par	Luddesdown
201	6		Nursted	Nurstead
	86	Toltingtrough, Lower	Gravesend Towne	Gravesend
202	132		West Street South Side	Gravesend
204	114		Gravesend, empty and exempt	
205	111		Northfleete	Northfleet, Ifield
207	221		Milton next Gravesend	Milton
210		Rochester City and Liberty		
	45		Rochester Cathedral, precinct	Rochester
			City of Rochester	Rochester
	40		Middle bor	Rochester
211	44		St Clement bor	Rochester
	45		South bor	Rochester
212	51		Northgate bor	Rochester
213	81		Southgate bor	Rochester
214	17		Bostall bor	Rochester
215	77		East bor	Rochester
216	312		Eastgate bor	Rochester
		SCRAY		
221	19	Newenden	Newenden township	most of Newenden. Adjacent to and counted with Selbrittenden
	182	Great Barnfield	Great Barnefeild	most of Hawkhurst and part of Cranbrook
224		Rolvenden		Rolvenden and part of Benenden
	80		Beneden bor	Benenden
225	76		Maytham bor	Rolvenden
226	34		Halden bor	Rolvenden
	27		Devernden bor, Devenden	Rolvenden

Pge	No of Entries	Hundred or other division	Hearth Tax Unit = Parish/Borough	Ecclesiastical Parishes prior to 1832
227		Selbrittenden		Sandhurst and part of Benenden, Hawkhurst, Newenden
	86		North bor	Benenden
228	35		East bor	Sandhurst, Newenden
229	82		West bor	Sandhurst, Hawkhurst
230		Cranbrook		part of Benenden, Biddenden, Cranbrook, Frittenden Goudhurst, Hawkhurst, Headcorn and Staplehurst
	90		Cruthole bor	Benenden, Hawkhurst
231	32		Kings Franchise bor	Staplehurst
232	116		North bor	? Frittenden, Headcorn, Staplehurst
233	287		Towne bor	Cranbrook
237	39		Abbots Franchise bor	Cranbrook
	84		Smithsditch bor	Cranbrook, Biddenden
239	118		Faire Crouch bor	Cranbrook, Goudhurst, Staplehurst
240		Barkley		part of Benenden, Biddenden, Cranbrook, Frittenden, Headcorn, High Halden and Smarden
	55		Hevenden bor	Benenden, Biddenden
241	123		Iborden bor	Benenden, Biddenden, Cranbrook
243	16		Wachenden bor	Biddenden
	27		Worchenden bor, Worsenden	Biddenden
	70		Omenden bor	Biddenden, High Halden, Smarden
244	31		Stephurst bor	Biddenden, Frittenden, Headcorn, Smarden
245		Blackborne		Woodchurch and part of Appledore, Bethersden, High Halden, Kenardington, Shadoxhurst, Smarden and Warehorne
	45		Novenden bor	High Halden
246	32		Povenden bor	Bethersden, Smarden
	55		Ridgeway bor	Woodchurch
247	29		Old Harlakenden bor	Shadoxhurst, Warehorne, Woodchurch
	17		Ingham bor, ? Engeham	Bethersden, Woodchurch
248	36		Great Kenardington bor	Kenardington, Warehorne
	21		Appledore Heath bor	Appledore
249	11		Little Kenardington bor	Kenardington
	31		Appledore Towne bor	Appledore

Pge	No of Entries	Hundred or other division	Hearth Tax Unit = Parish/Borough	Ecclesiastical Parishes prior to 1832
249	30		Hailes Bridge bor	Bethersden
250		**Marden**		**part of Goudhurst, Marden and Staplehurst**
	273		Gowtherst Great bor	Goudhurst
253	105		Elhurst bor	Marden
255	61		Laudenden bor, Loddenden	Staplehurst
256	55		Pattenden bor	Marden
	44		Dagswell bor	Marden, Staplehurst
257	25		Sutton bor	Staplehurst
	14		Frenches Liberty, Franchise Liberty	Staplehurst
258	24		Ruckherst bor, Rookherst	Goudhurst
		Milton		**Bapchild, Bobbing, Borden, Bredgar, Hartlip, Kingsdown, Lower Halstow, Milstead, Milton, Murston, Newington, Rainham, Rodmersham, Sittingbourne, Tonge, Tunstall, Upchurch and part of Bicknor, Iwade, Stockbury and Wormshill**
	206	Milton, East	Milton bor	Milton, ? Iwade
261	37		Milsted bor	Milstead, Wormshill
	40		Rodmersham bor	Rodmersham
262	9		Ringsdowne bor	Kingsdown
	46		Bredgar bor	Bredgar, ? Bicknor
263	24		Bapchild bor	Bapchild
264	13		Tong bor	Tonge
	24		Muston bor	Murston
	11		Tunstall Court bor	Tunstall
	115		Sittingbourne bor	Sittingbourne
266	73	Milton, West	Borden bor	Borden
267	72		Bobbing bor	Bobbing
268	43		Houltstreet bor	Hartlip
269	38		Ham bor	Upchurch
270	14		Otterham bor	Upchurch
	22		Goare bor	Upchurch
	32		Lucis bor	Newington
271	13		Elmsted bor	? Lower Halstow
	19		St Augustines bor	Newington
272	25		Wormedale bor, Wornedale	Newington
	29		Yelsted bor	Stockbury
273	28		Deane bor, Dane	Hartlip
	32		West Reynham bor	Rainham
274	31		Mackland bor	Rainham
	22		Tufton bor	Rainham

Pge	No of Entries	Hundred or other division	Hearth Tax Unit = Parish/Borough	Ecclesiastical Parishes prior to 1832
274	8		Meare bor	Rainham
275		**Tenham**		Doddington, Lynsted and Teynham, and part of Headcorn and Iwade
	54	Tenham, Upper	Bedmangore bor	Lynsted
276	14		Ockenfale bor, Okenfold	Doddington
	10		Headcorne bor	Headcorn. Detached and physically in Eyhorne
	6		Iwade bor	Iwade. Detached and physically in Milton
	66	Tenham, Lower	Bonepett bor, Bumpitt	Lynsted
277	26		Lewson bor	Teynham
278	38		Tenham bor	Teynham
	11		Downewell bor	? Doddington
279		**Faversham**		Badlesmere, Buckland, Davington, Eastling, Goodnestone, Isle of Harty, Leaveland, Luddenham, Newnham, Norton, Oare, Preston, Sheldwich, Stalisfield, Stone, Throwley, and part of Boughton Malherbe, Boughton under Blean, Faversham, Ospringe, Otterden, Selling and Ulcombe
	48	Faversham, Upper	Stalfield bor	Stalisfield, Otterden[306]
	48		Throwledge South bor	Throwley
280	18		Wilgate bor	Throwley
281	25		Kingsnorth bor	? Boughton Malherbe[307], Ulcombe. Detached and physically in Eyhorne
	10		Sillgrove bor, Selgrave	Sheldwich, Preston
	55		Argusthill bor	Sheldwich
282	13		Leaveland bor	Leaveland
	48		Eastling bor	Eastling
283	26		Badlesmeare bor	Badlesmere
284	19		Stupenton bor, Stuppington	Newnham, Norton
	52		Norton bor	Norton
285	2	Faversham, Lower	Buckland bor	Buckland, ? Stone
	18		Luddenham bor	Luddenham
	3		Chattam bor, Chetham	Ospringe
	3		Brimstone bor	Ospringe

[306] This borough includes some Otterden names whose property is located in Eyhorne hundred
[307] The maps show that part of Kingsnorth borough lies in Boughton Malherbe parish, but this is not noted by Kilburne or Hasted.

Pge	No of Entries	Hundred or other division	Hearth Tax Unit = Parish/Borough	Ecclesiastical Parishes prior to 1832
285	8		Ewell bor	Faversham
286	8		Goodnestone bor	Goodnestone
	21		Roade bor, Rode	Boughton under Blean,[308] Selling. Detached and physically in Boughton under Blean
	19		Davington bor	Davington
287	27		Oare bor	Oare
	12		Island of Hartey	Harty. Physically on the Isle of Sheppey
	18		Preston bor	Preston
288		Isle of Sheppey (Milton)		Eastchurch, Minster, Leysdown, Elmley, Warden and part of Queenborough
	48		Seden bor, ?Sednor	? Minster, ? Sednor in Queenborough
	19		Ossenden bor, Oxenden	Minster
289	27		Warden bor	Warden
	16		Rydes bor	Eastchurch
290	47		Holt bor	Queenborough
	10		Laisdon bor	Leysdown
291	77	Liberty of Ospringe	Liberty of Ospringe	part of Ospringe. Physically within Faversham hundred
292		Boughton under the Bleane		Graveney, Hernhill and part of Boughton under Blean and Selling
	33	Boughton,	Harvill bor, ?Harefield	? Selling
	4	Upper	Meneham bor	? Boughton under Blean, ? Selling
	7		Wastell bor, ?Fostall	? Hernhill
293	40	Boughton, Lower	Setton bor	? Boughton under Blean, ? Selling
	37		Staple bor	Hernhill
294	20		Graveney bor	Graveney
	12		Waterham bor	Hernhill
295	19		Nash bor	Boughton under Blean
	36		Milstreet bor	? Boughton under Blean
296	268	Ashford Towne	Ashford Towne	Most of Ashford. Physically in Chart and Longbridge
299		Chart and Longbridge		Hinxhill, Kennington, Kingsnorth, Sevington, Willesborough and part of Ashford, Bethersden, Great Chart, Hothfield,

[308] The maps show that part of Boughton under Blean parish lies in Faversham hundred, but this is not noted by Kilburne or Hasted.

Pge	No of Entries	Hundred or other division	Hearth Tax Unit = Parish/Borough	Ecclesiastical Parishes prior to 1832
				Mersham, [Shadoxhurst] and [Smarden]
299	56	Chart	Shelvington bor in Great Chart, ? Singleton	Great Chart
300	32		Bucksford bor	Great Chart
301	21		Chelvington bor, ? Chilmington	Great Chart
	4		Worting bor	Great Chart
	16		Swinford bor in Hothfield	Hothfield
	53		Hothfield Great bor	Hothfield
302	51		Shippenden bor in Bethresden	Bethersden
303	15		Rumden bor in Bethresden	Bethersden, ? Smarden
	25		Street bor in Bethresden	Bethersden
304	10		Snoad Hill bor in Bethresden	Bethersden
	22		Rudlow bor in Ashford	Ashford
305	57	Longbridge	Mersham bor	Mersham
306	34		Kingsnorth bor	Kingsnorth
	78		Kenington bor	Kennington
307	54		Lacton bor	Willesborough
308	4		Hewett bor	Ashford, Willesborough
	4		Hennard bor, Henwood	Ashford, Willesborough
	12		Sevington bor	Sevington
309	24		Hinxell bor, Hinxhill	Hinxhill
309		**Calehill**		**Charing, Egerton, Little Chart, Pluckley, and part of Bethersden, [Great Chart], Headcorn, [Hothfield], Lenham, Smarden and Westwell**
	30	Calehill, Upper	Sanpett bor, Sandpett	Charing
310	11		East Lenham bor	Lenham
	17		Well bor	Westwell
	18		Acton bor	Charing
311	35		Sandhatch bor	Little Chart, ? Westwell
	28		Feild bor	Charing, Egerton
312	27		Highslade bor	Charing, Westwell
	20		Nash bor	Westwell
	56		Charing Towne bor	Charing
313	38		Little Chart bor	Little Chart
314	88	Calehill, Lower	Hollingherst bor, Hallinghurst	Smarden
315	49		Holynes bor	? Smarden
316	49		Pluckly bor	Pluckley
317	42		Sednor bor	Egerton
	10		St John's bor	?
318	13		Greenehill	Egerton, Pluckley
	14		West Kingsnorth bor	Pluckley

Pge	No of Entries	Hundred or other division	Hearth Tax Unit = Parish/Borough	Ecclesiastical Parishes prior to 1832
318	24		Standford bor	Pluckley, Bethersden
319	49		Edgley bor	Egerton
		Bircholt Barony		part of Brabourne and Hastingleigh
	30		West Brabourne bor	Brabourne
320	12		Bockham bor	Brabourne
	16		Hastingly bor	Hastingleigh
	37		East Brabourne bor	Brabourne
321		Felborough		Chilham, Godmersham, Molash and part of Challock and Chartham
	43	Felborough, Upper	Markett bor	Chilham
322	14		Eaststeward bor, Esture, East Stour	Chilham
	24		Shottenton bor, Shottenden	Chilham
323	9		Boreland bor	Chilham
	12		Northearne bor, Northerne	Chilham
	9		Dane bor	Chilham
	58		Moldash	Molash
324	72	Felborough, Lower	Shamford bor, Shalmsford	Chartham
325	13		Ruttenton bor, Rattington	Chartham
326	28		Godmersham bor	Godmersham
	41		Hinxhill bor, Hinksell	Godmersham
327	25		Dorne bor	?Godmersham
	37		Challock bor	Challock
328	21		Persted bor, Pested	Challock
		Wye		Boughton Aluph, Brook, Crundale, Eastwell, Wye and part of Brabourne, Challock, Hastingleigh, Waltham and Westwell
	143	Wye, Upper	Bewbridge bor	Wye
330	41		Cuckoldscombe bor	Wye ? Brook
331	22		Trimworth bor	Crundale
	31		Brensford bor, ? Bromford	?Wye, ?Brook
	19		Towne bor	Hastingleigh, Waltham, Wye
332	8	Wye, Lower	Lennacar bor	Eastwell
	6		Febing bor	?Boughton Aluph, ?Wye (det)
	4		Deane bor	Westwell
	19		Socombe bor	Boughton Aluph
333	15		Gotly bor, Goatland	Boughton Aluph
	9		Wilmunton bor, Wilmington	Boughton Aluph
	16		Shottenden bor	Westwell

Pge	No of Entries	Hundred or other division	Hearth Tax Unit = Parish/Borough	Ecclesiastical Parishes prior to 1832
334	41	**Isle of Sheppey**	Queenborough Towne	Queenborough
335		**SHEPWAY** **Bircholt Franchise**		**Smeeth, and part of Aldington and Mersham**
	23		Lushington bor, Lustington	Smeeth
	10		Southward bor	? Mersham
	13		Coate bor	Aldington
336	31		Hearst bor, Copperhurst	Aldington
	38		Stock bor	Smeeth
337	14		Stonested bor, Stonestreet Green	Aldington
		Stowting		**Elmsted, Monks Horton, Stowting and part of Sellindge, Stanford, Stelling and Waltham**
	26	Stowting, Upper		Elmsted, Stelling, Waltham
338	51		North bor	? Stowting
	44	Stowting, Lower	South Horton bor	Monks Horton, Stanford
339	4		East Horton bor	Sellindge
	51[309]		Stowting bor	Stowting
340		**Loningborough**		**Acrise, Elham, Lyminge, [Paddlesworth], and part of Stelling and Upper Hardres**
	32	Loningborough, Upper	Carterwood bor, Canterwood	Acrise, Elham
341	122		Towne bor	Elham
342	76		Bladben bor, Bladbean	Elham, ? Stelling, Upper Hardres
343	32		Boyke bor	Elham
344	42[310]	Loningborough Lower	Lyminge bor	Lyminge
345	25		Eachinghill bor, Etchinghill	Lyminge
	28		Sipton bor, Sibton	Lyminge
346		**Street**		**Hurst and part of Aldington, Bonnington, Lympne, Sellindge and Stanford**
	15	Street, Upper	Giminge bor	Stanford

[309] The names of six people who were charged are repeated in the non-chargeable list and the second entries have not been counted.

[310] As above, several names in all the boroughs in the lower half of Loningborough hundred are repeated and the second entries have not been counted.

Pge	No of Entries	Hundred or other division	Hearth Tax Unit = Parish/Borough	Ecclesiastical Parishes prior to 1832
346	18		Willopp bor	Aldington det.[311]
347	13		Stonestreet bor, Stone Street	Lympne
	17		Summersfeild bor	Sellindge
	25	Street, Lower	Selling bor	Sellindge
348	12		Bellery Key bor, Billerica	Lympne (formerly Court at Street)
	3		Hast bor, Hurst	Hurst
	23		Bonington bor	Bonnington
349		Oxney		Stone and part of Ebony[312] and Wittersham
	27		Church bor	Stone
	15		Chrissenden bor, Kyrsmonden	? Wittersham
	20		Palster bor, Palstre	Wittersham
350	9		Knock Barnett bor, Knock	Stone
	5		Ownam bor, Onenhamme, ? Odiam	? Ebony
	37		Oxney Stone	Stone
351		Heane		Postling, Saltwood and part of [Lympne]
	23	Heane, Upper		Postling,
	28	Heane, Lower	Castle bor	Saltwood
352	10		Thorne bor	Saltwood, ? Lympne
		Folkestone		Alkham, Capel, Cheriton, Hawkinge, Newington, Swingfield and part of Acrise, Folkestone, [Hougham] and Lydden
	4	Folkestone, Upper	Evering bor, Everden	Alkham
	18		Alkham bor	Alkham
	6		Chilton bor	Alkham
	10		Standing bor, Standen	Hawkinge
353	18		Foxhall bor, Foxhole, Foxholt	Swingfield, ? Acrise
	4		Lidden bor	Lydden
	13		Hawking bor	Hawkinge
	9		Coldam bor, Cauldham	Capel, ? Hougham
354	34		Folkestone, Upper, not charged	

[311] Willop lies in a detached portion of Aldington parish to the east of Botolph's Bridge. This area appears to be in the Liberty of Romney Marsh, for which there is no normally no hearth tax data.

[312] The maps show part of Ebony in Aloesbridge hundred, but this is not noted in Kilburne or Hasted.

Pge	No of Entries	Hundred or other division	Hearth Tax Unit = Parish/Borough	Ecclesiastical Parishes prior to 1832
354	18[313]	Folkestone, Lower	West Brook bor	Newington
	21		East Brooke bor	Newington
355	11		Orping bor, ?Arpinge	Newington
	11		Argrow bor, Argrove	Hawkinge
356	12		Ashell bor, Asholt, Ashley	? Folkestone, ? Newington
	12		Broadmead bor	Folkestone
	10		Upingwell bor, Uphill	Hawkinge
357	20		Cheriton bor	Cheriton
		Ham, Upper		Orlestone and part of Ruckinge, [Shadoxhurst] and Warehorne
	5		Rooad bor	?
	7		Warhorne bor	Warehorne
358	5		East Ham bor	? Ruckinge
	16		Orlestone bor	Orlestone
	25		Super Snoad bor, ?Sibersnoth	Orlestone
359		St Martin and Longport, Upper		Midley and part of Broomhill, Ivychurch and Old Romney
	12		Doddington bor	?
	10		Southreeve bor	?
	1		Orleston	?
		Newchurch, Upper		Bilsington, and part of Ruckinge
	14		Huningherst bor	Ruckinge
360	6		Church bor	? Ruckinge
	19		Bilsington Church bor	Bilsington
		Aloesbridge, Upper		Brenzett, Brookland, Fairfield, Snargate and part of [Ivychurch]
	29		Brook bor	?
361	12		Missell ham bor, Misleham	Brookland
	9		Little Chapham bor, Chasthamme	?
	14		Flotham bor, Flodham	Snargate
363		ST AUGUSTINE Bleangate		Chislet, Herne, Hoath, Reculver, Stourmouth, Sturry, Swalecliffe and part of Westbere
	44	Bleangate, Upper	Stroud bor	Herne

[313] The names of several people charged in all the boroughs in the lower half of Folkestone hundred have been repeated in the non-chargeable list, and the second entries have not been counted.

Pge	No of Entries	Hundred or other division	Hearth Tax Unit = Parish/Borough	Ecclesiastical Parishes prior to 1832
363	25		Hampton bor	Herne
364	21		Thornden bor	Herne
	65		Haw bor	Herne
365	30		Belting bor	Herne
366	17		East Stower Mouth bor	Stourmouth
	13		Brookgate bor in Reculver	Reculver
	11		Reculver Street bor	Reculver
367	42		Hoath bor	Hoath
	11		West Stowermouth bor	Stourmouth
368	22	Bleangate, Lower	Earnbough bor, Armsborough	Chislet
	19		Bleangate bor	Chislet
	19		Westbeech and Ore bor	Chislet
369	26		Hatch bor	Chislet
	22		Craft bor	Chislet
370	17		Westbeere par and bor	Westbere
	8		Buckwell bor in Sturry	Sturry
	11		Blaxland bor in Sturry	Sturry
	44		Sturry Street bor	Sturry
371	13		Buckland bor in Sturry	Sturry
	15		Hoath bor in Sturry	Sturry
372	12		Coakett bor in Sturry	Sturry
	6		Swackliff par and bor	Swalecliffe
		Whitstable		**SS Cosmus and Damian in the Blean, and part of Seasalter and Whitstable**
	20	Whitstable, Upper	Whitstaple bor	Whitstable
373	10		Grimgill bor	Whitstable
	9		Bullinge bor	Whitstable
	15		Bourne bor	Whitstable
374	57	Whitstable, Lower		SS Cosmus and Damian in the Blean
	20		Sessalter bor, Seasalter	Seasalter
375		**Westgate**		**Archbishop's Palace precincts, Harbledown, Milton, St Dunstan's, Thanington, and parts of Holy Cross Westgate Without, St Alphage, St Gregory's, St Mary Northgate, St Paul's, St Stephen's Hackington, Seasalter, Westbere and Whitstable**
	33		Hackington bor	Hackington
	49		St Dunstane par	St Dunstan's
376	94		Holy Cross Westgate par and bor	Holy Cross (Westgate Without)
378	48		St Michael Harbledown bor	Harbledown

Pge	No of Entries	Hundred or other division	Hearth Tax Unit = Parish/Borough	Ecclesiastical Parishes prior to 1832
378	8		Tunford bor	Thanington
379	31		Harwich bor	Whitstable, Seasalter. Detached and physically in Whitstable hundred
	2		Rushbourne bor	Westbere. Detached and physically in Bleangate hundred
	36		Staplegate bor	Extra-parochial [314]
380	15		St Grigoryes bor	St Gregory's, Canterbury
	12		Archbishop's Pallace precincts	Archbishop's Palace (within City)
	31		Cockering bor	Thanington
381	81		Longport bor	St Paul's, Longport (detached part of Westgate)
382	63	Christ Church Precincts	Christ Church precincts	Christ Church under Westgate, but within City
383		Downhamford		Adisham, Ickham, Littlebourne, Stodmarsh, Wickhambreaux, and part of Staple and St Stephen's Hackington
	14	Downhamford Upper	Seton bor in Ickham par, Seaton	Ickham
384	19		Bromling bor in Ickham par, Bramling	Ickham
	20		Cottnam bor in Ickham par, Cottenham	Ickham
	37		Staple bor	Staple. Detached and physically in Wingham hundred
385	37		Adsham bor	Adisham
	6	Downhamford Lower	Shourt bor	St Stephen's, Hackington. Detached and physically in Westgate hundred, but cannot be mapped
386	21		Stadmarsh bor	Stodmarsh
	24		Wickhambrucks, North bor	Wickhambreaux
	32		Wickhambrucks, South bor	Wickhambreaux
387	84		Littlebourne bor	Littlebourne
388		Wingham		Ash, Goodnestone, Wingham, Womenswold and part of Eythorne and Nonington
	53	Wingham, Upper	Wingham Street bor	Wingham
389	21		Winghamwell bor	Wingham

[314] For the complex situation in Canterbury see Appendix V.

Pge	No of Entries	Hundred or other division	Hearth Tax Unit = Parish/Borough	Ecclesiastical Parishes prior to 1832
389	13		Rowling bor, Rolling	Goodnestone
390	47		Goodnestone bor	Goodnestone
	19		Wimblingswould bor	Womenswold, Nonington
391	10		Eythorne bor	Eythorne. Detached and physically in Eastry hundred
	12		Twittham bor	Wingham, Goodnestone
	63	Wingham, Lower	Chilton bor	Ash
392	43		Overland bor	Ash
393	9		Wenderton bor	Wingham
		Preston		**Elmstone and Preston**
	12		Elmeston bor	Elmstone
	5		Dureson bor	Preston
394	14		Blackin bor	Preston
	38		Inn bor	Preston
395		**Ringslow (Thanet)**		**Minster, Monkton, St Lawrence Ramsgate, St Nicholas at Wade**
	28	Ringslow	St Nicholas at Wade	St Nicholas at Wade
	33		Moncton par	Monkton
396	93		St Lawrence East bor	St Lawrence Ramsgate
397	69		Minster Street bor	Minster
398	36		Way bor	Minster
	45		West bor	St Lawrence Ramsgate
399		**Cornilo**		**East Langdon, Great Mongeham, Little Mongeham, Northbourne, Ripple, Sholden, Sutton**
	21	Cornilo, Upper	Northbourne bor	Northbourne
400	39		Great Mongeham bor	Great Mongeham, ? Little Mongeham
	25		Finglesham bor	Northbourne
401	26		Shoulden bor	Sholden
	30	Cornilo, Lower	Ashley bor	Northbourne
402	4		In Ticknes, Tickenhurst	Northbourne
	22		In Sutton	Sutton
	15		In Ripple	Ripple
	20		In Marten and East Langden	East Langdon
403		**Eastry**		**Barfreston, Betteshanger, Chillenden, Ham, Knowlton, Tilmanstone, Worth, and part of Denton, Eastry, Eythorne, Nonington, Staple, Waldershare, Woodnesborough and Wootton**
	46	Eastry, Upper	Eastry and Street	Eastry
404	7		Hacklings	Worth
	10		Hamden and Selson	Eastry

Pge	No of Entries	Hundred or other division	Hearth Tax Unit = Parish/Borough	Ecclesiastical Parishes prior to 1832
404	5		Felderland	Eastry, Worth
	18		Word Street	Worth
	9		Craythorn bor	Tilmanstone
405	12		Socken Langden, South Langdon	Eythorne
	7		Barnsole	Staple, Woodnesborough
	6		Geddings	Wootton. Detached, and physically in Denton in Kinghamford hundred
	26		Tilmanstone Street bor	Tilmanstone
406	17	Eastry, Lower	Coldfryday bor	Woodnesborough
	21		Chillenden bor	Chillenden
	12		Barfreston bor	Barfreston
407	13		Each bor	Woodnesborough
	17		Easole bor	Nonington
	23		Nonington	Nonington
408	40		Hamwell bor	Knowlton, Woodnesborough
	29		Denton par	Denton. Detached and physically in Kinghamford hundred
409	4		Waldeshare (Appleton bor)	Waldershare. Detached and physically in Cornilo hundred
	7		Ham and Bettshanger	Ham, Betteshanger
		Kinghamford		Barham, Bishopsbourne, Kingston, and part of Denton and Wootton
	6		In Giddens	Wootton
	36		Barham	Barham
410	30		Bishopsbourne bor	Bishopsbourne
411	22		Out Elmested bor, Out Elmstead	Barham
	22		Shelvinge bor, Shelving	Barham
	12		Barton bor, Burton	Barham
412	47		Kingston par	Kingston
		Bewsborough		Buckland, Coldred, Ewell, Guston, Oxney, Poulton, River, Shepperdswell, St Margaret at Cliffe, West Cliffe, West Langdon, Whitfield and part of Charlton, Hougham, Lydden, and Waldershare.
	28	Bewsborough, Upper	Shepperdswell bor, Sibbertswold	Shepherdswell
413	18		Gustone bor	Guston
	3		Westcliff bor	West Cliffe
	36		St Margaretts Atcliff bor	St Margaret at Cliffe, ? Oxney
414	8		Whitfield bor	Whitfield

Pge	No of Entries	Hundred or other division	Hearth Tax Unit = Parish/Borough	Ecclesiastical Parishes prior to 1832
414	8		Waldersheire bor	Waldershare
	20		West Langdon bor	West Langdon
415	5		Coldred bor	Coldred
	36	Bewsborough, Lower	Hougham par	Hougham, Poulton[315]. Detached by Cinque Port of Dover
	24		Buckland and Charlton	Buckland, Charlton
416	36		River par	River
	26		Ewell par	Ewell
417	10		Lidden par	Lydden
		Bridge and Petham		Bridge, Lower Hardres, Nackington, Petham, Patrixbourne and part of [Chartham], [St Stephen's Hackington], Upper Hardres and Waltham
	10	Bridge and Petham, Upper	Blackmansbury bor	Bridge
	31		Bridge bor	Bridge
418	6		Cheyney bor, Cheney	Patrixbourne
	14		Patrixbourne bor	Patrixbourne
	5		Nackington	Nackington
419	14		Lower Hardres	Lower Hardres
	33		Upper Hardres	Upper Hardres
	4	Bridge and Petham, Lower	Shipcourt bor in Waltham, Sheep Court	Waltham
420	24		Savintoune bor, Sappington	Petham
	15		Granaker bor, Grandacre	Waltham
	10		Temple bor	Waltham
421	9		Cotterell bor	Petham
	19		Hanvelle bor, Hanville	Waltham
	27		Broadway bor	Petham
422	6		Stonestreet bor	Petham
		SCRAY Tenterden		Tenterden, and part of Ebony
430	94		Towne bor	Tenterden
432	53		Castweasle bor	Tenterden
433	83		Boresyle bor	Tenterden
434	20		Shrubcoate bor	Tenterden
	35		Dumborne bor	Tenterden
435	11		Reading bor	Ebony

[315] The maps suggest that Poulton is wholly in Folkestone, but this is not recognised in the hearth tax, or in Kilburne or Hasted.

ABBREVIATIONS

CCA	Canterbury Cathedral Archives
CKS	Centre for Kentish Studies
DoE	Department of the Environment
DNB	Dictionary of National Biography
FFHS	Federation of Family History Societies
KCC	Kent County Council
NMR	National Monuments Record
OS	Ordnance Survey
PRO	Public Record Office
RCHME	Royal Commission on the Historical Monuments of England
VCH	Victoria History of the Counties of England

BIBLIOGRAPHY

Andrewes, J., 'Land, Family and Community in Wingham and its Environs. An Economic and Social History of Rural Society in East Kent from *c.* 1450 - 1640', unpublished PhD thesis (University of Kent, 1991)

Arkell, T., 'The incidence of poverty in England in the later seventeenth century', *Social History*, 12 (1987), 23-64

Arkell, T., 'Printed instructions for administering the Hearth Tax', in *Surveying the People*, ed. by Schürer and Arkell, pp. 39-41

Arkell, T., 'An examination of the Poll taxes of the later seventeenth century, the Marriage Duty Act and Gregory King', in *Surveying the People*, ed. by Schürer and Arkell, pp.130-80

Armstrong, A., ed., *The Economy of Kent, 1640-1914*, (KCC, Woodbridge, 1995)

Barnwell, P. S. and A. T. Adams, *The House Within: Interpreting Medieval Houses in Kent* (RCHME, London, 1994)

Beckett, J. V. et al., *Nottinghamshire Hearth Tax, 1664:1674*, Thoroton Society Record Series, 38 (Nottingham, 1988)

Berry, W., ed., *Kent County Genealogies* (1830)

Braddick, M. J., *Parliamentary Taxation in Seventeenth-Century England* (Woodbridge, 1994)

Bunce, C. R., *Ancient Canterbury Records of Alderman Bunce, 1800-1801*, republished from the Kentish Gazette 1800-1801

Chalklin, C. W., 'The Compton Census of 1676 - the dioceses of Canterbury and Rochester', in *A Seventeenth-Century Miscellany*, Kent Records, 17 (1960)

Chalklin, C. W., *Seventeenth-Century Kent* (London, 1965)

Chalklin, C. W., 'The Making of Some New Towns, c. 1600-1720', in *Rural Change and Urban Growth, 1500-1800* , ed. by C. W. Chalklin and M. A. Havinden (London, 1974), pp. 229-52

Chalklin, C. W., 'The Towns', in Armstrong, *Economy of Kent, 1640-1914*

Chandaman, C. D., *English Public Revenue 1660-1688* (Oxford, 1975)

Clark, P., 'Migration in England during the late seventeenth and early eighteenth centuries,' *Past and Present*, 83 (1979), 57-90

Clark, P. and P. Slack, *English Towns in Transition* (London, 1976)

Clark, P. and L. Murfin, *The History of Maidstone* (Stroud, 1996)

Coleman, D. C., 'The Economy of Kent under the Later Stuarts', University of London unpublished PhD thesis (1951)

Coleman, D. C. and J. Gibson, 'Naval Dockyards under the Later Stuarts', *Economic History Review*, Ser. 2, 6 (1953-4), 134-55

Collier, S., *Whitehaven, 1660-1800* (RCHME, London, 1991)

Cooper, N., *Houses of the Gentry, 1480-1680* (New Haven & London, 1999)

Dobson, M. J., 'Original Compton Census Returns - The Shoreham Deanery', *Archaeologia Cantiana*, 94 (1978), 61-73

Dobson, M. J., 'The last hiccup of the old demographic regime: population stagnation and decline in late seventeenth and early eighteenth-century south-east England', *Continuity and Change*, 4 (1989), 395-428

Dobson, M. J., 'Population, 1640-1831', in Armstrong, *Economy of Kent, 1640-1914*

Dobson, M. J., *Contours of Death and Disease in Early Modern England* (Cambridge, 1997)

Doubleday, H. A., ed., *The Complete Peerage*, by G.E.C., vol. IX (1936)

Du Boulay, F. R. H., *The Lordship of Canterbury* (London and Edinburgh, 1966)

Dulley, A. F., 'People and homes in the Medway Towns: 1687-1783', *Archaeologia Cantiana*, 77 (1962), 160-76

Dyer, A. D., 'The market towns of south-east England, 1500-1700', *Southern History*, 1 (1979), 123-34

Eaves, D., 'Wingham: its vernacular buildings pre 1700', unpublished Diploma thesis in Local History (University of Kent, 1982)

Edwards, D. G., ed., *Derbyshire Hearth Tax Assessments, 1662-70*, Derbyshire Record Society, 7 (1982)

Evans, N., ed., *Cambridgeshire Hearth Tax, Michaelmas 1664*, British Record Society, Hearth Tax Series I (London, 2000)

Evelyn, J., *The Diary of John Evelyn*, ed. by Guy de la Bédoyère (Bangor, 1994)

Everitt, A., *The Community of Kent and the Great Rebellion, 1640-60* (Leicester, 1966)

Everitt, A., 'The making of the agrarian landscape of Kent', *Archaeologia Cantiana*, 92 (1976), 1-31

Everitt, A., *Continuity and Colonization: the Evolution of Kentish Settlement* (Leicester, 1986)

Fiennes, C., *The Illustrated Journeys of Celia Fiennes*, ed. by C. Morris (Exeter, 1982)

Gibson, J., and A. Dell, *The Protestation Returns 1641-42 and other contemporary listings* (FFHS, 1995)

Gibson, J., *The Hearth Tax and other later Stuart Tax Lists and the Association Oath Rolls* (FFHS, 2nd edition, 1996)

Glasscock, R. E., *The Lay Subsidy of 1334*, British Academy Records of Social and Economic History, new series, vol. ii (1975)

Gravett, K., *Timber and Brick Building in Kent* (London and Chichester, 1971)

Guillery, P. and B. Herman, 'Deptford Houses: 1650 to 1800', *Vernacular Architecture*, 30 (1999), forthcoming

Harris, J., *The History of Kent*, 1 (London, 1719)

Harrison, W., *The Description of England* (Dover edn., Washington and New York, 1998)

Hasted, E., *The History and Topographical Survey of the County of Kent*, 12 volumes, (1797-1801, 2nd edn reprinted, Canterbury 1972, with an introduction by A. Everitt)

Hastings, P., *Upon the Quarry Hills: A History of Boughton Monchelsea (Boughton Monchelsea, 2000)*

Hatcher, J., *The History of the British Coal Industry, vol. 1, before 1700: Towards the Age of Coal* (Oxford, 1993)

Hoskins, W. G., 'The Rebuilding of Rural England, 1570-1640', *Past and Present*, 4 (1953), 44-59

Hoyle, R., *Tudor Taxation Records* (London, 1994)

Hull, C. H., ed., *Economic Writings of Sir William Petty*, 2 vols (Cambridge, 1899)

Husbands, C., 'Hearth, wealth and occupations: an exploration of the hearth tax in the later seventeenth century' in *Surveying the People*, ed. by Schürer and Arkell, pp. 65-77

Husbands, C., 'Regional change in a pre-industrial economy: wealth and population in England in the sixteenth and seventeenth centuries', *Journal of Historical Geography*, 13 (1987), 348-9

Hyde, P. and D. Harrington, *Hearth Tax Returns for Faversham Hundred 1662-1671* (Lyminge, 1998)

Inderwich, F. A., *Inner Temple Admissions 1547-1660* (n. ed. pb. 1877)

Inderwich, F. A., *Calendar of Inner Temple Records, vol. II, 1603-1660* (1896)

Johnson, M., *Housing Culture* (London, 1993)

Jordan, W. K., 'Social Institutions in Kent, 1480-1660', *Archaeologia Cantiana,*75 (1961), 32-56

Kelsall, A. F., 'The London House Plan in the Later 17th Century', *Post-Medieval Archaeology*, 8 (1974), 80-91

Kilburne, R., *A Topographie or Survey of the County of Kent* (London, 1659)

Laithwaite, M., 'A Ship-Master's House at Faversham, Kent', *Post-Medieval Archaeology*, 2 (1968), 150-62

Lambarde, W., *A Perambulation of Kent, 1570* (Bath, 1970)

Lansberry, H. F. C., ed., *Sevenoaks Wills and Inventories, in the reign of Charles II*, Kent Records, 25 (Maidstone, 1988)

Laslett, P., *The World We Have Lost* (London, 1965)

Machin, R., 'The Great Rebuilding: a Reassessment', *Past and Present*, 77 (1977), 33-56

McCrae, S. G. and C. P. Burnham, *The Rural Landscape of Kent* (Wye College, 1973)

Meekings, C. A. F., ed., *Surrey Hearth Tax 1664*, Surrey Record Society, 17 (1940)

Meekings, C. A. F., ed., *Dorset Hearth Tax Assessments, 1662-1664* (Dorchester, 1951)

Meekings, C. A. F., *Analysis of Hearth Tax Accounts 1662-1665*, List and Index Society, 153 (1979)

Mills, D. Nash, *The Nash Families in Goodnestone-next-Wingham*, Faversham Papers, 55 (1997)

Newman, J., *West Kent and the Weald*, 2nd edn (The Buildings of England, Harmondsworth, 1980)

Newman, J., *North East and East Kent*, 3rd edn (The Buildings of England, Harmondsworth, 1983)

O'Neill, B. H. St J., 'North Street, Folkestone, Kent', *Antiquaries Journal*, 29 (1949), 8-12

Parkin, E. W., 'The Ancient Cinque Port of Sandwich', *Archaeologia Cantiana*, 100 (1984), 189-216

Parkinson, E., ed., *The Glamorgan Hearth Tax Assessment of 1670*, South Wales Record Society (Cardiff, 1994)

Pearson, S., *The Medieval Houses of Kent: an Historical Analysis* (RCHME, London, 1994)

Pearson, S., 'Boughton Monchelsea Buildings' in Hastings, *Upon the Quarry Hills*

Pearson, S., P. S. Barnwell and A. T. Adams, *A Gazetteer of Medieval Houses in Kent* (RCHME, London, 1994)

Pepys, S., *The Shorter Pepys*, ed. by Robert Latham (London, 1985)

Petty, W., *Economic Writings of Sir William Petty*, ed. by C. H. Hull, 2 vols (Cambridge, 1899)

Platt, C., *The Great Rebuilding of Tudor and Stuart England* (London, 1994)

Power, M. J., 'East London housing in the seventeenth century', in *Crisis and Order in English Towns, 1500 – 1700*, ed. by P. Clark and P. Slack (London, 1972), pp. 237-62

Power, M. J., 'Shadwell: The Development of a London Suburban Community in the Seventeenth Century', *The London Journal*, 4 (1978), 29-46

Ruderman, A. W., 'Hearth Tax', *Journal of Kent History*, 13 (1981), 2-3

Ruderman, A. W., *A History of Ashford* (1994)

Quiney, A., *Kent Houses* (Woodbridge, 1993)

Schürer K., and T. Arkell, eds, *Surveying the People* (Local Population Studies Supplement, Oxford, 1992)

Sheail, J., *The Regional Distribution of Wealth in England as indicated in the 1524/5 Lay Subsidy Returns*, ed. by R.W. Hoyle, List and Index

Society, Special Series, 28, parts 1 and 2, and 29, parts 1 and 2 (Kew, 1998)

Short, B., 'The South-East: Kent, Surrey and Sussex' in *Agrarian History*, 6, ed. by J. Thirsk, pp. 270-313

Smith, J. T., *English Houses, 1200-1800, the Hertfordshire Evidence* (RCHME, London, 1992)

Spufford, H. M., 'The significance of the Cambridgeshire hearth tax', *Proceedings Cambridgeshire Antiquarian Society*, 55 (1962), 53-64

Spufford, M., 'The limitations of the probate inventory', in *English Rural Society, 1500-1800*, ed. by J. D. Chartres and D. Hey (Cambridge, 1990)

Stoate, T. L., *Cornwall Hearth and Poll Taxes 1661-1664* (Bristol, 1981)

Stoate, T. L., *Devon Hearth Tax Return, Lady Day 1674* (Bristol, 1982)

Styles, P., 'Introduction to the Warwickshire hearth tax records', *Warwick County Records: Hearth Tax Returns*, 1 (1957)

Thirsk, J., ed., *The Agrarian History of England and Wales: 1500 -1640*, 4 (Cambridge, 1967); *1640-1750*, 5 (Cambridge, 1984)

Thirsk, J., 'The Farming Regions of England', in *Agrarian History*, 4, ed. by J. Thirsk, pp. 55-64

Victoria History of the Counties of England, *Kent*, III (London, 1932)

Wallenberg, J. K., *The Place-Names of Kent* (Uppsala, 1934)

Webster, W. F., ed., *Nottinghamshire Hearth Tax 1664:1674*, with an introduction by J. V. Beckett, M. W. Barley and S. C. Wallwork, Thoroton Society Record Series, xxxvii (Nottingham, 1988)

Whiteman, A., ed., *The Compton Census of 1676: a critical edition*, British Academy, Records of Social and Economic History, NS 10 (Oxford, 1986)

Wight, J. A., *Brick Building in England from the Middle Ages to 1550* (London,1972)

Williams, P., *The Later Tudors, 1547-1603* (Oxford, 1995)

Winzar, P., 'Peirce House, Charing: the house and its owners', *Archaeologia Cantiana*, 111 (1993), 131-200

Withycombe, E. G., *The Oxford Dictionary of English Christian Names* (1989)

Witney, K. P., *The Jutish Forest* (London, 1976)

Wrigley, E. and R. S. Schofield, *The Population History of England, 1540-1871: a Reconstruction* (London, 1981)

Zell, M., *Industry in the Countryside* (Cambridge, 1994)

Personal name Index.

Adle *See* Adley
Adleton: John, 207
Adley *(Adle, Adly)*; Elias, 285;
  John, 331; Thomas, 39
Adlow: Francis, 97
Adman: Goodwife, 421; Henry,
  95; John, 331; Nicholas, 331;
  Robert, 314, 315, 330
Admans: Robert, 333; William,
  381
Adnett *(Admitt, Adnitt)*: Richard,
  348; Thomas, 348
Adoe: John, 307
Adren: Widow, 283
Adrian: Francis, 278
Adsly *(Adsley)*: Anthony, 193;
  Geoffrey, 196; Robert, 196;
  Thomas, 196
Adson *(Adsonn)*: John, 223;
  Thomas, 88
Ady Edmund, 97; Edward, 263;
  Gregory, 269; Henry, 173; Mr,
  173; Mrs, 262, 275; Simon, 111
  Cf. Eady, Hady
Adyson: John; junior, 166; senior,
  165
Aelst: John, 341
Afford George, 254
  Cf. Foord
Affrey: Edward, 396
Ager: Edward, 313; Mr, 380
Agge: Geoffrey, 70
Aggs: John, 3
Aieles *(Aiele)*: Edmund, 157;
  George, 157; senior, 157; Simon,
  395; Widow, 157
Akers: Henry, 337; William, 43,
  308
  Cf. Acres
Akerst *(Acurst)*: William, 65, 260
Alard: Edward, 72
Alay: Thomas, 224
Albert: Richard, 155

Albery: Thomas, 374
Albourne *(Alborne)*: John, 137;
  Widow, 137; William, 252
Alchin *(Allchin, Allichin)*: Henry,
  80; John, 80, 154; Nicholas, 284;
  Richard, 43; Robert, 70;
  Thomas, 41, 164; Widow, 80,
  209, 210; William, 75, 235
Alchorne: John, 105
Alcock *(Alcocke)*: Anthony, 149;
  Richard, 150; Samuel, 308, 336;
  Stephen, 217; junior, 217;
  Thomas, 144; Widow, 156
Alcone: Captain, 258
Aldcroft: William, 431
Aldersey *(Aldersea)*: Farnham, 187;
  John, 287; Terry, 242, 262, 263;
  Thomas, 23
Alderson: Mrs, 5; Richard, 289;
  Widow, 12
Alderston: John, 396; junior, 397
Aldey: Edward, 382; Mr, 436
Aldrey: Widow, 321
Aldridge *(Aldridg, Alridge)*:
  Ambrose, 265; Augustine, 194;
  Edward, 196; Goodman; junior,
  364; senior, 364, 382; Jeremiah,
  19; John, 39; Martin, 192;
  Thomas, 381, 382
Alewood: Tryman, 21
Aleword: John, 80; Widow, 80
Aleworth: John, 29
Alexander *(Allexander)*: James, 445;
  Mr, 19; Robert, 123; Thomas,
  268
Alford: Edward, 9; Gilford, 7;
  Widow, 13
Alfrey: Edward, 399; John, 154
Aliard: Robert, 84
Allard: Henry, 216; Iden, 179;
  Richard, 244; Robert, 183;
  William, 176
Allchurch: William, 216

B

Beard: Abraham, 185; junior, 183; Ann, 185; Daniel, 269; Henry, 388, 394; Isaac, 190; James, 187; John, 57, 152; Richard, 114, 161; Thomas, 389; William, 405

Beardsworth: John, 42; Widow, 43

Beare *See* Beere

Beareman *(Bearman)*

Bearman. John, 285; Thomas, 166 *Cf.* Barman, Burman

Bearton: Robert, 50

Beast: William, 193

Beat: William, 381

Beates: Robert, 273

Beatman: Widow, 358

Beaver: Michael, 187

Beawmont: William, 54

Beck *(Becke):* John, 217; Widow, 155

Beckenham: Wolssi, 63

Beckett: Abraham, 175; John, 78, 122, 178, 192; Philip, 115; Robert, 188; Thomas, 113, 127, 130, 258; Widow, 55, 164; William, 134, 178

Beckhing *See* Beeching

Beckinsall: William, 120

Beckley: Thomas, 27

Beckman: Gabriel, 187

Bedam *See* Bedham

Beddingfield *(Beddingfeild):* Humphrey, 337; Peter, 335; Timothy, 336; Widow, 411

Beddington: Widow, 96

Bedford: John, 35; Thomas, 63, 83; William, 372

Bedgeant: Thomas, 344

Bedham *(Bedam, Bedum):* Thomas, 176, 177; William, 192

Bedoe: Humphrey, 392; John, 392

Bedum *See* Bedham

Bedwell: Edward, 179; Henry, 404; John, 190

Bee: Edward, 123

Beech. Family, 251; George, 364; Thomas, 19, 20; William, 247, 364, 407 *Cf.* Beach

Beecham *(Beechum):* Family, 381; George, 446; John, 160; William, 417

Beecher: Daniel, 34; Henry, 51; James, 44, 51; Joan, 51; Peter, 126; Richard, 21, 140; Robert, 55; Widow, 55, 122, 142; William, 55, 117

Beeching *(Beckhing, Beechen, Beechin):* Abel, 106; Christopher, 444; Henry, 433; James, 240, 252; John, 156, 299, 350; Nicholas, 316; Richard, lxxv, lxxvi, 230, 245, 313, 432; Samuel, 431; Simon, lxxv, 309, 313; the elder, lxxv; Thomas, 160, 304; Widow, 253; William, 224

Beekman: Daniel, 187

Beeland *(Beland):* Richard; senior, 237; Simon, 236

Beeles *See* Beale

Beere *(Beare, Beer):* Francis, 31; George, 401; Henry, 347; John, 343; Philip, 416; Richard, 406; Suckling, 72; Thomas, 416; Widow, 322

Beereling: Goodwife, 278

Beesam. John, 175 *Cf.* Beeson

Beeson *(Beesam):* John, 175; Mary, 442

Beeste: Roger, 16

Beeston: Mr, 129

Beetchar: Thomas, 42; Widow, 43

Beets: Thomas, 71

Begford: Richard, 194

Beland *See* Beeland

Richard, 191; Robert, 316;
Thomas, 37; William, 109
Boulden *See* Bolden
Boulding *See* Bolding
Boules *See* Bowles
Boult: Widow, 393
Boulten *See* Bolton
Boulter: John, 152
Boulton *See* Bolton
Bounds *(Bound):* John, 266; Ralph,
284
Bount: John, 446
Bourder *See* Border
Bourman *See* Booreman
Bourne: Bethulia, 312; Cheyney,
260; Daniel, 302, 312; Edward,
211; Henry, 122; James, 114,
115; John, 125, 148, 249, 329,
434; Mr, 175; Nicholas, 290;
Richard, 244, 301; Robert, 141,
244; Thomas, 55, 94, 270, 363,
446; Walter, 142; Widow, 150,
409; William, 160, 276
Bousar: John, 340
Bowden: John, 184; Thomas, 203
Bowen *(Bowens, Bowin):* Abel, 103,
314; George, 13
Bower *See* Bowyer
Bowers: John, 10, 194; Ralph, 17;
Widow, 6, 13; William, 195
Bowes: James, 288; Richard, 12
Bowin *See* Bowen
Bowl *(Boule, Bowell):* Daniel, 202;
John, 207, 209; Thomas, 263,
414; William, 265, 384
Bowles *(Boules):* Charles, 194;
Henry, 251; John, 133, 136, 171;
Michael, 2; Robert, 230;
Thomas, 2; Widow, 136, 260;
William, 196
Bowman: George, 191; William;
junior, 159; senior, 159

Bowyer *(Bower, Boyer):* Aaron,
234; George, 4; John, 9, 192,
287; Richard, 25, 58; Sarah, 14;
Stephen, 25; Thomas, 16;
William, 87
Boxer: Richard, 256
Boyce: John, 307; Thomas, 15
Boycon *See* Boykin
Boycott *(Boykett):* Francis, 105;
George, 327; Widow, 371;
William, 277, 310
Boyden: Bonham, 122; John, 6
Boyer *See* Bowyer
Boykett *See* Boycott
Boykin *(Boycon):* Abiezer, cviii,
392; Bartholomew, 393;
Gervase, 368; James, 344; John,
351; Widow, 408
Boyman: William, 415
Boys: Anthony, 267; Edward, 297;
Family, lxxxiv, lxxxix; Francis,
459; John, lxxxiv, lxxxv,
lxxxviii, 147, 200, 374, 390, 407,
409; Margaret, 224; Mr, 389;
Richard, 80; Robert, 264, 412,
418; Widow, 226, 291; William,
xxxix, 98, 221, 318
Brabourne *(Brabon, Braborne):*
Benedict, 136; John, 57, 252
Brace: Edward, 265
Bracey: John, 360; William, 360
Bracking: William, 30
Brad: Thomas, 46; Widow, 246
Braddock: Thomas, 290
Bradds: Widow, 152
Bradfeild: George, 285
Bradfoote: Mary, 431
Bradford: Ann, 215; George, 114;
John, 285, 294; Margaret, 191;
Samuel, 295; Thomas, 85
Bradley *(Bradly):* James, 270; John,
386; Nathaniel, 118; Robert, 9;

Buckwell: Henry, 232; John, 233; Robert, 390

Budd: Richard, 26; Thomas, 75, 199

Buddell: William, 29

Buddle: James, 416; William, 416

Budds *(Buds):* After, 179; James, 205; John, 225, 254; Richard, 277, 410; Samuel, 277; Thomas, 226, 227, 410; Widow, 383; William, 258

Budgen: Thomas, 108; Widow, 256

Budgin: Moses, 24; Nicholas, 87; Robert, 376; William, 55

Bueden: John, 241

Buffeild: Mr, 172

Buffett: John, 117

Buggin *(Buggen):* Edward, 133; Mr, 89; Richard, 139

Buggs: Richard, 163; Widow, 253

Builting: Nicholas, 363, 365

Bulard: Lawrence, 119

Bulfinch: Thomas, 192; Widow, 172

Bull: Jacob, 169; John, 127, 212, 281, 321; Mr, 319; Mrs, 319; Widow, 6, 13, 303

Bullen: John, 211; Leonard, 48; Richard, 288; William, 278

Buller: Mr, 79; William, 397

Bulley *See* Bully

Bulling: Arthur, 89

Bullocke *(Bullock):* Edward, 441, 443; John, 230, 231; Robert, 369; Widow, 385

Bully *(Bulley, Buly):* John, 418; Robert, 73; Samuel, 71; Widow, 418

Bulman: James, 363

Buloe: Richard, 197

Bulteele: Susan, 30

Buly *See* Bully

Bunce. Cyprian R., 450; Elizabeth, 409; Henry, 259; James, 27, 103, 243, 267, 281, 282, 289, 404; John, 97, 109, 281, 431; Matthew, 95, 279; Mr, 258; Thomas, 347, 431, 444 *Cf.* Bance, Bence

Bunch: Matthew, 2

Bunckley *(Bunckly):* George, cxi, 301

Bundock: Nicholas, 116

Bungor: William, 103

Bungurst: Nicholas, 217

Bunker: Nicholas, 219

Bunkley: John, 247; Thomas, 247

Bunn: John, 214

Bunnett: Nicholas, 217, 254; Stephen, 215

Bunnyer: Thomas, 111

Bunting: John, 99; Mr, 83; Reynold, 263, 272; Widow, 170

Bunton: Thomas, 99

Bunyard: Arthur, 191; John, 310

Bur *See* Burr

Burbridge *(Burbidge):* Isaac, 110; James, 169; John, 24, 110, 185, 190; Thomas, 62, 176, 184, 214; William, 311

Burch *See* Birch

Burchall: John, 171

Burcham: Richard, 231

Burchatt *See* Birchett

Burcher: John, 258

Burchett *See* Birchett

Burchley *See* Birchley

Burchwood *See* Birchwood

Burd *See* Bird

Burden *(Burdon):* Christopher, 130; Family, 421; Henry, 160; Herbert, 226; Jacob, 147; John, 233, 236; Martin, 233; Nicholas, 7, 252; Richard, 224, 431; Robert, 67, 197, 198; Thomas,

C

367, 395, 440; Widow, 18, 147, 158, 173, 367; William, 100, 161, 172

Chamking: John, 388

Champe *(Champ):* Edward, 288; John, 189, 190, 267; Richard, 288; Thomas, 6, 150; William, 260

Champen: William, 274

Champes *(Champs):* John, 175; Thomas, 235; Widow, 41

Champion: George, 176; Philip, 144; Thomas, 99, 214, 296, 455; William, 294

Champlin: William, 24

Champneys: Richard, 244

Chandler *(Chantler, Chaundler, Chauntler):* Blaze, 6; Ezechiel; senior, 91; Ezechiell, 91; John, 181, 206, 207, 238, 366; Richard, 377; Robert, 6, 38; Samuel, 440; Thomas, 439; Widow, 235, 243, 377

Chantler *See* Chandler

Chaplaine *(Chaplin):* Edward, 357; John, 346

Chapman: Abraham, 258; Anthony, 300; Daniel, 322; Dorothy, 42; Edmund, 45; Edward, 12, 71, 74, 77, 91, 140; senior, 11; George, 79, 337; Henry, 41, 60, 61, 323, 445; James, 60; Joanne, 21; John, 52, 54, 102, 120, 169, 197, 198, 206, 207, 240, 241, 260, 266, 282, 300, 301, 311, 354, 405; Margaret, 27; Margery, 101; Mary, 326; Mr, 172; Nicholas, 76, 300; Peter, 291; Richard, 87, 254; Robert, 54; Simon, 326; Stephen, 246, 302, 303, 356, 357; Thomas, 29, 38, 77, 109, 252, 255, 271, 279, 282, 356; Tobias,

86, 87; Widow, 60, 101, 306, 326; William, 18, 41, 52, 54, 83, 90, 171, 291, 331; senior, 84

Chardy: William, 125

Charles: James, 70; John, 70, 192, 195; Ralph, 119; Widow, 113

Charleton *See* Charlton

Charlewood *See* Charlwood

Charley: Thomas, 43

Charlton *(Charleton):* Abraham, 112; Edward, 100; George, 177; John, 55, 176, 177, 179, 192; junior, 180; senior, 180; Josias, 222; Mr, 175; Thomas, 29, 107; William, 148, 180, 181; junior, 180

Charlwood *(Charlewood):* Robert, 46; William, 45, 58

Charnell: George, 414

Charr: Thomas, 28

Charrett: Thomas, 120

Chart: George, 58; John, 159

Charwood: Thomas, 50

Charye: Thomas, 156

Chase: John, 73; Matthew, 73

Chaser: John, 431

Chatborne: William, 211

Chatsfield *See* Checksfield

Chatten: Widow, 240

Chaundler *See* Chandler

Chauntler *See* Chandler

Chaxell: Goodman, 134; John, 131; Thomas, 134

Chaxsfield *See* Checksfield

Cheater *See* Jeater

Checksfield *(Chatsfield, Chaxsfield, Checksfeild, Chexfield):* Andrew, 71; John, 126, 144, 152; Robert, 317

Chedwick *See* Chadwick

Cheene: Widow, 179

Cheese: Robert, 190; Thomas, 238; William, 27

D

384; Robert, 448; Stephen, 443;
Widow, 408
Daley See Dally
Daling See Dalling
Dalke: John, 76
Dall, Dalle See Dale
Dallender: Mr, 174
Dalling (Daling, Dallin): George,
50; Robert, 38
Dally (Daley, Daly): Alexander, 75;
Christopher, 410; Edward, 327;
Jane, 322; Mary, 38; Robert,
327; Thomas, 49
Dalton: Abraham, 78, 83; John,
58, 75, 82; Richard, 92; Thomas,
46; William, 93, 146
Daly See Dally
Dalyson: Captain, cv; Maximillian,
174
Damant: Philip, 121
Dammar: Richard, 152
Damon: Thomas, 287
Damsell: William, 68
Danck See Dankes; Henry, 320
Dancye: Mrs, 417
Dandie See Dandy
Dandy, 14; Mary, 360; Richard,
337
Dane (Dany): Andrew, 278; Anne,
235; David, 164; Family, 261;
Giles, 349; Godfrey, 134;
Henry, 287; Isaac, 55; James,
167; John, 96, 279; Jonas, 279;
Michael, 151; Robert, 287, 293;
Thomas, 57, 100, 134, 143, 328;
Widow, 384; William, 150
Danes (Dannes): Robert, 102;
Samuel, 14
Danford: Henry, 311; Thomas,
282
Danggerfell: William, 15
Daniell: Edward, 183; Francis, 247;
James, 136; John, 4, 64, 123,

201, 258; Nicholas, 419;
Richard, 119; Stephen, 15;
Thomas, 136, 234, 259, 275;
Widow, 64, 256, 278
Dankes See Danck; James, 194;
Richard, 130; Thomas, 274;
William, 67
Dann (Danne): Clement, 159;
Elisha, 193; George, 176; Isaac,
158; James, 256, 257; John, 112,
161; Joseph, 256; Richard, 144,
145; Robert, 141, 280, 328;
Stephen, 130; Thomas, 104, 125,
128, 133, 139, 244; junior, 329;
senior, 329; Widow, 256;
William, 112, 133, 142, 160, 174,
183, 269, 280
Cf. Denn.
Dannes See Danes
Dannett: William, 41
Dansey: Robert, 273
Danton: George, 51; William, 404
Dany See Dane
Danzey: Elizabeth, 189
Dapp: Widow, 236
Darbers: John, 401
Darby (Darbey): John, 364;
Matthew, 158; Philip, 189;
William, 189, 289
Darell See Darrell
Darker: Arthur, 68; Family, 81;
John, 67; senior, 48; Thomas, 68
Darley: Widow, 376
Darling (Darlin, Darlinge):
Edward, 205; George, 84;
Matthew, 35; Peter, 35; Robert,
81; William, 373
Darnall (Darnell, Durnal): Alice,
204; Thomas, 204, 205
Darne: William, 389
Darnham: George, 131
Darrell (Darell): Family, lxxiii;
John, 313

Death: Thomas, 84, 91, 253
Debley: Richard, 241
Deborbene: Peter, 439
Decoates: Margaret, 444
Decroe: Anthony, 377
Dednam: James, 180
Deeds *(Deedes)*: George, 316; John, 94
Deering *See* Dering
Deerum: John, 188
Defraine: Widow, 69
Dehamell: John, 448
Deines: George, 38
Delabew: Peter, 438
Delapier: Peter, 438, 442
Delaroh: James, 376
Delawne: William, 275
Delber: John, 87
Deley: Widow, 86
Delilier: Arnaud, 442
Dell: Richard, 421
Dellver: Henry, 22
Deloe: Peter, 449; Stephen, 448
Delonoy: Peter, 19
Delton: Henry, 62, 85; James, 24; John, 85; Robert, 85, 230
Delve: Robert, 84
Delver: Henry, 23; John, 85, 86; Richard, 87; Robert, 84; Widow, 82
Demow: Jacob, 448
Dence: Widow, 430
Dench: John, 8
Dendy: Robert, 158
Denew: John, 380, 438; Samuel, 438
Denham *(Dennan)*: John, 432; Thomas, 37, 118; Widow, 48
Denis: Anthony, 438
Denman: John, 29
Denn *(Denne)*: Christopher, 403; David, 388, 392; junior, 387; senior, 387; Henry, 398; James,

414; John, 297, 418, 437, 458; Jonathan, 387; Katherine, 381; Margaret, 342; Mary, 442; Michael, 387; Mr, 412; junior, 216; senior, 216; Mrs, 376; Peter, 410; Samuel, 413; Thomas, 192, 388, 410, 443; Vincent, 442; Widow, 69; William, 343, 419, 438 *Cf.* Dann
Dennan *See* Denham
Dennard: Nathaniel, 264
Denne *See* Denn
Dennett: John, 230; Nicholas, 150; Stephen, 150; Thomas, 146, 221, 229; William, 350
Dennis: David, 38; Edward, 164; George, 40, 161, 187; Henry, 127, 136, 171; senior, 127; Humphrey, 86; John, 72, 126, 148, 186, 347, 388; Philip, 44; Robert, 84, 179; Thomas, 118, 196, 336; William, 126, 128
Dent: Widow, 59
Denton, 117; Robert, 342; Stephen, 147; Thomas, 157
Denward: William, 411
Denwood: Edward, 419
Deprose: John, 135
Deputy: Robert, 65
Deray: Julian, 448
Dering *(Deering, Deringe)*: Christopher, cvii, 1; Edward, xxxix, 316; Elizabeth, cvii; Heneage, cvii; Henry, 270, 318; James, 447, 448; John, cvii; Jonas, 449; Mary, 225; Widow, 313
Deringe *See* Dering
Derling *(Derlin)*: Robert, 86; Thomas, 92
Derrick: Henry, 116; John, 274; Richard, 153

E

Eades *(Eeedes):* Henry, 361;
  Margery, 298; Richard, 201, 204
  Cf. Adds
Eady: William, 208
  Cf. Ady, Hady
Eager: Widow, 23
Eagle: John, 203, 207
Eagles *(Egles):* Abraham, 184;
  David, 138; Isaac, 270; Thomas,
  101; Widow, 49; William, 110
Eaglesfield: William, 166
Eaglestone *(Egleston, Eglestone):*
  John, 157; Richard, 290; Robert,
  155; Tobias, 101
Ealy: Matthew, 101
Earbie: Richard, 7
Eares: Francis, 370
Earle *See* Early
Earles *See* Earls
Earlidge: Jacob, 63; Thomas, 62,
  63
Earls *(Earles):* James, 95; William,
  96
Early *(Earle):* Elizabeth, 21; John,
  32, 108, 143; Mr, 129; Thomas,
  244, 251; Widow, 134, 237, 240
Earme: John, 460
Earne: John, 297, 456
Earstfeild: Thomas, 361
Easden: Elizabeth, 196; Richard,
  289
Easdey: John, 381
Easdowne: George, 201; James,
  115; John, 124, 200
Easland: Richard; senior, 157
Easman: Widow, 315
Eason *(Easonn):* Andrew, 272;
  Ann, 195; Bartholomew, 122;
  John, 132, 148, 193, 271;
  Michael, 373; Richard, 216;
  Robert, 192; Roger, 325;

Thomas, 131, 182, 192, 415;
  Widow, 366; William, 122
East: John, 14, 389; Thomas, 350
Easterfield *(Easterfeild, Esterfeild):*
  William, 248, 249
Eastes *(Easts):* Nicholas, 389;
  Richard, 413; Robert, 414;
  Thomas, 401
Eastgreege: John, 261
Eastland: Edward, 318; George,
  171; John, 135, 162, 171; junior,
  52; Philip, 351; Richard, 64, 136;
  William, 153
Eastmore: William, 32
Eastry: Richard, 185; Roger, 190
Easts *See* Eastes
Eaton *(Eatten, Etten):* Francis, 359;
  Henry, 21; John, 66, 261, 305,
  380; Matthew, 6; Paul, 269;
  Richard, 59; Robert, 331;
  Thomas, 9, 17, 417; Widow, 23,
  69, 267; William, 150, 307
Ebbolt: William, 74
Ebbott: William, 79
Ebbs: Richard, 185
Ebbutt: John, 74; Thomas, 74, 75
Ebsworth: Adrian, 215
Edborow: Richard, 272
Eddenden; Richard, 313
  Cf. Iddenden
Eddisforth: Frances, 383
Edger: Thomas, 85
Edgerton *See* Egerton
Edgett: John, 66
Edgford: Mr, 436
Edghill: Adam, 29; William, 10
Eding: Mr, 415
Edlin: Richard, 6
Edlings: Richard, 3
Edlow: Joseph, 58; Walter, 51
Edmans: Nicholas, 260
Edmeades *(Edmeads, Edmed):*
  James, 201; John, 180; Nicholas,

192; Margaret, 165; Peter, 439; Robert, 155; Widow, 76, 155, 348; William, 74, 154

Fennell: Henry, 393; John, 407

Fenner, 317 *(Vennar, Venner):* Edward, 107, 317; George, 88, 191; Henry, 37, 176, 190; John, 110, 212; Joseph, 315; Rest, 443; Robert, 113, 191; Thomas, 174, 296; Widow, 135, 156

Fennes *(Fenes):* Henry, 161; Mr, 11

Fepes: John, 15

Ferall *See* Ferrall

Fereg: Richard, 194

Fereles: Widow, 173

Feres: William, 307

Ferman *(Farman):* John, 193; Thomas, 33; William, 196

Ferminger: Goodman, 421

Ferne *(Farne, Fearne):* Andrew, 302; Elizabeth, 264; Henry, 36; Joan, 271; John, 300, 326, 400; Robert, 311, 389; William, 400

Fernes *(Farnes):* John, 51, 111, 135; Nicholas, 195; Samuel, 142; William, 96, 236

Ferost: Edward, 246

Ferrall *(Ferall, Ferrell):* John, 37; junior, 133; senior, 133, 137; Stephen, 100, 251; Thomas, 234; Widow, 257

Ferree *See* Ferry

Ferrer: William, 438

Ferris *(Farris, Pharise, Phariss):* John, 35, 96; Richard, 370; Robert, 371; Thomas, 95; Widow, 96, 312

Ferry *(Ferree):* Cornelius, 377; James, 353; Nicholas, 447; Samuel, 437

Fesant: Thomas, 5

Fescue: John, 163

Fesey *(Fesie):* Daniel, 11, 14

Fetherstone *(Fetherston):* Arthur, 257; Henry, 319; John, 161; Widow, 96, 106

Fettyplace *(Fettiplace):* John, 203; Thomas, 208, 209

Feverstone: John, 81

Fewby: Thomas, 208

Fidge: Deborah, 442; Richard, 313; Robert, 442; Thomas, 94, 440, 460

Fidlyn: Nicholas, 57

Field *(Feild):* Ann, 124; Edward, 179; Henry, 124, 215; John, 261, 399; Nathaniel, 249; Richard, 182; Sarah, 192; Thomas, 126, 261, 447; Widow, 7, 110, 202, 287; William, 124, 143, 273, 358

Fieldcooke: John, 291

Fielder, 60 *(Feilder):* George, 3; Henry, 9; John, 154; Mark, 89; junior, 66; senior, 68; Mrs, 68; Richard, 66; Thomas, 36, 68, 69, 76; senior, 68; Widow, 71

Fiffee: David, 27

Figg *(Figge):* Alan, 121; John, 121; Nicholas, 171; Thomas, 99, 108 *Cf.* Fagg.

Figgett: Henry, 121

Filcock *See* Philcock

File: John, 328; Widow, 374

Fill *(Fille):* Jasper, 50; John, 385; Stephen, 384; William, 223

Filler *(Fyler):* John, 128; Richard, 407

Fillips *See* Phillips

Fillmer *See* Filmer

Fills: Widow, 280

Filly: Thomas, 246

Filmer *(Fillmer):* Ann, 111; Elizabeth, 265; Henry, 262; James, 108; John, 235, 281; Richard, 284; Robert, 96; Thomas, 94, 97, 98, 100;

Fullagat: John, 106
Fullager *(Fiullagar, Fullager,*
Fulliger): Christopher, 104, 244,
276; James, 315; John, 232;
Matthias, 269; William, 232
Fuller: Abraham, 248; Ann, 84;
Anthony, 48; Bartholomew,
222; Edmund, 69; Edward, 38;
Elizabeth, 96; Gabriel, 271;
George, 152; James, 101; John,
27, 68, 79, 90, 140, 179, 193,
228, 231, 397; Jonah, 239;
Nicholas, 153, 192; Richard, 50,
76, 115, 391; Robert, 87, 241,
260, 448; Samuel, 232, 431;
Susan, 188; Thomas, 194, 221,
249, 384, 397; junior, 249;
Thomasin, 327; Widow, 154,
349; William, 4, 46, 48, 63, 151
Fulligar *See* Fullager
Fulman: Fortunatus, 56; John,
142; Richard, 143; Robert, 143;
Thomas, 141; junior, 56; senior,
56; Widow, 56
Funnell *(Funiell)*: John, 63;
Widow, 49
Furby: William, 431, 433
Furlonger: Peter, 90
Furly: Alexander, 291
Furminger *(Firminger, Forminger)*:
Benjamin, 108; Henry, 247;
John, 365; William, 240
Furnager: Thomazin, 358
Furner: James, 215; John, 127, 242;
Thomas, 159, 184; Widow, 127,
129; William, 158, 300
Furrant: Thomas, 50
Fuson *(Fusonn)*: Gregory, 176;
Widow, 173; William, 175
Fusse: Richard, 249
Fusty: Edward, 203
Fuzard: John, 10
Fyler *See* Filler

G

Gabe: Richard, 146
Gabriell: Richard, 433; Thomas,
153; Widow, 433
Gadd: John, 267
Gadge: John, 203, 211
Gadsby *(Gadesbey)*: Edward, 302;
Robert, 302, 311; Widow, 244
Gage: Widow, 388
Gaine: John, 7
Gaines: William, 7
Gale: John, 258; Silvester, 399
Gales: John, 360
Gallant: Joseph, 3; Richard, 376
Gallard: John, 150
Gallat: John, 158
Galliard: Thomas, 441
Gallup: Nicholas, 206
Gamball: John, 213; William, 115,
200
Gambrill: James, 214
Game: Edward, 128; William, 9
Gammage: Widow, 121
Gammon *(Gamon)*: Alexander,
343; Elias, 412; Francis, 325,
408; James, 271; John, 28, 123,
256; Mr, 3; Nicholas, 343;
Richard, 139; Stephen, 273;
Thomas, 210; William, 6, 248
Gaping *(Gapeing)*: David, 66;
James, 69
Garaman: William, 171
Gardner *(Gardiner)*: Avery, 27;
Christopher, 127; Family, 342;
George, 48; Henry, 115, 400;
James, 32, 126; John, 48, 86,
131, 319; Mark, 127, 158;
Nicholas, 61; Peter, 244;
Phineas, 415; Richard, 14, 146,
270, 384; Robert, 154, 338;
Stephen, 131, 311; Thomas, 114,
284; Widow, 77, 119, 238, 338,
341, 411; junior, 48; William, 47

Gorden: Mark, 406

Gore *(Goore):* Christopher, 259; John, 191, 195; Robert, 233; Thomas, 317; Widow, 233; William, 231

Goreeke: James, 380

Goreham *See* Gorham

Gorger: Richard, 174

Gorham *(Goram, Goreham, Gorram):* Christopher, 186; Edward, 35, 102; John, 37, 312; Martin, 127; Richard, 107, 108; Robert, 158; Thomas, 246, 420, 448; Widow, 420; William, 127

Gorly *(Gooreley):* Edward, 398; John, 97, 197; William, 383

Gorredge *(Gorage, Gorridge):* John, 238; Robert, 54; William, 231

Gosbey *(Gosbie, Gosby):* Elizabeth, 196; Thomas, 305, 336

Goseling *See* Gosling

Gosford: Robert, 182

Goshage *See* Gossadge

Gosley: John, 197

Gosling *(Goseling, Goslin, Goslyng):* Ellen, 184; Family, 73; John, 94, 163, 181; Thomas, 31, 349; Widow, 67, 173, 176, 182; William, 130

Gosney: John, 114

Gossadge *(Goshage):* John, 37; William, 64

Gostling: Isaac, 160; Thomas, 115

Gostry: Thomas, 213

Goteer *See* Gooteer

Goudge: John, 39

Gould: Mr, 36; Thomas, 296

Goulden *See* Golding

Goulder: Bartholomew, 403; George, 368; John, 342, 369; Peter, 346; Roger, 403; Stephen, 372

Goulders: Henry, 271

Gouldford: Edward, 230

Gouldhatch: Robert, 304

Goulding *See* Golding

Gouldock: Widow, 117

Gouldring: John, 109

Gouldwell *See* Goldwell

Gour *See* Gower

Goures *See* Gowers

Gourley: Thomas, 51, 324

Gover: John, 191; Thomas, 97

Govett: Widow, 14

Gower *(Gour):* George, 105; Goodman, 128; Richard, 250

Gowers *(Goures):* Henry, 173; Thomas, 198

Gowles: Henry, 217

Gowll: Thomas, 455

Grace: Edward, 19; Richard, 380; Widow, 17, 73

Gradduck: Widow, 313

Grainsden *See* Gransden

Gramplett: Widow, 173

Gramsden, Grandsden *See* Gransden

Grandson: Nicholas, 115

Granely: Widow, 119

Granesden *See* Gransden

Granger: John, 398

Gransbury: Widow, 154

Gransden *(Grainsden, Gramsden, Grandsden, Granesden):* James, 307; John, 38, 39, 160, 202, 204; Thomas, 199; William, 201

Grant *(Graunt):* Geoffry, 331; Henry, 396; James, 371; John, 103, 222, 266, 397; Nicholas, 192; Paul, 264; Ralph, 219; Richard, 224; Thomas, 97, 390, 400; Walter, 440; Widow, 96, 376; William, 259

Grasham: Richard, 117

Gratnall: Michael, 380

Gratwick: Mr, 61; Tobias, 58

Gumry: Widow, cxi
Gunman: Christopher, 10
Gunn: Francis, 28; Richard, 235;
    William, 431
Gunning: Arthur, 200; Dr, 436;
    Peter, 382; Robert, 199
Gunter: William, 90
Gunton: Edward, 217, 220
Gunvill: Thomas, 266
Gurner: Widow, 405
Gurnett: Richard, 73
Gurney: Edward, 276; Joan, 30
Gurr *(Gurre):* George, 153, 162;
    Thomas, 253; William, 435
Gutfale; John, 137; Nicholas, 137
    Cf. Gutsall
Gutsall *(Gutsole):* James, 138;
    Nicholas, 138; William, 178
    Cf. Gutfale.
Gutteridge: Samuel, 328
Gutterson: Daniel, 327
Guy: James, 20; Robert, 239
Gyes: Henry, 16
Gyles *See* Giles
Gymber: William, 123
Gynder *See* Ginder
Gynner *See* Ginner
Gyssom: William, 118
Gytupp: Godfrey, 92
Gyver: Geoffrey, 92

H

Hackeng *See* Hacking
Hacker: Matthew, 193; Richard,
    377; Robert, 11; Widow, 13, 377
Hackett; James, 163; John, 40;
    Widow, 76
    Cf. Huggett
Hacking: Thomas, 356; William,
    177
Hackman: Widow, 12
Hackmore: Simon, 215
Hackney: Edward, 75

Hacksupp: Mr, 46
Hackwell: Joseph, 25
Hadd: James, 176
Haddeson: John, 16
Haddock: Samuel, 194
Haddon: Alexander, 88
Hadds *(Hads):* Edward, 95; Philip,
    252; Widow, 210
Hadister: Edward, 30
Hadloe *See* Hadlow
Hadlow *(Hadloe, Hadlowe):*
    Clement, 113; Daniel, 112;
    Edward, 98, 151, 270; Hamond,
    175; Henry, 174; James, 177;
    John, 198, 395; Lawrence, 193;
    Leonard, 155; Michael, 331;
    Robert, 206, 207; Simon, 197;
    Thomas, 69, 80, 271; Widow,
    102, 154, 261; William, 78, 79,
    209, 249
Hadlowe *See* Hadlow
Hadman: Richard, 233
Hads *See* Hadds
Hadsall *See* Hodsall
Hadswell: Henry, 48
Hady *See* Ady; Thomas, cxi
Haffall: Richard, 86; Robert, 377;
    Thomas, 86
Haffell *(Haffell)*
Haffenden *(Haffleden, Halfenden):*
    George, 242, 336; Goody, 435;
    John, 244; Margaret, 229;
    Richard, 433; Robert, 133;
    Thomas, 240, 244, 251, 433;
    Widow, 254, 319, 433
Haffleden *See* Haffenden
Hafin: Daniel, 83
Hagbin: Ingram, 327
Hager: Edward, 25
Hagskins: John, 17
Haies *See* Hayes
Hailock *See* Haylock
Haimes *See* Hamms

Edward, 15, 299; Family, 444;
George, 375; Henry, 290, 383,
436; James, 333, 422; John, 53,
64, 162, 309, 324, 326, 404, 408;
Mrs, 64, 407; Peter, 186;
Richard, 52, 333, 383, 436, 439;
Robert, 156; Thomas, 51, 201,
204, 323, 355, 371, 398, 407,
413, 417; Widow, 142, 277, 319,
342, 367, 371, 389, 406; William,
52, 365, 394
Harrow: Samuel, 18
Hart *(Harte, Hearte):* Arthur, 255;
Bartholomew, 445; Edward,
312, 411; Family, xxxix; Henry,
322, 335, 347, 351; James, 52,
343; John, lxxxvii, 24, 27, 79,
284, 313, 350; junior, 390;
senior, 390; Joseph, 275; Mary,
329; Miles, 26; Nicholas, 237;
Richard, 7, 198, 439; Robert,
327, 329, 371; Sarah, lxxvi;
Skyre, 165; Thomas, 4, 29, 103;
Timothy, 359; Widow, 100,
257, 316; William, 79
Harte *See* Hart
Hartell: George, 376
Hartenbrook: Nicholas, 13
Hartford: Widow, 204
Harthrop *See* Hartrupp
Hartland: Peter, 40
Hartley *(Hartly):* Henry, 192;
John, 269; Richard, 204; Robert,
234
Hartly *See* Hartley
Hartnap *See* Hartnapp
Hartnapp *(Harnupp, Hartnap,*
Hartnop, Hartnupp, Hattnup):
Gabriel, 143; Henry, 193; John,
239; Matthew, 238; Ralph, 140;
Widow, 144; William, 38
Hartnop *See* Hartnapp

Hartnupp *See* Hartnapp
Cf. Hartrupp
Harton *See* Horton
Hartopp *See* Hartrupp
Hartover: Christopher, 2
Hartredge *See* Hartridge
Hartridge *(Hartredge):* James, 137;
Margaret, 133; Michael, 144;
Robert, 189; Thomas, 147;
William, 136, 250
Hartrope *See* Hartrupp
Hartropp *See* Hartrupp
Hartrum *(Hartum):* James, 172;
John, 131; William, 131
Hartrupp *(Harthrop, Hartopp,*
Hartrope, Hartropp, Hartupp):
Isaac, 144; Jonas, 192; Richard,
198; Robert, 175, 346; Widow,
217; William, 73, 176, 271
Cf. Hartnupp
Hartsole: George, 227
Hartstone: John, 82
Hartum *See* Hartrum
Hartupp *See* Hartrupp
Hartwell: Ralph, 155
Harty: Lieutenant, 395; Thomas,
253
Harvey *(Harvie, Harvy, Harvye):*
Dudley, 14; Elizabeth, 442;
Henry, 405; John, 19, 68, 72;
Lawrence, 354; Matthew, 172;
Peter, 150; Richard, 162, 401;
senior, 234, 235; Robert, 21, 57;
Samuel, 224; Stephen, 74;
Thomas, 163, 235, 268, 283, 351,
401; Valentine, 415; William,
174, 240, 244
Harvie *See* Harvey
Harvill: John, 34; William, 90
Harvy & Harvye *See* Harvey
Harwar & Harward *See* Harwood
Harwing: James, 2

366; Widow, 24, 59, 176;
William, 129

Heather *(Hather, Hether, Heyther):*
Ann, 221; Clement, 4; John,
238; Robert, 86

Heaths: Widow, 12

Heaver: Henry, 50; Margery, 51

Hebb: Thomas, 86

Hedgcock *(Hedgecocke, Hidgcock):*
Clement, 446; Edward, 299;
John, 337, 412; Mrs, 186;
Richard, 397; Robert, 326;
Thomas, 247, 311, 357; Widow,
69; William, 345, 355

Hedger: Joan, 69; John, 20

Hedgman: Andrew, 146

Hedly: Widow, 59

Heed *See* Head

Heeler *(Heiler):* John, 287; Joseph,
293

Heeley *(Heale, Healy, Heely):*
Francis, 61; Gervase, 181;
Robert, 147; Widow, 385;
William, 191

Heiler *See* Heeler

Heines *See* Haines

Helbey *(Helbie, Helby):* Edward,
189; Moses, 172; Stephen, 122,
189

Helder: Widow, 134

Hellin: Daniel, 10

Hellman: Thomas, 414

Hells: Edward, 16

Hemaway: William, 372

Hembry: Benjamin, 253; James,
251; Widow, 253

Hempson: William, 192

Hemsley: William, 250

Hemsted: Widow, 372

Henbey: John, 32

Henden: John, 240, 242, 350

Henderson: John, 43; Thomas, 35

Hendy: Anne, 432

Hene: Joan, 34

Heneker *See* Henneker

Henfold: Henry, 200; John, 199

Hengar *See* Henger

Henge: Gilbert, 39; Nicholas, 64

Henger *(Hengar):* John, 63;
Widow, 61, 86

Henham: George, 159; Gregory,
299; Widow, 159

Henis *See* Hennis

Henley: John, 107; Mary, 139;
Samuel, 116; William, 174, 247

Henman: Abraham, 79; Adam,
379; Henry, 95, 96; John, 185,
242, 364; Robert, 299; Thomas,
81; Widow, 264

Henmarch: James, 78

Henneker *(Heneker, Hennicar,
Henniker):* Elizabeth, 219; Ellen,
95; Frances, 219; Henry, 279;
John, 94, 316, 317; Mary, 219;
Richard, 245; Thomas, 323, 407;
Walter, 268; William, 94, 318

Hennicar & Henniker *See*
Henneker

Hennis *(Henis):* George, 192, 219

Henry: Daniel, 15; Evans, 15;
James, 405; Mr, 17; Widow, 17

Henslie: Widow, 8

Hensom: Widow, 145

Henson: Widow, 203

Hensy: Joshua, 16

Henwood: Widow, 143

Hepenstall: Robert, 19

Herbert *(Harbert):* Caleb, 193;
Edward, 149; James, 289;
Richard, 341; William, 119
Cf. Hubbert.

Hercy: Robert, 264

Hereford: John, 193

Herett: John, 49

Herington *See* Herrington

Heritage: Edward, 347

High *(Hy, Hye)*: Gregory, 46;
Henry, 74; Richard, 47; Robert,
14
Higham *(Hyam, Hyham)*: James,
94, 269; Mary, 224; Widow, 96;
William, 96, 256
Highdowne: Edward, 281
Highland *(Hiland, Hyland)*:
Anthony, 127; Edward, 252;
George, 209; John, 134, 177;
Richard, 178; Thomas, 245, 361
Highstead *(Highsted)*: Joseph, 310;
Thomas, 284; Widow, 104
Highwood *(Hywood)*: Robert, 153;
Thomas, 135
Higinges *See* Higgens
Hiland *See* Highland
Hilby: John, 247
Hild: John, 404
Hilder: Henry, 54
Hile: John, 344
Hill *(Hile)*: Andrew, 23;
Christopher, 190; Daniel, 64;
David, 421; Harmond, 63; John,
22; Matthew, 14; Nicholas, 10;
Philip, 351; Richard, 184, 377;
Thomas, 123, 344, 400, 414;
Widow, 12, 215; William, 4, 9,
112
Hillary: Robert, 228
Hillen: Thomas, 281
Hilles *See* Hills
Hilliard *(Hillyard, Hilyard)*: John,
219; Widow, 101; William, 120
Hillman: Thomas, 285
Hills *(Hilles)*: Abraham, 67; Adam,
169; Alexander, 38; Andrew,
231, 244, 394; Arthur, 8; Avery,
443; Christopher, 290; Daniel,
184, 218; David, 254; Edward,
38, 107, 176, 253, 266, 273, 321;
Francis, 49; George, 78, 159,
290, 314, 315; Henry, 209, 247,

346, 363, 365, 366, 367;
Hercules, 216, 324; James, 111,
375; John, 21, 28, 38, 44, 100,
115, 177, 182, 183, 190, 200,
203, 241, 262, 278, 284, 291,
302, 315, 335, 347, 348, 356,
367; Lancelot, 75; Mary, 205;
Matthew, 74, 391; Michael, 326;
Mr, 64; Mrs, 208; Nathaniel, 25;
Nicholas, 292, 310; Norton,
375; Peter, 73; Pheobe, 224;
Phillis, 191; Richard, 46, 102,
123, 126, 182, 195; Robert, 38,
76, 268; Rowland, 114; Samuel,
394; Simon, 161, 284, 306;
Stephen, 30, 281, 311; Thomas,
30, 44, 95, 98, 162, 203, 250,
268, 306, 309, 311, 312, 313,
316, 318, 408, 431; Thomasine,
447; Walter, 130; Widow, 72,
109, 110, 180, 190, 204, 283,
292, 295, 298, 311; William, 104,
105, 123, 157, 175, 214, 239,
246, 250, 251, 259, 277, 281,
305, 306, 380, 396; Williams,
336
Hillyard *See* Hilliard
Hilton: Henry, 343; James, 194;
Stephen, 420; William, 325
Hilyard *See* Hilliard
Hince: Widow, 6
Hinchway: Absolom, 395
Hinckley: Edward, 153; James,
110, 275; Simon, 98
Hincton *See* Hinton
Hind *(Hinde, Hine)*: Edward, 97;
Elizabeth, 438; James, 68; John,
160; Robert, 176; William, 386
Hindes *(Hines, Hynes)*: Giles, 271;
Henry, 256; John, 227; Widow,
103, 186; William, 83
Hinge: John, 158; Richard, 39;
Thomas, 44, 158

Hoysted *(Hoystead)*: Joseph, 310;
Thomas, 310; William, 277
Hubart *See* Hubbert
Hubbard *(Hubberd, Hubord)*:
Alexander, 193; Christopher,
108; David, 301; Edward, 117;
Elizabeth, 102; Francis, 66;
George, 165; James, 177, 245;
John, 230, 236, 248, 445;
Nicholas, 131; Paul, 445;
Richard, 189, 270; Robert, 389;
Samuel, 216; Thomas, 69, 114,
131, 300, 333; Widow, 17, 56,
61, 131, 342, 407
Hubbell: Robert, 148
Hubberd *See* Hubbard
Hubberden: Robert, 397
Hubbert *(Hubart)*: Arthur, 299;
Christopher, 111; Henery, 139;
Henry, 140; James, 282; John,
198, 341, 413; Mr, 95; William,
106, 162, 244
Cf. Herbert
Hubble *(Hubel)*: Henry, 157; John,
156; Mark; junior, 157; senior,
157; Nicholas, 157; Robert, 157;
Thomas, 157; Widow, 48;
William, 156
Hubord *See* Hubbard
Huchford: Matthew, 154
Huchins *See* Hutchins
Huckley: Joseph, 11, 12; William,
11
Hucksted: John, 221
Huckstepp: John, 431; Stephen,
434; Thomas, 432, 433; Widow,
431; William, 435
Hudder: Robert, 31
Hudman: William, 442
Hudsall *See* Hodsall
Hudsford: Widow, 99
Cf. Hutsford.

Hudson: Andrew, 202;
Christopher, 75; Gunnner, 119;
Henry, 400; James, 380; John,
217, 270; Michael, 342; Richard,
441; Robert, 444; Sarah, 288;
Thomas, 201, 248, 399; Widow,
336
Cf. Hutson
Huens: Widow, 298
Hues *See* Hughes
Huett *See* Hewett
Huffam *(Huffham)*: George, 387;
Henry, 412, 415; Michael, 121,
394; Richard, 394; Stephen, 389
Hugbone *See* Hogben
Huges *See* Hughes
Hugessen *(Hugesson)*: John, 284;
William, 276
Hugett, Huggat & Huggate *See*
Huggett
Huggen: Thomas, 108
Huggens *See* Huggins
Huggett; Anthony, 133; Edward,
189; John, 138; Widow, 373;
William, 143, 144, 363
Cf. Hackett
Huggins *(Huggens)*: Daniel, 214,
215; Elizabeth, 187; George,
271; Henry, 57, 126; John, 74,
95, 161, 215; Thomas, 70, 109,
260, 290, 334; Widow, 71, 73,
78, 105, 157, 255, 330; William,
48, 109, 126, 322
Hughes *(Heuwes, Hewes, Hewis,*
Hues, Huges, Hughs): Alexander,
181; Henry, 11, 202, 204; John,
45, 67, 304; Phillip, 17; Richard,
13, 211, 234, 318; Robert, 302,
445; Sarah, 69; Simon, 15;
Thomas, 12, 25, 153, 219, 232,
392; Widow, 17, 419; William,
26, 392
Hughs *See* Hughes

89; Jane, 32; John, 14, 29, 279,
282, 365; Samuel, 21; Thomas,
28; Widow, 96
Hutchinson: Richard, 212
Huthum: John, 313
Hutley: Joseph, 5
Hutsford; William, 198
  Cf. Hudsford.
Hutson *(Huttson)*: Reman, 393;
  Thomas, 124; William, 115, 360,
  406
  Cf. Hudson.
Hutt: William, 212
Hutton *(Hutten)*: Christopher,
  235; Edward, 414, 415; Widow,
  138; William, 9, 207
Hy & Hye *See* High
Hyat *See* Hyett
Hyde *(Hide)*: Bernard, 50; Hannah,
  30; John, 40
Hyder *See* Hidar
Hyett *(Hyat)*: John, 12; Robert,
  289
Hyland *See* Highland
Hynes *See* Hindes
Hywood *See* Highwood

I

Idden *See* Iden
Iddenden; Richard, 313, 447;
  Widow, 108, 179
  Cf. Eddenden
Iddleton *(Idleton)*
Iden *(Idden)*: James, 110, 177;
  Living, 105; Richard, 105;
  Thomas, 164, 224, 319; Widow,
  177; William, 256
Idleton *See* Iddleton; John, 206;
  William, 73
Iffield *(Ifield)*: George, 114, 117;
  Henry, 157; Thomas, 157;
  William, 157

Iggleden *(Iggulden, Igleden)*: John,
  243; Joseph, 239, 245; Richard,
  228; Thomas, 246, 433; Widow,
  315
Ilcock: Thomas, 12
Iler: George, 231
Iles: Francis, 118; Thomas, 271;
  Widow, 119
Ilett; William, 189
  Cf. Ellett, Elliot
Illenden: John, 241; Joseph, 227;
  Lawrence, 228; Richard, 224;
  Thomas, 243
Illes: John, 272
Immett: William, 268
Impett: Henry, 320; John, 340,
  345, 346, 411; Michael, 387;
  Richard, 387; Robert, 388;
  Thomas, 387; Widow, 340;
  William, 388
Ince. *Cf.* Juce
Ines: Richard, 336
Inett: Mrs, 214; William, 214
Inge *(Innge)*: Henry, 148; John,
  134, 137; Stephen, 138; Widow,
  138; junior, 400; senior, 400;
  William, 406
Ingham: Widow, 205
Ingleton: Henry, 359; Widow, 398
Ingold: Widow, 13
Ingram *(Ingrom, Ingrome)*: Henry,
  63; John, 2, 12, 241; William, 53
Inkepenn *(Ynckpen)*: Robert, 143,
  299
Inman: William, 118
Inmeth *(Inmith)*: Thomas, 356
Inne: Widow, 394
Innever: Richard, 414; Thomas,
  414
Innge *See* Inge
Innges: John, 137
Inskipp: John, 145
Inward: Francis, 442

Jeddery: Stephen, 373
Jeff: Thomas, 350
Jeffard *See* Gifford
Jefferey *See* Jeffery
Jefferies *See* Jeffries
Jeffery *(Jefferey, Jeffrey, Jeffry):*
Abraham, 439; Alexander, 237;
Ann, 149; David, 45; Edward,
141, 143, 150; Francis, 286;
George, 189; Gervase, 234;
Henry, 54, 141; John, 41, 134,
140, 150, 192, 226, 307, 388,
431; Josias, 138; Mary, 218;
Reuben, 141, 150; Richard, 123,
142; Robert, 232; Samuel, 150;
Sarah, 400; Stephen, 287;
Thomas, 127, 141; Widow, 45,
59, 143, 150, 260, 365, 371, 400;
William, 107, 142, 150, 226, 279,
442
Jefford *See* Gifford
Jeffries *(Jefferies, Jeffryes):* Edmund,
168; John, 6, 193; Jonathan, 2;
Mr, 2, 5; Robert, 25
Jeffs: Thomas, 169
Jegoe: Elizabeth, 224
Jekin *(Jeakins, Jeikin, Jeking):* John,
191; Thomas, 176, 398;
Valentine, 414; William, 371
Jelfe: Widow, 120
Jell: Nicholas, 337; Thomas, 316;
Valentine, 414
Jellibrand *See* Gelibrand
Jellines: John, 16
Jemmett: Daniel, 306; James, 89;
Mr, 282; Richard, 57; Thomas,
110, 172, 297, 455; Widow, 329;
William, 305, 306
Jempson: William, 55
Jemson *(Jemsenn):* Thomas, 194,
217
Jenkenson: Ralph, 447

Jenkin *(Jenken):* Abraham, 307;
Henry, 348, 367, 445; Philip,
344, 345; Richard, 345, 346;
Thomas, 274, 321, 339, 340, 345,
354, 398, 405, 440; Widow, 278
Jenkins: George, 111; John, 42;
Perriman, 99; Richard, 190;
Thomas, 69, 95; Widow, 52;
William, 162
Jenman: John, 15; Richard, 193;
William, 192
Jenner *(Geyner):* Robert, 353;
Thomas, 236; William, 236, 237
Jennings: Abraham, 65; Alexander,
313; Alice, 30; Edward, 111;
George, 21, 449; Henry, 233,
313, 433, 434; James, 128;
Jeremiah, 255; John, 156, 171,
241, 256, 281, 357; Margaret,
432; Richard, 306, 322; Robert,
197; Samuel, 306; Simon, 122;
Thomas, 17, 20, 100, 171, 233,
443; Walter, 233; Widow, 95,
199, 314, 318; William, 80, 197;
Williams, 91
Jerland: Abraham, 32
Jervall: Robert, 228
Jervis *(Jervas, Jervice):* Anthony,
372; Benjamin, 363; Edward,
167; George, 239; Gervase, 312;
James, 434; John, 132; Ralph,
261; Richard, 180, 384; Thomas,
312; Widow, 433
Jesseman *See* Jessyman
Jessey: Stephen, 278
Jesson: Widow, 9
Jessupp *(Gessoppe, Jessopp, Jessup):*
Jasper, 56; John, 51, 52, 88;
Passwater, 131; Richard, 41;
Robert, 55; Widow, 51, 56, 122;
William, 89
Cf. Gissopp.

K

L

Mune *See* Munn
Munfort: Mr, 4; Widow, 5
Mungeham *See* Mongeham; John, 244
Munings: Richard, 447
Munn *(Mune):* George, 227; Henry, 160; James, 303; John, 178, 200, 225, 231, 232, 445; Joseph, 317; Matthew, 154; Stephen, 246; Thomas, 200; junior, 233; senior, 234; Widow, 74, 236, 242; William, 75, 178, 236, 252
Munnion *(Munion):* James, 43; John, 178; Thomas, 55
Munns *(Munnes, Muns):* Edward, 338; junior, 338; Gervase, 196; James, 158; John, 202, 205, 262, 265; Matthew, 338; Nicholas, 185; Richard, 165; Thomas, 219; Walter, 301; Widow, 392
Munson: Eleanor, 170
Munteth: Alice, 30
Murfield: Simon, 120; Thomas, 201
Murford: Richard, 101, 227
Murgin: Henry, 42; Jane, 154; Robert, 398; Thomas, 154; Widow, 42; William, 44, 66
Murrell: James, 8
Murrey *See* Murry; Henry, 88
Murrillian: David, 394
Murrin: George, 216
Murry *(Murrey):* Henry, 88, 353; William, 89
Murton *(Murten):* Arnold, 97; Daniel, 297, 456; John, 96; Joseph, 238; Nicholas, 271; Thomas, 296, 458; Widow, 12, 13
Musall *(Muzell):* Thomas, 173; William, 18
Musdred: John, 393

Musedar: Richard, 160
Musgrave: Henry, 252; Thomas, 7; Widow, 250
Musgreme: Widow, 64
Musgrove: Christopher, 29; Henry, 373; John, 254; Lawrence, 88; Mrs, 208; Robert, 64; William, 64
Muskerry: Lord, 149
Musred *See* Muzered
Mussard: Robert, 114
Mussery: Edward, 222
Mustard: William, 100
Muster: Mrs, 3
Mustred: Mrs, 188
Mutton: Edward, 325; Francis, 448
Muzell *See* Musall
Muzered *(Musred, Muzred):* James, 397; John, 363, 438; William, 419
    Cf. Musdred.
Muzzard: William, 185
Myland: Thomas, 21
Myles *See* Miles
Mylls *See* Mills
Myssam: John, 146

N

Nalder: Arthur, 196
Naman: Thomas, 404
Naper: Edward, 110
Napleton: Henry, 311; John, 267, 275, 294; Mr, 395
Napper: Thomas, 123
Narne: Mr, 353
Nasey: Widow, 322
Nash *(Naysh):* Aphery, lxxxvii; Edward, 12, 30, 268; Family, lxxxvii; George, 99; James, 221, 407; Joan, 38; John, lxxxvii, lxxxix, 256, 339, 340, 355, 390, 408; Joseph, 38; Mark, 368; Mary, 214; Matthew, 98;

O

Outridge *(Outrige)*: George, 385;
Richard, 368
Ovell: David, 388
Ovenden, 420; Daniel, 417;
Goodman, 421; John, 422;
Matthew, 17; Philip, 419;
Sampson, 327; Thomas, 343
Overie *See* Overy
Overstreete: Peter van, 37
Overton: William, 19
Overy *(Overie)*: George, 178; John,
36, 72, 167; Richard, 123, 387;
Robert, 363; Sarah, 41; Stephen,
388; Thomas, 133; Widow, 281,
388; William, 53; junior, 53
Owen, *(Owin)*: John, 32, 227;
Nathaniel, 43; Richard, 19;
Walter, 72; William, 413
Owens: Thomas, 198
Ower *(Owre)*: Boys, 397; Edward,
289; Mrs, 213
Owin *See* Owen
Owlett *See* Howlett
Ownsloe *See* Onsloe
Ownsted, *(Ounsted, Ownstead)*:
George, 61; John, 59, 81, 85;
Robert, 85, 86
Owre *See* Ower
Owsby: Thomas, 217
Owsnam: Andrew, 329
Owten *See* Horton
Owtrem: Mrs, 41
Oxburrough: William, 438
Oxenbridge: Edward, 62; Henry,
445; John, 249, 350; Nicholas,
437; Richard, 231; Thomas, 440;
Widow, 62
Oxenden *(Oxinden)*: Henry, xxxix,
389, 391, 408; Mrs, 388
Oxley: Ralph, 302; Solomon, 304;
William, 113, 266
Oxmond: John, 29
Oyler: Thomas, 240

Oyne: Widow, 402
Oynes: John, 342

P

Pace: George, 64
Pach: Widow, 287
Pack: Isaac, 127, 128; James, 164;
Jobb, 21; John, 108, 160;
Richard, 116, 279; Robert, 322;
Thomas, 119, 160; William, 149,
163, 202, 204
Packden: Anthony, 408; John, 407
Packenden: John, 170
Packenham *(Packnam)*: Edward,
31; Henry, 322; James, 197;
Robert, 183, 321; Thomas, 324
Packer: John, 259, 293, 295;
Philip, xxxix, lxiv, 54; Phillip, 1;
Thomas, 80, 395; Widow, 389,
391
Packham: Edward, 136; John, 111,
112, 350; senior, 104; Richard,
109; Thomas, 248; William, 248
Cf. Peckham
Packman: Edward, 90; John, 35,
378; Richard, 97; Robert, 99,
275, 418; Widow, 87, 110, 326
Cf. Peckman
Packs: George, 177
Packten: James, 447
Packwood: Mrs, 91
Paddock: Widow, 138
Padnar *(Padner)*: John, 186;
Robert, 181
Pagden: John, 265, 266; Margaret,
150; Nicholas, 265
Page *(Paige)*: Abraham, 180;
Ambrose, 151, 152; Edward,
260; Francis, 185; Henry, 345;
Humphrey, 415; Joan, 298;
John, 24, 92, 103, 106, 128;
Joseph, 367; Mary, 185;
Michael, 342, 344, 416; Mr, 36,

138, 148, 173; Robert, 128;
Stephen, 127; Thomas, 147, 148;
Widow, 137, 223; William, lxxx,
112, 126, 133, 155
Patteson *See* Pattison
Pattington: Dorothy, 24
Pattinson: Widow, 244
Pattison *(Patteson)*: Edward, 243;
Elizabeth, 432; James, 384;
Theophilus, 389; Thomas, 27,
190, 350, 361; William, 272, 434
Cf. Pattson
Patton *See* Patten
Pattoo: Anthony, 446
Pattoune *See* Patten
Pattson: John, 404
Paul *(Paule)*: Anthony, 193, 195;
John, 183, 246; Joseph, 223;
Robert, 215
Paulie&Pauly *See* Pawley
Pavely: John, 214
Pavye: John, 148
Pawley *(Paulie, Pauly, Pawly)*:
John, 107; Robert, 104, 129;
Solomon, 148; Thomas, 126;
Widow, 148; William, 147
Pawson: Family, 265
Paxford: Ann, 217
Pay *(Paye)*: Christopher, 374;
Edmund, 342; Isaac, 343; James,
304; Richard, 343; Roger, 249;
Thomas, 308, 421; Widow, 330,
370
Payle: Widdow, 256
Paylin: Simon, 205
Payne *See* Paine
Peacke *See* Peake
Peacock *(Peacocke)*: James, 115;
John, 70; Robert, 26, 206
Peader: Thomas, 37
Peake *(Peacke)*: Abel, 97; John, 41,
58, 255; Matthew, 444; Mr, 436;

Nicholas, 284; Richard, 85;
Robert, 19; William, 41
Peale: Roger, 449
Pearce *See* Peirce
Pearcey *See* Piercy
Pearles: Richard, 226; William;
junior, 66; senior, 66
Pearne: Henry, 67; John, 208;
Thomas, 208, 209
Pearson: Mr, 37
Pease: Henry, 203; Mark, 31;
Thomas, 30
Peate: James, 139; Richard, 216
Peck: William, 101
Peckden: Richard, 385
Pecke: Francis, 19; Widow, 208,
209
Cf. Pack
Peckham: Christopher, 233;
junior, 238; John, 95, 104, 149,
228, 350; Margaret, 136;
Reginald, 154; Reynold, 75;
Widow, 349
Peckman: John, 114; Joseph, 101;
Widow, 101
Cf. Packman
Peckworth: Widow, 208
Peeke *(Peke)*: Daniel, 398; James,
377; John, 447: Peter, 404;
Thomas, 382; William, 180
Peene: Alexander, 157; George,
191; Henry, 350; John, 180;
Nicholas, 344; Richard, 112;
Simon, 190; Stephen, 111;
Thomas, 113; William, 180, 240
Peerce *See* Peirce
Peere: Benjamin, 338
Peerles: Thomas, 257; Widow, 83;
William, 141
Pegler: Master, 159; Mr, 159
Pegrum: Richard, 168
Peirce *(Pearce, Peerce, Pierce)*:
Andrew, 328; Bartholomew,

Pepper: Alexander, 396; Widow,
    184; William, 260, 415
Pepys: Samuel, xvi, xx
Perch: George, 84; Thomas, 38
Percival *(Percivall, Piercevall)*:
    John, 61, 182; Richard, 185;
    Widow, 363; William, 366
Perfite: John, 219
Perin *(Perine)*: Richard, 137;
    William, 119, 267
Perins: Mary, 194
Perkin: William, 416
Perkins *(Pirkins)*: Edward, 214;
    Fne:, 13; George, 248; John,
    402; Michael, 36; Richard, 3, 9,
    80; Thomas, 17, 248; William,
    107
Perkinson *See* Parkinson
Perles: Richard, 225
Perley: John, 438
Perren & Perrene *See* Perrin
Perrett *See* Parratt
Perriman, 99; Thomas, 183
Perrin *(Perren, Perrene, Perring)*:
    Henry, 328; John, 332; Joseph,
    68; Nicholas, 59; Richard, 137;
    Thomas, 105, 135, 250; Widow,
    136; William, 250
Perrior: Edward, 59
Perritt See Parratt
Perry: Humphrey, 26; John, 73;
    Richard, 324; Stephen, 86;
    Thomas, 358
Perryer: Thomas, 42
Pescod: Widow, 13
Peters: Augustine, 31, 61; John, 3,
    103; Simion, 197; Thomas, 237;
    Widow, 235; William, 253, 265
Petley *(Petly* Pettley*)*: George, 62,
    146; James, 63; John, 392; Peter,
    20; Robert, 84 Roger, 30;
    Thomas, 38; William, 116
Petman: John, 371

Pett: Christopher, 14; George,
    395; Henry, 197; John, 18, 96,
    166, 178, 364, 389, 404; Mrs, 2;
    Peter, 191; Phineas, 191, 195;
    Robert, 129, 180; Thomas, 166,
    186, 268, 367; Vincent, 399;
    Widow, 294; William, 130, 167,
    194
Pettendell: Henry, 177
Pettenden: William, 275
Petter: George, 154, 155, 227, 228;
    John, 87, 228; Richard, 231;
    Samuel, 227
Pettett *(Pettet, Pettit, Pettitt)*:
    Elizabeth, 444; George, 415;
    Goodwife, 371; Henry, 405;
    James, 399; John, 330, 374, 399,
    401, 403; Joseph, 228; Michael,
    437; Richard, 401, 402; Thomas,
    271, 408; junior, 375; senior,
    375; Wesson, 67; Widow, 104;
    William, 271, 295
Pettingale: Richard, 189
Pettit & Pettitt *See* Pettett
Pettley *See* Petley
Pettman, 384; George, 333; John,
    441; Thomas, 46, 252; William,
    76
Pettock *See* Pittock
Pettoe: George, 133
Petts: Richard, 142
Petty: Christopher, 210, 272;
    George, 60; Robert, 40;
    Thomas, 38; William, xv, xvi,
    xix
Peyton: Thomas, xxxix, 408;
    William, 1
Pharise, Phariss *See* Ferris
Pharoe *See* Farroe
Phelpe: Stephen, 34
Phenice *See* Venice
Philbie: Richard, 3

Smallman: Widow, 132
Smallwood *(Smalwood)*: John, civ,
cv, 297, 459; Richard, 296, 458;
Thomas, 67, 432
Smalvill: John, 184
Smalwood *See* Smallwood
Smart: Mark, 259; Richard, 6, 336,
347; Stephen, 4; Widow, 300,
369; William, 6
Smeath: Widow, 412
Smeed: Ezekiel, 374; George, 354;
Thomas, 320; William, 265
Smeeths: Widow, 329
Smeke: William, 160
Smelt: Richard, 20
Smilson: Widow, 316
Smith *(Smyth, Smythe)*: Abraham,
310, 312, 315; Alice, 269;
Ambrose, 307; Amy, 378;
Andrew, 14, 286, 352; Ann, 208;
Anthony, 274, 346, 349; Attain;
senior, 251; Attained, 258;
Bartholomew, 24; Billington, 5;
Charles, 59, 194; Christopher,
10; Cuthbert, 6; Deborah, 339;
Edward, 3, 15, 44, 84, 118, 120,
171, 194, 259, 262, 306, 317,
330, 366, 395; Ezekiel, 10, 21;
Family, 286; Francis, 59, 117,
145, 147; George, 62, 82, 172,
180, 223, 298; Griffin, 94;
Henry, 61, 121, 183, 184, 210,
299, 370, 399; Humphrey, 209,
210; James, 44, 48, 172, 203, 219,
263; Jeremy, 181, 440; Joan,
218; John, 5, 7, 8, 30, 31, 36, 41,
47, 49, 51, 74, 76, 80, 82, 94,
109, 115, 118, 126, 129, 144,
163, 170, 175, 176, 192, 202,
206, 207, 258, 260, 284, 305,
322, 326, 347, 351, 353, 357,
360, 371, 373, 377, 382, 387,
398, 406, 420, 433; Jonas, 288;

Joseph, 8, 31, 205; Lawrence,
303; Leonard, 287, 405; Luke,
26; Mary, 186; Matthew, 25;
Mildred, 70; Mr, 12, 373; Mrs,
155, 402; Nathaniel, 205, 409;
Nicholas, 20, 411; Percival, 42;
Ralph, 403; Reynold, 309;
Richard, 8, 16, 37, 40, 46, 72,
108, 157, 160, 172, 233, 259,
266, 273, 286, 385, 448; Robert,
28, 52, 199, 233, 247, 248, 326,
395; Roger, 212; Samuel, 268,
338; Sarah, 400; Stephen, 234;
Susanna, 298; Thomas, 4, 29, 31,
37, 47, 61, 63, 65, 67, 72, 76, 77,
79, 124, 125, 126, 157, 170, 171,
172, 173, 175, 183, 185, 188,
192, 195, 200, 206, 207, 208,
209, 214, 216, 224, 233, 238,
256, 263, 264, 268, 273, 274,
288, 289, 290, 307, 318, 326,
353, 362, 383, 411, 434; Vincent,
369; Walter, 42; Widow, 12, 13,
39, 58, 68, 73, 83, 100, 103, 117,
131, 155, 178, 189, 196, 227,
251, 252, 283, 287, 290, 298,
305, 306, 361, 364, 365, 374,
375, 387, 400, 411, 433; William,
4, 13, 20, 27, 29, 31, 35, 38, 65,
106, 149, 165, 174, 182, 215,
245, 264, 285, 288, 290, 331,
332, 339, 386, 387, 401, 403,
409, 414, 444
Smithers: William, 65
Smithett: Andrew, 415
Smithie: John, 13
Smithson *(Smythson)*: Alexander,
391; Widow, 247, 310, 337;
William, 366
Smoothing: James, 107; Thomas,
187; Widow, 110
Smyth & Smythe *See* Smith
Smythson *See* Smithson

22, 26, 130, 174, 191, 327, 348, 351

Stoneham *(Stonham)*: Anthony, 223; Francis, 147; Roger, 228; Thomas, 41, 54; Widow, 229

Stonehorse: Edward, 325

Stonehouse: Christopher, 306, 379, 436; James, 107; Mary, 299; Robert, 100, 299; Stephen, 268

Stoner: Jeremy, 31; William, 28

Stonestreet: Henry, 94; John, 184; Margaret, 189; Widow, 306

Stonham *See* Stoneham

Stonnard *See* Stonard

Stookes *See* Stokes

Stoppell: Francis, 390

Storey *See* Story

Stort: Thomas, 315

Story *(Storey)*: John, 47, 154, 216; Richard, 7; Robert, 180

Stove, 11

Stow: Bartholomew, 21; John, 81; Samuel, 215

Stowell: Mr, 47

Strader: Gregory, 9

Straine *(Strayne)*: Edward, 281; Thomas, 259; William, 98, 274

Straite: Ann, 269

Strange, 217; John, 26, 31; Roger, 146; William, 432

Strangford: Philip, Viscount, 346, 364, 370; Viscount, xxxvii, xxxix, lxiii

Strart: Thomas, 275

Straton: Francis, 14

Strayne *See* Straine

Strayner: Tristram, 44

Strean: Thomas, 47

Streate *See* Street

Streater *See* Streeter

Streatfield *(Streatfeild, Streathfield, Stretfeld)*: Edward, 160; John, 56, 124, 145; Richard, 51, 55;

Robert, 60, 142; Sarah, 51; Stephen, 51; Widow, 55; William, 53, 125

Streator *See* Streeter

Stredupp: Lewis, 275

Stredwick *(Stredwicke)*: Afra, 445; Christopher, 411; Goodwife, 382; James, 381; Mary, 440; Nicholas, 445; Thomas, 392

Street *(Streate, Streete)*: David, 396; George, 92; Henry, 15; John, 33; junior, 34; Richard, 201; Stephen, 253; Widow, 19, 20

Streeteabbey: John, 33

Streeter *(Streater, Streator, Streter)*: Edmund, 361; George, 251; John, 251; Samuel, 222; Walter, 234

Streeting: Christopher, 372; Henry, 345; Robert, 286, 292; William, 323, 411

Streetly: John, 92; Thomas, 92

Streets: John, 275; Thomas, 284

Streter *See* Streeter

Stretfield *See* Streatfield

Stretton *(Streton)*: John, 121; Nathaniel, 225; Peter, 18; Thomas, 192, 225; William, 430

Streven: Roger, 399

Stringer: Abraham, 134; Edward, 42; Gilbert, 365; Joan, 242; John, 12, 134, 296, 388, 455; Mrs, 267; Stephen, 251, 391; Thomas, 47, 120, 251

Striting: John, 351

Stroakes: Thomas, 22

Strode: John, cx

Strong *(Stronge)*: Charles, 325; Francis, 8; Henry, 388; : Mary, 193; Richard, 388; Stephen, 442; Thomas, 381; Widow, 418

Strood *(Stroud)*: George, 233; Henry, 327, 347; James, 342;

T

W

183; Ingram, 400; John, 5, 29,
49, 89, 242, 388, 439; Marmion,
35; Mary, 374; Miles, 387;
Nicholas, 153; Richard, 181,
256, 303; Robert, 31, 269;
Samuel, 40; Stephen, 60;
Susanna, 192; Thomas, 111, 128,
190, 349, 370; Valentine, 209,
210; Widow, 63, 143, 151, 156,
257, 349, 388; William, 5, 28, 42,
74, 139, 266
Walklin See Wakelin
Wall: Abraham, 342; Frances, 146,
181; Mr, 270; Nicholas, li, 123,
171; Roger, 151; Samuel, 185;
Stephen, 192; Thomas, 107, 181,
317; Widow, 184; William, 44,
183, 189, 444
Wallance: George, 293
Wallard: Henry, 286, 294; John,
295; Mark, 286
Wallatt: William, 175
Wallenger: Jeremiah, 213
Waller *(Waler)*: Anthony, 65, 74;
Elizabeth, 102; Henry, 65, 79,
81, 292; John, 81; Mr, 11, 12;
Nicholas, 228; Richard, 12, 80,
149; Robert, 57, 300; Thomas,
33, 44, 228, 298; Widow, 299;
William, 10, 11, 80, 81, 127, 227;
junior, 80
Wallford: John, 245
Wallis: Aaron, 10; Anthony, 88;
Henry, 296, 457; John, 3, 56,
141, 147, 364; Richard, 76;
Robert; junior, 145; senior, 145;
Thomas, 56; Widow, 51, 87;
William, 53, 139
Wallison: Robert, 212
Walsall *(Walstall)*: Michael, 320;
Samuel, 217, 312
Walsbee *(Walsbie)*: John, 336;
Robert, 456

Walsingham: Edward, 165;
Francis, lxiv
Walsone: Thomas, 68
Walstall See Walsall
Walter: Anthony, 229;
Christopher, 224; Edward, 66,
230, 251; George, 116; Henry,
87, 90; Isaac, 230; senior, 239;
James, 44; John, 43, 70, 72, 75,
80, 151, 165, 175, 229, 250, 254,
257; Michael, 66; Mrs, 76; Peter,
240; Richard, 50, 255; Robert, 3,
165, 223; Stephen, 106, 132;
Thomas, 76, 105, 190, 215, 253,
255; junior, 182; senior, 182;
Widow, 157, 252; William, 57,
147, 150, 151, 248
Walteridge: William, 392
Walters: Captain, 31; Gabriel, 194;
William, 43
Walton: John, 6; Joshua, 209; Mr,
391; Thomas, 217; Widow, 6
Wamner: Richard, 52
Wamsley *(Wamseley)*: David, 156;
Robert, 295
Wandall: Joan, 31
Wanden: James, 188, 208
Wane See Wayne
Wanmar *(Wanmer)*: Robert, 51;
Thomas, 51
Wannam: Richard, 309
Wanstall *(Wansall)*: Edward, lxxxv,
390; Francis, liv, 120, 121;
Geoffrey, 339; James, 277; John,
296, 328, 387, 390; Mark, 280,
328; Michael, 326; Richard, 346;
Robert, 326; Sampson, 323;
Thomas, lxxxv, 323, 326;
Widow, 327; William, 328, 390,
418
Wantier: Abraham, 438
Ward: Andrew, 229; Anthony, 49;
Daniel, 35; Edward, 190, 352;

Place Name Index

C

D

F

L

M

N

S

T

Y

Subject Index

I

K

L

O

P